Praise for the First Edition of The Whole Internet

MicroTimes named Ed Krol one of 1993's top 100 industry leaders and unsung heroes. About *The Whole Internet* they wrote, "The book against which all subsequent Internet guides are measured. Krol's work has emerged as an indispensable reference to beginners and seasoned travelers alike as they venture out on the data highway."

The *Whole Internet User's Guide & Catalog* "is an encyclopedic compendium of all the places to explore, the short-cuts to get there, the reasons to linger, the treasures you might find, and the tools to make this free world-wide service worthwhile."

— Kevin Kelly, *WIRED*

"For the Internet novice with limited computer experience, the best introduction is Ed Krol's *The Whole Internet User's Guide & Catalog*."

— *The New York Times*

"*The Whole Internet User's Guide & Catalog* will probably become the Internet user's bible because it provides comprehensive, easy instructions for those who want to get the most from this valuable electronic tool."

— David J. Buerger, *Editor, Communications Week*

"*The Whole Internet User's Guide & Catalog* is currently THE definitive user guide to the Internet, and it frankly has no rivals. A simple recommendation—if you are interested in the Internet, buy it."

— Jack Rickard, *Editor, Boardwatch Magazine*

"*The Whole Internet User's Guide & Catalog* is the single best book on what's out there in the global electronic village. It does for the free Internet what Alfred Glossbrenner's books did for fee-based online databases. It's the first compendium on the world's largest computer network."

— Greg Goode, *Syndicated News Service*

"I recommend *The Whole Internet User's Guide & Catalog* very highly. Although there are many other competing works out there, this one covers almost everything anyone could want to know, is well written for both the novice and the experienced user, and is available now at a very reasonable price. All who are reading this review should have a copy on their desk and a copy in their public, academic, or special library for reference by other potential users."

— Dan Lester, *Associate University librarian, Boise State University*

"This is the kind of book that you get several extra copies of to give away when someone asks you 'What's Internet?' or to staff or colleagues when you want to give them the hint that they could be more effective in their work if they used Internet."

— Anthony M. Rutkowski, *SprintLink*

"In a word, it is a *must* for all Internet sites as a complement to much of the resource material and guides you would already have accumulated."

— Dr. Ian Hoyle, *Senior Research Scientist, BHP Research-Melbourne Laboratories*

"There is a new book out called *The Whole Internet* by Ed Krol. I highly recommend this book to anyone interested in learning more about the Internet."

— Scott Yanoff; the "Yanoff list," *Inet Services*

"I wasn't sure that an 'old hand' like me would learn much from an overview guidebook targeted at mere users, but there are whole chapters in here on subjects I've been meaning to find out about, such as gopher, wais, and www."

— Steve Summit, *Grizzled Internet Vet*

"Krol's style throughout the book is a breezy conversational style that is designed to not intimidate users but rather, make them feel at ease as they explore a potentially complex area."

— Naor Wallach, *Newsbytes News Network*

"*The Whole Internet User's Guide & Catalog*, published by O'Reilly & Associates and prepared by Ed Krol, covers the basic utilities used to access the network and then guides the reader through Internet's 'databases of databases'. The book also covers how to find software and how to deal with network problems and other troublesome issues."

— *UNIX Review*

"You can imagine that on Friday (the day I received *The Whole Internet*), the moment I laid it down, someone else was snapping it up. I had to guard it with my life! I think that pretty much speaks for itself."

— Phil Draughon, *Sr. Analyst, Distributed Systems, ACNS Networking*

"Still touted as the Internet bible...it has a superbly organized catalog and very good instructions. An excellent guide."

— *Knight-Ridder News Service*

"If you read just one technical manual this year, let it be *The Whole Internet User's Guide & Catalog*. Author Ed Krol, a University of Illinois computer administrator, has written a surprisingly clear and much-needed guide to services available on the world's largest and fastest-growing computer network."

— Beppi Crosariol, *Financial Times of Canada*

"*The Whole Internet User's Guide & Catalog* is not for computer experts, but for teachers, students, researchers, and business people who need to use the Internet. It is also for those who simply want to explore new means of accessing information, such as university library catalogs, electronic conferences, or electronic journals throughout the expanding world-wide network of computer networks."

— *Harvard Educational Review*

"The first half tells how Internet works and explains features most people will need. The second half describes services that are new even to people who've 'lived' online for years: whois, gopher, archie and others in development. There's a catalog of popular Internet resources (compiled using services described in the book), a brief but helpful glossary, and an invaluable Quick Reference Card."

— *Whole Earth Review*

"By far the easiest way to plumb the mysteries of the Internet is to acquire a new book called *The Whole Internet User's Guide & Catalog*. In addition to explaining the fairly complex process of creating an Internet address—Krol's is e-krol@uiuc.edu—the book shows you how to find the files you need and how to download them no matter how you are accessing the net."

— Jim Coates, *The Chicago Tribune*

"I recommend this book for anyone who is even thinking about using the Internet. It should also be mandatory reading for those (like managers) who need to be convinced about the value of Internet access, and why they should get access for their company or organization."

— Stephan M. Chan, *UniForum Monthly*

"It is for the rapidly expanding population of new networkers that Krol intends his book. His model reader, he explains, is a new graduate student in a nontechnical discipline who needs to use the Internet to do research. The emphasis is on finding your way around and getting what you need, not on the technical details of how the network functions. And yet the book is also an enthusiastic invitation to explore, to enjoy—and to marvel."

— Brian Hayes, *American Scientist*

The Internet "is about as close to mind-melding as it's possible to get—at present. *The Whole Internet User's Guide & Catalog* is an invitation to get on-line with a global intelligence."

> — *Curriculum Review*

"With its digital traffic growing exponentially, the Internet may soon join the telephone system and the interstate highway network as a fundamental utility for the twenty-first century. Commercial enterprises, some of them listed in the ample appendices, already are making the Internet available to users who do not have direct access at work or at school. Krol's book thus is as timely as it is readable: it opens gateways to a new electronic world."

> — *THE SCIENCES*

"Ed Krol's book will enlighten.... Two hours skimming through it taught me as much as I had picked up in months of trial, error, asking impertinent questions of busy people, and more error. *The Whole Internet* is a reference book, but Krol's touch is lighter than most computer-related prose."

> — Mike Holderness, *New Scientist*

The book "is highly recommended reading for anyone who has access to the Internet, whether they are signing on for the first time or have been using it for years."

> — Michael Laudone, *Library Software Review*

"*The Whole Internet User's Guide & Catalog*, by Ed Krol, is considered by many to be the bible of the Internet. A complete user's guide, it covers everything from the basics of E-mail and news groups to the newest developments."

> — *The Executive Educator*

"Krol's is the finest Internet guide I've seen. If you're new to the Internet, get a copy."

> — *Digital News & Review*

"Krol adequately explains to the PC user how to use the Telnet program to log onto a computer connected to the Internet, how to use the FTP (File Transfer Protocol) program to transfer files, and how to send e-mail using a Unix program. You'll also learn to use the fragmented white pages system, read network news, post articles, and use four timesaving programs that hunt down resources on the Internet."

> — Brent Helsop & David Angell, *PC Magazine*

THE WHOLE INTERNET
FOR WINDOWS 95

USER'S GUIDE & CATALOG

ED KROL & PAULA FERGUSON

O'REILLY & ASSOCIATES, INC.
103 MORRIS STREET, SUITE A
SEBASTOPOL CA 95472

THE WHOLE INTERNET FOR WINDOWS 95: USER'S GUIDE AND CATALOG
by Ed Krol and Paula Ferguson

Portions of this book appeared in a slightly different version in
The Whole Internet User's Guide and Catalog, second edition,
© 1992, 1994 O'Reilly & Associates, Inc.

Editor: Mike Loukides

Production Editor: Kiersten Nauman

Printing History:

      October 1995:   First Edition.

This book is printed on acid-free paper with 85% recycled content, 15% post-consumer waste.
O'Reilly & Associates is committed to using paper with the highest recycled content available
consistent with high quality.

ISBN: 1-56592-155-0   [11/95]

TABLE OF CONTENTS

PREFACE

This is a book about the Internet, the world's largest computer network. It's aimed at the "garden variety" computer user: not the expert or the computer aficionado, just someone who has a job to get done. To those of us who have been using the Internet for a long time, a lot of what we discuss has become commonplace. But to get a sense of what the Internet is, and why this book is important, we need to take a few steps back.

About twelve years ago, a minor revolution occurred when personal computers became common. Within a few years everyone had a computer at home or in the office. And, to be honest, most people thought that was adequate: a little help doing budget planning, a nice word processor for writing letters, and we were satisfied. Some visionaries talked about computers as information appliances: you could use your home or office computer to connect to the national news services, get stock reports, do library searches, even read professional journals or literary classics—but, at the time, these were far-reaching ideas.

Well, time has passed since computers first moved from behind the "glass wall" into our offices and homes. In those dozen or so years, another revolution, arguably more important than the first, has taken place. That revolution is computer networking. Personal computers are great, but computers become something special when they're connected to each other.

With the Internet, networking has come of age. The information resources that visionaries talked about in the early 80's are not just research topics that a few advanced thinkers can play with in a lab—they're realities that you can tap into from your home. Once you're connected to the Internet, you have instant access to an almost indescribable wealth of information. You have to pay for some of it, sure—but most of it is available for free. Through electronic mail and bulletin boards (called newsgroups in Internet lingo), you can use a different kind of resource: a worldwide supply of knowledgeable people, some of whom are certain to share your interests, no matter how obscure. It's easy to find a discussion group on almost any topic, or to find people interested in forming a new discussion group. While free advice is often worth what you pay for it, there are also lots of well-informed experts who are more than willing to be helpful.

In the three years since the first edition of the UNIX version of this book appeared, the Internet has become an even richer place. The Internet has surpassed critical mass largely because of the World Wide Web, which made the Internet friendly for the average person-on-the-street. When I first wrote, the Web was a promising experiment; since then, it has completely changed the face of the Internet. People are getting on because they are expected to be on-line. You can read about the Internet in *Time*, watch news items about it on your local TV station, and even see some advertisements giving electronic mail and World Wide Web addresses. There are also more (and better) resources: there's a whole world of multimedia resources, including museums, exhibitions, art galleries, and shopping malls, that didn't exist three years ago. Even the visionaries would be astonished by what we've achieved.

Well, then, where do you start? Getting a handle on the Internet is a lot like grabbing a handful of Jello—the firmer your grasp is, the more it oozes down your arm. You don't need to deal with Jello in this manner. To eat it, you just need the right tool: a spoon. And you need to dig in and start eating. The same is true of the Internet. You don't need to be an expert in telephone lines, data communications, and network protocols for it to be useful. And no amount of gushing about the Net's limitless resources will make the Internet useful. You just need to know how to use some tools and to start working with them.

As for uses, we've got millions of them. They range from the scholarly (you can read works analyzing Dante's *Divine Comedy*); to the factual (you can look at agricultural market reports); to the recreational (you can get ski reports for Aspen); to the humorous ("How do I cook Jello?"). It is also an amazing tool for collaboration: working with other people on your own *magnum opus*.

In a sense, the existence of this book is a tribute to the power and usefulness of the Internet. Mike Loukides, the editor, and I met via electronic mail. Network users were clamoring to get me to update a help guide I wrote a long time ago, *The Hitchhiker's Guide to the Internet*. I was about to volunteer when Mike sent me an electronic mail message and asked "How about doing it as a book?" This spurred a number of messages about outlines and time frames until both were finalized. The legalities and contracts were handled by the Postal Service; electronic contracts were too commercial for the Internet at the time, and are still too high-tech for courts to deal with. We were on our way.

Shortly thereafter, via the Net, I was shipped macro libraries to use in production, and began shipping chapters to Mike, all by e-mail. He would annotate, change, and ship them back to me by the same means. Occasionally, we would trade file directories, screen images, and illustrations. Except for the final review copies and illustrations, everything was handled via the Internet. The whole process was accomplished with fewer than ten telephone calls.

Think for a minute about what this means. Traditional Post Office service between Illinois (where I live) and Connecticut (where Mike lives) takes three days. If you want to pay extra, you can use a courier service and cut the time down to one day. But I can ship the entire book to Mike over the Internet in a few minutes.

Trying to write about the point-and-click interfaces of Windows 95 produced new challenges: how was I supposed to share screen images with Mike and the rest of O'Reilly's staff? The Internet was up to the task. I put up a World Wide Web server called WebSite on my Windows 95 computer—then anyone who knew the address could access the figures over the Net.* The uses for the Internet are changing as quickly as people can develop new software. New software introduces new functionality to the same old Internet.

We also gathered the information in the *Resource Catalog* without having to leave home. We watched newsgroups, followed e-mail discussions, and used various tools to acquire the information for the catalog, all of which are explained in the book. Before including any of the resources, we verified that they really existed by reaching out across the network and touching them.

It was almost a year before I finally met some of the amazingly professional people at O'Reilly & Associates, who helped me create my first book. It's always an interesting experience to finally meet network acquaintances, and in this case it was even more interesting, since I had spent thousands of hours with them electronically.

Audience

This book is intended for anyone using Windows 95 who wants access to the Internet's tremendous resources. It's a book for professionals, certainly, but not computer professionals. It's designed for those who want to use the network, but who don't want to become a professional networker in order to use it. If you're a biologist, or a librarian, or a lawyer, or a clergyman, or a high school teacher, or _____ (fill in your profession here), there's a lot of material and data available that will help you do your job. At the same time, you'll probably find recent Supreme Court opinions or chromosome maps much more interesting than the network itself. You want to use the network as a tool; you don't want to make the network your life. If this description fits you, you need this book. It will get you

---

* WebSite is available from O'Reilly & Associates.

started and point you towards some interesting resources. If, after this, you find that networking becomes your life—well, that's your decision. The Internet has a way of becoming habit-forming.

Very specifically: while I was writing this book, my model audience was a new graduate student in a non-technical discipline (i.e., not computer science or any form of engineering) who needed to use the Internet to do research. Of course, this presumes an audience ranging from Italian scholars to sociologists to physicists, with a correspondingly wide range of computer experience. I do assume that you're computer literate—if you weren't you probably wouldn't even be looking at this book—and that you are familiar with the basics of using Windows 95.

This book is also intended for the experienced network administrator: the one whose job it is to keep a company's or campus's networks working reasonably well. No, you're not supposed to read it; you probably know everything in here already. If you have this job, you probably spend most of your time answering the same fifty questions. When a new crop of students or employees arrives, you might not get any work done for weeks. With any luck, this book answers most of their questions. From the beginning, we were trying to write a book that would answer as many questions as possible. If you are a network administrator, this book is intended for you—so you can give it away, or post a note on your door saying, "Go to the bookstore, buy this book, and read it before bugging me!"

As with all Nutshell handbooks, O'Reilly & Associates is interested in hearing from readers. If you have any comments or suggestions, please send them to nuts@ora.com. (If you don't know what this e-mail address means, read Chapter 5, *Electronic Mail.*)

What Software Is Discussed

I assume that you have Windows 95 installed on your computer. That means, at a minimum, that you have basic network support for LAN and dial-up connections, plus Telnet and FTP applications, plus a version of Microsoft Exchange with Internet e-mail disabled.

That's enough to get going, but you certainly don't want to end there. At a minimum, you also want Microsoft's Internet Jumpstart Kit, which includes the Internet Explorer (Microsoft's World Wide Web browser), Internet support for Exchange (Microsoft's e-mail client), and an installation wizard that makes set-up easier. Here's how you can get the Internet Jumpstart Kit:

- It's pre-installed on new computers that are ordered with Windows 95.

- It's part of the Microsoft Plus! package, which you can buy for under $50.

- It's available for free via FTP; Appendix B, tells you how to get it and install it.

There's no two ways about it; you want the Internet Jumpstart Kit.

This book covers all the applications that are shipped with Windows 95 or the Internet Jumpstart Kit. However, the Internet has a long history of independent software development; you should investigate alternatives to Microsoft's offerings, if only to learn what's available. This book discusses a number of these packages, including:

- Netscape Navigator, for browsing the World Wide Web and reading news (trial version available for free)

- Trumpet for reading news (shareware)

- Eudora for e-mail (free)

A newsreader, for which Netscape or Trumpet will suffice, is one significant omission in Microsoft's offering.[*] Gopher, WAIS, and Archie clients are also omitted—one can argue that they're no longer necessary. I think they still belong in the complete Internet user's toolkit, so I've discussed popular freeware versions.

Whether you use Microsoft's applications or scrape together your own set is ultimately up to you. Experimenting with new tools (or "toys") is a big part of the Internet tradition; I recommend you try it.

Approaching This Book

Of course, there are many ways to approach the Internet; likewise, there are many ways to read this book. Here are a few suggestions. If you:

Are completely new to the Internet
> Start at the beginning and read to the end. You might want to pay particular attention to the *Resource Catalog* and Appendix A, *Getting Connected to the Internet.* You'll also find Chapter 6, *The World Wide Web*, of interest. The Web is the most user-friendly Internet application now available; it's what all the media hype is about. But, basically, you ought to read the entire book. If you want, you can skim Chapter 3, *How the Internet Works*, and Chapter 4, *What's Allowed on the Internet?*, which explain how the Internet works and what's allowed, but please revisit these later.

Are familiar with the Internet, but not a user
> Skip to Chapter 5; in this chapter, we start discussing the basic utilities that you use on the Internet.

Are an experienced Internet user
> Page through the book front to back. Pay special attention to things which are unique to Windows 95.

Have used the Internet casually
> Read the first four chapters to get the background you may have missed; then scan the Table of Contents for chapters whose topics are unfamiliar to you. Do

---

[*] Although a newly announced beta version of the Internet Explorer has a newsreader built into it.

make sure you are familiar with the World Wide Web (Chapter 6). Many of the following chapters describe how to do other things through the Web interface.

Want to get connected to the Internet
Look at Appendix A, which discusses various ways of getting a connection, and Appendix B, *Setting Up Your Internet Connection*, which discusses configuring your computer for Internet access.

Want to know what's available before committing yourself
Look at the *Resource Catalog*.

Use Windows 3.1
Read the whole book except for Appendix B and the material on Microsoft's Internet Explorer and Exchange. The other tools described will work for Windows 3.1. Configuration, unfortunately, is completely different.

Conventions

The following typographic conventions are used in this book:

Italic is used for the following cases:

- Names of the USENET newsgroups; for example, *rec.music.folk*.

- UNIX program names and filenames on the Internet; for example, */etc/hosts*.

- "Variables"—place holders that the reader will replace with an actual value—are printed in *italic*. For example, in the command **ftp** *hostname*, you must substitute the name of a computer on the Internet for *hostname*.

- Explanatory comments within code examples.

Bold is used to indicate commands that are typed at a prompt, i.e., when the **mget** command is issued within FTP. **Bold** is also used for the following cases:

- Input typed literally by the user; for example, **get hosttable.txt**.

- Internet names, addresses, and domains; for example, **ora.com**.

- Menu titles, menu items, folders, and references to icons are printed in **bold**. For example, "Select **Save As** from the **File** menu. Click the **Home** button."

- **Edit —> Copy** should be interpreted as "pull down the **Edit** menu and select Copy."

- Labels for areas on the screen to be filled in by you are in **bold**. For example, enter the destination for your e-mail message in the **To:** box.

Constant Width   is used within examples to show output from the computer.

Constant Bold   is used within examples of interactive sessions to show commands or other text that would be typed literally by the user.

Constant Italic | is used in examples to show variables for which a substitution should be made that applies to your specific situation.

UPPERCASE type | or capitalization of initial letter is used to show names of services or protocols such as BITNET or Archie. UPPERCASE is also used to discuss filenames on personal computers; for example, SYSTEM.INI.

Acknowledgments

A whole host of people helped with this book. First and foremost is my wife Margaret. Without her support and help, it never would have come to pass. She read and corrected most of it, searched Gopher for resources, and tried things to see if my explanations really were sufficient for a computer professional to use the Internet. Also, she took over enough of the running of our home to give me time to devote to the project.

Next comes my daughter Molly, who did without me in many ways for the better part of a year while I was writing. (This is Molly's second experience with computing fame—she was the toddler with a penchant for emergency-off switches, after whom "Molly-guards" are named in the "Hackers Dictionary.")

Then there is Mike Loukides, the editor, project leader, confidence builder, and cheerleader, who dragged me, sometimes kicking and screaming, to the finish line. In the beginning, Mike helped me to think through just what the book needed to contain, and then made sure that everything made it in. Near the end, when Tim O'Reilly asked us to beef up the coverage of a couple of topics, Mike did most of the restructuring and wrote a significant part of the new material.

A large number of other O'Reilly people had a hand in getting this out in a timely fashion. Paula Ferguson quickly became an expert on Windows 95 configuration, and also wrote the chapters on the World Wide Web, Gopher, and WAIS. Stephen Spainhour had the inglorious task of fixing lots of "little pieces": the introduction to the *Resource Catalog*, the Service Provider list, and the section on Eudora in Chapter 5. David Futato pulled together the list of service providers, with help from Jane Ellin.

Next are all the people at the University of Illinois who helped. George Badger, the head of the Computing and Communications Service Office, for the support I needed with the project. Beth Scheid for picking up some pieces of my real job while I was preoccupied with book-related problems. The real technical people, who answered some bizarre questions and made some of the examples possible: Charley Kline, Paul Pomes, Greg German, Lynn Ward, Albert Cheng, Sandy Seehusen, Bob Booth, Randy Cotton, Allan Tuchman, Bob Foertsch, Mona Heath, and Ed Kubaitis. The faculty of the Graduate School of Library Science was also involved, especially Greg Newby, who had a number of suggestions about how to approach the searching tools of the Internet.

Two people were my test audience: Lisa German, a recent library science graduate, and Pat King, a then neophyte system administrator. They knew little about the Internet when they began reading the book as it was written, chapter by chapter. They pointed out all the things that were used before or were just plain explained too technically. Lisa also spent many hours visiting most of the notable servers on the Internet, searching for resources. It's pretty amazing what someone with a knowledge of common cataloging words and phrases can do with a search tool, but I guess that's what librarians are trained to do.

A large group of people read the book, or just pieces of it, checking for technical errors, inconsistencies, and "useful stuff that I left out." These included Andrew Schulman, Eric Pearce, Robin Peek, Jerry Peek, Mitch Wright, Rick Adams, Tim Berners-Lee, Susan Calcari, Deborah Schaffer, Peter Deutsch, Alan Emtage, Mike Cornell, Chris Schulte, Martyne Hallgren, and Jim Williams. The book would not be anywhere near as useful without their help.

The interior design of the book, which is a departure from O'Reilly & Associates' previous books, was sparked by a comment of Dale Dougherty's. He thought it a shame that the standard dry "technical book" interior didn't live up to the whimsical promise of Edie Freedman's cover. Tim O'Reilly picked up on that comment, and insisted on a redesign to make the book and catalog more accessible to a non-technical audience. Edie actually developed the design (with her usual flair) and selected all of the illustrations for both the chapter dividers and the catalog. Her design work was not just something that happened after the book was done, but an integral part of how it turned out. The design was updated by Nancy Priest, and then implemented in **troff** by Lenny Muellner, something no sane person should be asked to do. It included the illustrations of Chris Reilley. The text was copy-edited by Kiersten Nauman, who corrected more typos than I thought existed.

Kiersten also served as the Production Editor on this book, and did a wonderful job of editing the *Resource Catalog* and bringing it up to date. Marcia Ciro implemented the design for the Catalog in Quark, Sheryl Avruch and Nicole Gipson verified the resources, and Edie put in a late night to solve a last-minute crisis. Production was very much a team effort: Sheryl, Nicole, Jane, David, and Mary Anne Weeks Mayo all deserve great thanks. Additionally, Clairemarie Fisher O'Leary wrote the colophon and Ellen Siever created the table of contents. Nancy Priest, Corrie Willing, and Kismet McDonough-Chan performed the quality-control reviews, and Seth Maislin wrote the index.

Also, thanks to Microsoft for letting us be part of their beta program. This allowed us early access to the software.

Finally, I'd like to thank the people at Yoyodyne Software Systems, especially John McMahon and Stuart Vance, whose domain I invaded.

Ed Krol

We'd Like to Hear from You

We have tested and verified all of the information in this book to the best of our ability, but you may find that features have changed (or even that we have made mistakes!). Please let us know about any errors you find, as well as your suggestions for future editions, by writing:

O'Reilly & Associates, Inc.
103 Morris Street, Suite A
Sebastopol, CA 95472
1-800-998-9938 (in the US or Canada)
1-707-829-0515 (international/local)
1-707-829-0104 (FAX)

You can also send us messages electronically. To be put on the mailing list or request a catalog, send e-mail to:

info@ora.com   (via the Internet)
uunet!ora!info   (via UUCP)

To ask technical questions or comment on the book, send e-mail to:

bookquestions@ora.com (via the Internet)

## CHAPTER ONE

WHAT IS THIS BOOK ABOUT?

Something for Everyone
What You Will Learn
What You Need
What an Internet Connection Means
How This Book Is Organized

If you wanted to tinker with horseless carriages in the early 1900's, you fell in with other tinkerers and learned by doing. There were no books about automobiles, no schools for would-be mechanics, no James Martin courses. The market was too small for these training aids. In addition, there were good reasons to fall in with a group of experts: early cars were so unreliable that they could hardly be called transportation. When your car broke down, you needed to fix it yourself, or have some good friends come to the rescue. You fiddled and asked questions. Soon you could answer questions for a novice. Eventually, you might become a highly regarded mechanic. When you got to this level, your car might actually be useful transportation instead of an expensive hobby.

Ten years ago, the Internet was in much the same state. The network had only a few thousand users. All of these users either had ready access to experts or were experts themselves. And they needed expertise—the network was slow and unreliable. Its major purpose was not to do anything useful, but to help people learn how to build and use networks.

In the past ten years, the number of Internet users has increased ten thousand-fold; thousands of new users are being added daily. These people use the network for their daily work and play. They demand reliability, and don't want to be mechanics. They want to be chemists, librarians, meteorologists, kindergarten teachers, and students, who happen to use the network. So now they demand documentation—something to read on the train to work to improve their job skills. They are computer-literate, but not network-literate. This book is about network literacy.

As we all know, the Internet has experienced incredible growth in the past few years. You can hardly go a week without seeing articles about it in *Time* or *Newsweek*, and newspaper ads frequently list Internet addresses.

One reason for the explosive growth of the Internet has been the many Windows users who have come on-line. With the release of Windows 95, I expect this trend to continue. Windows 3.1 was a pretty hostile environment for the beginning Internet user. You had to find and install your own networking support, and the operating system itself wasn't terribly reliable; you often had to reboot because something obscure went wrong. Windows 95 changes all that. Not only is it a more reliable operating system with improved multi-tasking, it also comes with networking support built-in. For the first time, networking is as easy and reliable for the Windows user as it has been for UNIX users. You won't have the system hang on you at awkward moments; you don't have to hunt for networking tools; and if you do go hunting for some fancy experimental application, you're much more likely to find that it works properly with everything else. With Windows 95, it is easier than ever for Windows users to get on the Internet without becoming computer experts.

Something for Everyone

The usefulness of the Internet parallels the history of computing, with a lag of about ten years. About twelve or thirteen years ago, personal computers brought computing from the realm of technical gurus to the general public: "the rest of us," as Apple said in their advertisements. The Internet is currently making the same transition.

As with personal computers (or, for that matter, automobiles), the Internet made the transition from an expert's plaything to an everyday tool through a feedback loop. The network started to become easier to use—in part because the tools were better, in part because it was faster and more reliable. Of the people who were previously scared away from the Internet, the more venturesome started to use it. These new users created a demand for new resources and better tools. The old tools were improved, and new tools were developed to access new resources, making the network easier to use. Now another group of people started finding the Internet useful. The process repeated itself; it's still repeating itself.

Whatever their sophistication, Internet users are, as a whole, looking for one thing: information. They find information from two general classes of sources: people and computers. It's easy to forget about the Internet's "people" resources, but they're just as important (if not more so) as the computers that are available. Far from being a machine-dominated wasteland, where antisocial misfits sporting pocket protectors flail away at keyboards, the Internet is a friendly place to meet people just like yourself. You're a potential network user if you are:

- A science teacher who needs to remain current and develop curricula

- A Unitarian-Universalist minister in a town of fundamentalists, looking for some spiritual camaraderie

- A criminal lawyer who needs to discuss a case with someone who has a particular kind of legal expertise

- An eighth grader looking for others whose parents don't understand real music

And so on. For all of these people, the Internet provides a way of meeting others in the same boat. It's possible—in fact, it's usually easy—to find an electronic discussion group on almost any topic, or to start a new discussion group if one doesn't already exist.

The Internet also provides these people with access to computer resources. The science teacher can access a NASA-funded computer that provides information—past, present, and future—about space science and the space program. The minister can find the Bible, the Koran, and the Torah, waiting to be searched for selected passages. The lawyer can find timely transcriptions of U.S. Supreme Court opinions in Project Hermes.[*] The eighth grader can discuss musical lyrics with other eighth graders or can appear to be an expert among adults.

This is just the beginning. Sure, you will still find a lot of things about computer internals and the network itself, but this is quickly being eclipsed by information about non-computer-related fields. A large part of this book is a catalog of information sources that you can access through the Internet. In creating this catalog, we picked as broad a range of sources as possible to show that the Net really does have something for everyone. If we cataloged every resource on the Internet, the book would be huge—and by the time we finished, it would be out of date. We tried to pick a few gems, fairly stable resources which we hope will be good examples of what's out there. Since one person's gem is another's muck, we grouped the catalog by subject.

The nice thing about the Internet is that you play on your terms. When trying something new in person, you're likely to be plagued by doubts. You hear about a bridge gathering at the community center, and wonder whether you're good enough, whether you're too good—maybe even whether your ex-spouse will be there. On the network, you can:

- Devote as much or as little time as you like

- Become casual acquaintances with someone, or fast friends

- Observe discussions or take part in them

- Walk away from anything you find objectionable, or stand fast and fight every wrong

If you like, you can make your collected works of poetry available to anyone who would like to read them. There is very little risk, so you might as well try.

---

[*] See "Supreme Court Rulings" in the Law section of the *Resource Catalog*.

What You Will Learn

Just as there is no one use for the network, there is also no one way to use the network. If you learn everything in this book, you will become a competent network user. You will know how to access every common thing on the network, and you'll know how to get the software needed to do the uncommon things. However, this book provides only one path. There are different software packages and philosophies of use which you may like better—nothing's wrong with them.

In particular, here's what we'll cover:

- How to send electronic mail to other people who use the Internet. The Internet provides worldwide e-mail delivery. We'll cover Microsoft Exchange and Eudora, another popular e-mail tool.

- How to access network resources using the higher-level tool that everyone is talking about, the World Wide Web. We'll cover Microsoft's Internet Explorer and Netscape Navigator, the state-of-the-art Web browser. We'll also talk about their less spectacular but still very useful cousin, Gopher.

- How to read and participate in group discussions (USENET news). There are discussion groups for topics ranging from the obscure to the bizarre to the practical.

- How to log on to other computers on the Internet (Telnet). Many computers are "publicly available" for various kinds of work. Some of these computers allow anyone to use them; for some, you have to arrange for an account in advance. Some of these computers can be used for "general-purpose" work; others provide some special service, like access to a library catalog or a database.

- How to move files from one computer to another (FTP). There are many public archives scattered around the network, providing files that are free for the taking. Many of these archives provide source code for various computer programs, but other archives hold recipes, short stories, demographic information, and so on. You name it, you can probably find it, or something reasonably close.

- How to locate various network resources, ranging from people to software to general databases, using all the common tools currently available. One of the Internet's problems is that it's too rich; there are so many resources available, it's hard to find what you want, or to remember where you found it. A few years ago, the network was like a library without a catalog. The "cataloging" tools are just now being put into place. We'll tell you how to use some new and exciting tools (and some older, less exciting tools) to locate almost anything you might possibly want, ranging from people and software to sociological abstracts and fruit-fly stocks.

With the tools I've just mentioned, you'll have the network at your fingertips. As I said earlier, getting Internet tools used to be a problem for Windows users: you had to buy them (often from many different sources), or hunt up public domain (free) equivalents. The free software was good, but presented its own difficulty: if you weren't already on the Net, you couldn't get software that was only available from the Net.

Windows 95 breaks this vicious cycle. Internet support, together with the most basic tools (FTP and Telnet clients) are integrated into Windows 95 directly. By itself, this would give you a very 1985-ish view of the Internet. The other important parts—a World Wide Web browser (Internet Explorer), an Internet e-mail driver for Microsoft's e-mail program (Exchange), and an installation wizard—are a part of a package called the Internet Jumpstart Kit. There are many ways to get the Internet Jumpstart Kit: if you buy a computer with Windows 95 installed, you already have it; if you buy the Microsoft Plus! package, it's included; and you can get it via anonymous FTP (see Appendix B, *Setting Up Your Internet Connection*).

I've let the Windows 95 and Internet Jumpstart Kit offerings guide my coverage in this book. I opted, first, to include any product which came with the Windows 95 distribution. You already have them, so they are a good place to start. Next, I included features that came with the Internet Jumpstart Kit. If you're running Windows 95, you probably like Microsoft products (or were forced into liking them by your IS department), and might like to stick with one vendor. In case you'd prefer to "roll your own" collection of tools, I've covered the most important alternatives to the Microsoft products. I've also covered the few essential pieces that are missing from the Microsoft offerings. All the non-Microsoft tools are available from the Net; either free or as shareware.*

For the most part, what you can do on the Internet is defined by the network itself, not by the software you run on your computer to gain access. As you become more experienced, you may hear about different tools that might be more convenient for doing what you want to do. Go ahead and use them. Experimentation is an important part of the Internet culture. You will probably find the transition easy, since the basic functions will be that same. It's like buying a new car. If you know how to drive, you can sit down in any kind of car and use its basic function—driving. It's only when you start dealing with the ancillary features, like setting the clock, that you may need the owner's manual.

What You Need

You need three things to explore and use the Internet: a desire for information, the ability to use a computer, and access to the Internet. Desire for information is the most important. Information is what the Internet offers: what you want, when you want it—not "details at noon, six, and eleven, stay tuned." Without that desire, this book's contents won't impress you. If I say, "Let's check the agricultural markets, the special nutritional requirements of AIDS patients, ski conditions,

---

* One drawback of the non-Microsoft tools is that many aren't yet available as 32-bit (Windows 95) applications. You can still use 16-bit versions; we expect 32-bit versions to be available in the near future.

and home beer recipes," and you reply, "So what?" then you're not ready. If your response is, "Wow," then the Internet is for you.

You use the Internet with a computer. You don't have to be a computer scientist to use it. You do need to be able to operate a computer, run existing programs, and understand what "files" are. Some computer jargon might help, but mostly you need a couple of very basic buzzwords:

bit The smallest unit of information. A bit can have the value 1 or the value 0. Everything in computing is based on collecting hunks of bits together, manipulating them, and moving them from place to place. For example, it takes eight bits to represent a standard alphabetic character.

K A suffix meaning "about 1000," derived from the Greek kilo. For example, 8.6K characters means 8600 characters. In computing, K may refer to 1000 or 1024 depending on the context—but who cares? For our purposes, "about 1000" is good enough.

click
A verb meaning "to select something with a mouse." Sliding a mouse around on the desk moves an arrow on the screen. Programs that use a mouse frequently display simulated "push buttons" on the screen. You activate those buttons by positioning the arrow on the button you want to push, and pressing the button on the mouse. This is commonly called "clicking" that button.

If I did my job in writing this book, you will learn anything else you need to know along the way. How's that for going out on a limb?

Finally, you need an Internet connection. This book is oriented toward someone who has a connection and needs to know how to use it. That connection can take a variety of flavors, ranging from a full time connection via a local area network (LAN) to a dial-up connection using some software called SLIP or PPP. All the software to do either of these kinds of connections comes with Windows 95—it just needs to be configured correctly to fit your environment. If you don't have a connection, Appendix A, *Getting Connected to the Internet*, discusses how to get one; Appendix B tells you how to configure your computer. If you already have a connection and just want to get on with using the Net, you can skip the next section.

What an Internet Connection Means

If you ask someone, "Are you connected to the Internet?" you might get some strange answers. The question has a good, precise answer, but that's not what many people think about. For many people, the question, "Are you connected" is similar to the question "Do you shop at J.C. Penney's?" Shopping at J.C. Penney's means different things to different people. To some, Penney's is a store at the mall; to others, it is a catalog; and to still others, it is an Internet site. Whether the answer to the question is "yes" or "no" probably depends on whether the respondent has been able to get what he or she wanted at Penney's, not the means by which the purchases were made. The same is true of Internet connections. If I ask,

"Are you connected?" the question you are likely to hear is, "Can I do the Internet things I want to do?" For example, it's common to hear CompuServe users talk about their "Internet connection" because they can send e-mail to Internet people. In fact, CompuServe users don't really have an Internet connection; they can only get at a few of the Internet's many services in a fairly limited way. Before you get started, it's important to know what a connection means. Once you know that, you can figure out whether or not you already have one; if you don't have one, you can determine what kind of connection service you want to buy and how much you should pay.

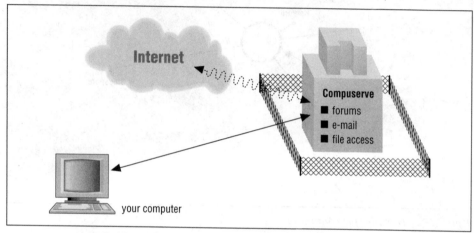

Figure 1–1: Connecting through an on-line service

What do you get when you connect to a traditional on-line service, like CompuServe, and how is the Internet different? Describing CompuServe is the easy part. It has a corporate headquarters, an accounting office, a stock price, and so on. It has a list of services that it offers. You get some software (in the case of CompuServe, WinCIM), subscribe, and then use that software to access CompuServe's resources—but whatever you do, you do through CompuServe and WinCIM. If you want to make data (software, your intimate diaries, product reviews) available to someone else, you make arrangements with CompuServe to put it on their computers. If you want to get someone else's data, you can only get stuff that he or she has made available by prior arrangement with CompuServe. And whatever you do, you do through WinCIM, software that CompuServe provides.

The Internet is much more nebulous—and that's its beauty. The Internet is really like a giant office LAN (local area network—like Novell). Just as your office computer can use a LAN to grab a file from your co-worker, an Internet user can grab a file from a site in Singapore, or can make files available to users all over the world. You don't have to make special arrangements, pay extra fees, or anything; you can "just do it." Your neighbor is as close to you as someone in London.

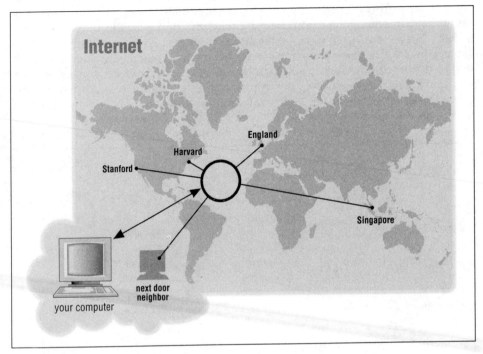

Figure 1–2: True Internet connection

Furthermore, the services that CompuServe offers are defined by its board of directors and the software it offers, WinCIM. They don't change often. The Internet gets new services all the time; someone says "I just invented this; here's some software you'll need if you want to play with it." That's how the World Wide Web got started; in 1992, Tim Berners-Lee and some others wrote some software, gave it away, and the rest is history. In the past year, a half-dozen completely new services have appeared, including live audio and virtual reality.

Why is this possible? Well, it's really possible because of what the Internet isn't. The Internet isn't a corporation that owns bunches of computers that provide certain services—the Internet really is only a mechanism for computers to communicate: at any time, in any place. It's just a way to get data from one place to another, with a minimum of fuss. My computer can contact yours as easily as I can call you on the telephone—in fact, easier. Once our computers can talk, the possibilities are endless. We've already mentioned e-mail and the World Wide Web, but they're nothing compared to what will be available in a few years.

The glue that allows computers to communicate over the Internet is called TCP/IP. To be on the Internet, you must have a TCP/IP-style connection. (Right now, treat TCP/IP as a buzzword; I'll describe what it means in Chapter 3, *How the Internet Works*.) A TCP/IP connection to the Internet is like a Vulcan mind meld on *Star*

Trek. Your computer is part of the network; your computer knows how to contact every computer on the Internet. If you're a home user, you get a TCP/IP connection by using some software called PPP—which is part of Windows 95. (If you're on a LAN, then your LAN needs to be connected to the Internet, which is a more complicated proposition—but it's someone else's job to worry about that.) TCP/IP and PPP are just the pipe that connects your computer to the rest of the world.

My account has been fairly heavily biased against the older on-line service vendors, like CompuServe and America Online. To give them their due, these services are getting a lot better at offering gateways to the Internet. Gateways are "magic doors" between incompatible networks which allow you to do some things through the door, but not everything you might want. If you are currently using one of these providers and are only marginally interested in the Internet, probably the easiest thing is to use their gateway service. It may cost a fair amount if you use it much, and you won't get to do everything you might want, but you also won't have to set up a new account and reconfigure everything in the world. Of course, you'll only get those Internet services that the gateway provides. You certainly won't have access to any new services—the older on-line services are just beginning to offer the World Wide Web, and that's already three years old. If you like playing with the latest toys (and who doesn't?), organizations like CompuServe don't have much to offer.

Getting Connected?

Here's the big surprise: You may already have an Internet connection and not know it. Most Internet users have a connection through work or school: their corporation or university is connected to the Internet, and they use it for work or for pleasure. If your company has an Internet connection, and you have a computer in your office, getting on the Net should be simple. Ask your LAN administrator whether or not the company is on the Internet, and (if so) how you can get your office system hooked up. If you're lucky, you may not have to do anything at all—you might be able to sit down, launch Internet Explorer (see Chapter 6, *The World Wide Web*), and go to work. Don't think this is unrealistic: there are *a lot* of people who are this lucky. If you're unlucky and the administrator says that your company or school is not on the Internet, ask the obvious question, "Why not?" For a small company, some relatively inexpensive Internet connections can give you the kind of worldwide corporate network that, previously, only companies like EXXON or IBM could afford.

If you're not already connected, there are many ways to get connected. These range from large, fairly expensive solutions that are appropriate for large corporations or universities to relatively low-cost solutions that are appropriate for very small businesses or home use. No matter what level you're at, Internet access always comes via an "access provider," an organization whose job it is to sell Internet access. There are access providers for every level of service from expensive dedicated Internet connections to inexpensive dial-up connections for home users. Appendix A lists many (though not all) access providers and the types of service they provide. It also gives you some hints as to how an individual may be able to get connected for little personal cost.*

How This Book Is Organized

This book is organized like a high school woodshop class. First, you talk about the history and theory of carpentry. Then, you discuss tool use and safety, one tool at a time. Next, you go on a field trip to the lumberyard to get a feel for what you have to work with. By the time the class ends, you can make a wine rack, a gun rack, a bookshelf, or whatever might suit you.

In Chapters 2 through 4, we'll start with some history and theory. We'll keep the background material to a minimum—just enough so you can understand why the Internet is like it is. We'll discuss how the Internet works: not a lot of "this bit moves here," but mostly hand-waving and conceptual explanations. This isn't really required reading and can usually be safely skipped, but it's fairly short, and I think it's important. If you get into a bind and have to guess at what is going on, or what to do next, nothing helps more than a feel for how things work. If you would like to know more about the history of the Internet or its technology, there are other books which go into more detail.†

Most of the book (Chapters 5 to 15) discusses how to use the tools that allow your computer to do things on the Internet. I will start with e-mail, the World Wide Web, and News, because these are the most popular services; then, I will talk about some tools, like Telnet, FTP, and Archie, that still have a place in the complete Netter's tool box. Their popularity has waned, but these tools are still effective and they are often the quickest and most efficient means of accomplishing specific tasks. I've tried to focus on what you're likely to do and why—not just which knob to turn and which button to push, but why you need the buttons and knobs. A lot of attention is paid to some relatively "fuzzy" but ultimately practical issues: what's allowed and what isn't, what's polite and what isn't, what's the best way to find the kind of information you want.

The final large section of this book is a *Resource Catalog*: a list of things you can find on the Internet. It's organized by subject, so you shouldn't have trouble finding topics that interest you. We found these resources by using the tools explained in this book and also by just looking around. The list is not complete, but no list is. Père Marquette didn't throw a dart at a map of the world and decide to look for Indians to convert where the dart landed. He started in a place where he knew

---

* The definitive guide to buying an Internet connection is Susan Estrada's book, *Connecting to the Internet*, published by O'Reilly & Associates.

† The best of these is probably Douglas Comer's book, *Internetworking with TCP/IP: Principles, Protocols, and Architectures* (Prentice Hall, 3 volumes). Technically, it's quite advanced, but it's the standard work on the topic. Additionally, O'Reilly & Associates' *TCP/IP Network Administration* by Craig Hunt provides a complete guide to running a TCP/IP network for practicing system administrators. Finally, O'Reilly's *Networking Personal Computers with TCP/IP*, also by Craig Hunt, is another good reference on the subject.

there were Indians and began walking from there. This is your place to start. Find someplace interesting and begin to look and wander. It's amazing what you will find.

If you still think this thing called the Internet is for you, press on, and you can find out what it really is.

CHAPTER TWO

WHAT IS THE INTERNET?

How Did the Internet Get Started?
What Makes Up the Internet?
Who Governs the Internet?
Who Pays for It?
What Does This Mean for Me?
What Does the Future Hold?

In the last chapter, I talked a lot about how the Internet was different from the traditional on-line services, like CompuServe. However, I didn't say much about what the Internet was—in fact, you probably realized that I said much more about what the Internet was not.

Let's start from the bottom up. On your computer, you have a bunch of files on your disk: programs, documents, and so on. Now, what if your neighbor writes a Word document and wants you to read it? She can put it on a floppy, trot over to your front door, and hand it to you. You can then stick the floppy in your computer and read the file. This was the earliest form of computer networking; it's now called the "Sneakernet."

Of course, people often want to share their work with one another. The more you want to share, the less effective Sneakernet is. For office situations, people developed local area networks (LANs), like Novell and Appletalk. With a LAN, you don't need to carry diskettes back and forth; you can access other people's files just as if they were on your desktop computer. However, if you want to send something to a friend in Reno, you still need to make a diskette and put it in the mail. That's the long-haul version of Sneakernet, and it's even less convenient.

The Internet really is nothing more than a worldwide LAN. Or, perhaps, a worldwide extension of your hard disk. If you're connected to the Internet, you can access all sorts of files (software, encyclopedias, magazines) as if they were on your own disk. Likewise, you "publish" your own material (software, documents, etc.) so that other people can use them. Your computer becomes a lot more interesting when you can trade files with people around the world. It's a lot easier to play with new software, collaborate on projects, or just keep in touch with friends. A lot of people who never write letters have no trouble sending e-mail. Ultimately, the network and what you can do with it are a whole lot more interesting than your computer by itself. The Internet breaks down barriers between you and other computer users: barriers that were created by operating systems, traditional network services, and hardware. As a Windows 95 user with an Internet connection, you can share files with Macintosh users or UNIX users; you can exchange e-mail with CompuServe and America Online users; you can work from your office, or from your home.

It sounds like an oversimplification to say that the Internet is a worldwide LAN. The technology is complicated, but to a user, the effect is the same. In fact, it really isn't an oversimplification to say that the Internet is a mechanism for connecting all the world's office LANs into one big network. Of course, the problem with connecting all the world's LANs is that they're all different: one uses Novell, one uses Appletalk, and so on. A Novell network can't talk to an Appletalk network without an intermediary, and neither can talk to the Internet.

To connect networks into one whole, the networks need to obey a set of standards. Standards are important because they are shared (non-proprietary). If two networks follow the same standards, they can communicate with each other, even if they are using software from different vendors. No one can say "You can't join the Internet because you didn't buy your software from me." For the Internet, the most important protocols are called TCP (Transmission Control Protocol) and IP (Internet Protocol); they are the glue that connects the local networks together. Another standard, called PPP, is a special kind of glue that lets home users take part. The Internet's standards (and its culture) arose in the research and UNIX communities during the 1970's and 1980's. To understand the Internet, it helps to have a sense of how it developed.

How Did the Internet Get Started?

The Internet was born about 25 years ago out of an effort to connect a U.S. Defense Department network called the ARPAnet and various other radio and satellite networks. The ARPAnet was an experimental network designed to support military research—in particular, research about how to build networks that could withstand partial outages (like bomb attacks) and still function. (Think about this when I describe how the Net works; it may give you some insight into the design of the Internet.) In the ARPAnet model, communication always occurs between a source and a destination computer. The network itself is assumed to be unreliable; any portion of the network could disappear at any moment (pick your favorite catastrophe—these days, backhoes cutting cables are more of a threat than bombs). It was designed to require the minimum of information from the computer clients. To send a message on the network, a computer simply had to put its data in an envelope, called an Internet Protocol (IP) packet, and "address" the packets correctly. The communicating computers—not the network itself—were also given the responsibility for ensuring that the communication was accomplished. The philosophy was that every computer on the network could talk, as a peer, with any other computer.

These decisions, like the assumption of an unreliable network, may sound odd, but history has proven that most of them were reasonably correct. With these assumptions, the U.S. was able to develop a working network (the ancestor of the current Internet), and the academic and research users who had access to it were soon addicted. Demand for networking quickly spread. Although the Organization for International Standardization (ISO) was spending years designing the ultimate standard for computer networking, people could not wait. Internet developers in the U.S., the U.K., and Scandinavia, responding to market pressures, began to put their IP software on every conceivable type of computer. It became the only practical method for computers from different manufacturers to communicate. This was attractive to the governments and universities, which didn't have policies saying that all computers must be bought from the same vendor. Everyone bought whichever computer they liked and expected the computers to work together over the network.

At about the same time that the Internet was coming into being, Ethernet local area networks (LANs) were developed. LAN technology matured quietly until roughly 1983, when desktop workstations became available and local networking exploded. Most of these workstations came with Berkeley UNIX, which included IP networking software. Widespread availability of Internet software created a new demand: rather than connecting to a single large time-sharing computer per site, organizations wanted to connect their entire local network to the ARPAnet. Connecting their network would allow all the computers on that LAN to access ARPAnet facilities. At about the same time, many companies and other organizations started building private networks using the same communications protocols as the ARPAnet: namely, IP and its relatives. It became obvious that if these networks could talk together, users on one network could communicate with those on another; everyone would benefit.

One of the most important of these newer networks was the *NSFNET*, commissioned by the National Science Foundation (NSF), an agency of the U.S. government. In the late 80's the NSF created five supercomputer centers at major universities. Up to this point, the world's fastest computers had only been available to weapons developers and a few researchers from very large corporations. By creating supercomputer centers, the NSF was making these resources available for any scholarly research. Only five centers were created because they were so expensive—they had to be shared. This created a communications problem: they needed a way to connect their centers together and to allow the clients of these centers to access them. At first, the NSF tried to use the ARPAnet for communications, but this strategy failed because of bureaucratic and staffing problems.

In response, the NSF decided to build its own network, based on the ARPAnet's IP technology. NSFNET connected the centers with 56,000-bits-per-second* telephone lines. It was obvious, however, that if they tried to connect every university directly to a supercomputing center, they would go broke. You pay for these

---

* This is roughly the ability to transfer two full typewritten pages per second. That's slow by modern standards, but was reasonably fast in the mid 80's.

telephone lines by the mile. A communication line from each campus to the closest supercomputing center, like spokes on a bike wheel, adds up to many miles of phone lines. Therefore, they decided to create regional networks. In each area of the country, schools would be connected to their nearest neighbor. Each chain was connected to a supercomputer center at one point, and the centers were connected together. With this configuration, any computer could eventually communicate with any other by forwarding the conversation through its neighbors.

This solution was successful—and, like any successful solution, a time came when it no longer worked. Sharing supercomputers also allowed the connected sites to share a lot of other things not related to the centers. Suddenly these schools had a world of data and collaborators at their fingertips. The network's traffic increased until, eventually, the computers controlling the network, and the telephone lines connecting them, were overloaded. In 1987, a contract to manage and upgrade the network was awarded to Merit Network Inc., which ran Michigan's educational network, in partnership with IBM and MCI. The old network was upgraded with faster telephone lines (by a factor of 20) and faster computers.

The process of running out of horsepower and getting bigger engines and better roads continues to this day. Millions of Windows and Macintosh users have come on-line in the last few years. The World Wide Web made the Internet friendly to people who weren't computer professionals. The Web's influence, together with media attention, attracted new Internet users, and network traffic soared. Visionaries talk about new applications (like video conferencing) that will increase the network's workload even more. To meet these demands, there are some experimental links that carry traffic 20 times faster than the current system; a lot of work is going into a new version of the network protocols so that the Internet will be able to meet the requirements of the next decade. Unlike changes to the highway system, however, most of these changes aren't noticed by the people trying to use the Internet to do real work. You won't go to your office, log in to your computer, and find a message saying that the Internet will be inaccessible for the next six months because of improvements. Perhaps more importantly, the process of running out of capacity and improving the network has created a technology that's extremely mature and practical. The ideas have been tested; problems have appeared, and problems have been solved.

For our purposes, the most important aspect of the NSF's effort is that it allowed everyone to access the network. Up to that point, Internet access had been available only to researchers in computer science, to government employees, and to government contractors. The NSF promoted universal educational access by funding campus connections only if the campus had a plan to spread the access around. That way, everyone attending a four-year college could become an Internet user.

The demand keeps growing. Now that most four-year colleges are connected, people are trying to get secondary and primary schools connected, along with local libraries. People who have recently graduated from college know what the Internet is good for, and they talk their employers into connecting corporations to the

Internet. All this activity points to continued growth, new networking problems to solve, evolving technologies, and job security for networkers. Many people are going further: after getting a network connection at work, the next logical step is to get a connection directly to their home.

What Makes Up the Internet?

What comprises the Internet is a difficult question; the answer changes over time. Seven years ago the answer would have been easy: all the networks, using the IP protocol, cooperated to form a seamless network for their collective users. This would include various federal networks, a set of regional networks, campus networks, and some foreign networks.

More recently, some non-IP-based networks saw that the Internet was good. They wanted to provide its services to their clientele. So they developed methods of connecting these "strange" networks (e.g., BITNET, DECnets, America Online, CompuServe, etc.) to the Internet. At first these connections, called gateways, merely served to transfer electronic mail between the two networks. Some, however, have grown to translate other services between the networks as well. Are they part of the Internet? Maybe yes and maybe no. It depends on whether, in their hearts, they want to be.

The Microsoft Network (MSN) is a new kind of creature that provides the features of the older networks, like CompuServe, but is also a full-fledged Internet service provider, providing a direct connection to the Internet for those who want it (See Figure 2-1). If you sign up for MSN by itself, you get bulletin boards, chat groups, and added value information services. If you connect to both, you get the MSN features plus the Internet, with full access to the World Wide Web and all the other Internet Services. MSN is discussed in Appendix D, *The Microsoft Network*.

It should be clear that MSN is not the Internet, but just another service provider that can connect you to the rest of the Net. As such, it's fundamentally no different from the guy down the street who offers Internet service from his basement; it's just bigger. You don't have to use MSN; Windows 95 can be used with any organization that offers Internet access. That's the beauty of the Internet: it levels the distinction between big players and small players, linking thousands of different networks into one whole. As a Windows 95 user, you can join whichever network will give you the best service.

Who Governs the Internet?

In many ways the Internet is like a church: it has its council of elders, every member has an opinion about how things should work, and you can either take part or not. It's your choice. The Internet has no president, chief operating officer, or Pope. The constituent networks may have presidents and CEOs, but that's a different issue; there's no single authority figure for the Internet as a whole.

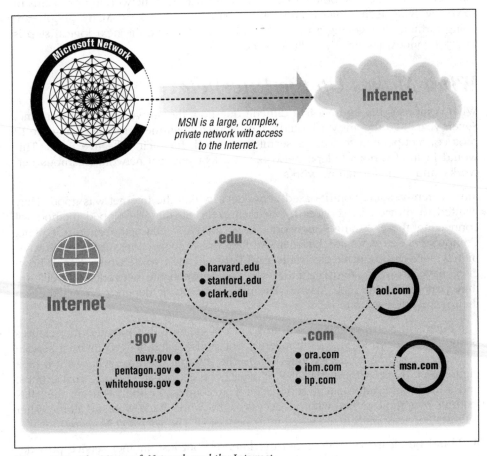

Figure 2–1: The Microsoft Network and the Internet

The ultimate authority for where the Internet is going rests with the *Internet Society*, or ISOC. ISOC is a voluntary membership organization whose purpose is to promote global information exchange through Internet technology.[*] It appoints a council of elders, which has responsibility for the technical management and direction of the Internet.

The council of elders is a group of invited volunteers called the Internet Architecture Board, or the IAB. The IAB meets regularly to "bless" standards and allocate resources, such as addresses. The Internet works because there are standard ways for computers and software applications to talk to each other. These standards allow computers from different vendors to communicate without problems. It's not an IBM-only or Sun-only or Macintosh-only network. The IAB decides when a

---

[*] If you'd like more information, or if you would like to join, see "Internet Organizations" in the *Resource Catalog*.

standard is necessary and what it should be. When a standard is required, the IAB considers the problem, adopts a standard, and announces it via the network. (You were expecting stone tablets?) The IAB also keeps track of various numbers (and other things) that must remain unique. For example, each computer on the Internet has a unique 32-bit address; no other computer has the same address. How does this address get assigned? The IAB worries about this kind of problem. It doesn't actually assign the addresses, but it makes the rules about how to assign them.

As in a church, everyone has opinions about how things ought to run. Internet users express their opinions through meetings of the Internet Engineering Task Force (IETF). The IETF is another volunteer organization; it meets regularly to discuss operational and near-term technical problems of the Internet. When it considers a problem important enough to merit concern, the IETF sets up a "working group" for further investigation. (In practice, "important enough" usually means that there are enough people to volunteer for the working group.) Anyone can attend IETF meetings and be on working groups; the important thing is that the attendees work. Working groups have many different functions, ranging from producing documentation, to deciding how networks should cooperate when problems occur, to changing the meaning of the bits in some kind of packet. A working group usually produces a report. This report could be documentation available to anyone wanting it, or the report could be a recommendation people ought to follow, or it could be sent to the IAB to be declared a standard.

If you go to a church and accept its teachings and philosophy, you are accepted by it, and receive the benefits. If you don't like it, you can leave. The church is still there, but you get none of the benefits. Such is the Internet. If a network accepts the teachings of the Internet, is connected to it, and considers itself part of it, then it is part of the Internet. If a member network finds things it doesn't like, it can address those concerns through the IETF. Some concerns may be considered valid, and the Internet may change accordingly. Some of the changes may run counter to the religion and be rejected. If the network does something that causes damage to the Internet, it could be excommunicated until it mends its evil ways.

Who Pays for It?

The old rule for unraveling mysteries is to follow the money. Well, this won't help you to understand the Internet. No one person or organization pays for it; there is no Internet, Inc. that collects fees from all Internet networks or users. Instead, everyone pays for their part. Networks get together and decide how to connect themselves together and fund these interconnections. A college or corporation pays for its connection to a local or regional network, which in turn pays a national provider for its access.

There is a myth that the Internet is free. It's not; someone pays for every connection to the Internet. Many times these fees aren't passed on to the actual users, which feeds the illusion of "free access." The Government used to pay for the

NSFNET part of the Internet, but that subsidy ended in early 1995, by which time the subsidized part had become a very small part of the whole anyway. There are plenty of individual users who know very well that the Internet isn't free: many users pay monthly or hourly charges for Internet access from home at speeds up to 56K bits per second (the same as the original network backbones). Right now, the fastest growth areas for the Internet are probably small businesses and individuals, and these users are very aware of the price.

What Does This Mean for Me?

The concept that the Internet is not a network, but a collection of networks, means little to the end user. You want to do something useful: run a program or access some unique information. You shouldn't have to worry about how it's all stuck together. Consider the telephone system—it's an internet, too. Pacific Bell, AT&T, MCI, British Telecom, Telefonos de Mexico, and so on, are all separate corporations that run pieces of the telephone system. They worry about how to make it all work together; all you have to do is dial. If you ignore cost and commercials, you shouldn't care if you are dealing with MCI, AT&T, or Sprint. Dial the number and it works.

You only care who carries your calls when a problem occurs. If one switch breaks, only the company that owns the switch can fix it. Different phone companies can talk to each other about problems, but each phone carrier is responsible for fixing problems on its own part of the system. The same is true on the Internet. Each network has its own network operations center (NOC). The operations centers talk to each other and know how to resolve problems. Your site has a contract with one of the Internet's constituent networks, and its job is to keep your site happy. So if something goes wrong, they are the ones to gripe at. If it's not their problem, they'll pass it along.

What Does the Future Hold?

Finally, a question I can answer. It's not that I have a crystal ball—if I did, I'd spend my time on Wall Street instead of writing a book. Rather, these are the things that the IAB and the IETF discuss at their meetings. Most people don't care about the long discussions; they only want to know how they'll be affected. So, here are highlights of the networking future.

New Standard Protocols

When I was talking about how the Internet started, I mentioned the Organization for International Standardization and their set of protocol standards. Well, they finally finished designing it. Now it is an international standard, typically referred to as the ISO/OSI (Open Systems Interconnect) protocol suite. For a while it was assumed that because this was an international standard, the Internet would use it widely. This appears not to be the case, as the benefits are marginal and the grief would be great. Most people feel that "if it ain't broke, don't fix it."

However, there is one thing which is breaking and will need to be fixed. The Internet is running out of addresses. Every computer connected or every portal that allows a temporary connection to the Internet must have a unique address. There is room in the IP packet to address about 2 billion computers. That's far more computers than the 10 million currently connected to the Internet, but it is cause for worry. (The problem really has more to do with the number of networks that can be connected to the Internet, but explaining why is beyond the scope of this book.)

At first, with the crazy growth rates the Internet was experiencing, it appeared we would run out of addresses sometime in 1994. It didn't happen. By conserving and recycling addresses, we may have enough to last until the late 1990's. In the meantime, the IETF is formulating a plan which will allow a migration to a larger number of addresses without requiring everyone on the Internet to install new software on their computers on a particular day.

This effort is usually referred to in the community as either IPv6 (we are currently running IP version 4—don't ask me what happened to version 5) or IPng (IP next generation). IPv6 also provides support for increased security (a significant weakness of the current protocols), and some features that will make live video and other desirable services easier to implement.

Faster Wires

Currently, the Internet's "long haul" lines work at 45 Mbits per second. (This is roughly the speed needed to transfer the entire text of the Bible in one second.) Experimental lines working in the 1 Gbit (1 billion bits per second, or roughly 20 times faster) range are already in place. The people working on these technologies talk a language that, frankly, isn't much understood by everyone else—it's full of acronyms like ATM, SMDS, and SONET. As far as we're concerned, these are just ways to make the network go faster. They're important, but they don't affect you directly unless you have a million dollars or so to spend on networking.

There's also improvement on the home front. Three years ago, a 9600 bps modem was high-tech. Now, 28,800 bps modems are common, and a small but increasing number of home users have ISDN connections which allow 64 kbps or 128 kbps transfers. ISDN is probably in your future—and not too far off, at that. What do these numbers mean? Not much, if you're primarily interested in e-mail, but the Internet is moving toward multimedia applications, for which the bottom line is "faster is better." A Web page that takes a minute to download with today's fastest modems will take 10 or 15 seconds with ISDN.

International Connections

The Internet has been an international network for a long time, but it only extended to the United States' allies and overseas military bases. Now, with the less paranoid world environment, the Internet is spreading everywhere. It's currently in over 80 countries, and the number is rapidly increasing. Eastern European countries that are eager to establish Western scientific ties have wanted to participate for a long time but were excluded by government regulation. Now that the "Iron Curtain" has been raised, they're well represented. Third-world countries that formerly didn't have the means to participate now view the Internet as a way to raise their education and technology levels.

In Europe, the development of the Internet used to be hampered by national policies mandating OSI protocols, regarding IP as a cultural threat akin to EuroDisney. Outside of Scandinavia (where the Internet protocols were embraced long ago), these policies prevented development of large-scale Internet infrastructures. In 1989, RIPE (Reseaux IP Europeens) began coordinating the operation of the Internet in Europe; today, about 25 percent of all hosts connected to the Internet are located in Europe.

At present, the Internet's international expansion is hampered by the lack of a good supporting infrastructure, namely, a decent telephone system. In both Eastern Europe and the third world, a state-of-the-art phone system is non-existent. Even in major cities, connections are limited to the speeds available to the average home anywhere in the U.S., 28,800 bits per second. Typically, even if one of these countries is "on the Internet," only a few sites are accessible. Usually, this is the major technical university for that country. However, as phone systems improve, you can expect this to change too; more and more, you'll see smaller sites, even individual home systems, connecting to the Internet.

Commercialization

Many big corporations have been on the Internet for years. For the most part, their participation has been limited to their research and engineering departments. The same corporations used some other network (usually a private network) for their business communications. Marketing via computer network was unheard of. After all, this IP stuff was only an academic toy. The IBM mainframes that handled their commercial data processing did the "real" networking using a protocol suite called System Network Architecture (SNA).

Businesses are now discovering that running multiple networks is expensive. Some are beginning to look to the Internet for "one-stop" network shopping. They were scared away in the past by policies which excluded or restricted commercial use. Most of these policies have fallen by the wayside. Now, corporations may use the Internet as a tool to solve any appropriate business problems.

Relaxation of the strictures against commercial use should be especially good for small businesses. Motorola or Standard Oil can afford to run nationwide networks connecting their sites, but Ace Custom Software can't. If Ace has a San Jose office and a Washington office, all it needs is an Internet connection on each end. For all practical purposes, they'll have a nationwide corporate network, just like the big boys.

The same is true of marketing on the Internet. L.L. Bean can afford to do a nation-wide mailing of their catalog, but the Cass Lake Bait'n More can't. The Internet can be the great equalizer when it comes to marketing. For very little money Bait'n More can have just as impressive an on-line catalog as L.L. Bean, and compete.

Privatization

Right behind commercialization comes privatization. For years, the networking community has wanted the telephone companies and other for-profit ventures to provide "off-the-shelf" IP connections. That is, just as you can place an order for a jack in your house for your telephone, you could do this for an Internet connection. You order, the telephone installer leaves, and you plug your computer into the Internet. Except for Bolt, Beranek and Newman, the company that used to run the ARPAnet, there weren't any takers. The telephone companies have historically said, "We'll sell you phone lines, and you can do whatever you like with them." Federal government stayed in the network business by default; no one else was interested in the job.

Now that the Internet is big business, the phone companies have started to change their attitude. They and other profit-oriented network purveyors complained that the government ought to get out of the network business—and that has happened. NSFNET, the staple of the Internet, has been shut down. In its place are three Network Access Points, or NAPs, where anyone who wants to be a network provider (and who can afford it) is guaranteed a connection to the Internet. This guarantees continued competition among Internet providers by preventing some well capitalized company from buying up a majority of the Internet and turning it into a monopoly. We are still not to the point where every employee of a tele-phone company knows it is in the Internet business, but that day is quickly approaching.

Since the Clinton administration started talk of the "national information infrastruc-ture," even more players have become involved. Cable TV companies have real-ized that they also own a lot of wire capable of carrying digital signals; that wire already extends into many homes in the U.S. So they've proposed solving the pri-vatization problem by creating their own network, with no government investment required. Their network would piggyback on their existing investment in cable TV. It remains to be seen what will come of this initiative; they've obviously got reli-gion (and money to spend), but they may be writing their own bible. It is clear that cable TV companies are interested in applications that haven't been seen on the Internet yet: interactive home shopping, video games, and so on. It's less clear that they understand the traditional uses of data networking, or that the network can't stop working every time a thunderstorm rolls through.

Although most people in the networking community think that privatization is a good idea, there are some obstacles in the way. Most revolve around funding for the connections that are already in place. Many schools are connected because the government pays part of the bill. If they had to pay their own way, some schools would probably decide to spend their money elsewhere. Major research institutions would certainly stay on the Net, but some smaller colleges might not, and the costs would probably be prohibitive for most secondary schools (let alone grade schools). What if the school could afford either an Internet connection or a science lab? It's unclear which one would get funded. The Internet has not yet become a "necessity" in many people's minds.

Part of the solution to the funding problem comes from a change in the way that government subsidies are distributed. We are quickly moving from the era when the network itself was the project, to an era when the network is a tool to be used in "real" projects. Therefore, rather than funding a network connection to a campus, school, agency, or corporation, subsidy money is moving to project budgets. The people who run the projects can then buy Internet services from a variety of vendors in the open marketplace. This makes a lot of people nervous, because it threatens an existing flow of money (something near and dear to the recipients' hearts). On the other hand, it is probably the only practical way to merge public money and private money into one pool big enough to keep the Internet expanding into the more rural parts of the world.

Well, enough about the history of the information highway system. It's time to walk to the edge of the road, hitch a ride, and be on your way.

CHAPTER THREE

HOW THE INTERNET WORKS

Moving Bits from One Place to Another
Making the Network Friendly

I t's nice to know a little about how things work. It allows you to make sense out of some of the hints you'll see in this book, so they don't seem like capricious rules to be learned by rote. Lest you be scared away, we will explore the guts of the Internet with a maximum amount of hand-waving. We'll never say something like "This field is three bits long"; we won't even think about it! If you want to know more, several books on the Internet's implementation are available.*

In this chapter, we will look at packet-switched networks (like the Internet) and how, by putting TCP/IP on top of such a network, something useful happens. We will talk about the basic protocols that govern Internet communication: TCP and its poor cousin, UDP. These are the network's building blocks. But if you only had the basic protocols, the Internet would be fairly boring, because it would be frustrating and hard to use. When you put the Domain Name System and a few applications on top of the basic protocols, the Internet becomes easily usable.

If you decide that this techno-speak isn't your cup of tea, feel free to skip the beginning of this chapter. Do read the section on the Domain Name System. You'll use it indirectly throughout your Internet career.

---

* Douglas Comer's *Internetworking with TCP/IP: Principles, Protocols, and Architecture*, Volumes I, II, and III (Prentice Hall) is the best source for in-depth information about how the Internet works. However, it is extremely detailed.

Moving Bits from One Place to Another

Modern networking is built around the concept of "layers of service." You start out trying to move bits from here to there, losing some along the way. This level consists of wires and hardware, although not necessarily good wires. Then, you add a layer of basic software to make it easier to work with the hardware. You add another layer of software to give the basic software some desirable features. You continue to add functionality and smarts to the network, one layer at a time, until you have something that's sophisticated and user-friendly. Let's start at the bottom and work our way up.

Packet-Switched Networks

When you try to imagine what the Internet is and how it operates, it is natural to think of the telephone system. After all, both are electronic, both let you open a connection and transfer information, and both are primarily composed of dedicated telephone lines. Unfortunately, this is the wrong picture, and causes many misunderstandings about how the Internet operates. The telephone network is a circuit-switched network. When you make a call, you get a piece of the network dedicated to you. Even if you aren't using it (for example, if you are put on hold), your piece of the network is unavailable to others wishing to do real work. This leads to underutilization of a very expensive resource—the network itself.

A better model for the Internet, strangely enough, is the U.S. Postal Service. The Postal Service is a packet-switched network. You have no dedicated piece of the network. What you want to send is mixed together with everyone else's stuff, put in a pipe, transferred to another post office, and sorted out again. Although the technologies are completely different, the Postal Service is a surprisingly accurate analogy; we'll continue to use it throughout this chapter.

The Internet Protocol (IP)

A wire can get data from one place to another. However, you already know that the Internet can get data to many different places, distributed all over the world. How does this happen?

The different pieces of the Internet are connected by a set of computers called routers, which connect networks together. These networks are sometimes Ethernets, sometimes token rings, and sometimes telephone lines, as shown in Figure 3-1.

The telephone lines and Ethernets are equivalent to the trucks and planes of the Postal Service. They are the means by which mail is moved from place to place. The routers are postal substations; they make decisions about how to route data (or packets), just like a postal substation decides how to route envelopes containing mail. Each substation or router does not have a connection to every other one. If you put an envelope in the mail in Dixville Notch, New Hampshire, addressed

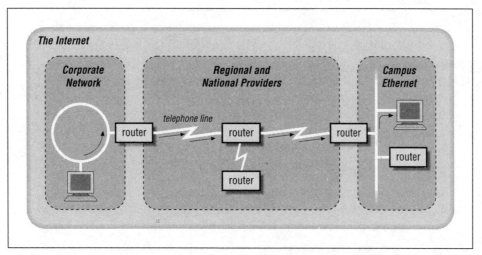

Figure 3-1: Internet hardware

to Boonville, California, the Post Office doesn't reserve a plane from New Hampshire to California to carry it. The local Post Office sends the envelope to a substation, the substation sends it to another substation, and so on, until it reaches the destination. Each substation only needs to know what connections are available, and what is the best "next hop" to get a packet closer to its destination. The Internet works in a similar manner: a router looks at where your data is going and decides where to send it next. The router decides which pipe is best and uses it.

How does the Net know where your data is going? If you want to send a letter, you can't just drop it into the mailbox and expect delivery. You need to put the letter into an envelope, write an address on the envelope, and stamp it. Just as the Post Office has rules that define how its network works, there are rules that govern how the Internet operates. The rules are called protocols. The Internet Protocol (IP) takes care of addressing, or making sure that the routers know what to do with your data when it arrives. Sticking with our Post Office analogy, the Internet Protocol works just like an envelope (Figure 3-2). Some addressing information goes at the beginning of your message; this information gives the network enough information to deliver the packet of data.

Internet addresses consist of four numbers, each less than 256. When written out, the numbers are separated by periods, like this:

```
192.112.36.5
128.174.5.6
```

(Don't worry; you don't need to remember numbers like these to use the network.) The address is actually made up of multiple parts. Since the Internet is a network of networks, the beginning of the address tells the Internet routers what network you are part of. The right end of the address tells that network which

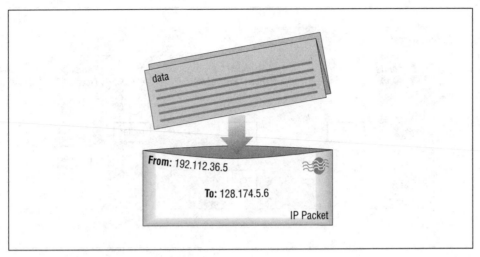

Figure 3–2: IP envelopes

computer or host should receive the packet.[*] Every computer on the Internet has a unique address under this scheme. Again, the Postal Service provides a good analogy. Consider the address "50 Kelly Road, Hamden, CT." The "Hamden, CT" portion is like a network address; it gets the envelope to the correct local post office—the one that knows about streets in a certain area. The address "50 Kelly Road" is like the host address; it identifies a particular mailbox within the Post Office's service area. The Postal Service has done its job when it has delivered the mail to the right local office, and when that local office has put it into the right mailbox. Similarly, the Internet has done its job when its routers have gotten data to the right network, and when that local network has given the data to the right computer, or host, on the network.

For a lot of practical reasons (hardware limitations, in particular), information sent across IP networks is broken up into bite-sized pieces called packets. The information within a packet is usually between one and approximately 1500 characters long. This prevents any one user of the network from monopolizing it, allowing everyone equal access. It also means that when the network is overloaded, its behavior becomes slightly worse for everyone; it doesn't stop dead while a few heavy users monopolize it.

One of the amazing things about the Internet is that on a basic level IP is all you need to participate. It wouldn't be very friendly, but you could get work done if you were clever enough. As long as your data is put in an IP envelope, the

---

[*] Where the network portion ends and the host portion begins is a bit complicated. It varies from address to address, based on agreements between adjacent routers. Fortunately, as a user you'll never need to worry about this; it only makes a difference when you're setting up a network.

network has all the information it needs to get your packet from your computer to its destination. That's a start. But if all you had was IP, you'd be faced with several problems:

- Most information transfers are longer than 1500 characters. You would be disappointed if the Postal Service carried postcards, but refused anything larger.

- Things can go wrong. The Postal Service occasionally loses a letter; networks sometimes lose packets, or damage them in transit.

- Packets may arrive out of sequence. If you mail two letters to the same place on successive days, there's no guarantee that they will take the same route or arrive in order. The same is true of the Internet.

So, the next layer of the network will give us a way to transfer bigger chunks of information and will take care of the many distortions that can creep in because of the network.

The Transmission Control Protocol (TCP)

TCP is the protocol, frequently mentioned in the same breath as IP, that is used to get around these problems. What would happen if you wanted to send a book to someone, but the Postal Service only accepted letters? What could you do? You could rip each page out of the book, put each page in a separate envelope, and dump all the envelopes in a mailbox. The recipient would then have to make sure all the pages arrived and paste them together in the right order. On the Internet, TCP rips up the book and then pastes it back together for you.

TCP takes the information you want to transmit and breaks it into pieces. It numbers each piece so receipt can be verified and the data can be put back in the proper order. In order to pass this sequence number across the network, it has an envelope of its own which has the information it requires "written on it" (Figure 3-3). A piece of your data is placed in a TCP envelope. The TCP envelope is, in turn, placed inside an IP envelope and given to the network. Once you have something in an IP envelope, the network can carry it.

On the receiving side, the TCP protocol collects the envelopes, extracts the data, and puts it in the proper order. If some envelopes are missing, it asks the sender to retransmit them. Once it has all the information in the proper order, it passes the data to whatever application program is using its services.

This is actually a slightly utopian view of TCP. In the real world, not only do packets get lost, they can also be changed by glitches on the telephone lines that transmit them. TCP also handles this problem. As it puts your data into an envelope, it calculates something called a checksum. A checksum is a number that allows the receiving TCP to detect errors in the packet.[*] When the packet arrives at its

---

[*] Here's a simple example, if you're interested. Let's assume that you're transmitting raw computer data in 8-bit chunks, or bytes. A very simple checksum would be to add all of these bytes together. Then stick an extra byte onto the end of your data that contains the

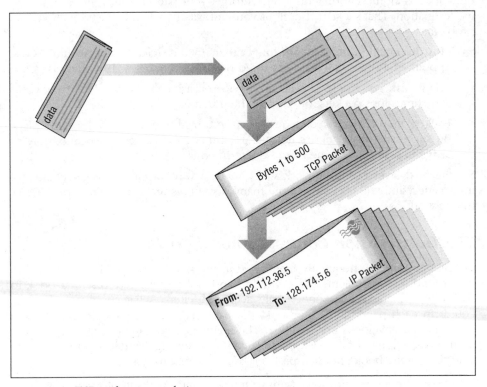

Figure 3-3: TCP packet encapsulation

destination, the receiving TCP calculates what the checksum should be and compares it to the one sent by the transmitter. If they don't match, an error has occurred in the transmission. The receiving TCP throws that packet away and requests a retransmission.

Other Transmission Protocols

TCP creates the appearance of a dedicated wire between the two applications, guaranteeing that what goes in one side comes out the other. You don't have a dedicated link between the sender and receiver (other people can use the same routers and network wires in the gaps between your packets), but, for all practical purposes, it seems as if you do.

---

sum (or, at least, as much of the sum as fits into 8 bits). The receiver makes the same calculation. If any byte was changed during transmission, the checksums will disagree, and you'll know there was an error. Of course, if there were two errors, they might cancel each other out. But more complicated computations can handle multiple errors.

Ideal as this may sound, it is not the best approach for every program to use. Setting up a TCP connection requires a fair amount of overhead and delay; if this machinery isn't needed, it's better not to use it. If all the data you want to send will fit in one packet, and you don't particularly care to guarantee delivery, TCP may be overkill.

It turns out that there is another standard protocol that does away with this overhead. This protocol is called the user datagram protocol or UDP. It is used instead of TCP in some applications; that is, instead of wrapping your data in a TCP envelope and putting that inside an IP envelope, the application puts your data into a UDP envelope, which goes in the IP envelope.

UDP is a lot simpler than TCP because it doesn't worry about missing packets or keeping data in the right order. UDP is used for programs that only send short messages and can just resend the message if a response does not come in a short time. For example, assume that you're writing a program that looks up phone numbers in a database somewhere else on the network. There is no reason to set up a TCP connection to transmit 20 or so characters in each direction. You can just put the name into one UDP packet, stick that into an IP packet, and send it. The other side of the application gets the packet, reads the name, looks up the phone number, puts that into another UDP packet, and sends it back. What happens if the packet gets lost along the way? Your program should handle that; if it waits too long without getting a response, it just sends another request.

Using the Net Over a Modem

TCP and IP were designed back when computers were big and expensive. Once you connected one to the Net, it stayed connected and stayed put. Now computers are cheap and portable. People want to use the Internet from wherever they happen to be, and connect when they are using it. They also want to use a regular modem that can work over a standard telephone line. To make this style of usage possible, a set of protocols was developed to allow IP connections out through the serial port of a computer. This protocol was called SLIP, for "Serial Line Internet Protocol."

SLIP worked but, as more and more people used it, some design deficiencies were discovered. Fixing the problems within SLIP was not possible, so a design team got together and designed a completely different protocol called the Point to Point Protocol or PPP. For all practical purposes, SLIP and PPP do the same thing—just PPP does it better.

SLIP and PPP are both still in use today. Most Internet service providers will accept either one. The preference is towards PPP, although Windows 95 can be configured to use either. Once you've made a connection with either SLIP or PPP, you are essentially a part of the service provider's local area network. Then the other protocols I've discussed join the provider's LAN to the other networks that make up the Internet.

Making the Network Friendly

Now that we have the ability to transfer information between places on the network, we can start working on making the Internet more friendly. This is done by having software tailored to the task at hand, and using names rather than numerical addresses to refer to computers.

Applications

Most people don't get really excited about having a guaranteed bit stream between machines, no matter how fast the lines or exotic the technology that creates it. They want to use that bit stream to do something useful, whether it's to move a file, access some information, or play a game. Applications are pieces of software that allow this to happen easily. They are yet another layer of software, built on top of the TCP or UDP services. Applications give you, the user, a way to do the task at hand.

Applications can range from home-grown programs to proprietary programs supplied by a vendor. Many Internet applications that are common today started out as home-grown experiments. Originally, there were three standard Internet applications (remote login, file transfer, and electronic mail) and everyone had to know how to use them. Over time, experiments like Gopher and the World Wide Web were so successful that they became standardly available applications. Chapters 5 through 14 of this book describe how to use most of the common Internet applications.

One problem with talking about applications is that your local system determines how the application appears to you. You might be discussing the World Wide Web with two friends and discover that you all use different application programs to do the same things. You might be using Internet Explorer from Microsoft, one friend might be using Mosaic, and the other Netscape Navigator. All three pieces of software do approximately the same thing. Don't become confused—and don't fall into the trap of thinking that you need a book that discusses exactly the software you have on hand. That's not true. Applications that do the same thing usually work more or less the same way. The user interface (commands, dialog boxes, etc.) may differ, but the principles will be the same.

It also means that even though you are using Windows 95, the messages and screens you see may be slightly different from the examples in the book. So, don't worry if the book says the message is "connection refused" and the error message you receive is "Unable to connect to remote host: refused"; they are the same. Try to distill the essence of the message, rather than match the exact wording.

You'll understand why applications behave the way they do if you know just a little about how applications are built. An application consists of two pieces of software that cooperate: the client, which runs on the computer that is requesting the service, and the server, which runs on the computer providing the service. The network, using either TCP or UDP services, is the medium by which the two communicate.

The client, which is the program that runs on your system and requests services from other systems on the Internet, must:

- Create a TCP network connection with a server
- Accept input from you in a convenient manner
- Reformat the input to a standard format and send it to a server
- Accept output from the server in a standard format
- Reformat that output for display to you

The server software runs on the machine delivering the service; if the server isn't running, the service isn't available. On multitasking systems, like UNIX, Windows NT, or Windows 95, which can run multiple programs at the same time, the servers are often called daemons. (On Windows 95 and Windows NT, daemons appear to be called services.) These are system jobs which run in the background all the time. If servers run on computers which can run only one program at a time, these machines must be dedicated to that singular purpose.

Daemons (or services) are "silent helpers" that wait for their services to be required and when they are, spring into action when they are needed. When a typical server is ready to accept requests it:

- Informs the networking software that it is ready to accept connections
- Waits for a request in a standard format
- Services the request
- Sends the results back to the client in a standard format
- Waits again

A server must be able to handle a variety of clients, some running on the same kind of computer, and some running on IBM/PCs, Macintoshes, UNIX workstations—whatever happens to be out there. To make this possible, there is a set of rules for communicating with the server. This set of rules is generally called a protocol. In this case, since it is a protocol used between pieces of an application, it is called an application protocol. Anyone can write a client on any type of computer. As long as that client can communicate across the network to the server and can speak the protocol properly, it can access the service. In practice, this means that your Windows 95 computer can use Internet tools to do work on an incredible number of different systems, ranging from UNIX workstations to IBM mainframes.

The Domain Name System

Fairly early on, people realized that numerical addresses were fine for machines communicating with machines, but human beings prefer names. It is hard to talk using these host addresses (who would say, "I was connected to 128.102.252.1

yesterday . . . " ?) and even harder to remember them. Therefore, computers on the Internet were given names for the convenience of their human users. The preceding conversation becomes "I was connected to the White House yesterday . . . " All of the Internet applications let you use system names, rather than host addresses.

Of course, naming introduces problems of its own. For one thing, you have to make sure that no two computers connected to the Internet have the same name. You also have to provide a way to convert names into numerical host addresses. After all, names are just fine for people, but computers really prefer numbers, thank you. You can use a computer name where an address is called for, but a program needs some way to look that name up and convert it into an address. (You do the same thing whenever you look someone up in the phone book.)

In the beginning, when the Internet was a small folksy place, dealing with names was easy. The NIC (Network Information Center) set up a registry. You would send in a form (electronically, of course), and the NIC would add it to the list of names and addresses they maintained. This file, called the hosts file, was distributed regularly to every machine on the network. The names were simple words, every one chosen to be unique. If you used a name, your computer would look it up in the file and substitute the address. It was good.

Unfortunately, when the Internet went forth and multiplied, so did the size of the file. There were significant delays in getting a name registered, and it became difficult to find names that weren't already used. Also, too much network time was spent distributing this large file to every machine contained in it. It was obvious that a distributed, on-line system was required to cope with the rate of change. This system is called the Domain Name System or DNS.

The Domain System Structure

The Domain Name System is a method of administering names by giving different groups responsibility for subsets of the names. Each level in this system is called a domain. The domains are separated by periods:

```
ux.cso.uiuc.edu
nic.ddn.mil
yoyodyne.com
```

There can be any number of domains within the name, but you will rarely see more than five. As you proceed left to right through a name, each domain you encounter is larger than the previous one.

In the name **ux.cso.uiuc.edu**, **ux** is the name of a host, a real computer with an IP address (Figure 3-4). The name for that computer is created and maintained by the **cso** group, which happens to be the department where the computer resides. The department **cso** is a part of the University of Illinois at Urbana Champaign (**uiuc**). **uiuc** is a portion of the national group of educational institutions (**edu**). So the domain **edu** contains all computers in all U.S. educational institutions, the domain **uiuc.edu** contains all computers at the University of Illinois, and so on.

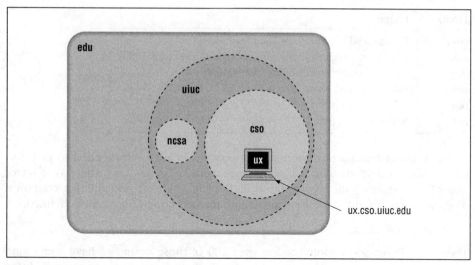

Figure 3–4: Domain authority

Each group can create or change whatever lies within it. If **uiuc** decided to create another group called **ncsa**, it could do so without asking anyone's permission. All UIUC has to do is add the new names to its part of the worldwide database, and sooner or later everyone who needs to know will find out about the new name (**ncsa.uiuc.edu**). Similarly, **cso** can buy a new computer, assign it a name, and add it to the network without asking anyone's permission. If every group from **edu** on down plays by the rules and makes sure that the names it assigns are unique, then no two systems anywhere on the Internet will have the same name. You could have two machines named **fred**, but only if they are in different domains (for example, **fred.cso.uiuc.edu** and **fred.ora.com**).

In practice, being the name administrator for a group requires certain skills and isn't very much fun. Somewhere around the enterprise level (**uiuc**) or one level below it, there is a person who is responsible for maintaining all lower levels. There is a locally defined procedure for requesting that a name be created or changed.

It's easy to see where domains and names come from within an organization like a university or a business. However, where do the "top-level" domains like **edu** come from? They were created by fiat, when the domain system was invented. Originally, there were six highest-level domains (see Table 3-1).

Table 3–1: Original High-Level Domains

Domain	Usage
com	Commercial organizations (i.e., businesses)
edu	Educational organizations (universities, secondary schools, etc.)
gov	Governmental organizations, non-military
mil	Military (Army, Navy, etc.)
org	Other organizations
net	Network resources

As the Internet became an international network, a way was needed to give foreign countries responsibility for their own names. To this end, there is a set of two-letter domains which correspond to the highest-level domains for countries. Since **ca** is the country code for Canada, a Canadian computer might be named:

```
hockey.guelph.ca
```

There are almost 300 country codes; over 200 of those countries have some kind of computer networking. There is a list of the country codes in Appendix C, *International Network Connectivity*, in case you want to see where mail you received came from.

The United States has its own country code, although it hasn't been used much up to now; in the U.S., most network sites use the "organizational" domains (like **edu**), rather than the "geographical" domains (like **va.us**—Virginia). But, as networking becomes more pervasive, the **us** domain will show up more and more. Just consider the problem of networking schools—how many **washington.hs.edu** might be requested? To reduce confusion, public schools will probably be allocated geographically, with names like **washington.hs.district123.il.us**.

One more thing to note: a computer may even have both kinds of names, just for completeness. However, there's no way to "convert" between organizational names and geographical names. For example, even though the name **ux.cso.uiuc.edu** happens to be in Urbana, Illinois, U.S.A., there is *not* necessarily a name **ux.urbana.il.us**. Even if there is, they aren't necessarily the same computer.

Domain name lookup

Now that you know how domains relate to each other and how a name is created, you might wonder how to use this marvelous system. You use it automatically, whenever you use a name on a computer that knows about it. You never need to look up a name or give a special command to find out about some name, although you can if you want. All computers on the Internet can use the domain system, and most do.

When you use a name like **ux.cso.uiuc.edu**, the computer needs to turn it into an address. To do so, it starts asking DNS servers for help, starting at the right end and working left. First, it asks the local DNS servers to look up the address. At this point, there are three possibilities:

- The local server knows the address, because the address is in the local server's part of the worldwide database. For example, if you're in the computer science department of the University of Illinois, your local server probably has information about the computers in your department.

- The local server knows the address because someone else has asked for the same address recently. Whenever you ask for an address, the DNS server keeps it on hand for a while, just in case someone else wants the same address later; this is called caching, and makes the system a lot more efficient.

- The local server doesn't know the address, but it knows how to find out.

How does the local server find out? Its software knows how to contact a *root* server. This is the server that knows the addresses of name servers for the highest level (rightmost) zone (in this case, **edu**). It asks the root server for the address of the computer responsible for the **edu** zone. Having that information, it contacts that server and asks it for the address of the **uiuc** server. Your software then contacts that computer and asks for the address of the server for **cso**. Finally, it contacts that machine and gets the address of **ux**, the host that was the target of the application.

Domain name system hints

There are a few common misconceptions that you may encounter while dealing with names. Here are a few "truths" to prevent those misconceptions from taking root:

- The pieces of a domain-style name tell you who is responsible for maintaining the name. It may not tell you anything about who maintains the computer corresponding to that IP address, or even (despite the country codes) where that machine is located. It would be perfectly legal for me to have the name **oz.cso.uiuc.edu** (part of the University of Illinois' name space) point to a machine in Australia. It isn't normally done, but it could be.

- The pieces of a domain name don't even necessarily tell you on what network a computer is located. Domain names and networks often overlap, but there's no necessary connection between them; two machines that are in the same domain may not be on the same network. For example, the systems named **ux.cso.uiuc.edu** and **ux1.cso.uiuc.edu** may be on different networks. Once again, domain names only tell you who is responsible for allocating the name.

- A machine can have multiple names. This is especially true of machines that offer services, where the service may be moved to a different computer in the future. My Sun workstation may be known by **ek.cso.uiuc.edu**. It also might be the computer where you can go to get publicly available files at the University of Illinois. So my workstation might also have the name **ftp.uiuc.edu** (**ftp** being the name of the file-moving program). Sometime in the future, this service might be moved to some other computer. When this happens, the name **ftp.uiuc.edu** would move along with the service (my computer gets to keep its old name **ek.cso.uiuc.edu**). People wanting the particular service use the same name, regardless of which computer is providing it. Names that symbolically refer to a service are aliases for the unique canonical name (or cname) of a computer. You will see symbolic names frequently as you wander about the Internet. The most common ones are shown in the following table.

Table 3-2: Common Names and Meanings

Domain	Usage
archie	File archive search server
ftp	Anonymous FTP (public file archive)
gopher	Gopher server
listserv	Mailing list manager
majordomo	Mailing list manager
mail	E-mail server
nntp	USENET news server
pop	Post office protocol (e-mail retrieval)
smtp	Mail transport service
www	World Wide Web server

- Names aren't necessary for communication. Unless the error message you receive is "host unknown," the name worked fine. A message like "host unknown" means your system could not translate the name you gave it into a host address. Once your system has the address in hand, it never uses the name again.

- It is better to remember names than host addresses. Some people feel that the name system is "just one more thing to go wrong." The problem is that an address is tied to a network. If the computer providing a service is moved from one building to another, its network, and hence its address, is likely to change. The name doesn't need to. The administrator only needs to update the name record so that the name points to the new address. Since the name still works, you don't particularly care if the computer or function has changed locations.

The Domain Name System may sound complicated, but it's one of the things that make the Internet a comfortable place to live. Pretty soon, you'll start realizing, "Yes, this resource is at the University of Virginia; this person works for IBM in Germany; this is the address for reporting bugs in Nutshell Handbooks (nuts@ora.com)," and so on. The real advantage of the domain system is that it breaks the gigantic worldwide Internet into a bunch of manageable pieces. Although hundreds of thousands of computers are "on the Net," they're all named, and the names are organized in a convenient—perhaps even rational—way, making it easier for you to remember the ones you need.

CHAPTER FOUR

What's Allowed on the Internet?

Historical Perspective
Legal Implications
Network Ethics
Ethics and the Private Commercial Internet
Security Consciousness

In earlier chapters, I told you very generally what the Internet is good for, where it came from, and how it works. Now it's time to get to the real nitty-gritty. We will talk about what you are allowed to do on the network; in the next chapter, we will start discussing how to do it.

What you are allowed to do is a very complex issue. It is influenced by law, ethics, and politics. How these interrelate, and which is paramount, vary from place to place. The Internet isn't a network; it's a network of networks, each of which may have its own policies and rules. Lest you give up before starting, the rules are reasonably uniform, and you'll be safe if you keep a few guidelines in mind. Fortunately, these guidelines aren't terribly restrictive; as long as you stay within them, you can do whatever you want. If you feel yourself getting near the edge, contact your network provider to determine exactly what is allowed and what isn't. It may be possible to do what you want, but it's your responsibility to find out. Let's look at the issues so you can see where the borders are.

Historical Perspective

When the Internet was young, the big issue as to whether what you wanted to do was legal depended on whether or not your application was commercial. This was because many of the networks in the Internet were sponsored by Federal agencies. Under Federal law, an agency may only spend its budget on things that it is charged to do. For example, the Air Force can't secretly increase its budget by ordering rockets through NASA. These same laws applied to the network—if NASA funded a network, it had to be used for space science. As a user, you didn't have any idea which networks your packets were traversing, but they still had to fall within the scope of each network's funding agency.

This gave rise to a set of Acceptable Use Policies (or AUPs) which detailed what you could and couldn't do. These AUPs also gave rise to a lot of confusion about anti-commercial aspects of the Internet. At the time, commercial activity on the Internet was unacceptable unless there was some direct benefit to the research and education community.

The Federal government has been trying to extricate itself from the networking business so that commercial firms will take over running the Internet's networks. This has had the effect of removing any commercial restrictions that Federal law placed on network use. The government's involvement now consists of trying to ensure that there is a wealth of competing Internet providers who can compete on an even footing and that the infrastructure is sound. You can now use the Internet for any commercial activities you want. Some service providers, however, do limit your activity; for example, a provider funded by the state for primary school access will probably place restrictions on what you can do. However, it's no longer a Federal issue.

These days, network culture is a bigger restriction than legal issues. Commercial activity has not only been accepted, it's been welcomed. However, the network has a culture of its own, and activity that disregards that culture (like junk e-mail) will get you into trouble. You don't have to worry as much about the law, but you also won't gain any friends.

Legal Implications

It would be naive, however, to say that the Internet is beyond the law. Three areas of the law affect you and the Internet:

- The Internet is not just a nationwide network, but a true global network. When shipping anything across a national boundary, including bits, export laws come into effect and local laws change.

- Whenever you are shipping software (or, for that matter, ideas) from one place to another, you must consider intellectual property and license issues.

- Although the Internet is global, local jurisdictions may try to exert authority over your Internet usage.

Export Laws

Whether you know it or not, exporting bits falls under the auspices of the Department of Commerce's export restrictions.* The Internet, being a virtually seamless global network, makes it very easy to export things without your knowledge. Because I'm not a lawyer, I won't get very technical, but I will try to sketch what is required to stay legal. If, after reading this, you think you might run afoul of the law, seek competent legal help.

---

* This is strictly a U.S.-centric discussion. Other laws apply to servers in other countries.

Export law is based on two points:

1. Exporting anything requires a license.
2. Exporting a service is roughly equivalent to exporting the pieces necessary to provide that service.

The first point is fairly obvious: if you ship, carry, transfer a file, or electronically mail anything out of the country, it needs to be covered by an export license. Luckily, there is a loophole called a general license that covers most things. The general license allows you to export anything that is not explicitly restricted and is readily available in public forums in the United States. So anything you can learn from walking into a conference or classroom that does not have security restrictions is probably covered by the general license.

However, the list of restricted items has a lot of surprises and does cover things that you can learn as a student in any university. Networking code and encryption code might be restricted, based upon their capabilities. Many times, one little item is of concern, but by the time the regulations are written, they cover a much wider area. For example, during the Persian Gulf War, it was a lot harder to knock out Iraq's command and control network than anticipated. It turned out they were using commercial IP routers which were very good at finding alternative routes quickly. Suddenly, exporting any router that could find alternate routes was restricted.[*]

More recently, Phil Zimmerman has been the subject of a criminal investigation for "exporting" cryptographic software via the Internet (a package called PGP). Zimmerman does not know who actually made PGP available outside the U.S., and it's widely felt that he's being harassed for developing the software.[†] Nevertheless, being the subject of a Federal investigation is not pleasant, especially if you're not guilty. If you give away software (or anything else) via the Internet, be careful. E-mailing a copy of PGP to your friend in Estonia would be a BAD IDEA.

The second point is even simpler. If exporting some hardware, say a supercomputer, is not allowed, then remote access to that hardware within this country is prohibited as well. So, be careful about granting access to "special" resources (like supercomputers) to people in foreign countries. The exact nature of these restrictions depends, of course, on the foreign country and (as you can probably imagine) can change quickly.

When investigating their potential for legal liability, the consortium that runs the Bitnet (CREN) came to the following conclusions:[‡] A network operator is responsible for illegal export only if the operator was aware of the violation and failed to

---

[*] This story may actually be a network "urban legend." Everyone on the Net talked about this situation, but when I tried to verify it I could not find a definitive source.

[†] See O'Reilly & Associates' *PGP: Pretty Good Privacy*, by Simpson Garfinkel, which includes a complete account of PGP's history and the legal controversy surrounding it.

[‡] The actual legal opinions are available on the network; see the *Resource Catalog* under Law: Corporation for Research and Educational Networking.

inform proper authorities; the network operator isn't responsible for monitoring your usage and determining whether or not it's within the law. So network personnel nationwide probably aren't snooping through your packets to see what you are shipping overseas (although who knows what the National Security Agency looks at). However, if a network technician sees your packets, and if the packets are obviously in violation of some regulation, then the technician is obliged to inform the government.

Property Rights

Property rights can also become an issue when you ship something to someone else. The problem gets even more confusing when the communication is across national borders. Copyright and patent laws vary greatly from country to country. On the network, you might find a curious volume of forgotten lore whose copyright has expired in the U.S. Shipping these files to England might place you in violation of British law. Know who has the rights to anything before giving it away.

The law surrounding electronic communication has not kept pace with the technology. If you have a book, journal, or personal letter, you can ask almost any lawyer or librarian if you can copy or use it in a particular manner. They can tell you if you can, or whose permission you need to obtain. Ask the same question regarding a network bulletin board posting, an electronic mail message, or a report in a file available on the network, and they will throw up their hands. Even if you knew whose permission to obtain and obtained that permission via mail, it's not clear whether an e-mail message offers any useful protection. Be aware that this is a murky part of law which is likely to be hammered out in the next decade.

Please note that property rights can be a problem even when using publicly available files. Some software available for public retrieval through the Internet must be licensed from the vendor. For example, a software vendor might make updates to its product available via anonymous FTP. So you can easily get the software, but in order to use it legally you must hold a valid software maintenance license. Just because a file is there for the taking doesn't mean that taking it is legal.

Localized Attempts at Legal Control

Some people use the Internet and think "This is Cyberspace, so real-world laws don't apply." Others think that if a lawmaking body puts its mind to it, it can regulate anything, including the Internet. Both of these groups are underestimating their foe, and if they try and fight, the battle will be long and bloody.

The bulletin board (BBS) community has given the legal community a number of opportunities to enforce intellectual property laws. BBSs that carried pirated software have been subject to (at least) a raid from a law enforcement agency and temporary impoundment of equipment. There is no reason to believe that these laws will not be enforced just as rigorously on the Internet. It is true that local raids frequently have no long-term impact on the availability of pirated software, since some copies might be available in other countries, out of reach of the authorities. Still, if you are on the receiving end of a police action, it is a not particularly enjoyable experience—even if you are eventually acquitted.

From a law enforcement perspective, the problem is that any attempt to control Net traffic is essentially local. Even if "local" means the entire U.S., that's still only one corner of the world; an agency may be able to shut down a few sites, but others will certainly spring up that aren't within its sphere of action. The result is that attempts to legislate content are burdensome and without effect. For example, consider Senator Exon's amendment to the Telecommunications Act of 1995,* which provides heavy fines for sites that make obscene material available. Limiting access to hard-core pornographic material may or may not be a noble goal, but the bill can only affect servers in the United States. Other sites worldwide can still provide these files, and no U.S. authority can stop them. From the recipient's perspective, there's no difference between a server in Kansas and a server in Morocco. On the Internet, everything is next door.

There is no easy fix for this problem. The fact of network life is that a pornographic file, as it traverses the network, is just a bucket of bits; it doesn't look intrinsically different from any other file. There's no easy way to tell (aside from setting someone up to look) whether a file is a "dirty" picture, pirated software, or the text of the Bible. Software that can make this kind of judgment is years away. A regulatory agency can't control what passes over the Net, because it can't tell what those bits represent; and it can't control the servers, because most of them lie outside its jurisdiction. Although there are great political gains to be made from passing lots of laws, the technical fact is that the laws won't have any real effect, except for allowing politicians to crow about what they've accomplished.

Regardless of any attempts to regulate Internet traffic, there is such a thing as "responsible use." Using an account at your public library or school to hunt down digitized centerfolds will have some unintended side effects. Some governing board won't appreciate your efforts, and your fellow citizens or students may lose their Internet access. No mayor or school administrator likes to see a TV special titled "Tax Dollars Fund Pornography Distribution."

It's important to realize that the Internet has many political supporters, including members of Congress, the Clinton administration, educational leaders, Federal agency heads, teachers, and local school board members. They support the Internet because it benefits the country: it increases the United States' ability to compete in international research and trade, and improves educational opportunities, particularly in remote areas. Speeding communications allows the research and educational process to speed up; because of the Net, our researchers and their students can develop better solutions to technical problems.

---

* As of this writing, this bill has not been definitively passed; if it is passed, President Clinton is likely to veto it (for reasons pertaining to cable television deregulation).

As is typical in the political world, there are also those people who see these benefits as drivel. The few thousand dollars the local schools spend on the Net could be better spent improving the putting greens on the golf course. And, as I've already said, there is no shortage of politicians willing to grandstand.

The bottom line in the politics of networking is that political support for the network is broad, but relatively thin. Any act that can cause political waves might radically change it, probably for the worse.

Network Ethics

For the novice network user, the apparent lack of ethics on the network is fairly disquieting. In actuality, the network is a very ethical place; the ethics are just a bit different. To understand this, consider the term "frontier justice." When the West was young, there was a set of laws for the United States, but they were applied differently west of the Mississippi river. Well, the network is on the frontier of technology, so frontier justice applies here, too. You can delve safely, provided you know what to expect.

The two overriding premises of network ethics are:

- Individualism is honored and fostered
- The network is good and must be protected

Notice these are very close to the frontier ethics of the West, where individualism and preservation of lifestyle were paramount. Let's look a bit more at how these points play off each other on the network.

Individualism

In normal society, everyone may claim to be an individual, but for normal people, individualism doesn't suffice: people also need to belong to groups that share their concerns. If you love medieval French poetry, you naturally want a group of friends who share your enthusiasm. But try to start that group. Unless you're in a large city, you probably won't be able to find enough interested people to support a chain of discussions. In short, you don't have the "critical mass" needed to maintain a specialized group. In order to get at least some interaction for your love, you join a poetry society with more general interests—perhaps one on medieval poetry in general. Maybe there's only one poetry society in town, and it spends most of its time discussing bad pseudo-religious verse. That's the problem with critical mass. If you can't assemble enough people to form a group, you suffer. You may join a larger group out of necessity, but it may not be what you want.

On the network, critical mass is two. You interact when you want and how you want—it's always convenient, and no driving is required. Geography doesn't matter. The other person can be anywhere on the network (virtually anywhere in the world). Therefore, a group, no matter how specific, is possible. Even competing groups are likely to form. Some groups may choose to "meet" by e-mail, some on bulletin boards, some by making files publicly available, and some by other means. People are free to operate in the manner they like. Since no one needs to join a large group to enjoy critical mass, everyone is part of some minority group.

Consequently, if you feel that the Net seems like a consortium of incredibly specific special-interest groups, you're probably right. Find the special-interest groups that excite you and get started. But the freedom to organize special-interest groups comes with the responsibility to respect other people's groups. No one wants to hear "This topic should not be discussed on the network." If I said that about French poets, you could attack my favorite group, cross-dressing male adventurers. People understand that others couldn't care less about the information they live and die for. Many Internet users are nervous (justifiably) that support for outside censorship could arise and, eventually, succeed in making the Net less useful. Indeed, the Exon Amendment (whether or not it becomes law) proves that such support has already arisen.

Of course, individualism is a double-edged sword. It makes the network a nice place for finding diverse information and people, but it may tax your commitment to freedom of speech. As painful as it may be, in practice "live and let live" will help you preserve your sanity. You may not like what other people are doing, but they may not appreciate you, either.

Protecting the Internet

Frequent users find the Internet extremely valuable for both work and play. Since Internet access frequently comes at little or no personal expense, they view this valuable resource as something that must be protected. The threats to the Internet come from two sources:

- Excessive use for unintended purposes
- Political pressures

A school's connection to the Internet has a purpose. A company's connection to the Internet has a purpose. Chances are no one will prosecute a person who uses these connections for unintended purposes, but it is still discouraged by other means. If you use an employer's computer for a bit of personal use, like balancing your checkbook, it will probably be ignored. Likewise, small amounts of network time used for unintended purposes will likely be ignored. (In fact, many seemingly unintended uses, such as a high school student playing a game across the network, might actually qualify as intended. She must have learned a lot about computing and networking to get that far.) It is only when someone does something blatant, perhaps organizing a nationwide multiuser dungeon game day on the network, that problems occur.*

---

* Even if you are paying for your own connection, these arguments still apply. Your cost is determined as a share of your Internet provider's costs. It only takes a few wasteful people doing stupid things to make the provider's costs go up—and, consequently, your own.

Unintended use also takes the form of ill-conceived supported usage. The network was not built to be a substitute for inadequate local facilities. For example, using an exported disk system halfway around the world because your employer wouldn't buy a $300 disk for your workstation is unacceptable. You may need the disk to do valuable research, but the cost of providing that storage across the network is outrageous. The network was designed to allow easy access to unique resources, not gratuitous access to common ones.

Heavy network users and network providers are not stodgy. They enjoy a game as well as the next person. They are also not stupid. They read discussion groups. They work on the network regularly. If performance goes bad for no apparent reason, they investigate. If they find that the traffic in a particular area has gone up a hundredfold, they will want to know why. If you are the "why" and the use is unacceptable, you will probably get a polite mail message asking you to stop. After that, you may get some less polite messages; finally, someone will contact your local network provider. You may end up losing your network access entirely, or your employer or campus may have to pay higher access fees (which, I assume, they will not be happy about).

Self-regulation is important because of the politics that surround the network. No reasonable person could expect the network to exist without occasional abuses and problems. However, if these problems aren't resolved within the network community, and are therefore thrown into newspapers and Congress, everyone loses. To summarize, here are some areas that are considered politically damaging to the network and should be avoided:

- Excessive game playing
- Excessive ill-conceived use
- Hateful, harassing, or other antisocial behavior
- Intentional damage or interference with others (e.g., the Internet Worm[*])
- Publicly accessible obscene files

It is difficult to justify funding Internet connections to grade schools if all Congress wants to hear about is the latest overblown media report on smut and frivolity on the Internet.

---

[*] The Internet Worm was a program which used the Internet to attack certain types of computers on the network. It would gain unauthorized access to computers and then use those computers to try to break into others. It was a lot like a personal computer "virus," but technically it is called a worm because it did not cause intentional damage to its hosts. For a good description, see *Computer Security Basics* (Russell and Gangemi), O'Reilly & Associates, Inc.

Ethics and the Private Commercial Internet

In the previous few sections, we talked about the political and social climate that the Internet created. However, the climate is changing. Every day the percentage of Internet funding which comes from the Federal government grows smaller and smaller because of increased commercial usage. It is the government's goal to get out of the networking business and allow private industry to provide Internet services. The obvious question is: If the government is getting out of the Internet business, do I still have to play by its rules? There are two issues to be dealt with, one personal and one commercial.

On the personal side, even though the Federal government might be out of the network funding business, most people would rather have someone else pay for their connection. So, if you get your connection through a school, employer, Free-net, or whomever, they may still require you to follow a set of policies. "Freedom's just another word for nothin' left to lose,"[*] and you may have to give up some freedom to prevent losing your subsidized network connection. It's your responsibility to find out what your network provider considers "acceptable use."

The commercial issue is how to do business in tune with the Internet's culture. Although the culture is under stress and changing all the time, there is still a lot of sentiment on the Internet against blatant commercialism. Sending an e-mail message advertising a product to everyone on the Internet (known as *spamming*) is an affront to most users, as is posting a message to all 10,000-plus known newsgroups. It will probably hurt sales by creating a large group of people who would rather not do business with a boorish company. It can backfire in other ways. If 100,000 people send you an e-mail complaint, they'll certainly make your life miserable. They may overload your service provider, forcing him to cancel your connection. This has happened. The Internet makes it very easy to get a very large number of people mad at you at once.

The Internet culture isn't necessarily opposed to advertising, but it demands that you view advertising as an information service. You can make marketing data available, but you can't force it on people. There would be nothing wrong, in terms of policy or culture, with an auto manufacturer putting up a server with pictures of its cars, technical data sheets, and information about options. If an Internet user wanted to buy a car, he could comparison shop from his terminal, decide what he wanted, and visit one dealer, rather than three, to do a test drive. Most users would be excited by this kind of service, and some resources are beginning to provide it.[†] In the future, you might even be able to do your test drive over the

---

[*] Kris Kristofferson and Fred Foster, *Me and Bobby McGee*, 1969.

[†] The *Global Network Navigator* (GNN), for example; for information, send e-mail to *info@gnn.com*.

Internet via a virtual-reality simulation. Even so, we're all trying to avoid a situation in which we're deluged with unsolicited e-mail selling everything from vinyl siding to sexy underwear.

Privacy

The Internet views privacy as a personal matter; that is, if you want privacy, it's your job to do something about it. Providing a guaranteed secure channel between two people is overkill for most users, who don't really care. Consequently, the Internet doesn't make any guarantees about privacy. This doesn't mean that every message you send over the Net will be read by someone other than the recipient. It probably won't be.

You may think that nothing you have to send over the Internet is that secret, so this isn't an issue. What about your credit card numbers? Everybody is talking about doing catalog shopping across the Internet and if you read the news media every credit card number which is sent is stolen. The problem is blown way out of proportion. Credit card fraud on the Internet is no worse than it is in the rest of the world. Think about how secure your credit card is next time you lay it on the little tray in a restaurant and the waiter takes it to the back room to run it through the machine. How many imprints did he make?

In any case, to set peoples' minds at ease, the community is trying to beef up security in the area most likely to be used for these kinds of transactions, the World Wide Web. The solution is known but it takes some time to spread the proper software around. By the middle of 1996, this will no longer be a concern.

If you are worried about privacy in personal dealings on the Internet, such as sending e-mail or locking files on your computer, you can fix the problem yourself. You can install and use a package like PGP (Pretty Good Privacy). PGP is a freely available encryption package that allows you to encrypt files before you send them (or make them available on a server). Of course, anyone who receives your encrypted messages will need to install PGP as well.

PGP also supports "digital signatures"; you can add an identifier to your mail that can't be forged. You can use a digital signature without encrypting the message itself. In this case, recipients without PGP can read the message; they just can't be sure that it really came from you. It's fairly easy to forge e-mail, so investigating digital signatures is a good idea, even if you feel the need to encrypt your messages themselves.

Security Consciousness

Earlier I said that the Internet's ethics were a lot like "frontier justice." Well, there wasn't a lot of respect for private property on the frontier, and, unfortunately, the same is true on the Internet. Many users on the Internet feel that if a file or a computer happens to be available, it's fair game. After all, if you didn't want to be on the Net, you shouldn't have connected. This view, of course, has no basis in law, but a lot of things on the frontier didn't either. So you should know a little about how to protect yourself.

A computer connected to the Internet is not, in itself, a much different security problem than a machine you can dial in with a modem. The problems are the same; it's the magnitude of the problem that changes. If you have a dial-up modem, anyone can dial the number and try to break in. There are three mitigating factors: the computer's phone number probably isn't widely known; if the intruder is outside your local calling area, he has to pay for the experience (or have stolen something else to get there); and there is only one interface which can be attacked.

If you are on the Internet, the mitigating factors are gone. The general address of your network is easily found, and an intruder would only have to try a few host numbers before stumbling onto an active one. In principle, this is still no worse than computer services that provide dial-in access to their machines through toll-free 800 numbers. The problem is that those services have staff who worry about security, and there is still only one point to break in from: the serial port. On the Internet, someone could try to break in through the interactive terminal port, the file transfer port, the e-mail port, etc. It's easy for someone to pull a workstation out of the box and put it on the Internet without thinking about security at all. He or she plugs the machine in, turns it on, and it works. The job is done, until someone breaks in and does something bad. In the long run, it is less time-consuming to put a little thought into security beforehand than to deal with it after the fact.

Luckily, most break-ins on the network occur on computers that are connected to the Internet continuously. Nothing frustrates a hacker more than investing a lot of time trying to break into a computer, only to have his efforts thwarted when the computer drops off the network. However, although you may connect to the Internet only occasionally today, more and more people are getting continuous connections to the Internet so they can publish information on the World Wide Web. When you begin doing that, you increase your risk—not because the Web is risky in itself, but because someone can now attack your computer in the wee hours of the morning, when you're in bed.

Start by having the right attitude toward security. Believe that it is your workstation's responsibility to protect itself, and not the network's job to protect it. A network provider can restrict who may talk over your connection. However, that probably isn't what you want, because it strips away much of the Internet's value. Most of this book describes how to reach out to random places and find good things. A network conversation is a two-way pipe. If a remote machine can't talk to you, you can't talk to it either. And if that computer has a resource that you might find useful next month, it's your loss. In order to take advantage of the Internet, you must be a part of it. This puts your computer at risk, so you need to protect it.

Security on the Internet is really a group effort by the whole community. One technique that break-in artists use is to break into a chain of computers (e.g., break into A, use A to break into B, B to break into C, etc.). This allows them to cover their tracks more completely. If you think your li'l ol' machine won't be a target because it is so small, dream on. Even if there's nothing of use on your computer, it's a worthwhile intermediary for someone who wants to break into an important system. And some people are out to accumulate notches on their keyboard, counting how many machines they have broken into. Size does not matter.

Discussing security and rumors of security problems is a little difficult. Imagine the following news story:

> At a news conference today, officials of the ACME Safe and Vault Company announced that their locks will unlock with any combination . . . .

To solve the problem of investigating a purported problem, finding a solution, and informing people without making the problem worse, the government has funded an organization named CERT: the Computer Emergency Response Team (see the *Resource Catalog* under "Computing"). CERT investigates security problems, works with manufacturers to solve them, and announces the solutions. It also produces a number of aids to allow people to assess the security of their computers. They prefer to work with site security personnel but will, in an emergency, field questions from anyone. If you feel you are out in the woods alone and must talk to someone about security, you can contact them via e-mail at:

    cert@cert.sei.cmu.edu

There are four ways in which network machines become compromised. In decreasing order of likelihood, these are:[*]

1. Valid users choosing bad passwords

2. Valid users importing corrupt software

3. Illegal users entering through misconfigured software

4. Illegal users entering through an operating system security flaw

You can draw one very important conclusion from this list. It is well within your ability to protect your system. Let's look at what you can do to stay out of trouble.

Passwords

Passwords are obviously the front line of defense against hostile attacks. You can configure Windows 95 to require a password when you start using it. Your Internet service provider will require a password when you start a SLIP or PPP session. You will also need a password to access e-mail on a POP server. Some passwords can be "remembered" by your computer; others, you have to type every time they're needed.

---

[*] See *Computer Security Basics* (Russell and Gangemi) for a general discussion of security issues, and *Practical UNIX Security* (Garfinkel and Spafford) for UNIX-related system administration issues. Both are published by O'Reilly & Associates.

Most people choose passwords for their convenience. Unfortunately, what is convenient for you is also convenient for the hacker. CERT believes that 80 percent of computer break-ins are caused by poor password choice. Remember, when it comes to passwords, computers break in, not people. Some program spends all day trying out passwords; it's not going to get tired when the first three passwords don't work. But you can easily make it very hard to guess the right password. Most password crackers don't pick random letters; they pick common words from the dictionary and simple names. So, pick a good password which:

- Is at least six characters long

- Has a mixture of uppercase, lowercase, and numbers

- Is not a word

- Is not a set of adjacent keyboard keys (e.g., QWERTY)

It is hard for many people to conceive of a password that will meet all the above criteria and will still be easy to remember. One common memory tool is to pick the first letters of a favorite phrase, like *FmdIdgad* (Frankly my dear, I don't give a damn).

Finally, be careful about techniques to bypass password requirements. Exchange, the e-mail package, gives you the option of having it remember your account and password information. If you take advantage of this, anyone who can get physical access to your computer will be able to read your mail or write messages that appear to come from you. Anytime you tell your computer to remember or bypass a password, you add a little more risk.

Importing Software

The following story illustrates the second most common source of security problems:[*]

```
Two Cornell University undergraduates were arrested for computer
tampering. They tampered with a Tetris-style game on a public
server at the school. When played, the game would appear
to work normally, but would cause damage to the machine running it.
It was spread throughout the world by computer networks.
The FBI is investigating and expects further charges to be filed...
```

This is a classic "Trojan horse" program: something threatening hidden in a gift.

Whenever you put software on your machine, you place it at risk. Sharing software can be a great benefit. Only you can decide whether the risk is worth it. Buying commercial software entails minimal risk, especially if you buy from reputable vendors. On the network, there are no assurances. You find a computer

---

[*] This story is a paraphrase of an article in the newsgroup *clari.biz.courts*, February 26, 1992.

that has good stuff on it. You want that stuff. You download it and install it. What can you do to make using it as safe as possible? Here are some rules of thumb:

- Try and use official sources. If you are after a bug fix to Windows 95, it's safer to get the code from a machine whose name ends with **microsoft.com** than **hacker.hoople.usnd.edu**.

- Before installing the software on an important, heavily used system, run it for a while on a less critical computer. If you have one machine on which you do your life's work and another which is only used occasionally, put the new software on the second machine. See if anything bad happens.

- Do a complete backup of your files before using the software.

- Use a virus checker to test the integrity of any software you get from the Net. But don't rely on virus checkers too much; the people writing viruses are generally a step ahead of the people writing the checkers.

Remember: only files that are executed can cause damage. Executable files are the most dangerous; source code is much safer. Data files are never a threat to a computer—though you should be aware that data files may be inaccurate.

System Software Flaws

Operating system flaws are either found and fixed, or work-around procedures are quickly developed. A computer manufacturer doesn't want his product to get a reputation as an "easy mark" for break-ins. The bigger problem comes after the manufacturer takes corrective action. You need to get the update and install it before it will protect anything. You can only install software updates if you know that they exist. Therefore, you need to keep up with the current state and release of your operating system. The easiest way to do this is to maintain a dialog with your campus, corporate, or vendor software support staff. For some obvious reasons, vendors don't make public announcements like, "Listen, everyone, Release 7.4.3.2 has this terrible security problem." It's also worth watching newsgroups and mailing lists on which your system is discussed. You'll find a number of Windows95 newsgroups listed under the grouping *comp.os.ms-windows.win95*.

What If My Computer Is Violated?

The first question to ask is, "How will I know if my computer is violated?" Someone who breaks in tries to be as discreet as possible, covering his tracks as he goes. Once you discover him, you should take corrective action. So, how do you discover a break-in? Most people don't take advantage of security information provided regularly by their computer. Let's say that your machine tells you, "Last login 06:31 26 Jan 1995." Can you remember when you last logged in? Probably not exactly. But you might notice that a login at 6:30 A.M. was strange, given your usual work habits. This is how many break-ins are discovered. The process often starts when someone simply "feels" that something is wrong. For example:

- I don't think I logged in then.

- The machine feels slow today.

- I don't remember deleting or changing that file.

If something like this happens, don't say, "Oh, well," and move on. Investigate further. If you suspect that you have been the target of a break-in, there are a few things you should investigate:

- Examine any log files which might exist for servers you are running.

- Check the task bar for unusual tasks running.

- Get a file list of your top-level hard drive, and look for directories which appear to be too big or to have changed unusually. Look for unfamiliar files or strange modification dates.

However, before you can investigate, you must know what the log file, sizes of directories, etc., normally look like. If you don't know what "normal" is, you're certainly in no position to decide whether or not something is abnormal! Therefore, you should check these things *now*, and continue to do so regularly. If you perform these checks periodically, you'll make sure that nothing suspicious is going on, and you'll stay familiar with your system.

If you see anything that looks suspicious, get help from either your campus or corporate security department. If you don't have one, ask your vendor. Act quickly to get help; do not try to proceed on your own. Don't destroy anything before you get help. Don't do another disk dump onto a standard tape or diskette backup yet; the backup tape you are overwriting may be the last uncorrupted one around. Don't assume that closing one hole fixes the problem. When a break-in artist gains access, the first thing he will do is cover his tracks. Next, he'll create more holes to maintain access to your system.

All of this may sound frightening, but don't let fear paralyze you. After all the cautions I've given, paralysis might sound like a good option. However, the non-networked world is full of dangers too; if you become overzealous about eliminating danger, you'll spend the rest of your life in a concrete-lined underground shelter (oops, can't do that, radon). Most people structure their lives to keep danger to a manageable level. This is a safe, healthy response; healthy adults don't intentionally subject themselves to dangers that they could easily minimize, and they try to live with the dangers that they can't minimize. They wear seat belts; they don't stop traveling. In the network's world, you need to do the same thing. Make sure your password is good, be careful about installing public domain software, watch your system so that you'll be aware of a break-in if one happens, and get help if you need it.

## CHAPTER FIVE

ELECTRONIC MAIL

When Is E-Mail Useful?
Hints for Writing E-Mail
How E-Mail Works
Acquiring E-Mail Addresses
Choosing an E-Mail Package
Exchange—Windows 95's E-Mail Package
Sending Other Documents in E-Mail Messages
Unusual and Non-Standard Features
Mail Lists and Reflectors
Accessing Mailing List Archives
The Eudora E-Mail Package

Most neophytes to electronic mail (e-mail for short) are hesitant at first. But, after sending a few messages (frequently followed by a telephone call to ask whether the mail arrived), most e-mail users quickly become comfortable with the system. Your confidence, too, will grow after you've gotten past the first few awkward messages; you'll be using e-mail frequently and with authority, customizing the system to meet your own needs and establishing your own mailing lists. Soon you will find that e-mail means much more than faster letters and memos. You can take part in electronic conversations about mystery writers, the stock market, or just about anything else you'd like. You might even decide that your telephone is superfluous.

How quickly you become comfortable with electronic mail has a lot to do with your knowledge of the medium and some basic technical decisions you make in choosing and using your e-mail software. To get enough background to describe good e-mail software, we will start by discussing general facilities of electronic mail, mail addressing, and how e-mail works. After that, using Microsoft Exchange as an example, we will look at what features exist in e-mail packages. Finally, we will talk about how to use those features in concert to move files, take part in discussions, and deal with problems that you might run across.

Exchange is an excellent mailer; you should be aware, though, that it can't be used for Internet mail unless you install Microsoft's Internet Jumpstart Kit. Different ways to acquire the Internet Jumpstart Kit are described in Appendix B, *Setting Up Your Internet Connection*. If you're interested in other options, there are many alternatives available. We provide a brief overview of Eudora, one widely used e-mail package that happens to be free.

When Is E-Mail Useful?

Like any other tool, e-mail has its strengths and weaknesses. On the surface, it appears to be just a faster way of delivering letters or their equivalent. To know when e-mail is appropriate, think about how it differs from other communications media. In some ways, e-mail is very similar to the telephone; in other ways, it's similar to traditional postal mail. Table 5-1 makes a quick comparison.

Table 5-1: Comparison of Communication Techniques

Factors	Telephone	E-Mail	Post
Speed	High	Moderate	Low
Synchronized	Yes	No	No
Formality	Varies	Moderate	Varies
Accountability	Low	Moderate	High
Conferencing	Small group	Any to all	One-way only
Security	Moderate	Low	High

First, let's think about how quickly each medium gets a message from one point to another. The telephone offers immediate delivery and works at a fairly high communication speed. The time it takes to deliver e-mail ranges from seconds to a day; and, as I'm sure you know, postal delivery can be overnight in the best case, but often takes several days. The price you pay for the quick communication of the telephone is that the caller and the sender must be synchronized; that is, they must both be on the phone at the same time. E-mail and postal mail are both asynchronous; the sender sends when the time is ripe, and you read it at your leisure. This comes in handy if you are trying to communicate over a long distance (e.g., across many time zones), or when daily schedules are quite different.

The delivery time for e-mail consists of two parts: the time it takes the network to deliver the message to your mail computer, and your delay in reading it once it arrives. The first part is a function of how your mail machine is connected to the network; it can only be changed with an outflow of money. The second part is under your control. If you don't check your e-mail regularly, then quick delivery is meaningless. Your messages just sit there waiting for you to come and look through them. Electronic mail becomes more useful as the delay in machine-to-human delivery is reduced. Try and keep it under a few hours. When e-mail is delivered (and read) quickly, it can become almost as convenient and fluent as a personal conversation.

Formality and accountability are closely related. On the telephone, formality varies: with some people you are very formal, with others, very casual. The same is true of postal mail. You have a lot of time to construct messages and multiple formats to choose from (handwritten notes, typed business letters, etc.). These formats and other cues (e.g., a perfumed envelope) give signals, both to yourself and to your reader, regarding the purpose of the note. E-mail is always typed, and there is no chapter in any high school typing book on the format of an e-mail letter.* Also, individuals are somewhat hidden in e-mail (i.e., the big boss's e-mail address looks just like everyone else's). Since e-mail often flies between parties at a rate approaching a conversation, and since most people are more comfortable being friendly than combative, many people tend to drift into informality in their electronic messaging. This can be a problem when it comes to accountability, the necessity of writers to take responsibility for their messages. There's also the possibility that someone may forward your message into the wrong hands.

Written media tend to hold writers more accountable for their actions than spoken media. If you are having a telephone conversation and make some comments you wish you hadn't, you can later claim that you didn't say them or that the hearer misunderstood (or take comfort knowing that only one person heard them). If you try and do this with e-mail, someone will have saved a copy of the message in a file and will trot it out to be rehashed. The only factor that reduces e-mail accountability is that the sender's identity can be spoofed. I could send you an e-mail with the return address **president@whitehouse.gov**, offering you a seat on the Supreme Court. It is also possible to forge paper mail, but it is a lot more difficult: I would have to mimic stationery, postmarks, signatures, etc. Digital signatures, which are discussed briefly in Chapter 14, *Other Applications*, make it impossible (or at least very difficult) to forge e-mail; however, these signatures aren't yet in widespread use.

Next, we need to examine group communications. The telephone is a fine medium, but only for small groups. Conference calls allow groups to talk with each other, but as the group gets larger, scheduling and setup become prohibitively difficult. On the other end of the spectrum, bulk mail is easy to use and can reach millions with little difficulty. The problem with junk mail (aside from being a nuisance) is that all messages originate from one point and go to the whole group. Communications from any other point cannot easily be sent to the whole group. E-mail allows you to set up arbitrarily large groups, and any member of the group can communicate with the whole at any time. This makes it very useful, both for disseminating information and for querying a group.

Finally, the security of e-mail is low, compared to the other media. If I am careful with the post, a letter could remain within locked boxes or the Postal Service until it gets into the recipient's hands. If it is opened along the way, damage to the envelope normally makes the intrusion obvious. Telephone tapping by normal folks requires access to the facilities at one end or the other to intercept a conversation. Once a conversation makes it outside your building and into the telephone network, it is technically difficult for anyone to intrude without the phone company's help.

---

* If you want some hints about e-mail style and usage, see O'Reilly & Associates' *Using Email Effectively*, by Linda Lamb and Jerry Peek.

E-mail, however, takes a fairly predictable route through computers, and the security may be questionable on some of them. Also, there are error modes where a message might be undeliverable and a computer, not knowing what else to do, delivers it to a mail administrator. Administrators will not normally snoop or spread your message around, but still, if security is an issue, having your mail fall into the hands of someone else—even a responsible administrator—is unsuitable. Privacy-enhanced mailers try to encrypt the message to combat these security deficiencies, but they are not in general use. As a general rule, you can't trust e-mail's security, and therefore you shouldn't use it when security is an issue. The most widely used privacy package is PGP, which is discussed in Chapter 14, *Other Applications.*

Hints for Writing E-Mail

If you read much e-mail, you'll see a lot of messages that should never have been sent—and that the sender probably wishes he or she hadn't sent. To prevent making such mistakes yourself, you should develop some e-mail etiquette. Creating good habits while you're beginning can prevent big embarrassments later on. Here is some advice:

- Never commit anything to e-mail that you wouldn't want to become public knowledge. As was discussed previously, you never really know who may end up reading your e-mail message. This may be on purpose (e.g., if a co-worker covers someone's e-mail while he's on vacation), or by mistake, either yours or a misbehaving computer's. The threat does not end when the mail is deleted from the mail system. E-mail messages are frequently caught in system backups and sit on tapes in machine rooms for years. With enough effort, an old message might be found and resurrected. (This was how much of Oliver North's connection to the Iran-Contra affair was documented.)

- Don't send abusive, harassing, threatening, or bigoted messages. While abuse, harassment, and even bigotry are hard to define, there's one good rule of thumb: if a message's recipient complains, stop. E-mail can usually be traced to its originating machine, and systems on the Internet are liable for the misdeeds of their users. You don't want your system administrator (or the system administrator of your e-mail link) to receive complaints about your activity. It could come back to haunt you.

- Writers frequently approach e-mail as a friendly conversation, but recipients frequently view e-mail as a cast-in-stone business letter. You might have had a wry smile on your face when you wrote the note, but that wry smile doesn't cross the network. Also, you can't control when the message will be read, so it might be received at the worst possible moment. Consider sitting around after work having a drink with a co-worker and saying, "You really blew that sale." You could judge his frame of mind before speaking, so you could be sure your co-worker will take it as a joke. That same thing in e-mail, which he reads after just being chewed out by the boss, comes off as "YOU REALLY BLEW THAT SALE!!!"

- Be very careful with sarcasm. Consider this exchange with the big boss (a real hands-on manager):

```
You worked with Sam a while ago. What would you think of promoting
him to regional sales manager?
```

To which you respond:

```
He's a real winner!
```

Does he get the promotion? The answer could either mean that he won the last three "Salesperson of the Year" awards, or that he hasn't sold anything for the past three years. There is no body language, nor perhaps any personal knowledge on the recipient's side (e.g., she may not know that you are quite the wisecracker). Some help is available for these situations. For example, inserting a "smiley" face into a message denotes "said with a cynical smile." So:

```
He's a real winner! :-]
```

means he couldn't sell his way out of a paper bag. Another symbol is the wink, meaning, "it's better left unsaid, but catch my drift." For example:

```
Sam and Bertha spent a long time in her room last night, working on
the presentation. ;-)
```

A sentence whose meaning is left to the reader. ;-) There are many others which are used less frequently. In general, their meanings are pretty discernible, so you'll have to figure them out for yourself. :-(

Aside from basic e-mail etiquette, there are a couple of style guidelines that, if followed, make e-mail easier to read and understand:

- Keep the line length reasonable (less than 60 characters). You want it to display on most terminals. If the note gets forwarded, it might be indented by a tab character (usually 8 columns). Messages that consist of a single extremely long line are particularly obnoxious. You have an ENTER key; use it! This may be especially hard if your mail package automatically goes to a new line when one gets too full. Frequently, these new lines are not inserted in the text; they only show up on your screen. When the message gets to its destination, it may be strangely formatted. It may appear as one long line or, as Microsoft Exchange handles it, there'll be strange characters like "=" inserted at the ends of lines.

- Use mixed case. All uppercase sounds harsh, like shouting. UPPERCASE CAN BE USED FOR EMPHASIS, as can *asterisks* and _underscores_!

- Read your message before you send it, and decide if you'll regret it in the morning. On most systems, once you send it, you can't get it back.

How E-Mail Works

Electronic mail differs from the other applications we are looking at because it is not an "end-to-end" service: the sending and receiving machines need not be able to communicate directly with each other to make it work. It is known as a store-and-forward service. Mail is passed from one machine to another until it finally arrives at its destination. This is completely analogous to the way the U.S. Postal Service delivers mail; if we examine that, we can draw some interesting conclusions.

The U.S. Postal Service operates a store-and-forward network. You address a message and put it into a post box. The message is picked up by a truck and sent to another place and stored there. It is sorted and forwarded to another place. This step is repeated until it arrives at the recipient's mailbox. If the recipient's mailbox happens to be in a place where the U.S. Postal Service cannot deliver directly (e.g., another country), you can still send the message; the U.S. Postal Service will pass the message to the postal service of that country for delivery.

We can infer a couple of things about the Internet from this analogy. First, if you correctly address a message, the network will take it from there. You needn't know much about what's going on. We can also infer that messages can be moved between the Internet and other mail networks. This is true, but the address required is more complex in order to get to and through the foreign network.

Just as with the Postal Service, if the destination and source are not on the same network, there needs to be a place where the e-mail from one network is handed to the e-mail service of another. Points of connection between e-mail networks are computers called application gateways. They are called gateways because they can be viewed as magic doors between worlds; they are application gateways because they know enough about the e-mail applications on both sides to reformat messages so that they are legal on the new network. To send mail through a gateway, you frequently have to give an address which contains both information about how to get to the gateway, and information about how to deliver the mail on the other side. We'll discuss addressing further below.

Finally, before you can put a postal letter into a mailbox, you put it in an envelope. The same happens to e-mail, except that the "envelope" is called a mail header. The header is the **To:**, **From:**, **Subject:** stuff on the front of the message. Just as an envelope may get changed *en route* (e.g., a hand-scribbled "not at this address" here, a yellow sticker with a forwarding address there, etc.), the mail header gets stuff stuck into it while the message is traveling to help you figure out what route it took, just in case it doesn't get through.

It's All in the Address

Whether or not your e-mail gets to its destination depends almost solely on whether or not the address is constructed correctly. (E-mail sometimes fails because machines or pieces of the network are unavailable, but usually the network tries to send mail for days before giving up.) Unfortunately, e-mail addresses are a bit more complex than the simple host addresses that I introduced in Chapter 3, *How the Internet Works*. They are more complex for several reasons:

- The world of e-mail is bigger than the Internet
- E-mail needs to be addressed to a person, not just a machine
- Personal names are sometimes included as comments in e-mail addresses

Let's start with the Internet's addressing rules. On the Internet, the basis for all mail is the domain name of the machine which is acting as a mail agent (the machine that's handling the addressee's mail—say **ux1.cso.uiuc.edu**). In fact, this is all that the network, per se, worries about. Once it has delivered a message to the named machine, the network's task is over. It's up to that computer to deliver it the rest of the way, but the machine requires more information about further routing: at the minimum, the name of a user, but possibly extended information for routing the mail to another kind of network. For example, the address krol@uxc.csu.uiuc.edu means, "the user named **krol** on the host **uxc.cso.uiuc.edu**." Most of the addresses you see will be like this.

Some people will not know enough to give you a complete e-mail address. They will say things like "Send me e-mail, I'm johnw on the Microsoft Network." Now you have to figure out what that means in the world of e-mail addressing. Luckily, most of these colloquially named networks have a direct mapping into Internet addresses. You just need to know that the translation of what Johnw said earlier is to send e-mail to **johnw@msn.com**. Table 5-2 shows common e-mail network names and their translations into Internet addresses.

Table 5-2: Addressing Users of Other Networks

Network	Send Mail To	Notes
Alternex	*user*@ax.apc.org	
ALAnet	*user*%ALANET@intermail.isi.edu	American Library Association
America Online	*user*@aol.com	User name lowercase, spaces removed
Applelink	*user*@applelink.apple.com	
ATTmail	*user*@attmail.com	
BIX	*user*@bix.com	
CGNet	*user*%CGNET@intermail.isi.edu	
Chasque	*user*@chasque.apc.org	
Comlink	*user*@oln.comlink.apc.org	
Delphi	*user*@delphi.com	
Econet	*user*@igc.apc.org	
Ecuanex	*user*@ecuanex.apc.org	
eWorld	*user*@on-line.apple.com	
Genie	*user*@genie.geis.com	

Table 5-2: Addressing Users of Other Networks (continued)

Network	Send Mail To	Notes
GeoNet	*user*@geo1.geonet.de	For recipients in Europe
	user@geo2.geonet.de	For recipients in the United Kingdom
	user@geo4.geonet.de	For recipients in North America
Glasnet	*user*@glas.apc.org	
Greenet	*user*@gn.apc.org	
Microsoft Network	*user*@msn.com	
Nasamail	*user*@nasamail.nasa.gov	
Nicarao	*user*@nicarao.apc.org	
NIFTY-Serve	*user*@niftyserve.or.jp	
Nordnet	*user*@pns.apc.org	
Peacenet	*user*@igc.apc.org	
Pegasus	*user*@peg.apc.org	
Prodigy	*user*@prodigy.com	Alphanumeric ID rather than name
Pronet	*user*@tanus.oz.au	
Web	*user*@web.apc.org	

It would be nice if all the e-mail gateways in the world were that simple. Unfortunately, they're not. Here are the more difficult addressing problems:

Bitnet

Bitnet addresses normally have the form *name@host.bitnet*. Try this first, it may work. If it doesn't, change this address to something like *name%host*, and use that for the login name part of the address. Use the address of a Bitnet-Internet gateway for the machine name side (for example, **cunyvm.cuny.edu**). Separate the two with an "at" (@) sign. For example, rewrite the address **krol@uiucvmd.bitnet** as **krol%uiucvmd@cunyvm.cuny.edu**.[*] If you are going to do this regularly, find out the best gateway for you to use from someone local.

CompuServe

CompuServe addresses consist of two numbers separated by a comma. Change the comma to a period and use that on the left-hand side of the address. To the right of the @ use **compuserve.com**. So, a CompuServe address of 76543,123 would be addressed **76543.123@compuserve.com**.

Fidonet

Fidonet addresses consist of a first and last name, and a set of numbers of the form a:b/c.d. Separate the first and last names with a period (.) and send to p*d*.f*c*.n*b*.z*a*.fidonet.org. For example, send mail to Willie Martin at **1:5/2.3** by

---

[*] This is a non-standard format for an address, known as the "BBN hack," but it is in common use, is easy for people to understand, and it works. The standard way of doing this would be **@cunyvm.cuny.edu:krol@uiucvmd**.

using the address **willie.martin@p3.f2.n5.z1.fidonet.org**. Some machines still may have trouble with an address like this. If yours does, try sending the above address to the gateway machine: **willie.martin%p3.f2.n5.z1.fidonet.org@ zeus.ieee.org**.

Sprintmail

Complete Sprintmail addresses look like "John Bigboote" /YOYODYNE/TELE-MAIL/US. If the address is used within Sprintmail, it can be abbreviated to John Bigboote/YOYODYNE. These first two parameters are the person and an organization. When someone gives you a Sprintmail address, this is all they will provide. The positional parameters need to be plugged into a command like the following:[*]

```
PN=John.Bigboote/O=YOYODYNE/ADMD=TELEMAIL/C=US/@sprint.com
```

Even if the person only gives you the first two parts of the address, the complete address should be used when sending it to **sprint.com**.

MCImail

There are multiple ways of addressing MCImail. MCI mailboxes have both an address and a person's name associated with them. The address looks a lot like a phone number. If that's what you have, then use that number on the left side of the @, and use the gateway name **mcimail.com** on the right side. For example: **1234567@mcimail.com**. If you are given the name of a person on MCImail, you can send mail by addressing it to **firstname_lastname@mcimail. com**, like: **John_Bigboote@mcimail.com**.

UUCP

Change the UUCP address, which looks like *name@host.uucp*, to *name%host*. Use that for the login name portion of the address. Use the address of a UUNET-Internet gateway as the machine name. Internet service providers provide these gateways for these constituents. Of course, you should separate the two with an "at" sign. For example, a user receiving mail via uucp from PSI, Inc. should be sent mail through **uu.psi.com**, like **john_w%yoyodyne@ uu.psi.com**. You can ask your e-mail or system administrator for a good gateway for you to use.

Many people also give UUCP addresses in the form: *. . .!uunet!host!name*. This is a UUCP "path"; it means "You figure out how to get the mail to the system named **uunet**, and then **uunet** will send it to **host**, which will deliver it." Convert this to: *name%host@gatewaymachine*. You pick the proper gateway by examining the UUCP path address. If it has **uunet** as part of the address you could use **uunet.uu.net**, if it has **uupsi** as part of the address you could use **uu.psi.com**, etc. On very rare occasions, you may see gateway names other than **uunet** or **uupsi** in the path; you will have to figure out the Internet

---

[*] This is called an X.500-style address. X.500 is an ISO standard form of addressing that no one really likes, but it will probably be around for a long time.

address of the gateway. Giving addresses as "paths" is, fortunately, becoming less common.

Acquiring E-Mail Addresses

Once you decide to jump into the e-mail world, you have to start collecting e-mail addresses. There is no national registry of e-mail addresses. There are a few specialized servers that you can peruse to try and find someone's address. These servers are known as white pages servers because they provide the electronic equivalent to the white pages section in the telephone book. (Chapter 11, *Finding Someone*, tells you how to use the most common servers.) But the easiest and best way of acquiring these addresses is via information given to you directly, be it as a business card, a phone call, a postal letter, an e-mail message, or a newsgroup posting.

This method of acquiring e-mail addresses has two advantages over all others:

- You are fairly sure it is an e-mail address which is current and checked regularly. An address found in an index might be an old e-mail address used at a previous employer, or an address on a machine which no longer exists.

- If you consistently have problems getting to the person's e-mail address, the address he gives out to all interested parties will probably reflect the best way to get to his machine. For example, if Joe's business card gives his e-mail address as **joe%bizarrenet@bizarregate.com**, that's the address you should try first.

Sometimes when you try to glean e-mail addresses from mail you receive, you will see an address which looks like:

```
John Bigboote <johnb@yoyodyne.com>
```

The full name "John Bigboote" is a comment; the actual address is **johnb@yoyodyne.com** inside the brackets. Adding comments to the e-mail address is a really nice thing to do. As in the example above, the comment is usually the addressee's name. Adding the name as a comment makes it clear to other recipients who got the message. This is especially true if the person's e-mail address is computer generated, like **ajzxmvk@uicvmc.bitnet**. Wouldn't you like to know who reads that mail! If you get a message as part of a mail distribution list, and if the list's manager has included comments, you can look at the **To:** field and easily see who else got the message—even if the e-mail addresses themselves are not recognizable. (You might want to squirrel away some of those addresses in case you want to send one of them a message later.)

Choosing an E-Mail Package

You should think about several questions when deciding what e-mail software to use:

- With whom are you going to be exchanging mail?

- How closely are you "tied" to them?

- What do you like in a user interface?

- How much do you travel?

- Are you happy sending text, or do you want to send other data?

- Where do you get network support from?

Many facilities are common to all mailers. Other features (like digitized pictures and voice) can only be used when the sender and recipient both use similar mail software and operating system utilities. If your goal is to transfer all kinds of files between a small circle of friends with as little trouble as possible, then you and your friends should agree on a single mail system and use it. If that is not a big concern, then you should pick the e-mail software that you find the easiest to use, and with which you can feel at home.

Microsoft's Exchange and other packages, such as Qualcomm's Eudora, are what is known as POP mail clients. POP stands for Post Office Protocol, and describes the "dialog" between two computers. POP clients don't transfer e-mail to other Internet hosts directly; they let some larger computer with a full-time, dedicated connection act as their Internet mail server.* This means that your machine is not required to be available for e-mail transfers all the time; you can have a dial-up Internet connection, or you can turn off the computer when you go home. Whenever you ask for e-mail, you computer contacts the server and downloads all the mail that has accumulated for you.

For example, your machine may be named **johnspc.yoyodyne.com**, but your e-mail address might be on the computer **mail.yoyodyne.com**. While your computer is turned off, people can continue to send e-mail to **johnb@mail.yoyodyne.com**, where it will accumulate. When you come into work and connect your computer to the Internet, it will check regularly (say, once every 20 minutes) with **mail.yoyodyne.com** to see if any mail has arrived. If it has, it will download your mail to **johnspc.yoyodyne.com** and delete it from the server. You may then use Exchange's nice familiar interface to do whatever you may want to do.

If you always use one computer to check your mail, POP mail programs are just fine. It was designed for people who use one computer exclusively and may only connect to the Internet occasionally. You can then read, think, and queue new messages to be sent while disconnected from the network. The next time you connect to the Net, the queued mail is sent. This minimizes the amount of time you are actually connected to the e-mail server, and therefore tends to lower costs. For the traveler it also lets you dial up in Chicago, download 20 messages, read and respond to them at 30,000 feet over Cleveland, queue your responses, and, finally, send the queued mail and pick up a new batch when you arrive in Washington, D.C. Your mail goes with you on your personal computer.

---

* Exchange can also be used with many on-line services, such as CompuServe, as well as with Internet providers.

Many POP clients allow you to operate them in remote mode. This allows you to leave messages you don't want to deal with at once on your mail service computer. This is useful if you have multiple personal computers (one at home and one at the office) which you read mail from. You can configure either Exchange or Eudora to work this way.

However, POP mailers aren't appropriate for everyone. If you don't have a personal computer and mooch connectivity as you travel ("Pardon me, John Warfin, but could I use your computer to check my mail?"), they present a bit of a problem. You don't want to be downloading your messages to John Warfin's computer. You want to peek at the messages and leave them on the mail server when you get back to your home system, where you can download them to your computer. For these situations, using a mainframe-based e-mail package (with which you contact the server directly and manipulate your messages in place), is more appropriate. Or, if your Windows 95 machine stays put while you travel, you can use the remote access facility to read mail on your desktop machine—which in turn collects mail through POP. Which solution is available or best is purely dependent on your corporate or Internet providers environment.

Exchange—Windows 95's E-Mail Package

Microsoft Exchange is a very complete and complex mail package. The whole issue of e-mail can be very intricate. However, it needn't be daunting. Ninety percent of your e-mail needs can be satisfied with a good grasp of the basics. We will start by looking at the basic ways of reading and sending messages. Afterwards, we will look at some of the bells and whistles.

Before you start using Exchange, you must give it information about how to access your Internet service provider. This process is covered in Appendix B. Once you have finished configuring Exchange, you can start the program by double clicking on the **Inbox** icon on your desktop.[*] Exchange rewards you with a dialog box, asking for your password, as shown in Figure 5-1.[†] This password may be different from the password you give when you boot up Windows 95, and the password assigned to your POP mail account by your Internet service provider's computer. It is the password to a Personal Information Store. A Personal Information Store gives the appearance of a special disk directory. It contains information about your e-mail; that is, the mail you have downloaded, your service provider's POP mail password, nicknames you have given people, etc. Most Windows 95 computers will have a single Personal Information Store. If more than one person uses the same computer, everyone will have their own Personal Information Store, to keep e-mail separate and private.

---

[*] If you don't see this icon, you can use **Find** under the **Start** button to search for Exchange.

[†] The password is set when you configure Exchange; see Appendix B for more information.

Personal Folders Password   ☒

Enter the password for 'mailbox'.   ┌─────────┐
                                                                    │   OK   │
                                                                    └─────────┘
<u>P</u>assword: [   ]   ┌─────────┐
                                                                    │ Cancel │
                                                                    └─────────┘
☐ <u>S</u>ave this password in your password list   ┌─────────┐
                                                                    │ <u>H</u>elp   │
                                                                    └─────────┘

Figure 5–1: Exchange Password dialog

If your computer is located in a secure place and you are not particularly worried about someone reading your e-mail (or writing mail which looks like it came from you), you can check the box **Save this password**. . . before you click **OK**. Windows 95 will store your password and use it whenever necessary; you won't have to type the password each time you use Exchange. However, anyone who can walk up to your computer will have access to your e-mail. This may be fine for a computer at home, but perhaps not for one in a fairly public part of an office.

Fill in the blank with your password, click **OK**, and Exchange will query your service provider and see if it has received any new mail. If it has, the mail is moved to your computer for reading. Once your e-mail has been moved to your computer, Exchange will display the main window, shown in Figure 5-2.

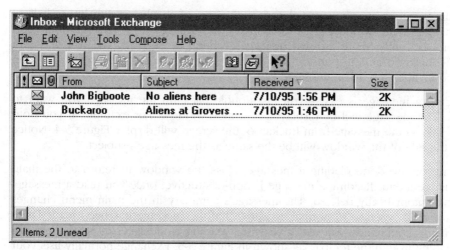

Figure 5–2: Main Exchange window

Most of the commands you need for reading or writing mail are available through the toolbar shown in Figure 5-3. Note that some functions in the toolbar, such as deleting a message, will have their buttons shaded and unavailable until you have selected a message by clicking.

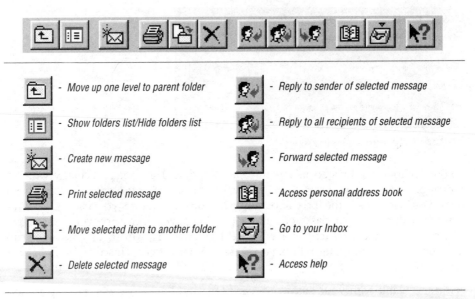

Figure 5–3: Exchange main toolbar

Reading Your Mail

As messages arrive, they are placed at the top of the list in the lower half of Exchange's main window. This list displays the messages in reverse chronological order.* Currently, there are two messages waiting to be read. The first was sent from Buckaroo at 1:46 p.m. on July 10, 1995. The latter one was sent from John Bigboote at 1:56 p.m. on the same day.

Reading a message is easy—you just double click on the message you want to read. The message will be displayed in a new window. For example, if you double-click on the message from Buckaroo, the screen will display Figure 5-4. Notice that the title of the window will be the same as the message's subject.

When you are done reading a message, close the window to return to the main Exchange menu. Reading a message is non-destructive; once you read a message, it isn't automatically deleted. The message's summary in the main menu changes from a bold typeface to normal, to show that the message has been read. There are many commands you can give while reading a message; most of them are available through the toolbar, as shown in Figure 5-5. Exchange normally lists your messages chronologically, most recent first. If you get a lot of e-mail, you may find it more convenient to sort mail by sender or by subject. To do so, click on the **From** or **Subject** button above the message list. (The **Received** button sorts the

---

* You can change this by pulling down **View** and selecting **Sort**. Then check **Ascending** for **Received**.

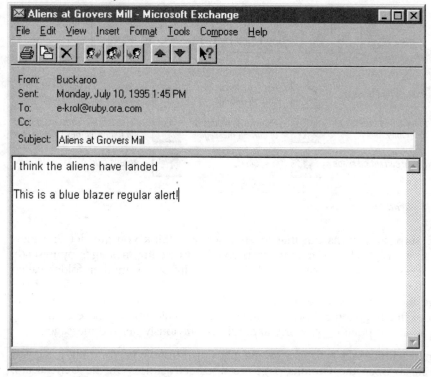

Figure 5–4: Buckaroo's message

messages in the default chronological order.) Sorting messages by subject is usually the most helpful.

Deleting messages

Unless you consciously delete them, messages keep accumulating in your **Inbox** until you run out of space. You can delete a message by clicking the **Delete** icon while you're reading it. If you click this icon, Exchange will not only delete the message, it will also open the message before the deleted one. If you don't like this feature, you can change it by pulling down the **Tools** menu and selecting **Options**. On the **Read** tab, there is a section called **After Moving or Deleting an Open Item**. This section lets you specify what to do when you delete an item you're reading.

The **Delete** button also appears on the main Exchange window (see Figure 5-2), but is shaded. It doesn't make sense to delete a message until you have selected the message you want to delete. If you select a message by clicking on it, the message will be highlighted and the **Delete** button will become active. If you push it now, it will delete the selected message.

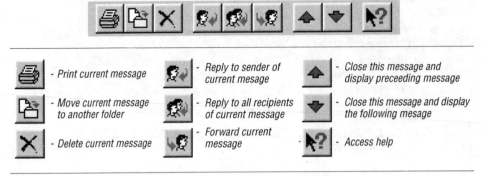

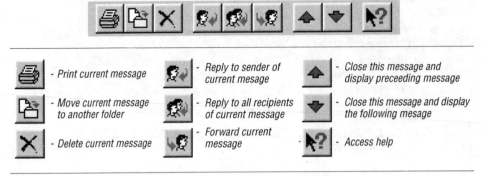 - Print current message

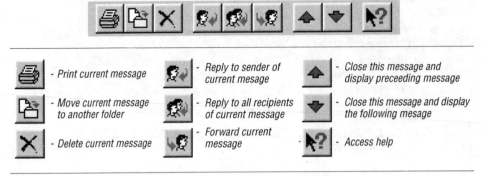 - Move current message to another folder

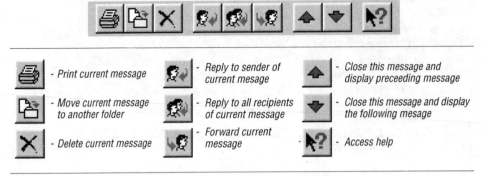 - Delete current message

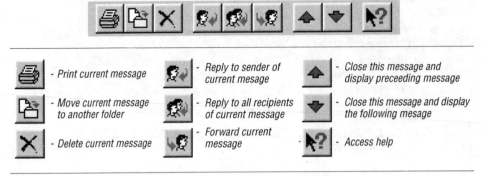 - Reply to sender of current message

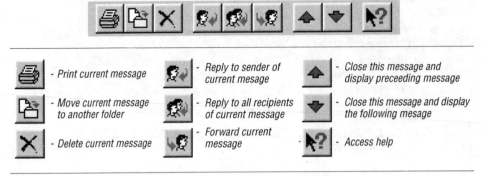 - Reply to all recipients of current message

 - Forward current message

 - Close this message and display preceeding message

 - Close this message and display the following message

 - Access help

Figure 5–5: Read Message toolbar

Now the surprise: it turns out that, even when you think you are deleting messages, you aren't. Exchange tries to keep you from deleting messages by mistake. Deleted messages are actually moved from your **Inbox** to another folder called **Deleted Items**, where they accumulate. You can go in there and delete them; Exchange then asks if you really want to delete the message forever. If you say yes, you've finally gotten rid of the bugger. We'll discuss folders more completely later on, so at this point don't worry about these previously deleted messages.

If deleting each message twice seems like too much trouble (and I think it is), you might want to open the **Options** page we discussed earlier. On the **General** tab, there is an option labeled **Empty the "Deleted Items" folder on exiting**. If you check that, messages are deleted forever when you quit Exchange.

Folders

Folders let you save messages in an organized way. For example, you could have a folder for each project you're involved with, and another folder for personal mail. As mail arrives, you can file it in the appropriate folder for future reference. These filed messages can be examined from within Exchange, using the same features you use to read incoming mail.

The **Inbox** is just a special folder where Exchange puts incoming mail. You can view the folders in your Personal Information Store by clicking the **Show/Hide Folders List** icon. Exchange responds by displaying your folders on the left side of its main window, as shown in Figure 5-6. The left-hand part of the window contains the Personal Information Store at the highest level; it contains four folders. We've already talked about **Inbox** and **Deleted Items**. **Outbox**, like its desktop counterpart, is the queue of messages that are waiting to be sent to your mail service. When a message is actually sent, it is moved into the **Sent Items** folder, which

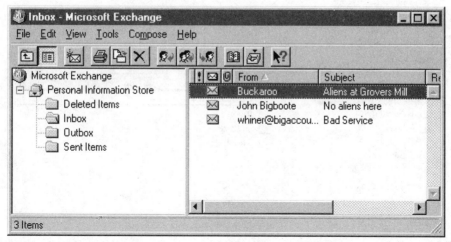

Figure 5-6: Folder tree

contains a copy of every message you have ever sent using Exchange. You'll want to clear out the **Sent Items** folder periodically.

Notice that the **Inbox** folder's icon is different from the others. **Inbox** was open when you clicked **Show Folders**, so its icon shows an open folder; the right-hand side of the screen shows the messages contained in that folder. To view the contents of another folder, just click on the folder name. Its contents will appear on the right. If you click **Show Folders** again, the folder panel on the left will disappear, and the screen will list the messages contained in the last folder you opened.

When you get comfortable with e-mail, you'll want to store messages in your own folders, organized as they make sense to you. Creating a folder is not hard, but it does require several steps. First, you must decide where you want to put the new folder. Click on the folder which will contain the new folder (i.e., its parent folder), so that it is highlighted.

In Figure 5-7 we are about to create a new folder at the same level as **Inbox** and **Outbox**; to do so, we clicked on **Personal Information Store.**[*] Next, we pull down the **File** menu and select **Create Folder**. Windows 95 will then ask you what to call the new folder with the dialog box shown in Figure 5-8. We entered *Blue Blazers* and clicked **OK**. Our new folder is now created and is shown in Figure 5-9. Now, we need to move some messages into it. We position ourselves at the **Inbox** by clicking on its folder. This displays the **Inbox**'s contents on the right side of the window. We can then select the message from Buckaroo by clicking on it once.

---

[*] Notice that the folders contained in the Personal Information Store are displayed on the right half of the screen. A folder may contain any combination of other folders and mail messages.

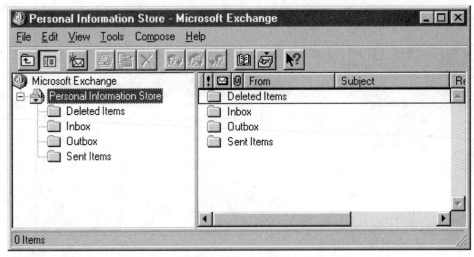

Figure 5-7: Preparing to create a folder

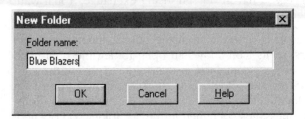

Figure 5-8: Folder Naming dialog

After you select a message, you move it by clicking the **Move Item** icon*—the one that shows a piece of paper being put in a folder. Exchange responds (Figure 5-10) by asking where you want to move the message. Since all your folders are part of your Personal Information Store, it knows you must want to put it somewhere in there, but it doesn't know quite where. To see what a folder contains, you must first click on the plus sign to the left of its name. We can see the cursor arrow pointing to the plus sign in preparation to peek inside.

Clicking the plus sign opens the folder, as shown in Figure 5-11. Notice that the plus sign has changed into a minus sign. You can hide the folder's contents by clicking the minus again—but we won't. Instead, we'll select a destination folder by clicking on it; to transfer the message, press **OK**.

---

* This is Move *Item* because it can be used to move any item such as a folder from one point to another.

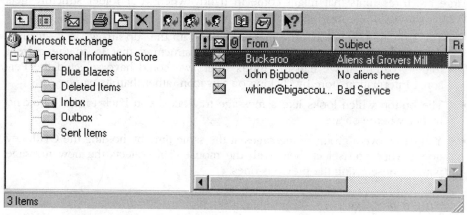

Figure 5-9: Selecting a message for transfer

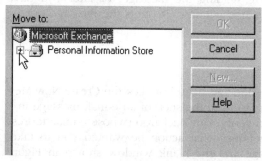

Figure 5-10: Opening a folder

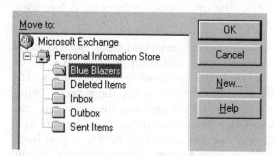

Figure 5-11: Completing the transfer

If you glance back to Figure 5-4, you will notice the **Move** icon is also available while you are reading a message. If you want to store the message you are reading in another folder, just click on the icon; then proceed as we just discussed.

Here are three hints that might come in handy when your folder structure gets complex and you are moving many things around:

- The **Up One Level** icon—the manila folder with the "up arrow" in it—causes you to move up one level in your folder structure, that is, to the current folder's parent. If we had the **Inbox** open, we could have selected the Personal Information Store by clicking on this icon rather than its name.

- The button which looks like a message tray takes you back to the **Inbox** no matter where you are.

- You can move a group of messages at the same time by holding the CTRL key down while you select them with the mouse. This selects the new message without unselecting the previous ones.

Printing a message

To print a message, click on the **Print Message** icon (which looks like a printer). You can use this icon while you are reading the message, or after you have selected a message in the main Exchange window. It prints the message on the Windows 95 default printer.

Sending Messages

Sending a message is not much more difficult—you just click the **Create New Message** button (the envelope with a star) to form the shell of an e-mail message in a new window. Let's say you wanted to verify with Buckaroo (whose e-mail address you know to be **buckaroo@blueblazer.org**) what action he wanted you to take. You would press **Create New Message** and the blank window shown in Figure 5-12 would appear.

Notice that this window has two toolbars. The upper one contains basic functions for composing messages, as shown in Figure 5-13.

The second toolbar, shown in Figure 5-14, contains extended features. The icons in this toolbar allow you to change the font, style, and color of text you enter in messages. These features, although nice, cannot be used unless the recipient's mail reader can handle Microsoft rich text messages. At this point, there aren't many mail readers with this capability, so you're better off ignoring the extended features. It's no use sending Buckaroo a message he can't read. Just to make sure you don't make a mistake, Exchange will only use the extended features if you have declared in a nickname (covered a bit later in this chapter) that the recipient can handle rich text messages. Otherwise, Exchange only sends normal, non-fancy mail messages.

Let's get back to our message to Buckaroo; the aliens have landed and there's no time to waste.

Place the mouse in the **To:** field and click the left mouse button. This selects the field; you can now fill in Buckaroo's address (see Figure 5-15). The address list

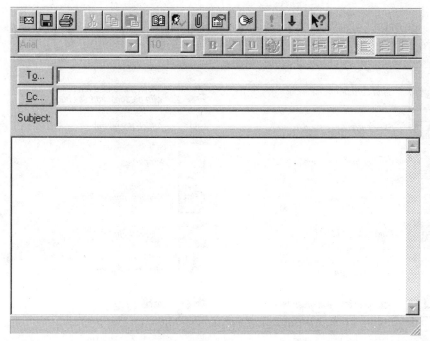

Figure 5–12: New (empty) mail message

can be one or more addresses separated by semicolons.* If any addresses are not full domain names, (i.e., **ed** instead of **krol@ux1.cso.uiuc.edu**), then Exchange assumes that they're aliases or nicknames you have created.

Next, select the **Subject:** field and fill that in. Subjects are optional, but as you have seen already, the sender's name and message subject are the only information the recipient gets to decide whether to read your message now or later. It is usually a good idea to provide a pointed, well-thought-out subject. Finally, you are ready to enter the text of your message in the big white area. Click in this area and type away.

When you are satisfied that the message really says what you want to say, and that you won't regret sending it later, you can send it on its way by pushing the **Send Current Message** button (which shows the letter speeding on its way).

---

* Yes, semicolons! Most e-mail packages (and the Internet standard form for messages) use commas, but Exchange converts the semicolons to commas as it sends the message.

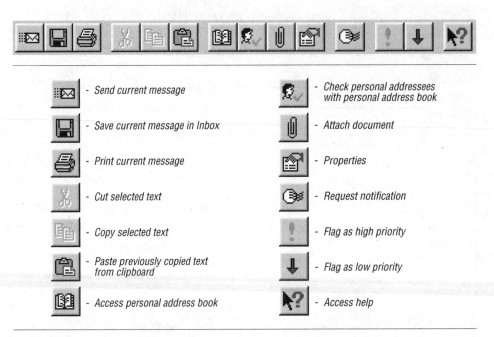

Figure 5–13: Main message composition toolbar

Figure 5–14: Extended Composing Toolbar

Carbon copies

Just as in a paper memo, it is frequently useful to differentiate between those to whom the message is primarily directed, and those who receive it for their information. You can do this by using the line beginning with **Cc:** when you create a new message. Anyone listed on the **Cc:** line will also receive a copy of the message, just as if he or she were listed on the **To:** line.

Some e-mail packages have the ability to send blind carbon copies of messages. Blind carbon copies, or bcc's are sent to a list of readers, just like carbon copies. However, the record that lists the recipients is automatically deleted from the outgoing mail. Therefore, none of the recipients will know who (if anyone) received the additional copies.

Exchange allows you to send bcc's, but the feature to do this is usually turned off. If you need it, you may activate it by pulling down the **View** menu and selecting

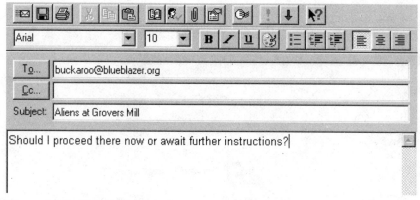

Figure 5–15: New Message window

the **Bcc box** option. Once selected, an additional blank area labeled **Bcc:** will appear under the **Cc:** line. You can fill in this area with secret addressees, separated by semicolons, as you like.

Forwarding

Forwarding e-mail has two slightly different meanings. First, forwarding means automatically sending all mail received by a particular account on one computer to another. This kind of forwarding is particularly useful if you have accounts on several different computers. That way, you don't have to check mail on different computers constantly.

You can't do automatic forwarding from a POP client like Exchange, but most systems that route e-mail (such as the one where your POP account resides) can. If you find yourself in this situation you can probably log into your POP account as a time-sharing user (using Telnet) and issue a command or two to set up automatic forwarding. The commands you need depend on the kind of computer that is acting as your mail server. You may need to get some help to set it up.*

Forwarding also means taking a message you have received and sending it on to someone else. This is another big boss tool: she forwards you the original message, adding something like, "Take care of this, Sam." Suddenly, it's your problem. If you would like to forward a message to someone else using Exchange, you first must select (or read) the message. For example, your superior gets a complaint from Mr. Whiner (Figure 5-16a). She decides you should deal with it. So she clicks the message once to highlight it. Next she clicks the **Forward** button (the arrow pointing to someone's back).

---

* Since most mail servers are still UNIX computers, you probably need to create a file called *.forward* in your default directory. The file should contain one line, which is the e-mail address where you want your mail sent.

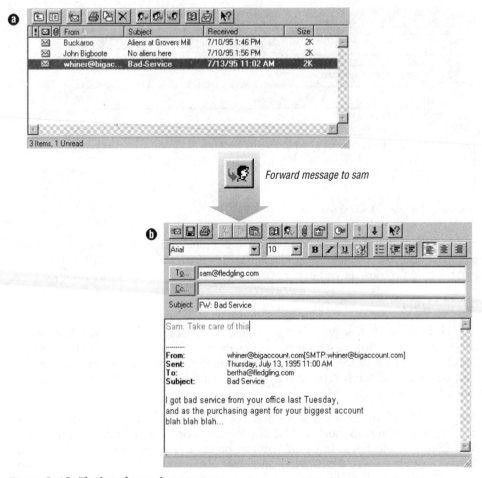

Figure 5-16: *The boss forwards a message*

Clicking **Forward** creates a new message window. This window is just like the message composition window you saw previously, but certain areas such as the **Subject:** and the body will already be filled in with information from the received message. The subject is prefixed with "FW:" to tell the recipient that this is a forwarded message. You need to fill in the **To:** and **Cc:** fields as before.

The headers and body of the original message are automatically copied into the new message, preceded by dashes. It's a good idea to delete any chunks of the original message that are irrelevant. It is customary to add some commentary about the forwarded message. Bertha added, "Sam, take care of this" (see Figure 5-16b). Exchange tries to make it clear what text was forwarded and what text you have added by showing your additions in blue, and in a slightly larger font—but the recipient won't see this fancy stuff. He or she will get plain text, with no special fonts or colors. When the message is ready, press the same old **Send** button and it will be on its way.

Reply

Replying means sending a response to the person who sent you a particular message. It saves you the trouble of typing in the e-mail address. Exchange copies the **From:** (or **Reply-To:**) field from the original message to create the **To:** line of a new message; to create the new **Subject:** line, it copies the original subject and adds "RE:" to show that this is a response to an earlier message. Just like **Forward**, **Reply** copies the text of the message to which you are replying into the new message window, preceded by a line of dashes.

Replies can be tricky. Your mailer may not be able to convert the original **From:** field into a reasonable address. Whether or not a reply will work correctly depends on whether the sender's return address is complete and acceptable to your mailer. If it doesn't work, you might need to look at the **From:** address and modify it, based on your experience (see "Acquiring E-mail Addresses" earlier in this chapter).

Like most mailers, Exchange has two commands for generating replies. One button, **Reply to Sender**, sends a message back only to the original sender; it looks like an arrow pointing to someone's mouth. The other button, **Reply to All**, has two heads. **Reply to All** sends a message to everyone listed in the **From:**, **To:**, or **Cc:** field. People who received blind carbon copies will not get a reply, because there's no record that they received a message.

Back to poor Sam, who's spent the last hour on the phone with Mr. Whiner, who is finally pacified. Now, let's watch Sam tell Bertha that everything is okay. Figure 5-17a shows the message received by Sam. Since this message is from Bertha, Sam can depress one of the **Reply** buttons to set Bertha's mind at ease. Bertha's address was automatically placed in the **To:** field; the reply's subject was copied from the original message prefixed with "RE:". Bertha's message, which included Mr. Whiner's, was included in the body of the new message, and Sam tacked the word "Done" on the front (see Figure 5-17b).

One more thing about replies. They have a way of getting very long, as people start replying to replies to replies. It is good form to delete portions of the message that are redundant. You can delete this text, or make other changes in the text, by using the standard Windows copy, cut and paste functions available under the **Edit** menu or through command keys (CTRL-C, CTRL-X and CTRL-V respectively). For example, the text of the Whiner message could have been deleted, because Bertha could remember the context from her message and the subject.

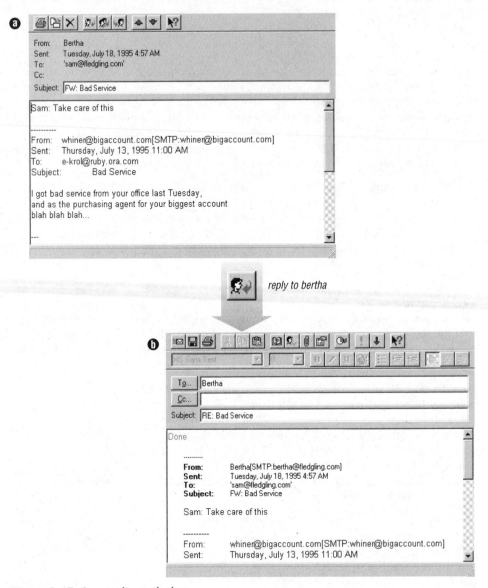

Figure 5-17: Sam replies to the boss

Aliasing (or nicknames)

Aliasing is the ability to define nicknames for people. If you don't like typing complete Internet addresses (and who does?), you can decide that **edk** is shorthand for **krol@ux1.cso.uiuc.edu**; if you then use **edk** as the recipient of a message, your system will substitute the complete address for you. Don't decide on aliases arbitrarily: pick some convention and stick to it. Having an alias doesn't do you any good if you can't remember it. You may need to remember an alias even though you haven't used it for a long time. It is common to use a first name, followed by the last initial, as an alias. It is also common to have nicknames that are tied to "functions," rather than to specific people (e.g., secretary or boss); over time, the person may change, but the function will remain the same.

Exchange stores aliases in your Personal Address Book. The Personal Address Book is a database for tracking people you contact frequently. In addition to e-mail addresses, you can use the address book to remember phone numbers, postal addresses, and more. For e-mail, only a few fields really matter. You can access your Personal Address Book by clicking the **Address Book** icon.

NOTE

The **Address Book** icon also appears in the message composition window. If you click on it there, you will get a different Address Book screen, which allows you to select addressees for the message under construction. To do alias maintenance, you must enter your Address Book from the main window.

Clicking on that icon for the first time will yield an empty address book screen, with the toolbar shown in Figure 5-18.

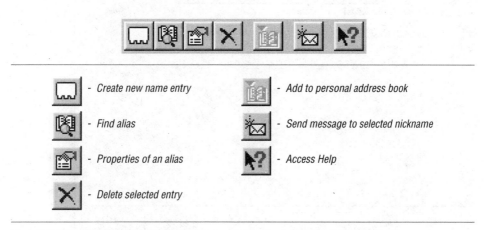

    - *Create new name entry*   - *Add to personal address book*

    - *Find alias*   - *Send message to selected nickname*

    - *Properties of an alias*   - *Access Help*

    - *Delete selected entry*

Figure 5-18: Address Book toolbar

To create an alias, select the icon that looks like a Rolodex card. You'll see a screen (Figure 5-19) that allows you to select what kind of Address Book entry you want to make. We have selected **Internet Mail Address**, which is used to create nicknames for a single Internet e-mail address. Once selected, click **OK** and we can finish the job. Figure 5-20 shows the main screen where nickname maintenance is done. There are many choices (**Business, Phone Numbers**, etc.). You can

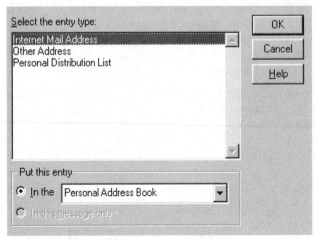

Figure 5–19: Choose address entry type

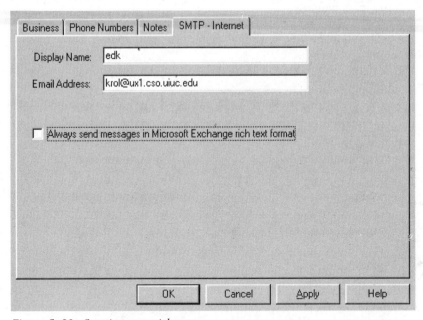

Figure 5–20: Creating new nickname

explore these, if you like, by clicking on the tab. But for Internet e-mail nick-names, the only one of any use is **SMTP - Internet**. As you can see, there are only a few things to specify. **Display Name** is the nickname you want to create for this e-mail address. **E-mail Address** is, obviously, the e-mail address you want associated with the **Display Name**.

The checkbox labeled **Always send ... Microsoft Exchange rich text format** is the hardest thing to understand. Checking this box tells Exchange that this recipient's mail program can understand an extended mail format which allows you to add colored text, special fonts, and other features. It should only be checked for people who always use Microsoft Exchange or another compatible mailer. Rich text messages will be unintelligible to people without compatible software. At this point, that's just about everyone.

When you have entered and verified the items, click **OK** to create the alias entry. The new entry is shown on the screen we visited on the way in (Figure 5-21).

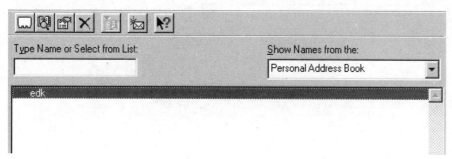

Figure 5-21: Alias ready for use

Once you have created an alias, there are two ways of using it. The first is to click on the alias in the Address Book, and then select **New Message**. This will create the new message window, with the **To:** line containing the selected alias. The second is to type the alias name into the **To:** or **Cc:** field of a message. When you type a name in which doesn't have an at sign (@) in it, Exchange will assume that it is a nickname in your address book. When you send the message, it will look up the name and substitute the actual e-mail address.

If you enter a name which is not a known alias, Exchange will bring up the error screen shown in Figure 5-22. Here, Sam tried to use the alias **bertha**, which was not found. There are three ways to proceed, depending on what exactly went wrong:

1. Sam did not mean to invoke a nickname; he might have just forgotten to finish typing the name. He should click **Cancel**, add **@fledgling.com** to Bertha's name, and click **Send** again.

2. Sam might have thought he had a nickname already, but didn't. He can instantly create one by clicking **Create a new address ...** and **OK**.

3. Sam might have misspelled the nickname. Exchange tries to show nicknames that were close to the one he entered. In this case, there aren't any (**No Suggestions**). If there were, Sam could click on the proper one and click **OK**.

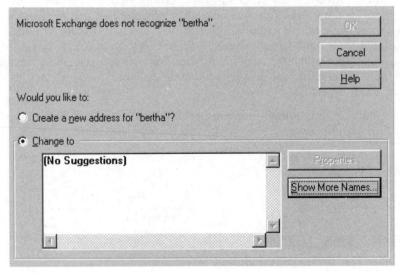

Figure 5–22: Alias error dialog

Mailing lists

With e-mail, it's just as easy to send a message to a group of people as it is to send a message to a single person. The facility that makes this possible is called a mailing list. It allows an alias or nickname to stand for a group of recipients; for example, the alias **staff** can be defined as "all employees." When you send e-mail to the name **staff**, the mail is actually delivered to everyone in the group.

Using Exchange, you can create groups with your address book. Start by clicking **New Name**, as before. When you are asked to choose an entry type, pick **Personal Distribution List** (see Figure 5-19) instead of **Internet Mail Address**. A personal distribution list is a mail alias that stands for an arbitrarily large group of people.

After you click **OK**, Windows 95 shows you a blank window used to define a mailing list. In the **Name** section, type whatever nickname you want to use for the list. In Figure 5-23, we enter the string **staff** to create a mailing list for staff members. This list is created as soon as you close this window by hitting the **OK** button. Don't do that quite yet, since the list is empty. At this point, you want to add some members to the list. To do so, click **Add/Remove Members**.

Figure 5-24 shows the window used to modify the membership in a list. The left-hand side of the screen is a list of all the aliases you have in your address book. The right-hand side of the screen shows all those who are currently members of the list. When you come here after creating a new list, the right hand side will be empty. The figure shows what it would look like after adding **akida** and **buckaroo** to the staff list; we're now about to add **new jersey**. We add items by selecting the name on the left and clicking the button labeled **Members ->** in the middle. When

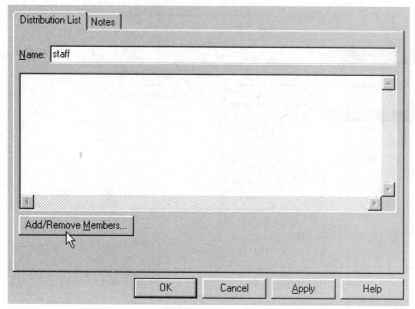

Figure 5-23: Starting to create the staff list

you click the button, the selected name appears on the right-hand side. (Alternately, you can double-click on the name on the left-hand side.)

Names added to the right-hand list appear in the same format as they would in the **To:** field of a message (names separated by semicolons). This is convenient for two reasons. First, it allows you to delete people from the list by hand. Second, it allows you to add people without aliases to the list. That is, there is nothing to prevent you from going in there and typing in another address:

```
akida; buckaroo; krol@ux1.cso.uiuc.edu
```

When you are done modifying the list, click **OK** to save the changes permanently. You can then use the mailing list named **staff** just like any other alias. Enter it on the **To:** or **Cc:** line of a message, or select it from the **Address Book** menu. In your address book, mailing lists appear in bold type and are flagged with an icon (Figure 5-25). The name **staff** is emboldened and an icon has been added to indicate that this is a list of recipients, rather than an individual.

Sending Other Documents in E-Mail Messages

It is often useful to include other files in your e-mail messages. This can be easy if the file is just text; you just paste the desired text into the composition window.

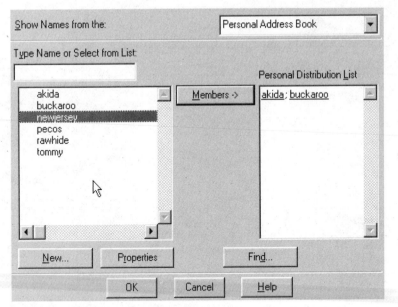

Figure 5–24: List members add and remove

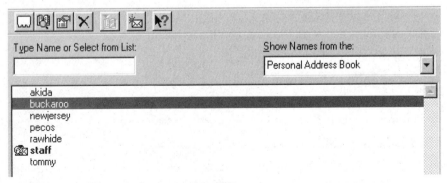

Figure 5–25: Address Book menu with staff list

But what about a binary file, like an audio file? Or a spreadsheet? To send other files as "attachments" (rather than just pasting the file into your message), you use a facility called MIME. MIME mail packages, including Exchange, allow you to mail files as separate entities along with a message. That is, when you send a message to someone, you can say: "Send this file, too." When the message is read, the receiving mailer asks the recipient where the file should be stored. These files can be either binary or ASCII, and system information about the file is preserved in the move. For example, you could send a message saying "Take a look at the spreadsheet I've enclosed and get back to me," and attach an Excel spreadsheet. When the recipient reads the message, he can start Excel and examine the spreadsheet.

Of course, the recipient also needs a MIME-compatible mailer, otherwise he'll get a weird (and probably useless) message. While you shouldn't take MIME for granted, it is an Internet standard, and most Internet mailers support it. Generally, there's a good chance your recipient will be able to handle a MIME message.

MIME: Multimedia Internet Mail Extensions

MIME stands for Multimedia Internet Mail Extensions. These extended messages are not limited to things like spreadsheets: you can even send digitized voice and pictures. The ability to create or display any of these depends on your computer having the appropriate hardware and, most likely, some additional software. You could send a message describing the new remote-control toy you're trying to market, attached to a video of the toy chasing the dog around the living room. The recipient could read the message and—without doing anything extra—watch the video. (Of course, he might curse you for sending him a gigantic file, especially if he pays for connection time.)

These features are both a blessing and a curse, wrapped up in one package. The blessing allows people with little technical know-how to send all kinds of files as part of their e-mail. The curse is that they don't realize they are using features that aren't universal, and that some recipients may not be able to decipher their messages. Sending an Excel spreadsheet isn't helpful if the recipient doesn't use Excel.

Receiving MIME attachments in Exchange

You don't have to do anything special to receive an e-mail message containing attached documents in Exchange. Exchange will download them and flag them on the main Exchange menu. A paperclip next to the sender's name (as shown in Figure 5-26) indicates a MIME attachment. You read John Bigboote's message just like any normal message, by double-clicking on it. You'll see a combination of normal text and icons representing MIME attachments (see Figure 5-27). In this message, there are two attachments: one named *overthruster.gif* and the other named *ATT00000.txt*. The GIF file* is a graphic image; the other file is text.

Notice that the text file has a rather screwy name. This is because some MIME mailers, like Exchange, expect to receive all the plain text of a message before any of the attachments. Others send attachments interspersed with text. If Exchange finds any plain text after an attachment, it treats the text as if it were an attached file, and makes up a strange filename for it. In practice, the filename doesn't matter; to view either attachment, just double-click on it. Windows 95 launches the proper program to act on the file. If you want to save an attachment on your disk, you can just click on its icon and drag it to a disk directory.

If you do anything with the message, the attached files go with it. If you move the message to another folder, the attachments go, too. If you delete it, they're gone. Forward the message and the attachments get sent as well.

---

* GIF is a standard format for computerizing images.

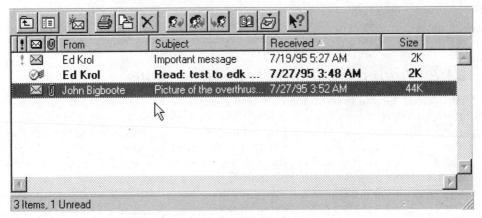

Figure 5-26: Recognizing messages with attachments

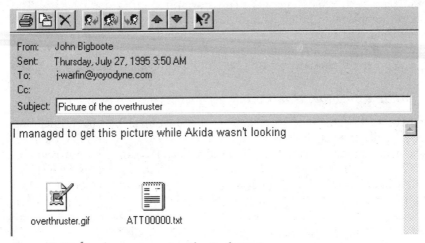

Figure 5-27: Reading a message with attachments

External documents

If this sounds too simple, it is—usually. There are a couple of gotcha's in MIME mail. The first is external documents. External documents are a way of sending a pointer to a file, rather than the file itself. For example, imagine that I have written a five megabyte treatise on the meaning of life. A few of my friends might be interested in it, but most won't be. If I included the document in e-mail to all of my friends, they would quickly cease to be my friends. What I really want to do is say, "Here it is, if you want it." That's what an external part does. It allows me to encode in a message all of the information necessary for Exchange to grab the file from some site on the Internet, if the recipient wants it.

External parts are all flagged with the icon shown in Figure 5-28. They could be files, World Wide Web documents—you don't care. The important distinction is that other kinds of documents are included in your message; with external parts, only the information on how to fetch the document is included.

This has two implications. First, the content of the external document can change over time. Each time you click on the external part icon, your computer may get a new copy. Nothing prevents someone from changing the document on the server where it resides. Second, an external document can be fetched only while your Internet connection is up and running. If you download your mail before catching a plane, you can't read the attachment until you you have landed and connected to the Internet again.

draft-ietf-uri-url-mailserv
er-02.txt

Figure 5-28: External part icon

You can include external parts in messages you send to other people, but be careful that they make sense. If you think about it, an external part is the equivalent of a Windows 95 shortcut: it's an icon which tells Windows 95 that the file resides elsewhere. There are two problems, however. Unless your computer is connected to the Internet continuously and set up to act as a server, the recipient won't be able to access the information that the external part is referencing. Second, shortcuts are a peculiar kind of external type that can only be assured of working if the recipient is running Exchange as well.

However, an external part does have a good chance of working if it lives on someone else's computer: for example, a Web page or an external part from someone else's e-mail message. To include an external part like this in a message that you're composing, just drag it from its old location and drop it into the message composition window.

Unknown MIME types

Another problem common to all MIME messages is that you may receive files which your computer doesn't understand. MIME mailers are supposed to understand how to decode different kinds of files. If things work correctly—and they often do—MIME will leave the decoded file on the recipient's computer, with no additional work on the user's part. However, there's still a compatibility problem. Each kind of file is defined as a particular MIME type, and there are many of them. A MIME-compliant mail package must be able to handle messages in the MIME format, but isn't required to handle all possible message types. In general, the sender's and recipient's mail packages each have a set of MIME types that they know about; some of them will overlap and some will not. When Exchange encounters an unfamiliar message type, it displays the icon shown in Figure 5-29.

ATT00009.att

Figure 5–29: Unknown type icon

It could be that Exchange didn't know how to decode the attachment, or it could mean that this particular file type has never been specified to Windows 95. In either case, a document in this state will require special handling. If you're lucky, you'll recognize the file type yourself; you can save the attachment and start the appropriate application by hand. In the worst case, the attachment is useless. You may have to send a message back to the sender and request more information about the file.

Sending attached documents

Attaching documents to messages takes longer to talk about than to do. You begin the message as you would any other message: fill in the **To:**, **Cc:**, and **Subject:** fields, then type in your message. When you are ready there are two ways to attach a file. The easy way is to drag and drop the file you want to include into the message composition window. If you want more control, click on the paper clip icon in the new message window. This brings up a dialog box (Figure 5-30) which allows you to specify the file. The entry box labeled **Look in:** lets you choose the directory where the file resides. The large white area shows the contents of the directory named in the **Look in:** field.

To attach a file, click on its filename. In this example, I clicked on **twi95**, and its name appeared in the **File name** box. Next, check the bottom of the window where it says **Insert as** and make sure **An attachment** is selected. When you are satisfied with your selection, click **OK**, and the file is attached.

You will return to the message construction window. Now, the message (Figure 5-31) will include an icon showing the kind of attachment. This icon means that the attached document is in HTML format for use on the World Wide Web. Now you can do whatever you want with a message: add more text, attach more documents, or send it.

Inclusion of Text Files

This is actually trickier than it sounds. You rarely find files which are just text. They tend to be Word or WordPerfect documents. These documents have all kinds of binary control information built into them; to send them in total, you need to

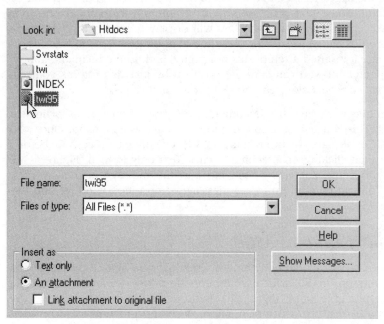

Figure 5–30: Attachment specification dialog

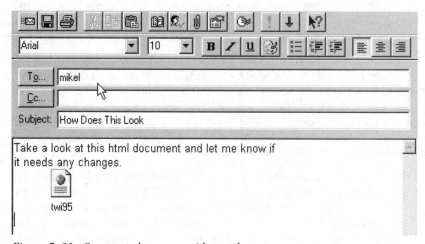

Figure 5–31: Constructed message with attachment

send them as MIME attachments. If you only want to insert the text into your message, there are two techniques you can use.

First, you can use the standard **Copy** and **Paste** functions. Use the appropriate software to view your file; then use the mouse to copy part of it (or the whole thing) into your e-mail message. This technique works fine for the most part, but you do need to be careful. Some text processors treat an entire paragraph as one long line. Exchange accepts this, and the window will display normally. But when you send the message, Exchange breaks the long line at appropriate points and inserts an = sign wherever it inserted a return. It's not pretty, and, to the recipient, annoying. In a short paragraph, you can cure the problem by inserting returns yourself. Unfortunately, this cure gets old pretty quick for long inclusions.

The other technique is to save the document you want to include as plain text with line breaks. This is usually an option under the **Save as** command. Once you have the text file, you can go through the MIME attachment process as before. However, rather than clicking **An attachment**, click **Text only** instead (Figure 5-30). This will copy the entire contents of the file into the message at the currently selected point. You can then return to the message composition window, and further edit the file.

Sending Binary Data as ASCII

Before the days of MIME, sending anything non-textual was quite a problem. You had to run a utility on the file which would encode the non-printable characters as sequences of printable ones; then you would send the encoded file to the recipient. He would then use a complementary decoding program to reconstruct the original file. Except in a few special cases, this is no longer necessary.

The biggest exception is that some non-Internet on-line networks (e.g., CompuServe) cannot accept MIME messages. So, if you are trying to pass information through CompuServe, you must still encode the file by hand and verify that the intended recipient can decode it.

There is no single best way to encode a file; however, there are many choices, which all work. Some common encoding programs are **uuencode** and **btoa**; the corresponding decoders are **uudecode** and **atob**. A utility called WinCode implements uuencode and uudecode; it's available on the Net (see the *Resource Catalog* under "Computing" for Windows shareware archives). **uuencode** is widely used on UNIX systems and is also available for the Mac, so it's a good choice.

One word of warning. If Windows 95 does not understand the format of a file, or if the file appears to be the wrong type, Exchange will MIME encode it again even though you may have encoded it already. For example, if you and your friend decide to use uuencoding, but you name the encoded file *program.exe*, Exchange may automatically encode the file with something called *base64*. In this case, unless your friend has additional software and can figure out what has happened, he may find the file useless.

Unusual and Non-Standard Features

The following features are found in some e-mail packages, but not all. It's intended partly as a "shipping list" so you'll know what's available when you're choosing a mailer, and partly so you'll understand what's happening as you read mail.

Signature Files

Signature files are a way to append additional standard information to outgoing mail messages. They are often used to include information about who you are and how you can be contacted. So, if you don't think:

```
From: johnb@yoyodyne.com
```

conveys a lot of information about yourself, you could set up a file which gives your name, postal address, phone number, fax number, other e-mail addresses, etc. For example, such a file might look like:

```
John Bigboote        | Yoyodyne Industries
johnb@yoyodyne.com   |
(212)333-4444        | "The Future Begins Tomorrow".
---------------------------------------------------
```

Remember, if the recipient cannot get e-mail back to you, the information in your signature file might be the only way to get in touch with you. Keep it short and useful, however. It is really pushing it (and irritating) when your signature includes your dog's and kid's names, pictures of your favorite cult icons, and takes up 15 to 20 lines. It is considered good "netiquette" to limit your signature file to no more than four lines.

Many mailers have a signature feature that automatically adds a signature to the end of each message. There is no signature file feature in Exchange. The best you can do is make a text file and then attach it at the end of each message.

Notification

Notification tries to give you some confidence that your mail has been delivered. In Exchange, you can request notification by clicking **Read-Receipt** (it looks like a postmark) on the message composition window. Because this feature is not standardized, it means different things depending on the recipient's mail package. If the recipient uses Exchange, you will receive confirmation when the recipient displays the message. The confirmation will be flagged with the notification icon, which looks like a postmark with a check on it (see Figure 5-26). It doesn't mean that he actually read or understood it. It does mean that you'll know he's lying if he says, "I just read it this morning," when you received confirmation two days ago!

If the recipient doesn't have a Microsoft package, **Read-Receipt** will return a message when the message is delivered to the first host on its way to its destination. It in no way tells whether she actually received it or read it.

Priority

The composition window's menu bar has two buttons that let you assign a priority to your message. The exclamation point is high priority, and the down arrow is low priority. Priority is another feature that only works with other Microsoft mail packages. The message will only be flagged with a priority if you use an alias to address the message, and that alias has the Microsoft rich text format option checked.

Worse than that, priority does not have anything to do with how fast the messages are delivered. They are delivered over normal channels at the same old speeds. The priority is only displayed on the recipient's **Inbox** menu as a hint that he ought to treat the messages accordingly—they have no bearing on whether he will.

Message Cancel

Message cancel is available on some LAN-based e-mail packages. It allows you to take back a message you wish you hadn't sent. On the Internet, the sad truth is that it's almost always impossible to cancel mail. There's really only one exception: you can delete the mail after you click **Send**, as long as the message is still in your **Outbox**; that is, before Exchange has delivered the mail to your server. You do that by moving to the **Outbox**, selecting the message, and deleting it in the normal manner. Once the message leaves your **Outbox** and gets sent to your Internet service provider, there's nothing you can do but start apologizing.

When E-Mail Gets Returned

When e-mail cannot be delivered, you normally get a message telling you why. This takes the format of a really ugly, strange message in your **Inbox**, from something called the *Mail Delivery Subsystem* (Figure 5-32) with the subject "Returned Mail".

Figure 5-32: E-mail returned

At this point, all you know is that your mail didn't go through; you have no idea why. To find out, you have to wade through the cryptic message that was returned, and look for clues.

There are three common reasons for e-mail to fail:

- The mail system can't find the recipient's machine
- The recipient is unknown at that machine
- The mail system can find the machine, but the machine isn't accepting mail for some unknown reason

Let's investigate these causes, one at a time.

Unknown hosts

When you send a message to someone, the network tries to make some sense out of the stuff to the right of the @. If it can't make sense of it, or if it can't look up the address of the named machine, the mailer that gives up sends you a message that the host is unknown. Let's assume we were trying to send a message to **johnb@yoyodyne.com**, but misentered the computer host name as **yoyodyne.org**. Our first indication of this would be a "Returned Mail" message. We can read it like any other message: As your message travels to its destination, it passes through a number of mail handlers. One of these intermediate handlers didn't like the message you sent. Since you have no control over these intermediate computers, the messages might differ from what is shown. The wording will usually be similar. In this case, we're in luck: the mail forwarder generated a "Subject:" header that tells you fairly explicitly that the name server could not find **yoyodyne.org**.

Had this intermediate host not been so nice, the next place to look is the text of the message (Figure 5-33). Look for the section marked "Transcript of session". Here, you find a message that the host **yoyodyne.org** is not found on the network. Sometimes the wording "Host Unknown" is used.

After this, you will usually find the unsent message itself. This mailer was nice enough to wrap it up as a MIME attachment with the subject line as the attachment name.

What should you do when something like this happens? First, check the address: is **yoyodyne.org** correct? (In this case, it isn't: it should be **yoyodyne.com**.) Second, check whether the address is complete. When presented with an incomplete name like **yoyodyne**, Exchange usually assumes it is an address book alias and, if the alias isn't there, gives you an error. But if you are replying to a message, Exchange just assumes that the return address is correct, which is not always the case. It passes the message to the mail server, which will notice the incomplete name and (most likely) assume that the suffix should be the same as its own. So, on a machine named **ux1.cso.uiuc.edu**, the address **yoyodyne** will be expanded to **yoyodyne.cso.uiuc.edu**. This frequently is a good assumption because in business most mail is directed within the same organization. However, if the mail came from outside it will fail.

A variant of this problem occurs when people give out partial addresses, assuming that you'll be able to figure out the rest. For example, someone might give you an

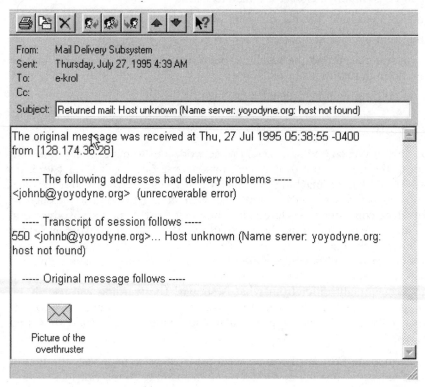

Figure 5–33: Error in mail host name

address like **joe@turing.cs**. He is assuming that you know he's in the Computer Science department of the University of Illinois (Urbana-Champaign), which is the domain **uiuc.edu**, and that his complete e-mail address is therefore **joe@turing.cs.uiuc.edu**. If you simply use the address **joe@turing.cs**, the mail-forwarding software will get confused—in this case, really confused. To a computer, **turing.cs** looks exactly like the complete name of **turing** in the country formerly known as Czechoslovakia (**.cs** was Czechoslovakia's country code).* If you're lucky, **turing.cs** doesn't exist, and you'll get an "unknown host" message. If you're unlucky, **turing.cs** does exist, and you'll be even more confused. (If you're really unlucky, **joe@turing.cs** will even exist, and he'll get your mail.) The moral of the story is twofold. First, you may need to finish the address yourself from your own knowledge of where the person really resides. Second, when you give your address to someone, always give a complete address; don't assume that your correspondents will be smart enough to figure it out.

---

* In fact, don't assume that the **.cs** country code won't work, just because the country doesn't exist. There may still be computers that honor it.

One last warning: you might find a returned message where the unknown host has multiple highest-level domains:

```
yoyodyne.com.cso.uiuc.edu
```

If you run across something like this, you have run into a misconfigured mail server. **yoyodyne.com** was a perfectly fine address. Some mailer along the way decided it wasn't and tried to complete it by tacking on its own domain, **.cso.uiuc.edu**, really screwing things up. In this case, there is nothing you can do. Find someone who knows about mailers and ask for help.

It's also possible that your computer just doesn't know about the system you're trying to send to. Some mailers have lists of valid hostnames; these lists are not updated continuously. The target machine may not be in the list. If you think this may be the problem, talk to whoever manages the mail system you are using.

If none of these hints apply, you have no recourse other than calling the recipient to see if some other address might work better.

Unknown recipients

Now, let's assume that your mail made its way to the correct host. Eventually, a machine forwarding your mail makes contact with the destination machine and tells it the recipient's name. What happens if the destination machine hasn't heard of the message's addressee? In this case, the returned message will have a subject like:

```
Subject: Returned mail: User unknown Status: RO
```

and a session transcript similar to this:

```
    ----- Transcript of session follows -----
While talking to yoyodyne.com:
>>> RCPT To:<johm@yoyodyne.com>
<<< 550 <johm@yoyodyne.com>... User unknown
550 johm@yoyodyne.com... User unknown
```

This failure is frequently caused by mistyping the username in the address. (That's what happened above. I mistyped **john**.) It is also possible that the username is correct, and the hostname is incorrect, but legal. For example, if you address a message to **johnb@ux2** rather than **johnb@ux1**, you may get a "User unknown" message. The machine **ux2** exists, but there is no user **johnb** on it. (In the worst case, the wrong person may receive your mail: some "johnb" that you've never met, but who happens to have an account on **ux2**.)

Mail can't be delivered

The previous examples show the most frequent ways of failing, but if you're clever you may find others. You may see the message:

```
----- Transcript of session follows -----
554 <johnb@yoyodyne.com>... Service unavailable
```

This message tells us that, although the machine was located and in communication, it wasn't accepting e-mail at this time. In this case, your best bet is to wait a while and try again, perhaps during normal working hours. (Or, if you tried during working hours, try again during off-hours.) Some machines are set up so that they won't accept mail on weekends or some other arbitrary time.

Another kind of failure can happen when someone's mailbox gets "full" because he hasn't bothered to read mail for a long time. In this case, you'll get a "Mailbox Full" message.

In the previous cases, you would receive notification of the problem almost immediately. For example, if the destination host is unknown to the network, you will receive notification as soon as a system that's handling the mail tries to look up the destination and fails. This should happen in minutes or, at most, a few hours. There is an additional common failure mode in which the problem might not be known for days: the machine is known to the network, but unreachable. In these cases, the sending machine may try to send the mail for two or three days (or more) before it gives up and tells you about it. The subject of one of these messages would resemble:

```
Subject: Returned mail: Cannot send message for 2 days
```

If you then delve into the body of the returned message you will find that it was or "Timed Out," which means the mail forwarding computer tried for a while and gave up.

```
----- Transcript of session follows -----
421 deadhost.cso.uiuc.edu (TCP)... Deferred:
    Connection timed out during user open
    with deadhost.cso.uiuc.edu
```

This message can mean several different things:

- The network may be faulty, making it impossible to contact the remote system.

- The remote system may be dead; for example, it may be having severe hardware problems. Or its owner may have turned it off and left for vacation.

- The remote system may be misconfigured; it isn't uncommon for someone to change the configuration of their system and forget to "tell" the network.

The message does not imply that the host was completely unreachable for the entire two days. After a few failures, the sending machine might only try to send the message every few hours or so. If the machine is having hardware problems, the network's chances of contacting it when it's working may be very small.

Don't be confused if you get multiple messages back about the same message you sent. In two days you might get one like the above; on the third day, you might receive another message saying that the network gave up.

Failures involving multiple recipients

So far, all of the examples of failures have been for mail destined for one person. It's easy to become confused when something goes wrong with mail sent to several recipients. The returned mail might look like this:

```
----- Transcript of session follows -----
While talking to ux1.cso.uiuc.edu:
>>> RCPT To:<willie_martin@ux1.cso.uiuc.edu>
<<< 550 <willie_martin@ux1.cso.uiuc.edu>... User unknown
550 willie_martin@ux1.cso.uiuc.edu... User unknown
```

If the original message was addressed:

```
krol@ux1.cso.uiuc.edu; willie_martin@ux1.cso.uiuc.edu
```

how do you know who got the mail, and who didn't? You can figure out the answer by looking at the "unsent message" section. The message was destined for both **krol@ux1.cso.uiuc.edu** and **willie_martin@ux1.cso.uiuc.edu**. The "Transcript of session" tells us it is complaining about **willie_martin**, not **krol**. You can conclude that **krol** received the message safely, and that there's something wrong with **willie_martin**'s address. You only need to resend the message to **willie** when you correct his address. You should assume that all the recipients which were not listed in the Transcript of session error message received the file correctly and you must resend it only to those listed.

Peeking a bit deeper

Along the way, I have mentioned mail headers a number of times. Exchange does its best to shield you from them, but they are still there. On any message you receive, you can ask to see its mail header by selecting the message, then clicking **Properties**. This will show you the applet shown in Figure 5-34. The **General** tab, which comes up first, doesn't tell you much. If you select the **Internet** tab, you will see the mail headers; from them you can figure out how the mail was sent. This can be useful because it will tell you which computer objected to your e-mail and sent you the rejection letter.

Last ditch help

By convention, every computer that exchanges mail should have a mailbox named **postmaster**. Mail addressed to **postmaster** should be read by the e-mail administrator for the host computer. If you need any help with a particular machine, you can send a request to:

postmaster@_hostname_

Here are some things you might send a message to **postmaster** about:

- Help finding the e-mail address for someone you know to be using that host

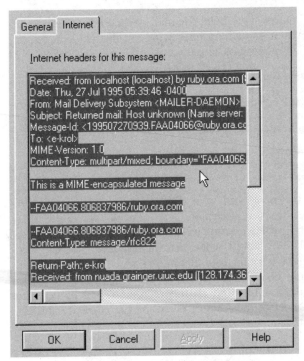

Figure 5–34: Internet properties--header information

- Help finding the proper gateway for sending e-mail to external networks
- Complaints about the actions of someone on that host (e.g., harassing messages)

Mail Lists and Reflectors

In an earlier section, we discussed aliases and learned how to define an alias with multiple recipients. For example, I can define a personal distribution list named **aliens** for a few suspicious people:

```
johnb@yoyodyne.com; johnw@yoyodyne.com
```

After I have created this list, I can send a message to **aliens**, and it will be delivered to both **johnb** and **johnw**. This is a natural way to implement group discussions through electronic mail. It works fine for small groups, or for personal groups that only you use. As the group grows and other people want to use the same group definition, it turns into a maintenance nightmare. Whenever anyone is added to or deleted from the group, everyone who wants to use the alias must change his or her own personal definition. "Everyone" never does, so someone gets left out and doesn't receive a message, and there is hell to pay.

You really want a centrally maintained mailing list, so that you can make a single change that is effective for everyone. As long as you (or some other responsible person) maintains the **aliens** mailing list, everyone—senders and recipients—will be happy. This is typically implemented by a mail reflector. A mail reflector is a special e-mail address set up so that any message sent to it will automatically be resent to everyone on a list. For example, let's assume that we've set up a mail reflector for **aliens**, rather than a simple alias. Now I can send a message to **aliens@yoyodyne.com**. The mailer on **yoyodyne.com** will take my message and resend it to **johnb** and **johnw**. It doesn't take much of a machine to act as a mail reflector, but it does take someone with system administrator privileges to set one up.* In this section, we'll tell you how to use lists that other people have set up; we won't discuss how to create your own.

In the tradition of computing, we need to make things even more complex. The mail reflector we discussed above works well for a private (though large) group. What if, rather than a private list of people, it was a list available to anyone who wanted to take part in a discussion? Suppose we want to allow anyone in the world who is interested in discussing pencil collecting to access the address **pencils@hoople.usnd.edu**. From there, the mail will be forwarded to all the other participating collectors. You will receive everyone else's messages automatically; likewise, anything you send to this address will be broadcast to pencil lovers worldwide.

For this to work, there must be a method for saying, "Please add me to the list." Sending that message to **pencils@hoople.usnd.edu** is not a reasonable solution. It sends the message to everyone on the list. Doing this may work, but it is considered bad form (making you appear to be a geek among pencil collectors everywhere). Worse, the person who manages the list may not get your message at all. The list maintainer may be an e-mail administrator who doesn't care at all about pencil collecting.

Unfortunately, the correct way to subscribe to a list depends on how the list is maintained. Historically, the Internet uses special addresses for administrative requests. Whenever you create a public mail reflector, you create a second mailbox on the same machine. This mailbox has the same name as the mailing list, with the suffix **–request** added. This special mailbox is "private"; anything it receives isn't broadcast, but instead is sent to the mailing list's maintainer. So the correct way of subscribing is to send a message to:

```
pencils-request@hoople.usnd.edu
```

This is still a bit of a chore for the list maintainer, who must read the requests and edit the list manually. A nice utility named **listserv** for maintaining lists (and more) without human intervention grew up in the BITNET community on IBM/VM

---

* One of the reasons for this is that if you create multiple mail reflectors, which have each other as members, they could send messages to each other forever.

machines.* Since BITNET **listservs** were accessible to both the BITNET and the Internet communities, they grew quite popular. So popular, in fact, that there has been a proliferation of **listserv**-like software running on all sorts of computers. Luckily, these packages, like **mailserv**, **majordomo**, and **almanac**,† accept similar command sets, so signing up for mailing lists isn't quite as confusing as it might have been.

To subscribe to a mailing list that's managed by one of these automatic packages, you send a specially formatted message to a special address on the computer that runs the mailing list. The "addressee" is often—but not always—the name of the program that's managing the list. For example, to subscribe to a pencil collector's list, you might send a message to **listserv@hoople.usnd.edu**. The messages would consist of one line, with no subject:

```
subscribe pencils your name
```

where **subscribe** is a keyword and **pencils** is the name of the group. Your name in the above example is strictly for documentation and the format doesn't really matter—though many groups won't let you sign up without giving your name. Be sure you send the subscription request from the account where you want to receive the mailings! The list processor gets your e-mail address directly from the message headers, so if you use the wrong account, the mail will go to the wrong place. Once you have subscribed, whenever anyone sends a message to **pencils@hoople.usnd.edu**, you will get a copy.‡

If the mailing list were managed by **majordomo**, the address might be **majordomo@hoople.usnd.edu**; the message you'd send to subscribe would have the same command, but you would replace your name with your e-mail address. Similarly, if the mailing list is managed by **almanac**, you would send your subscription request to an address like **almanac@hoople.usnd.edu**. You'd send the same message, except that **almanac** doesn't require your personal name: the message would be simply **subscribe pencils**. (**almanac** has another good feature: you can send the message **send mail-catalog** to a server to get a list of all mailing lists the server manages.)

No matter who manages the list, the following rules apply:

---

* BITNET is a message and file retrieval network which has been around for a long time within the educational community. It used to be a real network, with phone lines of its own. While BITNET probably still has a few phone lines, it now uses the Internet to handle a lot of its traffic.

† **almanac** appears to be most heavily used by Federal governmental information services. It looks like a good program, though, so expect it to spread.

‡ A few mailing lists add an additional step: they require "subscription confirmation." This means that they will send you a standard message, requesting that you forward it back to them—possibly with some additional information. In any case, the message you receive should contain precise instructions about what to do.

- The address you send your request to probably serves many different lists: **listserv@hoople.usnd.edu** could maintain mailing lists for pencil collectors, cat lovers, and fans of obscure Baroque composers.

- The address to which you send the subscription request and the address to which you send actual list postings are different.

- Many lists do not repost mail to the submitter, so you may not get the warm fuzzy feeling of seeing your message sent back to you. If you really want a copy, send a carbon copy to yourself.

Finding Out About Mailing Lists

Now that you can get on to a list, you need to know how to find out what lists are available. There are thousands of mailing lists out there, on just about every conceivable topic. The *Resource Catalog* in this book doesn't attempt to cover mailing lists; however, there are general lists of mailing lists available over the Internet; these are listed in the *Resource Catalog*, under the heading "Publicly Accessible Mailing Lists" in the section on "Internet Information." The easiest list to use is the World Wide Web site **http://www.neosoft.com/internet/paml**; this list is updated monthly, and organized by subject. (See the next chapter to find out how to use the World Wide Web.)

Once you've discovered a few lists that interest you, don't hesitate to sign up. You should probably be aware, however, that some lists have a lot of traffic; if you get carried away, you can easily end up with hundreds of e-mail messages a day.

Dropping Your Subscription

Now that you can get on a list, how do you get off it, or unsubscribe? Mailing lists can be as annoying as any other form of junk mail. Unsubscribing is known in the **listserv** parlance as **signoff**, and is done by sending the following command to the list server **listserv@hoople.usnd.edu**:

```
signoff pencils
```

This subscribe/signoff pairing was viewed as a bit obscure by the developers of **majordomo** and **almanac**, who chose the obvious:

```
unsubscribe listname
```

for their lists. Of course, if you want to unsubscribe to an Internet-style mailing list, just send a message to the administrative (**list-request**) address.

If you want more information about what any of these automated mailing list packages can do, send the message:

```
help
```

to any list server you can find—no matter what type of server it is. It will mail a help guide back to you.

This has been a lot of information. Let's summarize it with a table. In the table below, *hostname* is the computer that manages the list, and *list* is the name of the list.

Table 5-3: Subscribing to Mailing Lists

List type	Subscription Address	Subscription Message	Termination Message	Posting Address
listserv	listserv@*hostname*	Subscribe *list* yourname	Signoff *list*	*list*@hostname
majordomo	majordomo@*hostname*	Subscribe *list* e-mail-address	Unsubscribe *list*	*list*@hostname
Internet	*list*-request@hostname	Anything	Anything	*list*@hostname
almanac	almanac@*hostname*	Subscribe *list*	Unsubscribe *list*	*list*@hostname

If this seems complicated, remember that there are exceptions! (Not what you wanted to hear.) When you subscribe to a mailing list, the first message you receive will probably be a "form letter" describing the list in detail and telling you how to sign off. If you're likely to forget, save this message in a file!

If you think about what happens when a mail reflector is in operation, you will realize that it isn't terribly efficient. If five people from the Yoyodyne corporation all subscribe to the **aliens** mail reflector at **hoople.usnd.edu**, five messages will be sent from **hoople.usnd.edu** to **yoyodyne.com** for every original message sent to **aliens@hoople.usnd.edu**. This sends unneeded, extra traffic across the Internet. There is a way to get around this suboptimal behavior and, also, make the list more responsive to local personnel changes. The system administrator for **yoyodyne.com** can create a local mail reflector that only resends messages to its employees (Figure 5-35).

Then he subscribes the **Yoyodyne** reflector's address to the national reflector at **hoople**. So, when a message gets sent to **aliens@hoople.usnd.edu**, one message is sent to **aliens@yoyodyne.com**, which resends it to the five subscribing employees.

Moderators and List Etiquette

A few final pieces of trivia about mailing lists. First, some lists are moderated. With a moderated list, the messages are not automatically transmitted. Instead, a moderator screens the messages to determine whether they are appropriate. This is usually not a big deal, but may lead to delays in reposting. Inappropriate or grossly impolite postings will be screened out—though the meaning of "inappropriate" depends on the tastes of the moderator and the expectations of the particular list.

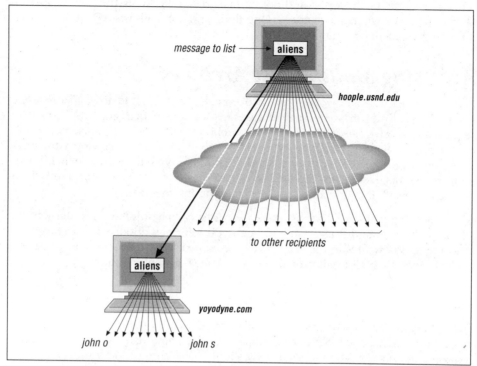

Figure 5-35: Local mail reflectors

Many mailing lists have their own etiquette rules. Some are free-for-alls, some have very strict standards about the behavior of their members. The form letter you get when subscribing will tell you what expectations the list has, if any. Be sure to obey these rules; don't make inappropriate postings.

Finally, be careful when responding to list messages. Some messages require personal responses to the original sender; for others, it's more appropriate to send your response to the list. For example, consider a meeting announcement requesting an RSVP. Your RSVP should be sent to the person requesting the information—don't expect everyone on the list to care that you're coming. However, replies to requests for information of general interest (e.g., "Anyone know how to make a million dollars legally?") should probably be sent to the list. Be careful about using your mailer's **reply** command. Sometimes, your reply will go to the entire list by default; other times, replies are sent to the originator by default. What happens depends on how the mail reflector was set up: it should set the message's **From:** line to the address of the reflector, and should insert a **Reply-To:** line containing the address of the original sender. If this is done, and if your mailer works correctly, the reply should go to the original sender. However, not all mail reflectors are set up correctly, and not all mailers handle **Reply-To**: lines properly.[*] Only experience will tell for certain. One thing about e-mail lists: you'll hear about it if you do something obnoxious.

Accessing Mailing List Archives

Earlier, we discussed how you can use e-mail to send a file to someone. The reverse is also true in some special cases: you can, on occasion, use e-mail to request and receive files from mailing list archives. You send the list server a special message, telling it which file you want it to send. Upon receiving your message, the server gets the file and sends it back to you through the mail. This approach works even when the list server is on a weird network or you're hidden behind a firewall. E-mail reaches many places the Internet doesn't.[†]

We'll cover the major mailing list packages: **listserv**, **majordomo**, and **almanac**. In all cases, the mailing list itself should keep you informed about what archives are available and how files in those archives are named—the response you get when you subscribe to the list will probably have some of this information.

Listserv File Retrieval Commands

The **listserv** commands for requesting files are similar to the commands used for mailing-list maintenance. Send your request to the name **listserv** on the machine providing the service. The message body should have lines of the form:

> **get** *filename filetype*

where *filename* and *filetype* are the two components that make up an IBM/VM filename.[‡] For example, assume you want to get an available list of files about BITNET network nodes. This list is in the file *bitnode filelist*, and is available from the server **bitnic.bitnet**. To get the file, you would send the message:

> **get bitnode filelist**

to the address **listserv@bitnic.bitnet**. There are a couple of funny things that you'll notice the first time you try to fetch something from a **listserv** server. You will receive at least two messages back: a message acknowledging the request and telling you it will be sent, and a message that contains the requested data. The data may arrive in multiple messages, because BITNET has a limit on the size of an individual message. If the file you want is too long, it will be divided into smaller chunks. Finally, with a **listserv** request, you don't have to worry about

---

[*] To check this, you need to use the **Properties** menu, as mentioned previously, and look at the header fields manually.

[†] See also the discussion of the FTPmail source (check subhead title) in Chapter 9, *Moving Files: FTP*. FTPmail is a more general file retrieval mechanism; here, we're limiting the discussion to mailing list archives.

[‡] There is more about this in Chapter 9, in the section "Target: IBM/VM Systems."

upper- and lowercase letters. **listserv** servers are not case-sensitive. All requests are converted into uppercase before being serviced.

Majordomo File Retrieval

The commands for file retrieval using **majordomo** are the same as those for **listserv**, with two differences:

- The files available are list-dependent
- The filenames are case-sensitive

On **listserv** servers, the files available to be fetched sit on the server in one big pool, so they all have unique names. The authors of **majordomo** considered this a problem, so **majordomo** software maintains a separate pool of files for each individual mailing list. Therefore, the server needs two pieces of information: the name of the file and the list that it came from.

The second difference is a result of **majordomo**'s UNIX background. On UNIX systems, upper- and lowercase characters are different. Therefore, the file *REPORT* is a different file than *report*. You must type the filename you want precisely.

Now that we've covered the background, let's look at the command you need:

    get *listname filename*

listname is the name of the mailing list, and *filename* is the file you want sent. You put this in the body of the mail message and send it, just as with **listserv**.

Almanac File Retrieval

almanac servers work a little differently. **almanac** servers are organized in terms of topic-oriented "folders." To get a list of the folders available at an **almanac** server, send the following message:

    send catalog

Folders can have many files (and other folders) within them. Once you know which folders are available, you need to look inside the folders that interest you. To do so, send a command like:

    send *foldername* catalog

Finally, when you have a catalog that contains a file you want, send a request like this to get the file:

    send *foldername filename*

So, to get the document *0001* from the folder *ers-reports*, send the command:

    send ers-reports 0001

Many folders and files have aliases, or shortened names that make requests more convenient. The catalog will show any aliases that are available. Aliases can be used instead of the file or folder name. You can also use wildcards to request multiple files or groups of files. For example:

```
send ers-reports "*"
```

retrieves all the files in the folder *ers-reports.* Beware—commands like this may retrieve many, many files. If you are paying for connection time, you may have a big bill!

For more information about what **almanac** does, send it a "help" message.

The Eudora E-Mail Package

E-mail programs were some of the earliest programs in use on the Net. There are many available, both commercially and free. As an alternative to Exchange, we will show you the basics of one of the most popular e-mail programs on the Internet—Eudora.

Eudora is a full-featured Internet mail client from Qualcomm Incorporated. Two versions of Eudora are available: Eudora Light, which is free, and Eudora Pro, which isn't. Eudora Pro contains more features than the freeware version, which is sort of a tester, and it is better documented and supported, but Eudora Light is still an excellent mailer. Like Exchange, Eudora is a POP mail client, and it does all the things that an Internet mailer should do. It handles ASCII mail messages, MIME attachments, aliases and address storage, and mailbox and folder accessories for storing your mail. This section will give you a brief overview of the features of Eudora Light.

There are versions of Eudora Light for Macs and Windows available at many sites on the Net. The latest version is always available at **ftp.qualcomm.com** in *Eudora/windows* (see Chapter 9 for FTP information). Get the *readme* file first to determine which subdirectory contains the freeware version (1.5 at this writing). You can either download the *.zip* version of the program (which will require PKUNZIP or WinZip to uncompress) or the uncompressed executable. Create a directory for the file and put it there. You should also download a copy of the Eudora help document. It will be a *.doc* file in the same directory as the program. It is a Microsoft Word file, and your best source of information on Eudora.

Choose **Run** from the **Start** menu and run the executable. The self-extracting file will produce four files: *Eudora.exe, Eudora.ini, Eudora.hlp,* and *Readme.txt.* All of these files can remain in the same directory. Installation on Windows 95 requires nothing else. The installation instructions in the readme file were written for Windows 3.1 and tell you to set a variable for a temporary directory in the AUTOEXEC.BAT file by adding the line:

```
SET TMP=C:\TMP
```

A temp variable is already set in this file in Windows 95, so this step is not necessary. You can add *Eudora.exe* to your **Start** menu, and it is ready to run.

When you run Eudora for the first time, the **Settings** window will come up. You must supply the name of your POP account, usually your full e-mail address. After you input this information, the window will close. Eudora will connect to your POP mail server[*] and ask you for your password. Your POP account password is supplied by your network administrator.

Open **Settings** again by selecting **Settings** from the **Special** menu. Now you can set many other options to make the mailer work best for you. You may specify your return address, especially if it is different from your POP account; your real name to include in outgoing messages; and SMTP, phonebook (Ph), and finger servers, if you have them.

In the **Checking Mail** section of **Settings**, specify how often the program should check for new mail on your mail server. If your connection time is costly, you may want to select the **Skip Big Messages** checkbox. Lengthy messages that would take a long time to download will then be left on your mail server to be read at another time. If you would like to leave all your messages on the server and simply copy them to your computer, check the **Leave Messages On Server** box. This is a helpful option if you access your mail from many different machines and need to keep a central organization of your mail messages. If your machine is secure, you can check the **Save Password** box, and Eudora will automatically log you in when it connects to the mail server. Eudora will also remember your password every time you start the program unless you choose **Forget Password** from the **Special menu** on the main window. You will have to type your password in every time you start Eudora (not every time the program checks your mail server) with this selection. It is a good security measure if you need it.

There are a few other important settings you should make as well. In the **Attachments** window of **Settings**, specify the directory where you want any mail attachments to be placed. The default is the directory from which you run Eudora. You might want to make a subdirectory for attachments. You should check the box to use MIME encoding for your attachments; BinHex is an encoding format that is common for Macintoshes, but not for Windows.

In the **Getting Attention** window of **Settings**, choose how you would like to be notified when you have new mail. You can select an alert dialog box, have the mailbox open automatically, or choose a sound to play. If you have the Plus! package, browse the sound files that come with the Desktop Themes. There are plenty of interesting sounds to choose from.

---

[*] Your network connection must already be up for Eudora to connect to your mail server. Eudora Light does not start your dial-up connection automatically when you open it.

Reading and Storing Mail with Eudora

Figure 5-36 shows the main Eudora window with the listing from the **In** mailbox. The functions of the toolbar icons (enlarged in Figure 5-37) are pretty straightforward. The messages are listed in the order they're received. There are four columns for each listing. The first shows the status of each message: a black circle if the message is unread, an R if the message has been replied to, up or down arrows indicating the priority,[*] and possibly other symbols. The second column lists the name of the sender. The third column shows the time and date at which the message was sent. The fourth column shows the approximate size of the message in kilobytes. The last column shows the message subject.

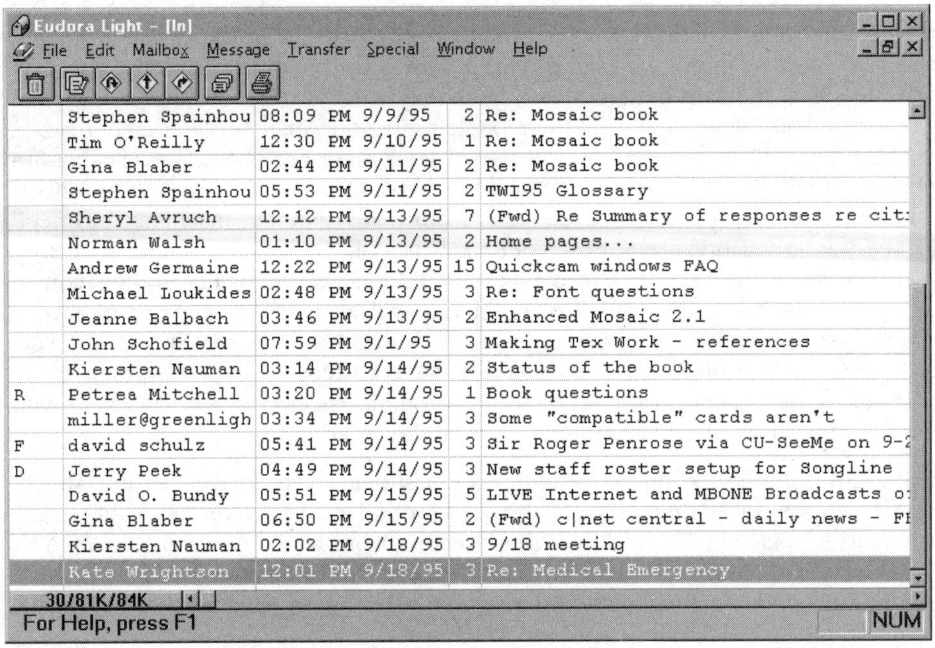

```
Eudora Light - [In]                                              _ □ ×
File  Edit  Mailbox  Message  Transfer  Special  Window  Help    _ 🗗 ×

       Stephen Spainhou 08:09 PM 9/9/95    2 Re: Mosaic book
       Tim O'Reilly     12:30 PM 9/10/95   1 Re: Mosaic book
       Gina Blaber      02:44 PM 9/11/95   2 Re: Mosaic book
       Stephen Spainhou 05:53 PM 9/11/95   2 TWI95 Glossary
       Sheryl Avruch    12:12 PM 9/13/95   7 (Fwd) Re Summary of responses re cit:
       Norman Walsh     01:10 PM 9/13/95   2 Home pages...
       Andrew Germaine  12:22 PM 9/13/95  15 Quickcam windows FAQ
       Michael Loukides 02:48 PM 9/13/95   3 Re: Font questions
       Jeanne Balbach   03:46 PM 9/13/95   2 Enhanced Mosaic 2.1
       John Schofield   07:59 PM 9/1/95    3 Making Tex Work - references
       Kiersten Nauman  03:14 PM 9/14/95   2 Status of the book
  R    Petrea Mitchell  03:20 PM 9/14/95   1 Book questions
       miller@greenligh 03:34 PM 9/14/95   3 Some "compatible" cards aren't
  F    david schulz     05:41 PM 9/14/95   3 Sir Roger Penrose via CU-SeeMe on 9-2
  D    Jerry Peek       04:49 PM 9/14/95   3 New staff roster setup for Songline
       David O. Bundy   05:51 PM 9/15/95   5 LIVE Internet and MBONE Broadcasts o:
       Gina Blaber      06:50 PM 9/15/95   2 (Fwd) c|net central - daily news - FF
       Kiersten Nauman  02:02 PM 9/18/95   3 9/18 meeting
       Kate Wrightson   12:01 PM 9/18/95   3 Re: Medical Emergency

  30/81K/84K  ◄│
For Help, press F1                                                NUM
```

Figure 5-36: The main Eudora window

To read a message, double-click on it, and it will be displayed in a child window of the Eudora window. Word wrap in Eudora works silently, so when there is a long line in a message, it is broken between words without inserting an equals sign, as Exchange does. You can go to the next message, using the down arrow key, and the previous with the up arrow key. (Or you may use ALT plus the arrow keys; you can choose in the **Miscellaneous** section of **Settings**.) To close a

---

[*] Priorities are not a universal mail feature. Eudora's priorities will be read by other people running Eudora and possibly some other mailers, but not all. Eudora's and Exchange's priorities are not compatible. See the discussion of priorities in the section "Unusual and Non-Standard Features" earlier in this chapter.

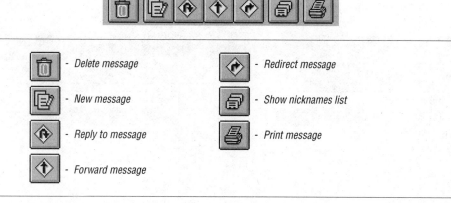

🗑 - Delete message		➦ - Redirect message	
▣ - New message		⬗ - Show nicknames list	
⬆ - Reply to message		🖨 - Print message	
⬆ - Forward message			

Figure 5-37: Main Eudora Toolbar Icons

message, select **Close** from **File** menu or simply close the window. The trash icon deletes the message, i.e., puts it into the **Trash** mailbox, which will be emptied upon exiting Eudora. If you check the **Automatically open next message** box in the **Miscellaneous** section of **Settings**, when you delete a message the next unread message will open.

Eudora stores messages in mailboxes and folders. There are three default mailboxes: **In**, **Out**, and **Trash**. All new mail retrieved from your mail server goes into the **In** mailbox. The **Out** mailbox stores any outgoing mail that you have composed until it can be transferred to your server on the next mail check. It will not store messages for long if you have **Immediate Send** checked in the **Sending Mail** section of **Settings**.

To create a new mailbox, select **New** from the **Mailbox** menu. A dialog box will pop up asking you for the name of the new mailbox. If you select the **Make it a folder** checkbox, you create a new subdirectory in the Eudora directory. Mailboxes are only files that store mail messages. Folders are directories that contain Mailboxes or other folders. When you create a new folder, you must then create a new mailbox in that folder to store messages in. All folders and top-level mailboxes (mailboxes that reside in the Eudora directory) are shown in the **Mailbox** and **Transfer** menus. The listed folder items contain submenus of all the mailboxes and subfolders that reside in them.

You can organize your folders and mailboxes by opening the Mailboxes window from the **Window** menu. The Mailboxes window, shown in Figure 5-38, shows all of your existing folders and mailboxes in two side-by-side windows. The listbox above each window shows which folder is being displayed (**Top Level** is the regular Eudora directory). You open a different folder by double-clicking on its icon or by selecting it from the listbox. The buttons underneath these windows allow you to **Rename** or **Remove** selected items or create new mailboxes and folders in the open folder. If you want to move a mailbox or folder into another folder, open its folder in one window and select it. In the other window, open the target folder, and press the appropriate **Move** button.

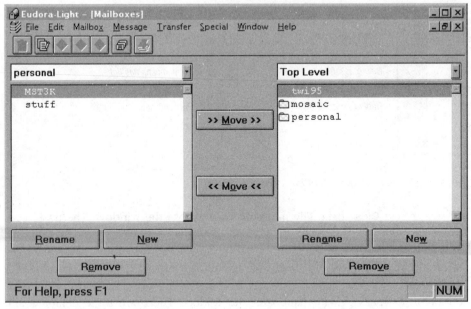

Figure 5–38: Mailboxes window

You can move messages from one mailbox and save them to another by using the **Transfer** menu. Just select the desired mailbox from the **Transfer** menu (or create a new one), and the open message or highlighted messages will be moved there.

Sending Mail

Figure 5-39 shows the message composition window. This is the window where you write and edit mail messages. When you press the new message button on the toolbar (or the corresponding **Message** menu items), the composition window appears with a mostly empty header section (only the **From**: line is filled in with your name) and a blank area below for typing in the message. If you are replying to or forwarding a message, the **To**: line is filled in with the recipient, and the **Subject**: line is filled in with an **Re**: to indicate that it is a reply. You can put new recipients on the **To**:, **Cc**:, or **Bcc**: lines by typing them in. Multiple addresses should be separated by commas (not semicolons as in Exchange). The text of the message being replied to or forwarded is put into the message indented with greater-than signs (>). You can edit this text as you need to and add new text to the message.

The toolbar of the composition window controls some useful options for the outgoing message. The first box enables you to set the priority of the message for

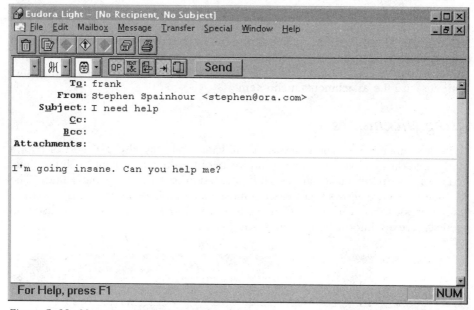

Figure 5-39: Message composition window

highest to lowest. A blank indicates normal priority and is the default. The second box allows you to to turn off signature file inclusion (your signature file will be inserted at the end of the message by default). You can make a signature for your mail messages by selecting **Signature** from the **Window** menu. A blank screen will open where you can enter the text of your signature. Remember, you can only use ASCII text, and you should keep it under five lines. When you close the window, you will be asked to save the signature; click **Yes**. Your signature is saved in a text file called *Signature.pce* in the Eudora directory.

The next box on the toolbar selects whether to use MIME or BinHex encoding for attachments. Unless you know your recipient can handle BinHex files, leave this set to MIME as it is a much more common mail encoding protocol. The next button, when pressed, will send any text file attachments as a separate attached file instead of including it in the body of the message. Choosing this option may be helpful if you are sending a long text file to someone. The next button turns on word wrap. If your line goes over the standard 80 column width, the line will be broken automatically. The next button converts tabs in the body of a message into spaces. Many applications treat tabs differently, and this option will enable columns of your text to line up properly when they are viewed with other programs. The next button will make a copy of your message and leave it in your **Out** mailbox. And finally, pressing the **Send** button delivers your message. Most of these functions can be set in the Settings window as your defaults.

If you wish to attach a file to your mail message, go to the **Message** menu and select **Attach File**. Choose the file you wish to attach from the window that appears and click **OK**. The file will be automatically encoded and identified by MIME. You will not see the contents of the file in the composition window, even if it is an inserted text file. The **Attachments**: line in the header shows the full path-name of the file. You cannot add to or alter the attachments by editing this line. You must use the **Attachments** menu item.

Using Nicknames

Trying to remember e-mail addresses is difficult. You may also get tired of typing out long addresses over and over again for people you send e-mail to all the time. In Eudora, you can make aliases and store addresses by using nicknames. The Nicknames feature allows you to assign more memorable or shortened names to e-mail addresses. You can also add notes to each nickname you create in case you need some extra information about the addressee.

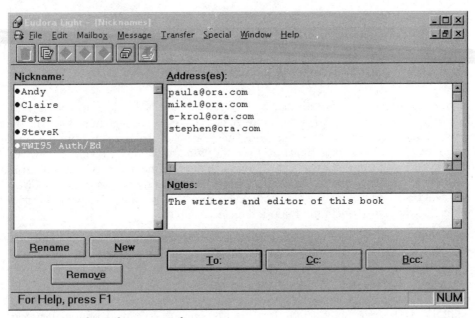

Figure 5–40: The Nicknames window

The easiest way to make a nickname is by choosing **Make Nickname** from the **Special** menu when you have a message open or selected. You will get a dialog box asking you what you want to call the nickname. Type in the name and press **OK**, and a new nickname is created from the address of the sender of the message. You can set up several nicknames by choosing **Nicknames** from the **Window** menu. This will open the Nicknames window shown in Figure 5-40.

In this window you can create new nicknames, edit existing ones, or choose nicknames to put on the **To:** or **Cc:** list of a message you are composing. To make a new nickname here, press the **New** button. A dialog box will ask you what to call the nickname. Enter the name and press OK. The new nickname will show up highlighted in the **Nickname** list, and the cursor will be placed in the addresses window. Type in the appropriate address or addresses (you can make lists) for the name. You can add comments about the name in the Notes window. When you exit the Nicknames window you will be asked to save the current list. Press **Yes**, and the new nicknames will be saved.

You can use any of the nicknames you create in Eudora's recipient list. The recipient list is a list of nicknames for frequently used addresses that becomes available from the **Message** menu. By using the recipient list you don't even have to type in the nickname. When you compose a new message, you simply go to the **Message** menu, select **New Message To**, and then select the nickname of the recipient. The nickname will be put into the **To:** list for the new message, and the message will be sent to the address associated with that nickname. You can place a nickname on the recipient list by checking **Add to recipient list** in the naming dialog. You can use the recipient list for addressing messages when replying, forwarding, or redirecting mail as well.

Features of Eudora Pro

Although Eudora Light is a perfectly useful mailer, you will probably want the advanced features of Eudora Pro. Eudora Pro is available at retail software outlets, and you can also upgrade from Light to Pro over the Internet (see Qualcomm's web page at **http://www.qualcomm.com/quest**). The advanced features of Eudora Pro include: built-in spell-checking, automatic display of attachments, uuencoding and uudecoding, rules-based message filtering, on-line help and multiple nicknames and signature files. Eudora Pro is a truly full-featured electronic mail program. Upgrading is easy, and all of your files and settings from Eudora Light are retained.

## CHAPTER SIX

THE WORLD WIDE WEB

Getting Started
Navigating the Web with Internet Explorer
Navigating the Web with Netscape Navigator
Working with Other Services
Creating Your Own Home Page
Windows 95 on the Web
Where the Web Is Going

The World Wide Web, or WWW, is the newest information service to arrive on the Internet. The Web is based on a technology called hypertext, which allows documents to be connected, or linked, to one another. When you are viewing a document that contains these links, you can view any of the connected documents simply by selecting the appropriate link. Linked documents on the Web are stored on host computers spread throughout the Internet; the Web lets you navigate the Internet by following such links. The World Wide Web is currently the most powerful and flexible Internet navigation system around.

The Web is also the fastest growing information service on the Internet. Since the first publicly available Web servers appeared on the Internet in early 1993, the number of sites providing information over the Web has been growing exponentially. In October 1993, there were just over 500 WWW sites on the Internet; as of now there are hundreds of thousands of sites. By September 1993, the WWW was responsible for 1% of the traffic on the NSF backbone; as of January 1995, the Web accounts for at least 18% of the traffic and it is the second busiest service on the Internet.

The World Wide Web originated at CERN, the European Particle Physics Laboratory, but it would be a mistake to see the Web as a tool designed by and for physicists. Tim Berners-Lee, an Oxford University graduate who came to CERN with a background in text processing and real-time communications, wanted to create a new kind of information system in which researchers could collaborate and exchange information during the course of a project. Berners-Lee used hypertext technology to link together a web of documents that could be traversed in any manner to seek out information. The Web does not imply a hierarchical tree, the structure of most books, or a simple ordered list. In essence, it allows many possible relations between any individual document and others. Berners-Lee implemented hypertext as a navigation system, allowing users to move freely from one document to another on the Net, regardless of where the documents are located.

There were many implementations of hypertext systems before the World Wide Web. What Berners-Lee did, in cooperation with others at CERN, was to define an Internet-based architecture using open, public specifications and free sample implementations. Because the specifications are public, anyone can build a Web client or server. Because there are sample implementations and the code can be obtained for free, developers can choose to build or refine parts of the system. Both factors encourage other people to contribute to the project, and as is true of many things on the Internet, the WWW effort has turned into a collaborative project involving people and organizations from around the world.

In order to navigate the Web, you need a Web client (called a browser, in the Web's terminology).[*] A WWW browser interprets and displays hypertext documents; it knows how to find and display a document pointed to by a link. The first WWW browser was a line-mode browser implemented by the team at CERN. However, it was Mosaic, a browser developed at the National Center for Super-computing Applications (NCSA), located at the University of Illinois at Urbana-Champaign, that took the Internet community by storm, and is in large part responsible for the tremendous growth of the Web.

Mosaic originated as part of a package of tools for scientific visualization. When Marc Andreessen, the undergraduate student working on the tools, started building Mosaic, he looked around on the Internet and discovered he didn't have to start from scratch. He found the WWW and saw that it was intended to serve a community similar to the one served by NCSA, so he based his work on what had already been started at CERN.[†]

It is hard to point out any single new feature that Mosaic introduced, either as a hypertext browser or a WWW client. Rather, Andreessen made available a solid program with the right number of features for users to feel amazed and empowered by their ability to navigate the riches of the Internet. Mosaic was the first widely available graphical Web browser; it demonstrated to the world at large the power of combining text and graphics. With an easy-to-use interface that let you click on links to navigate the Web, Mosaic made the Internet accessible to a broader group of users.

The first version of Mosaic was developed for UNIX-based systems running the X Window System. As excitement about the Web grew in the Internet-user

---

[*] More precisely, a browser is any program for reading hypertext. Web clients are basically hypertext readers, so they're called browsers.

[†] Eventually, Marc Andreessen left the University of Illinois and founded Netscape Communications Corporation, where he developed the Netscape Navigator. Netscape is similar to Mosaic (and to Internet Explorer), but adds many new features. Netscape will continue to be the leading-edge browser for the foreseeable future, so it's worth trying even if you have Internet Explorer.

community and the press, NCSA expanded its Mosaic development efforts and created Microsoft Windows and Macintosh versions of the browser. NCSA made Mosaic freely available on the Internet "for academic, research, and internal business purposes only," which helped make Mosaic and the Web so popular. NCSA also made it possible for commercial software developers to license the Mosaic source code. As a result, there are a number of commercial WWW browsers on the market that have evolved from Mosaic, including Microsoft's Internet Explorer.

But enough hype and history about the Web; what you really want to do is start exploring. To do so, you need a Web browser that runs on your PC. Internet Explorer is a Web browser from Microsoft. If you recently bought a PC with Windows 95 already installed, there should be an icon (**The Internet**) on your desktop that starts Internet Explorer. Internet Explorer is one of the tools provided with the Microsoft Plus! package. Internet Explorer is also included as part of the Internet Jumpstart Kit. See Appendix B, *Setting Up Your Internet Connection*, for information about how to get the Internet Jumpstart Kit for free.

If you don't want to use Internet Explorer, there are a number of other WWW browsers, both commercial and public domain, that you can choose from. Netscape Navigator is available on the Internet for free evaluation.[*] You can download Netscape via anonymous FTP from **ftp.netscape.com** (see Chapter 9, *Moving Files: FTP*). You want Netscape Navigator 1.22 for Windows 95; retrieve the file *n32e122.exe* from */netscape/windows*.

Mosaic, the graphical browser that started the WWW revolution, is freeware; it is available via anonymous FTP at **ftp.ncsa.uiuc.edu**. Other commercial browsers include Enhanced Mosaic from Spyglass, AIR Mosaic from Spry (which is included as part of "Internet In A Box"), and WebSurfer from NetManage.

In this chapter, I'll start by discussing Microsoft's Internet Explorer. After introducing the Web, I'll go on to discuss techniques that are common to all browsers, using Internet Explorer for the examples. Even if you don't plan to use Internet Explorer, you should read this material, as you'll need to know many of the techniques to use any Web browser. I'm also including a section on Netscape Navigator that covers the basics of navigating with Netscape, as well as some of its special features, since I expect many of you will want to check out this popular browser.[†] Then I'll talk about using the Web as an interface to other Internet services, such as FTP and Telnet. I close the chapter with some thoughts about where the Web is going.

---

[*] After the evaluation period, a license fee is due to Netscape if you continue using Netscape Navigator. However, if you are a student, faculty member, or staff member of an educational institution, or an employee of a charitable non-profit organization, you can use Netscape Navigator for free.

[†] As this book went to press, both Microsoft and Netscape announced new versions of their Web browsers. This chapter describes Internet Explorer 1.0 and Netscape Navigator 1.2. For information about the features in the new versions, see Appendix E, *Internet Explorer 2.0 and Netscape Navigator 2.0*.

What Is Hypertext?

Hypertext is a method of presenting information where selected words in the text can be "expanded" at any time to provide other information about the word. That is, these words are links to other documents, which may be text, files, pictures, anything. For the sake of illustration, let's assume that your library has a hypertext card catalog. If you pull up the card for a particular book, it might look like:

```
TITLE:    The river and the prairie : a history
            of the Quad-Cities, 1812-1960
AUTHOR:   Roba, William Henry.
PUBL.:    (Davenport, Iowa) : Hesperian Press,
DATE:     1986

SUBJECT:  Quad Cities (Iowa-Ill.)--History.
          Davenport (Iowa)--History.

FORMAT:   157 p. : ill., map ; 24 cm.
CONTENTS: Includes bibliographical references and notes.
```

If the italicized words are links, you can expand the author's name and get a biographical sketch. If you expand *prairie*, you might end up in a hypertext Oxford English Dictionary and see:

```
prairie ('pre&schwa.rI). Also 8, 9 parara, pararie, praira,
9 praire, prairia.   a. A tract of level or undulating grass-
land, without trees, and usually of great extent; applied
chiefly to the grassy plains of North America; a savannah,
a steppe.
```

Since this is another hypertext document, there are links in it as well. You can plunge deeper by expanding *savannah*, ending up in a hypertext encyclopedia positioned at a whole article on savannahs—complete with pictures and possibly even movies. You can repeat the process as long as you like, getting deeper and deeper into a topic.

The amount of hypertext on the Net has exploded in the past few years. Many museum exhibitions, magazines, and other hypertext presentations are available, including the well-known *Global Network Navigator* (GNN), formerly published by O'Reilly & Associates and now published by America Online, Inc.

Getting Started

What is WWW about? As I've said, it's an attempt to organize all the information on the Internet, plus whatever local information you want, as a set of hypertext documents. You traverse the network by moving from one document to another via links. For example, when you start Internet Explorer by double-clicking on **The Internet** icon, you should see something like Figure 6-1.*

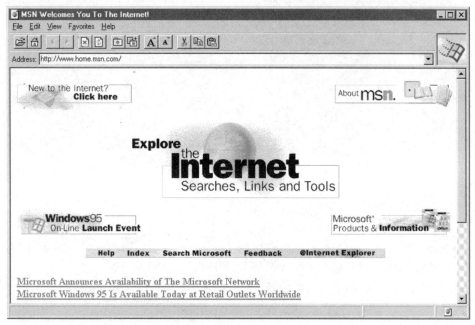

Figure 6–1: The Microsoft Network home page

This is Internet Explorer's current home page. Your home page is the hypertext document you see when you first enter the Web. The various images you see in Figure 6-1 are all links to other hypertext documents, as is the underlined text at the bottom of the screen. To distinguish textual links from plain text, the browser highlights the text by underlining it and using a different color. You can also tell that something is a link by moving your mouse around in the document; when the pointer changes to a hand cursor you are over a link to another document. To see what happens when you·select a link, click on the **Microsoft Products and Information** image. Now you should see something like what is shown in Figure 6-2. From Microsoft's home page, you can access all kinds of information about Microsoft

---

* Your system needs to be connected to the Internet before you can explore the World Wide Web. If you haven't set up your Internet connection yet, see Appendix B for information on how to do so. If you have an Internet connection but your system is not connected when you start Internet Explorer, you'll be prompted to establish a connection.

Figure 6-2: Microsoft's home page

products and services. You navigate from one page to another by selecting links; it's as simple as clicking on the word or graphic with your mouse.

You may be wondering about Internet Explorer's home page, especially if you aren't using the Microsoft Network for your Internet connection. Like any Web browser, Internet Explorer is set up to show you a particular Web document when you first start the browser. It so happens that Microsoft has chosen to use its MSN page as Internet Explorer's home page. This page is *not* part of the Microsoft Network; it's simply a Web document maintained by Microsoft that describes MSN. So just because you see this page does not mean you are using MSN, and as I'll explain later, you can change Internet Explorer's home page to be another document anywhere on the Web.

Any of these hypertext pages can be changed, hopefully for the better, at any time. It's important to realize that the Internet Explorer home page, Microsoft's home page, and everything else that's available on the Web is not built into your browser. They are just hypertext documents that can be modified at will. Some screens aren't even documents in the traditional sense (i.e., files that exist on some system's disk); they are generated "on the fly" by gateways between the Web and other services. Therefore, don't be surprised if you see images that don't match the sample screens. The Web is constantly changing; that's part of its beauty.

Now you may be asking what's so great about this. What is it about the World Wide Web that has made it so popular?

First, the Web is based on hypertext documents, and is structured by links between pages of hypertext. There are no rules about which documents can point where—a link can point to anything that the creator finds interesting. So a text about chemistry might point to a periodic table entry for Lithium, which might in turn point to some other articles discussing the properties of Lithium, which might point to an FTP server containing spectral data for various Lithium compounds. With the power of browsers like Internet Explorer and Netscape Navigator, documents can also contain illustrations and sound.

Second, the Web does an impressive job of providing a uniform interface to different kinds of services, such as FTP and Gopher. What does this mean in practice? It means that if you know how to use your Web browser, you can do just about anything there is to do on the Internet. And, it's simple. There are really only two Web commands: follow a link (which we've already demonstrated) and perform a search (which we'll discuss momentarily). No matter what kind of resource you're using, these two commands are all you need.

Simple as the Web is, it's still flexible. For example, the Web also allows you to read USENET news (see Chapter 7, *Network News*). If you read any news, you've probably noticed that each posting contains references to other messages. The Web restructures news postings as hypertext, turning these cross-references into links, so you can easily move between original postings, follow-ups, and cross-references, just by selecting links.

Finally, the Web eliminates the barrier between your data and "public data." If you set up a WWW server and an appropriate hypertext editor, you can integrate your own personal notes into the Web. (Your notes, of course, remain private, but they can have links to public documents.) Ten years ago, a few dozen boxes full of index cards was *de rigeur* for anyone writing a dissertation or an academic book. With the Web, a few hypertext documents make all that obsolete. Rather than copying a quote and sticking it into an index box, you can just create a link from a notes file to the document you're quoting. I touch on writing hypertext later in this chapter, when I discuss the Internet Assistant for Microsoft Word.

The best way to see the power of the Web is to look at some real hypertext documents. So let's start.

Navigating the Web with Internet Explorer

Starting Internet Explorer is very simple; just double-click on **The Internet** icon on your desktop. When the browser starts up, you'll see the home page shown earlier in Figure 6-1.

Let's start with a tour of the screen. Like all Windows 95 applications, Internet Explorer has a menu bar across the top of the screen. The toolbar, as shown in

Figure 6-3, is below the menu bar. The buttons on the toolbar provide single-click access to some commonly used commands.

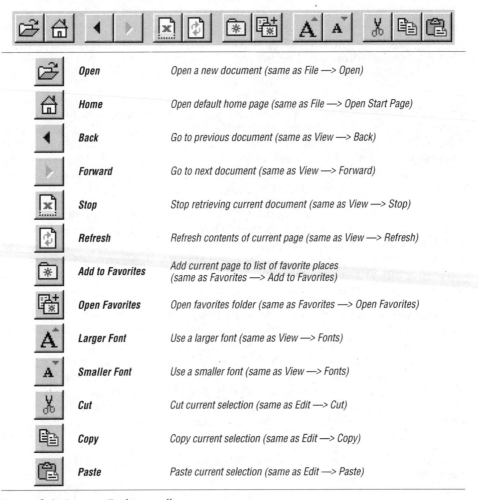

	Open	*Open a new document (same as File —> Open)*
	Home	*Open default home page (same as File —> Open Start Page)*
	Back	*Go to previous document (same as View —> Back)*
	Forward	*Go to next document (same as View —> Forward)*
	Stop	*Stop retrieving current document (same as View —> Stop)*
	Refresh	*Refresh contents of current page (same as View —> Refresh)*
	Add to Favorites	*Add current page to list of favorite places (same as Favorites —> Add to Favorites)*
	Open Favorites	*Open favorites folder (same as Favorites —> Open Favorites)*
	Larger Font	*Use a larger font (same as View —> Fonts)*
	Smaller Font	*Use a smaller font (same as View —> Fonts)*
	Cut	*Cut current selection (same as Edit —> Cut)*
	Copy	*Copy current selection (same as Edit —> Copy)*
	Paste	*Paste current selection (same as Edit —> Paste)*

Figure 6–3: Internet Explorer toolbar

The Windows 95 logo to the right of the toolbar becomes animated when Internet Explorer is loading a document. Underneath the toolbar, you see an **Address** field. The address is actually the Uniform Resource Locator, or URL, for the document you're viewing. It's a technical explanation of exactly where the document was found, and what kind of document it is. (URLs are discussed later in this chapter.)

Below the **Address** field is the document area; this area is where Internet Explorer displays the different pages you find on the Web. At the right side of the screen, you see a scroll bar that you can use for looking at documents that are longer than one page. If the document is too wide, Internet Explorer also puts a scroll bar at the bottom of the screen. However, scrolling left and right is terribly inconvenient; it's easier to resize the screen so it's wide enough to display the whole document.

At the bottom of the screen is the status bar. When you are moving your mouse around in the document area, the browser displays information about linked documents in the status bar as you pass over the links.

Like all Web browsers, Internet Explorer starts by finding a home page somewhere on the Internet.* The default home page is the "MSN Welcomes You To The Internet!" page shown in Figure 6-1. As I explained earlier, this page is about the Microsoft Network, but it's not part of MSN. And as I'll show you later, you can create your own home page, or select another home page anywhere on the Net. The home page consists of illustrations and text. Underlined text is a link to another document, as are many of the graphics.†

If you click on the **Explore the Internet** graphic, you'll see another page that contains hypertext links to Web documents where you can begin your exploration. You can distinguish hypertext from regular text because the hypertext is displayed in a different color and underlined. Now click on the **Links to other sites** graphic, and Internet Explorer displays a list of subjects, as shown in Figure 6-4.

If you scan the topics, you're bound to find one that interests you. Click on that link to see a list of Web documents on that subject. Just keep following links to locate information on specific topics. Congratulations! You're well on your way to using the Web to find fun and useful information.

Now, let's say you follow a link, then decide that it wasn't what you wanted. To return to the previous page, click on the **Back** button on the toolbar (i.e., the one with the left-pointing arrow). When you see the old page again, you'll notice that the link you selected is now a different color. This is a notice that you've already followed that link. It doesn't mean that you can't look at the same link again; you certainly can. It's just a notification that you've been there before. After you've played with Internet Explorer for a while, you'll starting seeing "already visited" links on pages you can swear you've never visited. You're not going crazy, and Internet Explorer isn't making a mistake; it just means you've visited this link before, but you took another route.

You can use the **Back** button repeatedly to step back through the pages you've already seen. And once you've clicked on the **Back** button, you can also use the **Forward** button (with the right-pointing arrow) to move through the pages in the opposite direction.

---

* Internet Explorer refers to the home page as the "start page." This terminology is not common in the Web community, however, so I am going to use the standard "home page" and let you make the translation.

† Again, Internet Explorer uses a non-standard term, "shortcuts," to refer to links to other documents. I'm going to use the term "links" to be consistent with other browsers. However, later in the chapter I will be describing something that is legitimately called a *shortcut*. It's a file on your desktop that takes you directly to a Web document.

Figure 6-4: Subject listing of links to other sites

As you travel the network with Internet Explorer, you can get quite far from where you started. Fortunately, if you want to get back to your home page at any time, all you have to do is click the **Home** button (i.e., the one with the house on it). Internet Explorer stores the address of your home page, so when you click **Home**, the browser immediately retrieves this document. When you are navigating the Web, you can travel far and wide and still never be far from home.

As you're browsing the Web, you will probably come across some documents other than the hypertext, or HTML, documents we've seen so far. Part of the beauty of the Web is that it supports multimedia: movies, full-color images, and sounds. The one drawback to multimedia on the Web is that the files can be quite large. A one-minute MPEG movie can be a megabyte or more, a four-minute sound clip might be two megabytes, and large full-color graphics are typically 200K or so. Depending on the speed of your network connection, it can take a while to download a multimedia file, but the wait is often worthwhile.

We've already seen a few images, and often, the pictures you see on Web pages are miniatures of larger images. When you click on a "thumbnail" image that is a link to a full-size image, Internet Explorer transfers the larger image and displays it for you right in the browser window. This works for both GIF and JPEG images, the two common formats on the Web. If your PC is equipped with a sound card and speakers, you can listen to any audio files you find on the Web. When you click on a sound file, Internet Explorer downloads it and plays it for you.

Navigation Tools

As the amount of information available on the Web continues to increase so rapidly, it becomes harder and harder to find the information you are interested in. To help with this problem, Internet Explorer gives you access to some on-line resources that can aid you in finding interesting Web documents.

As you use these resources to navigate the Web, you're likely to find documents that you want to visit again. While following links and using **Back** and **Forward** are useful for simple navigation, these tools can be cumbersome when you want to cover a lot of distance quickly. Internet Explorer provides other tools that make it easy to navigate directly to particular documents. For example, when you find a document that you really like, you can add it to your list of "favorite places." Once you've added the document to the list, you can view it simply by selecting the document from the **Favorites** menu. The browser also has a history feature that lets you go back to any page you've visited in the current session, just by choosing the page from a menu.

Search tools

Search tools offer a way to locate Web resources on a particular topic. As the Web has grown, the development of effective search mechanisms has become a hot research topic, so there are a number of search tools to choose from. Most search engines work by storing information about Web documents in a database. The actual information stored varies from tool to tool; some tools just use the document title, while others use the title, headings, links, and content keywords. When you perform a search, the search engine checks the database and returns links to the relevant documents. Obviously, the effectiveness of a search engine is highly dependent on the information it stores.

Like all things on the Web, the way you access a search tool is to follow a link to one. From the MSN home page, there are links to three different search tools. You can find them by clicking on the **Explore the Internet** graphic, followed by the **Internet Searches** graphic. Now you should see the Web document shown in Figure 6-5, which you can use to perform your search. Both InfoSeek and Lycos are search tools that maintain large databases of Web pages. You probably want to experiment with each of these tools and see which one you prefer. The Yahoo search takes a different approach, which I'll describe in the next section on Internet indexes.

To perform a search, enter your topic or keywords in the appropriate text entry area and click **Search**. Let's try a Lycos search. Enter the keywords *rock climbing* in the Lycos search field and click **Search**. The Lycos search engine searches its database and returns information about what it found. In our search, Lycos reports finding over 300 documents that matched the keywords. However, Lycos only returns the "top" 15 documents, based on how many times the keywords appeared in the document and how close they are to one another. Figure 6-6 shows one of the documents located by the "rock climbing" search.

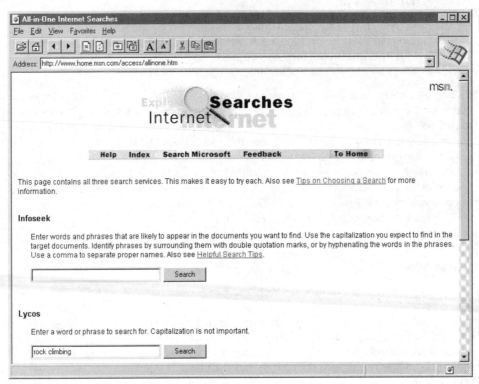

Figure 6–5: The all-in-one Internet search page

As you can see in Figure 6-6, the search results include a link to the matching document; "The Climbing Archive" is underlined, showing it's a link. If it looks like what you want, you can immediately check it out by clicking on it.

Internet indexes

The various search tools provide one means of locating Web resources on a particular topic. Internet indexes offer another approach; they are an easy way to get a feel for the kinds of things that are available on a particular subject. I've already shown you one such index, Microsoft's "Cool Links," in Figure 6-4. This index provides a fairly small sample of what's available on the Web; there are a number of other, more extensive, directories available. One common feature is that most of these directories are organized by subject. With so much information available on the Web, it's impossible to index every document. Essentially, an index is only as good as the people who maintain it, adding new Web documents as they appear and updating references to existing documents.

Perhaps the biggest and most popular directory is Yahoo, which currently features over 44,000 entries. You can get to this directory by clicking on the **categories** link

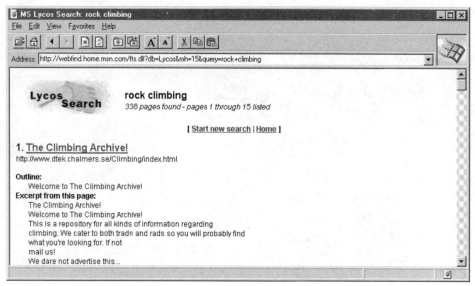

Figure 6–6: Lycos search results

in the Yahoo description on the "All-in-One Internet Searches" page.[*] Now your Internet Explorer window should look something like Figure 6-7.

As you can see in Figure 6-7, the Yahoo index provides an initial list of high-level subjects. Select a subject and you'll get a list of topics within that subject. As you keep narrowing down your topic, you'll eventually get to a page that provides links to relevant resources all over the Web. Follow these links to explore the resources. Often, Yahoo index pages include both links to Web resources as well as subtopics of a particular topic, as shown in Figure 6-8.

If you're in the mood to browse around the Web, Yahoo is a great place to start, as you can focus your browsing in a particular area. But if you have a specific topic in mind, you may not want to spend the time figuring out where that information is categorized. That's where Yahoo's searching mechanism comes in handy. Enter your keywords in the search field shown in Figure 6-7 (or the Internet search page) and click **Search**. Yahoo will return a page listing the documents in the directory that match your keywords.

I told you that there are a number of Internet indexes available on the Web, but so far I've only shown you one. Let's find some more. Select Yahoo's **Computers and Internet** subject, followed by the **Internet** subheading. Now you should see a link to **Indices to Web Documents**. This page contains links to countless Web directories, including something familiar: the *Whole Internet Catalog*, a part of the *Global*

---

[*] While you can search the Yahoo index from the Internet search page, I think Yahoo is more interesting as an index, so that's what I'm going to show you.

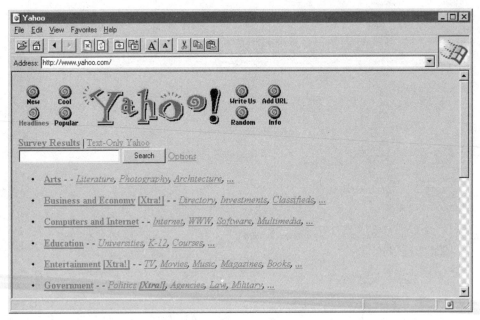

Figure 6–7: The Yahoo Internet index

Network Navigator. GNN is an on-line magazine; it's updated frequently with news and articles of interest to the Internet community. The *Whole Internet Catalog* is an on-line version of the *Resource Catalog* in this book, with an additional twist: once you've found a resource, you can click on a link and access it.

Favorite places

By now, you've probably spent a lot of time clicking on items and following links. Hopefully, you've found some interesting Web documents that you'd like to visit frequently. When you already know exactly what you want, you won't want to be constantly mousing around and searching for these documents.

To solve this problem, Internet Explorer provides the concept of a favorite place. Your list of favorite places is a permanent list of documents that you find interesting and can access with a single menu selection. Once you've found an interesting document, adding it to your list of favorite places is easy. Just click the **Add To Favorites** button on the toolbar, or select **Add To Favorites** from the **Favorites** menu. When you do so, Internet Explorer displays the window shown in Figure 6-9.

For now, just click **Add** to add the document to your list of favorite places. As I'll explain shortly, you can arrange your favorite places in separate folders. Later, when you want to go to one of your favorite places, just go to the **Favorites** menu and select the appropriate page. As you can see in Figure 6-10, all of your favorite

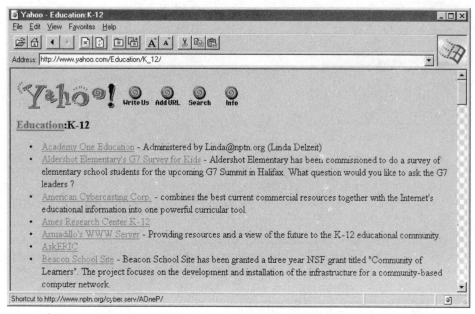

Figure 6–8: K-12 education resources

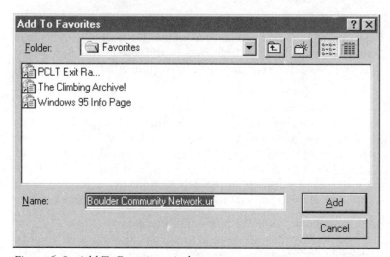

Figure 6–9: Add To Favorites window

places are listed in this menu. What's particularly handy about the list of favorite places is that it lasts between sessions; once you add something to the list, it stays until you delete it.

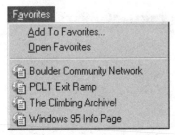

Figure 6–10: Favorites menu

Once you've accumulated a list of a dozen or more favorite places, you may want to think about organizing the documents into separate folders. For example, you could organize your favorite documents by subject, with a folder for PC-related pages, one for community information, and another for recreational documents.

To reorganize your favorite places, click the **Add To Favorites** button to open the window shown in Figure 6-9. This window is actually a variant of the standard Save dialog; to create a new folder, just click the **Create New Folder** button and give the new folder an appropriate name. Now you can move the relevant Web documents into the folder using drag-and-drop; select a document, drag it over the folder, and drop it. You can create as many folders as you need by repeating this process. When you are done, click the **Cancel** button.

The folders within your list of favorite places appear as submenus of the **Favorites** menu, as shown in Figure 6-11, so you can still access the documents with a single menu selection. Notice that you can have both folders and documents in your list of favorite places. In fact, you can even nest folders within other folders, if you need that level of organization.

The addresses of your favorite documents are actually stored in separate files on your system. If you click the **Open Favorites** button on the toolbar, or select **Open Favorites** from the **Favorites** menu, Internet Explorer opens the *Favorites* folder on your desktop. This folder contains a file icon for each document in your list of favorite places. If you've organized your favorite places into folders, you'll see those folders inside the *Favorites* folder. Since each favorite place is stored in a separate file, there's no one file you can edit to modify your list of favorite places.

While you can add documents to your list of favorite places and rearrange those documents using the **Add To Favorites** window, there are some things that you can only do from the desktop. For example, if you want to delete a document from your list, you have to drag its file from the appropriate folder to the **Recycle Bin**. Internet Explorer doesn't provide a way to modify the address of a favorite document. If you find that a document has moved (and it happens fairly often), your best bet is to delete the old file and add the new location to your list of favorite places.

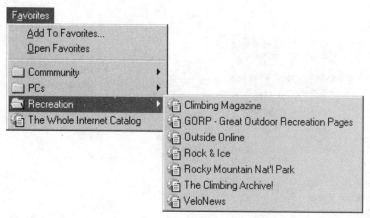

Figure 6-11: Favorites menu with folders

The file type of the files in your *Favorites* folder (and any subfolders) is associated with Internet Explorer. This means that if you double-click on one of the file icons, the system uses Internet Explorer to retrieve the document and display it. Essentially, the address files are shortcuts to the actual documents on the World Wide Web. Each time you add a document to your list of favorite places, Internet Explorer creates a shortcut and stores it in the *Favorites* folder (or a subfolder).

You can also create a shortcut to a Web document by selecting **Create Shortcut** from the **File** menu. In this case, Internet Explorer stores the shortcut directly on your desktop, instead of putting it in the *Favorites* folder. The advantage of having the shortcut on your desktop is that you can start Internet Explorer and immediately see the document you want with two quick clicks of your mouse. As I'll explain shortly, you can achieve the same effect by changing your home page to be the Web document you visit most often. However, if there are two or three different Web documents that you visit all the time, you might want to store them as shortcuts on your desktop, as you can only have one home page.

History

Internet Explorer keeps track of the documents you have seen and lets you move back to your previous selections. At the simplest level, you can use the **Back** button to move to the previous document. Once you've moved back, you can also move forward again by using the **Forward** button. (Moving forward doesn't make sense until you've moved back at least once; Internet Explorer won't let you try it.)

You can also see a list of the last nine pages you've visited by looking at the **File** menu, as shown in Figure 6-12. You can return immediately to one of these pages simply by selecting it from the menu. If you select **More History**, Internet Explorer opens the **History** folder, where it stores shortcuts to the last 300 documents you have visited. If you double-click on one of these shortcuts, Internet Explorer retrieves the document for you.

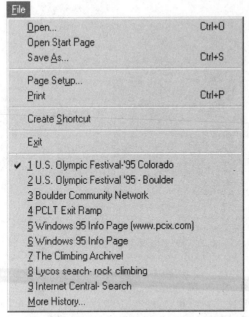

Figure 6-12: Document history on the File menu

There's one final history mechanism that you need to know about. The **Address** field in the Internet Explorer window is actually a combo box. If you click on the arrow in this field, you'll see a list of all the different home pages you've visited. (In this case, "home page" means the top-level entry point into the Web documents for a particular company or organization.) To return to one of these pages, simply select it from the list.

Searching Through a Document

So, you've found an interesting document, and Internet Explorer has displayed it on your screen. But it's ten pages long, and you're only interested in part of it. How do you find what you want? Go to the **Edit** menu, and select **Find**. You'll see the Find window, as shown in Figure 6-13.

Type your search word (or phrase) into the text entry area. If you want your search to start at the top of the document, click the **Start from top of page** check box; if capitalization is important in your search, click the **Match case** box. When you are ready, click **Find Next**. Internet Explorer then finds your string, highlights it, and puts it at the top of the display. If you find something you didn't expect and want to continue down the document, press **Find Next** again.

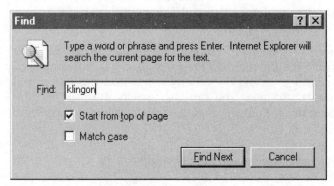

Figure 6–13: The Find window

Saving and Printing Files

To save a Web document on your system, select **Save As** from the **File** menu. Internet Explorer displays the standard Windows 95 Save As dialog, as shown in Figure 6-14.

Figure 6–14: The Save As dialog

Select the directory where you'd like to save the file and enter a filename in the **File name** field. The **Save as type** combo box lets you choose how you want to save the file. You can save it as plain text or as HTML. If you save it as plain text, you will only get the textual part of the document, without any fancy fonts or graphics. This is useful if you want to use the text in another program or extract snippets of it. HTML is the internal language used to format Web documents. It allows you to save most of the formatting of the document, but you can only view it later from a Web browser. If you view it with Notepad or Microsoft Word, you'll see a lot of funny things inserted in the text which I'll demystify later in the chapter. When you're ready, click the **Save** button to save the file.

Printing a document is similar—but even simpler. When you select the **Print** option in the **File** menu, you'll see the standard **Print** dialog shown in Figure 6-15. If there's more than one printer available on your system, select the printer you want to use from the **Name** combo box. You can also specify the page range if you don't want to print the entire document, as well as the number of copies you want.

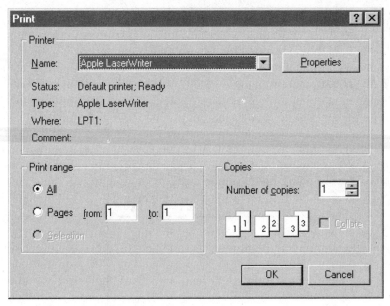

Figure 6-15: The Print window

If you want to adjust how the document is displayed when it is printed, select **Page Setup** from the **File** menu. The Page Setup window lets you control the page margins and the header and footer that are used on each page. You can print specific information as part of the header and footer using special characters. For example, &u inserts the URL, &w inserts the window title, and &p inserts the current page number. For a complete list of the special characters, press the F1 key while the cursor is in one of the header or footer fields.

Filling Out Forms

As you're exploring the Web, you may come across other documents like the Internet search page that allow you to enter all sorts of information. These are known as forms. Some of these forms are surveys, while others allow you to subscribe to a service or order products over the Web. The information you enter in the form is sent back across the Internet to the Web server that provides the document. For example, Figure 6-16 shows a portion of the *GNN* Subscriber Information form. You can fill out this form to subscribe to the *Global Network Navigator* on-line magazine; the form is available from the *Whole Internet Catalog.*

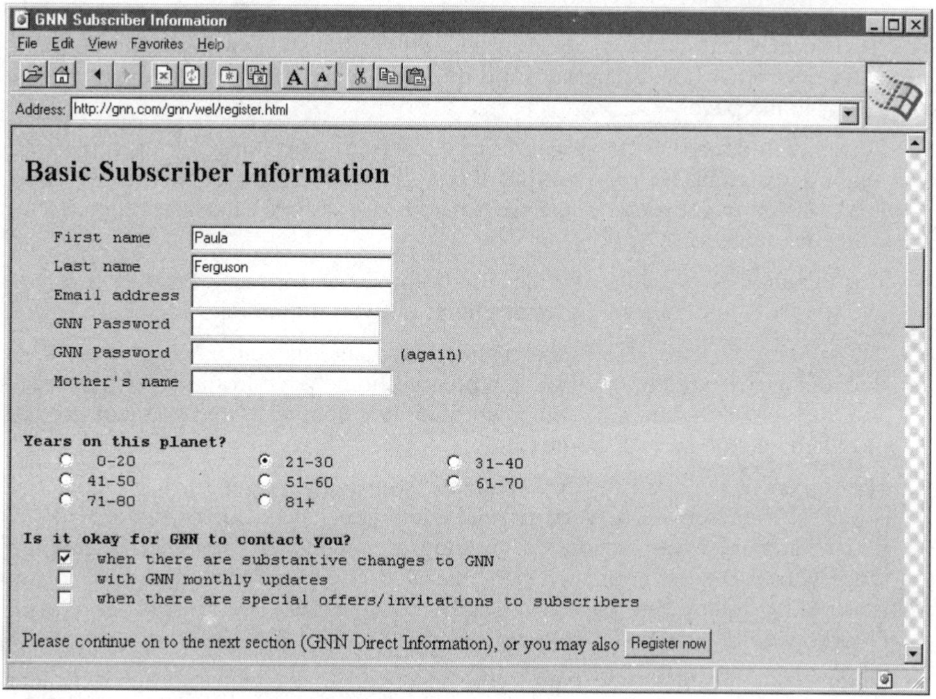

Figure 6-16: GNN Subscriber Information form

Filling out forms is a fairly intuitive process. Sometimes there are blank fields for you to fill out; sometimes you're asked to pick one of several items. Using your mouse to move from one field to another, fill in the appropriate text and make your selections. When you are done, you have to click on a button to send the information. This button is often labeled **Submit**; on the *GNN* form, the button is labeled **Register Now**.

One word of caution about the information you provide in forms. At this time, transferring information over the Web is not a secure process. While a small number of companies have set up secure Web sites that protect the information you enter, most transactions are not protected in this way. While it's conceivable that someone could intercept sensitive information, like your credit card number, I'd say the real chance of that is incredibly rare. The media has made this out to be a bigger problem than it really is; sending your credit card number over the Web is no worse than giving it to someone over the telephone or faxing it. And this situation should improve as more secure servers spring up. As with any credit card transaction, you'll want to make sure you're dealing with a reputable site: **landsend.com** is fine, but you might be wary of **joesjunk.com**.

Changing Your Home Page

When Internet Explorer starts, it presents you with the default "MSN Welcomes You To The Internet!" home page. However, you're not stuck with this home page; you can select other home pages around the Net. There are many reasons to select a different home page:

- You may find another home page that's more to your liking; for example, you might like starting with the on-line *Whole Internet Catalog* or the Yahoo directory. Or you might prefer some specialized subject index that's appropriate for your own interests.

- The server that provides the default home page for your browser may be overloaded—and therefore inconvenient, or even impossible, to use.

- If you want to learn HTML, the markup language in which World Wide Web documents are written, you can download a home page from somewhere else, and customize it—i.e., add your own favorite resources. Then you can use the modified version as your home page.

- Many Internet service providers maintain Web home pages for their clients as a part of their service. If your provider lets you have your own home page, you should read the section on creating a home page later in this chapter. Once you've created your own personal Web page, you may also want to use it as your default home page, especially if you've included links to all of your favorite Web documents in your home page.

To change your default home page, you first need to be viewing the document you want to use as your home page. Navigate to this document using your list of favorite places or whatever technique you find convenient. Now select **Options** from the **View** menu. The **Start Page** tab is shown in Figure 6-17. Simply click on **Use Current** to tell Internet Explorer to use the current page as your default home page. Now, when you start Internet Explorer, or when you click **Home** on the toolbar, you'll see your new home page.

A Few Hints

I've covered the basics of what you need to know to use a World Wide Web browser like Internet Explorer. However, since these browsers are the ultimate in power tools, a few formal hints are in order. You would probably figure out most of these yourself, but I can get you pointed in the right direction. Note, however, that I'm not going to tell you about every single feature of Internet Explorer; some of the more obvious features I'll leave for you to experiment with on your own.

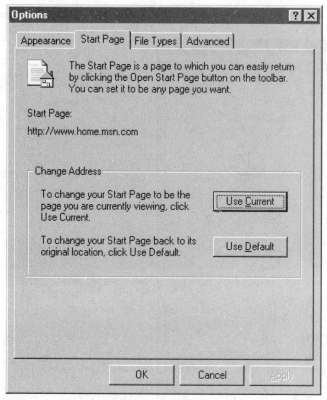

Figure 6–17: Start Page Options tab

Canceling

If you get tired of waiting for Internet Explorer to load a Web document, or if you decide you've made a mistake, you can cancel the operation by clicking on the **Stop** button on the toolbar.

Minimizing delays while loading images

If you're using Internet Explorer over a medium-speed link (e.g., between 9600 and 28,800 baud), you'll find it takes a fair amount of time to load graphics. For many documents, that isn't a problem; for example, *GNN* includes many graphics, but it's organized in relatively short chunks, so that waiting for them to "come down the line" isn't burdensome. However, there are documents that contain so many graphics that you can easily spend 10 minutes or more waiting. The worst offenders in this regard tend to be the exhibitions and museums.

To eliminate the time it takes to load the pictures, select **Options** from the **View** menu. The **Appearance** tab, shown in Figure 6-18, contains the **Show pictures** box.

If you remove the check mark in this box, Internet Explorer will stop showing you pictures in the Web documents you view.

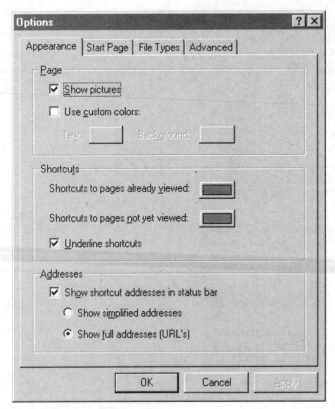

Figure 6–18: Appearance tab

Now, when you load a document that contains embedded graphics, you'll see icons instead of pictures. To download a picture, click the right mouse button over the icon and select **Show Picture** from the popup menu that appears. You can read the text, figure out which illustrations should be interesting, and get those as desired. If the graphic is also a link to another document, you can click on the icon with your left mouse button to follow the link, just as before.

To return to normal image loading, go back to the **Appearance** tab of the Options window and select the **Show pictures** box again.

Using the popup menu

Internet Explorer provides quick access to some of its functionality through a popup menu. If you click the right mouse button in the document area, you'll see the popup menu. The contents of this menu varies, depending on where you clicked the right mouse button. For example, if you click over a hypertext link, you'll see menu items that let you open the linked document, open the linked document in a new window, put a shortcut to the linked document on the clipboard, or add the linked document to your list of favorite places.

When you click the right mouse button over an image, the popup menu lets you save the image, copy it to the clipboard, or use it as the background wallpaper on your screen. If the image is a link to another document, you can also use the popup menu to open the linked document, put a shortcut to the linked document on the clipboard, or add the linked document to your list of favorite places. Being able to save images that you find on the Web can be useful, especially if you are writing your own Web documents. Just be careful that you don't reuse images that are copyrighted.

If you click the right mouse button over the background of the document area (i.e., not over a hyperlink or an image), you'll see menu items that let you select all of the text in the document, create a shortcut to the document, add the document to your list of favorite places, or view the HTML source of the document. The **View Source** option opens the HTML source for the document in Notepad. This is useful if you want to create a Web page that mimics the style of a document that you've found, as you can modify the source however you'd like.

Manipulating text

You can select text in a Web document just as you would in a word processing application, even though you can't edit the contents of the document area. Simply drag the left mouse button over the text; Internet Explorer highlights the selected text so that you can see what you've selected. You can also use **Select All** on the **Edit** menu to select all of the text in a document.

After you select some text, all you can really do is copy it to the clipboard; use **Copy** on the **Edit** menu. But once you've copied the text to the clipboard, you can paste it into any application that allows you to do so, such as a word processor, or the New Message window in Microsoft Exchange.

Using drag-and-drop

Internet Explorer supports a few drag-and-drop operations. For example, instead of copying selected text to the clipboard and then pasting it in another application, you can simply drag the selected text to the other application and drop it. The browser also supports dragging hypertext links. If you drag a hypertext link to the desktop or to a folder, Internet Explorer creates a shortcut to the linked document.

You can also drag a link to Exchange's New Message window. When you send the message, the link is sent with the message as a MIME attachment. If the recipient is also using Exchange, she can click on the attachment to start Internet Explorer and view the document.

Document tracking

By default, Internet Explorer stores shortcuts to the last 300 documents you have visited. These shortcut files are kept in the **History** folder; they are accessible through the **More History** option on the **File** menu. If you have limited space on your hard drive, you may want to reduce the number of shortcuts that are saved. To do so, select **Options** from the **View** menu. On the **Advanced** tab, change the value of the **History** field. You can also remove all of the shortcuts from the **History** folder by clicking the **Empty** button.

To cut down on the amount of information that it has to retrieve from the network, Internet Explorer caches HTML documents and graphics files on your system. Unlike shortcut files, which simply store the address of a Web document, each file in the cache contains an entire HTML document or graphical image. Before Internet Explorer retrieves a document from the network, it checks to see if the document is in the cache, and if it is, the browser displays it immediately. Using a cache can greatly improve performance, especially if you have a slow Internet connection.

The only drawback to the cache is that the HTML documents and image files can be quite large. The cache exists between Internet Explorer sessions; it takes up space on your disk even when you aren't using the browser. Internet Explorer limits the maximum size of the cache to ten percent of the size of your hard drive, but you may want to set this limit lower if you have limited space on your drive. You can control the maximum size of the cache on the **Advanced** tab of the Options window by moving the slider in the **Cache** section. You can also remove all of the files in the cache by clicking the **Empty** button. If you don't want Internet Explorer to use caching at all, set the **Update Cache** option to **Never**. You should only do this if you have very limited disk space.

When things go wrong

Sometimes when you try to open a connection, things don't go quite right. For example, it might take a *really* long time to connect to the server. It may be that you're connecting to a distant server, and it's going to take a long time to connect. Or you may be dealing with a slow or overburdened network. If the server is actually down, you'll eventually get an error message from Internet Explorer that the connection failed.

If Internet Explorer tells you that it cannot access the server you want, you can use the **Refresh** button (or **Refresh** on the **View** menu) to tell Internet Explorer to try again. Obviously, if the server isn't responding, trying again won't work and your best bet is to try later. But if the problem is on your end, **Refresh** may help. For example, if your connection to the Internet is congested, or momentarily flaky, a retry might be all you need to set things right.

People often change the locations or names of their documents, which means, of course, that the address, or URL, has also changed. The more polite folks out there will leave a document that points to the new URL. If not, however, you'll simply get an error message that the URL couldn't be found.

The important thing to remember about Internet Explorer (and the Web in general) is that when things don't work out, it's hardly ever your fault. Just accept the fact that you can't get access right now, and try again later.

Navigating the Web with Netscape Navigator

If you've decided not to use Microsoft's Internet Explorer Web browser, you may want to check out Netscape Navigator, a popular commercial Web browser. Actually, even if you have Internet Explorer, you may still want to try out Netscape, as it is the most innovative Web browser available today. While Netscape Navigator is a commercial product, you can retrieve the browser from the Internet and evaluate it before you decide whether or not to buy it. Netscape Navigator is available via anonymous FTP at **ftp.netscape.com**. For information on how to download software using anonymous FTP, see Chapter 9.

Getting Started

After you have downloaded the latest release of Netscape Navigator, you'll need to unpack the self-extracting archive and then install the browser.* Follow the instructions provided with the software in the *Readme.txt* file; basically, you just need to run the Setup program. This program installs the browser on the desktop, so you can double-click on the **Netscape Navigator** icon to use the browser. If you are using auto-dial, the Connect To window should appear automatically when you start Netscape; otherwise you'll need to make sure your Internet connection is up before you start the browser. When you start Netscape Navigator, you should see a window that looks something like Figure 6-19.

As you can see, Netscape's interface looks quite similar to that of Internet Explorer. Like all Windows 95 applications, Netscape has a toolbar located beneath the menu bar. This toolbar is shown in Figure 6-20.

The **Netsite** field underneath the toolbar displays the address of the document you're viewing, and the buttons below it provide quick access to a few Web pages maintained by the Netscape folks. For example, the **What's New!** button brings up a document that lists interesting new Web sites, while the **What's Cool!** button presents a page of "cool" Web sites, as judged by the Netscape "cool team." The **Handbook** button retrieves Netscape's on-line handbook, which contains both tutorial and reference material on using Netscape Navigator. The Netscape icon to

---

* You want Netscape Navigator 1.22 for Windows 95. This version of Netscape is in the */netscape/windows* directory; the file you want is *n32e122.exe*.

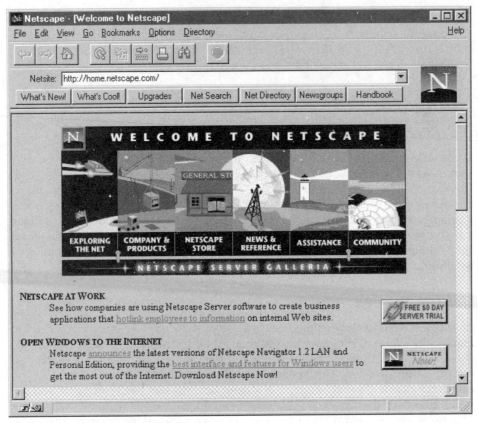

Figure 6–19: Netscape Navigator home page

the right of these buttons becomes animated when the browser is loading a document.

Just like Internet Explorer, Netscape has a large document area with scroll bars that it uses to display Web documents. The status bar at the bottom of the screen contains a few items: a security indicator, a message area, and a progress indicator. If the key in the status bar is broken, it means you are viewing a document on an insecure Web server; if the key is whole, you are dealing with a secure Web server. When Netscape is used with a secure Web server, the information transmitted between the browser and the server is protected. The message area displays information about linked documents as you move your mouse around the document area. If Netscape is loading a document, the message area provides status reports about the retrieval, while the progress indicator shows this information graphically.

We looked at Netscape's home page in Figure 6-19. As with any Web browser, you navigate by clicking on links. Netscape provides the standard **Back** and **Forward**

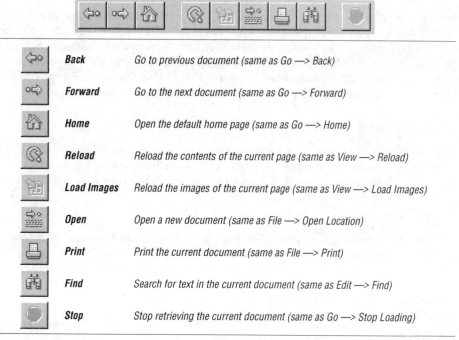

Figure 6–20: Netscape Navigator toolbar

buttons for viewing documents that you've already seen before. And when you've traveled far afield, you can click on the **Home** button to return to the Netscape home page or another home page anywhere on the Internet (if you've changed your home page, as I'll explain later).

Much of Netscape's functionality is the same as Internet Explorer's. For instance, you can use the **Find** item on the **Edit** menu to search through the text of a Web document. You can also save and print Web documents using the **Save As** and **Print** commands on the **File** menu. One additional feature that Netscape offers is the ability to e-mail the address of the current Web document to another person; select **Mail Document** from the **File** menu.

Filling out forms with Netscape Navigator is performed exactly as you would with Internet Explorer; use your mouse to move from field to field and fill in the appropriate information. Pressing ENTER when you are done entering the information in one field automatically moves you to the next. However, Netscape is a very security-conscious Web browser. When you click on the button to send the information, Netscape brings up a window warning you that submitting the information is not protected. Netscape *does* have security features built in; if you are dealing with a secure Web server, Netscape can protect the information it transmits.

Navigation Tools

Netscape Navigator offers a number of tools to help you explore the World Wide Web. For example, Netscape gives you quick access to various Internet indexes and search tools with buttons in its main window. Netscape's bookmarks facility is akin to Internet Explorer's favorite places, letting you keep track of Web documents that you want to visit often. Netscape also allows you to easily open multiple windows, so that you can view more than one page at a time.

Internet indexes

The **Net Directory** button on Netscape's interface takes you to a page that provides access to a number of Internet indexes. This page includes a link to the Yahoo index described earlier, as well as links to all of the high-level subjects in Yahoo.

Search tools

As you might guess, clicking the **Net Search** button causes Netscape to display a document that contains links to a number of Web search tools. One of these tools is the Lycos search engine described earlier. Netscape also offers links to the Info-Seek and WebCrawler search tools, so you can experiment with the different tools and decide which one you prefer.

Bookmarks

Once you start exploring with Netscape, you'll want to keep track of the interesting Web documents you find, so you can visit them frequently. Netscape uses the concept of a bookmark for this purpose. When you find an interesting document, you create a bookmark for it. Then you can access the document by selecting it from a menu.

To create a bookmark for the Web document you are currently viewing, select **Add Bookmark** from the **Bookmarks** menu. Later, when you want to see the document again, go to the **Bookmarks** menu and select the document. As you can see in Figure 6-21, all of your bookmarks are listed in this menu. Each time you add a bookmark, the document is added at the bottom of the menu. These bookmarks last between sessions; once you create a bookmark, it stays until you delete it.

After you have more than a dozen or so bookmarks, you may want to think about organizing them into separate folders. This will make it easier for you to find your favorite documents, especially if you organize the bookmarks by subject. To reorganize your bookmarks, select **View Bookmarks** from the **Bookmarks** menu. This command opens the window shown in Figure 6-22.

As you can see, your bookmarks are stored as documents in a single folder. To create a new folder, select **Insert Header** from the **Item** menu in the Bookmarks windows. Netscape brings up the Bookmark Properties window that allows you to change the name of the header (folder) to something appropriate. Now you can

Figure 6-21: Bookmarks menu

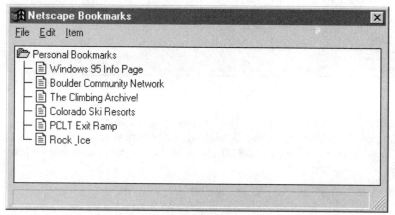

Figure 6-22: Netscape Bookmarks window

move bookmarks into the folder using drag-and-drop; select a bookmark, drag it to the folder, and drop it. Repeat this process to create as many folders as you need. When you're done, you might have something that looks like Figure 6-23.

Your bookmark folders appear as submenus of the **Bookmarks** menu, so you can still get to the documents with a single menu selection. You can also tell Netscape to retrieve a bookmark from the Bookmarks window by double-clicking on the bookmark, or by selecting the bookmark and using **Go To Bookmark** on the **Item** menu.

Netscape makes it easy to maintain your bookmarks. As you continue to add bookmarks, you can reorganize them to your heart's content using drag-and-drop. You can even create folders within folders, if you need that level of organization. If you want to delete a bookmark, select it in the Bookmarks window and then choose **Delete** on the **Edit** menu. If you find that the address of a document has changed, you can modify the bookmark by selecting it and then picking **Properties** from the **Item** menu. Netscape brings up the Bookmark Properties window, from which you can change the address of the document.

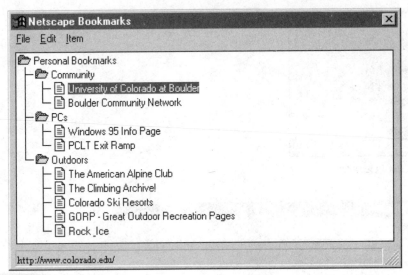

Figure 6–23: Netscape Bookmarks window with folders

Unlike Internet Explorer, Netscape Navigator does not store each bookmark in a separate file. Instead, it keeps all of the bookmark information in a single HTML file, *Bookmark.htm*. You can view this HTML file with Netscape by selecting **View in Browser** from the **File** menu.

One advantage to the single-file approach is that you can share your bookmark file with other people. Say, for instance, that you're working on a research project with a colleague. You've spent some time navigating the Web, finding documents relevant to your research. If you've created bookmarks for these documents, you can e-mail your bookmark file to your research partner and then she can import it into Netscape using **Import** on the Bookmarks window's **File** menu.

History

Like any Web browser, Netscape Navigator keeps track of the documents you have seen, so that you can move back to your previous selections. Netscape lists your document history on the **Go** menu, as shown in Figure 6-24.

You can immediately view one of these pages by selecting it from the menu. As your document history gets longer, Netscape truncates the number of pages it lists in the **Go** menu. However, you can view your complete document history for the current session by selecting **View History** from the menu. Netscape displays the history in a separate window; the documents listed here are all of the different pages you've visited in your Web exploration. You can go to any of these pages by selecting it and clicking the **Go To** button.

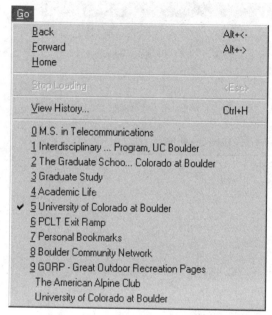

Figure 6–24: Document history on the Go menu

Multiple windows

You can have multiple Netscape windows on your screen, which is convenient if you want to look at several documents at the same time. To open a new Netscape window, select **New Window** from the **File** menu. This command opens a new window with the same history as the previous window. The new window displays the oldest document in the history, which is typically your home page.

Changing Your Home Page

When you start Netscape Navigator, you see the default Netscape home page. However, as with any good Web browser, you can change the default home page to a page of your own creation or another page anywhere on the Web. To change your home page, select **Preferences** from the **Options** menu. Netscape displays the Preferences window; the **Styles** tab shown in Figure 6-25 should be visible.

With Netscape, you have the option of starting with a blank page or an actual home page. If you choose to start with a blank page, the document area will be empty each time you start Netscape. You'll need to navigate to the Web document you want to see, probably using a bookmark. This feature is also useful if you want to look at Web pages on your system, as you can do so without being connected to the Internet.

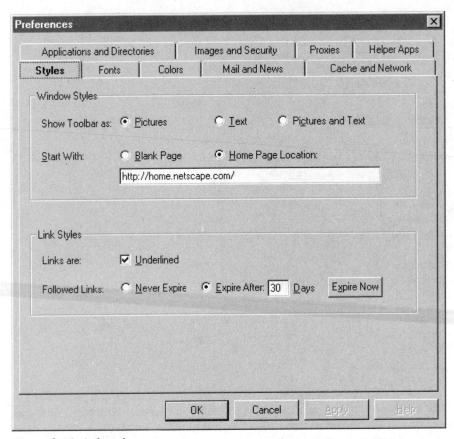

Figure 6-25: Styles tab

If you want to start with a home page, enter the address of that page in the text field on the **Styles** tab. The easiest way to do this is to use the clipboard; it saves you from having to type the address and possibly making a mistake. For example, if you are viewing the page you want to use as your home page, do the following:

1. Select the address in the **Netsite** field in Netscape's window.

2. Copy the address to the clipboard using **Copy** on the **Edit** menu.

3. Open the Preferences window and select the **Styles** tab.

4. Delete the address of the current home page from the text field.

5. Click the right mouse button over the text field to bring up the popup menu. Select **Paste** from this menu to paste the address of your new home page.

6. Click the **OK** button.

Now, when Netscape Navigator starts, or when you click **Home** on the toolbar, you'll see your new home page.

A Few Hints

When I described using Internet Explorer to navigate the Web, I gave you some hints for getting the most out of the browser. Many of those hints also apply with respect to Netscape Navigator. For example, you can tell Netscape to stop loading a document by clicking the **Stop** button on the toolbar.

However, in some cases, the names of the buttons or menu items in Netscape are different from those in Internet Explorer. One important case of this involves asking the browser to reload a Web document. While Internet Explorer uses the **Refresh** button for this purpose, Netscape uses the **Reload** button. Netscape also has a **Refresh** item on the **View** menu, but this item simply redraws the current document without reloading it from the network.

Where the command names are different in the two browsers, I'm going to tell you exactly how to use the hints with Netscape. But just as with Internet Explorer, I'm not going to tell you about every feature of Netscape. I'll leave some things for you to explore on your own, especially the myriad of configuration options available through the **Preferences** item on the **Options** menu.

Minimizing delays while loading images

If you have a slow connection to the Internet, you may want to eliminate the time it takes Netscape to load images by turning off automatic image loading. To do so, remove the check mark next to **Auto Load Images** in the **Options** menu. Now, when you load a document, any embedded images are replaced by icons, so Netscape can load the document much more quickly. If you decide you do want to see the images in a particular document, click the **Load Images** button in the toolbar and Netscape retrieves them. You can also load a single image by clicking the right mouse button over the icon and selecting **Load this Image** from the popup menu.

Using the popup menus

The document area in Netscape Navigator has a popup menu that gives you quick access to common functions. Click the right mouse button in the document area to post the popup menu; the active items in the menu vary depending on where you click the mouse button. One advantage of using the popup menu is that you don't have to move your mouse outside of the document area to the toolbar or the menu bar.

If you click the right mouse button over a link, the popup menu lets you open the linked document, create a bookmark for the link, open the linked document in a new window, save the linked document, or copy the address of the link to the clipboard. When you post the menu over an image, you can view the image, save the image, or copy the address of the image to the clipboard. If the image is a link to another document, the popup menu also lets you do all of the things you can do with a link.

Some of the items in the popup menu are active regardless of where you click the right mouse button (i.e., over a link, over an image, or over the background). You can always use the popup menu to go **Back** or **Forward** and to create a shortcut.

The final item on the popup menu, **Create Shortcut**, creates a shortcut to the current Web document, just like with Internet Explorer. If you choose this item, Netscape posts a dialog box that asks you to confirm the name and address for the shortcut. After you confirm this information, Netscape stores the shortcut file directly on your desktop, so that you can access the document by double-clicking on the shortcut.[*]

Netscape's Bookmarks window also has a popup menu associated with it. If you post the menu over a bookmark, you can select items to go to the bookmark, to create a shortcut to the bookmark, or to view the bookmark's properties. When you click the right mouse button over a folder in this window, you can open or close the folder (depending on its current state) or view the properties of the folder.

Document tracking

By default, Netscape keeps track of all of the Web documents you have visited in the past 30 days, so that it can display links to these documents in a different color. Netscape stores this history information in a file, which can grow quite large if you do a lot of exploring. If you want to minimize the size of this file, you can decrease the number of days Netscape stores this information. To do so, select **Preferences** from the **Options** menu. On the **Styles** tab, shown in Figure 6-25, change the number of days in the **Expire After** field. You can also clear the history file and start over by clicking the **Expire Now** button.

Just like Internet Explorer, Netscape Navigator saves recent HTML documents on your system (known as caching) to cut down on the amount of information it has to retrieve from the network. Netscape uses both a memory cache and a disk cache. You can control the size of these caches from the **Cache and Network** tab of the Preferences window. If your system has limited memory and you are running a number of applications at the same time, you may want to reduce the size of Netscape's memory cache. If you have a small hard drive, you may want to reduce the size of the disk cache. To clear either of the caches, click the appropriate **Clear Now** button.

---

[*] If you have both Internet Explorer and Netscape Navigator on your system, Windows 95 will use the last browser you installed to open all of your Web shortcuts, regardless of which browser you used to create them. You cannot have Internet shortcuts specific to different browsers at the same time. If you want your shortcuts to use a particular browser, make sure it's that last browser you installed on your system.

Getting the big picture

As you're browsing the Web, you are bound to come across documents other than HTML documents. As I said earlier, one of the best things about the Web is that it supports multimedia, including images, sounds, and movies. Just like Internet Explorer, Netscape can display GIF and JPEG images right in the browser window. If your PC is equipped to handle sounds, you can also listen to audio files using Netscape. When you click on a sound file, Netscape plays the sound through an external program that comes with the browser, Netscape Audio Player.

Movies are the one multimedia type that isn't handled automatically. If you find an MPEG movie on the Web and you want to view it, you'll need to download a special MPEG viewer program to do so. The best place to find an MPEG viewer is through Netscape's home page; click on the **Helper Apps** link under **Assistance**. The "Helper Applications" page has links to archive sites for various applications, as well as links to documents that explain how to configure Netscape to work with helper applications. After you have an MPEG viewer, you'll need to configure Netscape. Select **Preferences** from the **Options** menu and then use the **Helper Apps** tab to tell Netscape to use the MPEG viewer for movies.

Working with Other Services

If Web clients like Internet Explorer and Netscape Navigator could only read hypertext documents, they would be interesting and useful—but not that interesting or that useful. While the amount of hypertext on the Net is growing explosively, there are still are large number of more prosaic services: Gopher servers, FTP servers, Telnet servers, and so on. And in many cases, Web documents contain links to these services. In this section, we'll discuss how other services behave when you access them through the Web using Netscape Navigator.[*] It's actually quite simple; for most services, the Web presents a very clean, nicely usable interface.

Searchable Indexes

As you travel through the Web, you'll find lots of searchable indexes. These indexes are different from the Web search engines presented earlier. Web search engines search WWW resources, while searchable indexes present many different kinds of resources, including Veronica searches, WAIS searches, and CSO phone book lookups. I describe all of these resources later in the book. What's nice is that the same user interface is used for all searches, no matter what their type. In many cases, you don't even need to know what kind of search you're making.

---

[*] While I could have used Internet Explorer for these examples, I chose not to. Internet Explorer's interface for FTP and Gopher servers is somewhat deficient; it doesn't use graphical icons to represent different file types.

If you encounter a searchable index while using Netscape or Internet Explorer, you'll see something like what you see in Figure 6-26. The text **Enter Search Keywords**: tells you that you're looking at something you can search. Move the cursor into the editing window and type the keywords you want to search for, then click the **Begin Search** button. When the search is done, you'll see a Web page that contains links to all of the relevant items, so that you can immediately view these items.

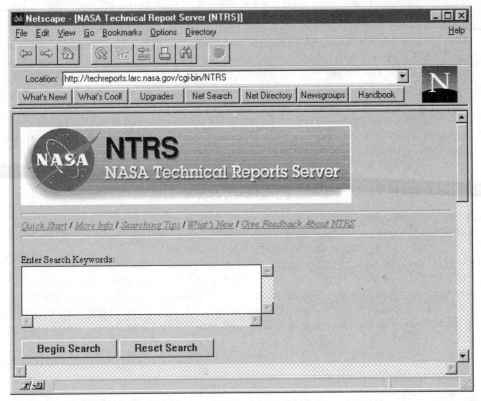

Figure 6–26: A searchable index

The location of the keyword entry area varies from page to page, depending on the author's design; you won't always find it in the same place, and may need to look around. By the way, if you think that Figure 6-26 looks suspiciously like a form, you're right. Most searchable indexes are implemented as forms and, as such, always have a **Submit** button (here labeled **Begin Search**). However, there is an older search feature that you may run across; it looks similar, but lacks the **Submit** button. In this case, pressing the ENTER key in the editing window submits your search.

FTP Servers

The World Wide Web is a great way to access FTP servers; you'll find these poking up frequently in various resource lists and indexes. The File Transfer Protocol (FTP) is designed to move files from one computer to another; FTP servers are the oldest kind of Internet file repositories. There are FTP servers for recipes, legal opinions, and, most important, free software.

In Chapter 9, I tell you everything you need to know about moving files with FTP, so I'm not going to go into much detail here. Basically, I just want to show you what FTP servers look like when you access them with a Web browser, since you're likely to encounter them as you explore the Internet. I also provide a bit of additional information about how to navigate within an FTP server, so that you should be able to download files from the Internet with a Web browser, even before you read Chapter 9, *Moving Files: FTP*.

When you come across an FTP server with Netscape, you'll see something like what's shown in Figure 6-27.

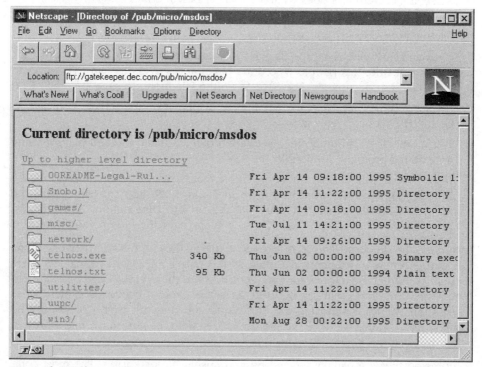

Figure 6-27: Netscape viewing an FTP archive

The title of the "document" tells you what directory you are currently in. Below the title, you see a list of files in the directory, along with information about when the files were created. Each filename has an icon next to it, telling you something about the file's contents. The icons and filenames are all links, so you can click on them to move around the directory structure. Netscape automatically inserts an **Up to higher level directory** link at the top of the file list to make it easy to move up in the directory structure.

Figure 6-28 shows the icons you'll see when using Netscape to access FTP servers (some of these are shown in the previous figure).

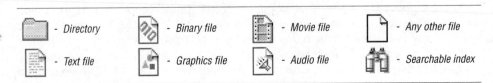

- *Directory*   - *Binary file*   - *Movie file*   - *Any other file*

- *Text file*   - *Graphics file*   - *Audio file*   - *Searchable index*

Figure 6-28: Netscape FTP server icons

If you follow a link to a directory, Netscape displays the items in that directory. If you select a file, Netscape does what it can to display the file:

- If it's a text file, Netscape displays the file on the screen. Use **Save As** on the **File** menu to save it.

- If it's an HTML file, Netscape displays it, complete with links that you can click on. This feature lets people who don't have Web servers use an FTP server to maintain Web documents. Use **Save As** on the **File** menu to save it.

- If it's a graphics file, Netscape attempts to display it on the screen. Use **Save As** on the **File** menu to save it.

- If it's a movie or an audio file, Netscape downloads the file and plays it using an external program, if possible.

- If it's a binary file or any other type of file that Netscape doesn't recognize, the browser pops up the window shown in Figure 6-29. You can either save the file or cancel the transfer. If you click the **Save to Disk** button, Netscape displays the standard Save As window so you can save the file on your system.

To reduce the amount of time it takes to transmit files across the network, large files like executable programs are often stored in a compressed format. As there are many different techniques for data compression, there are a variety of different compression programs that can be used. Netscape handles compressed files just as it treats binary files, so moving the files across the network isn't a problem. The problem arises after you have the file on your system, as you must uncompress it before you can use it.

Compressed files are usually flagged by an unusual file extension. The most common compression utilities are listed in Table 6-1.

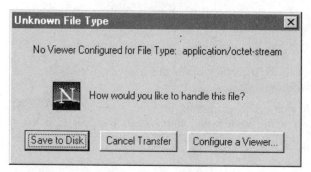

Figure 6-29: Unknown File Type window

Table 6-1: Common Compression Programs

Compression Program	Decompression Program	Typical Platform	File Extension	Typical Filename
compress	uncompress	UNIX	.Z	*rfc1118.txt.Z*
gzip	gunzip	UNIX	.z or .gz	*textfile.gz*
StuffIt	unsit	Macintosh	.sit	*program.sit*
PackIt	unpit	Macintosh	.pit	*report.pit*
PKZIP	PKUNZIP	PC	.zip	*package.zip*
zoo210	zoo210	PC	.zoo	*picture.zoo*

If you are looking at the files available on an FTP server and see these file extensions, that's a hint that the files are probably compressed. The extension gives you a hint about what utility should be used to uncompress it. The program you need to uncompress the file varies depending on what kind of computer you are using and what kind of compression was used. This is only the tip of the iceberg; there are about as many compression programs as there are types of computers.

If you're browsing around FTP archives that store free software for PCs, you shouldn't have any problems. For the most part, PC programs are compressed using PKZIP, which means you'll need PKUNZIP to uncompress them. Fortunately, this is a free program which is itself available in a number of FTP archives. Some PC software is actually provided as a self-extracting archive, so you don't need a separate decompression program; all you have to do is run the self-extracting archive file. If, however, you've found a compressed text file or other document, you may have to do a bit more work to locate the appropriate decompression program for your PC.

Here are the steps that you'll need to follow if you want to download a compressed PC program from an FTP archive using Netscape:

1. Click on the link to the file you want to retrieve.

2. Specify that you want to save the file on your system by clicking the **Save to Disk** button.

3. Select a directory in which to save the file and click **OK**.

4. When Netscape is done retrieving the file, open the folder on your desktop that contains the compressed file.

5. Double-click on the file. If it is a self-extracting archive, it will be unpacked automatically. If it's a PKZIP compressed file, the system will ask you for a program to associate with *.zip* files. Specify PKUNZIP and this program will be used to uncompress the file.

Gopher Servers

A Gopher server provides a menu-driven interface to files, most of which are ASCII text. Before the appearance of the World Wide Web, Gopher represented a major step forward in the direction of user-friendliness on the Internet. Rather than forcing you to remember an arcane set of commands that had to be entered on the command line, Gopher allowed you to maneuver using a set of menu choices. Gopher servers remain popular; you'll see them in a number of Internet resource lists. I cover Gopher in detail in Chapter 12, *Tunneling through the Internet: Gopher.*

While there are specialized Gopher clients, a **WWW** browser like Netscape Navigator also functions as an effective client. Actually, Netscape uses the same interface for Gopher servers as it does for FTP servers. The only difference is that you get descriptive phrases, instead of just filenames. When you encounter a Gopher resource, the Netscape window should resemble Figure 6-30.

Netscape offers a graphic representation of the Gopher menu system, using the same icons as it does for FTP servers. From the viewpoint of navigating a Gopher menu system, the most important of these is the folder icon. This indicates a menu option that, when selected, opens another menu. Notice that when you are using Netscape to view a Gopher menu, you are not offered the **Up to higher level directory** link to return to a previous menu. Instead, you can move up the menu hierarchy by clicking the **Back** button. Netscape handles all other Gopher resources the same way it handles files when it is serving as an FTP client.

Reading Network News

USENET news is the Internet equivalent of a bulletin board system (BBS) like those on CompuServe or other dial-up services. The discussions that take place via network news are organized into topic areas called newsgroups. With news, you can read and post messages on any number of useful, interesting, and bizarre topics, using a program called a newsreader. I discuss USENET news in detail in Chapter 7.

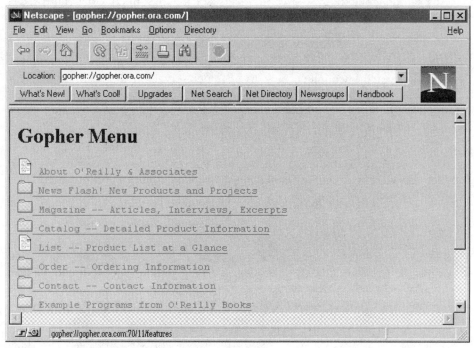

Figure 6–30: Netscape viewing a Gopher menu

Most Web browsers provide rudimentary news-reading capabilities, so that if you encounter a link to a newsgroup, you can read the messages posted there.[*] However, you probably won't find that many links to newsgroups when you're exploring the Web. Frankly, reading news isn't one of the Web's strong points. It has a few good features that you won't find elsewhere, but many basic newsreader features are missing. For example, using most browsers, you can only read news; you can't reply or post messages. Unless you're the type who insists on using a Swiss Army Knife for everything, you're better off using a program that is designed to read news.

Netscape Navigator, however, is an exception to this rule. Netscape has been designed to serve as a fully functional newsreader, as well as a Web browser. In fact, the news-reading capabilities in Netscape are so good that I describe them in detail in Chapter 7. If you're anxious to see what news is all about now, click on

---

[*] Internet Explorer does not provide news-reading capabilities by itself; you'll get an error message if you follow a news link. If you are using MSN as your service provider, however, you can read news through MSN. Version 2.0 of Internet Explorer corrects this deficiency; see Appendix E for information about reading news with Internet Explorer.

the **Newsgroups** button in Netscape.* Netscape's news interface is fairly self-explanatory, so you should be able to start exploring without much trouble.

Using Telnet Servers

Occasionally, you'll encounter a link to a Telnet server on the Web. Telnet is a "terminal emulation" protocol that lets you log into another computer on the Internet; it's often used to access public services like library card catalogs and other databases. Telnet services are covered in Chapter 8, *Remote Login*.

If you select a Telnet resource while using a Web browser, the browser should run the Windows 95 Telnet program and connect you to the resource.† Now you can do what you want with the Telnet session, as well as continue exploring the Web with your browser.

Using WAIS Servers

WAIS (Wide Area Information Service, pronounced "wayz") is another fairly new service on the Internet. WAIS is a tool for searching through indexed material and finding articles based on what they contain. There are many WAIS resources available through the World Wide Web; these resources appear as searchable indexes. As I've already explained, using searchable indexes is quite easy.

It is also possible to use the Web to perform more comprehensive WAIS searches, including searches of the WAIS directory of servers. In fact, I've found that Web browsers make perfectly adequate WAIS clients. For a complete discussion of WAIS, including a demonstration of using a Web browser as a WAIS client, see Chapter 13, *Searching Indexed Databases: WAIS*.

Going Directly to a Resource

Although the World Wide Web spreads further every day, it doesn't encompass the entire Internet. There are many resources that you can't reach by following links. And there are also many resources for which you would rather *not* follow links. After all, if you know you want anonymous FTP to **ftp.uu.net**, why should you have to follow links through three or four Web documents to find it? It's easier to go directly to the FTP server you want than to look around until you find some page with a link.

---

* To read news, you need to have access to a news server. Your Internet service provider should provide you with the name of your news server; you need to supply this information to Netscape for the news-reading functionality to work. Select **Preferences** from the **Options** menu. On the **Mail and News** tab, enter the name of the news server in the **News Server** field.

† If you want Netscape to be able to run the Telnet program, you need to specify the location of Telnet. Select **Preferences** from the **Options** menu. On the **Applications and Directories** tab, click the **Browse** button next to the **Telnet Application** field to select the Telnet program from the **Windows** folder.

Before we can go to an arbitrary resource on the Net using a World Wide Web browser, we have to answer two questions:

1. How do you do it? (What's the command?)

2. How do you name the resource you want?

The first question is mechanical and fairly simple. Every Web browser has a command for moving to resources directly. The second is more involved; we'll need to introduce the concept of a URL, or Uniform Resource Locator. Fortunately, URLs are standardized, so they're the same for all Web browsers, and for other tools as well.

I've mentioned URLs a few times, but I haven't told you what they mean. Actually, if you simply enter a URL that someone has given you, you don't really need to know much about its syntax. Indeed, companies have begun printing URLs in their advertisements, people are putting them on their business cards, and URLs are passed around by e-mail quite frequently.

Opening other resources

Both Internet Explorer and Netscape Navigator have **Open** buttons on their toolbars; these buttons are what you use to open a resource directly. If you click on Internet Explorer's **Open** button, you'll see the window shown in Figure 6-31.

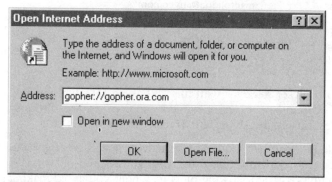

Figure 6-31: Open Internet Address window

Type the URL of the resource you want into the editing window and click **OK**. Now, the browser accesses the resource and displays it appropriately.

Uniform resource locators

A URL is an address that identifies a server on the network and a particular document on that server. It also indicates which type of service (or protocol) a Web browser must use to retrieve the information. URLs are not pretty to look at, but you may find that understanding the syntax can be extremely helpful. They contain a wealth of information and you may need to construct them yourself in some cases. The most common form of a URL is:

```
service://server/path/file.type
```

Table 6-2 shows valid services and examples of URLs using each type.

Table 6-2: Services and Sample URLs

Service	Function	URL
http	Use the HyperText Transfer Protocol	http://gnn.com/gnn/GNNhome.html http://info.cern.ch
ftp	Use the File Transfer Protocol	ftp://archive.umich.edu/msdos ftp://ftp.cica.indiana.edu/
file	Open a local file or use FTP	file://archive.umich.edu/msdos file://ftp.cica.indiana.edu file:///c:/windows
gopher	Open a Gopher menu	gopher://gopher.ora.com
telnet	Open a Telnet session	telnet://nyplgate.nypl.org
news	Use the Network News Transfer Protocol	news:comp.infosystems.www
mailto	Send mail to a user	mailto:jdoe@anyco.com

For instance, take a look at the URL for the *GNN* home page:

```
http://gnn.com/gnn/GNNhome.html
```

The document that a Web browser retrieves with this URL is an HTML file named *GNNhome.html*. That file is found on a server named **gnn.com**, in the directory */gnn*. The browser retrieves it using the HyperText Transfer Protocol (HTTP).

When entering a new URL, be sure that you type it exactly as it was given to you. If you can use the clipboard to copy and paste the URL you should do so, as it will keep you from making typos. The following hints may help you avoid making errors in entering URLs, or diagnose the errors you've made:

- A URL can consist of three readily identifiable components: a protocol or service, which is followed by a server name, which is followed by a filename. In the case of USENET news, the server name is skipped because a local server is assumed. In the case of Telnet, only a server name is provided.

- Spaces are not allowed within a URL.

- The HTTP service is different from the HTML file format. The HTTP service name tells the browser how to transfer the file; in other words, it tells the browser to contact a Web server. The HTML file type tells the browser how to interpret the file once it receives it.

- Some HTML files have the extension *.html*, while others use *.htm*. This variance is due to the three-character extension limitation under DOS and Windows prior to Windows 95. If your Web browser tells you that an *.htm* file doesn't exist, you might try *.html* instead.

- The name of the service or protocol is usually followed by the `://` characters and the server name. This is not true of news, e-mail, or local files, though, because their URLs do not include the server name.

- The forward slash (/) is generally used as the path separator instead of the backslash (\). (The forward slash is the path separator on UNIX systems; the backslash is the path separator on Windows systems.) A backslash is translated to a forward slash when used as a pathname separator. However, you cannot use `:\\` in place of `://` to separate the service from the server host name. Because of this, the first and second URLs below are valid, while the third URL is not:

      http://hoohoo/docs/DEMO.html   *good*
      http://hoohoo\docs\DEMO.html   *good*
      http:\\hoohoo\docs\DEMO.html   *bad*

- Case is important. The two URLs below are different, because most Internet servers are UNIX systems, which are case-sensitive filenames.

      http://gnn.com/gnn/gnnhome.html
      http://gnn.com/gnn/GNNhome.html

By the way, do you find the process of constructing a URL laborious and confusing? There's a solution. Once you've constructed the URL and visited the item you want, just add it to your list of favorite places or create a bookmark for it.

Displaying local files

You can use a Web browser to display a file on your local hard disk by specifying the **file** service and omitting the server name. The drive can be specified using a colon (:) or bar (|). The following are valid URLs:

      file:///c:/netscape/ch3.htm
      file:|c:/netscape/ch3.htm
      file:///c|/netscape/ch3.htm

However, both Internet Explorer and Netscape Navigator make it even easier to view a local file. With Netscape, simply select **Open File** from the **File** menu. Netscape brings up a standard Open dialog that lets you select a file on your system. With Internet Explorer, click the **Open** button on the toolbar and then click **Open File** to browse the file system.

Creating Your Own Home Page

If your Internet service provider offers you space to store a Web home page, you'll want to spend a little bit of time creating one. Having a home page on the Web is akin to having a personal billboard in cyberspace; it's the status symbol of the Internet age. People are starting to give out the address of their home page in the same breath as their e-mail address, and URLs are becoming more and more common on business cards.

A personal home page occupies a unique niche on the World Wide Web; it represents the Web at its most basic and at its most eccentric. We can lay the blame for this multiple-personality disorder on evolution. From its simple text-based roots in CERN, the WWW home page has rapidly grown into a flexible self-publishing tool. It can now serve as anything from a conservative, professional-looking front door on the Net, to a medium of personal expression that intersects with autobiography, e-zines, and science fiction.

Before you decide what to put on your home page, you may want to think about the attitude you want to project. Do you want to come across as professional or do you want to get up close and personal? Do you want to act as an information kiosk, providing links to other Web resources that interest you? The attitude you decide on will dictate a lot about the various aspects of designing your page. If you're creating a professional page, you'll want your photograph to be professional and your links to be clearly identified. If you're being more personal, you can embed lots of links within text, make inside jokes, show off your homemade computer art, and so on.

To create a home page, you need to know a little bit about HTML, the markup language used to format Web documents. Creating an HTML document involves inserting tags into a text file to format the text and define hypertext links. HTML provides a number of formatting tags, including things you would expect, like headings, paragraphs, and bulleted lists. There are also tags to specify text attributes, such as bold and italic text, and to insert graphics into a document. Perhaps the most important tag is the anchor tag (<A>), which is used to define hypertext links to other documents. Many tags come in pairs; their action starts at the tag and ends at the tag preceded by a slash. For example, <I>*says this all should be in italics*</I>.

Unless you are going to be creating lots of hypertext documents, that's probably about all you need to know about HTML. If you do need to become fluent in HTML, or you are just curious, there are lots of on-line resources that cover HTML. For example, check out the following:

```
http://www.ncsa.uiuc.edu/General/Internet/WWW/HTMLPrimer.html
```

One of the nice features of the Web is that you can always get the source of the document you are viewing. So if you find a Web page that you really like, or one that has an interesting format, you can save the HTML source and see just how the author created the effect.

The next step beyond creating your own home page is to become a full-fledged Web publisher by running a Web server on your system. If you have a dedicated connection to the Internet, and you have information that you think other people would be interested in, you may want to consider running a Web server. There are currently three commercial Web servers that run under Windows 95: WebSite from O'Reilly & Associates and Commerce Builder and Communications Builder from The Internet Factory.

Using a Text Editor

You can create an HTML document using a text editor, such as Notepad, or any word processor that can write plain ASCII files, such as Microsoft Word. Here's a basic template for a home page; all you need to do is fill in the blanks.

```
<HTML><HEAD>
<TITLE>YourName's Home Page</TITLE></HEAD><BODY>
<H1>YourName's Home Page</H1>
<IMG SRC="YourPicture.gif"> picture title
<H2>Where I work/go to school</H2>
I work at <A HREF="URL here">company/school name</A>.
<H2>Hobbies</H2>
<UL>
<LI>description
<LI>description
<LI>description
</UL>
<H2>Personal Hot List</H2>
<UL>
<LI><A HREF="URL here">description</A>
<LI><A HREF="URL here">description</A>
<LI><A HREF="URL here">description</A>
</UL>
<ADDRESS>YourName (YourEmailAddress@host.domain) </ADDRESS>
</BODY></HTML>
```

This template uses an inline image, a bulleted list, and some links. All of the text inside angle brackets (<>) is HTML code; be sure you don't accidentally remove any of the tags. After you've filled in the template and customized it as you wish, you can view the document with a Web browser and make sure it looks like you want it to.

Although you can create your home page from scratch, there's really no reason to. Another easy way to create your home page is to find a home page already on the Web that is formatted in a way you like. Save the document on your system in HTML format and then edit the file with a text editor. Simply by removing all of the original content and replacing it with your own information, you have your own home page. If the original document included a photograph, make sure you use your own photo.* Again, be sure to view the document with a Web browser to make sure it looks right.

Using an HTML Editor

While HTML is a relatively simple markup language, it is easy enough to make mistakes. What you really want is a tool that helps you to add all the extra stuff without memorizing and typing all the commands. There are two ways of doing this: with a special editor or with a conversion package.

HTML editors simplify the process of creating Web documents by inserting the appropriate HTML tags for you when you click on buttons or select menu items. A number of good HTML editors have appeared in the past year; some are commercial products while others are freeware or shareware.

Another dynamic area of HTML generation is in creating programs to convert other, more common rich text formats into HTML. For example, it's easy to convert Word Perfect or Microsoft Word documents with different fonts and styles into HTML. The documents look the same, but they still don't have links to other documents. You have to add these by hand if you want them.

Microsoft Internet Assistant for Word is an add-on product to Microsoft Word that combines the features of an HTML editor, a conversion tool, and a Web browser. For more information about Internet Assistant, visit the following URL:

http://www.microsoft.com/msoffice/freestuf/msword/download/ia/default.htm

You can download Internet Assistant from this Web page, install it, and try it out. Once you've installed the package, select **Browse Web** from the **File** menu. You should see a document like the one shown in Figure 6-32.

When Word is in Web browsing mode, you can read Web documents and follow hyperlinks just as you would with any Web browser. These documents can be either local documents on your system, or Web pages on the Internet. Like any good Web browser, Internet Assistant allows you to move backward and forward, open particular documents, and keep track of favorite places.

When you want to create a Web document with Word, you switch to an HTML edit mode. In this mode, you create a document using Word styles as you would normally do. When you are done creating the document, you can convert these styles to HTML, so that the document is suitable for publishing on the Web. The nice thing about Internet Assistant is that you never have to look at the HTML tags unless you want to. Internet Assistant also makes it easy to create hyperlinks to both local documents and remote URLs, insert pictures, and insert HTML tags that don't correspond to standard Word styles.

---

* If you want to use a photograph on your home page but you don't have access to a scanner, you can take your picture to a copy shop that provides image-scanning services. Be sure to get the scanned photo on floppy disk in GIF or JPEG format, as that's the format that Web browsers use.

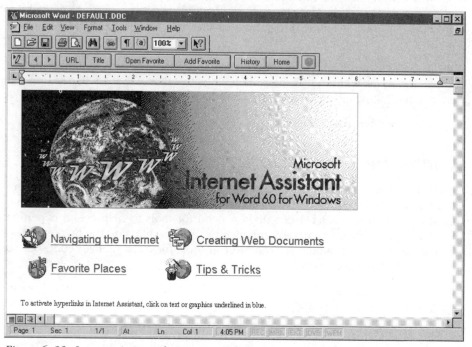

Figure 6–32: Internet Assistant browsing window

Windows 95 on the Web

Now that we've done a fair bit of exploring, I want to steer you towards a few Web sites that I think you'll find interesting. These sites contain helpful and interesting information about various aspects of Windows 95.

We already looked at Microsoft's Web site back in Figure 6-2. This site contains a wealth of useful information, but unless you explore it fully, you may not find the best stuff. The "Support" area contains product support information for all of Microsoft's products. You can read frequently-asked questions and their answers, and often download free software add-ons.

You may also want to check out the document on "Using Third-Party Internet Applications with Windows 95." Here's its URL:

```
http://www.windows.microsoft.com/windows/pr/inetapps.htm
```

Another interesting area is Microsoft's free software archive for Windows 95. Use the following URL to take a look:

```
http://www.windows.microsoft.com/windows/software.htm
```

From this document, you can get a collection of "Power Toys" for Windows 95. And if you purchased the diskette version of Windows 95, you can download the Windows 95 CD-ROM Extras, programs that are only on the CD-ROM version of Windows 95.

O'Reilly & Associates maintains a Windows Web site that contains a number of feature articles about Windows 95, as well as links to other Windows 95 sites on the Web. See the following document:

```
http://www.ora.com/windows/
```

Where the Web Is Going

In the first edition of this book, I ended this chapter with a discussion of where the Web was going. I made a few predictions, some of which have borne fruit, and some of which haven't. I described a need for tools to help create hypertext documents, and now there are a number of hypertext editors on the market. I also predicted that the Web would spur interest in tools for collaborative work, but so far these tools have not emerged.

When I first wrote about the Web, I said that it consisted mostly of textual documents, and that there was a significant need for browsers that could make intelligent decisions about processing different kinds of files. There's been tremendous progress in this area, especially with the current generation of Web browsers like Netscape Navigator and Internet Explorer.

At this point, the World Wide Web has become the most important information delivery systems on the Internet. It has been immensely successful, in large part because of Mosaic and the next generation of Web browsers, which have encouraged people of all kinds—not just physicists—to build hypertext documents.

Just as the Web continues to grow, Web-related research and development is happening in both industry and academia. Here's a brief survey of some of the interesting areas that are being explored today.

Document Rendering

One problem with HTML is that it doesn't give an author complete control over the presentation of information. Although the author can specify various visual attributes, the Web browser that displays the document has ultimate control over its appearance. While this setup works well for simple hypertext documents, it is not sufficient in situations where layout and format are critical. For example, the Internal Revenue Service has made tax forms available on the Web. Obviously, the layout of these forms needs to be precise, so using HTML is not an option.

Some Web authors are solving this problem by supplying documents in Adobe's Portable Document Format (PDF); you'll recognize these documents because they have a *.pdf* file extension. PDF gives the author complete control over color, graphics, fonts, and structure, independent of the computer platform used to display the document. In order to view PDF documents, you need Adobe's Acrobat Reader software, which is available free on the Internet. You can set up your Web browser to use Acrobat Reader to display PDF documents. For more information, use the following URL:

```
http://www.adobe.com/Acrobat/AcrobatWWW.html
```

More immediately, there's something of a political battle between HTML "purists," who believe that the author should *not* be able to specify appearance, and those who would like to add this ability. Netscape falls into the latter group; their extensions (discussed shortly) give users more control over a document's appearance.

Program Execution

Another deficiency of the Web is that the current specifications don't support running programs within a Web browser. A number of groups are working on solutions to this problem; the most noteworthy effort is the HotJava browser and Java programming language being developed by Sun Microsystems.

HotJava is a WWW browser that can execute applets, which are programs written in the Java programming language that are included in Web documents. Some examples of applets include: animated text, dynamically updated stock data, and rotatable, 3D chemical models. And games for that matter. You shouldn't have to use a server that's shared by thousands of people to move your starship around; that computation should be done on your local computer (after all, it's more powerful than the supercomputers of only a decade ago).

Although executing some random code from the Web on your machine seems like a recipe for disaster, Java is designed to be "safe"—that is, you can execute a Java applet on your computer with some confidence that it won't do anything hostile. The Java language is designed so that a Java program can't be a "Trojan horse."

For complete information about HotJava and Java, see the following document:

```
http://java.sun.com/
```

This Web page provides access to an alpha-level release of HotJava for Windows 95. Expect a beta-release in the not-too-distant future. Netscape has also announced that its next release, Netscape Navigator 2.0, will support Java applets. A beta release of this version is available for Windows 95.

HTML Extensions

The amount of hypertext on the Internet continues to increase daily. As people become more experienced at creating hypertext, they often want to be able to do more sophisticated formatting than HTML allows. As a result, there is work underway to change the HTML specification to support such features as tables, figures, and mathematical equations. Today, the majority of Web browsers support HTML

2.0, which is in final review as an Internet standard, while the specification for HTML 3.0 is still in the development stage. For details about the various HTML specifications, use the following URL:

```
http://www.w3.org/hypertext/WWW/MarkUp/MarkUp.html
```

Unfortunately, the standardization process can take a long time. Many developers have become impatient waiting for new features in the HTML specification, so they have created their own HTML extensions. These extensions work on a browser-by-browser basis. The best-known extensions are those supported by the Netscape Navigator browser. The Netscape extensions provide the ability to center text and graphics, create floating images, make text blink, specify background patterns, create tables, and specify text and background colors, among other things. Some of these features are useful, while others can be more annoying than anything else.

As you are exploring the Web, you are bound to come across documents that proclaim they are "Netscape enhanced." What this means is that these documents use the Netscape HTML extensions. If you aren't viewing the document with Netscape, at best you just won't see the enhancements, and at worst the document may look like gibberish. For more information about the Netscape extensions, see the following document:

```
http://home.netscape.com/home/services_docs/html_extensions.html
```

Internet Explorer also supports some of these HTML extensions, like background patterns, centered text, and text and background colors. For details about the Internet Explorer extensions, using the following URL:

```
http://www.windows.microsoft.com/windows/ie/htmlext.htm
```

Visualizing Web Space

The idea behind the Virtual Reality Modeling Language (VRML) is to create a language for describing multi-participant interactive simulations. This language allows authors to create virtual reality "scenes" that are connected by the Internet and hyperlinked with the World Wide Web. As a user, you would be able to walk around in a virtual world and push open doors to other parts of the Web that are linked to this world. For more information about VRML, point your browser to the following URL:

```
http://vrml.wired.com/
```

Commerce on the Web

One of the main reasons the Web has grown so rapidly in the past few years is that more and more companies are jumping on the Web bandwagon. These companies have seen the tremendous potential of the Web and they are eager to provide on-line information about their products and services. The obvious next step is to allow users to make purchases using the Web, as some companies have already started doing. Today, you can order flowers, CDs, computer software, and take-out Chinese food over the Web.

However, before commerce on the Web can really take off, there are a number of security-related issues that need to be resolved. As I mentioned earlier, there are very few secure servers on the Web today. Many of the companies that provide on-line ordering are not yet comfortable transmitting credit card numbers and passwords over the Web; they may require you to set up an account by phone first.

Work on WWW security issues is considered high-priority by many of the key players in Web development, so it shouldn't be too long before you start seeing some readily available solutions. For details about the various security issues and the work that is being done, see the following document:

```
http://www.w3.org/hypertext/WWW/Security/Overview.html
```

How Can I Help?

In July 1994, CERN and MIT made an agreement to create the World Wide Web Consortium (W3C). This consortium exists to shape the future of the WWW by developing common standards for Web technologies. The W3C is run by the Laboratory for Computer Science at MIT; in Europe, MIT collaborates with CERN, the original developer of the Web, and INRIA, the European W3C center. Membership in the W3C is open to any interested organization. For complete information about the W3C, including membership information, see the following URL:

```
http://www.w3.org/hypertext/WWW/Consortium/
```

The W3C is intended to serve as a repository of WWW information, including specifications and protocols. The consortium plans to provide reference implementations of these specifications to promote vendor-neutral standards and ensure interoperability. In addition, it may develop prototypes and sample applications that demonstrate the use of new Web technologies.

## CHAPTER SEVEN

NETWORK NEWS

Newsgroups and News System Organization
Getting Started
Reading News
Posting Articles
A Summary of Trumpet Commands
Other Hints and Conventions
A Different Approach: Netscape Navigator

Let's say you wake up one morning, and three issues are really bothering you. Your Western Digital Ethernet card won't work in your new Pentium machine, your laser won't lase and you can't figure out why, and you don't know where to stay on your upcoming trip to Disney World. You want to get back in bed. Wouldn't it be nice to ask the world to solve your problems?

Actually, you can. The Internet makes it easy to discuss your favorite obscure hobby with obscure hobbyists worldwide. On the surface, e-mail discussion groups (which were covered in Chapter 5, *Electronic Mail*) seem to provide all you could possibly want for worldwide discussions. As you get into it, however, you find that there is a problem with the volume of messages. There are discussions you take part in for work and those you participate in for recreation and enjoyment. Having these messages mixed in with the messages from the big boss, to which you need to react immediately, is an information disaster waiting to happen. Network news[*] is a way to take part in even more discussions, yet keep them organized and separate from your mail.

News is ideal for browsing and doesn't require a lot of commitment. If you're marginally interested in an obscure hobby, you can drop in and read up on the latest discussions once a month, or once a year. Of course, something about network news turns lots of these marginal interests into all-consuming passions. If e-mail is the application that forces people to use the Internet the first time, net news is the application that keeps them coming back.

Network news is the Internet equivalent of a discussion group or a bulletin board system (BBS) like those on the Microsoft Network, America Online, or other private dial-up facilities. To the user, network news organizes discussions under a set

---

[*] Also called USENET. Technically, there's a difference between Network News and USENET, but the terms are pretty much interchangeable.

of broad headings called newsgroups. A newsreading program presents those discussions in an orderly way: a menu of classical music discussions, followed by a menu of pencil collecting discussions, followed by a menu of chemical engineering items, etc. Inside each newsgroup, there are usually multiple discussions going on under specific subjects. In the classical music newsgroup, you might see discussions of Beethoven's Ninth Symphony, breaking in reeds for an oboe, and Bach's children. All of these discussions will be going on simultaneously. The newsreader helps you keep everything in order. It keeps track of the items you have already seen and only displays new items that have arrived since your last session. Once the newsreader has shown you what articles are available for any topic, you can select and read the items that interest you. If you forget where you have seen something, some newsreaders allow you to search for an article based on its author, subject, or an author-given synopsis. Your newsreader may also allow you to view or discard certain items automatically, based on the author's name or the article's subject.

No newsreader comes with Windows 95. Microsoft's answer to news is to provide it to you as a World Wide Web application through the Microsoft Network.[*] Appendix D, *The Microsoft Network* shows you some examples of how news looks on the Microsoft Network, but if you aren't reading news there, you need to find a newsreader on your own. As with most Internet applications, there are many newsreading programs from which you can choose. You could use Trumpet, one of the most popular newsreaders in the community.[†] You could also use Netscape Navigator (see Chapter 6, *The World Wide Web*), which has a news interface built in. This is one respect in which Netscape has an advantage over other Web browsers. Other browsers (like Mosaic) have bare-bones support for News; Netscape has reasonably nice support.

I will cover both of these packages in this chapter, but most of the discussion will center on Trumpet. There tends to be a lot of similarities between different newsreaders, so looking at the commands and features of Trumpet will give you a start on whatever newsreader you finally decide to use. There is no best newsreader. Despite these similarities, nowhere on the Internet are flame wars so evident as when users discuss which newsreader is best. Ignore them; choose a newsreader that works for you.

The important thing is not whether or not you use Trumpet, Netscape, or some other program, but rather that you use a reader that supports threads. This feature separates the cream from the milk. Some newsreaders show you articles in the order they were received, regardless of the topic of the discussion. People are usually interested in only certain discussions within a group, and they like to follow

---

[*] Version 2.0 of Microsoft's Internet Explorer does provide a way to read news. See Appendix E, *Internet Explorer 2.0 and Netscape Navigator 2.0*, for information about reading news with Internet Explorer.

[†] Trumpet is a shareware program available across the network. You can get an evaluation copy via anonymous FTP from **ftp.trumpet.com.au**. If you like it and want to continue using it, you must register your copy with its author.

them to completion, rather than jumping from topic to topic chronologically. Threaded newsreaders, including Trumpet, show you the articles in the order they were received *within* a discussion, so consecutive articles focus on the same topic.

Newsgroups and News System Organization

Newsgroups are organized hierarchically. A newsgroup name consists of a few words, separated by dots—for example, *rec.music.folk*. This kind of notation should be familiar to you by now. The name becomes more specific as you read from left to right. So *rec.music.folk* is a *rec*reational discussion, one which most people take part in for fun, in the general category of *music*. Specifically, it's a discussion of *folk* music; *rec* is the most general category; *music* is a subtopic within *rec*, and *folk* is a subgroup of *music*.

Now the big question: "Which newsgroups are available to me?" Well, it depends, mostly on which computer your newsreader uses for its news server. To understand this, we need to look at how news works. Figure 7-1 shows what the news system looks like to users. There is a newsreader, which interrogates a news server to receive menus of articles, and calls for the articles themselves as required. The server collects news from a number of places: USENET, local news sources, mail reflectors, and Clarinet. It holds these articles for a certain preset period (controlled by the server's administrator), and eventually discards them.

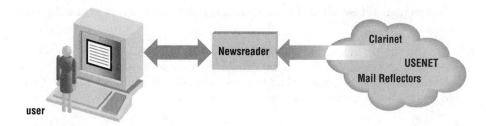

Figure 7–1: User's view of the news system

Most of the server's newsgroups come as part of USENET, a set of newsgroups generally considered to be of global interest, which are available for free. USENET is one of the most misunderstood concepts around. It is not a computer network. It does not require the Internet. It is not software. It is a set of voluntary rules for passing and maintaining newsgroups. Also, it is a set of volunteers who use and respect those rules. (If you want the whole story, get the article "What Is USENET" that's listed under "USENET News" in the *Resource Catalog.**)

USENET is made up of seven well-managed newsgroup categories. The rules for how to use, create, and delete groups have been around since before the Internet. (Yes, USENET predates the Internet; in those days, news was passed via regular dial-up connections. There are still many sites that participate in USENET in this fashion.) The seven major news categories are:

comp
> Computer science and related topics. This includes computer science proper, software sources, information on hardware and software systems, and topics of general interest.

news
> Groups concerned with the news network and news software. This includes the important groups *news.newusers.questions* (questions from new users) and *news.announce.newusers* (important information for new users). If you are new to USENET, you should read these for a while.

rec
> Groups discussing hobbies, recreational activities, and the arts.

sci Groups discussing scientific research and applications (other than computer science). This includes newsgroups for many of the established scientific and engineering disciplines, including some social sciences.

soc
> Groups that address social issues, from the politically relevant across the spectrum to socializing

talk
> The *talk* groups are a forum for debate on controversial topics. The discussions tend to be long-winded and unresolved. This is where to go if you want to argue about religion.

misc
> Anything that doesn't fit into the above categories, or that fits into several categories. It's worth knowing about *misc.jobs* (jobs wanted and offered) and *misc.forsale* (just what it says).

Servers may also have newsgroups they create locally. Any server administrator can create whatever groups he or she likes, corresponding to the interests of the server's users. These might include discussions of campus events, local network outages, and employee announcements. Although these are local groups, they can still be passed to other servers that want to carry them. In a large corporation,

---

* It is also reprinted in *The USENET Handbook* (Mark Harrison, published by O'Reilly & Associates), which surveys a number of newsreaders, and provides a lot of historical and cultural background.

each department might have its own news server; the servers would be able to pass the employee-announcements group among themselves. Of course, the servers wouldn't pass groups like this to the outside world. Local newsgroups are named by the local server's administrator, who must choose names that don't conflict with other newsgroups.

Now we start getting to the confusing part. To a user, the news system looks like Figure 7-1. In actuality, it is implemented as shown in Figure 7-2. A server's administrator makes bilateral agreements with other administrators to transfer certain newsgroups, usually over the Internet, among one another. A site that provides your server with one or more newsgroups is known as a news feed. Certain servers will provide feeds for some groups, other servers for other groups. A server administrator may make any arrangements for news feeds from any servers that are necessary to provide the set of groups to be offered. Over the years, this has caused some useful local groups to be distributed almost as widely as the core USENET groups.

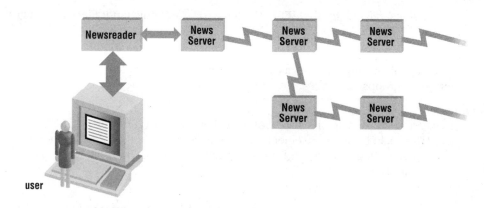

Figure 7–2: Implementation of the news system

These widespread local groups are known as alternative newsgroup hierarchies.[*] Since they look like the USENET newsgroups (except that they have different names), the term USENET is frequently expanded to include these groups as well. The most common alternative newsgroups are:

alt Groups that discuss alternative ways of looking at things. There are a lot of truly bizarre newsgroups here (including one that tracks the wanderings of an itinerant West-coast evangelist). In a few groups, the postings lack any coherence at all, and make you wonder what, er, stimulants were influencing the authors. However, there is also a lot of useful information. Some important

---

[*] If you are interested in a complete list of all official and alternative newsgroup hierarchies, you might check out the newsgroup *news.groups*. These lists are posted regularly there.

groups (like *alt.www*) were created here initially. When their topic was obviously important, they went through the voting process required to create an "official" newsgroup. On the whole, though, discussions tend to be out of the mainstream.

bionet
Groups of interest to biologists

bit The most popular BITNET *listserv* discussion groups

biz
Discussions related to business. This newsgroup hierarchy allows postings of advertisements or other marketing materials; such activity is not allowed in other groups.

hepnet
Discussions primarily of interest to the High Energy Physics community

ieee
Discussions related to the IEEE (Institute of Electronic and Electrical Engineers)

info
A group of mailing lists on a wide variety of topics, which are transformed into newsgroups

gnu
Discussions related to the Free Software Foundation (FSF) and its GNU project. This includes announcements of new FSF software, new developments to old software, bug reports, and questions and discussion by users of the Foundation's tools.

k12
A group dedicated to teachers and students, kindergarten through high school

schl
Discussions among the educational community

vmsnet
Discussions of Digital Equipment's VAX/VMS operating system and DECnet

de, fj, nz, pl . . .
Newsgroups created to serve the needs of a particular country's people. Sometimes in the language of that country (and if so, requiring special software to display non-roman characters)

austin, ba, ne . . .
Newsgroups created to serve particular geographic regions in the U.S. and Canada. (*ba* is the San Francisco bay area; *ne* is New England)

Several of these groups are *gatewayed*; in particular, the *bit*, *info*, and *gnu* groups. This is another way of creating newsgroups. The output of a mail reflector or a list server can be converted into a newsgroup. This allows people who would rather use the organizational facilities of news to take part in a mail-reflector-style discussion without subscribing to the mailing list themselves. A few computers subscribe to a mailing list, reformat the mail so it's appropriate for the news system, and then distribute it to anyone who wants a news feed.

Finally, several commercial information services are distributed via network news. One example of this is Clarinet, which is a news hierarchy that broadcasts articles from the traditional wire services, plus syndicated columns. For a server to offer this service, the organization that owns it must contract with Clarinet for the service; this contract places limits on where the server can distribute the Clarinet newsgroups. The distribution is usually limited to a particular corporation, campus, or work group. These newsgroups are prefixed by the header *clari.*

All of these groups generate an amazing amount of network traffic; a typical server subscribes to over 7500 newsgroups and receives about 150 megabytes a day. This leads to other limitations on which newsgroups are available from any particular server. A server administrator may choose not to accept a certain group because it is very active and eats up too much disk space. This also limits the amount of time old news items will reside on a server. It's possible to go back and read news items you passed by earlier, provided that the server hasn't yet deleted (or expired) the article. The amount of time that any article remains on the system depends entirely on how long the administrator feels those items can be stored. It varies from a few days to months and may be different for each group. This also means that if you go away on vacation, some items may come and go before you get a chance to read them. Luckily, many important work-related newsgroups have their conversations archived at various places. The locations of these archives are usually announced via the group.

Last, we must deal with (how can I write this delicately?) censorship. Some administrators decide that some groups (especially in the *alt* category) are not for consumption by the server's clientele. So they choose not to carry them. If you are offended, you have two choices: find another server or beat up on your administrator.

This point is very fuzzy and leads to much animated discussion about basic freedoms. There are many reasons that an administrator might decide not to offer a group; strictly speaking, censorship usually isn't among them. A server administrator is the steward of a machine. That computer is owned by someone, and it has a purpose, aside from being a news server. The administrator walks a fine line between accepting as many newsgroups as possible and not diverting too many machine resources to news. If you look at this logically, on most servers (other than perhaps at the Kinsey Institute) the group *sci.engr.chem* has a lot more to do with the machine's intended purpose than *alt.sex.* Hence, if disk space runs low, the group to be cut is *alt.sex.* If you use that machine as a news server, you are using someone else's property. There is no basic freedom to use other people's property. You can suggest that *alt.sex* (or any other group) be carried, but not demand it.

Some newsgroups are moderated. Moderation may seem like censorship to some people, but it's better to think of it as editorial selection. All items in the group are reviewed by a moderator, who relays the postings that are of genuine interest to the rest of the group. A moderated group is thus more like a magazine or journal than a free-for-all discussion. As you might expect, moderated groups have much higher "quality," albeit at the cost of spontaneity. Posting to a moderated group is no different than posting to any other group. The news servers know which groups are moderated and who moderates them; your news item will be forwarded to the moderator automatically. In turn, he or she will approve or reject your posting. When it is approved, you'll see it in the newsgroup.

Getting Started

The first thing you need to do is get and configure Trumpet. You can get it by going to **ftp.trumpet.com.au** with anonymous FTP. Move to the directory *wintrump* (**cd wintrump**) and download *wtwsk10a.zip* (**get wtwsk10a.zip**). You now have the software, but it is a "zip" file which contains multiple files and needs to be broken apart with PKUNZIP using the DOS command:

```
pkunzip -e wtwsk10a.zip
```

This will yield the file *wt_wsk.exe*, which is the executable file for Trumpet.[*] Before you start Trumpet, your network connection must be available. If you are dialing in with SLIP or PPP, you must connect manually. (See Appendix B, *Setting Up Your Internet Connection.*) The current version of Trumpet is only a 16-bit (Windows 3.1) application, so they cannot automatically initiate an Internet connection.

Now comes the hard part. You must configure the software to know where your news server resides. When you start Trumpet the first time, it will ask you to fill in the form shown in Figure 7-3. You need to fill in the top three lines, and you should fill in the first five. Here is how to configure each line (most of the information is provided by your Internet service provider):

News Host

> The computer which provides your news service. The name of your news server should be provided by your Internet service provider. A common name for a news host may contain the string "nntp," such as **nntp.yoyodyne.com**.

Mail Host

> A computer you can use to send e-mail responses to news posting. It may be known as an SMTP host as well. It may be the same or different from your **News Host**. Again, your service provider will tell you what host to use.

---

[*] This is an evaluation copy which can be registered with the owner (instructions are in the documentation files which also get created by PKUNZIP). Note that the filename may change as future revisions are released.

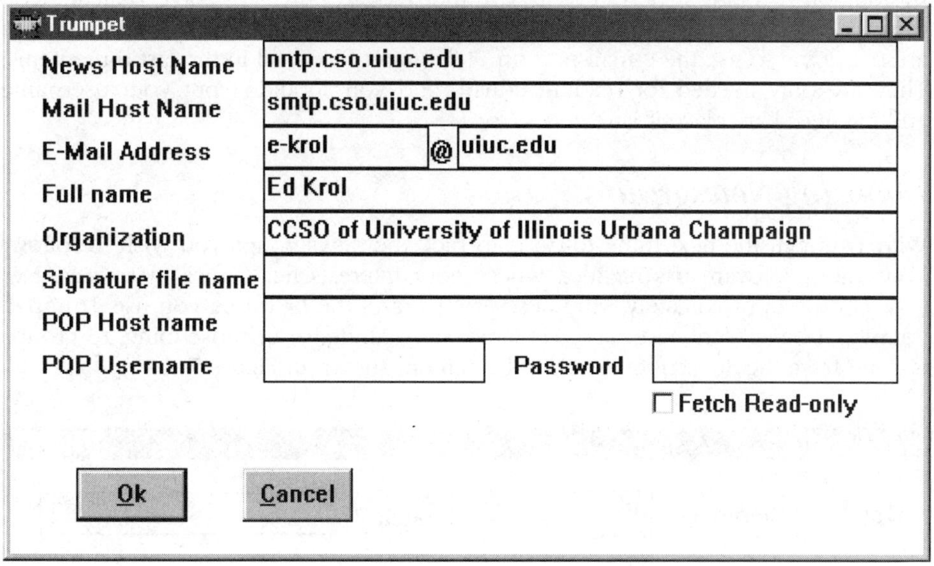

```
Trumpet                                                    _ □ ✕
News Host Name   nntp.cso.uiuc.edu
Mail Host Name   smtp.cso.uiuc.edu
E-Mail Address   e-krol        @  uiuc.edu
Full name        Ed Krol
Organization     CCSO of University of Illinois Urbana Champaign
Signature file name
POP Host name
POP Username                         Password
                                              □ Fetch Read-only

         Ok            Cancel
```

Figure 7–3: Trumpet configuration menu

E-Mail Address

Your e-mail address. It is used to provide the return e-mail address for messages you respond to via e-mail.

Full Name

Your name, as you want it to appear in the news postings you create.

Organization

The organization (employer, etc.) to which you belong. Often left blank or filled with a flippant remark, like "Disorganized." This information is logged by servers, so they have some idea of who is using their services.

Signature file name

The name of a file (a complete file string is a safe way to do it) which will be appended automatically to every news item or e-mail message you send with Trumpet.

POP Host name

The name of the host computer where you receive e-mail (usually, the name after the @ in your e-mail address).

POP Username

The user name on your e-mail account (usually, the name before the @ in your e-mail address).

Password

The password for the e-mail account you entered in the previous two areas.

In addition to being a newsreader, Trumpet has an e-mail package built in. You can use it if you'd like, but it is not as fully featured as Exchange or Eudora. If you are not going to use the e-mail portion of Trumpet, don't fill in the last three items. They are only needed for reading e-mail, and you shouldn't put your username and password anyplace it isn't necessary.

Choosing Newsgroups

With Trumpet, the next thing to do is to pick the newsgroups you wish to follow. Your client software has no idea where your interests lie. Typical network news servers offer approximately 7500 newsgroups, and the first time you use Trumpet, you won't be subscribed to any of them.[*] Subscribing, or unsubscribing, to groups is done from the Subscribe/Unsubscribe screen, shown in Figure 7-4.

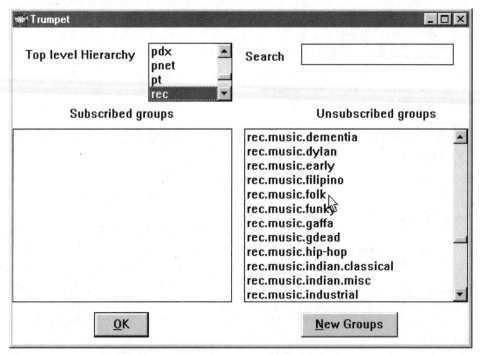

Figure 7-4: Subscribe/Unsubscribe screen

After you finish the configuration screen, you will come here automatically, but you can get here anytime you want to change the status of a group by selecting **Subscribe** under the **Group** menu.

---

[*] Consider yourself lucky. Some newsreaders will assume you are subscribed to all of them, and unsubscribing is a daunting task.

At the top is a pull down list which shows you all of the top level news categories available from your server. Clicking on a particular category, such as *rec* as shown, will display all the available groups within that hierarchy in the two windows below.

In the lower window, Trumpet shows that we aren't subscribed to any groups under *rec* (the left half is empty). The groups you can choose are shown on the right. To move a group from unsubscribed to subscribed (or vice versa) just click on the group name. In the example, we have positioned the cursor arrow over the group *rec.music.folk* in the unsubscribed list. When we click on this, it will disappear from the right side, and appear in the list of subscribed groups. You can continue this process until you have subscribed to all the groups you care to read. When you have had your fill, press the **OK** button. You can then start reading the articles in those groups.

At times, you may not know the name of the group you are interested in, and scrolling down each list to find it can be time-consuming. You can have Trumpet search the groups it knows about by entering a string in the **Search** box in the upper right, as shown in Figure 7-5.

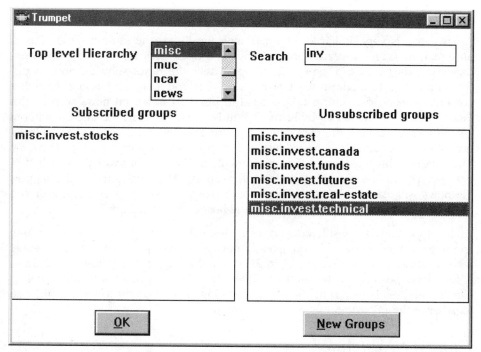

Figure 7-5: Searching for a group

We are looking for a group about investing. We don't know if one exists, what its name is, or what hierarchy it might be in. So, we type a likely word in the **Search** box. First "i," which causes no obvious changes, because many groups contain an "i" in their names. As we continue adding letters, the lists get shorter and shorter until finally, after "inv," only the groups in the *misc.invest* area appear. You can then subscribe as before. To return to the normal mode or look for another string, just erase the **Search** box and start again.

The button marked **New Groups** lets you find out about new groups that have been created since the last time you checked. New groups are created all the time, so you should check for new groups every month or so. To view the recently created groups, push this button and they will appear.

Reading News

Now we're through with preliminaries: selecting the newsgroups that you're interested in. Once you're through with this somewhat messy process, you can start the fun part: reading news and creating your own news items.

What Is a News Item?

A news item is very similar to an e-mail message. It has the same general parts as an e-mail message: a header and a body. The body of a news item is the message's text, just as you'd expect. The header tells the news software how to distribute the item throughout the Internet, and tells you something about the item's contents. The header information is used to build an index on news servers; this index allows the clients to build menus and search for items of interest without having to pass around the complete set of articles. Thus, the header has information about the submitter, the subject, a synopsis, and some indexing keywords. The header is built when you create a new item. You needn't worry about its format, but you do need to provide the information. (The program you use to post the news will ask you for the information it needs.) You will see a header if you save an item in a file for later use, since the header is saved as well.

Each news item is considered part of a discussion thread. The act of creating (posting) a new article on a completely new topic creates a new thread. People who want to add their "two cents" to the discussion then make follow-on postings. A follow-on posting creates another article, but tells the news software that it is part of the thread created by the original posting. This allows it to be logically tied together in the presentation.

Using a Newsreader

The Trumpet newsreader has three distinct phases of operation: group selection, article selection, and reading. In the group selection phase, you pick which newsgroup, of all of the ones to which you are subscribed, you wish to examine. Then, you are shown the set of articles available. You pick one in which you are interested, and the text of that article is displayed.

Let's continue on and assume that we are subscribed to *misc.invest.stocks* and *rec.music.folk*. When you start Trumpet (or have just finished the initial subscription dialog), you will see the screen shown in Figure 7-6.

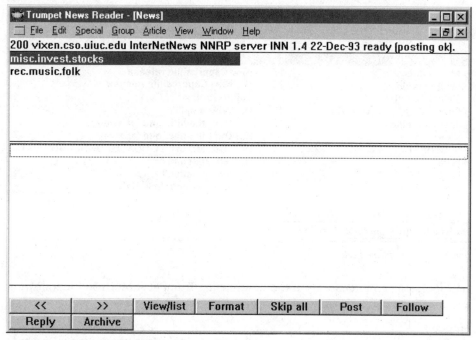

Figure 7–6: Group selection

It shows all of the groups you are subscribed to at the top of the window. To select any group, double-click on the group. This will bring up a dialog box, which says **Scanning**.

At this time, Trumpet compares its information on which articles you have already seen and dismissed with the ones your server has available. This may take a while, because it must download the table of contents of the newsgroup. If the newsgroup is very active, it takes a long time. It will then display on the lower half the subject lines of those articles which are available that you haven't read or thrown away. This is shown in Figure 7-7. The format of the listing is pretty simple. The line highlighted in the group selection area (*rec.music.folk*) is the group that is displayed on the bottom. The line highlighted on the bottom half of the display is the current news item ("Ralph McTell US Tour Postponed"). The subject line of the current news item is also displayed on the very top line of the window.

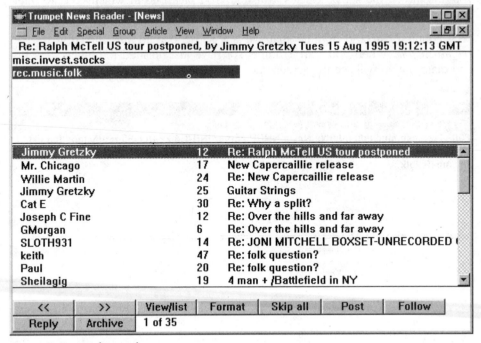

Figure 7-7: Articles to select

Let's look a little more closely at the news items. Trumpet shows you the following information about each entry:

Author

The name of the person who posted the article. Most news senders include their login name as the name in this field. Some newsreaders allow you to post news with a *nom de plume* (e.g., Mr. Chicago). These pseudonyms are frequently used in discussions where anonymity promotes a more complete expression of opinion (as in *alt.sex*).

Size

The number of lines of text in the article. Some newsreaders fail to provide this information when posting, so you will sometimes see a ? in the size field.

Subject

The subject of the article, as typed by the submitter. Notice that some items have the same subject, but with an **Re:** prefixing it. The second posting is by Mr. Chicago. It is a 17-line item on a new record released on the Capercaillie label. The next item, by Willie Martin, is a follow-on posting to Mr. Chicago's. This is what makes a threaded newsreader worthwhile. The **Re:** prefix is a clue to let you know that all of these postings are related to the first. It didn't matter that other items were posted between these two; since they are of the same thread, they appear consecutively. This lets you follow the discussion without interruption.

Now look at the very bottom line of the window. It says that the current item is number 1 of 35 new items in this group. You can view the subject lines of all 35 by scrolling up and down in the window. As you change the current item, either by clicking on another item with the mouse or by moving up and down with the arrow keys, the first number will change.

Now we are ready to read a news item. Let's say we want to read the fourth entry, the question about "Guitar Strings." We can either make it the current item and push the **View/List** button at the bottom or just double click on the item. Either way will show you the contents of the posting, as shown in Figure 7-8.

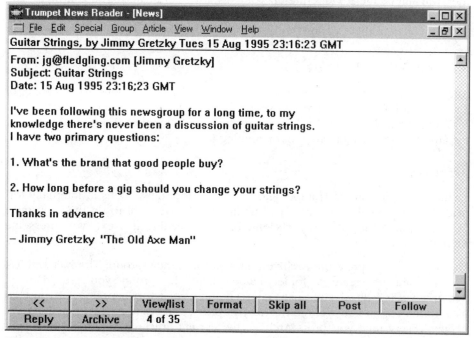

Figure 7-8: The Guitar String question

When you finish reading a news item, the easiest thing to do is press **View/List** again, and Trumpet will return you to the article selection screen. However, that's not your only option. You may also go directly to reading either the preceding article or the following article by using the **<<** or **>>** buttons. This is especially useful when following a thread.

Regardless of where you go after you read an article, Trumpet remembers that you've read it. It will mark the article as "read" on the screen by putting ">>" before the author's name, as shown in Figure 7-9.

» Jimmy Gretzky   **25   Guitar Strings**

Figure 7-9: Article marked as read

Once the newsreader marks an article as "read," it discards it from all future sessions. The next time you start Trumpet, you won't see Jimmy Gretzky's article again.

What about the articles you don't read? Most of the time, you will read less than 10 percent of the articles presented in a group. If you just leave Trumpet and return, they will still be there, cluttering up your window. Fortunately, you can press **Skip All** when you are done with a group. It will mark all of the items shown as read, so you won't see them again.

Saving News Articles

After reading a news article, you will often want to print it, mail it to someone, or just save it for later. There are two ways of doing this in Trumpet. One is designed for filing away old articles for future reference, and the other is designed for using the article in some other program or printing it.

Archiving

The archiving feature of Trumpet allows you to store news items in internally formatted folders, so that you can read them later. If you want to do this, you must first select an item, either by clicking on it or reading it. Next, you press the **Archive** button.

The first time you press the **Archive** button within a newsgroup, Trumpet will ask if you want to create a folder named after the group you are in (e.g., *news:rec.music.folk*). If you answer yes, nothing seems to happen—you just go back to the screen you were at before you pressed the button. But something did happen! Every time you press **Archive**, the current article is appended to a specially formatted folder (very much like folders in Exchange).

Once you get to these folders, they are quite easy to use. How you get there, however, is not obvious—the folders are part of the e-mail system built into Trumpet. To access them, you must select the **Mail** option from the **Window** menu. Selecting this will bring up a screen which looks very much like the article selection screen, except the **Archive** button will be missing and the newsgroups will be replaced by the folders you have created (Figure 7-10). You also use it in the same manner as article selection. You click on the archive file you want to access (in the example we picked, *news:misc.invest.stocks*). To read an article, you double-click on it, or select it and press **View/List**.

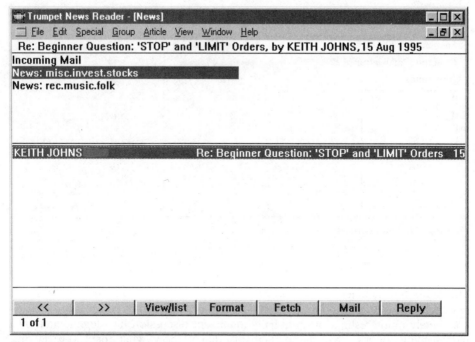

Figure 7-10: Viewing archived items

It is possible to delete things from an archive folder once you no longer have a need for them. You do this by selecting the item and using the **Delete** item from the **Article** menu. It will ask you to confirm that you really want to delete it. Once you say yes, it's gone.

Once you are done reading your archives and want to go back to today's news, just select the **News** menu item to return there.

Saving items to files

If you want to save an item in a file by itself, choose the **Save** or **Append** command under the **Article** menu. The **Save** command will create a new file and copy the article into it, and the **Append** command appends the current item to the end of a file. Trumpet will ask you the name of the file through the dialog box shown in Figure 7-11. The directory shown in the second line of the entry is the default, which will be used if an incomplete file string is used. For example, if I just type in the name *gretzky.txt*, Trumpet will store the file in *c:\wintrump\gretzky.txt*. If I wanted the file to go in a different directory, I could have easily typed in the complete directory path for where I wanted it to go, such as *\c:\gretzky.txt*. Remember that Windows applications frequently look for files with certain filename extensions, such as *.txt*, so be careful what you pick for a name.

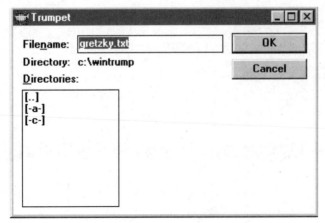

Figure 7-11: Saving an article

Controlling What You Read

There are few needles in the haystack. For every news item that's truly worth reading, there are many that are a waste of time: either they're on a topic that's completely uninteresting, or an initially intelligent discussion has degenerated into name-calling, or it's clear the participants didn't know what they were talking about in the first place. So you shouldn't be surprised to learn that all newsreaders support some commands to limit the number of articles that are inflicted on you.

Subscribing and unsubscribing

When we first used Trumpet at the beginning of this chapter, we visited a screen that allowed us to subscribe to a number of newsgroups. Just as with a magazine, you can change your subscription status at any time: you can subscribe to new groups and unsubscribe to groups you're currently receiving. You can do this by asking to see that same subscription screen we used before, by selecting **Subscribe** under the **Group** menu.

There is a shortcut for unsubscribing to the group you are currently reading. No selection windows are involved. Just pull down **Group** and select **Unsubscribe**, and it's gone.

Catching Up

Eventually, when you are reading twenty or thirty groups regularly, you will go on vacation. You will come back to find thousands of articles in those groups waiting for you to scan. When confronted with this daunting task, you may decide that you really *do* need to read all the messages in some of those groups; but for most of them, you'd just as soon flush all of the old articles. Most newsreaders provide you with a feature to do this; it is generally called catching up.

With Trumpet you catch up on a group-by-group basis with the **Catch up** command in the **Group** menu. Whatever group you have currently selected, this command will mark all current entries in it as having been read and will move you to the next group. The effect is exactly the same as the **Skip all** button (or its synonym, **Read all**) under the **Group** menu, which can also be used for this purpose, but it will skip the lengthy "scanning" process, so it is much faster.

Going Back

In life, it's been said that you can never go back. On USENET, however, it may be possible. There are two scenarios in which this commonly happens. The first is when you glance at a newsgroup and mark it all as having been read, then come back the next day and really need to see one of the previous articles.

If the article still resides on your news server, it's possible to read it again, by using a command under the **Group** menu. There are three commands: **Unread 10**, **Unread 20**, and **Unread all**. These change the status of the last 10, 20, or all of the articles on the server from having been read to not yet read, so they will reappear.

If the article of your dreams is no longer on the server, things get a bit chancier. Your best hope is to read any periodic postings or FAQs which describe the newsgroup. If you are really lucky, one of them will tell you about an archive for the group. You may need to use some other technology, such as the World Wide Web, Gopher or anonymous FTP to get at it, but you may be able to find an article again. If an archive exists, the FAQ will give you the details of its organization and access.

rot13

In an attempt to keep political pressures at bay, there was a voluntary rule that potentially offensive postings to widely read newsgroups should be encrypted with a code called rot13. The intent of rot13 isn't to keep any information confidential; it is just to prevent readers from accidentally seeing something they would rather have avoided.* If you go to the trouble of decoding the message, you deserve what you get.

You are most likely to see encrypted messages in groups like *rec.humor.* Such groups are read by a wide range of people, with many different tastes. In groups in the *alt* area, where some of these same topics are commonplace, it is not

---

* The code could be implemented with one of the coding rings found in cereal boxes. It's merely the alphabet rotated 13 letters: "a" mapped to "n", "b" to "o", "A" to "N", etc. All non-letters remain the same. (As we said, this code isn't designed to keep anything secret; it's just to allow readers to ignore offensive material.)

needed. The easily offended should not be wandering through the *alt* groups, anyway.

The use of rot13 encoding on the Net has fallen off considerably of late. USENET has been flooded by people who apparently care even less what others think about them than "old-timers" did (a frightening thought, if you ask me; USENET was never noteworthy for its politeness). You can now read a lot of pretty offensive stuff in newsgroups, out there in plain text. So you may never need to know how to read a rot13 message (Trumpet doesn't make it easy for you to create them), but just in case, it's only one command away.

A posting which is in rot13 will usually be flagged on the selection menu line:

```
Ed Krol          38       Joke offensive to some (rot13)
```

If you decide to live dangerously and read it, you will see a posting like this:

```
Lbh qvqa'g rkcrpg or gb trg
bssrafvir va cevag, qvq lbh?
------
Ed Krol    Speaking for myself not my employer
```

Now you're curious and want to see what this is all about. To decode the text, pull down the **Article** menu and select **Rot13**; this causes the screen to be repainted with:

```
Ed Krol: Joke offensive to some  Thu, 21 Nov 1991 16:24

You didn't expect me to get
offensive in print, did you?
------
Rq Xeby   Fcrnxvat sbe zlfrys abg zl rzcyblre
```

Notice that the entire text of the message is changed, including the signature (which was not encrypted to start with).

Features You'll Wish Trumpet Had

Although Trumpet is easy to use and perfectly serviceable, it does fall down on the list of available features. Here are a couple of facilities which you may find in other newsreaders but, unfortunately, are not found in Trumpet.

Auto-kill and auto-select

Some newsreaders allow you to automatically throw away articles (known as killing) whose subjects contain certain phrases or who have been penned by certain authors. This can be quite useful if there are topics frequently discussed which you know you will never want to read. For example, say you were reading *rec.humor* and notice that many jokes have a subject of "racial humor." Since you don't like racial humor, you could tell your newsreader to just throw away any articles which contain "racial" in the subject line.

There is another situation in which you might want to kill articles. Some groups have an internal structure. Although the group isn't divided into subgroups, the readers of the group have agreed to put certain codes into their subject lines to allow their messages to be categorized easily. For example, the group *rec.arts.tv.soaps.abc* (don't worry, there is also one for *cbs* and *nbc*) uses codes to indicate what soap opera is being discussed. Articles may have subjects like:

```
OLTL: Did Todd Get A Makeover?
OLTL: Luna's funeral
GH: Dr. Laura as AIDS ignoramus
AMC: How stupid can Hayley be
```

In this example, if the only soap you are interested in discussing is "One Life To Live," you could auto-kill all articles that do not contain the string "OLTL" in their subject. If a newsgroup has established conventions like this, someone regularly posts a key showing which flag strings to use.

Auto-selection is the opposite of killing. You set some criteria. If an article meets the criteria, the newsreader automatically displays the article for you when you select the group. Killing is far more frequently used. This is because judicious use of kill criteria saves you time. There are fewer items to scan, and it takes less time to download the newsgroup's table of contents from the server.

Searching

When Trumpet enters the "scanning" phase to look at a new newsgroup, it actually is being passed the header information for each article available. This includes author, subject, synopsis, and keyword information. Some readers allow you to say things like "Search for an article by Krol" or "Search for an article which has 'fleas' in the subject line." This allows you to easily find articles you may have run across or that people have suggested you read. Trumpet doesn't allow you to do this, so you have to scroll and scan by eye to find things.

Posting Articles

After reading news for a while, you might get your courage up enough to take part in a discussion. There are two basic ways of taking part: adding to an existing discussion thread or starting a new discussion.

Adding to an Existing Discussion

Let's start by adding a follow-up item to an existing discussion thread. This is a bit easier, because all the work of describing the thread (i.e., building the header) is done for you. It is like replying to an e-mail message. Remember Jimmy Gretzky's question:

```
I've been following this newsgroup for a long time, to
my knowledge there's never been a discussion of guitar
strings. I have two primary questions:

1. What's the brand that the good people buy?...
```

You, being a folk guitarist from way back, see this request for comments on guitar strings and wish to respond. So, while viewing this article, you press the **Follow** button, meaning "make a follow-on posting."

Trumpet will create the skeleton of the posting by copying things from the header of the old article (such as the subject and group information) to the new posting. It will also take the old text of the posting you are replying to and copy it into the body part of new posting, preceding each line with a >. Now you are ready to add your two cents.

Please, please, please delete irrelevant chunks of the old article. Some people just leave it there and add their information at the end, which makes follow-on messages longer and longer. All of the old discussion is there to the reader in the thread if they care to read it. Deleting this stuff is a bit of a trick, since you can't get at the **Edit** menu item by pulling it down from the posting window. If you want to use **Cut** and **Paste**, you can get at the **Edit** menu by pressing the right mouse button or by remembering the key short cuts (CTRL-X and CTRL-V).

If you are really into wholesale changes in a posting, you might find it more convenient to copy and paste the text into a word processor window, change it there, and copy and paste it back. One of the nice things you can do while it's in the word processor is spell check your work. Do remember to insert ENTER's manually at the ends of lines.

After that, you can just type what you want to add to the post, as shown in Figure 7-12. When you are done, just click **Post**, and it's on its way.

Starting a New Discussion

The only difference between a follow-on posting and creating a new thread is that for a new thread, you must supply the information to fill out the header. To begin a new discussion, use the **Post** button. Trumpet will create a new posting window (which looks just like the follow-on posting window), and will fill in the name of the current group. You can change that if you'd like, or add additional groups separated by commas (known as cross-posting). You don't have to be looking at the group, or even subscribed to it. After you type the group's name, enter the subject, keywords, and a summary of the article. These are the items which go in the header to allow searches. Finally, you need to tell the newsreader how far you want your posting disseminated. This exchange is shown in Figure 7-13. Remember that the **Subject**, **Keywords**, and **Summary** are the only things passed from

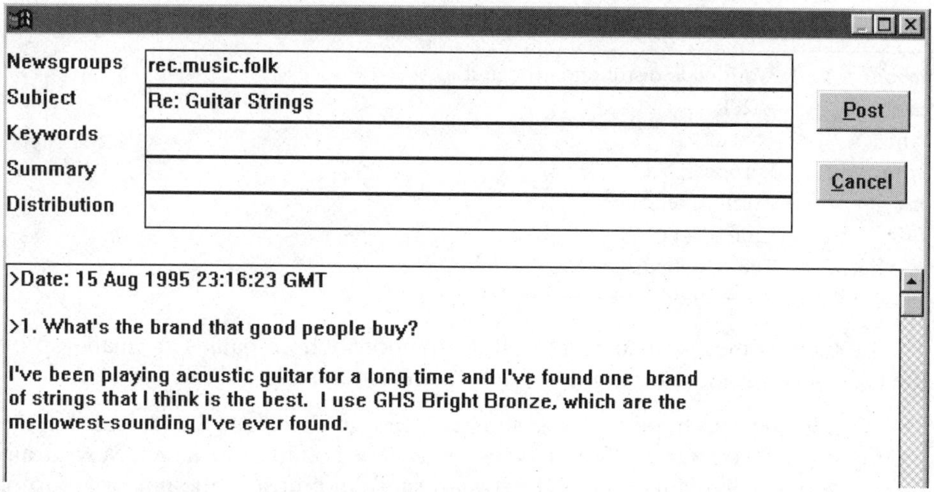

```
┌──────────────────────────────────────────────────────────────┐
│ ▓                                                    _ □ ✕     │
├──────────────────────────────────────────────────────────────┤
│ Newsgroups  ┌─────────────────────────────────────┐           │
│             │ rec.music.folk                      │           │
│ Subject     ├─────────────────────────────────────┤  ┌───────┐│
│             │ Re: Guitar Strings                  │  │ Post  ││
│ Keywords    ├─────────────────────────────────────┤  └───────┘│
│             │                                     │           │
│ Summary     ├─────────────────────────────────────┤  ┌───────┐│
│             │                                     │  │Cancel ││
│ Distribution├─────────────────────────────────────┤  └───────┘│
│             │                                     │           │
│             └─────────────────────────────────────┘           │
├──────────────────────────────────────────────────────────────┤
│ >Date: 15 Aug 1995 23:16:23 GMT                           ▲   │
│                                                               │
│ >1. What's the brand that good people buy?                    │
│                                                               │
│ I've been playing acoustic guitar for a long time and I've    │
│ found one  brand of strings that I think is the best.  I use  │
│ GHS Bright Bronze, which are the mellowest-sounding I've      │
│ ever found.                                               ▼   │
└──────────────────────────────────────────────────────────────┘
```

Figure 7–12: Following on to an existing posting

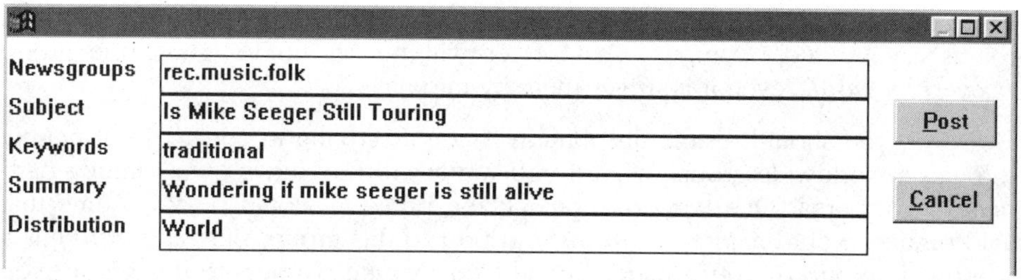

```
┌──────────────────────────────────────────────────────────────┐
│ ▓                                                    _ □ ✕     │
├──────────────────────────────────────────────────────────────┤
│ Newsgroups  ┌─────────────────────────────────────┐           │
│             │ rec.music.folk                      │           │
│ Subject     ├─────────────────────────────────────┤  ┌───────┐│
│             │ Is Mike Seeger Still Touring        │  │ Post  ││
│ Keywords    ├─────────────────────────────────────┤  └───────┘│
│             │ traditional                         │           │
│ Summary     ├─────────────────────────────────────┤  ┌───────┐│
│             │ Wondering if mike seeger is still alive│ │Cancel ││
│ Distribution├─────────────────────────────────────┤  └───────┘│
│             │ World                               │           │
│             └─────────────────────────────────────┘           │
└──────────────────────────────────────────────────────────────┘
```

Figure 7–13: Creating a new thread

news servers to the newsreaders, allowing them to build selection menus and kill or auto-select your article. Therefore, make your subject a good one. It is all the reader has to decide whether your posting is interesting or not. The actual text of an article is only sent from a news server to a newsreader when someone selects the article for reading. Readers pick which articles they want to read on the basis of the subject, so misleading subject lines can be really annoying.

The distribution line gives the news system some idea about how far you would like the posting passed. You should treat this as a statement of the minimum coverage required for the article. There is no guarantee that it will not be propagated farther than you think. Once you pick a distribution that goes beyond your local server, you are depending on remote servers' configurations to be correct. This is probably too optimistic.

There is no way to find out exactly what distribution lists are available for a server. There is a set of standard distributions that are available on most servers, but they describe only wide areas. They are shown in Table 7-1.

Table 7–1: Common Distribution Keywords

Keyword	Distribution area
world	Worldwide distribution (default)
att	AT&T
can	Canada
eunet	European sites
na	North America
usa	United States
IL,NY,FL . . .	The specified state

The problem comes with smaller, local distributions whose names are made up by the local server's administrator. Only your administrator can tell you for sure.

This is not quite as hopeless as it sounds. Most of the time, the default for the group is what you want. This is okay, even if it sounds too large. Newsgroup propagation is voluntarily arranged between sites, and most of the time a group of local interest is not sent too far, even if you specify "world" as the distribution. The person who runs a neighboring server for the Megabucks Corporation certainly doesn't want his disk filled up with discussions about the problems with dorm rooms on a remote campus. That server will be set up to ignore the group *hoople.campuslife,* even if it arrives there by mistake.

However, you should restrict distribution if you are trying to contact local people through a worldwide group. What if you wanted to find lunch-hour running partners in your area? One way to approach the problem would be to assume that avid runners would read *rec.running* and post to this group. But *rec.running* is a worldwide group. If you posted a request for jogging partners to this group, you would probably get snide replies like "Sure, meet on the steps of Paddington Station at noon." Quite a jog. What you want to do is post to that group, but use a limited distribution: "campus," "local," "hoople," or whatever your local distribution identifiers are. Similarly, if you're offering an old car for sale, you might want to restrict distribution to your state (unless you're willing to deliver the car); for example, IL, NY, or CA.

One final word of warning about the distribution. You cannot specify a distribution that does not contain your server. For example, you can't specify a distribution in Florida while sitting on a machine in New York. This is because news is distributed by flooding: it is "poured" into the system by your server to its neighbors, and flows outward. If you specify Florida in a message that's distributed from New York, about the time it gets to New Jersey, machines start saying "Why did you give this to me?" and throw it away.

After you've completed your post, press the **Post** button to pour it into the system.

Replying via E-Mail

You sometimes want to reply to the submitter of an item privately, through e-mail. This is useful when the comments you want to make are not of general interest, or should not be widely distributed. To make this easy, Trumpet has a mail facility built into it. To invoke it, use the **Reply** button while reading an item. The mail interface then proceeds much like a follow-on posting. For example, if you were reading the same Jimmy Gretzky item you have been reading throughout this chapter, and you pressed **Reply**, you would see something like Figure 7-14.

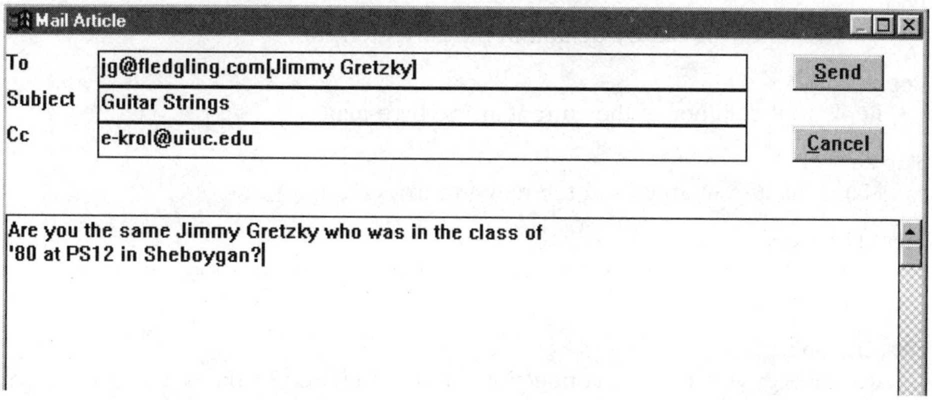

```
┌─────────────────────────────────────────────────────────────────────────┐
│ ▓ Mail Article                                                  _ □ ✕    │
│ To       jg@fledgling.com[Jimmy Gretzky]                      ┌─────────┐ │
│                                                               │  Send   │ │
│ Subject  Guitar Strings                                       └─────────┘ │
│ Cc       e-krol@uiuc.edu                                      ┌─────────┐ │
│                                                               │ Cancel  │ │
│                                                               └─────────┘ │
│ Are you the same Jimmy Gretzky who was in the class of                ▲ │
│ '80 at PS12 in Sheboygan?                                              ▒ │
│                                                                        ▒ │
│                                                                        ▼ │
└─────────────────────────────────────────────────────────────────────────┘
```

Figure 7-14: Replying by e-mail

Again, Trumpet automatically fills in the **To:** address, the subject, and the message you were reading when you clicked **Reply**. You should delete unnecessary parts of the message and fill in whatever you message is. When you are satisfied, click **Send** and it will be on its way.

You can also use Trumpet to read and reply to your other e-mail. However, Trumpet is not particularly great as an e-mail program; you're better off with Exchange or Eudora, which are discussed in Chapter 5.

A Summary of Trumpet Commands

The list below shows the most important commands available in Trumpet. It includes all of the commands that we have covered, and a few that we haven't. There are additional commands that we won't mention; those listed below are certainly all you need to get going, and may be all that you'll ever need. Further help is available in the **Help** menu. It is a bit terse, but it is complete.

<< While reading, moves to news item before the current one.

>> While reading, moves to news item after the current one.

Archive

Saves the current article in a folder for future reading from the Mail window.

Follow

Create a follow-on posting to the current article.

Format

Reformats the view screen. There are four formats; the one we use in examples is the default. Pushing this button moves you through the available formats.

Post

Creates a new thread by default in the current group.

Reply

Reply to the author of the current article by e-mail.

Skip all

Marks all current articles in the newsgroup as read.

View/List

Toggles between viewing the list of available articles and looking at one particular article.

File->Reconnect

Reconnects you if your connection to your newserver times out. Instead of using this button, you can quit Trumpet and start again.

File->Quit

Gets you out of Trumpet. Probably easier to use the close box in the upper right of the window.

Group->Unread *amt*

Allows you to reread articles which are normally hidden because you have seen them already; *amt* can be 10, 20 or all.

Group->Catch up

Marks the whole current group as having been read. It is faster than **Skip all**.

Group->Subscribe

Brings up the group subscription window to allow you to either subscribe or unsubscribe to groups.

Group->Unsubscribe

Unsubscribes you to the currently selected group.

Article->Save

Saves a copy of the current article in a file; the file will be overwritten if it exists, or created if it doesn't.

Article->Append

Saves a copy of the current article by appending it on the end of the named file; the file must exist or an error will be reported and no action taken.

Window->Mail

Gets you into the e-mail part of Trumpet; also used to read archive files.

Window->News

Returns from Trumpet's e-mail reading mode to reading news.

Other Hints and Conventions

Here are some other gems which are known to most experienced news users:

- If you start Trumpet and then go away for a long time, the connection between it and the server will time out. If you try to do anything at this time, you will get a bunch of ugly messages about "Timeouts," "No Connection..." and no commands will seem to work. To fix the problem, select **Reconnect** under the **File** menu.

- Read before you post. Get to know both the system and the group. If you see any postings marked **FAQ** (Frequently Asked Questions), read them. These postings may be in the group itself, or they may be in the special group *news.answers*. Your question may have already been discussed *ad nauseam*, and you will look like a novice by asking it again.

- If you are leery of posting for the first time, you might post to the newsgroup *misc.test*. It is designed to allow people to practice posting. If you post to it, you will get automatic e-mail responses from a variety of sites.

- Format your postings nicely. Use a descriptive subject. People will choose to read your postings based on the subject. Busy people tend to have less time to read news than they would like, so they choose items which don't appear to be a waste of time. A subject like "Question" will probably be ignored. Try "Guitar String Question." Never use "gotcha" subjects (e.g., "Subject: Sex", but in the body, "Now that I have your attention, I have a question about insects"). On the other end of the posting, signatures are fine, but keep them short.

- Be polite. You asked a question of the network. Someone took time to answer; a thank-you message back is appreciated. Disagreements are fine, but attacking someone personally for their postings is not good form (although common). This is known as *flaming*.

- Post and reply appropriately. Post to the smallest distribution that will get the job done. Read the whole thread before responding. If someone asks, "What's the answer?" and someone already said "The answer is 42," you don't add anything by repeating it. Some of this is inevitable because of the delays in news propagation, but avoid contributing to the problem intentionally. If the answer is not of general interest, reply by e-mail.

- Don't automatically include the article to which you are responding. Too many times, articles get longer and longer with each response, because people include all previous discussion. The people who are reading the group chose to read your posting based on the subject. If it is a follow-on posting, they probably have read the initial postings, too (they had the same subject). Please don't make them read it again. If you want to respond point by point, edit the discussion down until only the relevant sentences are included.

- Controversy is fine, but keep it in its place. There are groups designed for pro/con discussions, and there are groups where people of a like mind meet to commiserate. Don't post anti-gun sentiments on *rec.hunting*; it won't do anything but get you flamed. In any group, flag controversial opinions with IMHO (In My Humble Opinion); i.e., "IMHO, Mossberg makes the best firearms."

- Be patient; news takes a while to be distributed. When you post something, it goes into a queue on your server; it then needs to be indexed and passed on to the rest of the world. All of this is done by background tasks on the server. Your posting won't appear on your system immediately, and may take a day to get to the rest of the world. Also, don't expect responses immediately, even by e-mail. Some people feel guilty reading *rec.arts.disney* on company time. Therefore, a lot of people read recreational groups only on the weekend.

- As I said, there are many programs for reading news. Trumpet is typical, but don't be afraid to try another that might be more to your liking. It will have more or less the same features, and work more or less the same way.

- The biggest problem with reading news is that there is so much, and it is all so interesting. It is easy to become enamored with it. Be selective about which groups you read. News addiction may threaten you . . . .

A Different Approach: Netscape Navigator

Many people think that the Internet, USENET, and the World Wide Web are all the same thing. Although this is not the case, these people feel quite comfortable using a browser as their window to all there is to know, including USENET. For these people, Netscape Navigator and its internal newsreader might be just the thing.

Trumpet treats news in the traditional manner, as a series of text files sorted by subject and time. Netscape uses a graphical display. It tries to show you more about the structure of the discussion, which conveys a bit more information about how deep the discussion has gone and how the articles are related to one another. Some people may find this intuitively obvious, while others may find it confusing. Again, the choice is yours—there is no correct way of reading news.

Netscape requires some additional configuration before it can be used as a newsreader. First, pull down the **Options** menu and select **Preferences** and fill out the

Mail and News section. If Netscape complains about multiple news servers, some of which work and some not, after you have configured this area, find the *news/fat* file in the main Netscape directory and delete it. Netscape will complain next time you enter news, but the only server it will try to use will be the one you have configured.

Steering Netscape

When you're using Netscape, most of the decisions you make about what to read happen from the page you see when you enter the **Newsgroups** area. The first section of the page gives you some textual instructions about how to read news with Netscape. If you scroll down a bit, you will see a list of all the newsgroups to which you are currently subscribed (Figure 7-15).

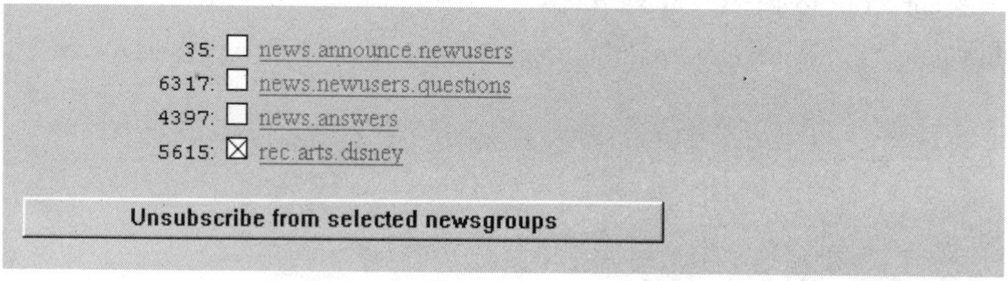

35: ☐	news.announce.newusers
6317: ☐	news.newusers.questions
4397: ☐	news.answers
5615: ☒	rec.arts.disney

Unsubscribe from selected newsgroups

Figure 7-15: List of current subscriptions

When you first begin reading news in Netscape, you will be subscribed to:

```
news.announce.newusers
news.newusers.questions
news.answers
```

Use this section of the screen to unsubscribe to these or any other newsgroups later. You do this by clicking the check box to the left of a name and then pressing the bar labeled **Unsubscribe from selected newsgroups**. In Figure 7-15, if we pressed this bar, we would unsubscribe to *rec.arts.disney*.

You subscribe to groups a bit further on down the page. There is a box shown in Figure 7-16 where you type in the name of the group to which you want to subscribe. Fill in the name and press the ENTER key. The box will go blank and the named group will appear in the list we looked at above. Netscape does not verify the existence of the group until you try to use it. If you don't get the name correct, it will not complain until you click on the group name to access it. It will then tell you the group is not available.

If you don't know the name of the group you want, and would like to scan the list of all available groups, press the button labeled **List Of Available Newsgroups** at the bottom of the page. It will take you to a place where you can see what groups are available, but it may take a while. Netscape must bring down the list, which is

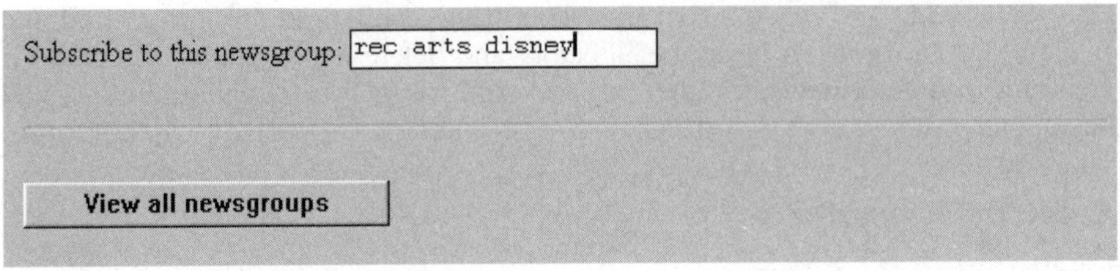

Subscribe to this newsgroup: [rec.arts.disney]

[**View all newsgroups**]

Figure 7-16: Subscribing in Netscape

a few hundred thousand characters, from the server. This page will give you a list of all of the high-level hierarchies, just like Trumpet. When you find the newsgroups you want, click in their respective white check boxes. When you are done, click **Subscribe to selected newsgroups**.

In Figure 7-17 we have entered this area. First we selected *rec* and then *rec.arts*.

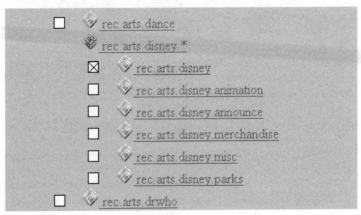

□   ☞ rec.arts.dance
  ☞ rec.arts.disney.*
☒   ☞ rec.arts.disney
□   ☞ rec.arts.disney.animation
□   ☞ rec.arts.disney.announce
□   ☞ rec.arts.disney.merchandise
□   ☞ rec.arts.disney.misc
□   ☞ rec.arts.disney.parks
□   ☞ rec.arts.drwho

Figure 7-17: Viewing the newsgroup list

You can see the newsgroups displayed in outline form. The ones which are the lowest levels of the outline have the white checkbox next to them. We have checked *rec.arts.disney*; when we push the button we'll be subscribed to it.

Remember that any time you are looking at a page with Netscape, including these pages that list newsgroups, you can use the **Find** button to search for a string. So, to search for groups about investing, you can use **Find** to look for the string "inv". The search only covers the page you're currently reading, not all USENET hierarchies—unlike the search feature in Trumpet.

One more thing. On the bottom of this page, there is a button labeled **Get new groups since last update**. It works just like the **New Groups** button in Trumpet—it queries the server and gets a list of groups recently created.

Scanning a Newsgroup in Netscape

Scanning a newsgroup in Netscape is patterned after Web browsing. The list of subscribed newsgroups are underlined and blue. That is, they look just like a Web hypertext link. If you want to read *rec.arts.disney*, click on it as you would on any other link. This will download the headers available for the available articles, and display them as shown in Figure 7-18.

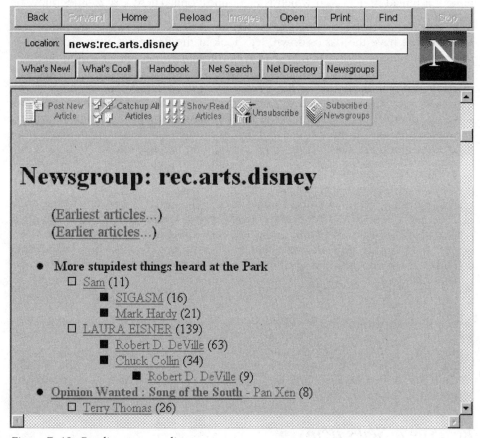

Figure 7-18: Reading rec.arts.disney

Look around the window to familiarize yourself with what is there. At the top, there is a bar of buttons which have some familiar functions, such as posting, catching up, etc. These buttons are duplicated on the bottom of the page as well, so you can scroll up or down to access them, whichever is more convenient. We'll talk about these later. Let's continue our window tour for now.

Beneath the buttons, Netscape displays the name of the newsgroup you are reading, and some links named **Earliest articles** and **Earlier articles**. Netscape's way of dealing with long lists is scrolling, which works fine for a long list, but not outrageously long lists. Recognizing that a newsgroup may have hundreds of unread articles, Netscape displays the most recent 100 articles, and creates pseudogroups for the older ones. If you haven't read an active newsgroup for a while, these may appear.*

Finally, we see the subject lines of the news postings. Let's look at the last news item on the page with the title beginning "Opinion Wanted . . . ." This is the beginning of a thread by Pan Xen which is eight lines long. There is a 26-line follow-on posting by Terry Thomas shown after it. To read any article, just click on it.

Now that we have the basics down, let's look at the first news item on the page, beginning "More stupidest things . . . ." It's a bit more complex. First, the title is in black and not underlined, which is different from other postings. This tells you that although this is the title of the thread, you can't see the original posting. You may have read the article already, or the article may have been from the news server (expired). If the problem is the former, you can probably see it by clicking **Show Read Articles**. If the article has been expired by the server, you would have to look for group archives.

Notice that Netscape gives you another dimension in threading. It shows you how the follow-on postings are related to each other, not just that they are related to the main posting. Here Sam and Laura Eisner both posted follow-ons to the original posting. Later SIGASM and Mark Hardy had a comment on Sam's thoughts, while Robert DeVille and Chuck Collin had something to say about Laura's. Obviously, some people don't know when to stop. Robert DeVille had yet another comment about Chuck Collin's posting.

When you are done reading a newsgroup, you have three actions you might want to take, all available as buttons from the bar across the top of the group. First, when you have scanned all the postings and decided there is nothing else to view, you might want to click **Catchup All Articles** so you are not bothered by them again. Second, if you decide this newsgroup isn't as great as you thought it was going to be, you can unsubscribe immediately by clicking **Unsubscribe**. Finally, clicking **Subscribed Newsgroups** gets you back to the newsgroup list, shown in Figure 7-15.

Reading a News Item

As we said, you read a news item by clicking on the link to it from the article selection page. Figure 7-19 shows you the screen used to read a news item. You will notice it already feels familiar, since it is patterned after the article selection page, although the action bar of buttons is a bit expanded. The new buttons help you select articles to read, without returning to the newsgroup's article list. You can either move with a particular thread or to the next thread at the click of a button.

---

* You can change this number under **Options->Preferences**.

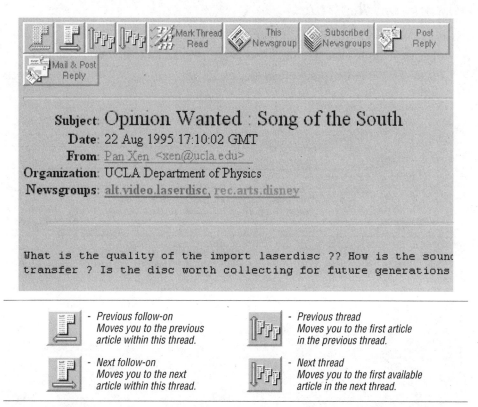

Figure 7–19: Reading an article in Netscape

In Figure 7-19, the first button is grayed out. Moving to the previous article doesn't make sense at this point, since there is no previous article in the same thread. As you move around, various buttons become inactive, depending on your position.

Another nice feature is a button labeled **Mark Thread Read**. Frequently, you will enter a thread thinking it's going to be great, and it turns out to be a real dud. After reading one or two items, you want to get rid of the whole thread. Mark it read, and move on to something more interesting.

If you don't want to proceed across the current thread or down the group, you also can return to the article selection page for the current group by clicking **This Newsgroup**. Or you can click **Subscribed Newsgroups** and return to the first page, where all of your subscribed newsgroups are listed.

Finally, there is one more hidden navigation feature you might want to know about. Notice that the newsgroups listed in the **Newsgroups** section of the header appear to be links (this article is cross-posted in both *alt.video.laserdisc* and *rec.arts.disney*). Although you are not subscribed to the *alt.video.laserdisc*, you can click on its name if you'd like to peek at it to see what is being discussed.

Posting and Replying

There are many ways in Netscape to post or reply via e-mail. You can:

- Click **Post Reply** while reading a news item to send a follow on posting.

- Click on the **From:** field of an item you are reading, to send e-mail to its author.

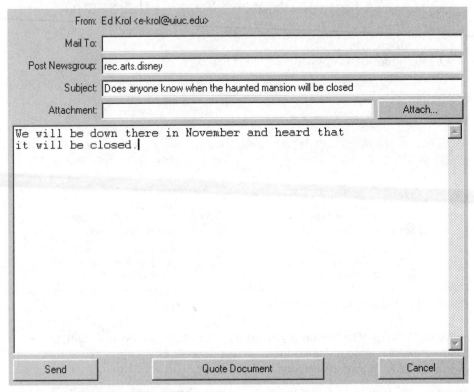

Figure 7-20: Post and reply window

- Select **Mail & Post Reply** while reading an article, to e-mail its author and post the same text.

- While scanning the article selection menu of a newsgroup, click **Post New Article**.

Any of these actions will present you the window shown in Figure 7-20. How you get to this window determines what fields get filled in automatically. In turn, the fields that are filled in determine how the message is handled. If **Mail To:** is filled in, the text you fill in gets sent via e-mail; if **Post Newsgroup:** is, the message gets posted; and if you fill in both, the message is sent via news and e-mail. If you are following-on, the subject will be filled in from the thread. If you are starting something new, you must fill it in yourself.

Next, fill in the text you want to send. Unlike Trumpet, Netscape doesn't automatically include the article you're replying to. If you want it included, click the **Quote Document** button at the bottom.

The other thing you can do is attach a document (either a file, or the URL of a Web document) as you could with Exchange. Selecting **Attach** will give you a dialog box to ask what you want to attach, and it will be pasted inside the posting.

Other than that, posting is just like Trumpet. When you've written your article, click **Send** and your thoughts are on their way. When you are done reading news in Netscape, you may return to browsing, or quit Netscape by selecting **Exit** under the **File** menu.

CHAPTER EIGHT

REMOTE LOGIN

Connecting a Remote Computer
Non-Standard Telnet Servers
Telnet Program Options
Telneting to IBM Mainframes

The three applications we've discussed already—e-mail, news, and the World Wide Web—are probably the core of what people want from the Net. But they're certainly not all that's out there. The next two chapters discuss two of the Internet's oldest applications: Telnet (remote login, or "keyboard-level" access to other computers) and FTP (file transfer protocol). As we've said, Telnet is the Internet's remote login protocol. It lets you sit at a keyboard connected to one computer and log on to a remote computer across the network. Since Windows machines are completely self-sufficient computers, there isn't (strictly speaking) a need to log in to remote computers. You can't run Windows over the network, and Telnet only gives you an old-style command-line interface, rather than a nice windowing system. However, before we relegate Telnet to the "dustbin of history," let's see what it's good for. It's still a very important application.

Telnet was really designed to let you log onto your account on a timesharing computer to do "regular work"—and it's still useful for that. These days, Telnet is most frequently used to access library catalogs and other large databases; the U.S. government makes a lot of information available via Telnet. In this case, you're logging in to the remote computers and executing a special application that lets you do lookups. (For example, the Weather Underground has a Telnet interface to give you weather reports for the whole country.) The Telnet interface also works well for BBS systems; as these join the Internet, I expect you'll see many new Telnet servers. Finally, Telnet is good for trying out new services. For example, let's say you want to try out Internet Relay Chat (IRC), a very popular application in some circles. Before you hunt down the software and install it, you can use Telnet to access a public chat server somewhere on the Net, play around for a few hours, and decide whether IRC is worth pursuing.

So, although Telnet isn't the Windows user's preferred way of working, it still has important uses on today's Internet. It's really the Internet's equivalent to Hyperterminal or PROCOMM—applications which, although they don't give you a state-of-the-art user interface, are nevertheless an important part of everyone's toolkit.

Connecting a Remote Computer

The hardest thing about using Telnet on Windows 95 is probably finding it—you won't find it under the **Start** button in the **Programs** menu, unless you put it there previously. The easiest way to get started is to use the **Find** menu to search for the string "telnet." Once you've found it, double-click on it, and you should see a blank window which represents a terminal screen containing 80 columns and 24 rows of characters.

The top of the screen will have the menu choices shown in Figure 8-1.

Figure 8-1: Telnet menus

Most of your dealings with Telnet will occur in the **Connect** menu (shown selected). The highlighted item, **Remote System**, is where you should go to begin a connection to a remote system. Select that menu item and you should see the dialog box shown in Figure 8-2. Type in the name or address of the computer you want to contact where it says **Host Name**, and click **Connect**. Telnet remembers the last host to which you connected, so your dialog box may have **Host Name** already filled in. If it is, you can select the name with your mouse and type over it. For now, you can ignore all the other features of this box; we will get to the rest in due course.

For example, let's say you found NASA Spacelink in the Aeronautics and Astronautics section of the *Resource Catalog* in the back of this book, and wanted to check it out. It tells you to **telnet** to **spacelink.msfc.nasa.gov** and login as **guest**. You need to click the **Host Name** entry area and type **spacelink.msfc.nasa.gov**, then click **Connect**. Don't worry if the computer's name doesn't fit into the entry area. As you type, the beginning of the name will disappear as you add more characters. The entire name is still there; the box is just too small. Your computer will contact the spacelink computer and reward you with the screen shown in Figure 8-3.

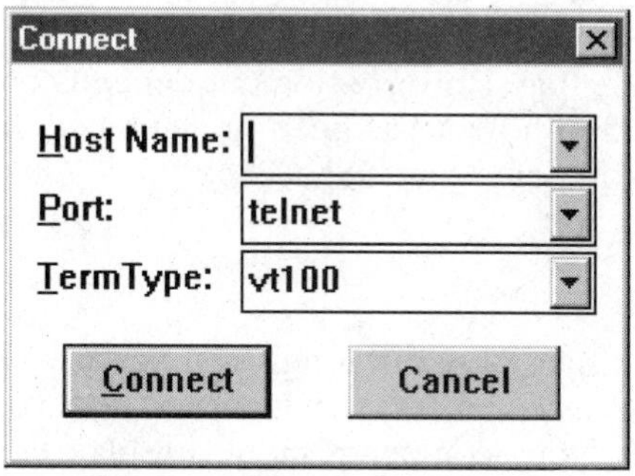
Connect
Host Name:
Port:
telnet
TermType:
vt100
Connect
Cancel

Figure 8-2: Connect dialog box

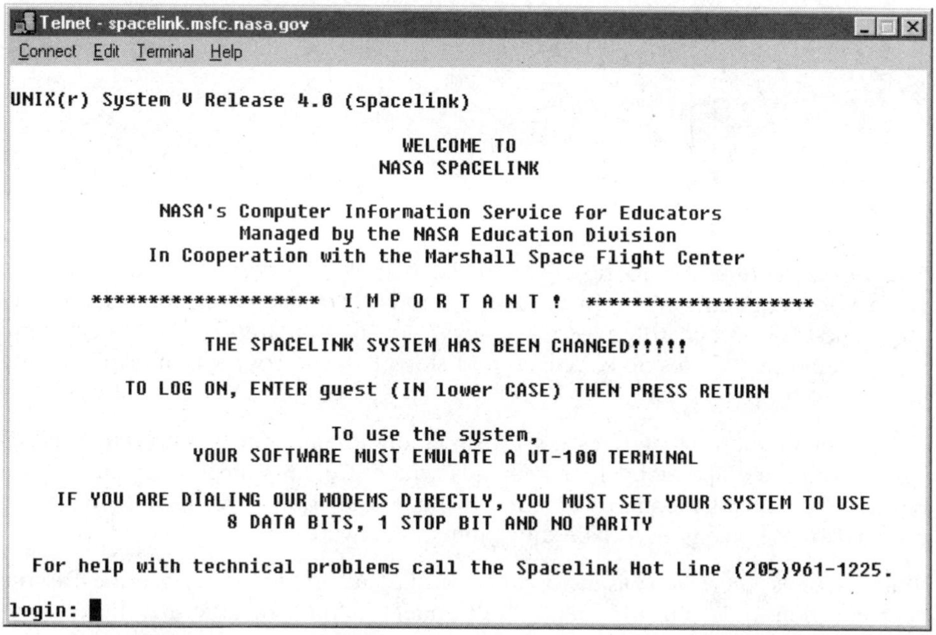
Telnet - spacelink.msfc.nasa.gov
Connect Edit Terminal Help
UNIX(r) System V Release 4.0 (spacelink)
WELCOME TO
NASA SPACELINK
NASA's Computer Information Service for Educators
Managed by the NASA Education Division
In Cooperation with the Marshall Space Flight Center
******************** I M P O R T A N T ! ********************
THE SPACELINK SYSTEM HAS BEEN CHANGED!!!!!
TO LOG ON, ENTER guest (IN lower CASE) THEN PRESS RETURN
To use the system,
YOUR SOFTWARE MUST EMULATE A VT-100 TERMINAL
IF YOU ARE DIALING OUR MODEMS DIRECTLY, YOU MUST SET YOUR SYSTEM TO USE
8 DATA BITS, 1 STOP BIT AND NO PARITY
For help with technical problems call the Spacelink Hot Line (205)961-1225.
login:

Figure 8-3: Remote connection made

Once you make this connection, anything you type into this window gets sent to the spacelink computer. So you are no longer using Windows 95 commands; you have to use whatever commands happen to be supported by the remote system. Since this is a public service site, the system has been set up to lead you through in a way that doesn't require much prior knowledge. The first thing you need to do is log in with the login name the resource catalog specified, **guest**. (If you read the introductory screen, which is always a good idea, it tells you the same information). Type **guest**, followed by a carriage return, and you are on your way.

Quitting a Connection

Quitting is a bit more of a problem than connecting. How you log out depends on what kind of computer the remote system is, and how it has been programmed. If you are lucky, the remote system will give you some hints. Spacelink does. After you have read the introductory pages of Spacelink:

```
Press ? for Help, q to Quit
```

will appear at the bottom of the screen. This is fairly typical. It tells you that if you need help about how to proceed, enter a question mark; if you want to leave, type **q**. If you are successful at logging out, your computer should display the message shown in Figure 8-4.

Figure 8–4: Logout successful

The words "connection to host lost" make it look like something went wrong; when you're quitting, it's normal. Your computer doesn't know what the logout command is. It just merrily passes whatever you type to the remote system, until that system sees this magic command and stops talking. Your system is just telling you that it stopped.

If the system you're using does not give you any hints about how to quit, there is a set of more or less standard commands which are sometimes recognized. In a pinch, you might try some of the following words: **quit**, **bye**, **logout**, **logoff**; or press CTRL-d. Remember to type the commands lowercase!

If all else fails, there is a distinctly antisocial last resort. This is to use the **Disconnect** selection under our old friend, the **Connect** menu. In Figure 8-1, this is shadowed because you are not connected anywhere. Once you make a connection, you are allowed to select **Disconnect**. Using **Disconnect** is the equivalent of hanging up the phone on the remote computer. It will eventually figure out that you have gone away, but it may not end the session gracefully. If you were entering information, you may lose some or all of the work you did. If you're being billed for your connection time, the meter will continue running until the remote machine figures out that you've gone. Use **Disconnect** only as a last resort, not as a standard operating procedure.

That's really all that Telnet is: a tool that lets you log in to remote computers. In the course of this chapter, we'll discuss a number of fancy options, and you'll see that you can use Telnet to access some special-purpose servers with their own behavior. But the simple Telnet operation shown above, along with an account on the remote computer, is all you need to get started.

Logging in to Private Accounts

Telnet can also be used to connect to private computers that you have permission to use. This is done in the same manner as our example above, although usually the login name will not be **guest** or something obvious, but your name or some seemingly garbage string like **ajzxmvk**. The remote system will also ask you for a password before it lets you in.

Once you do gain entry, there probably won't be a nice user interface to help you along. You might even be plopped into a command-line interface to something as arcane as UNIX. So, if your collaborator tells you to Telnet to his workstation to check something out, make sure she gives you enough information to get the job done. At the very least, you'll need a login name (account name) and a password.

Non-Standard Telnet Servers

Earlier, I mentioned that Telnet is often used to access special-purpose servers. Here's why. If I were writing an application, and I would be happy with the VT-100-style connection that the Telnet protocol supports, why not use Telnet as the client and write a special server that does what I want? All I have to do is make the server talk the Telnet protocol. On the positive side, it saves me the trouble of distributing a special client program to everyone who is going to use my application. It also gives the users an interface with which they are already familiar: anything that works with Telnet will work with the new application. On the negative side, it means that the server is virtually dedicated to the single application: anyone who Telnets to it will, by default, end up in my application.

To you, it also means that when you connect to a computer using Telnet, you won't get the normal login prompt. You get whatever the writer of the service wanted to give you: you may start out right in the middle of some application. So, you need to approach these services with a bit of caution. Here are a few notes to keep in mind when dealing with one of these beasties:

- Almost every special-purpose server is different. Some have good user interfaces; some have horrible user interfaces. What you get is what you get. Most have help facilities (some useful, some not so useful).

- Many servers will ask for a terminal type of some sort when you enter. If you look back at Figure 8-2, you will see that the Telnet software's **TermType** field is set to **vt100** by default; so when the server asks, tell it you are using a VT100.[*] If it complains about VT100 or does strange things, then fall back to

---

[*] Digital Equipment Corporation VT100 terminals were the industry standard for many years when people bought terminals. Now, every terminal emulation package knows how to act like one.

hardcopy or **dumb**. The only thing you will probably lose is the ability to move the cursor around. Some servers don't ask—they probably assume you are using a VT100 automatically.

- On their first screen, most servers will tell you how to log out, or terminate your session. Look for this information when you start a session; it will keep you from getting stuck. Of course, you can always use **Disconnect** (under the **Connection** menu) if you get in a real bind.

Telnet to Non-Standard Ports

There is a way to allow a Telnet client to access a service other than standard remote login without dedicating a computer to it. To understand how it works, you must understand how the same computer can offer WWW, e-mail, and network news and keep the services separate. This is accomplished by assigning each server a specific port number as identification.* When a client program wants to connect to some service, it must specify both the address (to get to a particular machine) and a port number (to get to a particular service on that machine). Frequently used applications have standard port numbers. If you refer back to Figure 8-2 again, you will see the Telnet program assumed you wanted to connect to the port called **telnet**. The **telnet** port is port 23. The standard port numbers for other services are built into this Telnet client; you can view them by clicking on the down arrow. To use an alternate port, choose one of the standard names from the list, or type the port number directly into the entry box.

Now, we can see how to use a standard client for another application—all we need is some way to make use of another port number. Private applications have to use an unassigned port that the client and server agree upon. If we write our non-standard server and tell it to listen to some other port (for example, port 10001), and if we can tell users to connect their Telnet client to port 10001 on our machine, we're home free. We've already seen this concept in another context: the World Wide Web's standard port is port 80, but many servers require you to use a special port number (often, 8080).

There are many non-standard Telnet applications scattered around the Internet. When applications are provided over non-standard ports, the documentation about the service (or the person telling you to use it) must tell you which port to use. For example, let's try to use the Weather Underground, which provides access to weather information for cities across the United States. Its entry in the *Resource Catalog* looks like:

```
Access:  telnet madlab.sprl.umich.edu 3000
```

This tells you to "connect to the computer named **madlab.sprl.umich.edu** using Telnet, but don't use the default port (23); use port 3000 instead." To access this

---

* These are "virtual" ports that are used by software to differentiate between various communications streams. Don't confuse them with terminal ports, SCSI ports, etc., which are actual hardware plugs.

service you must you click on the **Host Name** field and fill it in as before; then, you click on the **Port** field and enter 3000. Figure 8-5 shows the dialog box to access this service:

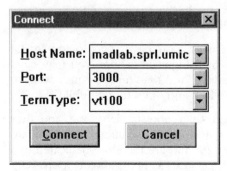

Figure 8-5: Selecting the Weather Underground

When you click on the **Connect** button you will be rewarded with the Weather Underground, shown in Figure 8-6.

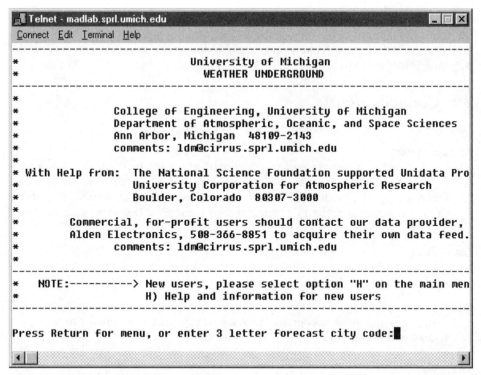

Figure 8-6: Weather Underground connected

There are two things worth noting about this session. First, rather than receiving the usual login prompt, you ended up right in the middle of an application. Every non-standard server has its own set of commands. You need to read the screens carefully to learn how to use them. Most servers tell you fairly early in the session how to log out and how to access its help facility. In this case, you enter a carriage return to get to the main menu and then an **H** to get to help information.

Second, because you never saw a login prompt, you never had to log in. Of course, the non-standard server can have its own login procedure; you may need to register with some authority to use the service, and that authority may want to bill you for your usage. But many services are free and open to the public.

In this example, we used Telnet to connect to a non-standard port and thus accessed a special service. In practice, you will see both solutions: non-standard Telnet servers that use the standard port (port 23) and are therefore dedicated to a particular task, and non-standard servers that use a non-standard port. Our *Resource Catalog*, and other databases of network resources, tell you when a non-standard port is necessary.

Telnet Program Options

We've discussed the most common ways of using the Windows 95 Telnet program, but there are a number of other features and options you might find useful from time to time. All of these features are available under the pull-down menus on the standard Telnet window.

The Connect *Menu*

You should be fairly familiar with the **Connect** menu by now.

Remote System

Used to select a remote system to which you want to connect. This is discussed at length in the text, but there is one thing to note. The Windows 95 Telnet program can only have one conversation going at a time. If you are already connected and you connect again, it forces a **Disconnect** of your current host before connecting to the new one.

Disconnect

Used to disconnect from a remote system in an emergency. It may cause some adverse effects on the remote system.

Exit

Terminates the Telnet program. Another way to exit is to press the keys ALT and F4 at the same time.

Recent Host List

Telnet keeps track of the last ten hosts you have visited and lists them under **Exit** on the **Connections** menu. If you look at Figure 8-1 again, you will see we have recently visited two hosts: **ux1.cso.uiuc.edu** and **uxh.cso.uiuc.edu**. If you want to go back to one of these places again, you can select it on this menu and bypass the **Remote Systems** dialog box.

The Edit *Menu*

The **Edit** menu shares many of the same functions as the edit menu of every other Windows application.

Copy
> Places a copy of the text you have previously selected with the mouse in a temporary area. If you like, you can then switch to a different application, and insert the selected text into a field.

Paste
> Copies whatever is in the temporary area (placed there with a previous **Copy** or **Cut** command) to the computer you are connected to in that window. It is as if you typed whatever text you are pasting to the remote system.

Select All
> Selects all the text that the Telnet program remembers. This includes what is shown on the screen and whatever has scrolled off the top, but is still in memory. The amount of text stored in memory is determined by the **Buffer Size** preference, discussed later. The entire window will change to reverse video as you click and drag through it with a mouse. You can then use the **Copy** menu to insert the text into another place.

The Terminal *Menu*

Since Telnet is an application which turns your computer into a terminal, the **Terminal** menu is the place where you make changes in how your computer acts locally.

Preferences
> Allows you to set default values for how your computer behaves when it connects to a remote system. Figure 8-7 shows the **Preferences** dialog box. In the area **Terminal Options**, you may select **Local Echo** by clicking its check box. Echoing is the process by which the characters you type appear on your screen. Usually, the remote computer is responsible for sending the character back to your terminal after it receives it. Hence, most of the time this option should remain unchecked. This is called remote echoing, and is generally considered more reliable, because you know that the remote system is receiving your keystrokes correctly. Local echoing means that the local computer (in this case, the Telnet client) sends the characters you type back to the display screen. It has the same effect as the half/full duplex switch on modems and computer terminals, if you have any experience with them.

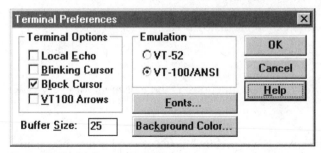

Figure 8–7: Preferences menu

How do you know whether local echoing should be on or off? If local echoing is turned off and it should be on, any characters you type won't be echoed; you won't see the commands you send to the remote system, but you will see the output from these commands. In this case, check the **Local Echo** option. If local echoing is turned on and it should be off, you'll see every character you type twice. In this case, you should uncheck the option.

Blinking Cursor and **Block Cursor** refers to how the application will call your attention to the typing point on the screen. You can set these as you like; what you do will not affect the performance of the program.

VT100 Arrows allows you to choose what character codes your computer sends when you press one of the four arrow keys to the right of the ENTER key. Start with this box unchecked; this will work fine on most Internet hosts. If the arrow keys don't seem to be doing the right thing, or if something like ^[[A appears when you press them, try checking this box and seeing if it helps.

Buffer Size controls how many lines of text the program will remember. It can take a value between 25 and 400, even though Telnet can only display 24 lines on the screen. If you set it to a value greater than 25, a scroll bar will appear on the right hand side of the terminal window. You can use that scroll bar to go back to text which has disappeared off the top of your screen.

The **Emulation** area allows you to specify the kind of terminal your Telnet client will mimic. This is used to fill in the **TermType** field in the **Connect** dialog box (Figure 8-2) whenever you try to connect to a host. I can't think of a situation where you will go wrong on the Internet leaving this set to *VT100/ANSI.*

The rest of the **Preferences** options are fairly obvious. **Fonts** and **Color** allow you to change the appearance of the text and background displayed. **OK** and **Cancel** allow you to update your **Preferences** to whatever you've set in this dialog box, or throw away any changes you have made since you entered this dialog box. Finally, **Help** will get you some help on all of these options.

Start Logging

Brings up the dialog box shown in Figure 8-8. This dialog allows you to specify a filename where everything displayed in the Telnet terminal window will be saved for your future enjoyment. For example, if you find a document on a remote computer that you really want to copy, but there seems no way to send a copy to yourself, you can start a log file and type the file on the screen. You can also do this by making the file buffer size huge and pasting the entire buffer into a file—but that doesn't work if the file is over 400 lines long. Logging places no limits on the amount saved.

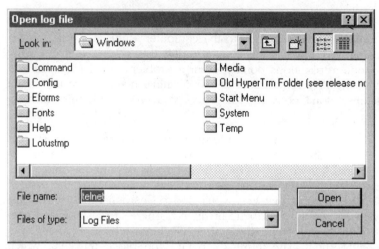

Figure 8-8: Logging dialog

The top half of the screen allows you to move about in the directory structure of your computer's files to decide where the file will reside. The **File name** area is where you specify the name the file will take. Once you have specified where and the name, click **Open** and logging will commence. Note that logging starts with the very next thing sent or received by your computer. Things already displayed on the screen will not be saved.

Stop Logging

Appears to do little. It stops the logging function that you started with **Start Logging**. It will give you no confirmation, so don't be concerned if you select it and nothing appears to happen. Note that your log file could become huge if you forget to stop logging when you're done.

The Help *Menu*

The **Help** menu is your standard Windows 95 help menu. There is nothing tricky or Telnet-specific about it.

Telneting to IBM Mainframes

If you've used computers for very long, you've probably come to expect IBM mainframes to exhibit their own behaviors, just to confuse the rest of the world. Telnet is no exception. As far as Telnet is concerned, we can divide IBM applications into two classes: line-mode applications and 3270 (or full-screen) applications. We'll consider each of them separately; unfortunately, the application you need to use these full-screen IBM applications is not included with Windows 95. You may discover there is something you want to do, but can't, with the standard software.

First, line-mode applications are more or less what you're used to. "Line mode" means that the terminal sends characters to the computer a line at a time. This is the way most common terminals behave, and it's the way Telnet normally behaves. So line-mode applications don't present a problem. You might have to check **Local Echo** in the **Preferences** area of the **Terminal** menu, since line-mode applications sometimes don't echo the characters you type. With this warning, you're all set.

Now for 3270 applications, which are (unfortunately) nowhere near as simple. First, what does "3270" mean? For a long time, IBM computers have used a proprietary full-screen terminal known as a 3270.[*] The 3270 was designed to make data entry (filling in forms, etc.) easier for the user and less of a load on the system. Therefore, it has many features that you won't find on garden-variety terminals: protected fields, numeric fields, alphabetic fields, etc. There are also several special-purpose keys, notably programmed function (PF) keys, which may have special commands tied to them. The terminal operates on block transfers, which means that it doesn't send anything to the host until you press either ENTER or a PF key; when you do, it sends a compressed image of the screen changes since the last transmission. Obviously, then, a 3270 application is going to require some special handling. It is usually possible to use a 3270 application in line mode, but it will be pretty unpleasant.

To use a 3270 application on its own terms, you really need a terminal emulator that can make your system act like a 3270 terminal. In many cases, the IBM mainframe that you're connected to will provide the terminal emulation itself. In this case, you can use Telnet to connect to the computer. When Telnet connects, the mainframe will ask you what kind of terminal you are using. After you tell the system your terminal type, you're ready to go.

---

[*] Actually, there are a whole series of 3270-class terminals with a variety of characteristics (screen width, etc.). The original terminal was called a 3270; later, improved versions were known by model numbers like 3278 or 3279. So if some documentation talks about "emulating a 3278," it refers to a particular flavor of the 3270 emulation that we're discussing.

If the host you contact does not provide some kind of 3270 emulation, you need to use a special version of Telnet that has an emulator built in. This version is frequently called tn3270. First, how do you know when you need tn3270? If you **telnet** to a system and see a message like this:

```
VM/XA SP ONLINE-PRESS ENTER KEY TO BEGIN SESSION.
```

you know you're talking to an IBM mainframe. Two flags should provides clues. One is the string "VM" in the message (or, it might say "MVS"); these are the names of IBM operating systems. The other clue is that the message is entirely in capital letters, which is common in IBM-land. (Of course, there are other operating systems that do all their work with uppercase letters.) In this case, you should be able to use the computer system with regular Telnet, but it will be cumbersome; tn3270 will probably work better.

You should also try tn3270 if something funny happens to your session:

```
Connection closed by foreign host.
```

Telnet managed to connect to the remote system, but something went wrong, and the remote system gave up. In this example, the remote system is so entrenched in the 3270's features that it quit and closed the connection when it found you were not using them. (Note: Many things can cause a connection to close immediately; this is only one of them.)

If you suspect that you require a 3270 emulation package, there is nothing you can do to operate in this manner until you get another software application.

CHAPTER NINE

MOVING FILES: FTP

Introducing Windows 95 FTP
Anonymous FTP
Browsing on a Remote Machine
Moving Files in Private Accounts
ASCII and Binary Transfers
Handling Large Files and Groups of Files
A More Friendly FTP
FTP Over the Web
Hints, Advice, and Problems
File Retrieval Using E-Mail

FTP is the acronym for "File Transfer Protocol." As the name implies, the protocol's job is to move files from one computer to another. It doesn't matter where the computers are located, how they are connected, or even whether they use the same operating system. Provided that both computers can "talk" the FTP protocol and have access to the Internet, you can use the FTP application to transfer files. Some of the nuances of its use do change with each operating system, but the basic command structure is the same from machine to machine.

Perhaps even more than Telnet, FTP can be considered ancient history. The Windows 95 FTP client betrays FTP's origins in the early days of the ARPAnet. There are better options around, and we discuss one at the end of this chapter. But even with modern clients, FTP begs the question: Why do I care? Can't I get any file I want with a Web browser? The answer, for the most part, is yes. WWW browsers let you access FTP archives with their familiar "point and click" interface. But there are a few things you can do with FTP that you can't do otherwise:

- You can upload files from your system to another system. (Of course, the other system needs to supply a place to put those files.) Although a "put" command is part of the HTTP protocol, I've yet to see a WWW browser that implements it.

- You can get large batches of files with one command. If you want a large batch of stuff, using FTP is a lot easier than clicking on (and saving) a dozen separate files. In fact, on a popular site that limits access to a certain number of users, you might find that getting a dozen files with a Web browser is nearly impossible. Before you're done, someone else will log in and the system won't serve you any more. That doesn't happen with FTP. (It doesn't even happen if you don't use a separate command for each file; all your transfers are done in a single FTP session with the server.)

- FTP is also more convenient for accessing "private" accounts—i.e., your personal files. You can build a username into a WWW URL and supply your password to get at your own files, but it isn't convenient.

FTP is a complex program because there are many different ways to manipulate files. Different ways of storing files (binary or ASCII, compressed or uncompressed, etc.) introduce complications. First, we'll discuss anonymous FTP, which is a special service that lets you access public databases without obtaining an account. Most public archives provide anonymous FTP access, which means that you can get files from the archive without arranging for a login name and an account in advance. Next, we'll look at moving files in private accounts for which you have a password. We'll discuss some common cases (accessing VMS, VM, DOS, or Macintosh systems) which require some special handling. Finally, we'll look at how to transfer files through e-mail (a service called **ftpmail**).

Introducing Windows 95 FTP

FTP is usually hidden in the *c:\windows* directory on a normally installed Windows 95 computer, and perhaps it should stay there. It pops up in the window shown in Figure 9-1, but has only limited Windows functionality; its window isn't even scrollable. At the top of the window are a number of buttons that let you cut and paste, and change fonts. However, when it comes down to the nitty-gritty of moving a file, you have to type a series of commands, just as you would have ten years ago. The commands you type will appear on the last line of the window following the string ftp>. As you type commands and FTP responds, you will fill the window from top to bottom. When the screen fills up, your earlier commands will roll off the top file screen, and you will be typing on the last line.

Before we get to those commands, let's look at the top menu bar of the FTP window shown in more detail:

Size pulldown menu
  This allows you to change the font size of the window. It will normally come up as **Auto**, meaning it picks a font depending on the window size.

Select
  Used to point out text to be copied later. To use it, click **Select** and drag the mouse across the text you want to select.

Copy
  Takes text previously selected and moves it to the temporary clipboard, so that you can paste it somewhere else.

Paste
  Takes text previously copied on the clipboard and pastes it at the current prompt. You cannot arbitrarily **Paste** text at a random point in the FTP

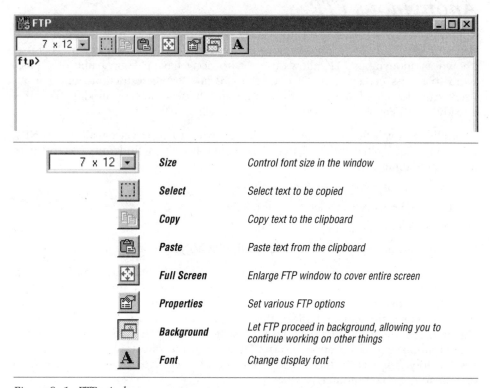

Figure 9–1: FTP window

window, because the computer is trying to read commands you type on the bottom line. You can use **Paste** most effectively to copy filenames into *your* FTP commands.

Full Screen
Enlarges the FTP window to cover the whole screen.

Properties
Allows you to examine and configure a number of program parameters, such as whether it should allow a screen saver to take over if you leave it idle. Normally, you should never have to muck around in here.

Background
Sometimes FTP transfers take a long time. Clicking this button lets the transfer proceed while you do other things on the computer.

Font
Allows you more complete control of the display than the **Size** pulldown menu; here, you're also allowed to change the font.

Anonymous FTP

The most frequent use of FTP is to contact public repositories of files on the Internet, and move a copy of one or more of them to your home computer. This use, known as anonymous FTP, allows users who don't have a login name or a password to access certain files. Of course, there are strong restrictions: anonymous users can download files, but they can't install new files or modify files that already exist.* Finally, there are strict limits on which files they can copy.

Typically, you will find out about the file you want to copy via e-mail or USENET, or through an Archie index search. No matter how you find out, you need to know three things:

- The name of a computer containing the file
- The file directory in which the file resides
- The name of the file

With this information, you can download the file to your computer.

Let's say you received a message from a friend that said, "grab the file *pkunzip.exe* in *NSF/genpubs* on **stis.nsf.gov**." Or perhaps your friend's message says: "Get **ftp://stis.nsf.gov/NSF/genpubs/pkunzip.exe**." Your friend is not trying to be obtuse; these messages are actually typical. But what do the messages mean, and how do you translate them into actions? The translation is simple: "Go to the computer named **stis.nsf.gov** using anonymous FTP, look in the directory *NSF*, then in the subdirectory *genpubs*. In there, you'll find the file *pkunzip.exe* which you should download to your computer."

Putting our translation into action is a bit more complex. Figure 9-2 shows what needs to be done. The first line begins "ftp>," which means that FTP is waiting for you to type a command. We start our FTP session by typing **open**, followed by the name of the computer (**stis.nsf.gov**) and a carriage return. FTP responds with "Connected to . . . ," which means that you found the computer and it's willing to talk. It then asks for your username, with the cryptic string "User (x.nsf.gov)(none)):", to which we respond **anonymous**. This is where anonymous FTP comes into play.

FTP responds by asking for a password. Of course, since you don't have a real account, you don't have a real password, either. That's OK; because you gave **anonymous** as your login name, FTP will accept any string as your password. It is considered good form to use your e-mail address as the password, so that the managers of the server have some idea who is using it, and can contact you if necessary. So, dutifully after the prompt "Password:" you type your e-mail address. It doesn't echo because FTP treats it as any other password, and doesn't print it for

---

* An archive manager can create directories that can be written by anonymous FTP users. Such directories are often used to let people submit articles or software for inclusion in an archive. If the archive manager has set up an incoming anonymous FTP directory, you can use FTP's **put** and **mput** commands to place files there.

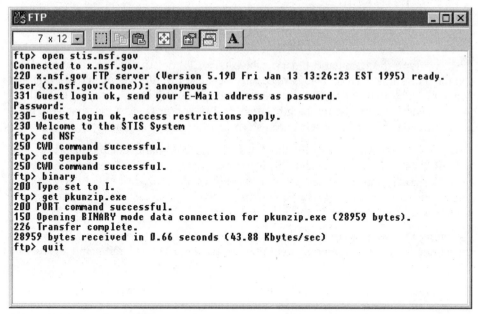

Figure 9–2: Anonymous FTP example

security reasons. After signing in as **anonymous**, you are allowed to see and retrieve only those files which are expressly permitted to the anonymous FTPers.

Finally, you are connected and welcomed with the message:[*]

    Guest login ok, access restrictions apply.

Now, position yourself in the proper file directory by using **cd**, the change directory command. Your friend's message told you to move down two levels of directories. First, we move to one called *NSF*, and then to the subdirectory *genpubs*. So we issue two separate **cd** commands (**cd NSF** and **cd genpubs**), each of which evokes the following response:

    CWD command successful

telling us it all worked fine.

We could have done all of this in one command; **cd NSF/genpubs** moves directly down two levels.[†] It has the same effect as the two separate commands, but it's

---

* Don't be confused by other messages. "Guest login ..." is the standard message you will always get. The "Welcome to STIS ..." is a message which the manager of this particular site decided to send you. It will vary from place to place.

† Note the "creeping UNIXism"; you use the "slash" character to separate directories in FTP even though we are doing this on a Windows 95 computer where you would expect to use the DOS backslash.

more convenient. It takes a bit longer to issue two commands. On the other hand, if you mistype something in the longer command, the whole command will be rejected and you will have to retype the whole thing. The whole directory string must be correct before any change is made.

Next, we type the command **binary**, which tells FTP not to change anything about the file as it's transferred. This is necessary because the file we are transferring is a program to be executed. (The file ending *.exe* should have clued you in to this.) We'll discuss this at greater length later on, but for now, assume that you must issue the binary command before transferring a file that isn't plain text.

Finally, you're ready to transfer the file with the command **get pkunzip.exe**. FTP tells us it is starting to transfer 28949 bytes (characters). You may have to wait here, depending on the speed of your Internet connection, but eventually, you are rewarded with the message "28949 bytes received." Success! The file *pkunzip.exe* should be waiting for you in the *C:\windows* directory.

Assuming that was the only file you wanted, issue the **quit** command. This closes the connection to the remote computer, stops the FTP program, and deletes its window.

FTP is fairly verbose; it gives you a lot of information about what it's doing. Unfortunately, the messages are rather arcane and inconsistent; FTP was designed before "user-friendliness" was invented. All of the messages begin with a "message number," which is eminently ignorable. However, the message texts (arcane though they may be) are worth scanning.

Remember, when you are using anonymous FTP, you are a guest on someone else's system. Sometimes, there will be usage restrictions posted:

```
230-Available for anonymous FTP only between 5 pm EST
230-and 8 am EST.
```

These are displayed when you first log in. Please observe them—if you don't, the server might become disabled for everyone.

The **get** command can also rename a file while transferring it. Imagine that you already have *pkunzip.exe*, but you've heard that there's a new version with some new features. You don't want to clobber the old version when you get the new one, since you don't know that the new one works yet. This command names your copy of file *pkunzip2.exe*:

```
ftp> get pkunzip.exe pkunzip2.exe
```

It's essentially like a DOS **COPY** command except the first file happens to be on some other computer. You can also **put** one of your files on a remote system, possibly renaming it in the process. **put** works as you'd expect:

```
ftp> put local-file
```

or, if you want to give the file a new name:

```
ftp> put local-file remote-file-name
```

Of course, you can't put a file onto a remote system unless you have permission to do so; with anonymous FTP, that usually won't be the case. However, some site managers create a directory (usually called *incoming*) where users can put contributions for the archive. (Note: Often, the *incoming* directory is set up so you can download the files in there but can't take them out until the system administrator moves them elsewhere.) **put** is more useful when you have a personal account on the remote system, which we'll discuss shortly.

Browsing on a Remote Machine

When you are using FTP, you may not have all the information about what files you want and where they are located. You usually need to browse around to figure out what you want to transfer and where it resides. There are a few useful commands and techniques to allow this. The basic commands to list directory information on the remote machine are **dir** and **ls**. Both commands have the same format:

```
ftp> dir directory-name local-file-name
ftp> ls directory-name local-file-name
```

Both commands list the files in directory *directory-name* on the remote machine, putting their output into a local file. Both arguments are optional. The second argument (the *local-file-name*) tells FTP to put the listing into the given filename on the local system. If you want the listing to appear on your terminal rather than saving it in a file, just omit this argument. Since that is what you usually want, the *local-file-name* argument is rarely used.

The first argument, *directory-name*, gives the name of the directories or files that you want listed. If it is omitted, FTP lists all the files in the current remote directory. If it contains what appears to be a complete file name, FTP will only tell you if that file exists.

A fairly common way of using the **ftp dir** command is to include "wildcard" characters in the first argument. This allows you to request a partial list of files, e.g., "all files ending in the extension *.txt*." However, there are no easy rules for wildcards; the wildcards are interpreted according to the rules of the remote system to which you have connected. Therefore, their meaning will differ somewhat, depending on what kind of computer you are trying to browse. Luckily, on *most* computer systems, the asterisk (*) is a wildcard that matches any group of characters. For example, on many machines the command:

```
ftp> dir test*
```

lists only files whose names begin with *test*. The biggest difference between systems is whether a wildcard can match across a period in the name. If the remote computer is running the UNIX operating system, it can; *test** would match filenames like *test.txt* and *test.exe*, in addition to filenames like *test1* and *testout*. (Under UNIX, there is no formal difference between a "name" and an "extension." A period may occur anywhere in a file name, even multiple times. It is just another character in a UNIX file name.) On remote computers running the VAX/VMS operating system, or any running the MS-DOS operating system, the filename and extension are considered different entities, so we would expect *test** to match only files without extensions (like *test1* and *testout*). However, that's not the whole story. Many servers on VMS and DOS machines interpret a wildcard without an explicit extension to have the extension .*. That is, the name *test** is interpreted as *test*.** (match any name starting with *test*, with any extension). Note that you can use a wildcard in either the name, the extension, or both. Therefore, you can use names like *test** to match files beginning with *test* with no extension. This sounds awfully confusing but—in practice—what you think is right usually *is* right. Remember to watch for the occasional surprise, and you'll be fine.

Now, back to the basic listing commands, **ls** and **dir**. Their output should be quite different. **ls**, by default, gives you a simplified listing of filenames with no additional information. It should look something like this:

```
ftp> ls
150 Opening ASCII mode data connection for file list.
nsfnet
CIC
campus
scott
```

The **dir** command produces more complete information:

```
ftp> dir
150 Opening ASCII mode data connection for /bin/ls.
total 2529
-rw-------   1 krol     cso      110 Oct 31 08:18 .Xauthority
-rw-r--r--   1 krol     cso      821 Nov 21 15:11 .cshrc
drw-------   1 krol     cso       68 Mar  4  1994 archive
```

This is a very common format for a directory output. It is produced on a UNIX computer; there are scads of them as FTP servers across the Internet. The name of the file is all the way on the right end of each line (file names *.Xauthority*, *.cshrc*, and *archive*). The left-hand string of characters and dashes are file status indicators, most of which you can ignore. The leading character is important: the *d* on the line listing *archive* means that *archive* is a directory. Therefore, you can **cd archive** to move down one level into the *archive* directory.

You can never be sure what the output of a **dir** command will look like until you try it. The output of this command looks like a full directory listing on the remote system. So, if you are connected to a computer running the VMS operating system, it will look like the output from a VMS **direct** command. If you are connected to a UNIX machine, it will look like the output from the **ls –lga** command. This is

because the client tells the server to send the directory information; the server exe-
cutes an appropriate command, and then sends the listing back to the client,
untouched.*

The ultimate in directory commands, which only works if the remote system is
running UNIX, is **ls −lR**. This is a "recursive" listing; it lists all the files in the current directory and, if there are subdirectories, lists the files in them, too. It continues until it has exhausted the subdirectories of the subdirectories, listing just about
every file you can get to with FTP. Output from **ls −lR** looks like this:

```
ftp> ls -lR
200 PORT command successful.
150 Opening ASCII mode data connection for /bin/ls.
total 2529
-rw-------  1 krol   cso    110 Oct 31 08:18 .Xauthority
-rw-r--r--  1 krol   cso    821 Nov 21 15:11 .cshrc
drwx------  3 krol   cso    512 Oct  3  1989 iab
-rw-r--r--  1 krol   cso   2289 Jan  5 12:34 index

iab:                        contents of iab directory above
total 51
-rw-r--r--  1 krol   cso  25164 Sep  1  1989 crucible
-rw-r--r--  1 krol   cso  14045 Oct  3  1989 iab
drwx------  3 krol   cso   1024 Jan  3  1990 ietf
-rw-------  1 krol   cso  10565 May 15  1989 inarc

iab/ietf:                   contents of subdirectory ietf of iab
total 416
-rw-r--r--  1 krol   cso  24663 Jan 17  1990 agenda
drwxr-xr-x  2 krol   cso    512 Jul 13  1989 reports

iab/ietf/reports:
total 329
-rw-r--r--  1 krol   cso  46652 Jul 13  1989 jun89
-rw-r--r--  1 krol   cso  53905 May 11  1989 mar89
-rw-r--r--  1 krol   cso  53769 Jun 15  1989 may89
-rw-------  1 krol   cso  47429 Dec 15  1988 nov88

226 Transfer complete.
```

Be careful: it may produce large amounts of output. Since this FTP client doesn't
have the ability to scroll the window back, it is a good idea to save the results of **ls
−lR** in a file with the command:

```
ftp> ls -lR filename
```

Now, you can do a few **dir** commands and see some files which are likely candidates to **get**, but you're still not sure exactly which file you want. You could **get**
the file, switch to another window and list it. If you find out that the file isn't what

---

* If you find yourself on some other kind of computer, you may find the implementers of
FTP were lazy and just made the **ls** command a synonym for **dir**.

you want, flip back to the FTP window and **get** again, list again . . . but that would be a pain. You really want to see what's in the file before you decide which to transfer it. There is a limited ability to do this in FTP, by using a minus sign (–) instead of a destination filename:

```
ftp> get source-file -
```

For example, let's list the file *index*:

```
ftp> get index -
200 PORT command successful.
150 Opening ASCII mode connection for index (2289 bytes).
The following archives are available at this site:

activism    Files related to activism in general, NOT to any
            particular "cause."

...lines deleted ...

226 Transfer complete.
2289 bytes received in 0.41 seconds (5.5 Kbytes/s)
```

The problem with this technique is that the entire file is transferred to your terminal, which can be more than you want to see. One solution is to try to suspend the output with CTRL-s. Typing CTRL-s stops your computer from sending characters to the screen. To see more, type CTRL-q, which lets your computer continue. You do have to be quick and may not catch what you want, so this approach is really only useful for short files. A bigger problem is that if your file is binary, this command will only spray garbage all over your screen; it won't show you anything remotely useful.

Some FTP servers have the ability to send you a prerecorded message whenever you move into a directory. In the following snippet of a session, you logged into an anonymous FTP server, and issued the command **cd pub/nic**.

```
331 Guest login ok, send e-mail address as password.
Password: krol@ux1.cso.uiuc.edu
230 Guest login ok, access restrictions apply.
ftp> cd pub/nic  move to the directory
250-######WELCOME TO THE SURANET NETWORK INFORMATION CENTER###########
250-SURAnet                            info@sura.net
250-8400 Baltimore Blvd.               301-982-4600(voice)
250-College Park, Maryland  USA 20740-2498    FAX 301-982-4605
250-    Many of the documents available in this FTP archive are geared
250-towards the new user of the Internet. SURAnet has provided several
250-"How To" guides for network navigation tools such as telnet, FTP,
250-and e-mail. These "How To" guides are available in the directory
250 CWD command successful.
```

The server responded with a message (all the lines beginning 250).* This helpful hint is provided by the server's administrator; such hints are becoming increasingly common. It frees you from having to do a **dir** command to look for files (such as *README* or *index*), downloading them, and reading them as three separate steps.

NOTE

The FTP client that comes with Windows 95 sometimes has trouble with these automatic help messages. In particular, it sometimes fails to give you the entire message until you type the next command; the FTP client then spits out the rest of the help file. You can suppress this feature by prefixing your password with a minus sign (e.g., I would type **-krol@ux1.cso.uiuc.edu** rather than **krol@ux1.cso.uiuc.edu**). You can then read the comments manually, using **get .message -**.

There are a number of commands in FTP that can be used to deal with filesystem directories—probably more commands than you'd ever need to use. There are so many commands because two sets of directories are involved during an FTP session: the working directory on your local machine and the directory on the remote machine. We've already seen the **cd** command for changing your remote directory. Moving around the local directory is easy:

```
ftp> lcd directory
```

The usage rules for **lcd** are the same as for the DOS **cd** command except you use / rather than \. The rules can be summarized as follows:

- If no directory is given, **lcd** sets your position back to the default directory (*c:/windows*).
- If the directory starts with a slash (/), **lcd** moves you to the specified directory regardless of your current position (absolute positioning).
- If the directory is **..**, **lcd** moves you up one level from the directory at which you are currently positioned.
- If the directory starts with an alphanumeric character, **lcd** looks for the directory as a subdirectory of the current one.
- If you want to change drives, you must include a directory as well as a drive letter (i.e., **lcd a:** will not work, but **lcd a:/** will).

The rules for the **cd** command, which changes the directory on the remote computer, are similar. There are two differences. If you issue a **cd** command with no argument, FTP will prompt you for it:

```
ftp> cd
(remote-directory) █
```

---

* The initial message is stored in the file *.message*; you can see it in the directory listing.

To return to your initial directory (the directory FTP put you in when you started), give the command **cd /**. It's important to remember this command because it's easy (too easy) to get lost while poking around someone else's FTP archive. The command **pwd** will tell you what directory you're currently in; that's also important information:

```
ftp> pwd
/pub/goodies
```

Unfortunately, this often isn't as helpful as you might like. UNIX has the concept of a link, which is (basically) a way of giving directories two or more names. They're very convenient for the person trying to organize his files, but they do mean that, sometimes, the output from **pwd** will be an unexpected surprise. If you see something unexpected, go back to the beginning (**cd /**) and start over.

Moving Batches of Files

The **get** and **put** commands that we discussed earlier can only transfer one file at a time. However, the ability to transfer groups of files is one real advantage of FTP. To do so, you can use the **mput** and **mget** commands. They have the following syntax:

```
ftp> mput list of files
ftp> mget list of files
```

The **mput** command takes the files in the list and moves them to the remote system. The **mget** command moves files from the remote system to the local system. In both cases, the filenames will be the same on both the local and remote systems. The list of files can be arbitrarily long and can include wildcards.

The actual rules for how wildcards are expanded are fairly complicated. You can usually use an asterisk (*****) to match zero or more characters and forget about the complexities; you can use a question mark (**?**) to match any single character.[*] Here's a typical session using **mget** and **mput**:

```
ftp> cd work                       change the remote directory
250 CWD command successful.
ftp> ls b*                         see what files are there
200 PORT command successful.
150 ASCII data connection for /bin/ls (127.0.0.1,1129) (0 bytes).
b.tst
bash.help
bsdman.sh
```

---

[*] The actual rules go something like this: When you're using **mput**, you're moving files from your local system to the remote system. The wildcards are expanded by your local (Windows 95) system, and use Windows 95's wildcard rules. When you're using **mget**, you need to locate files on the remote system. In this case, FTP uses the remote system to see what, if anything, matches the wildcards. Therefore, the wildcard rules that **mput** and **mget** obey may differ, and **mget**'s rules depend on the remote system, which is probably running UNIX.

```
226 ASCII Transfer complete.
remote: b*
29 bytes received in 0.03 seconds (0.94 Kbytes/s)
ftp> mget b*                        try to transfer the files
mget b.tst? yes                     first file: do I really want it?
200 PORT command successful.
150 ASCII data connection for b.tst (127.0.0.1,1133) (68112 bytes).
226 ASCII Transfer complete.
local: b.tst remote: b.tst
81927 bytes received in 0.41 seconds (2e+02 Kbytes/s)
mget bash.help? no                  second file; do I really want it?
mget bsdman.sh? no                  third file; do I really want it?
```

Now, let's try to **put** a group of files. This time, I'll explicitly put two filenames on the command, just to show you that it can be done.

```
ftp> mput login tblsz.c             now try to put some files
mput login? yes                     first file: do I really want it?
200 PORT command successful.
150 ASCII data connection for login (127.0.0.1,1139).
226 Transfer complete.
local: login remote: login
2785 bytes sent in 0.03 seconds (91 Kbytes/s)
mput tblsz.c? y                     second file: do I really want it?
200 PORT command successful.
150 ASCII data connection for tblsz.c (127.0.0.1,1141).
226 Transfer complete.
local: tblsz.c remote: tblsz.c
975 bytes sent in 0.04 seconds (24 Kbytes/s)
ftp>
```

Note that the command we just gave, **mput login tblsz.c**, does *not* mean "put *login* on the remote system with the filename *tblsz.c*," as it would if it were a simple **put** command. It means "copy all the files on the command line to the remote system, in the current remote directory, without changing their names." Also, note that we've ignored an important issue: do you have permission to put files on the remote system? For anonymous FTP, the answer is usually "no," unless the remote sites administrator has created a special directory, often called *incoming*, where anonymous users can leave submissions.

For both **mget** and **input**, FTP normally asks you whether or not you want to transfer each file; you have to type **y** (or **yes**, or ENTER) to make the transfer.

Typing **n** (or **no**)[*] cancels the transfer. Being prompted for each file is annoying (particularly if you're transferring a large group of files), but it helps prevent mistakes. If you really dislike being prompted, or you need to transfer a huge group of files, give the command **prompt**; that disables prompting. The whole group of files will be transferred without further intervention. Giving the **prompt** command again re-enables prompting.

---

[*] Actually, anything that doesn't begin with the letter **y** is taken as a no.

Here are a few things to watch out for:

- Remember that you don't get to specify a name for the destination file. All the names on the command line are interpreted as source files. It's particularly tempting to try to copy a group of files into a directory; watch out for this! You cannot use a command like the following:

  ```
  ftp> mput ch*.txt book
  ```

  where *book* is the name of a remote directory. Instead, you must first use **cd** to change the remote directory.

  ```
  ftp> cd book
  ...
  ftp> mput ch*.txt
  ```

  The same goes for **mget** commands.

- You cannot use **mput** or **mget** (or, for that matter, the regular **get** and **put**) commands to copy a directory. You can only use them to copy groups of plain files. Copying a directory yields unpredictable results. Some servers have various "fake outs" that will "do the right thing" (sort of), but you can't count on that.

- You may find that **mget**, with wildcards, doesn't always work properly; it appears to depend on whether or not the **ls** command is implemented correctly by the remote FTP server. *Caveat emptor.*

Moving Files in Private Accounts

FTP also allows you to manipulate files in a private account; that is, an account for which you have a login name and password. This usage is similar to what we have looked at already with anonymous FTP, but there are far fewer restrictions. In particular, you can freely use the **put** and **mput** commands I've been teasing you with. It assumes that since you have access to a personal account, you can do anything to the files which that account would allow you to do if you were sitting directly in front of the computer the account is on.

When FTP makes the connection with the remote computer, it asks you to identify yourself with a login name and password (see Figure 9-3). With some operating systems, like DOS and the Macintosh OS, FTP may not ask for a password; it may only demand a login name, since there is no password security on the system. On these machines, protection from unwanted access is usually handled by disabling the FTP server software.

After the remote system has accepted your login name and password, you are ready to start transferring files. FTP prints "ftp>" to prompt you for further commands. In the following example, I start by logging into the machine **uxh.cso.uiuc.edu** under the name **krol**. I transfer the file *comments* from the

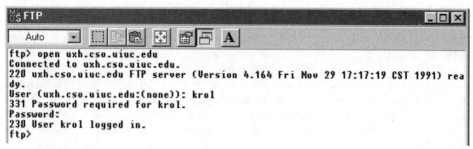

Figure 9–3: Signing on to a private account

machine **krol.cso.uiuc.edu** under login name **krol**'s default directory to the originating machine. Then I transfer the file *newver.txt* to **uxh.cso.uiuc.edu**, renaming
the new copy to *readthis* (as shown in Figure 9-4):

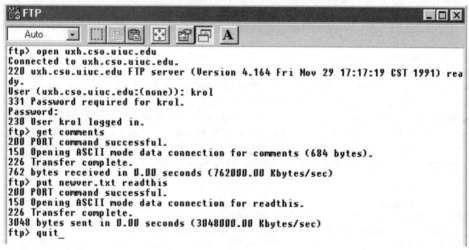

Figure 9–4: File transfer examples

ASCII and Binary Transfers

Now that you can move around and find files, let's think a bit more about how to
transfer data. FTP has two commonly used ways ("modes") of transferring data,
called "binary" and "ASCII." In a binary transfer, the bit sequence of the file is preserved, so that the original and the copy are bit-by-bit identical, even if a file containing that bit sequence is meaningless on the destination machine. For example,
if a Windows 95 computer transferred an executable file to an IBM VM system in
binary, the file could not be executed on the VM system. (It could, however, be
copied in binary mode from that VM system to another Windows 95 computer and
be executed there.)

ASCII mode is really a misnomer: it should be called "text" mode. In ASCII mode, transfers are treated as sets of characters; the client and server try to ensure that the characters they transfer have the same meaning on the target computer as they did on the source computer. Again, think of a Windows file being transferred to an IBM VM system. If the file contains textual data, the file would be meaningless on the IBM VM machine, because the codes used to represent characters on the Windows computer are different than those used on the IBM mainframe. That is, the bit pattern used to represent an "A" in Windows is not the same bit pattern as that used on the VM system. In ASCII mode, FTP automatically translates the file from a Windows text file to an IBM VM text file; hence, the file would be readable on the IBM VM machine.

If you are confused by this, think of giving someone a journal article published in German. Binary mode would be equivalent to photocopying the article, in which case it is useless unless the recipient understands German. However, if the recipient photocopies the article again and gives it to someone who reads German, it is useful even if the original recipient didn't understand it. ASCII mode is equivalent to translating the article before giving it to the other person. In this case, it becomes useful to the person who doesn't understand German, but probably loses some detail in the translation process.

In the example in Figure 9-4, some of the messages made a big point of saying that this was an ASCII transfer. This is appropriate, because the two files we were transferring were both text files. We don't know what kind of machine we're taking them from, and we don't care; we just want to make sure that we can read the files on our machine. To make sure that FTP is in ASCII mode, enter the command **ascii**. To put FTP into binary mode, enter the command **binary** (as we did in Figure 9-2). The command **image** is a synonym for **binary**; you'll find that a lot of FTP messages use the phrase *image mode*, or *I mode* when they mean binary. For example:

```
ftp> binary              now we're ready to transfer a binary file
200 Type set to I.       I stands for "image" or "binary"
ftp> put program.exe     transfer an executable (binary)
ftp> ascii               now we're ready to transfer a text file
200 Type set to A.       A stands for "ASCII" or "text"
ftp> get help.txt        retrieve a text (ASCII) file
```

Even if you are transferring files between identical machines, you need to be aware of the proper mode for the type of file you are transferring. The FTP software doesn't know the machines are identical. So, if you transfer a binary file in ASCII mode, the translation will still take place, even though it isn't needed. This may slow the transfer slightly, which probably isn't a big deal, but it may also damage the data, perhaps making the file unusable. (On most computers, ASCII mode usually assumes that the most significant bit of each character is meaningless, since the ASCII character set doesn't use it. If you're transferring a binary file, all the bits are important.) If you know that both machines are identical, binary mode will work for both text files and data files. Therefore, it is important to know what kind of data you want to transfer. Table 9-1 gives you hints for some common file types.

Many database and spreadsheet programs use a binary format to store their data, even if the data is inherently textual. Therefore, unless you know what your software does, we recommend trying binary mode first for database or spreadsheet files. Then see whether the file you transferred works correctly. If not, try ASCII mode. For word processing programs, there are a few additional clues. The so-called "WYSIWYG" word processors (word processors that have an elaborate display that matches the actual output very closely; WYSIWYG stands for "what you see is what you get") usually store documents in a binary format. Some of these programs have a special command for writing text files (i.e., "text only") that can be transferred in ASCII mode, but you may lose some formatting information. The simpler (and older) word processors that don't have fancy WYSIWYG display capabilities typically store data in an ASCII format.

Table 9–1: Common File Types and Modes

File	Mode
Text file	ASCII, by definition
Spreadsheet	Probably binary
Database file	Probably binary, possibly ASCII
Word processor file	Probably binary, possibly ASCII
Program source code	ASCII
Electronic mail message	ASCII
PKzip'ed file	Binary
Backup file	Binary
Compressed file	Binary
Binhexed or uuencoded* file	ASCII
Executable file	Binary, but see below
PostScript (laser printer) file	ASCII (with rare exceptions)
WWW (HTML) document	ASCII
Picture files (GIF, JPEG, MPEG)	Binary
Audio files (WAV, AU)	Binary

* **uuencode** is a UNIX utility analogous to BinHex for DOS and Windows systems, which we mentioned in Chapter 5, *Electronic Mail*. UNIX users frequently use it to encode binary files in an all-ASCII representation, which makes them easier to transfer correctly.

Executable files are generally binary files; however, there are exceptions. Programs that are compiled and executed directly by the processor are always binary. However, most operating systems provide at least one "scripting" language that allows you to write sequences of commands that are then interpreted by another program. You can think of these as files of commands like **autoexec.bat** on MS-DOS PC's, but you will find other kinds of files as well; Visual Basic and a popular language called perl fall into this category.

On the Internet, many hypertext files are stored in a format called HTML, which stands for "hypertext markup language." This is an ASCII format that's used by the World Wide Web (see Chapter 6, *The World Wide Web*). There are many places on the Net where various types of images (weather maps, satellite images, etc.) are available. The most important file formats for images are called GIF and JPEG, both of which can encode elaborate multicolor images, and MPEG, which is used for "movies." These are all binary formats, and should therefore be transferred in binary mode. You probably need extra software to view these files; that's also available through the Internet.

Many FTP implementations provide several additional modes (e.g., **tenex**, an obsolete operating system format, or **jis78kj**, a *kanji* character set for Japanese), but they are not commonly used.

Handling Large Files and Groups of Files

Network users often need to transfer extremely large files or large batches of files. You may need a large database, an archive of a discussion group, a set of reports, or the complete source code to your life's work. Each of these tends to be large.

To reduce the cost of storage and transmission across the network, large files are frequently stored in compressed format. There are many techniques for data compression, and consequently a number of different compression programs that can be used. Text files run through a good data compression program can be reduced anywhere from 30 to 70 percent in size. Chapter 6, which covers the World Wide Web, gives a good summary of compression and archiving techniques.

Moving compressed files across the network really isn't a problem. They should always be treated as binary files. The problem is that getting the file to the target system is only half the battle. After it is there, you must uncompress it before it is usable. This may or may not be easy, since there is no one standard for compression utilities, though most compression utilities are available (free or as shareware) on the Net.

Moving a Whole Directory

When you're using FTP, you often want to receive a whole file structure: a directory or collection of directories, not just a single file or a group of files. FTP really isn't designed to do this effectively. You can type **mget ***, but there is no standard command for moving a directory.

This problem is usually solved in the FTP server: the person maintaining the server will package groups of interesting files into aggregates, formally called archives. For example, someone who distributes a free software package usually needs to make dozens (maybe even hundreds) of files available. Rather than telling users to "FTP these 50 files," he or she usually uses a backup utility to package all of these files into a single file (see Figure 9-5). When someone gets the package, he or she must open it up to get the group of files contained in it. On PC-based systems,

PKZIP and PKUNZIP are often used to do the packaging. For example, let's say that some FTP site manager wants to make a set of pictures in GIF files available. The manager could package all the files with the extension *.gif* with the following commands:

```
C:\WEBSITE\HTDOCS> dir
CONMENU   GIF        3,372   05-15-95   2:06a conmenu.gif
CONDIA    GIF        3,059   05-15-95   2:07a condia.gif
SPACE     GIF        9,454   05-15-95   2:14a space.gif
LOGOUT    GIF        1,798   05-15-95   2:43a logout.gif
PREFS     GIF        4,448   05-15-95   8:15a PREFS.GIF
WXUGDIA   GIF        3,155   05-17-95   1:14p wxugdia.gif
WXUGCON   GIF       10,608   05-17-95   1:16p wxugcon.gif
LOGFILE   GIF        5,766   05-25-95   6:11a logfile.gif
INDEX     HTM          589   05-18-95  10:51a index.htm
          9 file(s)           42,249 bytes
          2 dir(s)       350,355,456 bytes free

C:\WEBSITE\HTDOCS> pkzip -a pictures *.gif
PKZIP (R)   FAST!   Create/Update Utility   Version 1.1   03-15-90
Copr. 1989-1990 PKWARE Inc.  All Rights Reserved.  PKZIP/h for help
PKZIP Reg. U.S. Pat. and Tm. Off.

Creating ZIP: PICTURES.ZIP
   Adding: CONMENU.GIF  storing    ( 0%), done.
   Adding: CONDIA.GIF   imploding ( 1%), done.
   Adding: SPACE.GIF    storing    ( 0%), done.
   Adding: LOGOUT.GIF   imploding (10%), done.
   Adding: PREFS.GIF    storing    ( 0%), done.
   Adding: WXUGDIA.GIF  imploding ( 1%), done.
   Adding: WXUGCON.GIF  storing    ( 0%), done.
   Adding: LOGFILE.GIF  storing    ( 0%), done.
```

PKZIP tries to compress the files, in addition to archiving them. That's what imploded means. The imploded files were compressed before they were stored in the file *pictures.zip*. GIF files don't compress very well, so there were not much savings to be gained. Many files weren't compressed; they were just "stored" as-is, because compression didn't make them smaller.

Some time later, you decide you want to pick up the "pictures" package and install it on your computer. You begin by using anonymous FTP to contact the server and retrieve *pictures.zip*:

```
ftp> open ux1.cso.uiuc.edu          Start an FTP to the server
Connected to ux1.cso.uiuc.edu.
220 ux1.cso.uiuc.edu FTP server (Version 5.60) awaits your command
Name (ux1.cso.uiuc.edu:(none)): anonymous   Log in as appropriate
331 Guest login ok, send ident as password.
Password:
230 Guest login ok, access restrictions apply.
Remote system type is UNIX.
Using binary mode to transfer files.      Note binary mode
```

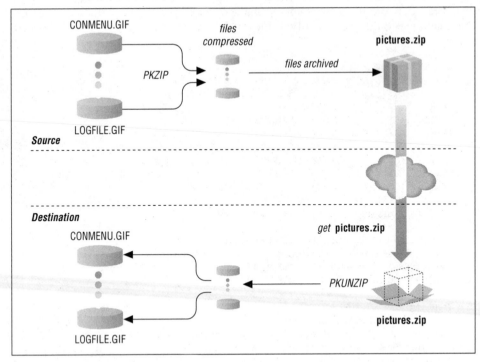

Figure 9–5: Moving many files

```
ftp> get pictures.zip                    Get the aggregate dump file
200 PORT command successful.
150 Opening BINARY mode data connection for pictures.zip (41660 bytes).
226 Transfer complete.
41660 bytes received in .5 seconds (92 Kbytes/s)
ftp> quit                                Quit FTP
```

You now have the ZIP file; you only need to undo the operation to it to get the original GIF files back.

```
C:\temp> pkunzip -e pictures.zip

PKUNZIP (R)    FAST!   Extract Utility    Version 2.04g  02-01-93
Copr. 1989-1993 PKWARE Inc. All Rights Reserved. Registered version
PKUNZIP Reg. U.S. Pat. and Tm. Off.

Searching ZIP: PICTURES.ZIP
 Extracting: CONMENU.GIF
  Exploding: CONDIA.GIF
 Extracting: SPACE.GIF
  Exploding: LOGOUT.GIF
 Extracting: PREFS.GIF
  Exploding: WXUGDIA.GIF
```

```
Extracting: WXUGCON.GIF
Extracting: LOGFILE.GIF
```

All the extracted files will be available in the directory where you executed the command, and the archive will be untouched.

Other archival utilities

As you travel the Internet, you will see archives created by packages other than PKZIP. These may be created by the UNIX backup package **tar** or the BACKUP utility on VMS operating systems. Unfortunately, most archival tools are specific to one operating system—if you're using Windows 95, you probably don't have a **tar** command, let alone a VMS BACKUP command. Therefore, as a rule, an archive is only useful if you're unpacking it on the same kind of computer that created it. (The archive might be stored on another kind of computer, which is not important—as long as it is treated as a binary file.)

However, all is not lost. If the Internet presents some problems, it also gives you a way to resolve these problems. If you have the time and energy to poke through the acres of free software that are available on the Net, you *may* be able to find a program that will unpack a strange archive format on your system.

Most often, you'll need to work with UNIX archives. These are created in two steps: the archive is made with a utility called **tar** and then compressed using a utility called **gzip**. Another common UNIX compression utility is **compress**. Windows versions of **gzip**, **compress**, and **tar** are readily available. You can find out how to locate software in Chapter 10, *Finding Files*. When working with other archival utilities, remember to perform the unpacking operations in the right order. The file name should give you a clue: if you see a file named *book.tar.gz*, you must get rid of the *.gz* first (using **gzip**), and then get rid of the *.tar* (using **tar**). Likewise, *book.tar.Z* should first be uncompressed with **compress** (to get rid of the *.Z*).*

A More Friendly FTP

If you think you will be doing a lot of FTP work, you might consider getting yourself a more modern client. One good client is WS_FTP.† Rather than using typed commands, WS_FTP lets you work with dialogs and buttons. You can get it with anonymous FTP from the host **ftp.halcyon.com** in the directory *pub/slip/ftp*. After you get the file *ws_ftp.zip*, extract the executable with pkunzip. If you install this

---

* Of course, you do need to be aware of file name length limitations so remember the long file name on the remote system before you move it to the local machine with a shorter name.

† This is a 16 bit application, so your network connection must be up and running before you use it. So, if you are using SLIP or PPP and have done no other network commands you may have to bring up the connection manually (see Appendix B, *Setting Up Your Internet Connection*).

client and start it, you'll be greeted with the window shown in Figure 9-6.

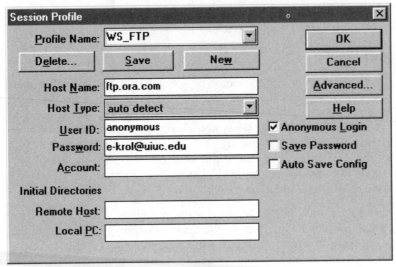

Figure 9-6: WS_FTP connection window

Here you have to fill in the blanks. In the example, I connect to host **ftp.ora.com**, login as **anonymous**, and give my password as **e-krol@uiuc.edu**. At the bottom, I could have filled in an **Initial Directory**: WS_FTP would automatically **cd** to this directory after logging in.

Figure 9-7 shows you the screen you get automatically after clicking **OK**, assuming that the server accepts your attempt to log in. This gives you a graphical view of both the local file space (in the left-hand pane) and the remote files (in the right-hand pane). Directories are shown above the horizontal line, files are below.

It's pretty easy to see how to use this tool: you click on a file to select it for transfer, and then push one of the arrow buttons between the panes. The left arrow is a **get** and the right arrow is a **put**. To change directories, click on the name and click **ChgDir**. The left panel changes the local directory; the right panel changes the remote directory.

After you have selected a file, you can browse through it by clicking on the **View** button. This is the easy way to decide whether you really want to transfer the file.

FTP Over the Web

As I described in Chapter 6, a World Wide Web browser like Internet Explorer or Netscape Navigator functions as an adequate FTP client for retrieving files. A Web browser provides a graphical representation of the contents of an FTP server; each filename has an icon next to it that tells you something about the file's contents.

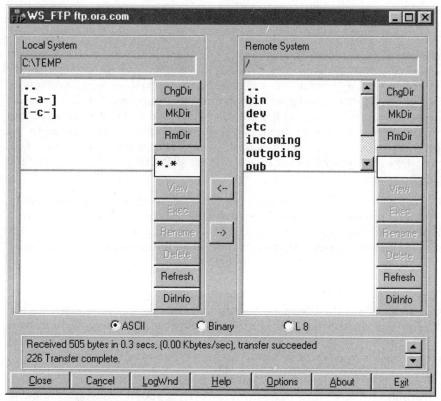

Figure 9–7: WS_FTP transfer window

The icons and filenames are all links, so you move around the directory structure by pointing and clicking with your mouse.

If you click on a link to a directory, the Web browser displays the items in that directory. If you select a file, the browser tries to handle it appropriately, including deciding whether to use ASCII or binary mode to download the file. If it's a text file, the browser displays it, which is useful for checking out *README* and *index* files. If you want to save the file on your machine, use the browser's **Save** command. When you select a binary file, or any other type of file that the browser doesn't recognize, like a PKZIP archive, the browser gives you the option to save the file on your system. This is how you use a Web browser to download software and other files.

But how do I get to an FTP site with a Web browser, you may be asking. The answer is simple. Use the browser's **Open** command and enter a URL for an FTP resource, which takes the following form:

```
ftp://server-name/remote-path
```

The *server-name* is the name of the server you want to access, and the *remote-path* is the file you want. If you don't specify the *remote-path*, the browser shows you the FTP server's root menu—that is, the directory you'd see when you log in. If you specify a directory, the browser shows you that directory; you can then use point-and-click navigation to find the file you want. And if you specify a file, the browser gets the file for you, without any further navigation. For example, to get the file *pkunzip.exe* in *NSF/genpubs* from **stis.nsf.gov**, use the URL **ftp://stis.nsf.gov/NSF/genpubs/pkunzip.exe**. To get UUNET's root directory, use the URL **ftp://ftp.uu.net**.

Web browsers assume that FTP servers are "well-behaved"—that is, they behave like UNIX FTP servers, which are a *de facto* standard. In particular, they need to accept an *anonymous* login. That's usually the case, but you may run into trouble with servers that require **ftp** or something else as the anonymous login name. Using a more general form of the URL can help:

```
ftp://username@server-name/remote-path
```

For example, to access the server **foo.bar.edu** that requires the login name **ftp**, use the URL **ftp://ftp@foo.bar.edu**. This syntax also allows you to use a Web browser to access a private FTP account. If the account requires a password, the browser should bring up a window that prompts you for the password.

All in all, a Web browser makes a decent FTP client. One particularly nice feature is that it handles the mechanics of anonymous FTP for you; it logs you in automatically. However, there are a few limitations worth noting:

- There's no equivalent to the **put** command; the Web is strictly for downloading files.

- Web clients don't handle groups of files: it's strictly one file at a time. There's no equivalent to **mget**. If you habitually collect lots of stuff, the standard FTP client might work better.

- After you start downloading a file, you have to wait until the retrieval is done before you can continue browsing the Web.

Actually, Netscape Navigator gets around this last limitation by using a separate process to download a file. When you retrieve a file with Netscape, the browser opens a separate window that keeps you informed about the status of the operation, so you can keep browsing at the same time. You can even perform multiple downloads simultaneously.

Hints, Advice, and Problems

Because using FTP is fairly straightforward, it is easy to get enthralled with the power it puts at your fingers and lose sight of its limitations. Here are a couple of hints that you may find useful:

- FTP allows you to create, delete, and rename files and directories on a remote system. Treat this ability as a convenience to use occasionally, rather than a technique to use all the time. If you are making a lot of changes on a remote system, instead of moving files, it is probably easier to use Telnet and do your changes as a timesharing session.

- Directions about anonymous FTP are frequently sketchy. Someone will tell you "anonymous FTP to **server.public.com** and get the *Whizbang* editor, it's really neat." Servers set up for distributing free software (or other large public archives) frequently have many, many files stashed in various directories. If you can't find what you are after, try looking for files in the default directory named *README*, *index*, *ls-lR*, or something similar. If you're lucky, you'll find information about how the server is organized.

- Some FTP servers allow you to put extensions on filenames that are really file reformatting commands to the server. The two most common ones are .**tar** and .**Z**. For example, if a file named *program* exists, and you issue the command **get program.Z**, the server automatically compresses the file before the transfer. With the .**tar** ending (e.g., **get pub.tar**), the file or directory is converted to a UNIX **tar** archive before it's transmitted. This makes it possible to transfer an entire directory tree with a single command. As you might expect, the server does nothing special if a file with the suffix already exists. For example, if *program.Z* already exists, the server will give it to you as is, without trying to compress it.

  These are extensions to the normal FTP service which will probably become more widespread in the future. Right now, they may work and may not. If you use a server regularly, you might give them a try to see if they work. Of course, you'll need to get Windows versions of the **tar** and **uncompress** utilities before this feature becomes useful.

Common Problems

So far, I've always typed the user name and password correctly. Of course, that only happens in books; in real life you won't always be so lucky. If you make a mistake, you'll get a "Login incorrect" message. There are two ways to handle this. You can exit FTP and try again; or you can give the **user** command, followed by your login name, to restart the login process. You'll be prompted again for your password, and can continue from there:

```
ftp>open sonne.uiuc.edu
Connected to sonne.uiuc.edu.
220 sonne FTP server (SunOS 4.1) ready.
```

```
Name (ux.uiuc.edu:(none)): krol          login name krol
331 Password required for krol.
Password:                                type the password incorrectly
530 Login incorrect.
Login failed.
ftp> user krol                           start again with the login name
331 Password required for krol
Password:                                this time, get the password right
230 User krol logged in.
ftp>
```

It's a bit confusing, because if your first attempt to log in fails, you get an "ftp>" prompt, but you can't do anything with it. You have to complete the login process before proceeding. If you're using WS_FTP, click the **LogWind** button.

There are, of course, other things that can go wrong. You can misspell the name of the computer you're trying to reach; this will probably earn you the message "unknown host" (or something of that sort). Check the spelling of the hostname. If the host you're trying to access has crashed, or is unreachable for some other reason, you'll see the message "host not responding," "host unreachable," "connection timed out," or something along those lines. In this case, your only solution is to wait and try again later. If the situation persists for a long time, try contacting whoever is responsible for the remote system. (You'll find more troubleshooting help in Chapter 15, *Dealing with Problems.*)

If you misspell the name of the file you're trying to transfer, you'll see a message saying "no such file or directory," or the equivalent. Make sure you typed the name correctly, and make sure that the file you want to download actually exists; we'll show you how to do that in the next section. If you try to get a file that you aren't allowed to take, you'll get a message that reads "access denied," or something like that.

One oddity of the Windows 95 version of FTP is that it handles long filenames strangely. This is a legacy of its MS-DOS heritage. You can download (**get**) files with long filenames (longer than eight characters) with no trouble. If, however, you try to **put** a file with a name longer than eight characters, you will likely get the message, "file not found," even if it exists:

```
ftp> put "long-file-name" longname
long file name: File not found
```

For the purposes of this FTP client, the long filename has been coverted to an eight-character name, with a three-character extension. You must use the converted name. You can find this name by selecting the file in the **My Computer** icon, pulling down the **File** menu and selecting **Properties**. This will yield the screen shown in Figure 9-8. There, you can see the field **MS-DOS Name**. If you use that name, it will work just fine; for example, **put longfi~1 longname**. This shouldn't be a problem with WS_FTP, since you'll see the filename on the screen.

Occasionally, you'll see a message like "control connection closed" or "control timeout." To discourage hogs, most FTP servers decide you've gone away if you're

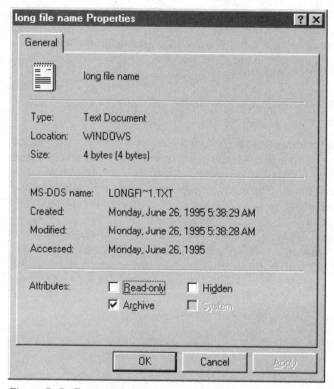

Figure 9–8: Properties menu

idle for some period of time (usually five minutes). This won't happen as long as the server is actually doing work for you. If you see this message, just log in to the server again.

Finally, remember that some files you may find on the Net are huge (all right, pretty big—over a million characters). Some systems place file size limits on their customers, or your disk may not have room for large files. Make sure you have room for the file before you start to transfer it. In the next section, we'll see how to find out just how big a file is.

Special Notes on Various Systems

FTP's biggest virtue is that it lets you move files between computers regardless of their type. In many cases, you don't need to know anything about the remote systems. In practice, however, whenever you have two systems, you usually end up needing to know something (certainly not much, but something) about the remote system.

The problems are relatively minor, and typically have to do with the way the remote system specifies filenames. As much as possible, FTP uses a uniform, UNIX-like notation for filenames and addresses. However, this can be confusing, since FTP doesn't try to interpret **dir** listings and other output generated by the remote system: it just sends the command's output back to you verbatim. Deciphering the output from **ls**, **dir**, or any other command usually isn't too difficult. It's fairly easy to find the filename, the file's size, and the last modification date, and that's usually all the information you care about. But you do need to know how to convert remote filenames into a form that FTP understands.

Here are a number of examples using FTP to access various kinds of systems that you will find as servers on the Internet. Remember that these are examples. There are many vendors of TCP/IP software for the Macintosh, Digital Equipment, and IBM computers. The server you are contacting might look a bit different from the examples we show here. Also, in most of the examples, the remote system tells you what kind of computer it is. This is not always the case. If you don't know what kind of system you're using, your best bet is to look for *README* files; there's often one that explains what archive you're looking at, what kind of a system you're using, and so on. If this doesn't work, do a **dir** and try matching the format to the examples.

Target: Digital Equipment VMS systems

VMS systems have a fairly feature-rich file structure. Logging into one presents no particular problems. Here we open a connection to **vaxb.cs.unsd.edu**:

```
Connected to vaxb.cs.unsd.edu.
220 FTP Service Ready
Name (vaxb.cs.unsd.edu:krol): anonymous    anonymous FTP
331 ANONYMOUS user ok, send real identity as password.
Password:
230 ANONYMOUS logged in, directory HSC1$DUA1:[ANON], restrictions apply.
Remote system type is VMS.
```

FTP was nice enough to tell you that it's talking to a VMS system, so you know what to expect. This is not always the case. The software necessary to take part in the Internet does not come automatically on VMS. A site wanting Internet access must buy a software package from one of several companies; the competing implementations are all a bit different. Another clue that you're communicating with a VMS server might be the word *multinet*:

```
220 FTP.unsd.edu MultiNet FTP Server Process 3.3(14)...
```

Multinet is the name of a popular software product for VMS systems; if you see it, you're probably dealing with a VMS server.

The complexity surrounding VMS lies in its file structure. We have been placed in a directory containing files accessible via anonymous FTP; the complete name of this directory is *HSC1$DUA1:[ANON]*. This name consists of two parts:

HSC1$DUA1 is the name of a disk; and *[ANON]* is a directory on that disk.*

Now that we have logged in, let's try a **dir** command to see what's available:

```
ftp> dir
200 PORT Command OK.
125 File transfer started correctly
Directory HSC1$DUA1:[ANON]

AAAREADME.TXT;9   2-MAY-1991 15:45:51    730/2    (RWED,RE,,R)
ARTICLES.DIR;1   28-MAY-1990 10:20:14   1536/3    (RWE,RE,RE,R)
LIBRARY.DIR;1    30-APR-1991 11:13:06   1536/3    (RWE,RE,RE,RE)
WAIS.DIR;1        1-OCT-1991 10:21:16    512/1    (RWE,RE,RE,RE)
Total of 4 files, 1448 blocks.
226 File transfer completed ok
```

Each file consists of a name (e.g., *AAAREADME*), an extension (e.g., *TXT*), and a version number (e.g., *9*). Ignore the version number;[†] you will almost always want the most recent version of a file, which is what you'll get if you pretend the version number doesn't exist. The extension tells you something about the file. *TXT* is the extension for text files, so these files may be read directly. Files with the extension *DIR* are directories. There are a number of other standard extensions, like *FOR* for FORTRAN files, *EXE* for executable files, *COM* for command files. The file-names will be listed in uppercase, but VMS doesn't care whether you use upper- or lowercase letters.

We see that the default directory for anonymous FTP has three subdirectories. Let's use **cd** to look at the subdirectory *wais.dir.* When you use **cd** to change directories, you use the directory name without the extension:

```
ftp> cd wais
200 Working directory changed to "HSC1$DUA1:[ANON.WAIS]"
```

Now our working directory is *HSC1$DUA1:[ANON.WAIS].* Notice that VMS specifies a subdirectory by listing each subdirectory after a period within the brackets. So this subdirectory is roughly equivalent to the UNIX path *HSC1$DUA1/ANON/WAIS.* Likewise, it's equivalent to the DOS path *\ANON\WAIS,* on a disk named *HSC1$DUA1:.*

Unfortunately, the people who sell TCP/IP software for VAX/VMS systems don't agree about how the **cd** command should work, particularly when you want to

---

* If we had been using regular FTP, rather than anonymous FTP, we probably would have been placed in a "default directory," which is similar to the UNIX "home directory." The home directory name would probably be *HSC$1DUA1:[KROL].*

† All right, we'll explain it. VMS has the peculiarity that it keeps old versions of your files, until you explicitly tell it to delete them. This can waste tremendous amounts of disk space, but it does make it easy to undo your mistakes.

move through multiple levels of directories. With some VMS FTP servers, you have to use a VMS-style directory specification, like this:

```
ftp> cd [x.y.z]
```

If the FTP server you're using expects this syntax, then to move up a level, you must use the command **cdup**; the UNIX-style **cd** .. will not work.

Other implementations expect you to specify multiple directories using the UNIX "slash" notation:

```
ftp> cd x/y/z
```

Which do you use? As I said, it depends on the software the FTP server is running. The easiest way to find out which syntax to use is to try one approach; if it doesn't work, try the other. No harm will be done if it doesn't work. If you want to be safe, you can move through one directory level at a time:

```
ftp> cd x
ftp> cd y
ftp> cd z
```

This strategy works in either case. And, once again, you must omit the *.dir* extension from the directory's name whenever you use it in a **cd** command.

get and **put** work in the usual way. You must specify the extension as part of the filename. You can include the version number, but it's easier to omit it (unless you want an old version for some special reason).[*] In this example, we will move two levels down the directory tree and retrieve the file *waissearch.hlp* from there:

```
ftp> cd wais/doc              Change to directory anon/wais/doc
200 Working directory changed to "HSC1$DUA1:[ANON.WAIS.DOC]"
ftp> get waissearch.hlp       get the file waissearch.hlp
200 PORT Command OK.
125 ASCII transfer started for
    HSC1$DUA1:[ANON.WAIS.DOC]WAISSEARCH.HLP; (1076 bytes)
226 File transfer completed ok
1076 bytes received in 0.35 seconds (3 Kbytes/s)
ftp>
```

As long as you aren't confused by the VMS-style file specifications, you should have no problems dealing with VAX/VMS systems.

Target: MS-DOS systems

As a Windows user, you're probably pretty familiar with DOS. But, as FTP servers go, DOS machines are the exception, so they need some coverage. The following notes should only be review. MS-DOS systems look very much like other network

---

[*] If you specify an old file version be sure to specify a local filename. If you don't, you will probably end up with a filename that has a semicolon in it.

servers. You log in using the normal procedure. Here, we'll FTP to **server.uiuc.edu**, a DOS machine:

```
Connected to server.uiuc.edu.
220-server.uiuc.edu PC/TCP 2.0 FTP Server by FTP Software ready
220 Connection is automatically closed if idle for 5 minutes
Name (server.uiuc.edu:): krol
331 User OK, send password
Password:
230 krol logged in
Remote system type is MSDOS.
```

Note that the remote system tells you that you are connected to a system running DOS. The **dir** command gives you a familiar, DOS-style file listing:

```
ftp> dir
200 Port OK
150 Opening data connection
        336            FS.BAT    Tue Dec 17 21:36:56 1991
          0            MBOX      Thu Nov 07 14:46:30 1991
        123            NS.BAT    Tue Jan 08 22:34:44 1991
<dir>                  NETWIRE   Tue Jun 11 02:37:34 1991
<dir>                  INCOMING.FTP  Tue Dec 17 21:42:24 1991
226 Transfer successful. Closing data connection
```

Filenames on a DOS computer consist of a filename (e.g., *FS*) and a three character extension (e.g., *BAT*). Subdirectories are flagged with the character string "<dir>" at the beginning of their line.

Under DOS, directories are disk-specific; you sometimes need to specify the disk on which the directory resides. Disks are identified by a single letter followed by a colon (:). The following **cd** command changed the "working disk" to the **h** disk:

```
ftp> cd h:
200 OK
```

If you now do another directory command, you will see a different set of files:

```
ftp> dir
200 Port OK
150 Opening data connection
<dir>                  SYSTEM    Wed Dec 31 00:00:00 1980
<dir>                  PUBLIC    Wed Dec 31 00:00:00 1980
226 Transfer successful. Closing data connection
```

Change directories within a disk with a normal **cd** command, like this:

```
ftp> cd public
200 OK
```

This command changes to the subdirectory *public*. You can also move down multiple directory levels at once with a command:

```
ftp> cd h:public/ibm_pc/msdos
200 OK
```

The trick is that DOS uses backslashes (\) to separate directory levels. However, when you access a DOS server with FTP, the server will try to be Internet-compatible and accept the slash rather than the backslash. If you use a backslash (as an experienced DOS user would expect), you'll get an error message:

```
ftp> cd h:public\ibm_pc\msdos
550 can't CWD: Error 2: No such file or directory
```

To add to the confusion, when you check the current directory, FTP prints the name using backslashes:

```
ftp> pwd
250 Current working directory is H:\PUBLIC\IBM_PC\MSDOS
```

Once you are positioned in the directory where the file you want lives, moving the file works as expected:

```
ftp> get config.bak
200 Port OK
150 Opening data connection
226 Transfer successful. Closing data connection
99 bytes received in 0.12 seconds (0.82 Kbytes/s)
```

The moral of the story is very simple. When you're accessing an MS-DOS system using FTP, use slashes instead of backslashes. With this in mind, you won't be confused.

Target: IBM VM systems

IBM VM systems require a little more special handling, mostly because VM doesn't have a hierarchical filesystem. On VM, you have disks; each disk can have multiple passwords (one for read-only access and one for read/write access); and filenames are short but have two parts. When you FTP to a VM system and log in, it looks like this:

```
Connected to vmd.cso.uiuc.edu.
220-FTPSERVE at vmd.cso.uiuc.edu, 14:46:14 CST MONDAY 12/16/91
220 Connection will close if idle for more than 5 minutes.
Name (vmd.cso.uiuc.edu:krol):          took the default name: krol
331 Send password please.
Password:
230 KROL logged in; no working directory defined. Remote system type
  is VM.
```

Once again, FTP was nice enough to inform you that the remote system is VM. It also tells you that, even though you are logged in, you can't get at the files you want. The message "no working directory defined," which you see when FTP confirms that you are logged in, tells you that you aren't ready to transfer files yet.

When you do a **cd** command on a VM system, you are really asking to get at another disk. Disks are functions of a login name and an address. So, to cram this into a **cd** command, you need to say:

```
ftp> cd login-name.disk-address
```

For example, the command:

```
ftp> cd krol.191
```

starts the connection to the disk addressed **191** of user **krol**. (You can find the names and addresses of the disks you normally use when logged in to a VM system by doing a **q disk** command.) A disk password is usually required; to supply the password, use the **account** command immediately *after* the **cd** command. Continuing the previous example:

```
ftp> cd krol.191
550 Permission denied to LINK to KROL 191; still no working directory
ftp> account j9876hoh
230 Working directory is KROL 191
```

Note that message 550 implies your **cd** command failed, even though it looked correct at the time. The **account** command, which you must give next, "fixes" the original **cd** command, so you can access files. Also, since your local system does not really know what the **account** command does on the remote computer, it makes no attempt to hide your password. Take precautions to make sure that others don't find out your password.

Now you have established a directory to work in. The output from a **dir** command looks like this:

```
ftp> dir
200 Port request OK.
125 List started OK
ACCNT    LEDGER    V    80    59      5 12/20/90  9:04:24 LEN
AGENDA   MEETING   V    73    34      2  9/24/91 10:23:01 LEN
ALL      NOTEBOOK  V    80  5174    233 12/10/91 15:17:11 LEN
```

Each filename on an IBM VM system consists of two character strings. Each string has at most eight characters. The first string is called the "filename" and the second is call the "filetype." Above, the filenames are in the first column (e.g., *ALL*), while the second column shows the filetype (e.g., *NOTEBOOK*).

If **dir** doesn't show you all the files you expect to see, it's because there is also a file mode (1 or 0) associated with a file. A file with the mode 0 is considered private and cannot be seen with the read password. If you give the write password, you can see all the files. Again, the read and write passwords are set by the owner of the disk.

The filename and filetype both must be specified if you try to move a file. Since both are variable length, you use a period (.) to separate the two. So:

```
ftp> get all.notebook mbox
```

transfers the file *all* of type *notebook* to the file *mbox* on the local machine.

If you're doing anonymous FTP and the remote host is a VM system, you still have to give a **cd** command before you can access any files. You don't have to give a second password with the **account** command. When you actually **get** files, you must (as you'd expect) give a complete, two-part filename.

Target: Macintosh

Using FTP to access a Macintosh server is fairly straightforward, once you get connected. Getting connected might be a problem if the Mac is on a network that dynamically assigns addresses. Many Macs are connected to Localtalk networks, which in turn are connected to the Internet through a gateway. Some Localtalk gateways assign Internet addresses to computers as they are turned on, taking addresses from a pool reserved for the Localtalk net. This means that the address or name of a machine might change from day to day; the address that works today might not work tomorrow. This isn't usually a problem with public archives; anyone who configures their Macintosh as a public server usually makes sure that its address is assigned permanently. (Otherwise, complaining users would make his life miserable.) You are most likely to run into addressing problems when someone tells you to "grab this file from my Macintosh" on the spur of the moment. The system's owner gives you a numeric IP address, letting you grab the file—as long as he doesn't turn the system off first. Newer Macintoshes usually don't have this problem, because they can handle Ethernet cards and be connected directly to the Internet.

When you get connected to a Macintosh, FTP may ask you for a name; even if it does, it will not require a password. The name is used for logging purposes only.

Here we'll FTP to a Macintosh, with the numeric IP address 128.174.33.56. We use the numeric address because this system doesn't have a domain name.

```
Connected to 128.174.33.56.
220 Macintosh Resident FTP server, ready
Name (128.174.33.56:krol):          send default name
230 User logged in
```

Doing a **dir** command will get a listing which looks like this:

```
ftp> dir
Accelerator
Administration/
Applications Combined
Article T3 connections
```

There are two things to note about this listing. One is that subdirectories, which in the Mac world are called folders, are flagged by the trailing slash (/). The second is that filenames can have spaces in them, which requires special handling. If a filename contains spaces, you must put the entire name within quotes. For example:

```
ftp> get "Applications Combined" applications
```

This gets the file *Applications Combined*, putting it into the file *applications* on the local machine. Aside from the Macintosh, most systems cannot handle names with spaces properly. Therefore, in this example, we made a point of specifying a local filename without a space.

Changing directories is handled in the usual way. The command:

```
ftp> cd Administration
```

changes the current directory to *Administration*. If we wanted to move through multiple folders and subfolders, we would list the whole path separated with slashes:

```
ftp> cd Administration/Personnel
```

File Retrieval Using E-Mail

In some cases, it may be more convenient to request a file via e-mail than to FTP it. Some people find it more convenient to send a mail message, then let the file arrive some time later; you may also have trouble accessing some server, because of your network setup (you're behind a firewall that won't let you **FTP** to Internet sites, for example), or for some other reason.

There are three cases to worry about:

- Specialized "Internet-style" servers that give access to a specific set of files at one location.

- General FTP-mail gateways (**ftpmail** and **bitftp**). These servers allow you to send a message describing what you want to get. The server then transfers the file to itself and mails it back to you. This differs from the previous two cases in that **ftpmail** can get any publicly available file anywhere on the Internet.

- Mailing-list archive servers; since these are closely tied to mailing lists, they are covered in Chapter 5.

Internet-Style Servers

The first method of retrieval is used by Internet information repositories that have to be widely accessible. To get a file from one of these Internet-style servers, send a mail message to the server in which the message body contains the command **send**, followed by the name of the file you want.

```
To: mail-server@rtfm.mit.edu
Subject:

send usenet/comp.mail.misc/Inter-Network_Mail_Guide
```

This message asks the machine named **rtfm** at MIT to send a copy of the file *usenet/comp.mail.misc/Inter-Network_Mail_Guide* back to the original send (i.e., the **From**: line of the requesting message). If you don't have enough information, or if your request fails, a message with the word "help" as the body requests information about what facilities are available through that server. One common pitfall: filenames on Internet servers are usually case-sensitive, so be careful to use capital and lowercase letters appropriately; you must match the filename exactly.

The FTPmail Application Gateway

You can also request a file through e-mail by using an FTP application gateway called **ftpmail**. **ftpmail** may be used to retrieve files from any FTP server on the Internet. Requests to use the **ftpmail** service are made by sending messages to an **ftpmail** server. The original server was **ftpmail@decwrl.dec.com**, but several more have appeared; we'll give you a list of known servers later. The server includes your subject text in the mail it returns to you, but otherwise ignores it—so you can use the subject line for your own reference. For example, let's assume that you are really into juggling and want to get a copy of the Juggling FAQ, available in the directory */pub/juggling* on the computer **cogsci.indiana.edu**. You might do the following:

```
To: ftpmail@decwrl.dec.com
Subject: juggling FAQ

connect cogsci.indiana.edu      ftp from this computer
chdir pub/juggling              move to target directory
get FAQ                         request the file
quit
```

You can get complete information about how to use **ftpmail** by sending it a message with the single word **help** in the body, but some of the more useful commands are listed here:

connect *hostname login password*
> Specifies the host to contact. Each request must have one **connect** statement in it. If you don't list a *hostname* with the command, **ftpmail** assumes that the file is located on the host **gatekeeper.dec.com** (which isn't a very good assumption). *login* and *password* are optional. If they are not given, they default to "anonymous" and your e-mail address.

binary
> Specifies that the files are binary and should be encoded into ASCII before being transmitted. By default, the files are encoded with the **btoa** utility.

uuencode

Specifies that binary files be encoded with **uuencode** rather than **btoa**.

compress

Specifies that binary files be compressed with the UNIX **compress** utility.

chdir *directory*

Change to the specified *directory* when the **ftp** connection is made to the server computer.

dir *directory*

Return a directory listing of the specified *directory*. If none is specified, return a listing of the current directory.

get *file*

Specifies the *file* to be sent to you from the **ftp** server via electronic mail.

chunksize *number*

Specifies the maximum number of characters which will be sent in any one message. If a message is larger than the number specified (the default is 64000), the file is split into as many messages as required for transmission. When you receive all the pieces, you have to reassemble them in order.

quit

Tells the server to terminate the request.

The **ftpmail** utility will be quite happy to mail you any file. It's up to you to tell it if it should treat it as a binary file or not. If it is binary and you don't tell it so, what you get will be useless.

Other FTPmail Servers

The original **ftpmail** *server at* **decwrl.dec.com** is very heavily loaded—obviously because it fulfills a need. However, it may take days for it to respond. Their help file says that it may take a week or more. Therefore, some other servers have appeared that you might want to try. Table 9-2 lists some FTP to e-mail gateways we know about. It's a good idea to use a server that's close to you. In particular, avoid the European servers if you're not in Europe.

Table 9-2: FTPmail and BITFTP servers

Server	Location
ftpmail@decwrl.dec.com	United States (West)
ftpmail@ieunet.ie	Ireland
bitftp@vm.gmd.de	Germany
bitftp@pucc.princeton.edu	United States (East)
bitftp@plearn.edu.pl	Poland

Now, how do you use these servers? Before doing anything else, get the **help** file. All of the servers respond to the single word "help" sent as the body of a mail message. That's the easy part.

Describing more than the **help** command is difficult. The problem is that the five servers we've mentioned have three different command sets! However, I can give you a couple of examples. That, plus the **help** file of the server you want to use, should get you started.

FTPmail to IEUnet

Here's how to get the file we retrieved earlier from the IEUnet server. Send the following message to **ftpmail@ieunet.ie**:

```
begin
send cogsci.indiana.edu:/pub/juggling/FAQ
end
```

By default, the file will come back **uuencode**d, unless you specify some other encoding with the **encode** command. You can include several **send** commands if you want. Note that the command includes the hostname, the directory, and the filename as a single string.

BITFTP

The three BITNET servers, fortunately, have the same user interface. Here's how to get a file from them. Send the following message to **bitftp@pucc.princeton.edu**, **bitftp@vm.gmd.de**, or **bitftp@plearn.edu.pl**:

```
FTP cogsci.indiana.edu
USER anonymous
cd /pub/juggling
get FAQ
QUIT
```

You can include more **get** commands if you wish.

CHAPTER TEN

FINDING FILES

How Archie Works
Contacting Archie
Using Archie from the Web
Special-Purpose Archie Clients
Contacting an Archie Client Remotely

Historically, one of the biggest problems on the Internet has been finding what you know already exists. Anonymous FTP servers sprang up early on, giving you the ability to fetch files from repositories on the network, but the existence of those files was largely communicated interpersonally. Part of the apprenticeship for a network guru was knowing enough people and attending enough conferences to find out where things were hidden. This worked just fine when the Internet was a small network used by computer professionals. Now that the Internet provides resources to the masses, the "good ol' boys" network no longer works. Plenty of new users don't have access to an experienced administrator with the right contacts. And there are now so many resources on-line that not even the best administrator could keep track of them all. You may know that such-and-such a database or public domain program exists, but finding it is like finding the proverbial needle in a haystack.

This sounds like a job for a computer. Enter Archie, a system which allows you to search indices to locate files that are available on public FTP servers. In its heyday it was revolutionary; it was the only place to turn if you were searching for programs, data, or text files. Although Archie still indexes about 1200 servers and 2.5 million files, most people will use other tools offered on the World Wide Web or Gopher to find and get files. Its use is now limited to searching for files whose approximate name you know and which you can't seem to find by other means.

Archie's downfall is that it is very hard to browse. You ask it either to find filenames which contain a certain search string, or to suggest files whose description contains a certain word. It returns the actual filenames that meet the search criteria and the name of the servers containing those files. Once you decide which of the files is most likely to meet your needs, you can easily move the file to your computer via anonymous FTP.

This two-step process dealing only in filenames and directories makes its use a last ditch utility rather than the utility of choice. Still, when all else fails, Archie can come through and save the day.

First, we'll look at how Archie works. It's so amazingly simple that it took years for someone to think of it. From there, we will move to how to use Archie. Like a lot of Internet services, Archie can be accessed in multiple ways. It's simplest to use Archie through a WWW gateway. It is a bit restrictive in what you can do, but it meets most people's needs. Then we'll discuss using an Archie client program **wsarchie** on your own computer. It is the best thing to do if you are going to do frequent Archie searches. Finally, we'll discuss use of Archie through Telnet and e-mail, which is more difficult to use, but offers the fullest functionality.

How Archie Works

If you were reading a murder mystery, this would be the time to unveil the killer. In the preceding chapters, I have given you all the clues necessary to build an Archie service. The answer to "whodunit?" is "some people at McGill University."[*]

The answer to "howdunit?" is "to ask, via the network, for people who were running servers to register them." The perpetrators run a program once a month which contacts those servers via FTP (Figure 10-1). When it contacts each server, it builds a directory listing of all the files on that server, using standard FTP commands (ls −lR, to be exact). When you come along some time later and say, "Find me a file which contains the string 'eudora' in its filename," Archie just scans all the merged directories and sends you the filenames that match your search string, together with the names of the servers where each file is available.

This is the basic service that was created. It became obvious that some people choose strange, non-intuitive names for their files, like a filename of *POPclient* for the e-mail program named Eudora. The Archie developers then asked for people to send information on the major packages they provide. They used this information to create a service called **whatis**, a set of alternative indexing keywords for files on the network that can be used to locate software or data files, even if the filename bears no resemblance to its contents. Since this service requires human intervention, it is a lot spottier, and is becoming pretty dated. As Archie's usage grew, the service changed to meet the increased demand. Currently, there are many Archie servers scattered across the Internet. Each server builds an index of the FTP archives close to itself, and then the servers share the information. This allows the updates to be more timely without severely loading the network. For the most part, however, you don't care about how the system works. The mechanics are hidden from you; all you need to do is contact any Archie server and look up the data you want.

---

[*] Archie development continues, but no longer at McGill; development work now takes place at a company named Bunyip.

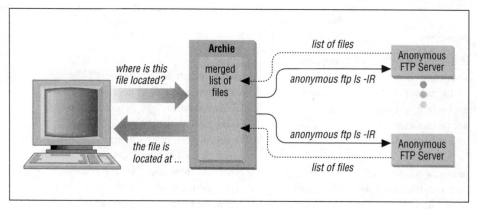

Figure 10-1: How Archie works

Contacting Archie

To use Archie, you must choose an Archie server. There are a number of equivalent servers; that is, each has the same information.* You only care about picking the server that will answer your queries fastest.

Start the search for a good Archie server with your service provider. If your provider recommends a particular server, try it first. Some providers set up private servers, available only to their clientele. If so, you're lucky: the private server will almost certainly give you excellent response. (As competition increases, service providers are offering more special services like this.) If your service provider has such an offering, it's probably mentioned in their documentation. If not, ask your system administrator (or your service provider's support staff), if there's a preferred Archie to use.

If you can't find the best Archie server from documentation (and I wouldn't look too long) or word of mouth, pick one of the systems listed in the following table. The "nice" way to pick a server is to choose one that is close to you on the network. This is not easy to do, since you probably don't know exactly where the wires providing your Internet connection go after leaving your campus or company. The best approximation you have is to pick one that is geographically close. Using a server in Australia from the U.S. might be cool, but it is a poor use of slow transoceanic network links. Table 10-1 shows a list of public Archie servers and their general locations.

---

* At least in theory. From time to time, differences between Archie servers creep in. They're usually resolved eventually; the Archie developers at Bunyip are working on ways to solve these problems. In the meantime, if you don't find what you're looking for, you can try another server—but only *after* you've made sure that everything else is correct (you're doing the right kind of search, you typed the search string correctly, etc.). The differences between servers are very minor.

Table 10-1: Available Archie Servers

Name	Suggested Usage Area	Name	Suggested Usage Area
archie.au	Australia	archie.nz	New Zealand
archie.univie.ac.at	Austria	archie.uninett.no	Norway
archie.belnet.be	Belgium	archie.icm.edu.pl	Poland
archie.bunyip.com	Canada	archie.rediris.es	Spain
archie.cs.mcgill.ca	Canada	archie.luth.se	Sweden
archie.uqam.ca	Canada	archie.switch.ch	Switzerland
archie.funet.fi	Finland	archie.ncu.edu.tw	Taiwan
archie.univ-rennes1.fr	France	archie.doc.ic.ac.uk	U.K.
archie.th-darmstadt.de	Germany	archie.hensa.ac.uk	U.K.
archie.ac.il	Israel	archie.sura.net	U.S. (MD)
archie.unipi.it	Italy	archie.unl.edu	U.S. (Central)
archie.wide.ad.jp	Japan	archie.internic.net	U.S. (NJ)
archie.kornet.nm.kr	Korea	archie.rutgers.edu	U.S. (NJ)
archie.sogang.ac.kr	Korea	archie.ans.net	U.S. (NY)

Archie is a very popular service. It is not unusual for a server to handle over 40 requests simultaneously. In order to protect the responsiveness of the service, some servers have limits on the number of concurrent requests that can be handled. If you try to use a server and hit one of these limits, you will get a message like:

```
Due to serious overloading on the archie server,
we have been forced to restrict the number of concurrent
interactive (telnet) sessions to 10.

Connection closed by foreign host.
```

The actual text of the message will vary from server to server, but the intent should be clear. If everyone uses a server close to them, it naturally spreads the load around and minimizes this irritation.

Using Archie from the Web

If you are doing occasional simple searches, the easiest way to use Archie is through one of the many available WWW forms. The nice thing about these forms is that they guide you through the search. You don't have to remember a lot of commands and parameters; just fill in the blanks and pull down selection lists.

There are many Web interfaces to Archie, all of them slightly different in format. Table 10-2 is a list of the ones we know about.*

Table 10–2: The URLs of Some Archie Gateways

Australia	http://www.gh.cs.su.oz.au/Utils/archieplexform.html
Austria	http://bau2.uibk.ac.at:81/archieplex-info/archieplexform.html
Germany	http://marvin.physik.uni-oldenburg.de/Docs/net-serv/ archie-gate.html
Portugal	http://s700.uminho.pt/CGI/archieplex/archieplexform.html
Taiwan	http://peacock.tnjc.edu.tw/NEW/archie/AA.html
United Kingdom	http://src.doc.ic.ac.uk/archieplexform.html
	http://web.nexor.co.uk/archieplex-info/archieplexform.html
United States	http://www.amdahl.com/internet/archieplex/
	http://hoohoo.ncsa.uiuc.edu/archie.html

Figure 10-2 shows one of the search forms.† Regardless of how you contact Archie, the procedure for making a search is:

1. Enter the name of the file in the **Search for:** box, and select the type of search you want.

2. Select a server appropriate to your area by pulling down the list labeled **Several Archie Servers can be used:**. Each form will have a default server listed; this one uses the server **archie.rutgers.edu**. Remember that the default is not necessarily the fastest.

3. Click **Submit** to start the query.

Let's say we heard about a file named *wsarchie* and wished to locate a copy. The default search type is a **Case Insensitive Substring Match**. That's appropriate for us; we aren't sure we have the entire file name, and we don't want to make any bets about capitalization. So we enter "wsarch" in the **Search for:** box, pull down the server list to **University of Nebraska**, which is fairly close to us, and press **Submit**. When the query is serviced, we get back the screen shown in Figure 10-3. At the top of the screen, it shows you which server was used. Next, it tells you the name of a computer on the Internet where a match occurred. The first match is on a computer named **ftp.halcyon.com**. There, you can find the file *wsarchie.zip* in either of two directories: *disk2/tiskwin* or *pub/fx/winsock*.

---

* In order to get an up-to-date list of gateways, contact **http://pubweb.nexor.co.uk/public/archie/servers.html**. Their functionality is basically the same, because it is provided by the Archie system, but the descriptive strings on the forms will vary somewhat. Some of the forms do limit your choices in parameters. So, if one doesn't do everything you want, you might look at others. For most searches, it won't matter which one you use.

† Archieplex was developed by Martijin Koster. This form is Copyright © 1995 by Amdahl Corporation, used with permission.

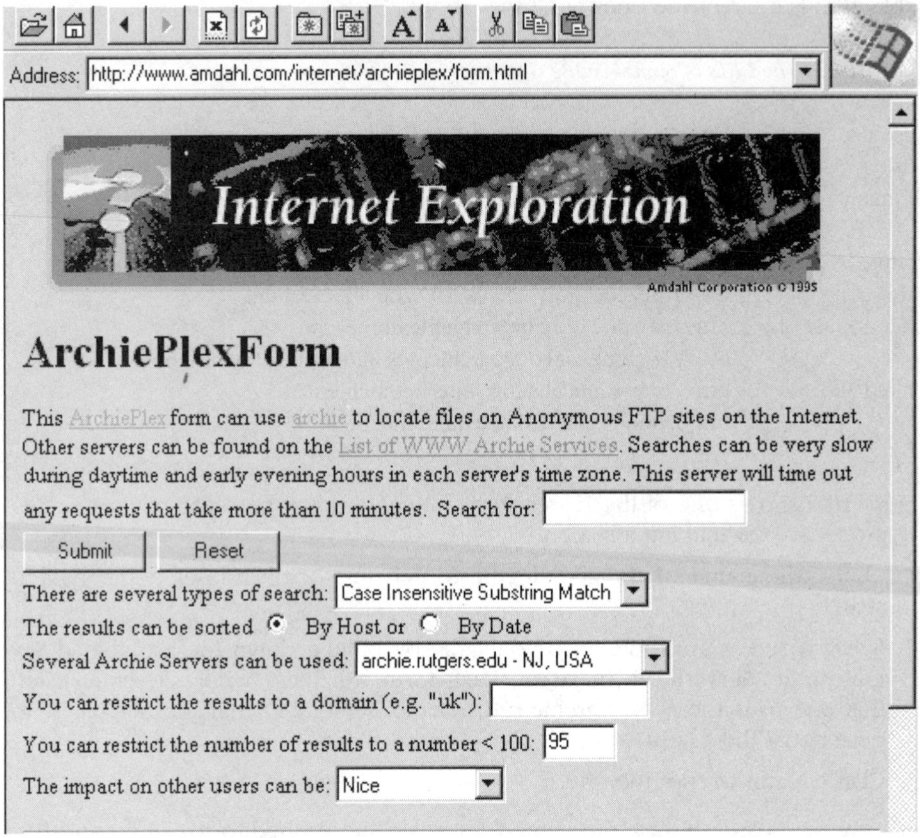

Figure 10-2: WWW Archie Query Form

With that information at your disposal, you should be able to contact that computer using FTP and login as **anonymous**. Next, issue a **cd** command to move to the directory in question. And, finally, issue a **binary** command, because *.zip* files require it, and **get wsarchie.zip**.* Or, much easier, you can use the World Wide Web's FTP interface and click on the filename to fetch it.

Why is it in two places on the same machine? Who knows? It may be the same program, placed in two locations for easy finding, or it could be different versions of the same program. Only the administrator of **ftp.halcyon.com** knows for sure. If you scrolled down the output a bit, you would find that many other anonymous FTP servers have the file you want. Which one should you explore first? This is a significant problem. There are lots of files out there, but you get little or no information to help you decide which file is best to use. Here are several suggestions:

---

* This process is described in gory detail in Chapter 9, *Moving Files: FTP*.

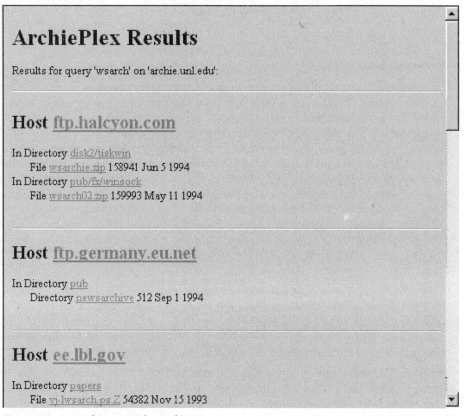

Figure 10-3: Archie via Web results

- Many programs have separate versions for DOS, Windows, UNIX, and the Macintosh operating systems. If a program does run on several kinds of computers, you have to decide which file contains the version you want. The only help Archie gives you is in the directories and filenames. There are no standards for these names, but most server administrators try to name directories in an intuitive, descriptive way. In this example, the first two entries are probably DOS programs (although it is possible that they could be for Windows), since they are stored in subdirectories of a directory whose names contain "win."[*] Filename suffixes provide another clue. Certain kinds of compression and file encoding techniques are common on certain kinds of computers. In particular, .ZIP, .ARJ, .ARC, and sometimes .LZH are frequently used on PCs. (There is a table of these in Chapter 9.)

---

[*] Unfortunately, "win" does not necessarily imply Windows. It can also stand for *winsock*, a standard way applications talk to TCP/IP on a computer. It was developed for Windows but it is also used with DOS. Windows 95's TCP/IP conforms to this standard, so most winsock programs will work with Windows 95.

- Multiple versions of the same software may be available. If you're lucky, a version number will be encoded in the filename, as in these examples:

  ```
  wsarch02.zip
  wsarch8.zip
  wsarch08.zip
  ```

  If some friends told you about the software, you might ask which version they were running. If you can't, you might pick the latest version possible. Again, there are no standards for how versions are encoded into the filename. You could guess that *wsarch8* is a later version than *wsarch2*, and you would almost certainly be right. Sometimes, the directory name provides another clue. If you found directories named */win/old* and */win*, you might presume that the newer software is in the latter directory. The files date can also serve as a version indicator; the later the date, the newer the version. However, you can only compare file dates when both files are on the same server. Some Johnny-come-lately server may have copied a bunch of old software fairly recently, giving it a newer creation date. Also, remember that the terms "alpha" and "beta" are used to denote test versions of software. Unless you are adventurous, stay clear of these.

- If you can, pick an official-looking server. (Remember the security discussion from Chapter 4, *What's Allowed on the Internet?*) Try to pick a server that is run by someone who should be in the business of delivering software, like a computer center, network provider, etc. In this case, though, neither of our two candidates seems to be more "official" than the other.

- If you can, pick a server that is close. Earlier, we said that you should pick an Archie server that's relatively close to you, to minimize the total network traffic and spread the workload among the different servers. The same reasons apply here.

  There's one other important reason to pick an FTP server that's local. If you speak English and grab *GrpIcon* from a server in Finland, you might find that everything has been translated into Finnish. If you pick up a file from a server that's not in your native land, the file might not be in your native language.

- File sizes may not be accurate. They depend somewhat on the kind of computer where the file resides. Some computers give their sizes in blocks rather than bytes, making files appear much smaller than they really are.

If I were trying to decide from which of the sites in the example to get *wsarchie.zip*, I would probably look in the */disk2/tiskwin* on the **ftp.halcyon.com** server. First, the server is run by **halcyon.com**, a network service provider. They have an interest in distributing reliable software to their clients. I don't really know exactly what version of the software I would be getting, but if I got it and unzipped it I could find out. I am presuming that it is newer from the creation date (relative dates on the same server are a bit more accurate since they are administered by the same person). Also, I trust the name *wsarchie.zip* a bit more than *wsarch02.zip*. By using a generic name, the Archie manager may be implying that this is the best file to take; after all, it's easier to search for. The more cryptic name may be an old version that's kept around for historical purposes.

Sometimes a search will match a word in a directory path, but not find a filename in that directory. This was the case at **ftp.germany.eu.net**. In that case, it said that in the directory *pub* there was a directory *newsarchive*. The match succeeded because the search string was contained in the directory name, but there was no filename given. This shows that what was found is a directory that might contain something useful. If you decide that a directory, such as one called *wsarchie*, is promising, you'll have to use anonymous FTP or (click on the directory) to find out exactly what it contains.

Searching by Filename

In our example, we searched for the file *wsarch* and found files named *wsarchie.zip*, among others. Obviously, we are not limited to specifying the filename exactly. How the string you specified relates to the filename is controlled by the pull down list labeled **There are several types of search:**.

The default for this server is **Case Insensitive Substring Match**. This means that an uppercase "A" and lowercase "a" will match each other. So, *wsarchie* would match:

```
WSarchie
wsarchie
WSArchie
```

The second bit of the phrase "substring match" says that the string we specified does not have to match the filename in its entirety. Even though we specified *wsarchie*, we got files named *wsarchie.zip*.

It's usually good to pick a minimal search string that will probably occur in a filename you are looking for and to use case-insensitive substring searching. You can never be too sure what people will name things. Version 8 of *wsarchie* may be found on the Net under each of the following names:

```
/msdos/08/wsarchie.zip
/wsarch08.zip
/wsarchie/version8.zip
```

You're more likely to succeed if you use a substring search, because it's more likely to find all possible matches.

There are other kinds of searching that may be used, depending on how much you know about the file you want. For example, if you are sure that you know exactly how the file is named, you can request an exact file match. With an exact match, you won't have to sort through accidental matches (like *newsarchive*) that are completely unrelated. Or, if the filename is really common and unrestricted substrings get you too many possibilities, you can use a regular expression match (essentially, a wildcarded match) to specify what you want more precisely. Table 10-3 shows the wildcards used in regular expressions.[*]

Table 10–3: Some Archie Regular Expressions

Character	Description
^	The string that follows must match the beginning of the filename
$	The preceding characters must match the end of the filename
[abc]	Matches one character from a set of characters abc
[a-d]	Matches one character from a range of characters a-d
.	Matches any single character
*	Matches any number of occurrences of the previous character
.*	Matches any group of zero or more characters (equivalent to * in most wildcard systems)
[^list]	Matches any character other than one in the list

With regular expressions you can specify a string like *wsarch[1-3].** which matches any filename that starts with *wsarch*, followed by the digit 1, 2, or 3, followed by anything. So *wsarch1.zip*, *wsarch3.zip*, and *wsarch2.arc* would all match.

Regular expressions are complex and most of the time they're overkill. For most purposes, a case-insensitive substring match is appropriate.

Controlling a Search Geographically

The newer Archie servers allow you to restrict a search to a particular geographic area—more formally, a particular set of domains. There are a few reasons why you'd want to do this:

- Some servers, by default, return only information about files within their domain. The Australian server may only return information about files on servers within Australia. An Australian looking for something obscure might need to search FTP sites worldwide.

- If you're looking for a popular piece of software, Archie may present you with a huge list of FTP archives, worldwide, where you might find it. Rather than wading through such a huge list, you might want to restrict the search to servers within your area.

- If you're looking for specialty software, you might have ideas about where to find it. For example, if you're looking for a version of Netscape that's been

---

[*] This is another creeping UNIXism. Regular expressions are a gory UNIX way to specify classes of search strings, like "look for one or more alphabetic characters followed by one character from the following set followed by this string exactly." They can be very complex. Should you need to know more about them, consult O'Reilly & Associates' *UNIX in a Nutshell* by Daniel Gilly.

translated into Japanese, you're most likely to find good, up-to-date software by searching the **.jp** domain.

To restrict (or broaden) an Archie search, you can enter a domain in the **You can restrict the results to a domain (e.g. "uk")** box. If you entered **uk** in that box (note no leading period), only sites whose names ended with ".uk" would be searched. If you want to search multiple domains, you can enter them all, separated by colons. For example, to search for files located in the United States, you would need to enter **us:com:mil:edu:gov**.

Typing this string each time you want to do a search in a particular area could get tedious, but luckily there is a short cut. Each Archie server has defined a list of mnemonics for groupings of commonly used domains. Some of the common ones available on many servers are shown in Table 10-4.

Table 10-4: Geographical Search Area Mnemonics

Mnemonic	English Meaning	List of Domains
africa	Africa	za
anzac	Australia & New Zealand	au:nz
asia	Asia	kr:hk:sg:jp:cn:my:tw:in
centralamerica	Central America	sv:gt:hn
easteurope	Eastern Europe	bg:hu:pl:cs:ro:si:hr
europe	Europe	bg:hu:pl:cs:ro:si:hr de:ie:pt:es:uk:at:fr:it:be:nl ch:cy:gr:li:lu:tr
mideast	Middle East	eg:il:kw:sa
northamerica	North America	edu:com:mil:gov:us:ca:mx
scandinavia	Scandinavia	no:dk:se:fi:ee:is
southamerica	South American	ar:bo:br:cl:co:cr:cu:ec:pe:ve
usa	United States	edu:com:mil:gov:us
westeurope	Western Europe	ch:cy:gr:li:lu:tr de:ie:pt:es:uk:at:fr:it:be:nl
world	The World	All of the above

So, instead of typing **us:com:mil:edu:gov** in the box, we could have typed **usa**.

Other Controls on Searches

Most of the other options you have available to you from these Archie Web pages are pretty obvious. You can use the radio buttons to choose whether you want the output sorted by date or host. Neither one is particularly useful; you usually have to scan a bunch of the output by hand to pick the best location. (Remember, comparing file dates isn't all that useful unless the files are on the same server.)

You can restrict how much output you want. There is a maximum of 100 matches on any given search, but that is usually too much to wade through. This client defaults to 95 matches, but if you are on the end of a slow line 20 might be enough. If you don't find what you want in 20 hits, you probably should use a different search string or type of search.

Finally, there is the question of citizenship. You can give your search a priority ranging from **Nicest** to **Not nice at all**. This page starts at **Nice**, which gets a reasonable response without being boorish about it. If you can't seem to get a search through at this priority, you will probably have better luck trying a different server. If your first server is that busy, raising your priority won't do much good.

Special-Purpose Archie Clients

At the time of this writing, only one Archie client for Windows, WSArchie, is available. The program is available from a number of anonymous FTP sites, including **gatekeeper.dec.com** in the directory */pub/micro/msdos/win3/winsock*. Get the file *wsarch08.zip* and extract the files using PKUNZIP. This will yield the executable *wsarchie.exe* which you can then run.[*]

When you launch WSArchie, it appears as shown in Figure 10-4. Before using it, you must configure it by opening the **User Preferences** dialog in the **Options** menu, shown in Figure 10-5. You can select the server you'd like to use for most of your searches from the **Default Archie Server** drop-down list box. You can also select the type of search you would prefer to use most frequently. Finally, you should enter your e-mail address in the **User ID** text box. This allows WSArchie to provide the Archie server with your e-mail address when you log in.

Using WSArchie is very similar to using the Web form gateway. You enter a search string, select some options, and press **Search**. The **Exact first** box is an interesting twist. If you select it, it means that Archie first performs an exact search and, if that fails to return any results, performs the search you've selected. (In theory, an exact search should be faster.)

Once you've submitted your query, assuming that the information is available from the server, WSArchie shows your position in the server's queue and the estimated time in seconds that is needed for the search. Once the Archie server completes the search, the status bar also informs you how much information (i.e., how many packets) is being received from the server.

---

[*] This is a 16 bit application so your network connection must be available before you start it. If you are using SLIP or PPP and have done nothing else with the network, you will need to start it manually (see Appendix B, *Setting Up Your Internet Connection*).

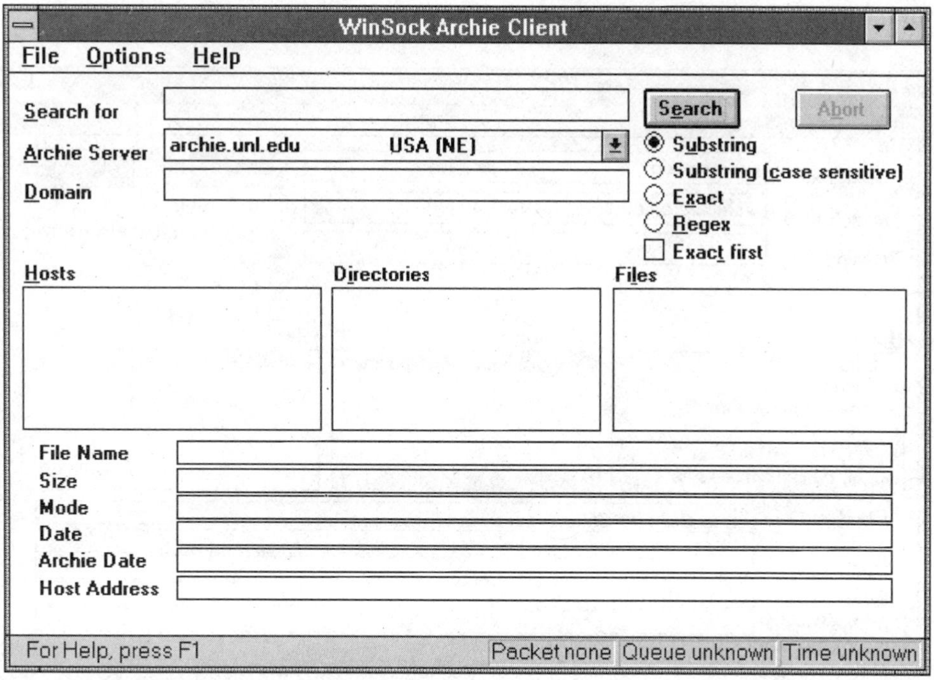

Figure 10–4: The WSArchie window

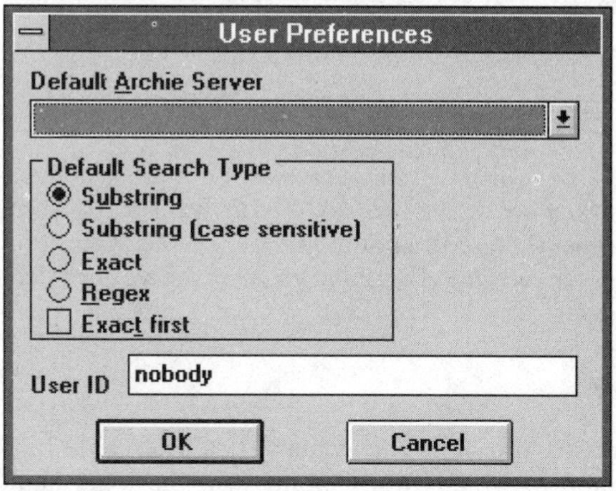

Figure 10–5: The User Preferences dialog

Figure 10-6 shows the results of a search for wsarchie.zip. All hosts having files or directories that match your search specification are displayed in the **Hosts** list box. When you select a particular host, WSArchie displays (in the **Files** and **Directories** list boxes) the files that meet the search criteria and the directories in which they are stored. Information on the file that you select in the **Files** list box is displayed in the lower third of the WSArchie window.

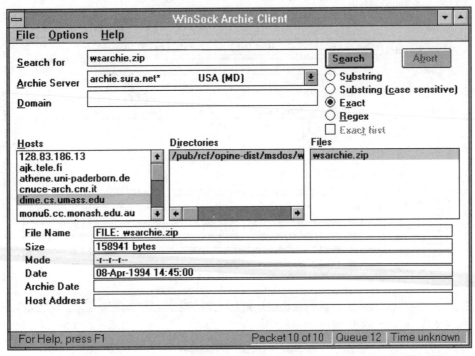

Figure 10–6: The results of a search using WSArchie

Contacting an Archie Client Remotely

Using the Web or an Archie client to contact Archie servers offers great convenience, but there are some things they won't let you do. If you want to do some obscure searches or find out some things about the Archie server, your only recourse will be to contact the server directly via Telnet, or to make your request via e-mail.

Using Archie with Telnet

After you decide which server to use, use Telnet to contact it. It will come back with a standard UNIX login prompt, to which you respond with the login name **archie**:

```
Welcome to Archie.info.AU (aka plaza.aarnet.edu.au)

We acknowledge the support of Sun Microsystems Australia
who donated an additional CPU module for this machine.
```

```
Public access services provided on this machine are
        archie       The Archie System
        de           Directory Service
        netfind      Network Search Utility

Unauthorized access to any other account is prohibited.

Local time is 11:19PM on Friday,  1 September 1995

login: archie
Last login: Fri Sep  1 23:09:18 from cant-t.remote.ds
SunOS Release 4.1.3 (PLAZA) #13: Sun Mar 5 00:29:45 EST 1995
# Bunyip Information Systems, Inc., 1993, 1994, 1995

# Terminal type set to `vt220 24 80'.
# `erase' character is `^?'.
# `search' (type string) has the value `sub'.
Archie.AU>
```

Some servers may ask you for a password. Reply with your e-mail address, as you would with anonymous FTP.

This initial screen gives you a lot of information that will help with your searches. Don't ignore it. According to this screen, Archie thinks you're using a VT220-style terminal, with 24 lines that are 80 characters long, and that you're doing "sub" searches, which is its parlance for "Case-insensitive substring searches."

To do a search, use the **prog** command or its synonym **find** to do an actual search. For example, we'll go fishing for files that may be of use in meteorology. After logging into Archie, we would issue the command:

```
archie> prog meteorology
```

Archie would give me an estimate of how long it would take and eventually would produce the output:

```
# Search type: sub.
# Your queue position: 1
# Estimated time for completion: 5 seconds.
working... O

Host ftp.une.edu.au    (129.180.4.7)
Last updated 01:50 30 Aug 1995

Location: /pub/faqs
  DIRECTORY drwxr-xr-x 8192 bytes 10:29 24 Aug 1995 sci.geo.meteorology


Host quartz.rutgers.edu    (128.6.60.6)
Last updated 22:09 12 Jul 1995

Location: /pub/internet/education
  FILE   -rw-r--r--  44117 bytes  01:41 14 Jul 1994  meteorology-
```

```
        resources-faq.gz
    . . .
```

You can see the output looks very much like the output produced by the Web gateway.

When you're finished searching, you leave Archie with:

```
archie> quit
```

This terminates the Telnet session and returns you to your local computer.

Controlling Archie

The search we just performed didn't demonstrate any new features; we could have done the same thing with a Web form or WSArchie. To get more control over Archie, you need some additional commands. Here is a fairly complete (but not exhaustive) list of commands:

find
> Synonym for the **prog** command.

help
> Displays a list much like this one.

list *regexp*
> Displays a list of anonymous FTP servers that are indexed in the Archie system. If a regular expression is specified, only servers which match the expression are displayed.

mail *destination*
> Sends the result of the last search to an e-mail address. The *destination* is optional. If given, it is taken to be an e-mail address to which the search results should be mailed. If no destination is specified, the value of the variable **mailto** is used as the destination.

manpage
> Displays the complete reference manual description of the Archie system.

prog *string*
> Searches the index of ftp sites for files which match the *string*. The match is controlled by settings of a variety of variables.

set *variable value*
> Used to set parameters for controlling your Archie session. The variable name is required (there is a list of variables in the next section). The value is required only if the variable is not a Boolean (on or off) variable. For Boolean variables, **set** *variable* turns the variable on. For other variables, the value is remembered and used appropriately.

show *variable*

> Displays the value of the specified variable. *variable* is optional. If it is not specified, Archie displays the value of all variables. **show**, with no variable name, is a good way to get a list of valid variable names or to find out your server's default settings.

servers

> Gets a current list of all the known Archie servers.

whatis *string*

> Finds the names of files matching *string* in the descriptive index.

unset *variable*

> Turns off a Boolean variable or clears the value of a string variable.

version

> Returns the version number of the Archie server you are using.

Of these commands, three deserve special attention. **help** takes you into the help subsystem. Once there, **?** gives you a list of all help topics. When you give a help command, you're put into the **help** mode, with the special prompt:

```
help>
```

Type the name of a help topic; to return to Archie's normal command mode, press ENTER on a line by itself, until you get back to the command prompt:

```
archie>
```

The **set** and **show** commands give you control over a number of variables, which in turn control how your **prog** and **find** commands (the basic Archie search commands) work. The **show** command tells you the current value of any variable. For example:

```
archie> show search
# 'search' (type string) has the value 'exact'.
```

This command tells you that the server is set to do "Exact match" searches.

You can change the way the search is conducted with the command:

```
archie> set search type
```

type indicates how Archie should conduct your search. It must be one of **sub**, **subcase**, **exact**, or **regexp**. These correspond to the same old search types we saw in the other interfaces (sub stands for "substring case insensitive," and subcase for "substring case sensitive," etc.).

Here's a partial list of the variables you can work with:

mailto *address*

> Sets a default e-mail address; this address is used whenever the **mail** command is given without a parameter.

match_domain

Specifies a list of top-level domains; the FTP server on which any file resides must belong to one of these domains for a match to occur. Explained more fully in the section on controlling a search geographically.

match_path

Specifies a list of directory components that must be in the pathname for a match to occur. Explained more fully in the section on restricting searches within certain directories.

maxhits *number*

Limits the amount of output to *number* entries. (*Number* must be between 1 and 1000.)

pager

Determines whether the output should stop whenever the screen is full. If **pager** is set, output will be held until you enter a carriage return when the screen is full. This is a Boolean variable. Use **set pager** to turn it on, **unset pager** to turn it off).

sortby *keyword*

Declares the sort order of the output. For a list of the kinds of sorting available, try **help set sort**.

search *keyword*

Sets the search type. This was explained more fully in the section on searching by filename in this chapter.

term *type row col*

Declares that you are using a *type* terminal (e.g., VT100) which has *row* rows on the screen and *col* columns. The type can be any one of the typical terminal abbreviations available in UNIX. *row* and *col* are optional. If they are omitted, the standard size for the declared terminal type is used.

We'll have more to say about using these after discussing the e-mail interface to Archie.

Using Archie by E-Mail

In addition to logging into an Archie server directly, you can use Archie via electronic mail. While it's less convenient than an interactive session, there are two reasons why you might want to use mail. First, you may be forced to: your network might not allow you to contact Archie via Telnet. This would be the case, for example, if your only connections to the outside world are through UUCP or Bitnet. Many of the servers that Archie indexes provide access through **ftpmail** (Chapter 5, *Electronic Mail*) for those networks which can't do FTP. Second, you may not care to wait around for Archie to do the lookup. If you hear about something great at 4:59 and have to run for the train, send an e-mail query—the answer will be there when you get to work the next morning. The same logic applies if Archie tells you that it's busy, or if it's unavailable for some reason.

The format of commands for using Archie by mail are the same as those available using Telnet. Of course, a few like **set term** don't make sense and a few new ones are available to make this kind of access more useful. These additional commands are:

path *e-mail-address*

> Tells Archie to send the responses to *e-mail-address* rather than the address given in the **From:** field of the requesting message. It is useful if you are traversing e-mail gateways and not enough information is conveyed to Archie in the **From:** field for the return trip. If you send requests and never receive an answer, try specifying a very explicit route back to your computer and see if it helps.

compress

> Causes the output sent to you to be compressed and **uuencoded** before being sent. It is suggested you use this option whenever you expect the output to exceed 45K bytes.

quit

> Causes processing to be terminated and any lines following this command to be ignored. Although not new, this is useful if you have a signature file, which Archie might try to interpret as commands.

To access Archie via e-mail, build a message with a series of commands in it and send it to:

`archie@`*server*

where *server* is one of the servers mentioned earlier. Commands must begin in column one of a line. You can have as many commands as you like in a message. Any command which cannot be understood is interpreted as **help**. So if you do anything wrong, you get help whether you need it or not.

For example, let's construct an e-mail message to search for files containing the word "meteorology." The message, ready to be sent, is shown in Figure 10-7. Notice that we specified the search type and the domain list explicitly. Since these settings vary from server to server, you could find out how these variables are set by sending a message with a number of **show** commands and wait for a reply, but why bother? It is probably faster to say what kind of search you want and send it off. Some time later, frequently overnight, you will receive a message back from the server, containing the results.

Additional Features Using E-Mail and Telnet

I said earlier that the Web and clients are a bit restrictive in what they let you do. Now, let's look at some of the features which are only available using e-mail or Telnet.

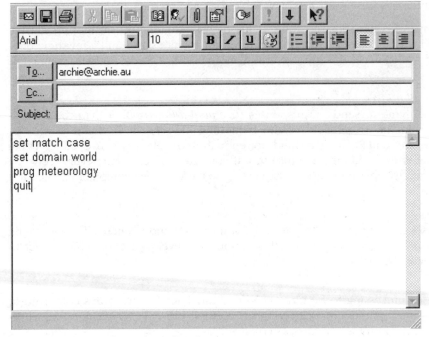

Figure 10–7: E-mail search ready to be sent

Restricting searches within certain directories

There is no way to specify part of a directory name in the **prog** command that you use to start the search. That is, if you say, **prog eudora**, Archie will find directories and files named *eudora*. But, Eudora is a package which runs on both Macintoshes and PCs. If you are interested in only the Windows version, you may not say **prog windows/eudora** (*eudora* in the directory *windows*). In most cases, this is reasonable: the directory structure depends entirely on the FTP server that has the file you want. If you know the directory in which a file resides, it's a good bet that you know the server, too, and don't need Archie.

If you really want to look for a file in a directory, you can, but it takes two commands. First, you must specify which directories to search. You do this by setting the **match_path** variable:

```
archie> set match_path path-list
```

The *path-list* is a list of strings separated by colons. One of these strings must be found in the directory path. This is always a substring match, ignoring case, regardless of the search type you have chosen. For example, to find the Windows version of Eudora, you'd like to restrict your search to directories named *pc* or *win*. To make this search, give these two commands:

```
archie> set match_path pc:win
archie> prog eudora
```

Of course, these aren't the only directories in which you might find the software; they're only good guesses. If you don't find anything, try a broader search. Remember to give the command **unset match_path** first; the **set match_path** stays in effect until it is changed to something else, or **unset**.

Searching the Descriptive Index

Archie also lets you search a descriptive index; this is called a **whatis** search. It searches the so-called "software descriptions database." When administrators place a file in their FTP archives, they may contribute an index entry for the file to help people find it. The index entry creates a relationship between a filename and a set of keywords. When you do a **whatis** search, your search string is used to examine the keyword list. The search is done with the command:

```
archie> whatis searchstring
```

If the search string matches any of the keywords in the descriptive database, Archie prints the name of the files associated with the keywords. (Searches of the descriptive database are always case-insensitive substring searches, regardless of your search type). Once you have a filename that sounds appropriate, you must do a filename search to find out where it is located.

Let's say you were looking for a gene sequence map for E.coli bacteria.[*] If you do a **prog coli**, Archie would return over 100 filenames. Most of the matches are obviously not what you want: the broccoli recipes, the horse colic database, etc. There are a few like *colidb* which might be good, but that's all you know. So you decide to try a **whatis** search to get more information:

```
archie> whatis coli

ECD         Escherichia coli db (M. Kroeger, Giessen)
NGDD        Normalized gene maps for E.coli, S.typh., etc.
                    (Y. Abel, Montreal)
```

The file *NGDD* looks like just what the doctor ordered. To find out where it lives you do a **prog** search, just like you did before:

```
archie> prog NGDD
# Search type: sub, Domain: edu:com:mil:gov:us.
# Your queue position: 2
# Estimated time for completion: 02:40
```

---

[*] As this example shows, Archie isn't just good for looking up software; it's good for finding all kinds of resources.

```
Host ncbi.nlm.nih.gov   (130.14.20.1)
Last updated 02:23  4 Mar 1992
 Location: /repository
   DIRECTORY rwxrwxr-x    512  Jun 25  1990   NGDD
```

This looks even more promising now. It comes from a reliable source, the National Institutes of Health (**nih.gov**). Notice, however, that what Archie found is not a file called *NGDD*, but a directory by that name. So you don't quite know what you really have. You need to anonymous FTP to **ncbi.nlm.nih.gov** and go to the */repository/NGDD* (**cd repository/NGDD**) directory. Do a **dir** command to see what files are there.

Remember one caveat. The **prog** index is up to date to within 30 days. The **whatis** index is not. Someone can create an entry, and sometime later delete the file. So you may occasionally find something with **whatis**, but not be able to locate it with the **prog** command.

As time goes on, the problem with updating the descriptive database has gotten worse. The **whatis** index depends too much on centralized human processing. So much so, that the Archie maintainers have stopped making changes to it. They have designed a new system that allows FTP system administrators to maintain their own information. Unfortunately, this new system isn't widely used yet. For now, Archie users are stuck with an index of pretty old information.[*]

Postprocessing Archie output

Archie's output normally looks like the examples in this chapter. This is fine for human consumption, but occasionally you might want to take Archie's output and use it as input to another program. In this situation, it would be more convenient if all the information about each file were printed on one line, rather than on multiple lines.

Two options give you "one line per file" output formats. They are controlled by the variable **output_format**. Normally, this variable is set to **verbose**, which produces the familiar format. By setting it to **terse**, you get a one line per file output like this:

```
Archie.au> set output_format terse
Archie.au> prog eudora
# Search type: sub, Domain: au, Path: win31:pc.
# Your queue position: 1
# Estimated time for completion: 02:29
working...
```

---

[*] This new system is part of the IAFA templates work being done in the IETF. The templates are forms to be filled out by the administrator of each archive and left on the system in a specially named file. They are gathered during the Archie data acquisition visit to each server, so they would be more up to date, and maintained by people much closer to the data. It is moving towards standardization, but it's not there yet.

```
tasman.cc.utas.edu.au  22:49  1 Nov 1993 512 bytes /pc/win31/
  mail/eudora
csuvax1.murdoch.edu.au  14:05 11 Nov 1993 512 bytes /pub/pc/
  windows/eudora
ftp.utas.edu.au  22:49  1 Nov 1993 512 bytes /pc/win31/mail/eudora
```

This is our same old search for Eudora for PCs and Windows in Australia. Same files, different format. The output is still fairly readable, particularly the date.

The command **set output_format machine** generates output that can be read easily by a computer, but isn't quite so convenient for humans. It gives additional information about file access modes, and displays the file's date in a numeric format. Otherwise, the output is fairly similar to what we saw above:

```
19931101224900Z tasman.cc.utas.edu.au 512 bytes drwxrwxr-x /pc/win31/
  mail/eudora
19931111140500Z csuvax1.murdoch.edu.au 512 bytes drwxr-xr-/pub/pc/
  windows/eudora
19931101224900Z ftp.utas.edu.au 512 bytes drwxrwxr-x /pc/win31/
  mail/eudora
```

CHAPTER ELEVEN

FINDING SOMEONE

Why Isn't There a Single Internet Directory?
CSO Directories
Finding a User on a Specific System
Whois
The USENET User List
X.500 Directory Services
Knowbot Information Service
Netfind
Four11
In Closing

Y ou would think that if the phone company can provide a "white pages" telephone directory of its customers, then the Internet should provide one, too. Well, it does. Just like the phone company, however, there are multiple "phone books" for various parts of the Internet. It is easy to find out Willie Martin's phone number if you know he lives in Chicago. If you don't know where he lives, the task becomes nearly impossible. The same is true of the Internet. You can probably find someone, but the more you know, the easier it will be.

Making a rare attempt not to be confusing, the technical community calls this service the *white pages*, named after the phone book. On the surface, it looks like building a global white pages service should be easy; after all, we have computers. But it's not as easy as it looks. There are a couple of reasons why there is no single service for the entire Internet. I'll discuss this first, then I'll discuss how to look people up.

Discussing how to use the white pages isn't as easy as it should be. There are many different kinds of white pages directories. On top of that, there are usually several different ways to interrogate each kind of directory. For example, one kind of white pages directory is named **whois**. On UNIX systems, there is a **whois** command for accessing these directories; you can also make **whois** queries through Telnet, Gopher, WAIS, and the World Wide Web. Most of the time, these services present white pages directories as simple index lookups.

Why Isn't There a Single Internet Directory?

There are three reasons why a single, unified Internet user's directory doesn't exist:

- Change of user location and work habits
- Lack of standards for directories
- Security and privacy concerns

These factors delayed the creation of such a directory. Slow progress is being made now that some of the fundamental problems have been solved. Let's examine these issues more closely.

Mobile Users

Let's consider the first point by comparing an Internet directory to the telephone directory. You want a phone. You call the company, pay them some money, give them some information, get a phone, and they put you in the directory. If you move, you cancel your service, and the company takes you out of the directory. If you stop paying your bill, the company discontinues your service and takes you out of the directory. You are forced to play the phone company's game: each time you get a new phone, you have to give them information and pay their fees. Under these circumstances, creating and maintaining a directory is easy: the phone company always has all the information it needs.

On the Internet, there is no one group to deal with, no one has to collect information, and in many cases no money changes hands. If my workstation is on the network and you want to be on, I can set up an account for you in five minutes. I'll set up an account for you and boom! you're an Internet user with all the capabilities of the millions of other users. Since there is no monthly charge for the account, there is no reason to turn your account off if you stop using it. It just sits there looking like the active accounts.

This illustrates how difficult it is to keep data accurate, but it's really only the tip of the iceberg. First, many people on the network have multiple accounts. Sometimes they are on co-located computers: everyone in the office has accounts on each other's workstations. Sometimes, they are widely separated: I may have an account at the San Francisco office, so that I can work while I am there. In either case, having an account on an Internet-connected machine makes me an Internet user. It doesn't mean I will ever use that account again. If you send an urgent e-mail message to my account at the San Francisco office, I probably won't read it until next year, when I'm there for the annual sales meeting.

A good directory needs someone to maintain it; in turn, the maintainer needs the cooperation, even if it's forced, of the user. On the Internet, the first part is easy. The second part is almost impossible. Many campuses and corporations maintain internal staff directories. Some of these include electronic access information, and some are on-line. That doesn't mean the information is up-to-date. Most of the information is gathered when a person is hired and deleted when that person retires or quits. Updating the information is optional and frequently not done.

Standards

When every community creates its own version of a directory service, the result is confusion. Every community has its own directory; you need one program to access Joe's Directory of Fishermen Online, another to access Mary's Directory of Physics Grad Students at the University of Omaha, and so on. After an awkward period, a standard technique emerges and is agreed upon. When the people providing the service (Joe and Mary) have converted to the standard, anyone can use the service, regardless of what he or she wants to look up: Joe's and Mary's directories will obey the same rules. But even after the standard has been settled, it can take a long time for everyone to put it into practice.

A long time ago (by computing standards, anyway) the Organization for International Standardization started to develop a standard for directory services called *X.500*. There were some non-standard servers already, built for special groups. As the X.500 standard took longer and longer to complete, more special directory services with their own facilities were built out of need. Now X.500 is a reality, but a lot of the other services are still operational and working just fine. Almost every campus or corporation has its own local service. The people who use them are reluctant to change—if it ain't broke, why fix it? The end result is that a standard exists, and now we're waiting for the Joes and Marys of the world to use it. In the meantime, we have to put up with confusion.

Security and Privacy

Remember when we discussed security and said that a common way to break into a system was to find a valid username and try common passwords? Since an e-mail address usually contains the recipient's login name, some people think making this information public is a breach of security. Therefore, as a matter of policy, some systems refuse to provide any information about users. Many organizations get around this security problem by making sure that e-mail addresses are different from login names.

The other side of the coin is personal privacy. Some people believe that they should be able to control whether or not their e-mail address and user name are publicly accessible. Some countries have very strict personal privacy laws that forbid any personal information to be released without express permission. This is not a problem for voluntary systems on which you ask to be included. Problems arise when you try to include people in directories automatically, without their consent. Most corporations and campuses have e-mail information gathered, but administrative procedures may not be in place to protect the users' privacy. Rather than deal with the administrative problem directly, these organizations solve the problem by refusing to give out any information.

Now that you understand some of the issues, let's look at what white pages directories are available, and how to use them. The facilities are not presented in any order of preference; rather, each one has its own place. You have to decide which one will be most likely to produce results, based on whatever information you already know. Remember, even the best on-line directory is out of date and gives only approximate information. If you really want to know for sure, gather the information yourself; that's much more accurate. If you need to know Jane Doe's e-mail address, give her a call, or look up her business card.

CSO Directories

CSO-style directories are one of the most prevalent on the Internet. A large number of colleges and universities use them to put their student and staff information on-line. To use these directories directly, you need a client called **ph**, which isn't easy to get. It's primarily available at sites running CSO directories, and is occasionally included as part of another package (Eudora, for example). Most people access CSO directories through Gopher, which does a lot more than white pages queries. Because they're usually accessed through Gopher, I'll defer a detailed discussion of CSO directories until Chapter 12, *Tunneling through the Internet: Gopher.*

Finding a User on a Specific System

finger is an old and widely used facility that examines the user login file (*/etc/passwd*) on a UNIX system. It lets you find out someone's login name (hence the e-mail address), plus his or her personal name, given that you know what computer your correspondent uses. **finger** also tells you whether or not the user you're asking about is currently logged in to the target machine. Although **finger** is closely tied to UNIX, there are clients that allow you to make finger-style queries from other types of systems as well.

There are a few different Windows versions of **finger** clients. In this discussion, I've used a **finger** client developed by Lee Murach. It is usually stored under the filename *finger.zip* or *finger31.zip*. This client is available from a number of anonymous FTP sites; see the *Resource Catalog* under "Computing" for a list of some of the sites.

When you launch **finger**, a window opens with a single menu, the **Host** menu, on the menu bar. The only thing that you can really do with it (other than exiting the program) is to select the **Host** option from the **Host** menu. This leads, as you might expect, to the Host dialog shown in Figure 11-1.

The user login ID is optional and specifies the name you want to look up. If you choose to enter a name in this text box, **finger** returns information on all users

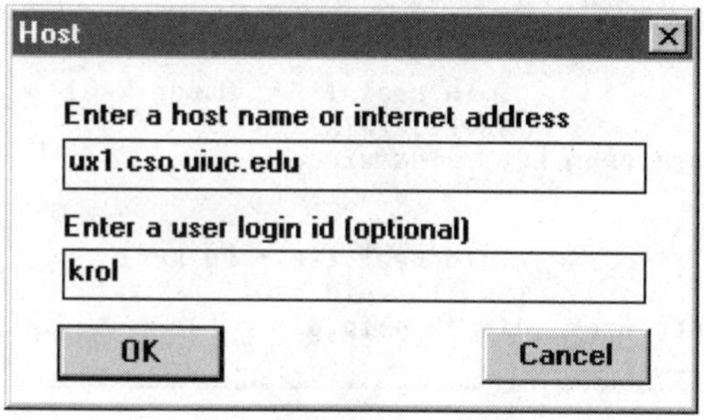

Figure 11-1: The finger host dialog

whose first or last name matches that name, or who have chosen that name as their login ID. The host name (or Internet address) identifies the computer where you want the inquiry to be made.

The mechanics of the search are confusing. The contents of the user login ID field must be one of the following:

- An exact match, case-sensitive, for a user's login name. It may help you to remember that UNIX login names are almost always all lowercase.

- An exact match, case-insensitive, for a user's first name, as listed in the system's accounts file.

- An exact match, case-insensitive, for a user's last name, as listed in the accounts file.

In practice, it's not that bad. If you use lowercase letters for everything, you'll be fairly safe: you won't inadvertently exclude login names, and you'll still find any first and last names that match.

For example, you know that Ed Krol uses the computer **ux1.cso.uiuc.edu**. To find his e-mail address, you might enter the following in the Host dialog, as shown in Figure 11-1:

```
Host name:        ux1.cso.uiuc.edu
User login id:    krol
```

As Figure 11-2 shows, this query found two Krols on the machine **ux1.cso.uiuc.edu**: the first is Marge Krol, with the login name *ajzxmvk*; the second, Ed Krol, with the login of *krol*. There is other information of interest here. If you were looking for a place to send e-mail, you might glean that sending mail to **ajzxmvk@ux1.cso.uiuc.edu** is somewhat futile. You performed the query on August 12, 1995, but the last time that login was used was in April 1995. Obviously, it's not regularly used. Ed Krol, on the other hand, has last used his account last Thursday, August 10, at 6:33. Using this one for e-mail would probably be successful.

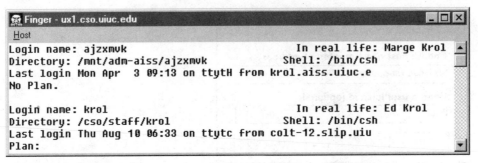

Figure 11–2: finger results

On the surface, the *ajzxmvk* login appears to be owned by a shiftless person with no plan. But since this is a UNIX system, "No Plan" actually refers to the file *.plan*. If the file *.plan* exists in the user's home directory, **finger** displays its contents. The file *.project* is treated similarly; if it exists, its contents are displayed at the end of **finger**'s report.

finger is often used to get a list of the people who are currently using a system. To do this, just omit the login name from the Host dialog. For example, entering the following in the Host dialog instructs **finger** to find out who's logged in to the system **uxc.cso.uiuc.edu**:

```
Host name:          ux1.cso.uiuc.edu
User login id:
```

The results of **finger**'s query are shown in Figure 11-3. Notice that the output looks quite different and gives information about the current login as well as some personal information.

```
Finger - ux1.cso.uiuc.edu                                    _ □ ×
Host
Login      Name            TTY Idle    When      Where
opr        System Operator b0  4:25 Sun 08:51
m-yang     yang ming hong  p1     4 Thu 12:50    rm125.mrl.uiuc.e
dehaan     Jason A. DeHaan p2  2:20 Wed 13:07    secondhome
n-crow     crow naomi      p3       Thu 12:50    acq19.library.ui
zinzow     Mark Zinzow     p5     9 Thu 12:12    suzie
gopher     Gopher Client   p6     4 Thu 12:50    VAX.LCLS.LIB.IL.
stafford   Gale Stafford   p7       Thu 11:04    ih-scmac
shenson    Stanley W. Henson p8 1:01 Thu 08:37   ithaca.cso.uiuc.
```

Figure 11–3: finger results for a system

You've probably noticed the big problem with **finger** already: if you don't know that Ed uses the computer **ux1.cso.uiuc.edu**, you can't look him up. In practice, that's what you're least likely to know.

finger as a general information server

finger's ability to display a *.plan* file provides a simple and effective way to distribute small amounts of information. It's often used for this purpose, playing a role as a very simple database server. For example, in the account for **quake@ geophys.washington.edu**, someone maintains a listing of recent earthquake information in the *.plan* file. So, if you use **finger** to inquire about that login, you get something like Figure 11-4.

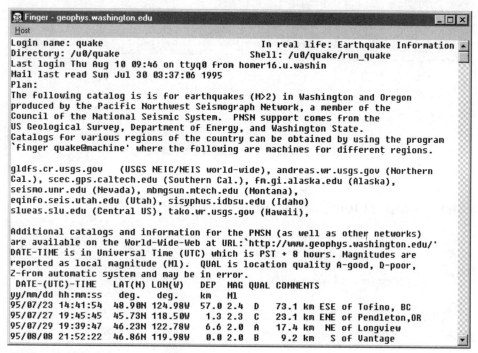

Figure 11-4: finger retrieving a plan

If you look through the *Resource Catalog*, you'll find a couple of organizations that provide similar information through **finger**.

finger and the World Wide Web

In the last chapter, you saw that, in addition to serving as a hypermedia browser, a Web client can double as an Archie client if it accesses a special ArchiePlexForm gateway. The versatility of Web clients, however, does not end there. Although a Web browser itself (like Netscape Navigator) is unable to communicate directly with a **finger** server, it can communicate with one through a *finger gateway*—an intermediary that translates between the hypertext protocol used by the Web and the protocol used by **finger**.

To access a **finger** gateway, use the following URL:

```
http://www.cs.indiana.edu/finger/gateway
```

If you are using Netscape, the window should resemble Figure 11-5.

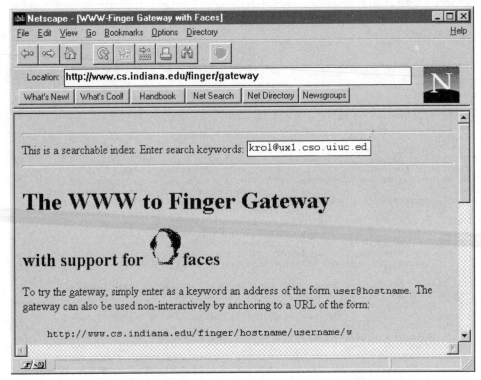

Figure 11–5: A finger gateway

When you enter an e-mail address in the search field, Netscape provides you with the **finger** information for that address, as shown in Figure 11-6.

When finger fails

Like most client/server software on the Internet, **finger** requires that a server be running on the target computer to service the request. If you try to use **finger** on an uncooperative host, you will get a message like "Cannot connect to remote server." In this case, there is nothing you can do. **finger** is simply unavailable on the remote computer. You might complain to the administrator—but, likely as not, the administrator has decided that running **finger** is a security risk (a point that's been hotly debated on the Net). Try other means to find the information you require.

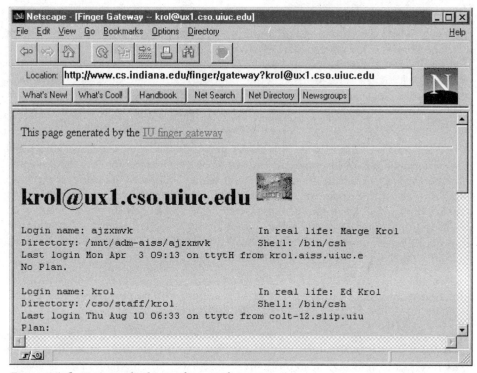

Figure 11-6: Netscape displaying finger information

Whois

whois serves three functions at once: it is the name of a particular white pages directory, a general kind of directory, and an application to access it. The confusion arises because **whois** was the original way of doing Internet directory lookups (on what was at the time the ARPAnet). When you are the only game in town, people aren't too accurate with names. You would say, "Gotta run, e-mail me, I'm in **whois**," and everyone would know how to look you up.

The original directory was maintained by the *Network Information Center* (NIC) of the Defense Data Network (DDN), and at its peak contained about 70,000 entries. In its prime you were automatically listed in the directory if you had any authority over an IP network or a domain name; in addition, anyone who wanted to be listed could get in the directory by filling out a form. Life was good and simple.

With the ARPAnet's decommissioning, the DDN NIC stopped supporting a global white pages directory for the Internet. The DDN NIC still exists, but it only supports a directory of people in a restricted part of the Internet called MILNET (used by the U.S. Department of Defense and its contractors). Currently, the Registration

Services portion of the InterNIC, the new Internet information provider, maintains the **whois** directory for non-military network and domain contacts.

This new **whois** directory is a little different from its predecessor. It doesn't accept random listings from people who want to be included; it is restricted to people with authority over some bit or piece of the Internet. It is restricted because the **whois** technology was never designed to support really huge directories (it doesn't "scale well"). You can still use these two **whois** directories to find someone, but they only really help if you're looking for someone connected with the networking infrastructure.

That's still not the entire story. When the initial database was split up, the DDN NIC wanted only DDN people, and Registration Services of the InterNIC wanted only network and domain contacts. No one wanted the network hangers-on, who requested to be listed for no particular administrative reason. These fell to yet another party, the Database Services section of the InterNIC, whose task is to begin building the big global white pages directory. They started by putting up these old records in yet a third directory. (This directory is really a WAIS database, but it is searchable through the **whois** interface.)

There are many ways to access these directories. I'll discuss the **whois** program and Telnet access in detail here. You can also get to these directories through the InterNIC's Gopher, WAIS, and World Wide Web servers.

There is a **whois** client for Windows available via anonymous FTP from the site **ftp.sunet.se** in */pub/pc/windows/winsock/apps/winwhois* or **bitsy.mit.edu** in */pub/dos/potluck/winsock/*. The program is stored with the filename *winwhois.zip*.

When you launch WinWhois, you'll see the window shown in Figure 11-7. Simply type the last name of the person you are looking for into the **Name to Query** field and click the **Make Query** button. WinWhois returns the matches it finds for the name you've entered.

What actually can you search for? Individual names are stored as:

```
last name, first name, titles
```

Matches always begin at the beginning of this text, so it is easiest to look up people by last name. If you are hazy about spelling, you can search on a portion of the last name by ending the search string with a period. For example, the search string "kro." matches all names beginning with the three characters "kro," as shown in Figure 11-8.

If you match more than one item, WinWhois gives you a shortened output format, shown above. The funny string in parentheses, like (EK10) for "Krol, Ed", is a unique identifier known as a *handle*. If you have someone's handle, you can get his or her complete record by entering the handle in the **Name to Query** field, preceded by an exclamation point. The exclamation point tells WinWhois that you want to look up a person by handle rather than name. If you omit it, the results are actually the same, although the search takes a little longer.

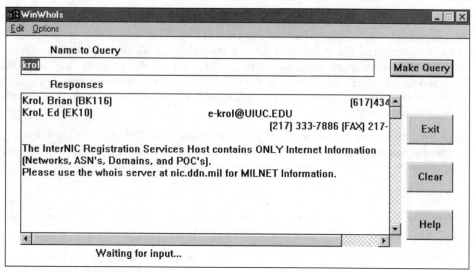

Figure 11–7: A whois query

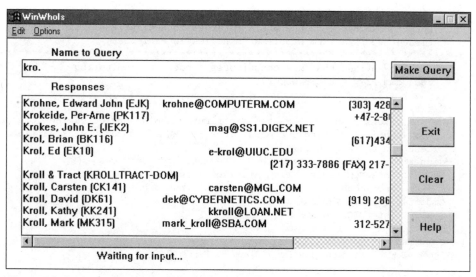

Figure 11–8: A whois query with multiple matches

By default, the WinWhois program looks up the **whois** server at **rs.internic.net**. You can specify an alternate server by selecting **Change hosts** from the **Options** menu. This is convenient because there are a number of **whois**-style services around. Some sites that got into the game early standardized on **whois** for their on-line phone books; you can access any of these special servers with WinWhois.

For a list of available **whois** servers, select **Get list of servers** from the **Options** menu.

So far, we've only discussed searching two of the three major **whois** directories. How do you get at the third? By pointing WinWhois at **ds.internic.net**. The server at **ds.internic.net** automatically searches all three directories in sequence. Because this server accesses all three databases, it's the best one to use for most requests—unless you know you're looking for someone involved with network management.

You can also access the Registration Services **whois** using Telnet. Start by Telneting to the **internic.net** address.* When you get there, give **whois** as a login name, and start making queries. For example, here's the output of a sample session:

```
BSDI BSD/386 1.1 (rs2.internic.net) (ttypc)


**********************************************************************
* -- InterNIC Registration Services Center  --
*
* For wais, type:                    WAIS <search string> <return>
* For the *original* whois type:     WHOIS [search string] <return>
* For referral whois type:           RWHOIS [search string] <return>
*
* For user assistance call (703) 742-4777
# Questions/Updates on the whois database to HOSTMASTER@internic.net
* Please report system problems to ACTION@internic.net
**********************************************************************
Please be advised that use constitutes consent to monitoring
(Elec Comm Priv Act, 18 USC 2701-2711)


6/1/94
We are offering an experimental distributed whois service called referral
whois (RWhois). To find out more, look for RWhois documents, a sample
client and server under:
gopher: (rs.internic.net) InterNIC Registration Services ->
        InterNIC Registration Archives -> pub -> rwhois
        anonymous ftp: (rs.internic.net) /pub/rwhois
Cmdinter Ver 1.3 Thu Aug 10 19:35:54 1995 EST
[vt100] InterNIC > whois
Connecting to the rs Database . . . . . .
Connected to the rs Database
InterNIC WHOIS Version: 1.0 Thu, 10 Aug 95 19:37:40


Whois: krol
Krol, Brian (BK116)                                       (617)434-3143
Krol, Ed (EK10)              e-krol@UIUC.EDU
                                 (217) 333-7886 (FAX) 217-244-7089
Whois: !ek10
Krol, Ed (EK10)          e-krol@UIUC.EDU
    University of Illinois
```

---

* Not every **whois** server allows Telnet access.

```
     Computing and Communications Service Office
     195 DCL
     1304 West Springfield Avenue
     Urbana, IL 61801-4399
     (217) 333-7886 (FAX) 217-244-7089

     Record last updated on 18-Jul-95.
Whois: ^D
[vt100] InterNIC > ^D
```

When you are done, you need to send two CTRL-D characters: one to end the **whois** session, and one to close the connection to the InterNIC.

In case you are wondering, the **rwhois** service mentioned in the above sample session is an experimental distributed **whois** service. The idea behind this service is that if the **whois** database you query doesn't have the information you are looking for, **rwhois** can "refer" you to another database closer to your goal. The client and server software for **rwhois** are still under development, so I'm not going to describe them any further.

The **whois** database contains more than just people. There are several other kinds of entries. Do you care? Yes, for two reasons. First, if you make broad searches, you will probably see some odd stuff returned. Second, you may occasionally need other kinds of information. After the information about users, the most useful data in the **whois** database concerns network and domain ownership. Let's try to find some information about the networks at the University of Illinois. This time, let's do it by e-mail. Construct a message like the one below and send it using your favorite e-mail program:

```
To:       mailserv@internic.net
Subject:
whois University of Illinois
```

In about a day, you'll get a response containing an answer to the request. It should look something like this:

```
From mailserv@internic.net Fri Aug 11 08:06:22 1995
Date: Fri, 11 Aug 1995 06:35:18 -0400
From: Mail Server <mailserv@internic.net>
To: krol@uxh.cso.uiuc.edu
Subject: Re: whois university of illinois

University of Illinois (GARCON) ARGUS.CSO.UIUC.EDU          128.174.5.58
University of Illinois (NET-NCSA-K12-NET) NCSA-K12-NET         192.17.6.0
University of Illinois (NET-UI-ISDN-NET) UI-ISDN-NET           192.17.7.0
University of Illinois (NET-UI-ISDN-NET2) UI-ISDN-NET2        192.17.16.0
University of Illinois (NET-UIUC-NCSA) UIUC-NCSA              130.126.0.0
University of Illinois (ASN-UIUC) UIUC                                 38
University of Illinois (ILLINOIS-DOM)                        ILLINOIS.NET
     ...
```

Our query was about the University of Illinois. But you can use the same technique to inquire about people, domains, and other networks.

The USENET User List

MIT maintains a list of the names and e-mail addresses of everyone who posts USENET news. This list is generated by automatically extracting names and addresses from all the news postings that pass through MIT—which includes just about all of the official and alternative newsgroups described in Chapter 7, *Network News*. The extraction itself is fairly simple. Most news messages contain a line like the following:

```
From: krol@ux1.cso.uiuc.edu (Ed Krol)
```

A newsreader uses this information to tell you that someone named Ed Krol posted the message. MIT's address service uses this line to infer that the e-mail address **krol@ux1.cso.uiuc.edu** will probably work if you want to contact Ed Krol.

To use this service, send an e-mail message to **mail-server@rtfm.mit.edu**. The body of the message should look like this:

```
send usenet-addresses/search-string
```

Search-string is the name that you are interested in finding. The *search-string* can only be one word without spaces. Matches will not occur on a partial word. So you can't use "kro" to find "krol." For example, to look up "Ed Krol" using the USENET address database, send a message like this:

```
To:        mail-server@rtfm.mit.edu
Subject:
send usenet-addresses/krol
```

Some time later, you'll receive a response:

```
From mail-server-bounces@bloom-picayune.MIT.EDU Fri Aug 11 09:28:15 1995
Date: Fri, 11 Aug 1995 10:58:08 -0400
From: mail-server@bloom-picayune.MIT.EDU
To: Ed Krol <krol@uxh.cso.uiuc.edu>
Subject: mail-server: "send usenet-addresses/krol"
Reply-To: mail-server@bloom-picayune.MIT.EDU
Precedence: junk
X-Problems-To: owner-mail-server@rtfm.mit.edu

-----cut here-----
"Marty A. Krol" <krol@uwindsor.ca>    (May 9 95)
krol@uwindsor.ca (Marty (Marcin) Krol)        (Apr 9 95)
krol@enet.net (Jim Krol)        (Mar 29 95)
krol@ux1.cso.uiuc.edu (Ed Krol)        (Jun 7 95)
krol@server.uwindsor.ca (Marcin Krol) (Nov 17 94)
krol@server.uwindsor.ca (Marcin (Marty) Krol)(Feb 26 95)
thomas.b.krol@den.mmc.com (Tom Krol)  (Jan 16 95)
Ed Krol <krol@ux1.cso.uiuc.edu>        (Jan 11 95)
```

```
Marcin Marty Krol <krol@SERVER.UWINDSOR.CA>   (Nov 23 94)
e-krol@uiuc.edu(Jun 14 95)
jarosk@evitech.evitech.fi (J.Krol)    (Jun 9 95)
krol@lreri.lviv.ua     (Jun 22 95)
   ...
```

Notice that the search found multiple Krols, and a few possible e-mail addresses for Ed Krol. You have to figure out, or guess, which address is most likely to reach the person you are looking for.

If your search request fails to locate anyone, the response will look like this:

```
From mail-server-bounces@bloom-picayune.MIT.EDU Fri Aug 11 09:26:39 1995
Date: Fri, 11 Aug 1995 10:58:33 -0400
From: mail-server@bloom-picayune.MIT.EDU
To: Ed Krol <krol@uxh.cso.uiuc.edu>
Subject: mail-server: "send usenet-addresses/ekrol"
Reply-To: mail-server@bloom-picayune.MIT.EDU
Precedence: junk
X-Problems-To: owner-mail-server@rtfm.mit.edu

-----cut here-----
No matches for "ekrol".
-----cut here-----
```

This service has a few minor limitations. First, it doesn't know about people who don't post news at all, or who only post to local newsgroups, or who post with restricted distribution that doesn't include the MIT campus.

More importantly, this service depends on information in the **From:** field of news postings. Many users use pseudonyms when they are posting messages. So, if Ed Krol has his newsreader configured to post with an alias like "Mr. Hockey," you won't find "Ed Krol" in this directory. If you happen to know that Ed's alias is "Mr. Hockey," though, you could look this up, instead.

But since most people, sooner or later, post something to USENET, this database is probably the best place to look up someone's e-mail address.

X.500 Directory Services

None of the services I have mentioned so far scale well. That is, **whois**-style directories work just fine for 70,000 entries, but would fail horribly if asked to list millions of users. As is often the case, the Internet is the victim of its own success; when **whois** was planned, no one thought that the database would ever have 70,000 entries, to say nothing of the millions of Internet users who aren't listed.

At the beginning of this chapter, I mentioned the X.500 directory service, adopted by the Organization for International Standardization (ISO). Unlike **whois**, X.500 scales very well. In fact, it is the only currently available technology which does, so it has been chosen for the global on-line Internet directory that the InterNIC is building. Unfortunately, although it solves the scaling problem, it creates a different problem: the standard offering is very cumbersome to use directly. I'll start by talking a bit about the philosophy of X.500, then move on to looking at how to do a search with an X.500 client.

Native X.500

Let's go back to our first analogy: the phone company. If you were looking up Willie Martin in Chicago, you could start at one end of a shelf of phone books and look at each one sequentially, but it would take all day. Instead, you would find the U.S. section of the shelf, within that find the Illinois section, then find the Chicago directory, and finally look up Willie. This is known as a tree structure. Figure 11-9 shows how to model a collection of phone books as a tree.

If you want to find a person, you start at the top and pick the most likely path. When you finally get to the node at the bottom, which has the directory information, you can look up Willie. The path from the top of the tree to the bottom should identify a particular Willie:

```
World, US, IL, Chicago, Willie Martin
```

This points to your Willie, not the one in Grovers Mills.

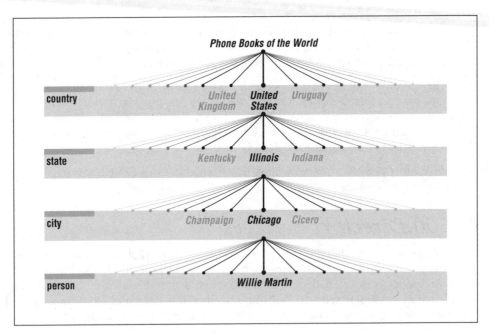

Figure 11-9: Phone book structure

X.500 views "the white pages problem" as a library of telephone books. Each participating group is responsible for its own directory, just as Ameritech is responsible for the Chicago phone book. Figure 11-10 shows the tree structure for the

X.500 directory service. The structure is very similar to our phone book model, though the labels for each level are different. The levels shown are fairly static. At the organization level, each one has responsibility for its own lower structure. This is analogous to the set of phone books for Illinois, where any changes to the books, or to their structure, are made by Ameritech.

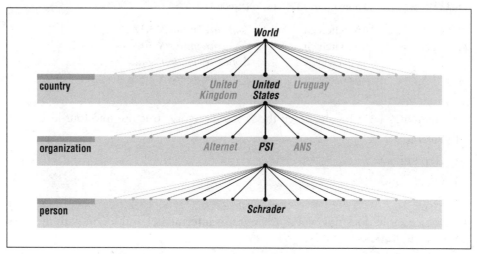

Figure 11–10: X.500 tree structure

Therefore, with the X.500 service, once you know the right organization, you can probably find the name you want without trouble. If you like, you can poke around and find out about the organization's internal structure, but you don't need to. Limiting your search to the organization will suffice for doing queries.

How does this work? If I were searching for my buddy Bill Schrader, who works for Performance Systems International, I would type something like:

```
c=US@o=PerformanceSystemsInternational@cn=Schrader
```

As you can see, direct X.500 has a fairly complex syntax. You might not have considered **whois** terribly "friendly," but X.500 is downright antisocial! To be fair, X.500 was designed to be used by computers, not people. As we know, computers aren't bothered by complexity.

X.500 access

The ISO usually decides that standard terminology isn't good enough to describe what they do, so they always develop their own language. X.500 clients are known as *Directory User Agents* (DUA). To do a white pages search, you need to get the DUA you are using to contact a *Directory Server Agent* (DSA), which actually does the search for you. A number of DUAs for Windows are currently available, as Table 11-1 shows; if you can't find one, though, you can access a public

DUA with Telnet, Gopher, and the WWW. We'll concentrate on Telnet access using the client at **ds.internic.net**[*], since it's generally easier to use than the Windows clients.

Table 11–1: X.500 Client Software for Windows

DUA	Anonymous FTP Site	Directory
SWIX22.EXE	ftp.switch.ch	*/software/msdos/X.500*
WDUAINST.EXE	ftp.switch.ch	*/software/msdos/X.500*
	naic.nasa.gov	*/software/windows-dua*
WINDUA.ZIP	ftp.switch.ch	*/software/msdos/X.500*

The InterNIC's DUA breaks down the X.500 directory structure into four levels:

1. Person
2. Department
3. Organization
4. Country

In practice, how does this work? Telnet to **ds.internic.net** and log in with the password **x500**. It looks like this:

```
              InterNIC Directory and Database Services

     . . .

   SunOS UNIX (ds)

   login: x500
   Last login: Mon Aug 14 12:27:10 from motif.jsc.nasa.g
   SunOS Release 4.1.3 (DS) #3: Tue Feb 8 10:52:45 EST 1994

   **********************************************************************

        Welcome to the InterNIC Directory and Database Server.

   **********************************************************************


        Welcome to the InterNIC X.500 Directory Service
```

---

[*] Older books on the Internet, including the first edition of this book, recommended the public client called **fred**, run by PSI, Inc. on the computer **wp.psi.com**. Fred appears to be dead. The computer is still there, but as soon as you give the password "fred" it cuts the connection. Use the InterNIC; it is more reliable.

```
Connecting to the Directory - wait just a moment please ...
You can use this directory service to look up telephone numbers and electronic
mail addresses of people and organizations participating in the Pilot
Directory  Service.

Select the mode you would like:

S Simple queries - if you know the name of the organization you want to search
  [this is how the interface always used to behave]

P Power Search - to search many organizations simultaneously

Y Yellow Pages - power searching but allows user to search for an entry
    based on criteria other than the entry name

U Enter search string in form of User-Friendly Name - e.g.,
    p barker, ucl, uk

I Brief instructions explaining the program modes and how to use the program

? The help facility - usage and topics

Q To quit the program

Enter option:
```

Once you give the login name **x500**, you are logged in without a password, and
the search software is available to you. Enter an **s** to enter simple query mode; this
means that the InterNIC DUA prompts you each step of the way as you complete
your query. It begins by asking you for the name of the person for whom you're
searching.

Let's say you want to look up your old friend Bill Schrader again. You remember
he changed jobs and now works for the firm "Performance something or other."
How do you find him? First, you need to find the organization's exact name. Let's
look at all the organizations that start with the letter "p." This can be done by
responding to the first two questions (person's name and department name) with
a RETURN, and typing "p*" when you're asked for the organization:

```
Enter option: s
?           for HELP with the current question you are being asked
??          for HELP on HELP
q           to quit the Directory Service (confirmation asked unless at the
            request for a person's name)
Control-C   abandon current query or entry of current query

Simple query mode selected
Person's name, q to quit, * to list people, ? for help
:-              type RETURN
Department name, * to list depts, ? for help
:-              type RETURN
Organization name, * to list orgs, ? for help
```

```
:- p*
Country name, <CR> to search `United States of America,' * to list
  countries, ? for help
:-                     type RETURN
United States
```

The **p*** says: "find all the entries starting with p of type *organization*." Note the use of the ***** as a wildcard to match any string of zero or more characters. The results of this search are:

```
Got the following matches.  Please select one from the list
by typing the number corresponding to the entry you want.

United States
    1 Pace University
    2 Pacific Northwest Laboratory
    3 Performance Systems International
    4 Portland State University
    5 Princeton University
    6 Princeton University Plasma Physics Laboratory
    7 United States Postal Service
```

Number three looks like a good candidate for Bill's employer. Let's display it by responding to the following query with a **3**:

```
Organization name, * to list orgs, ? for help
:- 3
United States
  Performance Systems International
    postalAddress         PSI Inc.
                          Reston International Center
                          11800 Sunrise Valley Drive
                          Suite 1100
                          Reston, VA 22091
                          US
                          PSI Inc.
                          5201 Great American Parkway
                          Suite 3106
                          Santa Clara, CA 95054
                          US
                          PSI Inc.
                          165 Jordan Road
                          Troy, NY 12180
                          US
    telephoneNumber       1-703-620-6651 (Corporate Offices)
                          +1 800-836-0400 (Operations)
                          +1 800-82PSI82 (Sales)
                          +1 518-283-8860 (Troy Office)
                          +1 408-562-6222 (Santa Clara Office)
    fax                   +1 703-620-4586
                          +1 518-283-8904
                          +1 408-562-6223
```

Yes, that's it. Now let's try to look up Bill:

```
Person's name, q to quit, * to list people, ? for help
:- schrader
Department name, * to list depts, <CR> to search all depts, ? for help
:-            type RETURN
Organization name, <CR> to search `Performance Systems International,'
           * to list orgs, ? for help
:-            type RETURN
Country name, <CR> to search `United States of America,' * to list
  countries, ? for help
:-            type RETURN
```

Notice that Performance Systems International became the "default organization" for this search because we displayed it in the previous search. So here we just had to press RETURN at the Organization prompt, rather than retyping the name. Here is the successful result:

```
United States of America
  Performance Systems International
     Reston
       William Schrader
          postalAddress        PSI Inc.
                               Reston International Center
                               11800 Sunrise Valley Drive
                               Suite 1100
                               Reston, VA 22091
                               USA
          telephoneNumber      +1 703-620-6651 x310
          fax                  +1 703-620-4586
          electronic mail      wls@psi.com

Person's name, q to quit, <CR> for `schrader', * to list people, ?
  for help
:- q
Do you want to quit the Directory Service (y/n)? y
If you have any comments, or have had any difficulties while using this
service, or if you would like further information, please contact:

  InterNIC Directory Services Help
  e-mail:        admin@ds.internic.net
```

The quit command, q, tells the client that you're finished. This ends the session and logs you out.

Remember that X.500 is a decentralized database. Every participating organization is responsible for its own server. Sometime a server may be unavailable. If this occurs you will get the message:

```
The search for `schrader' has failed, probably because a Directory
server is temporarily unavailable.

In the meantime, displaying organization details.
For information on people, try again a little later.
```

This means that the server that's responsible for the organization "Performance Systems International" was unavailable; you had better try other means to find your name. You might try the same query a few hours later, on the chance that PSI's server is only temporarily out of commission.

Knowbot Information Service

The Knowbot Information Service (KIS) is an experimental white pages meta-server. That is, it does not itself hold any white pages data. Instead, it knows about other servers, and allows you to query them all through one set of commands. You say "find krol" and it contacts **whois** servers, X.500 servers, **finger** servers, and so on. You don't have to think about what tool to use; Knowbot does that for you.

On the surface, this sounds so nice that you're probably wondering why I bothered talking about the other servers. The problem is that the Knowbot "ease of use" philosophy is somewhat constrained by practicality. KIS could easily be made to access every host on the Internet when looking for a person, but the search would take days. Therefore, you don't really escape the basic phone book problem: you need to know something about how to search before you can search effectively. A Knowbot can use **finger**, but only if you tell it what host to inquire on. It can use X.500, but only if you tell it an organization. In short, you have to know enough about these services to use them through KIS, but why bother? It is far easier to inquire with **finger** directly than to have a Knowbot do the search for you.

Nevertheless, Knowbots are useful, because they know how to access some unusual directories. One such service is the MCImail directory, which contains information about users of MCI mailboxes. Another unusual directory is the RIPE directory, which contains the names and addresses of Internet networking people in Europe. Let's see how it works.

KIS can be used with Telnet. You Telnet to port 185 of **info.cnri.reston.va.us**.

When Telnet makes the connection, you'll be asked to add your e-mail address to the KIS "guestbook"; if you want to be private, you can ignore this. The easiest way to use KIS is to type the name you want to find at the prompt. For example, let's look up "krol" again, this time using KIS:

```
                    Knowbot Information Service
     KIS Client (V2.0).    Copyright CNRI 1990.    All Rights Reserved.


     KIS searches various Internet directory services
     to find someone's street address, e-mail address and phone number.

     Type 'man' at the prompt for a complete reference with examples.
     Type 'help' for a quick reference to commands.
     Type 'news' for information about recent changes.
```

```
Backspace characters are '^H' or DEL

Please enter your e-mail address in our guest book...
(Your e-mail address?) > krol@ux1.cso.uiuc.edu

> krol
Trying whois at ds.internic.net...

The ds.internic.net whois server is being queried:

No match for "KROL"

The rs.internic.net whois server is being queried:

Krol, Brian (BK116)                                         (617)434-3143
Krol, Ed (EK10)                    e-krol@UIUC.EDU
                                (217) 333-7886 (FAX) 217-244-7089


The nic.ddn.mil whois server is being queried:

Krol, Ed (EK10)
   University of Illinois
   Computing and Communications Service Office
   195 DCL
   1304 West Springfield Avenue
   Urbana, IL 61801-4399
   (217) 333-7886
   Krol@UXC.CSO.UIUC.EDU
Trying mcimail at cnri.reston.va.us...
Multiple matches found, results may be incomplete.
<names deleted>

Trying ripe at whois.ripe.net...
<names deleted>

Trying whois at whois.lac.net...
No match found for KROL
> quit
```

You can make as many requests as you like in this fashion. If your request had not
been serviced at the NIC, the Knowbot would have gone ahead and tried a number of other places. Unless you tell it otherwise, it will try, by default, the following directories:

1. DDN NIC and InterNIC **whois** servers

2. MCImail

3. RIPE

KIS knows how to search in many more places, including most of the places we have visited in this chapter and some we haven't. You can get a list of all the directories it knows about with the command **services**:

```
> services
1.   nic   -- User and Point Of Contact (POC) DBs from internic (mostly US)
2.   mcimail   -- MCImail directory of users
3.   ripe   -- User and point of contact DB from European NIC
4.   latin-america-nic   -- User and POC for Latin America and Caribbean
5.   x500   -- Quipu directory lookup -- worldwide (specify country, org)
6.   finger   -- Unix finger service (specify an organization or machine)
7.   nwhois   -- Unix whois service (specify an organization or machine)
8.   quipu-country   -- Lists countries with x500 service
9.   quipu-org   -- Lists organizations with x500 service (specify country)
>
```

If you want one of these listed directories, like the combined Latin American directories, used in the search, add it with the **service** command:

```
> service latin-america-nic
```

When you are done, you can exit by typing **quit**.

Netfind

Netfind is a useful but intrusive way to find people. It isn't really a white pages directory; it's more like a private investigator. You tell Netfind to find someone, give it some idea of where to look, and it searches that general geographical area for you. On the surface this sounds really great, but it should be employed only in the most desperate cases. It's not extremely efficient—either of your time or of the computer resources on the Net. Finally, like a private investigator, it *is* intrusive, querying computers all across the Internet.

Netfind does its work in two phases. In the first phase, it takes the list of "hints" you gave and locates every domain in that geographical area. If the list is small enough, it uses a variety of means, like **finger**, to interrogate each machine in the area. If there are too many domains, Netfind shows you the list and asks you to pick a likely few, then does its **finger**ing within your selected domains. Of course, if you don't know where someone is, you might not know enough to pick likely domains.

The most common way to do a Netfind search is to Telnet to a Netfind server; alternatively, you can use Netfind through an integrated package like Gopher. As before, I'll concentrate on Telnet access here. To start, pick a server from Table 11-2 and Telnet to it.

Table 11–2: Public Netfind Access Sites

Computer Name	Location
archie.au	Melbourne, Australia
bruno.cs.colorado.edu	Boulder, Colorado
dino.conicit.ve	Venezuela
ds.internic.net	Plainfield, New Jersey
eis.calstate.edu	Fullerton, California
krnic.net	Taejon, Korea
lincoln.technet.sg	Singapore
malloco.ing.puc.cl	Santiago, Chile
monolith.cc.ic.ac.uk	London, England
mudhoney.micro.umn.edu	Minneapolis, Minnesota
netfind.ee.mcgill.ca	Montreal, Canada
netfind.elte.hu	Hungary
netfind.fnet.fr	France
netfind.icm.edu.pl	Poland
netfind.if.usp.br	Brazil
netfind.mgt.ncu.edu.tw	Taiwan
netfind.oc.com	Dallas, Texas
netfind.sjsu.edu	San Jose, California
netfind.uni-essen.de	Germany
netfind.vslib.cz	Czech Republic
nic.uakom.cs	Slovakia
redmont.cis.aub.edu	Birmingham, Alabama

Most of these sites expect you to log in as **netfind**. Once there, you enter a search string that looks something like this:

```
name hint hint hint...
```

Name is usually the person's last name, and the hints are keywords used to constrain the search to an area. In all the search strings you give, case is ignored. The hints can be city and state names (if you know them), or domain names, separated by spaces instead of periods. Let's look for "krol" at a university in Illinois:

```
Enter person and keys (blank to exit) --> krol university illinois
```

Netfind says the search is too broad, and it returns a list of hundreds of domains where it would be happy to look. Here's a carefully chosen chunk of the list:

```
cs.uiuc.edu (computer science department, university of illinois,
  urbana-champaign)
csl.uiuc.edu (university of illinois, urbana-champaign)
cso.uiuc.edu (computing services office, university of illinois,
  urbana-champaign)
cso.niu.edu (northern illinois university, dekalb, illinois)
csrd.uiuc.edu (university of illinois, urbana-champaign)
```

The search is too broad because it will look at the University of Illinois, Urbana; the University of Illinois, Chicago; Illinois State University; and so on. If you really wanted to narrow the search, you could do University of Illinois, Urbana, but there are still hundreds of domains there. The search becomes productive only if you know that this guy works for the Computing Services Office (CSO):

```
Please form a more specific query.
Enter person and keys (blank to exit) --> krol illinois university cso
Please select at most 3 of the following domains to search:
0. cso.niu.edu (northern illinois university, dekalb, illinois)
1. cso.uiuc.edu (computing services office, university of illinois,
   urbana-champaign)
2. corn.cso.niu.edu (northern illinois university, dekalb, illinois)
Enter selection (e.g., 2 0 1) --> 0 1
The domain 'cso.niu.edu' does not run its own name servers,
        and there is no aliased domain IP address/CNAME/MX record for
        this domain -> Skipping domain search phase for this domain.
------
Domain search completed.  Proceeding to host search.
SYSTEM: ux1.cso.uiuc.edu
        Login name: ajzxmvk               In real life: Marge Krol
        Directory: /mnt/adm-aiss/ajzxmvk   Shell: /bin/csh
        Last login Mon Apr  3 09:13 on ttytH from krol.aiss.uiuc.e
        No Plan.

        Login name: krol                  In real life: Ed Krol
        Directory: /cso/staff/krol        Shell: /bin/csh
        Last login Mon Aug 14 08:42 on ttysS from nuada.grainger.u
        No Plan.

FINGER SUMMARY:
- Remote mail forwarding information queries (SMTP EXPN) were not
  supported on host(s) searched in the domain 'cso.uiuc.edu'.
- Found multiple matches for "krol" in finger output, so unable to
  determine most recent/last login information or most promising
  electronic mail information.  Please look at the above finger search
  history and decide for yourself which is best.
```

If you know that much about "krol", you can look directly in the University of Illinois' on-line white pages server instead of **finger**ing every machine at the campus.

The bottom line is that if you have any clue about someone's whereabouts, it's probably better to use a few of the on-line white pages servers than Netfind. If, when you last heard of your buddy Willie Martin, he was a computer programmer at an Illinois university, it would probably be faster to try every on-line phone book in Illinois looking for "martin, wil*" than to use Netfind. If you look in a white pages directory for "martin, wil*", and it doesn't find someone, you can be reasonably sure he is not there and move on to another directory. With Netfind, you never know. You might look for Martin in an Illinois university, and it would return hundreds of departmental domain names, most of which hire programmers. You can waste a long time searching and still come up empty.

Even if you know someone's whereabouts, there's no guarantee that Netfind will work. Let's say that you know Willie is a chemist at the University of Illinois. There's no reason to believe you'll find him by searching the Chemistry department. He almost certainly has an account there—but he may not use his chemistry department account to read mail. He may read his e-mail on a computer in the cso domain. Or he may not read e-mail at all. Unfortunately, Netfind is really good at finding computers people never use. Your college Anthropology professor has probably been assigned an account for reading e-mail, but he may not even know the account exists. Netfind doesn't care; it will locate the e-mail address anyway. Netfind works best when you can make good educated guesses about where people are located and how they work; unfortunately, those guesses are often hard to make.

Four11

The Four11 White Page Directory is a relatively new on-line white pages service for Internet users. It claims to be the largest Internet white page directory, with over 1.1 million listings. Four11 gets its listings from "voluntary" registrations (you have to register to use the service), public sources like the USENET user list, and automatic registrations from Internet service providers.

Four11 is actually a commercial Web-based service, but all Internet users are provided a free listing and free basic searching capabilities. Use the following URL to access the Four11 directory:

```
http://www.four11.com/
```

As you can see from Figure 11-11, you have to enter your e-mail address and your Four11 password to be able to search the directory. To get a Four11 password, you'll need to register a listing with the directory. That isn't such a bad thing, since your friends and business acquaintances will be able to find your e-mail address there.

You can register by following the link for first-time users. Fill out the registration form with the pertinent information; you can include as little or as much personal information as you want. If you have a personal home page on the Web, you can include its URL in your listing. After you submit your information, you'll be allowed to search the Four11 directory and your password will be sent to you via e-mail within 24 hours. After you have your password, you can log in and search the Four11 directory using the form shown in Figure 11-12.

Enter as much information as you can about the person you are searching for. With the free searching provided by Four11, you are allowed to view up to 30 matches for a particular search. If your search returns more matches, Four11 tells you that you need to narrow your search.[*] You can use the * wildcard character in the Four11 search fields; if you're looking for your friend Tim Jones, but you aren't

---

[*] Another option is to upgrade your Four11 membership. That'll cost you money, but will give you more search options.

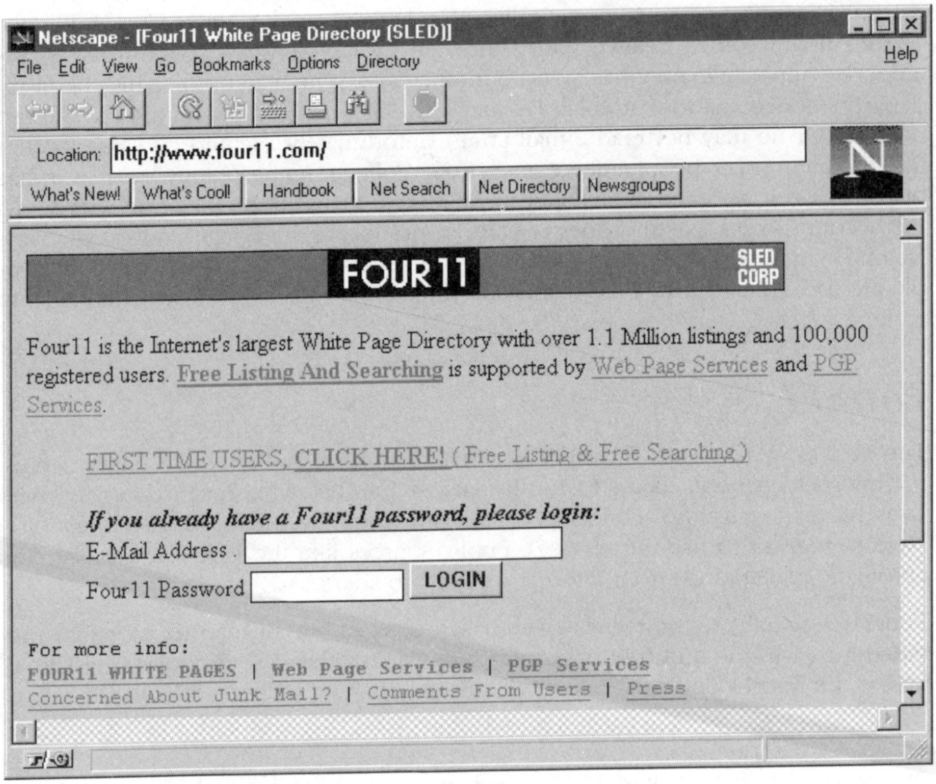

Figure 11–11: Four11 white page directory

sure if he's going by Tim or Timothy these days, you might try "tim*" in the **First** field.

Some of the search fields may not be too helpful in narrowing your search. For example, let's say you are looking for an old college buddy who you know has moved to Colorado. You might try entering his last name and the state abbreviation. That will work fine if your buddy has registered with Four11, but it won't work if the information has come from another source. Much of the information currently in the Four11 directory is based on the USENET user list, which only includes a user's first and last name and an e-mail address. As more people register with Four11, the information provided by the directory will become even more accurate, and you'll be able to narrow your search more effectively.

Of course, there's a problem with the voluntary registration process. The information in the Four11 directory is only going to remain accurate if individual people maintain their entries. If you register with Four11 and then your e-mail address changes a few months later, you'll need to update your entry. If you don't, your friends and colleagues won't be able to locate your new e-mail address.

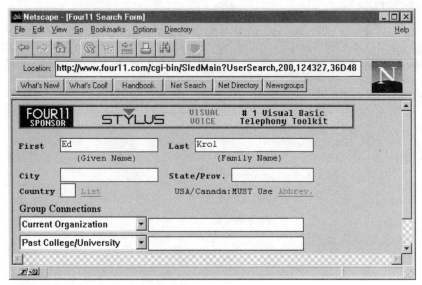

Figure 11–12: Four11 search form

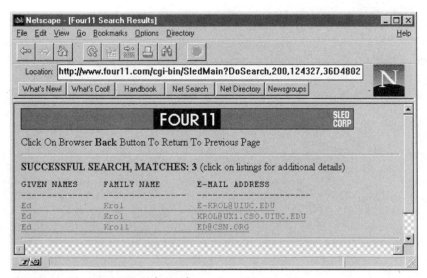

Figure 11–13: Four11 search results

Let's look up Ed Krol again. If we only enter "krol" in the **Last** field, Four11 says there are too many matches, so we also need to enter "ed" in the **First** field. As you can see in Figure 11-13, the search returns three matches.

In Closing

If you think that this is all very confusing—so many tools, so little time—you've got the picture. Directory services are a big problem, and there isn't any really good solution. The best you can do is to arm yourself with a good arsenal of weapons: learn which tools are available, be prepared to try all of them, and don't be too surprised if none of them work. You can usually find who you're looking for, if you look hard enough.

## CHAPTER TWELVE

TUNNELING THROUGH THE INTERNET: GOPHER

The Internet Gopher
Working with Gopher Resources
Searching with Gopher
Remembering Where You Are
The Web and Gopher
A Last Word

Tools like Telnet and FTP once were the major software utilities used to get information on the Internet. In most cases, they were command-line utilities: they placed the onus on you, the user, to understand the commands needed to get the software to operate, and to know where the data that you want resides. In recent years, a number of tools have been developed that aim at making the Internet more friendly by decreasing your need to know exactly where particular resources are located. These tools help you to search a variety of on-line resources.

To understand what each of these tools does, think of your local public library. It's convenient, and it has a fairly good collection on its shelves. It also belongs (most likely) to a system of cooperating libraries. The library in the next town belongs to the same system, and it has a lot of the same material as yours. But it also has some different materials. If your library doesn't have something, the neighboring library will honor your library privileges. You don't even need to visit the other library in person. You talk to your local librarian, arrange an interlibrary loan, and the materials you need are shipped from the next town to you.

This chapter discusses Gopher, a lookup tool that lets you prowl through the Internet by selecting resources from menus. If you want to use one of the resources that Gopher presents, it helps you access it. This is like helping you browse the remote library's card catalog and automatically sending the material you want. It doesn't really matter where the library is located, as long as it is part of the Gopher system.

In the next chapter, we'll look at Wide Area Information Service (WAIS). This service helps you search indexed material. You can search for particular words or phrases; it gives you a list of on-line files that contain those words. WAIS is like walking into a library with a quote ("These are the times that try men's souls"), and having the library automatically check out everything that contains it.

In Chapter 6, *The World Wide Web*, I discussed the newest arrival from the Internet's toolshop: the World Wide Web. On the surface, the Web looks like a variation on Gopher: it's another menu-based service that helps you access different resources. However, the Web is based on a much more flexible "hypertext" model that allows cross-references, or links, between related resources. Some of these related resources may also be different media. The Web allows pictures, text, and audio to all appear in a single document. And, unlike Gopher, the Web has the potential for more than just the passive consumption of information. The Web really offers a different paradigm for working: if you have access to a Web server and a hypertext editor, it supports all kinds of collaboration and joint authorship. The number of Web servers on the Internet is growing by leaps and bounds.

In the first edition of this book, I touted Gopher as one of the hot new Internet tools. But as the World Wide Web has taken off, the number of new Gopher servers has, in fact, leveled off. However, there's still a wealth of information available through Gopher servers on the Internet; universities, the K-12 community, and many government services only provide some information exclusively through Gopher. So it's definitely worth knowing what Gopher is all about. Best of all, you can use a Web client, like Internet Explorer or Netscape Navigator, to explore Gopher servers.

The Internet Gopher

Gopher, or more accurately, "the Internet Gopher," allows you to browse for resources using menus. When you find something you like, you can read or access it through Gopher without having to worry about domain names, IP addresses, changing programs, etc. For example, if you want to access the on-line library catalog at the University of California, rather than looking up the address and Telneting to it, you find an entry in a Gopher menu and select it. Gopher then "goes fer" it.

The big advantage of Gopher isn't so much that you don't have to look up the address or name of the resources, or that you don't have to use several commands to get what you want. The real cleverness is that it lets you browse through the Internet's resources, regardless of their type, just as you might browse through your local library, with books, filmstrips, and phonograph records on the same subject grouped together.

Let's say you're interested in information about the American West: history, climatological data, mineralogy, and so on. You can use Gopher to wander around the Internet, looking for data. By looking through a menu of "on-line catalogs" or "libraries" (the exact menu item will vary, depending on your server), you see that the University of California library catalog is available, and you know that its collection of Western Americana is very strong; so you access the catalog and try to

look up relevant books. (You may even be able to use Gopher to arrange interlibrary loans through the on-line catalog, if the library permits it.) A search of FTP
archives finds some data about the relationship between drought cycles and snow
pack, which is interesting; looking further, you could probably find some meteorological statistics from the time of the Gold Rush.* Yes, you still need to know what
you're looking for, and a little bit about where the resource might be located, but
Gopher makes the search less painful.

To think about how to use Gopher, it's best to return to our well-worn library
analogy. Think of the pre-Gopher Internet as a set of public libraries without card
catalogs and librarians. To find something, you have to wander aimlessly until you
stumble on something interesting. This kind of library isn't very useful, unless you
already know in great detail what you want to find, and where you're likely to
find it. A Gopher server is like hiring a librarian, who creates a card-catalog subject
index. You can find something by thumbing through the subject list, then showing
the card to the librarian and asking "Could you help me get this, please?" If you
don't find it in one library, you can electronically walk to the next and check
there.

Unfortunately, Gopher services usually did not hire highly trained librarians.
There's no standard subject list, like the Library of Congress Subject Headings,
used on most Gophers to organize things. The people who maintain each server
took their best shot at organizing the world, or at least their piece of it. It's the
same state we would be in if one library had things filed under a subject called
"Folklore, American" and another had the same works under "Funny Old Stories."
Each server is a bit different—you have to approach each one with an open mind.

Gopher does not allow you to access anything that wouldn't be available by other
means. There are no specially formatted "Gopher resources" out there for you to
access, in the sense that there are hypertext (HTML) documents, FTP archives, or
white-pages directories.† But, once you find something you want to "check out,"
Gopher also helps you with that. Gopher knows which application (Telnet, FTP,
white pages, etc.) to use to get a particular item you are interested in and does it
for you. Each type of resource is handled a bit differently. However, they are all
handled in an intuitive manner, consistent with the feel of the Gopher client you
are using.

If you've followed the discussion so far, you should realize that it doesn't really
matter what Gopher server you contact first. Your home server only determines

---

* I don't know if such a database exists—but you could certainly use Gopher to check. A
little experience will teach you a lot more than this book.

† Some files might only be available through Gopher, but that is strictly a security issue. If
you access those files through Gopher, they come to you via **ftp**.

the first menu you see. The other menus all come from whichever server is appropriate at that point. Each server, like each library, has a unique collection.[*] Popular files, like collections of frequently asked questions, may be in several places. Obscure collections of data might only be found through a single server. If you don't find what you want at your initial library, you can search elsewhere. When you find what you like, you get it by interlibrary loan. With libraries, this can take a while; with Gopher, getting material from somewhere else is instantaneous.

Finally, the system is smart enough to enforce licensing restrictions. Some software or resources (e.g., on-line newspapers) may only be licensed for use within a particular city or campus. You may access a remote Gopher server, but it may prevent you from accessing a particular resource because you are not local. This is annoying, but inability to enforce licensing has been a major stumbling block in the delivery of on-line information. Gopher seems to have taken a step in the right direction.

Gopher is a lot harder to talk about than to use. So, if you are mildly confused, just press on. Find a Gopher client and play with it! The information is there for the taking. It's there to be used. No one is watching you and laughing at your mistakes. So make some!

Finding a Gopher Client

To access the Gopher system, you need a Gopher client program for your PC. There are a number of public domain or shareware Gopher clients for Windows. Ultimately, the choice of a client isn't important; find one that suits your taste. You can get the software you need from the anonymous FTP site **boombox. micro.umn.edu**, in the directory *pub/gopher/Windows*. You can also use Archie to find other sources for the client software—in fact, that's a good way to practice. I've chosen to use a Gopher client called WSGopher to illustrate how Gopher works; the filename for this client is *wsg-xx.exe*, where *xx* indicates the version number.

Whichever client you decide to install, it will be pre-configured with the Internet address of a home server. Since all servers are public, it doesn't really matter where it points initially. You can start the client, get a menu, and browse the Gopher system. When you have some experience, you can decide which Gopher server you want to be your home and change the configuration accordingly.[†]

If you want to try Gopher before you download a Gopher client, you can access the system through one of the public Gopher sites. Pick a site from Table 12-1 that is geographically close to you, **telnet** to the computer name shown, and login

---

[*] In reality, the collection might be housed elsewhere, but you don't care—it will be fetched automatically should you request it.

[†] How you change the configuration varies from client to client. Check the documentation that comes with the client you have installed.

Where Gopher Was Born

The name "Gopher" is an interesting pun. It started out as a distributed campus information service at the University of Minnesota, home of the "Golden Gophers." Since its primary function is to "go fer" things, the name Gopher was coined.

The service was designed so that each piece of a bureaucracy could have control over its own server and data. That is, the school administration could have a computer in the administration building that could deliver information on administrivia. The athletic department could have a sports-schedule server in its offices. Each academic department could provide a server with a class schedule, and so on. There could be as many servers as there were groups who wanted to provide them.

Gopher's developers then created a special application that could guide students to the information, with no training required. To do this, they organized the system by topic, so that it looks like one large database, rather than hundreds of smaller databases. It can access files in FTP archives, phone numbers from white-pages servers, library catalogs, and other databases with special-purpose (Telnet-based) servers, whatever. Only Gopher knows where the data really is, how to access it, and that there are multiple servers providing it.

It didn't take much effort to see that if this could work for a bunch of servers in various departments, it could work for servers all over the world. All it took was the Internet to connect them all together. In the space of about four years, the Gopher system grew from one site to over 1300 sites.

using the corresponding login name. It automatically starts a non-graphical Gopher client for you when you login.

Public-access Gophers are fine for getting the flavor of the Gopher system, but you will be severely hampered in certain areas. Any use which either leaves the Gopher system, such as accessing Telnet resources; requires disk space, such as saving files you find; or involves e-mailing the results, will be prohibited. If you want to do these things, you should get a Gopher client for your own system.

I'm not going to explain how to use the public Gopher client in this chapter. If you want to check out Gopher this way, consult the on-line help system for a quick overview of using the client. It's actually quite simple and intuitive.

Table 12-1: Public Gopher Access Sites

Computer	Login	Location
consultant.micro.umn.edu	gopher	North America
ux1.cso.uiuc.edu	gopher	North America
gopher.msu.edu	gopher	North America
gopher.ebone.net	gopher	Europe
info.anu.edu.au	info	Australia
gopher.chalmers.se	gopher	Sweden
tolten.puc.cl	gopher	South America
ecnet.ec	gopher	Ecuador
gan.ncc.go.jp	gopher	Japan

How Gopher Works

When you first start up a Gopher client, it contacts its home server and asks for its main menu. The server sends the menu and some hidden information to your client. The hidden information tells your client what each item on the menu represents (e.g., a text file, a directory, a host, a white-pages server, etc.), the IP address of a server for that item, a port number to use, and a directory path to a file. The IP address could be the home server itself, if that's where the resource resides; it could just as easily be another server somewhere else. It doesn't matter; when you pick a menu item, the client always does the same thing. Your client saves its current position (in case you want to return) and contacts the new server. Then the process repeats itself.

Eventually, you will choose a resource rather than a menu. Your Gopher client will choose an appropriate utility for dealing with the resource you select, whatever it is. If it is a file, the client FTPs it for you. If the resource is a "login" resource (i.e., a system you can log in to), it creates a Telnet session. If it's a collection indexed by Archie or WAIS, Gopher uses Archie or WAIS to find out what's relevant. The Gopher client you are using allows you to speak to it in a screen-oriented, menu-driven fashion. It takes what you say and turns it into real commands for the appropriate application. So, if you are in Gopher, you never have to type an FTP **get** command.

Working with Gopher Resources

Getting started is easy. Start your Gopher client or **telnet** to one of the public-access clients. With WSGopher, the first menu looks like Figure 12-1. But regardless of the client you're using, you should see a menu similar to the one in Figure 12-1.

If your initial server resides at the University of Minnesota, you may find items in the menu about Minnesota campus events. If you use the University of Illinois'

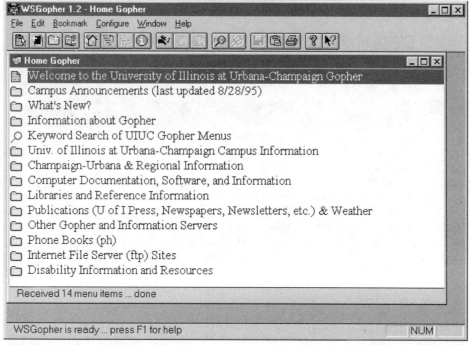

Figure 12–1: Initial Gopher menu

server, as in our example, you'll find items of interest to its students. In addition to these "local interest" categories, though, you should always find a few topics of general interest (for example, "Libraries and Reference Information") and a way to reach other servers ("Other Gopher and Information Servers"). You're also likely to find some introductory information; this is typically the first item in the list. Usually it is be pretty obvious what an item is from the menu entry. If it isn't, try accessing it and see if it looks interesting.

Gopher clients keep track of several different types of entities. The most important are directories and text files; we'll see the others later. All clients use some kind of flag to show you what kind of entity any menu item represents. The WSGopher client uses a folder icon to represent directories. A directory is really equivalent to another menu. That is, if you select a directory and access it, you'll see another menu—this time, one that's more specific to your topic.

With the WSGopher implementation, you select a menu item by clicking on the item or using the arrow keys to highlight the item you want. If you are interested in "Libraries and Reference Information," select this item. Notice that the item has a folder next to it, meaning that it's a directory; expect another menu when you access it. When you want to access this directory, or any other resource you've selected, press the ENTER key or simply double-click on the item. If you access

"Libraries and Reference Information," you'll see the menu displayed in Figure 12-2.

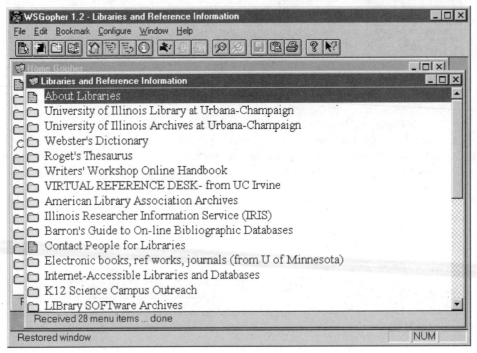

Figure 12-2: Libraries and Reference Information menu

As you can see from Figure 12-2, WSGopher opens a separate window for each menu that you access. While this feature is nice in that you can easily view the contents of a number of menus, you may also find that you quickly get buried in windows. To avoid this problem, simply close the windows for menus that you aren't interested in before you continue exploring the interesting menus.

If you find yourself somewhere you don't want to be, or if you decide that you're done with a topic, you can move back to where you came from by clicking the **Back** button on the toolbar. If you really get lost, you can get back to your home menu any time by clicking the **Home** button. There are many useful buttons on WSGopher's toolbar, shown in Figure 12-3.

The "Libraries and Reference Information" menu is longer than the first menu we looked at. Conveniently, WSGopher provides a scroll bar in the window, so that you can view all of the items in the menu. As you explore with Gopher, you may

	Fetch Bookmarks	Bring up the Bookmarks window (same as Bookmark —> Fetch)
	Add Bookmark	Add the current item to the bookmark list (same as Bookmark —> Add Bookmark)
	Add Directory Bookmark	Add the current directory to the bookmark list (same as Bookmark —> Add Directory Bookmark)
	Edit Bookmarks	Bring up the bookmark editor (same as Bookmark —> Edit Bookmarks)
	Home	Go to the home Gopher server (same as File —> Home Gopher)
	Top	Go to the top menu of the current Gopher server
	Back	Go to the previous menu (same as Window —> Back Track)
	Info	Show information on the current item (same as File —> Info on Item)
	Fetch	Fetch the current item (same as File —> Fetch)
	Cancel	Cancel the current transaction (same as File —> Cancel)
	Cancel All	Cancel all transactions (same as File —> Cancel All)
	Find	Find text in Gopher window (same as Edit —> Find)
	Find Next	Find next occurrence in a Gopher window (same as Edit —> Find again)
	Save	Save the current item (same as File —> Save Item)
	Copy	Copy the current item to the clipboard (same as Edit —> Copy)
	Print	Print the current item (same as File —> Print)
	Version	Get WSGopher version information (same as Help —> About WSGopher)
	Help	Get context-sensitive help (same as Help —> Context help)

Figure 12-3: WSGopher toolbar

find yourself in a menu with hundreds of items. The **Find** button provides an easy way to search for text in a menu. If you click the **Find** button, you'll see the window shown in Figure 12-4.

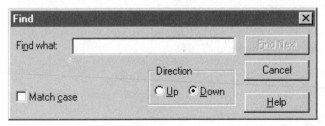

Figure 12–4: The Find window

Enter the string you are searching for and then click **Find Next**. WSGopher positions the cursor at the next menu item which contains that string. If Gopher can't find the string you're looking for, you'll get a message saying "Text not found."

Looking at Text Files

The menus we've looked at so far have shown us mostly directories. But a few of the items have been other things. For example, some of the items are preceded by file icons; these are text files. To read a text file, access it just like you accessed a directory: double-click on it or select it and press ENTER. For example, let's say you want to peek at the "About Libraries" item. When you double-click on the item, you'll see something like Figure 12-5.

Notice that the text-viewing window has a scroll bar, so you can look at the entire file. If you want a copy of a document you are looking at, you can save the document to your system by clicking the **Save** button on the toolbar. WSGopher brings up a standard Save window, so that you can store the file on your system.

In the next few sections, we'll visit a few other menus. These should give you a feeling for how to navigate through Gopher, and what kinds of information you're likely to find.

Moving to Other Servers

By poking around with Gopher on your home server, you might find 80 percent of everything you ever wanted to find. Now you need to find the other 20 percent. You can do this by poking around on other servers. Most Gopher main menus usually have an entry that looks something like "Other Gopher and Information Servers," as you saw in Figure 12-1. The wording may change from server to server. Sometimes it may be one level down in menus, underneath "Other Services" or something like that. It may be hidden, but it's always there.

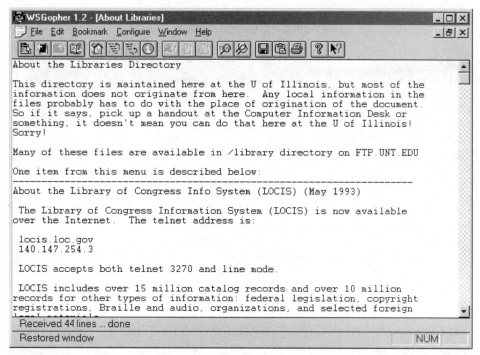

Figure 12–5: Viewing a text file

Moving from one server to another isn't different from any other search: you look through menus and pick a resource. So, after picking the "Other Gophers" entry, you may have to go through a few screens to find one you want. Some servers break them up alphabetically according to the server's name, while others break them up by geographical area, usually by continent. Move around until you find an entry you want to try; eventually you should see something that looks like Figure 12-6.

Notice that other servers are flagged as directories. If you think about it, this makes sense—if you access any of these servers, you get a menu of services. It's not important that the services are provided by another server.

From the list above, you might be able to gather that some servers are general, like the one we have been using. Other Gopher servers have a particular focus. On a focused server, you might not find any of the specific items we've seen so far, like the glossary of network terms or a general directory of white pages services. But you will always find a way to move to other Gophers. If your interests lie in the area of one of these special servers, you might consider making it your home base. The "Academe This Week" server would be an obvious choice if you're specifically interested in academia. It can place much of the information you need for day-to-day existence at your fingertips—and someone else maintains it for you!

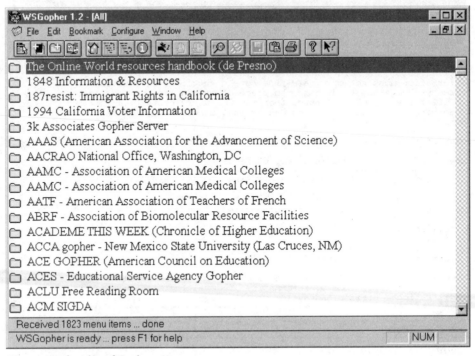

Figure 12–6: A list of Gopher servers

If you already have a particular Gopher server in mind, there's an easier way to get to it than going through a chain of Gopher menus. You can point the WSGopher client at a particular server by selecting **New Gopher Item** from the **File** menu. When WSGopher displays the window shown in Figure 12-7, enter the server's Internet address in the **Server name** field and click **OK**. Let's say you want to access the "Academe This Week" gopher, **chronicle.merit.edu**. To do so, just enter the Internet address in the window and click **OK**.[*]

Now you'll jump immediately to the "Academe This Week" main menu; you don't have to track the server down. Given the number of available Gopher servers, this is often a more effective way to get to a particular resource. It's how we list Gopher resources in the *Resource Catalog*.

---

[*] You can get the Internet address of a Gopher resource by clicking the **Info** button. When WSGopher displays the information about that resource, jot down the **Host** information. That's the same as the Internet address for the resource.

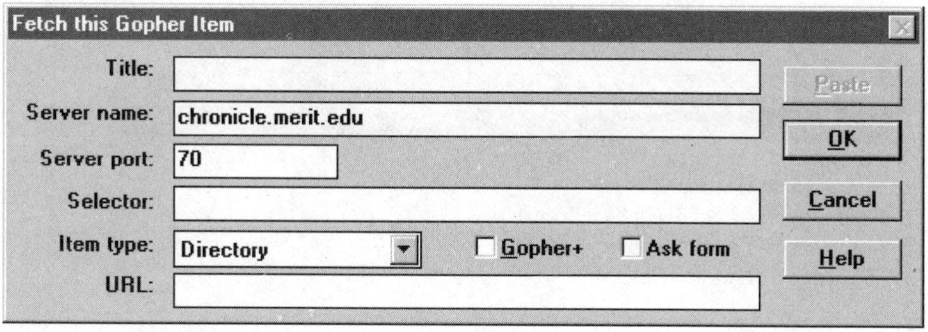

Figure 12–7: Opening a particular Gopher server

Searching with Gopher

Perhaps the nicest feature of Gopher is its search capability. Not only does Gopher support a number of different kinds of searches, but it returns the results of a search as a series of menu items as well. This means that, by selecting one of the items returned in a search, you can access that resource immediately (always assuming, of course, that a connection is available).

Index Searches

Let's say that you're a biologist, and are looking for strains of Drosophila (fruit flies) for a particular experiment. You go to the Indiana University Biology Archive (**ftp.bio.indiana.edu**), and see an item called "FlyBase." After selecting that item and poking around a little more, you get to a menu called "Stocks." That menu contains some icons we haven't seen before, as shown in Figure 12-8.

Both the magnifying glass and question mark icons refer to a type of entry that we haven't seen yet; these are *indexed directory* resources.[*] In a normal Gopher directory, you select the directory and see a menu of everything in it. An index is similar. When you select an indexed item, you get an opportunity to do a keyword search through a database.

First, you'll be asked for a search string; Gopher then searches for items that match your string and presents you with a special menu containing only the items it found, rather than a complete list of the directory's contents. For your experiment, you need a strain of Drosophila with purple eyes. So, after finding the "Stocks" menu, you select "Search Stock—center stocks" and you see the screen shown in Figure 12-9.

---

[*] The magnifying glass indicates a normal Gopher indexed search, while the question mark specifies an Ask form, which is a Gopher+ feature. While WSGopher supports Gopher+ functionality, not all Gopher clients do, so we're going to stick with the standard features.

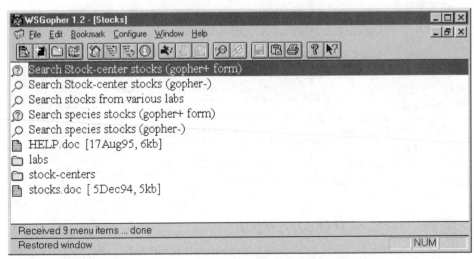

Figure 12–8: The Stocks menu of the Indiana University Biology Archive

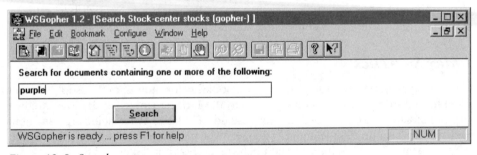

Figure 12–9: Search screen

Now you can type keywords. If you've previously performed a search, Gopher will remember the keywords you used last time and show them on the screen. This makes it easier to repeat your search if you don't get what you want the first time. If you want entirely different keywords, just backspace over your old keywords and start again.

In our case, we want to find out about Drosophila with purple eyes, so we type the keyword "purple" and then click the **Search** button. Now Gopher searches the index and builds a "custom" directory menu that only contains items matching your search criterion. In this case, you'll see the new menu shown in Figure 12-10.

This menu isn't any different from the other menus. You're looking at a list of files; if you double-click on one of the files, you can view it. If you're a biologist, you presumably know how to use this information!

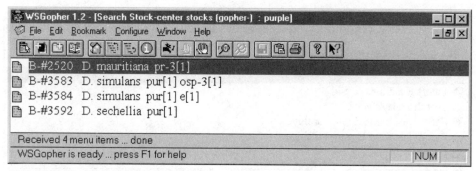

Figure 12–10: Search results

Indexed searches are a great feature, but there are some tricks. The Gopher interface is very general and, as with anything very general, there are several causes for confusion. First, you have no idea what kind of computer or software is really doing the search. Gopher can do searches through Archie servers, WAIS servers, and others. Each of these servers has its own search rules, and interprets keywords differently. Some, like Archie, only let you search for a single word. Some servers accept strings of keywords, but the meanings of these keywords may change as you move from index to index. For example, consider the string:

```
clinton and gore
```

Does this mean that for the search to match, the item must contain the words "clinton," "and," and "gore"? Or is the "and" a directive telling the server to find entries that contain the word "clinton" and the word "gore"? You don't know, and you can't tell beforehand. You don't want a list of every item containing the word "an"!

You may also find that the resources which are most useful to index also tend to have licensing restrictions. Most of the time, you're allowed to search the database, but you're not allowed to see the information that you find. For example, the University of Minnesota's Gopher server (**gopher.tc.umn.edu**) has the UPI press feed (derived from the Clarinet newsgroup) as an indexed resource. You can access it, as Figure 12-11 shows, by selecting the "Wire Service News" option from the "News" menu.

If you double-click on any of the indexed search icons, you can enter a string, like "clinton," in the search field. But, when you try to access a news article, you get an error message that reads something like, "Sorry, we don't allow off-campus access to this server." This is because the license that allows the University of Minnesota to have the UPI news feed on-line forbids them from distributing it off-campus. Gopher knows where you are coming from and enforces this restriction. A few restrictions are a minor price to pay. Keep in mind that the alternative to licensing restrictions is not unlimited access to data; in reality, the alternative is no data at all.

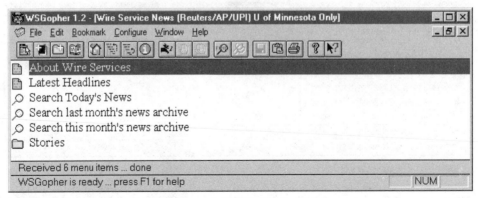

Figure 12–11: The University of Minnesota's Wire Service News menu

With a little experience, you will hardly notice the differences in how searches work. Here are a few hints to help you through:

- Gopher searches are always case-insensitive; uppercase and lowercase letters are considered the same.

- When you approach a new index, keep the search simple. If you want articles containing "clinton" and "gore," just look for "gore." He is likely to appear in fewer articles, hence the resulting menu will be shorter. If your search is too broad, no harm done, the menu will just be longer.

- If you use a particular resource regularly, take five minutes to experiment. Find an article and read it. Jot down a few terms from the article. Try a few searches with multiple keywords, including some with "and," "or," and "not" in between them. See what happens; are words like "and" considered part of the search string, or are they keywords? Remember that the rules change from resource to resource; that is, two different resources that you access from the same Gopher server may behave differently.

- If you move from Gopher server to Gopher server, the way a search is conducted for a similarly named resource may vary. If you always use a resource from the same Gopher server, the search semantics will remain the same.

Searching for Things in Menus

It is fairly easy to move around in one Gopher server and to move from one server to another server. This points to a problem: how do you find the item you want among the tens of thousands of Gopher menus available? Until two people at the University of Nevada at Reno built the Gopher equivalent to Archie (covered in Chapter 10, *Finding Files*, there was no way to know. With a typical hacker's sense of humor, they named their Archie-like facility Veronica, after the comic-book character.

Basic Veronica

Veronica acquires its data exactly like Archie: it visits Gopher servers worldwide and traverses their menus, remembers what is there, and builds a combined index of Gopher menus. The most amazing thing about Veronica is that you know how to use it already! It appears to be just another index search. You select it just like any other search menu item. It asks you for words to search for and builds you a custom menu. The menu items are items from all the Gophers worldwide which contain the words you are looking for.

To access Veronica, look around on any Gopher server for a menu item like this:

```
Search titles in Gopherspace using Veronica
```

Select this item; your next menu should look something like Figure 12-12.

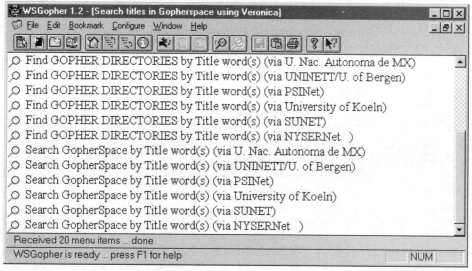

Figure 12–12: The Veronica menu

The first thing to notice is that there are several menu entries, associated with several different Veronica servers. The number of servers varies from place to place and from time to time. Some Gopher servers are smart enough to know when a Veronica server is unusable, and delete unusable servers from their menus dynamically. Others leave them all there and let you try and fail.

There are many servers, because they are heavily used; one server could not handle the searches for the whole Internet. How do you know which one to use? Well, there is no way to know beforehand which is the best. They all contain the same data, but you can't tell which are busy and which aren't. As with Archie, start by trying a server that's close to you; if that doesn't work, try one slightly farther away, until you reach one that responds.

When you select a Veronica server, Gopher asks you for your search words. Healthcare is a big political topic, and you'd like to follow the debate. So you are interested in finding a place where you can drop in occasionally and find out what's new. So you start by typing your search term, "healthcare."

If all goes well, you are rewarded with a menu of items related to health care, as shown in Figure 12-13. In fact, this search gave you more than you bargained for: many pages worth!

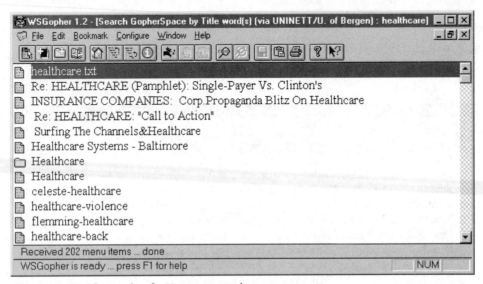

Figure 12–13: The results of a Veronica search

This many pages might be acceptable if you're only going to do the search once: your kid comes home and says, "I need a periodic table for chemistry quick!" You find it, you pick it up, look at it, and are done. But that's not the only way to use search information. If you occasionally want to find out what's new on a particular topic, you'd rather find a few collections of information than a long list of scattered resources. This means searching for a directory, rather than for individual resources. That's why the Veronica menu contained items like the following:

```
Find GOPHER DIRECTORIES by Title word(s) (via SUNET)
```

The first search we did found any item that matched our keywords; this item only searches for directories (which are, by definition, collections of things). The actual mechanics of the search are exactly the same in either case: Veronica asks you what to search for; you enter a string and click on **Search**.

If we did our healthcare search looking only for directory titles, we would get a more reasonable number in response, as Figure 12-14 shows. That's more to your liking. You don't need a complete list of healthcare resources; you just want a few places where you can poke around from time to time. These examples show basic

Veronica usage at its best. Frequently, though, you'll select a Veronica server and get a message like:

```
*** Too many connections - Try again soon. ***
```

If this happens, try another server or try the server later. Gopher remembers your search string, so you won't have to enter it time and time again.

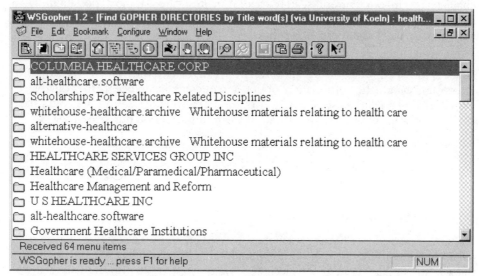

Figure 12–14: The results of a Veronica directory search

Advanced Veronica

When we talked about index searches earlier, we said you don't know what kind of software is actually doing the search for you. You couldn't try really sophisticated search strings unless you had inside knowledge of the index server. Well, Veronica servers are smarter than the average server. They all do limited Boolean and substring searches.

Boolean searches allow you to use the words "and", "or", and "not", together with parentheses, to allow you better control of the search. For example, if you were interested in healthcare as it relates to women or families, you could have used the search string:

```
healthcare and (women or family)
```

This string is interpreted as a mathematical expression; "healthcare and" applies to all the items within the parentheses. So the meaning of this expression is: return any items that contain both of the words "healthcare" and "women" or both of the words "healthcare" and "family". As a shorthand, the "and" is assumed between any two adjacent words, unless there is another directive present. That is, searching for "healthcare and women" is the same as "healthcare women". Why type it if you don't need it?

If you think carefully about the search we just did, you'll realize that it might exclude some entries we would like see because they contain "woman" (or even "womyn") rather than "women". To handle situations like this, use the wildcard character *. In our current search, "wom*" takes care of most possibilities—in addition to finding articles about the care of wombats. (Nothing's perfect.) The * may only be used at the end of a word.

If you actually perform the above search, you'll find that the fishing expedition lands a lot of information about "Preferred Family Healthcare, Inc." If I had to guess, this would be information about a particular insurance plan available to employees on a campus somewhere. Not too interesting to us, and we could have excluded it with the Boolean "not". So, we can further refine our search to:

```
healthcare (wom* or family) not inc
```

We want "healthcare and some word starting with 'wom' or healthcare and family, but if the menu item has 'inc' anywhere in it, ignore it."

Jughead—the searcher you never see

We have explored two kinds of searches in Gopher, an index search of a particular database and an index search of the whole Gopher community. What about something in the middle? Remember the note "Where Gopher Was Born"? The idea was that each department of a University could have its own Gopher server: one for administration, one for athletics, etc. All of these servers were part of one community. Using Veronica, there's no way to say, "Search only at the University of Minnesota's Gophers"; that's what Jughead is for.

Jughead is an indexing facility that indexes a particular set of Gopher servers. You'll rarely see the name Jughead. Rather, you will see another kind of index search in a Gopher menu (usually a site's main menu), like the option "Keyword Search of UIUC Gopher Menus" shown way back in Figure 12-1. For you, it's just another index search. The underlying technology is Jughead, but you use it just like you would use any other index item.

White-Pages Servers

In Chapter 11, *Finding Someone*, we discussed white-pages services, which are essentially electronic phone books. However, we omitted one important group of over 300 phone book servers: those available through Gopher. White-pages services are offered through Gopher in two ways: as normal index searches, and as

"CSO name servers."* If you find a menu item on a Gopher server called something like "Phone books" and follow it down through a bunch of geographic areas, you will eventually get to lists of white-pages servers for different groups of people, as shown in Figure 12-15.

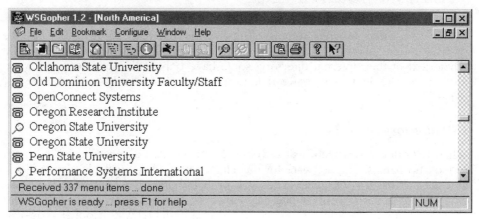

Figure 12–15: White-Pages servers

The items marked with a telephone icon are CSO-style servers; the ones labeled with a magnifying glass are Gopher index servers.

Gopher index white-pages searches

White-pages directories offered through the Gopher index facility work just like you would expect them to. You select the directory you want to use, it gives you a familiar dialog box, you fill in your search term, and Gopher looks up the name. For example, let's pick the Performance Systems International server and look up Bill Schrader, as we did in Chapter 11, *Finding Someone*. You type in the name and click on **Search**. Gopher looks up the name and returns some information about it in a menu item named **Raw Search Results**. If you select that menu item (often it's the only one), Gopher should show you the following text:

```
William Schrader (1)                    wls@psi.com


President

Chief Executive Officer
PSI Inc.
   Reston International Center
   11800 Sunrise Valley Drive
   Suite 1100
   Reston, VA 22091
```

---

* So named because they were developed from the CSnet name server code at the Computing Services Office of the University of Illinois, Urbana.

```
     USA

   Telephone: +1 703-620-6651 x310
   FAX:       +1 703-620-4586

   Locality:   Reston, Virginia
   ...
```

In principle, these searches are easy. The catch is that you can never be too sure of what you're allowed to search for. Some of these places have indexed the whole text of their internal directory; some have only indexed names; and some are somewhere in between. Keep it simple and search only for first and last names.

CSO directory searches

When CSO directories were first developed, you needed a special client program to look up names. The software for this client isn't widely available; if you're not at a site that has a CSO name server, you probably don't have access to it. (That's why we didn't cover it in Chapter 11.) However, Gopher knows how to perform CSO name-server lookups; so, once you're comfortable with Gopher, you can access these on-line directories too.

If you scroll around in the list of white-pages servers shown in Figure 12-15, you should find an entry for the "University of Illinois Urbana-Champaign." The telephone icon indicates that this entry is a CSO-style white-pages server. Actually, most of the CSO-style directories are for large universities, as that's where CSO servers are most popular. If you access one of these items, just like you accessed the file we used in the previous example, you can look things up in the selected directory.

For example, let's say that you accessed the server for the University of Illinois. Now you get the screen shown in Figure 12-16 for entering search criteria. The **Fields** combo box lists all of the different criteria you can search by.

When you select a field, WSGopher puts the field name in the **Search for:** box, so that you can type the words you want to search for following the field name. For example, Figure 12-17 shows what happens when you select **name**. You can constrain the search with any of the fields listed in the combo box. When you have filled in everything you want, click **Search** to start the search.

CSO's search rules make sense, but they're a little different from what you might be used to. Each word in the name is taken as an item, with the * wildcard character allowed. The words in the search string must all be found in the target for the target to match. Substrings don't automatically match. If you met Ed Krol over a beer, and tried to look up "Ed Krol" when you got thirsty, you would likely be drinking alone. "Ed" would not match "Edward" or "Edwin", and his first name is not Ed. Therefore, it is usually safer to search for wildcarded first names like "Ed*". Order and case are not important. That is, both "Ed* Krol" and "Krol Ed*" would match "Edward M Krol", because both "Ed" followed by any characters and "Krol"

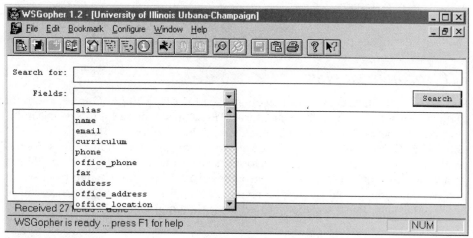

Figure 12–16: CSO search criteria

were in that name. You needn't match every word in an entry, like the middle initial M. After entering either of these strings, click **Search** to start the search. When it's finished, you'll see the results shown in Figure 12-17.

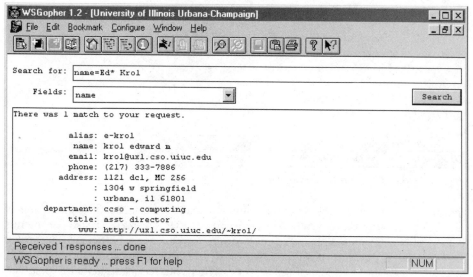

Figure 12–17: CSO search results

One quirk of CSO-style servers is that they only index entries based on certain fields in an item. You might think that you could find the person whose address is "1121 DCL" by searching by **address**. But you can't, because there is no index for the data based on the address. Your search must be based on the person's name, phone number, or e-mail address. You can use any of the other fields, however, to further constrain a search. Conversely, if you don't specify any search criteria, the CSO server searches the name field for the words you have entered.

FTP Through Gopher

You can use Gopher as an alternative interface for FTP. Using a Gopher client for FTP works just like using a Web client for FTP, so there's not a lot to say about this functionality beyond what we've already said in Chapter 9, *Moving Files: FTP*. Essentially, Gopher allows you to move files from an anonymous FTP server to your computer. If you look back at Gopher's main menu (Figure 12-2), you'll see an item labeled **Internet File Server (ftp) Sites**. The name may change from server to server, but you should be able to recognize which item we mean. Once you've selected this item, you'll see the Gopher menu shown in Figure 12-18.

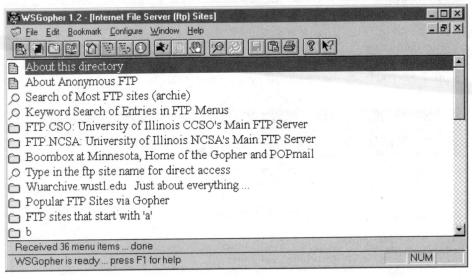

Figure 12–18: FTP sites through Gopher

The menu shown in Figure 12-18 contains a few different kinds of items. Some of the menus provide direct connections to various FTP sites. You'll also see menus that organize FTP sites alphabetically. If you're looking for a particular FTP server, you can search through these menus to find the server you want; the listings are annotated with the contents of the servers. When you access an actual FTP server, the directories are presented as menus (with folder icons). You can navigate among the directories just as you would menus. WSGopher uses different icons to indicate other files types, such as PC executables, text files, audio files, and graphic images Just as with a Web browser, you can view the text files and download executables. You can also configure WSGopher to use external viewers to display images and play sounds; select **Viewers** on the **Configure** menu.

Figure 12-18 also contains a few items that are flagged as searchable indexes. These are what really distinguish Gopher as an FTP client. They allow you to search FTP resources for the files you want. That is, rather than traversing a series of menus to find a server, you can use a Gopher-style indexed-directory search to find the file you want. You're actually using Archie—but, as you'd expect, Gopher hides the details of Archie from you.

It's convenient that most Gopher servers that provide access to FTP servers offer both interfaces: an Archie-like indexed directory, plus an alphabetical list of FTP servers. Archie's resource list is probably more reliable, but both are useful in their own way. The indexed list is obviously appropriate if you're looking for information about a particular topic and don't know where to find it. The alphabetical list may be easier if you already know where the data is (you don't have to try constructing an appropriate search), or if you've heard that the FTP server at **hoople.usnd.edu** has some great stuff and you'd like to check it out.

Using Telnet Through Gopher

Gopher can connect you to resources using **telnet** as an interface. You do this in the same fashion as every other resource: walking through the menus, and then selecting a resource that interests you. For example, while browsing through the "Libraries and Reference Information" menu shown in Figure 12-2, you notice the "Library of Congress Info System (LOCIS)" resource. This is an on-line, Telnet-style interface to the Library of Congress. The terminal icon next to the entry tells you that this is a Telnet resource.

When you select a Telnet resource, Gopher brings up a screen that indicates the address of the Telnet resource and provides any special instructions you'll need to use the resource.[*] Figure 12-19 shows the screen for LOCIS. Click the **Start** button to connect to the resource. Gopher starts the **telnet** program and connects to the resource. You can use the Telnet resource, as well as continue to navigate with Gopher, as you see fit.

Remembering Where You Are

By now you should have gotten good enough at moving around in Gopher to have experienced one of its frustrations: getting to somewhere through a long series of menus can be tedious. You start at your main menu, pick **Other Gophers**, pick **USA**, **North Carolina**, **NCSU Library Gopher**, **Library without Walls**. You did all

---

[*] Before you can access a Telnet resource with WSGopher, you need to select **Telnet/3270 Path** from the **Configure** menu and specify the location of the Telnet program on your system.

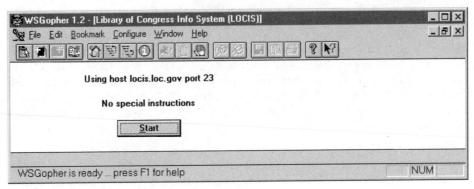

Figure 12–19: Accessing a Telnet resource

of this just so you can look at the resource you really wanted to use. This isn't so bad when you're just prowling around to find out what's interesting; but what if you find a resource you want to use every Friday? It gets mighty old mighty fast.

The solution to this problem is called a bookmark. Bookmarks are available in almost all clients; they let you "mark" a particular place, so that Gopher can return to it later—possibly in another session.

What if you find yourself doing Veronica searches regularly? Rather than searching through menus to find the Veronica items, you might place a bookmark on the directory where Veronica searches live. Creating a bookmark is a two-step process. First, position yourself at the menu item you want to remember. That accomplished, create the bookmark by clicking the **Add Bookmark** button on the toolbar. When you do, WSGopher displays the window shown in Figure 12-20.

WSGopher defines a number of categories for bookmarks. You can save your bookmark in one of these categories, or you can create your own category. The **Searches** category is a logical one for our bookmark, so we've selected it. Now we click **Create** to create the bookmark. WSGopher uses the item's menu string as its name when storing the bookmark.

You now have a bookmark. You can do a search now, move somewhere else, or quit. It doesn't matter what you do since you can always jump back to this directory. You do that by clicking the **Fetch Bookmarks** button on the toolbar. This command brings up the window shown in Figure 12-21.

Again, WSGopher wants you to select a category. If you select **Searches**, you'll see a number of bookmarks, including the one you just defined. If you want to jump straight to the Veronica directory, select the bookmark from the **Bookmarks** list and click **OK**. WSGopher comes with quite a few predefined bookmarks; these provide another good avenue for exploring the Gopher resources that are available on the Internet.

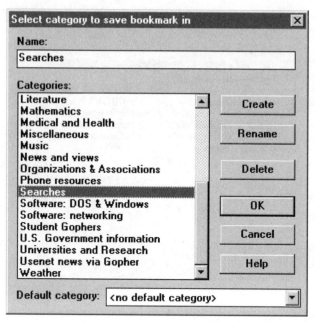

Figure 12–20: Creating a bookmark

Some time in the future, you might want to get rid of a bookmark. You may not need the resource any more, or the resource may have disappeared or moved. (The Internet in general, and Gopherspace in particular, is constantly in flux.) To delete a bookmark, use the **Edit Bookmarks** button on the toolbar.

Bookmarks are especially useful after Veronica searches. You might get back a bunch of articles you really think are great. You haven't a clue where they live. You might figure it out with the **Info** command, but why bother? Just set a bookmark on the articles you want to remember and you're done.

A variation of the bookmark command remembers how you got to a particular menu, rather than an item within the menu itself. This is the **Add Bookmark Directory** command on the toolbar. Why would you do this? Well, there's one obvious reason. Often you get to a directory that looks interesting; but you don't know that it really contains what you want until you look at some of the items within it. Now, when you're looking at those items, you can say "yes, this entire directory is something worth remembering" and simply click the **Add Bookmark Directory** button.

Pointing to Another Server

Earlier, we said that every Gopher client is configured with a "default server" that it contacts when it starts. You can tell WSGopher to go directly to another server by selecting **New Gopher Item** from the **File** menu. When WSGopher brings up the

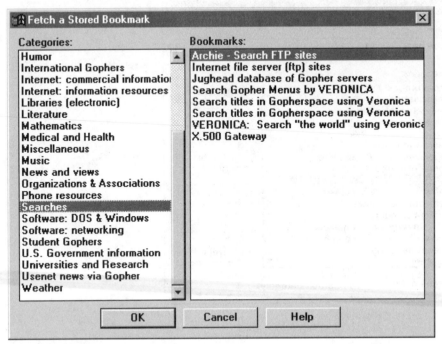

Figure 12-21: Fetching bookmarks

Fetch window (shown in Figure 12-7) enter the Internet address of the server in the **Server name** field.

The reason you want to go directly to a server is to get to where you want quickly. If you know that the information you want is offered by one particular server, you can go there directly, rather than hunting through a bunch of menus. With the thousands of servers out there, finding the one you want on a menu can be tedious. (The *Resource Catalog* in this book assumes that you'll be using Gopher this way.)

If the information you use regularly is on a particular server, you can change your home Gopher server by selecting **Home Gopher Server** from the **Configure** menu. WSGopher displays a window that lets you specify a new home server, as well as a backup server. It's a good idea to specify a backup server, in case your main server is unavailable.

How do you get Gopher server names, like **gopher.colorado.edu** and **gopher. internic.net**? The easiest way is to prowl around through the **Other Gopher and Information Servers** menu. When you find a particularly well-stocked server, use the **Info** command and scribble down its name.

The Web and Gopher

As I mentioned at the beginning of the chapter, you can use a Web browser, like Internet Explorer or Netscape Navigator, as an effective Gopher client. As you can see in Figure 12-22, Netscape Navigator's Gopher interface is quite similar to the one used by WSGopher. Gopher menus are depicted as folders; you navigate the menu system by clicking on the menus. One minor difference, however, is that with Netscape you access a menu with a single mouse click.

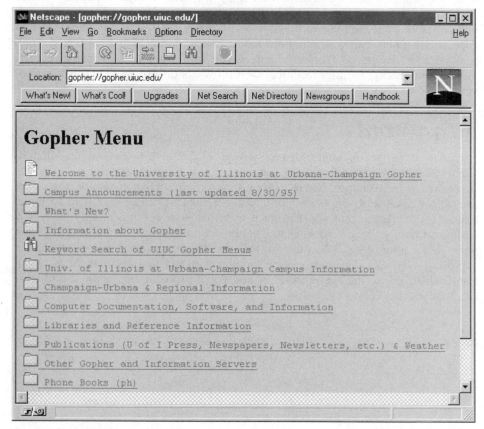

Figure 12–22: Gopher over the Web

In the course of exploring the Web, you may encounter some Gopher resources. If you want to open a Gopher resource directly, you need to enter a Gopher URL. These take the following form:

```
gopher://server-name
```

If you look at the **Location** field while you are exploring a Gopher resource, you may notice that Gopher URLs for items within a menu system can be rather ugly.

For that reason, you probably want to access a Gopher server using the URL for its main menu, and then navigate to particular resources using the menus. That's how we've listed Gopher resources in the *Resource Catalog*. Another way to get around the ugly URLs is to keep track of interesting Gopher resources using Netscape's bookmark facility, or Internet Explorer's list of favorite places.

So, if a Web browser makes such a wonderful Gopher client, you may be wondering why you should bother with a specialized Gopher client. It really depends on to what extent you use the Gopher system. If you are only an occasional Gopher user, you will probably be content with using the Web to access Gopher servers. However, if you make extensive use of Gopher resources, especially searches, you will probably want the full functionality of a Gopher client. For one thing, Gopher clients remember search strings between searches, while Web browsers do not. Another nice feature of Gopher clients is the **Info** command, which gives you information about a Gopher resource. Web browsers do not provide this functionality.

A Last Word

I hope I've given you some idea of what's available through Gopher—that is, almost everything. One thing that I can't give you is a better sense of how Gopher is organized: for example, where to look if you're an archaeologist, or a financial analyst, or a software developer, or a Dante scholar. Gopher may help to guide you to the resources, but you still have to know your resources fairly well. In a traditional library, there's no substitute for browsing through the stacks and seeing what looks interesting. The same is true for Gopher: there's no substitute for exploring. Not only will you become familiar with the various commands, you'll also find out where the "good stuff" is. And you'll probably find some useful services that you didn't know existed.

CHAPTER THIRTEEN

SEARCHING INDEXED DATABASES: WAIS

How WAIS Works
Getting Access
WAIS and the Web
Public WAIS Clients
What the Future Holds

The *Wide Area Information Service* (WAIS, pronounced "wayz") is a service that lets you search Internet archives, looking for articles containing groups of words. It's great for searching through indexed material and finding articles based on what they contain.

WAIS is really a tool for working with collections of data, or *databases*. To many people, databases connote a file full of numbers—or, once you've seen a little of what WAIS can do, a set of articles about some topic. Both of these definitions are too narrow. WAIS can deal with much more; the format of the information presented doesn't matter much. It doesn't really look at the data in the process of a search; it looks at an index. If someone takes the trouble to build an index, WAIS can select information and present it, regardless of its format. It's most common to see indexes for various kinds of text (articles, and so on), but you can build an index for anything. For example, someone could build an index from descriptions of great works of art; the data tied to the index could be the works of art themselves, stored in some standard graphical format (e.g., GIF). You could then search for "gothic," and up would pop Grant Wood's painting "American Gothic." There are many such indexes built from data that is available elsewhere (such as **whois** and **archie** indexes). Some of them are useful and some are not, but you can search them and frequently come up with what you want.

I dislike the "official" terminology used to discuss WAIS. The database language is overly abstract and prevents you from seeing what WAIS can do. Think of WAIS databases as private libraries devoted to a particular topic: for example, a library of architectural building standards and codes. Since this is an easier way to view things, that's how I'll discuss them throughout the chapter.

Like Gopher, WAIS allows you to find and access resources on the network without regard for where they really reside. In Gopher, you find resources by looking through a sequence of menus until you find something appropriate. WAIS does the same thing, but it does the searching for you. You tell it what you want; it tries to find the material you need. A WAIS command is essentially: "find me items about this in that library." WAIS then looks at all the documents in the library (or libraries) you gave it and tells you which documents are most likely to contain what you want. If you like, WAIS then displays the documents for you.

There are more than 500 free WAIS libraries that are currently on the network. Since they are maintained by volunteer effort and donated computer time, coverage tends to be spotty. For topics that inspire a lot of willing volunteers, coverage is good: as you'd expect, there are many libraries for computer science, networking, and molecular biology. Some literature libraries exist, such as Project Gutenberg's collection and various religious texts. Coverage in the social sciences is pretty thin at this time; however, libraries are always being added. There is a way to ask whether a library covers a particular topic, so you can easily check whether or not WAIS has any resources that are relevant to you.

Some commercial information products, like the Dow Jones Information Service, provide their product through a WAIS interface. You have to pay a fee to use services like this. Once you've arranged for payment, these services are no different than the free network WAIS services.

We'll introduce you to WAIS by discussing how it works. There are some good and bad points about how WAIS does its job. It takes a little practice to do what you want; you have to ask it the right questions. It's a bit easier to understand how to construct these questions if you know what WAIS does with them. Once that is behind us, we can do some searches.

How WAIS Works

WAIS is a distributed text-searching system. It is based on a standard (named Z39.50[*]) that describes a way for one computer to ask another to perform searches. WAIS was one of the first systems based upon this standard. At this point, it's also the most common.

To make a document available through a WAIS server, someone must create an index for that server to use in the search. For textual information, every word in the document is usually indexed. When you request a search from a WAIS client, it contacts the servers that handle the libraries you suggested. It asks each server, in turn, to search its index for a set of words. The server then sends you a list of documents that may be appropriate, and a "score" telling how appropriate it thinks each one is. The scores are normalized, so that the document that best matches

---

* Z39.50 is an American National Standards Institute standard for requesting bibliographic information. It has been under development for a long time within the library and computing communities.

your search criterion is given a score of 1000; others get proportionally less. So, if you say, "Find me documents that contain 'clinton and gore,'" WAIS looks in the index and counts how many times each document contains the word "clinton," the word "and," and the word "gore." The sum of these counts, weighted slightly by what the word is, is converted to a score for a document. After all the libraries have been searched, WAIS gives you the titles of the documents that received the highest scores. There's a limit to the number of documents it reports—usually between 15 and 50, depending on which client you use. You can then pick which documents to view, and WAIS will display them for you.

You should see a problem already. How many times can you conceive of selecting a document because it contained the word "and"? You might have thought that "and" meant the logical *and* operation in WAIS. In fact, there are no special words in WAIS; every word counts in the ranking. A document that contains 1000 matches for "and," but no matches for "clinton" or "gore" might just have the best score; or, more likely, a score high enough to place it in the top 10. Remember that WAIS is a relatively new facility, and all the kinks haven't been worked out yet. As the software matures, some of these problems will be resolved.

A second problem that may not be as obvious is that WAIS lacks "contextual sensitivity." You could ask WAIS to find articles containing the words "problem children," but it would also be just as happy with an item containing the sentence, "The children had a problem; they'd lost their lunch money." You can't tell WAIS that the words must occur in a certain order, and you can't provide any information about the context in which they occur.

Finally, once a search has taken you astray, you can't tell WAIS to exclude any "wrong turns" or portions of a source. That is, you can't give a command like, "find articles with the words 'problem children,' but throw out articles that contain references to lunch." There is also no way to ask, "What's been added to this source since last year?" This makes it hard to do searches repeatedly in a changing source. If your source is an index of papers from a journal, there is no way to say, "Look for the articles that have been published since the last time I checked."

So much for the bad aspects. Even with these flaws, you'll find that WAIS is one of the most useful lookup tools on the Internet. And it's possible that future versions of WAIS will solve these problems. WAIS has one really unique feature going for it: *relevance feedback.* Some clients allow you to find articles that are similar to the articles you've already found. Let's say your search for "problem children" turned up an article titled "Educational Problems In Gifted Children," in addition to the spurious "lunch money" article. "Educational Problems . . . " happens to be exactly what you're looking for. Relevance feedback allows you to take some text from that article and have WAIS extract good words from it to use in future searches. These searches can be done either within the same source or in a different source.

Getting Access

Accessing WAIS is a lot like accessing Gopher. In order to use it, you need a computer running a WAIS client program. You can install the client program on your own system, or you can access a computer that already has the client installed and run it there. There are a number of widely-available freeware and shareware WAIS clients for Windows, as shown in Table 13-1. You can get these clients from a number of anonymous FTP sites; see the *Resource Catalog* under "Computing" for a list of some of the sites. In this chapter, we'll use EINet winWAIS, a shareware Windows client, which we got from **ftp.einet.net**, in the directory *einet/pc*.

Table 13-1: Some Freeware and Shareware WAIS Clients

WAIS Client	Filename*	Type
EINet winWAIS	*ewaisxxx.zip*	Shareware
WinWAIS	*wnwaisx.zip*	Freeware
WAIS Manager	*waismanx.zip*	Freeware
WAIS for Windows	wwaisxxx.zip	Freeware

* One or more lowercase x's in the filename indicates a version number that is subject to change.

However, you can also perform WAIS searches without a specialized WAIS client. In this chapter, we'll take a look at two alternatives to running a WAIS client on your own computer. You can Telnet to a particular computer and login with a special ID, like "wais," and do some simple searches. Also, you can do WAIS searches using Gopher and the World Wide Web. For example, most Gopher servers have a line like this on the main menu:

```
9.   Other Gopher and Information Servers/
```

If you select this item, the next menu will have an entry:

```
6.   WAIS Based Information/
```

This item lets you use the Gopher index interface to search any WAIS source for which there is no charge. The only thing you can't do with this facility is search multiple sources at one time.

You might want to use one of these alternative methods the first time, to try things out. If you decide you want to use WAIS regularly, you might then want to get yourself a specialized WAIS client.

Formulating a WAIS Search

Now that we're through the preliminaries, let's get started. To get properly started, however, you need to make a leap of faith and forget how you would normally deal with computer databases. When many users try WAIS for the first time, they ask the question "What libraries of documents are out there, anyway?" This is the wrong approach. People are used to relying on the computer for some tasks and their brain for the others. The brain is usually responsible for scanning lists to look for interesting items. In order to use WAIS most effectively, you must trust WAIS and let it do the scanning for you.

When you start winWAIS, the first thing you'll see is the winWAIS*Question window, which appears in Figure 13-1. winWAIS, like most WAIS clients, maintains a list of questions. Basically, a question consists of two parts:

- A query, or list of keywords, that the client is to submit to a WAIS server.

- A list of the WAIS servers (referred to as "the sources," but you may prefer to think of these as the libraries) to which the query is to be submitted.

In other words, in using WAIS to gather information about a topic, you submit a "query" (or a list of keywords) to a "source" (or a WAIS server).

Both parts of a question appear in the winWAIS*Question window:

- The **Tell Me About** field contains your query—a list of keywords for which you'd like to search.

- The **Selected Sources** combo box lists the WAIS servers to which your query will be submitted. Since it is a combo box, though, only a single server is visible when the box is closed.

winWAIS allows you to save a question in a file on your system. When you are using a saved question, the name of the saved question file is shown in the title bar; in Figure 13-1, for example, an existing query named CHILD is being used. Once you save a question, it's easy to see what's new in a particular field every month. All you need to do is re-execute the question in its original form, or modify it (either by changing the keywords or changing the servers to which it is submitted), and issue it again. Items on the **File** menu allow you to maintain your list of saved questions. You can design a new question, open a saved question, save a question, or delete an existing question.

winWAIS also maintains a list of sources or libraries.[*] This is basically a list of WAIS servers that winWAIS knows how to locate and search. Maintaining the list of libraries, as well as selecting and removing individual libraries from questions, is handled by the **Select Sources** option on the **Edit** menu. This opens the Select WAIS Sources window, which is shown in Figure 13-2.

From this window, you can add a library to your question by selecting the source in the **Available Sources** list box and clicking **Select**. You can also remove a library by selecting the source in the **Selected Sources** box and clicking **Remove**. To define a new library, select the **New** button. If you select a source and click the **View** button, you can modify information about the source.

The **Ask** button on the upper-right side of the winWAIS window (Figure 13-1) submits your query. The results are displayed in the **Information Found** area.

---

[*] The list is a collection of .SRC files stored in a directory named *wais\sources*.

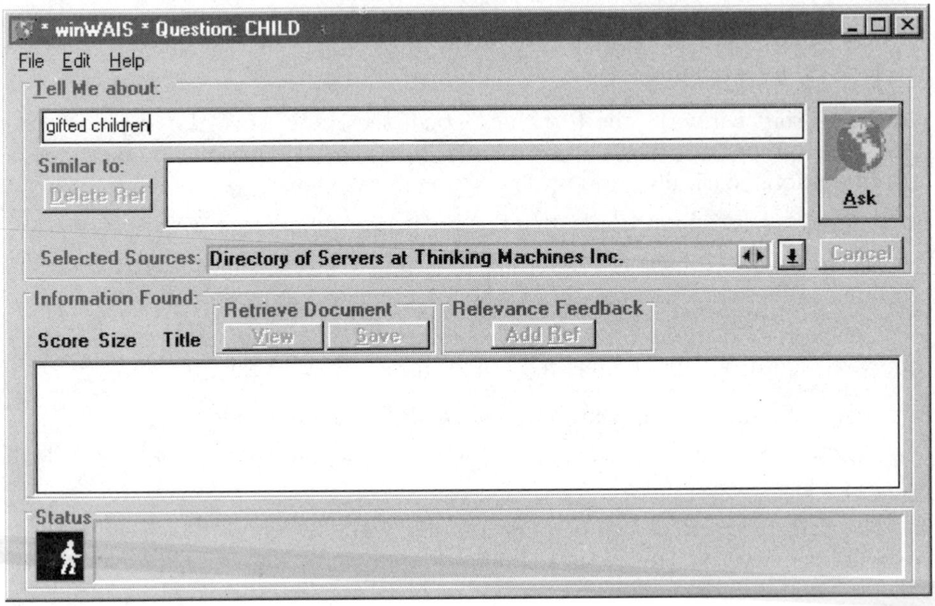

Figure 13-1: The winWAIS main window

Finding a Library

How do you go about gathering information on the WAIS libraries to which you submit your queries? If you want, you could get a list of all the public WAIS libraries in existence and add them to the list of sources in winWAIS. This master list of libraries is itself a WAIS library; it's called the *Directory of Servers*. If you know about this one library, you've got it all. But instead of reading the list of libraries yourself, you should start your search by asking WAIS: "What library do I look in for 'gifted children'?" To start the process, select the **New Question** option from the **File** menu. winWAIS opens the Select WAIS Sources window, shown in Figure 13-2.

The **Available Sources** list box lists all the libraries in winWAIS' list of sources. Since we want to query the Directory of Servers, make sure this library is listed in the **Selected Sources** list box. Remove any other libraries in that list box; they are extraneous to our initial search. Now click **OK**.

So, now it's time to compose a question. Before starting, we'll give you a clue. "Gifted children" is much too narrow a term; if you look for libraries that are appropriate for "gifted children," you're not likely to find any. This makes sense, if you think about traditional (books and paper) libraries: there are probably very few libraries in the world with "gifted children" in their name. If you had an index of important special collections, you'd probably find a few that contained the words "gifted children," but not too many. If you restricted your search to these

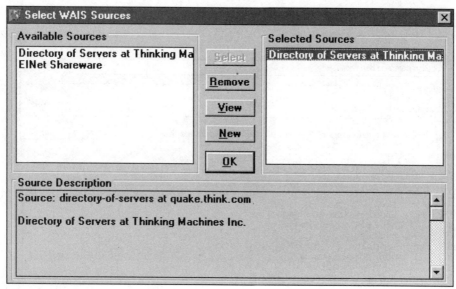

Figure 13-2: The Select WAIS Sources window

libraries, you'd miss many libraries with excellent social science collections, some of which may be more useful than the special-purpose libraries. WAIS is no different. The right way to find an appropriate library is to use really broad terms. Think about what kind of people would be concerned about gifted children. You might think of psychologists, educators, parents, etc. Since adding more terms to a search in WAIS makes it easier to match, try to search the Directory of Servers with your relevant terms:

```
education
parenting
behavior
```

Type your keywords into the **Tell Me About** field in the winWAIS main window. You're ready to run your query. So, with bated breath, click the **Ask** button. If you did things correctly, WAIS fills in the **Information Found** list box, as shown in Figure 13-3.

Look at the first result. The 1000 is its score; this score indicates that it fit your search criteria better than any other source, not that it was a perfect match—but you're more likely to find interesting articles here than anywhere else. The size is listed next: 1600 characters.* The name of the index, *MacPsych.src*, sounds promising. When you make your next search, looking for actual articles (rather than promising libraries), you'll want to define *MacPsych.src* as a source, so that it

---

* This is the size of the item you found. In this case, it is the size of the server descriptor. The 1600 characters have nothing to do with the size or completeness of the library itself.

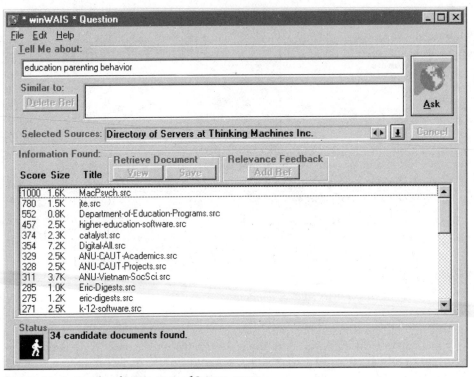

Figure 13–3: Results of a Directory of Servers query

appears in the **Available Sources** list; that allows you to add it to the **Selected Sources** list for your query. At the end of the line, you see the filename of this source. You can ignore this for now.

If you scroll down the list of prospective sources, you will find their scores fall off significantly after the top four. You decide to draw the pass-fail line there and use the top four for the real search:

```
MacPsych.src
jte.src
Department-of-Education-Programs.src
higher-education-software.src
```

Now that you've successfully used winWAIS to search for something, it's really tempting to select **Exit**, to exit winWAIS, or **New Question**, to create a new question. Don't be so hasty. You'll need this information again in a bit. The Directory of Servers is like the Yellow Pages telephone directory. It tells you what telephone numbers to call for different services, but it doesn't call them for you. The Directory of Servers likewise tells you where to look to find what you want. You'll need to take the sources you just found, and use them in the next search.

It's time to think about what we just accomplished. There are a couple of obvious questions which WAIS users ask at this point. First: "How do the Directory of Servers, the Available Sources, and the Selected Sources relate?" To make sense of this, you need to keep in mind what you know and what winWAIS knows. In the beginning, you know what you want to ask, but you don't know where to tell winWAIS to look. winWAIS knows how to look in all the servers listed in its library of sources, but you have to tell it which ones. The Directory of Servers solves this quandary by suggesting where you should send winWAIS looking. Once you've found out which libraries are useful, you can fill in the Selected Sources part of a question and send winWAIS off.[*]

The second question is simply "Why do we bother?" Why don't we just tell WAIS to "look everywhere"? There are several reasons. First, selecting sources is one way to narrow the search. If you ask WAIS to look up items about "cars," you could get articles on toys, automobiles, and Computer Aided Registration Systems (CARS). Selecting some suitable libraries, like "automobile-repair-records," focuses your search.[†] Wading through hundreds of articles to decide which are relevant is a waste of your time—that's what WAIS is supposed to do. Second, searching everywhere could take a long time. You don't go to the library and start at one end of the shelves looking at every title to find something of interest. You know that the automobile repair section starts at 629.28, so you start there and browse only that section.

Asking your question

Now that we've got these questions out of the way, let's get back to behavior problems: how do we compose an appropriate question? The real search is similar to the directory search with which we started. Unfortunately, as you may recall from Figure 13-2, none of the libraries that we'd like to query appear in the **Available Sources** list. Since they must appear here in order for winWAIS to access them, we must add them. To do this, select any one library in the **Information Found** list box that you'd like to add and click **View** in the **Retrieve Document** group box. winWAIS then opens the WAIS Source Description window shown in Figure 13-4, which describes the library and asks whether you want to add it to your source list.

The window offers you four options; the one you choose depends on whether this WAIS server appears to have useful information, and on what you want to do for the next phase of your query. If the information doesn't appear useful, click the **No, Don't Save This Source** button. If the information appears useful, you want to save it for use later. Before clicking **Yes, Save This Source**, be careful to check the options listed below.

---

[*] You may also find that searching the Directory of Servers leads you to another directory of servers: for example, *JANUS-dir-of-servers* (which happens to be a good place to look for legal and U.N.-related resources). That's okay; just add this new directory to your source list and ask a general question again.

[†] We used this for illustration; we don't think this library exists—yet.

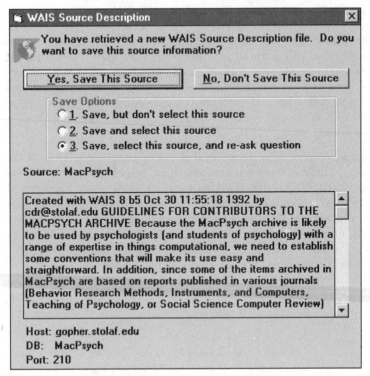

Figure 13–4: The winWAIS Source Description window

You probably don't want to save the source while the **Save, select this source, and re-ask question** button is selected; this clears the **Information Found** list box, and resubmits your query. Unfortunately, it's the default, so you need to deselect it. If you accidentally save your source while this option is checked, click **Cancel** (just beneath the **Ask** icon) and start over by resubmitting your query to the Directory of Servers.

You do want to check the **Save, but don't select this source** option. With this option checked, click **Yes, Save This Source**. winWAIS adds the library to the **Available Sources** list to make it available for searching. You can then repeat the procedure to add the other three top libraries to the **Available Sources** list.

The remaining option, **Save and select this Source**, moves the source into the **Selected Sources** list and kicks out the sources that are already there. This is useful if you only want to search a single server, but won't help you if you want to search several.

Once you've added all four to the list of available libraries, you're ready to create your query. Select **New Question** from the **File** menu. If winWAIS asks you about saving the current question, you can select **No**. When the Select WAIS Sources window appears, select each of the four libraries you just added to the **Available Sources** list and click **Select**. Now that all of these libraries are listed in the **Selected Sources** list box, click **OK**.

Next, enter your question in the **Tell Me About** field. Fill in some relevant keywords:

```
behavior problems in gifted children
```

Click the **Ask** button, and off you go. In a bit, the results return, as shown in Figure 13-5.

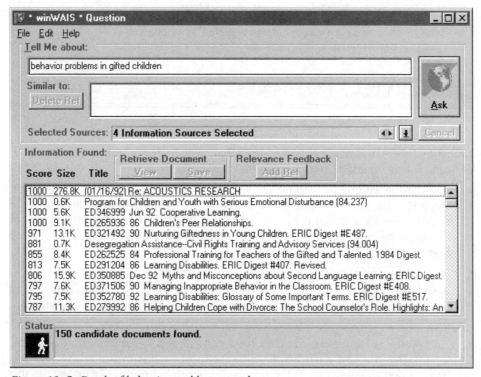

Figure 13–5: Result of behavior problems search

Now that's what you wanted: a list of articles that sound interesting. The item's size field tells you the size (in bytes) of what will be fetched. For each item that you decide looks interesting, you have two options. If you highlight that item and click the **Save** button, winWAIS immediately downloads a copy of the article and asks where you would like it stored. If you click the **View** button, winWAIS opens a view window that allows you to browse the article. For example, if you double-click "Children's Peer Relationships", winWAIS fetches the article (9,100 characters worth) for you and displays it in another window. This is shown in Figure 13-6.

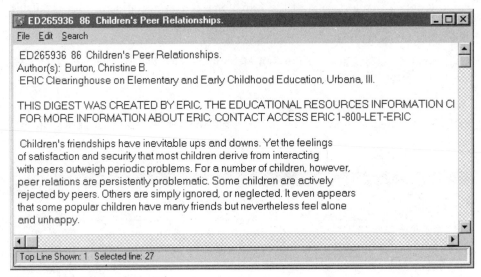

Figure 13–6: Viewing an article

Notice that the View window has a menu bar, which allows you to do a number of useful things, in addition to reading the article:

- **Save** on the **File** menu downloads the article and saves it on your computer. winWAIS asks you to specify a directory and filename. If you select the default, winWAIS stores it in the *wais\save* subdirectory, under the directory that contains winWAIS. The operation of this feature is identical to that of the **Save** button in the main winWAIS window.

- **Print** on the **File** menu downloads the article and prints it on your printer.

- **Relevance Feedback** on the **Edit** menu adds either the highlighted section of the article or the entire article to the **Similar To** list box in the winWAIS window.

- **Find** on the **Search** menu searches for and highlights a text string in the article. Optionally, you can have winWAIS locate those words in the article that you had defined as keywords. If the results of your searches are disappointing, this option can give you a good idea why.

Finally, with your problem solved, you can exit winWAIS. winWAIS asks you if you want to save the current question. If you do, click **Yes**, and then provide a filename. After you have saved a question, it appears in your question list when you select the **Open Question** option from the **File** menu. The next time you want to ask the same question and query the same sources, just select it.

Refining a Search

Relevance feedback lets you use the results of a search to further refine the search. You do this by selecting items, either in whole or in part, that you have already found and moving them to the **Similar To** area of the winWAIS window. If you want to use the whole article, you select the article in the **Information Found** list box and click the **Add Ref** button. The result of this action is shown in Figure 13-7. In this example, you selected "Children's Peer Relationships" as the most appropriate article to use.

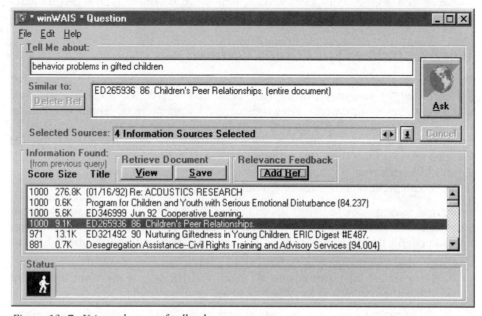

Figure 13-7: Using relevance feedback

To use a portion of an article as feedback, you must be viewing the document. Highlight the text you want and select the **Relevance Feedback** option from the **Edit** menu. winWAIS allows you to choose either the entire file or selected lines; choose the latter. When you return to the main winWAIS window, the article's entry in the **Similar To** section should refer to the selected portions of the document. You can select multiple pieces of the same article, or of different articles, in the same manner. When you are done selecting, click **Ask** to try the search again, with the added selection criteria.

From start to finish, there are a lot of steps. Here's a summary of how to go about a search:

1. Select the Directory of Servers.

2. Ask a general question of the Directory of Servers, to find any libraries that are relevant to your topic. Do this as often as necessary, until you find good libraries.

3. Select the libraries that look interesting.

4. Ask a specific question to find the articles (or other items) that you're searching for.

5. If you're not satisfied with the results, refine your search, possibly using relevance feedback, to get a new set of articles.

As we've said, formulating good WAIS searches can be tricky. You'll get the hang of it, with a little practice.

When Searches Don't Go as Planned

Sometimes your searches won't retrieve what you want; you may get articles that are unrelated, or you may find nothing at all. There are two possible problems: you used either inappropriate keywords or the wrong sources. That's one reason why most WAIS clients let you save your questions. Some questions are hard to construct. Once you have one that works, you may not want to let it go. Even if you don't want to ask the same question next time, you may find it easier to modify an old search than to start from scratch. It is not unusual to do a search many times, modifying it slightly each time until you get what you want.

Of course, saving your searches doesn't solve the problem at hand: searches that aren't effective in the first place. The only real solution is to keep trying until you find something that works. However, we can give you some hints about how to proceed:

- If the search results are reasonable, but not what you really want, refine the search, either by adding keywords yourself or using relevance feedback.

- View an article even if it isn't what you really want. It may give you some ideas about terms appropriate to the field you're searching. You won't find many matches for "God" in the Koran, but you will find "Allah." WAIS does not automatically try synonyms. This technique might also turn up some variant spellings ("behavior" versus "behaviour") or relevant synonyms (like "Llah").

- Search the article using the keywords that you selected. It might give you some insight into how the search is being conducted or how you might modify your query. winWAIS makes this particularly easy. While a document view window is open, select the **Find** option from the **Search** menu. winWAIS opens the Text Search window shown in Figure 13-8. Just click on **Use Wais Search Keywords**, then click **OK** to close the window. winWAIS begins searching for your keywords. Once it has located a keyword, you can press F3 to continue the search.

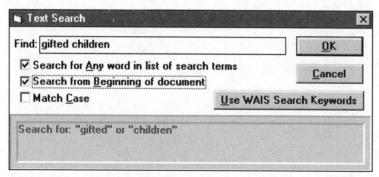

Figure 13–8: The Text Search window

- If WAIS doesn't find anything, and if you're confident about your sources, try a simple search first—a search for which you're sure there will be some articles. Look at the results; this may give you some clues about the best words to search for.

- If you keep getting irrelevant articles, try to limit the number of sources you use. A highly rated source can, on occasion, provide a lot of irrelevant articles. So you've got to find out which source is providing the irrelevancies, and eliminate it from your search. Unfortunately, not all WAIS clients tell you which source a particular document came from. You might be able to guess by checking whether the article's filename corresponds to the source's name. (This won't always help, but it's worth trying.) If you need to, you can delete a source and try the search again. If it's better, leave it out. If it's worse, put it back and delete another.

Adding Sources

Since winWAIS only searches sources or libraries that are in its source list, it is important to familiarize yourself with the methods for adding new entries to the list. In the process of composing the question about "behavior problems in gifted children," for example, your original list of available sources included only two entries, as shown in Figure 13-2. You learned that you could, however, dynamically add new sources or libraries to the list of sources once the Directory of Servers returned the results of your query. You did this by selecting the **View** button in the **Retrieve Document** group box and then selecting one of the **Save** options in the WAIS Source Description window. If the relationship between the Directory of Servers and your list of sources seems confusing, remember that the Directory of Servers is like the phone book's Yellow Pages; likewise, the list of sources is like a set of "speed dial" buttons. If you look up your favorite pizzeria in the Yellow Pages, you'll find it listed there; but you could just press the speed dial button on your phone (you probably programmed it last year). However, if you want to try a new pizzeria, you'll have to look it up in the yellow pages *and* program it into your phone.

To see why this analogy is relevant, think about what the Directory of Servers is. It's just another library (or database). The actual information isn't on your client—it's on a server in a remote part of the world. You can make WAIS searches on that server, and dig up any information it has. From time to time (fairly often, in fact), people create new WAIS libraries, tell the folks who maintain the Directory of Servers, and the new sources appear there. winWAIS doesn't know anything about these new sources, any more than your phone automatically knows about every number in the Yellow Pages. How could it? Before you can use the source, you have to look it up in the Directory of Servers, which knows where the source is located.

Notice that, as Figure 13-9 shows, if you highlight a source that is already in the list of sources and then click on the **View** button, the form of the WAIS Source Description window is somewhat different than the one shown in Figure 13-4. In particular, the window informs you that the source already exists in the source list, and that saving it updates the existing entry.

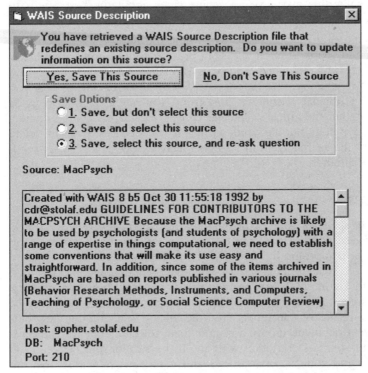

Figure 13-9: Updating an existing source

New Sources That Aren't in the Directory of Servers

Most of the time, you'll discover new sources through the Directory of Servers. However, you'll sometimes find one through other means. You might be prowling through a newsgroup, and see a message like this:

```
I just created a new and most wonderful source:

(:source
    :version  3
    :ip-name "nic.sura.net"
    :tcp-port 210
    :database-name "/export/software/nic/wais/databases/ERIC-archive"
    :cost 0.00
    :cost-unit :free
    :maintainer "info@sura.net"
    :description "ERIC (Educational Resources Information Center) Digests

Information provided by Educom

ERIC Digests are:

- short reports (1,000 - 1,500 words) on one or two pages, on topics
  of prime current interest in education.
- targeted specifically for teachers and administrators, and other
  practitioners, but generally useful to the broad educational community.
- designed to provide an overview of information on a given topic,
  plus references to items providing more detailed information.
- produced by the 16 subject-specialized ERIC Clearinghouses, and reviewed
  by experts and content specialists in the field.
- funded by the Office of Educational Research and Improvement (OERI),
  of the U.S. Department of Education (ED).

Created with WAIS Release 8 b4 on Apr 10 13:02:45 1992 by
lidl@nic.sura.net
 ")
```

Most of this message (everything following the first line) is a standard WAIS descriptor for the source. To tell winWAIS about this source, select the **Select Sources** option from the **Edit** menu. When the Select WAIS Sources window (shown earlier in Figure 13-2) appears, click on the **New** button. winWAIS opens a blank **Edit WAIS Source Definition** window, in which you can fill in the information necessary to add a source.[*]

If you fill in the template given for the "ERIC-archive" source shown in the previous example, it should look like Figure 13-10. Retyping the source by hand may be painful, but you can use the clipboard to cut from your original document into

---

[*] Before copying the source descriptor by hand, it might save you some work to search the Directory of Servers to see whether or not it's been "officially" added to the list. Anyone who creates a new library is supposed to tell the maintainers of the list. This doesn't always happen, but it's worth checking.

winWAIS. Although winWAIS does not have a **Paste** option on the **Edit** menu, you can press **Shift-Insert** to paste the contents of the clipboard into a winWAIS text box. When you are done adding or changing an entry for a source, you should click the **Check Host** button to make sure that the remote server responds, assuring you that you've entered valid information for the host address and the database. Clicking **OK** saves your changes.

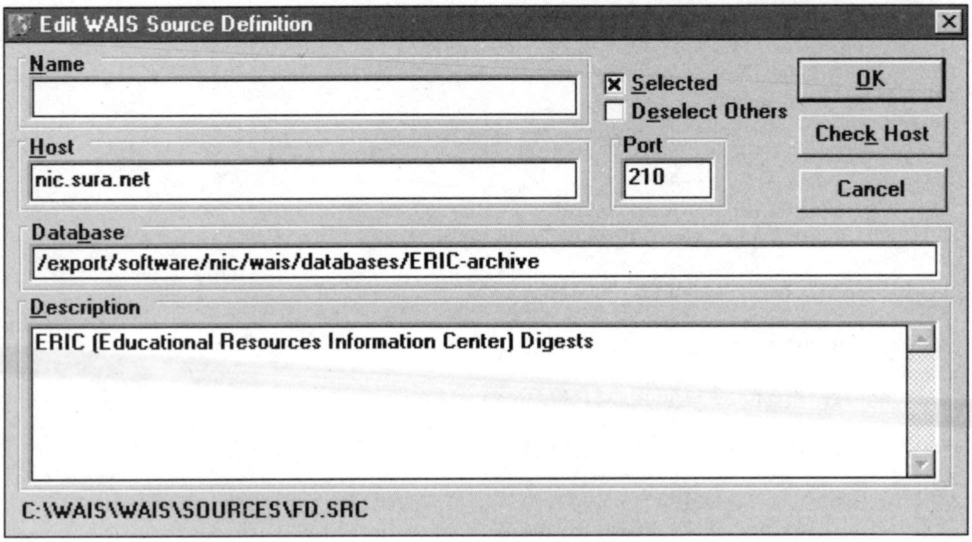

Figure 13-10: Add a new source

WAIS and the Web

As we mentioned in Chapter 6, *The World Wide Web*, there are many WAIS resources available through the Web. These resources appear as searchable indexes; they allow you to search specific databases like magazine back issues, scientific abstracts, and the *Encyclopedia Britannica*.

WAIS Inc., a company that produces WAIS software used by on-line services to publish large databases, also offers a way to perform comprehensive WAIS searches using the World Wide Web. To use a Web browser as a WAIS client, open the following Web document:

```
http://www.wais.com/newhomepages/wais-dbs.html
```

As you can see in Figure 13-11, this page lets you search the Directory of Servers, just as you would with winWAIS. Simply enter your keywords in the **Find** field and click the **Search** button.

The Directory of Servers page actually lists all of the available WAIS libraries; if you scroll down you'll see that all of the libraries are links. If you know which

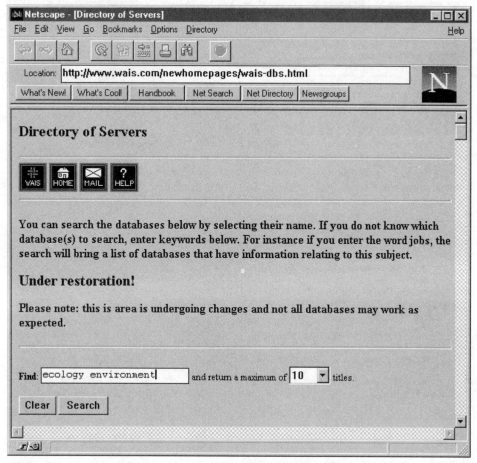

Figure 13-11: The Directory of Servers on the World Wide Web

library you want to search, you can select the link to the library and then search it directly.

As before, let's take a concrete example. Imagine that you're interested in gathering information about global warming and its effect on the environment. Since we're searching the Directory of Servers first, we need to think of some broad terms for this search. For example:

```
ecology
environment
```

Enter your keywords in the **Find** text box and click the **Search** button. After a few moments, you'll see a Web document like the one in Figure 13-12.

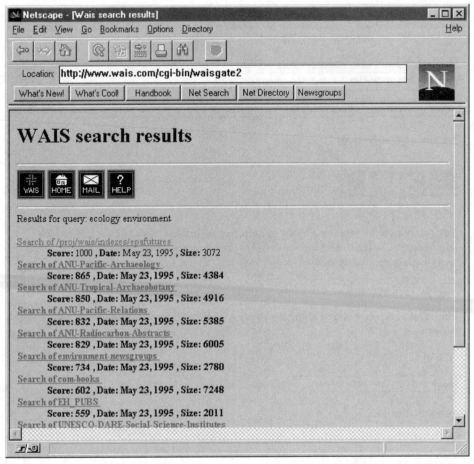

Figure 13–12: Results of Web directory search

This document lists the libraries that best matched the keywords, along with their scores, just like winWAIS. Each of the libraries is also link; if you click on a link, you'll see a description of the library, as shown in Figure 13-13. You can also search the library from this new document by entering your keywords in the search field. (One of the main drawbacks of using the Web as a WAIS client is that you can only search one library at a time.)

Let's finish our search now, by entering "global warming" in the search field and clicking **Submit Query**. As you can see in Figure 13-14, the Web interface to WAIS returns a document that lists matching articles. To view an article, simply click on the link to it. If your search didn't turn up anything of interest, you can refine it by entering new keywords and searching again. The Web interface also provides a

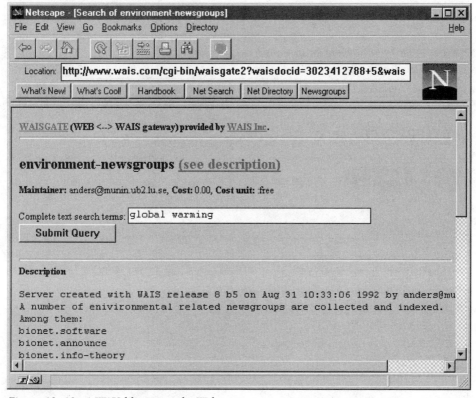

Figure 13–13: A WAIS library on the Web

limited form of relevance feedback. If you want to use an article for relevance feedback, click on the check box next to the article and perform your search again.

We've found that Web browsers make perfectly adequate WAIS clients. They don't let you do anything fancy, like save your queries or use a portion of a document for relevance feedback, but they get the job done.

Public WAIS Clients

Rather than downloading your own WAIS client or using the Web as a WAIS client, you can, as we already mentioned, use Telnet to access a WAIS client. For most Windows users, though, this method has one enormous disadvantage: it discards a Windows graphical interface for a command-based, line-oriented interface. Nevertheless, using this line-oriented, public WAIS client is not particularly hard. The first thing you must do is pick a likely prospect out of Table 13-2, the table of public WAIS servers, and **Telnet** to it.

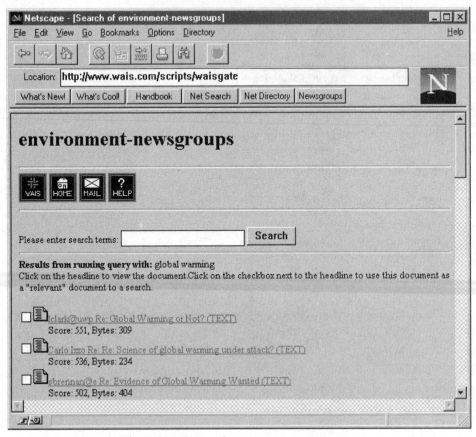

Figure 13–14: Results of a Web WAIS search

Table 13–2: Public WAIS Servers

Name	Login	Location
info.funet.fi	wais	Europe
sunsite.unc.edu	swais	Eastern US
quake.think.com	wais	Eastern US

When you are connected, use the login shown, and you will automatically be placed in **swais**. What you should see next is a list of all the available databases. Since there are over 500 WAIS libraries, the list is approximately 25 pages long, which makes it rather unwieldy. The best approach is to search the Directory of Servers as before, and locate the libraries you want to use (unless you know exactly which libraries you want). In this case, just find the libraries in the 25-page listing and select them.

Let's say that you're interested in finding information about specific classical music composers for a paper you're writing. After you Telnet to **quake.think.com**, you are presented with the entire list of sources. Since you don't really know which sources you want to search, you should start by searching the Directory of Servers. To do this, you need to select this source. You can use the down arrow key to move through the sources one by one, or type **J** to scroll a page at a time. The fastest way to select this source, however, is to search for it by typing **/** and then entering **directory-of-servers** at the **Source Name** prompt. Once you have highlighted the Directory of Servers, select it as the source you want to use by pressing the SPACE BAR. An asterisk appears in the display to flag the Directory of Servers as a selected source, as shown in Figure 13-15.

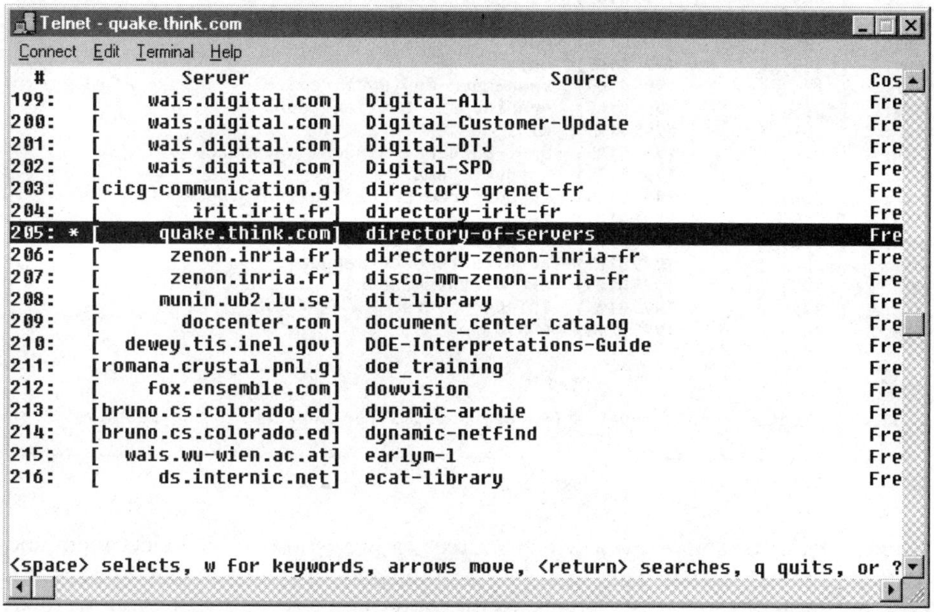

```
 Telnet - quake.think.com                                        _ □ ✕
Connect  Edit  Terminal  Help
  #             Server                    Source                    Cos ▲
199:  [      wais.digital.com]  Digital-All                         Fre
200:  [      wais.digital.com]  Digital-Customer-Update             Fre
201:  [      wais.digital.com]  Digital-DTJ                         Fre
202:  [      wais.digital.com]  Digital-SPD                         Fre
203:  [cicg-communication.g]   directory-grenet-fr                  Fre
204:  [          irit.irit.fr]  directory-irit-fr                   Fre
205: * [     quake.think.com]   directory-of-servers                Fre
206:  [        zenon.inria.fr]  directory-zenon-inria-fr            Fre
207:  [        zenon.inria.fr]  disco-mm-zenon-inria-fr             Fre
208:  [         munin.ub2.lu.se] dit-library                        Fre
209:  [          doccenter.com]  document_center_catalog            Fre
210:  [   dewey.tis.inel.gov]   DOE-Interpretations-Guide           Fre
211:  [romana.crystal.pnl.g]   doe_training                        Fre
212:  [       fox.ensemble.com]  dowvision                          Fre
213:  [bruno.cs.colorado.ed]   dynamic-archie                       Fre
214:  [bruno.cs.colorado.ed]   dynamic-netfind                      Fre
215:  [    wais.wu-wien.ac.at]  earlym-1                            Fre
216:  [        ds.internic.net]  ecat-library                       Fre



<space> selects, w for keywords, arrows move, <return> searches, q quits, or ?▼
◄ □                                                                        ► ▼
```

Figure 13–15: Selecting the directory-of-servers

Once you have chosen a source, you need to enter the keywords you want to search for. Press **w** to signal that you want to enter keywords; **swais** positions the cursor near the bottom left of the screen, and prompts you:

```
Keywords: classical music
```

You type in the words you are interested in, separated by spaces. We're looking for information on classical composers, so we'll start with "classical music." Why not just start with the name of one of the composers? At this point, we're still looking for music references in our electronic card catalog; we aren't yet looking for individual composers. Once we find some music references, we'll do a more specific search.

After typing the search string, press ENTER; that starts the actual search. When the search is completed, it returns a screen showing the results (Figure 13-16). This is really interesting. You found a number of sources and some of them are mighty odd. This is a good illustration of how WAIS works. You were looking for the words "classical" and "music." While some of the sources matched both words, others only matched one of the words, so they got lower scores.

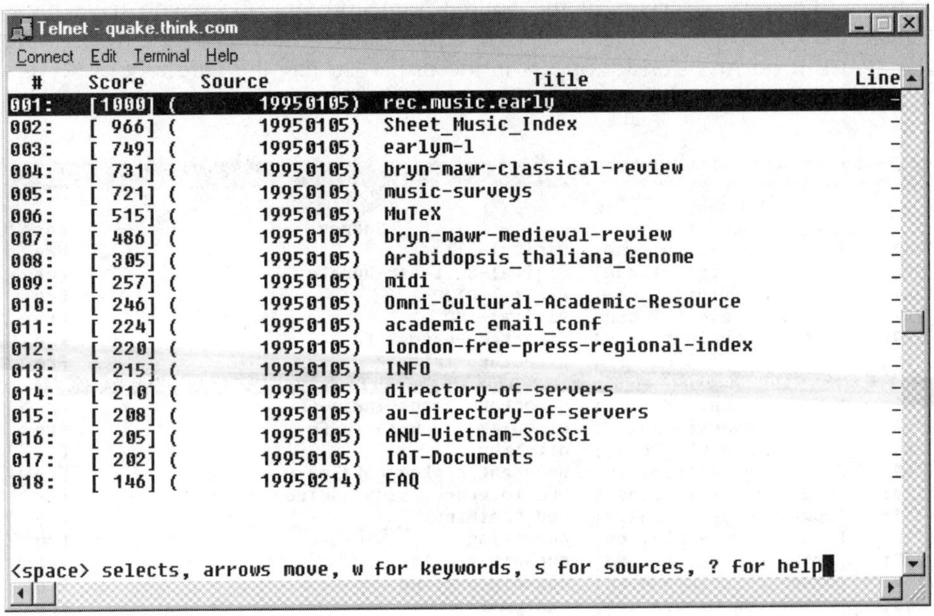

```
┌─────────────────────────────────────────────────────────────────────────┐
│ ⬛ Telnet - quake.think.com                                    [_][□][✕] │
├─────────────────────────────────────────────────────────────────────────┤
│ Connect  Edit  Terminal  Help                                            │
│   #      Score      Source             Title                    Line ▲   │
│ 001:   [1000] (      19950105)  rec.music.early                    -     │
│ 002:   [ 966] (      19950105)  Sheet_Music_Index                 -      │
│ 003:   [ 749] (      19950105)  earlym-1                          -      │
│ 004:   [ 731] (      19950105)  bryn-mawr-classical-review        -      │
│ 005:   [ 721] (      19950105)  music-surveys                     -      │
│ 006:   [ 515] (      19950105)  MuTeX                             -      │
│ 007:   [ 486] (      19950105)  bryn-mawr-medieval-review         -      │
│ 008:   [ 305] (      19950105)  Arabidopsis_thaliana_Genome       -      │
│ 009:   [ 257] (      19950105)  midi                              -      │
│ 010:   [ 246] (      19950105)  Omni-Cultural-Academic-Resource   -      │
│ 011:   [ 224] (      19950105)  academic_email_conf               -      │
│ 012:   [ 220] (      19950105)  london-free-press-regional-index  -      │
│ 013:   [ 215] (      19950105)  INFO                              -      │
│ 014:   [ 210] (      19950105)  directory-of-servers              -      │
│ 015:   [ 208] (      19950105)  au-directory-of-servers           -      │
│ 016:   [ 205] (      19950105)  ANU-Vietnam-SocSci                -      │
│ 017:   [ 202] (      19950105)  IAT-Documents                     -      │
│ 018:   [ 146] (      19950214)  FAQ                               -      │
│                                                                          │
│ <space> selects, arrows move, w for keywords, s for sources, ? for help▮ │
│ ◀ ▌                                                               ▶      │
└─────────────────────────────────────────────────────────────────────────┘
```

Figure 13-16: Search results of "classical music"

Now that you have an idea of which sources to use, you need to select them and perform another search. First, give the **s** command to return to the sources list. Currently, the Directory of Servers is the only selected source. If you were to search for composers, you would search the Directory of Servers again: not what you had in mind. You must do two things: first, get rid of the currently selected source, then select the sources you want. This is pretty easy. Press = to deselect all current sources, and get rid of any asterisks in the display. Next, select the sources you want, just as you selected the Directory of Servers initially. Scroll through the list until you find each source that you want; press the SPACE BAR to select it.

You need to change keywords, so press **w** again. Surprise, it positioned you after the keywords, "classical music," that you entered earlier. You need to clear these, by typing **CTRL-U**. After clearing the keyword list, enter the composers you are looking for:

```
Keywords: beethoven bach
```

You've finally set up the environment for doing the search you originally wanted.

Pressing ENTER signals the end of keyword entry and starts the search. The results are shown in Figure 13-17.

```
Telnet - quake.think.com                                              _ □ ×
Connect  Edit  Terminal  Help
  #      Score    Source                   Title                    Line ▲
001:    [1000] (          earlym-1)  Bruno Cornec <br List of Early Music Con   194
002:    [1000] (rec.music.early)  Bruno Cornec <br List of Early Music Con   194
003:    [ 754] (          earlym-1)  Bruno Cornec <br French mags EM CDs revi   167
004:    [ 754] (rec.music.early)  Bruno Cornec <br French mags EM CDs revi   167
005:    [ 672] (          earlym-1)  Dave Lampson <da Nimbus Clearance Sale     36
006:    [ 672] (rec.music.early)  Dave Lampson <da Nimbus Clearance Sale     36
007:    [ 656] (          earlym-1)  Bruno Cornec <br French mags EM CDs revi   148
008:    [ 656] (rec.music.early)  Bruno Cornec <br French mags EM CDs revi   148
009:    [ 639] (          earlym-1)  Cornec ESLOG p80 French mags Review Nov    108
010:    [ 639] (rec.music.early)  Cornec ESLOG p80 French mags Review Nov    108
011:    [ 607] (          earlym-1)  Bruno Cornec <br French mags EM CDs revi   128
012:    [ 607] (rec.music.early)  Bruno Cornec <br French mags EM CDs revi   128
013:    [ 574] (          earlym-1)  Don Cameron <dcc Re: Bach's temperament     3
014:    [ 574] (          earlym-1)  Greg Lewin <Greg Re: Bach's temperament     4
015:    [ 574] (          earlym-1)  BobH321 <bobh321 Concert Announce. - Mia   15
016:    [ 574] (rec.music.early)  Don Cameron <dcc Re: Bach's temperament     3
017:    [ 574] (rec.music.early)  Greg Lewin <Greg Re: Bach's temperament     4
018:    [ 574] (rec.music.early)  BobH321 <bobh321 Concert Announce. - Mia   15

<space> selects, arrows move, w for keywords, s for sources, ? for help█       ▼
◄ ▌                                                                    ► ▌
```

Figure 13–17: swais search results

You can view any one of these items by selecting it and pressing the SPACE BAR. You're done! If you want to get your own copy of the article, type **q** to get back to the list of articles; then type **m** to mail the article to yourself. You'll be prompted for your e-mail address. When you are done with **swais**, type **q** to exit from the program.

Those are all the commands you need to use the **swais** client, but there are a couple more which might make your life a bit easier:

/string
  Search for a particular string in the results.

r Use an article for relevance feedback.

What the Future Holds

The short answer is: I don't know. When the first edition of *The Whole Internet* was published, WAIS and WWW were the hot new tools. Lots of new WAIS resources were being created. Since then WWW has prospered, and WAIS fell on hard times. WAIS, Inc. was started to commercialize the technology, but really didn't accomplish much, at least as far as mere users were concerned. Thinking Machines, where WAIS was incubated, and which provided a home for the

Directory of Servers, went out of business. (Their hostname was recently revived, so don't worry about the examples that use **quake.think.com**; they work as of this printing.) WAIS drifted; people stopped creating new resources, and the older ones became harder to find, or disappeared entirely.

Recently, WAIS Inc. was bought by America Online, which promises (if nothing else) an infusion of money and public exposure. This is all for the good. WAIS is important because it's one of the few tools out there that support searching a large collection of heterogeneous databases efficiently. WAIS provides a way of searching databases, like sets of journal articles, easily. As such, it's really crucial for doing "industrial strength" research on the Net, as opposed to casual surfing. So I hope that WAIS will prosper in the future.

This doesn't mean that a WAIS client is in your future, though; in fact, WAIS Inc. only sells server products, not clients. It's probably more likely that you'll use various Web gateways to search WAIS resources, and that the Web will be a front-end to WAIS-based search engines. It's already being used that way; it's a good bet that Lycos and other Web search pages are based on WAIS technology. The client software isn't important: the technology will survive if people create new high-quality resources that are listed in a central directory of servers, and if the WAIS gateways (like the one at **www.wais.com**) improve so that you can search multiple databases with a single query.

CHAPTER FOURTEEN

OTHER APPLICATIONS

Time Services
Fax Over the Internet
Diversions
Audio and Video
PGP—Privacy and Encryption

I have covered all the standard, system-independent, and useful software that an average Internet user needs to make the network useful. There are many other Internet facilities that don't fit these categories. Some of them are useful, but system-specific. Some are useful to system administrators and software developers, but not to a "general purpose" user. And some are just plain useless. Notwithstanding these problems, no book on the Internet could be complete without introducing a few such applications.

This chapter is a brief introduction to the clutter of "miscellaneous" applications that you'll find. I've assumed that you'd probably rather not know about those facilities that are useful to large networked systems and are of interest primarily to system administrators. Those that are really useful to normal Internet users such as yourself are discussed in detail.

Time Services

Computers have had built-in clocks since the early days of computing. On large, multiuser systems, they were used for a variety of reasons, but mainly to help figure out what happened when something went wrong: did event A happen before event B, or after it? What if you start two jobs: one to create a file and one to use it, in that order. The second job fails because the file was not found. To see what happened, you check a log file to see whether the second job ran faster than the first and tried to use the file before it was created.

Before networking, time synchronization didn't matter much. Whenever you needed to compare two times, the times were all taken from the same clock. It didn't really matter if that clock was inaccurate; it would still tell you that event A took place before event B. With the advent of networks, the same problems existed, but you started to compare events that happened on different computers. Each computer's clock was set by a half-asleep myopic operator, who typed in the time from the wall clock when the system booted. Needless to say, there was a lot of error entering this data. So, the times on various computers were never quite the same. Did event A occur before B? You didn't really know, particularly if the times were close.

Initially, software was developed to synchronize the time clocks on computers running on the same local area network. With such software, each computer adjusts its clock slowly until the whole network reaches an average network time. From then on, the software continues monitoring to make sure the clocks stay synchronized, making slight modifications if needed.

This was good as far as it went. The next problem was: how do you synchronize clocks on computers that are widely separated? How do you keep a computer in California synchronized with a computer in Massachusetts? This problem is much harder: you have to account for the time the synchronizing messages take to reach their destination, including (if you really need accuracy) the time it takes for an electrical signal to travel down a wire at the speed of light. To handle this case, a more advanced service was developed: the *network time protocol*, or NTP.

NTP uses time servers at various points on the Internet. These time servers listen to time synchronization broadcasts from the U.S. Naval Observatory, and make them available to computers that need them. This is a really hard problem, considering that the network distributing the information has variable delays. So a lot of fancy computations are done to derive some statistically reasonable time to the requesting computer.

These are neat things, but in reality, using them may be beyond your control. However, a somewhat scaled-down client for Windows named TimeSync is readily available via anonymous FTP. It allows you to poll a time server on a single remote system, and adjusts your system clock accordingly.

Fax Over the Internet

These days, everyone seems to have access to a fax machine. To use one, you need a communications medium. Since the Internet is a communications medium, you would assume the technologies should merge: it should be easy to send fax transmissions over the Internet. Well, the technologies are indeed merging, but certainly not as smoothly nor as quickly as you would anticipate. The reason for this is, I think, primarily a "not invented here" phenomenon. The people who developed fax are making money hand over fist because it works fine over phone lines. They aren't primarily computer networking people, and they're perfectly happy sending fax transmissions over the phone. On the other hand, computer people have viewed fax as a lesser service, because the documents are not machine readable, merely machine transferable and displayable. That is, you can't fax a document to a computer and then edit it with a text editor. What's there is not text, but a picture of the page. It's only those of us who might find the facility useful who are tugging at the coat tails of the manufacturers saying, "Pardon me, but can you make fax work over the Internet?"

As I said, the technologies have merged to a limited extent. You can take a file (either a text file, or a file in any number of standard display formats) and send it via a modem to a fax machine. Likewise, you can receive a fax and have it placed in a file, where you can examine it with a display program. All the software you need is commercially available.

In 1993, a group of people got together and tried an experiment to provide Internet fax services on a wider basis. They recognized that the ability to send faxes over the Internet means that you can transfer the "fax" file by whatever means to another system across the Internet. Then you could view or re-fax it to its destination by placing a local phone call, saving long distance charges. If sites were already paying for Internet services, why not make it more useful?

This group has solicited sites in various geographical areas to act as fax gateways. If you volunteer, you allow a system on your site to receive faxes from anywhere in the world via the Internet, and then you relay these fax transmissions by phone to fax machines in your local calling area.

To send a fax via this service, you have to create a really strange e-mail address that contains the destination fax machine's phone number. For example, say you wanted to send a fax to Ed Krol, whose fax phone number is 1-217-555-1234.[*] You would send an e-mail to the following address:

```
remote.printer.Ed_Krol/1120_DCL@12175551234.iddd.tpc.int
```

The mailbox (the part to the left of the @) always starts with **remote.printer**. After **remote.printer**, you can put some text that will be printed on the fax's cover sheet. To get things through the e-mail system, where spaces in names are forbidden, use an underscore (_) in place of a space, and a slash (/) to signal a new line. So the address above puts the following text on the cover:

```
Ed Krol
1120 DCL
```

This address format is relatively new; if you have trouble getting it to work, try using an address like this one:

```
remote.printer.Ed_Krol/1120_DCL@4.3.2.1.5.5.5.7.1.2.1.tpc.int
```

Note that the phone number is listed in the host part of the domain name in reverse order.

---

[*] Don't send faxes here; I just made this number up!

No matter what the address looks like, the body of the mail message is just a normal e-mail message. The text of this message is printed on the recipient's fax machine.

International faxes are no different, except that the phone numbers are longer. If you send an international fax through the Internet, omit the international access code, but leave the country code on the phone number.

If this all sounds too good to be true, it sort of is. The area covered by volunteer gateways is constantly growing, but there is no guarantee that the area you want to reach is covered. And, like any volunteer service, it can be unreliable. If one of the relaying systems crashes while its owner is at work or on vacation, there's no staff to rush out and get it fixed. The best way to stay on top of Internet faxing is to send e-mail to **tpc-faq@town.hall.org** to receive the documentation. (The message itself can be null; all they care about is your e-mail address.) You can also send e-mail to **tpc-coverage@town.hall.org** to receive a list of the areas currently covered. If you would like to volunteer to serve as a gateway in your local area, this document will tell you how.

Diversions

Many ways to waste time, both yours and the network's, are available on the Internet. Some people read recreational newsgroups. Others talk to other people or play games. There is fairly wide disagreement about the validity of these uses. For this reason, I don't want to encourage you. But if I didn't tell you about them, you'd find out they exist on your own.

Conversations with Others

Several facilities allow you to "connect" to someone at another Internet site and type messages back and forth. These facilities are generically called *talk* (for two-way conversations) or *chat* (for group discussions). Of course, communications are what you make of them. Talks and chats can be business-oriented, helping you win the Nobel prize. Or someone may be giving you grief because your team lost the big playoff game. They can be used either way, so it is hard to condemn or restrict their use.

Talking

A fairly typical talk program is WinTalk, a freeware program from ELF Communications. You can download it from a number of anonymous FTP sites, including the following:

```
ftp.bhs.com
ftp.elf.com
```

To use talk programs, two people must agree to communicate with each other. The process starts when one person calls the other, using the talk program to set up the communications link. Let's say that Stephen wants to talk to David F. on **ora.com**. He opens WinTalk, which in its current version has no open window when it is running with no connections. It will show up on the taskbar at the bottom of the desktop. To make a connection, click the right mouse button on the WinTalk task icon and select **Talk** from the popup menu. In the Open Talk Connection dialog, type the address of the person you want to talk to, as in Figure 14-1. Then press the **Talk** button.

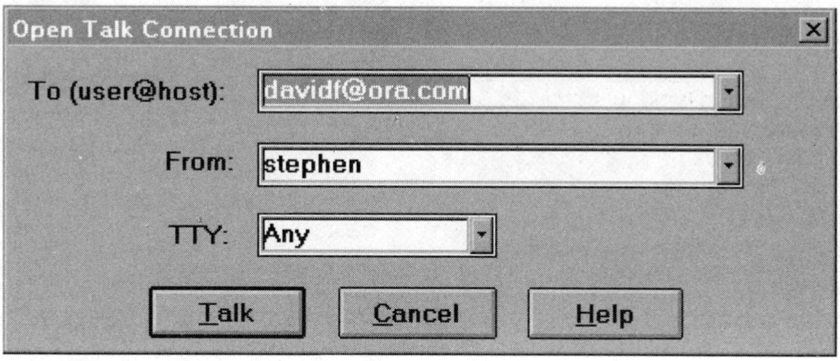

Figure 14–1: Opening a talk connection with WinTalk

The talk window with the vertically split screen will then open, and the message area on the bottom will say "Trying to connect to davidf@ora.com".

If David F. is logged in, a message appears on his screen informing him that **stephen@ora.com** wants to talk. Just in case David doesn't notice, the terminal's "bell" beeps a few times. If David wants to talk back, he must run his talk program and connect to **stephen@ora.com**.

When David responds, the talk window message area says "Connected!!" and the talk can proceed. Anything Stephen types to David is displayed on the top half of his screen and on the bottom half of David's corresponding screen, and vice versa. In this example, Stephen's screen looks like Figure 14-2. David typed everything that appears below the line; Stephen's replies appear above the line. It's a little hard to describe how this works, but you'll get used to it fairly quickly once you try.

WinTalk, like all talk programs, displays everything you type one key at a time as you type it. You can't edit something before you send it off as you can with mail. Talk programs don't even wait until you finish typing the line. So if you are a bad typist, the other person can see how slowly you type and every mistake you backspace over. This can be dangerous. Ill-advised comments still appear for an instant, even though they are erased. If you type "get off my case" while you're talking to the big boss, you're in trouble. Even if you change your mind and backspace over it, you've already dug your grave. It was displayed long enough for her to read it.

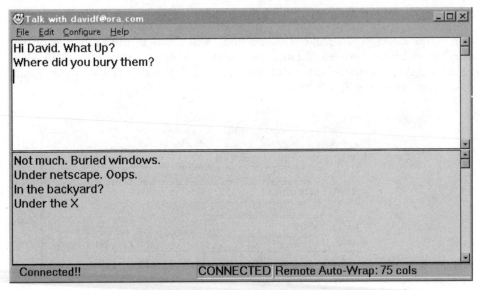

Figure 14–2: A talk session

Some talk programs are incompatible. If you have trouble communicating with someone using WinTalk, you might recommend that they try another talk program developed for whatever platform they're using. The problem is that older versions tend to send characters out in a manner that is specific to a particular vendor's hardware.

Chat

Chats are generalizations of talk where multiple people converse at once.[*] You can think of this as an electronic cocktail party without drinks. Groups gather to chat about various subjects. You can feel free to wander from group to group and take part as you like. Sometimes you might feel the need for a private conversation with someone in the discussion—i.e., drop out of the chat and revert temporarily to a two-person talk. All this is possible within the framework of chat facilities.

Some chat facilities are quite open, allowing discussions about any topic (or no topic) at all. Most Free-nets include chat facilities where users gather to discuss the local weather and whether the Peoria Rivermen will win their big game. Other topics (whatever is on anyone's mind) might be discussed in separate groups at

---

[*] You may have noticed that one of your Windows Accessories is a program called Chat. But this is not the same kind of utility that we are discussing here. In terms of purpose, Windows Chat more closely resembles the talk utilities we discussed earlier—it is used for communication between two people at two different computers. And Windows Chat is also of limited scope: it can be used as a talk program on a local Microsoft network, but not on the Internet.

the same time. At the other extreme, some chat facilities are "directed": they're restricted to a particular topic. One such facility is the discussion group in the SpaceMet resource, where people can gather to talk about space exploration. They are not so much restricted by charter as they are by audience. If you go to SpaceMet to try and talk hockey, you will feel as lonely as a social scientist at a computer science faculty cocktail party.

The most popular general chat facility is the *Internet Relay Chat*, or IRC. It consists of thousands of channels, each with a particular topic, with participation from all over the worldwide Internet. A person can be talking and listening on multiple channels at once, either to the whole channel or to a single person. To participate in Internet Relay Chat, you'll have to find a client program. One option is to contact a public client running on another system; or you can have your own client on your local computer. In the case of IRC, using a public client isn't a very good option. They exist, but they are very dynamic: they come and go all the time and are very hard to keep track of. It's really better to have your own client.

One of the best IRC clients for Windows is mIRC, written by Khaled Mardam-Bey. The latest version of mIRC is available at **ftp.demon.co.uk** in */pub/ibmpc/ winsock/apps/mirc*. Copies can also be found at **papa.indstate.edu** in the */winsock-1/winirc/* directory. You should also look at the newsgroup *alt.irc* to see how to become active. Discussions about client software, the locations of chat servers, and updated versions of the IRC FAQ are regularly posted to this group.

Figure 14-3 shows a sample session with mIRC. I'm participating in the "#friendly" channel in the window in the foreground. When you join and leave a channel, your coming and going is announced to the other participants. Each message is prefaced with the nickname of its sender (nicknames, rather than real names, are used throughout), and a list of participants in the channel is shown in the right-hand pane of the channel's window.

There are no standards for how chats should work, so each one is different. Fortunately, the software is pretty user-friendly, and on-line help is usually available. You only need to learn a few commands to function effectively on IRC, and because IRC is such a rich program, there are many more sophisticated commands and uses you can learn. New functionality in IRC clients has recently begun to include robust file transfer and video and audio communications. So, if you are interested, feel free to try one out.

Multi-Person Games

Computer games have been around for a long time. In fact, the UNIX operating system was invented in order to play a game called "Space Travel."[*] However, the past few years have spawned a number of person-to-person games played via the

---

[*] Maurice J. Bach, *The Design of the UNIX Operating System* (Prentice Hall: 1986).

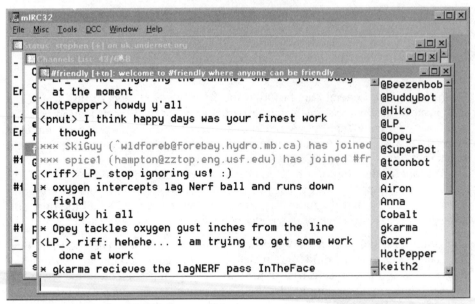

Figure 14–3: An Internet Relay Chat session using mIRC

computer. These range from traditional games, like Chess,[*] to real-time simulation games. The traditional games are not really a problem on the network, since they consume few resources. The others, however, have the ability to consume both computers and networks.

In real-time simulation games, each player is the commander of something (like the starship *Enterprise* or an F16 fighter). The players all take part in a simulated battle, complete with cockpit displays and visual effects. These games were really designed to be played over LANs because of their high-speed communication requirements. They require more speed than most Internet dial-up connections provide. As a result, if you play these games over the Internet, two things will happen:

- You will get other network users (and maybe some administrators) mad at you, because you're dragging the network's performance down.

- You will lose. You are at a competitive disadvantage, because the speed with which you can react to threats is limited by the speed of your link to the Internet.

Play if you must, but be discreet and considerate. There is no inalienable right to play games on the Internet.

---

[*] Take a look at the Recreation section of the online *Whole Internet Catalog* for the most up-to-date games listings.

MUDs

Multi-User Dungeons (MUDs) were created around 1980 as a network-accessible version of the Dungeons and Dragons adventure game. You could create a character, wander through the dungeon, meet other characters, fight various foes, and accumulate treasures and experience. They've changed a lot since then: there are still the original adventure-style games, but there are also MUDs that are oriented towards conversation, teaching, and even various kinds of experimentation. The thread that holds MUDs together is that they are games in which people interact with each other and their surroundings.

At the most basic level, they are text-based virtual worlds. Everything around you in the "game" is described with words. You can move around, manipulate objects, and interact with other users in a world that scrolls by on your screen.

There is more than one type of MUD. The different types are based on the kind of software used to run the MUD. There are perhaps a half dozen basic categories (MUD, MUSH, tinyMUD, MUSE, MOO, etc.) and many variations within each category. Each has its own client and server software, but they all support the same general type of multi-user space. You will notice the differences between the types by the commands that you use to move and act in each MUD. For example, a MOO and a MUSH might both describe a Star Trek sort of world, but what you can do will be different.

The majority of MUDs are still dungeon or combat games of some form. However, consider what it takes to build one of these dungeon games, and you'll realize that there are other possibilities, too. You build a world complete with a variety of objects and manipulate those objects with commands like "take axe," "look book," etc. It takes very little to turn a fantasy world into a poor person's virtual reality. The fact that you are interacting with other people in real time can really draw you into these worlds of text.

As an example of what can be done with a MUD, consider a MUD designed for teaching chemistry. If you give the commands "pour water into beaker" and "pour acid into beaker" in that order it's OK; if you give the commands in the other order, you get a message like:

```
The mixture foams and gets very hot, cracking the beaker.
Concentrated sulphuric acid splashes in your face!
```

It's arguably better to learn this way than by playing around with real chemicals. So, in addition to their role as diversions, some MUDs have found a home in education. Currently, most of the educational MUDs I know about are in the social sciences, computer science, or humanities. There are some MOO-style MUDs used as conferencing tools in molecular biology and genetics. If interest and discussion is any measure, many more MUDs for research and education will be springing up in the near future.

Lately, many new MUDs have been created primarily as social spaces as opposed to games. Each has some sort of theme or structure, such as a virtual house, hotel, or city. As users build the world that they'll inhabit for tens of hours a week, they develop strong social ties with each other, often developing into large and personally significant virtual communities. Another interesting feature of these social MUDs is that the notion of creating and becoming a character has crossed over from the gaming MUDs. Many people assume an identity in the MUDs that is quite different from their "real life" identity. (The theme of one MUD is that every user takes on the character of a furry animal.)

Many MUDs let players of sufficient experience modify the game. In the Dungeon games, you might be allowed to "dig" a new section of tunnel. In the chemistry MUD, you might be able to define a new experiment. Changing things usually means you need to learn a bit of programming in some language; it might be the C programming language, or some language specific to your MUD. Always check with your local wizard (i.e., a person on a MUD who has the authority to modify the software and exercise almost total control over what happens in a MUD) to see what you can do.

How do you get started in MUDing? Start with the FAQ posted to the newsgroup *rec.games.mud.announce* (or FTP it from the FAQ directories at *rtfm.mit.edu*). The first part gives you a general introduction to MUDs. The second part also tells you, in general, which software is used for what kind of MUD. For example, if you are into combat, you might look for DIKU sites (DIKU is a particular class of MUD that tends to be used for the traditional slaughter-and-pillage games). If not, you might look at tinyMUSHs. There is not always a correlation between the type of software that's used and the type of game that's played, but it's a start.

Once you have read the FAQ, you can look at the MUD newsgroups:

```
rec.games.mud.announce
rec.games.mud.diku
rec.games.mud.misc
rec.games.mud.moo
rec.games.mud.tiny
```

This is where you'll see announcements about MUD software, ongoing games, and so on. Many MUDs allow you to login as a guest, so you can explore a MUD to see how you like it. Also, there is usually a tutorial for new users that you should take when you first enter a MUD. Even if the first MUD you learn is not destined to be your eventual home, it will be fairly painless to make the transition to other MUDs of the same class (i.e., other MUDs using the same software). And—even if you're not enamored of the first MUD you play—you will find out about others from the adventurers you meet while playing.

Now, how do you do all of this? Well, it's possible to play a MUD with nothing but Telnet; all you need to do is Telnet to a special port on the MUD server. You are better off with a client on your local system. Again, there are many clients, and they're all slightly different; the best way to find out about them is to read the FAQ on MUDs, which is posted to the above groups. Also look out for more MUD variants, such as MUDs based on Gopher and the Web.

Audio and Video

It is either trivial or very difficult to send audio or video over the Internet, depending on how you look at it. If you only want to send a snippet of voice, a song, or a short video, it's easy. All these things are just files: rather large files, but nonetheless just files. For example, Carl Malamud produces an Internet radio show called Internet Talk Radio. He tapes interviews with well-known people within the networking community. He then places the digitally encoded interviews on a number of anonymous FTP servers. If you want to hear what the "Geek of the Week" said, you can download one of these files with FTP (or a higher-level tool like Mosaic, at **http://www.ncsa.uiuc.edu/radio/radio.html**) and play it through your PC. These are large files (15MB), but they're still just files: you download them and play them at your leisure.

The difficult thing about audio and video is doing it in "real time."[*] That is, it's very difficult to have a phone or video conference over the Internet. The problem is that the Internet was not really designed to do real-time conferencing. To understand, think about the telephone. When you dial a phone number, you are essentially renting a phone line all the way from your house to whomever you are calling. It is yours and you are paying for it whether you are talking or not. No one else can use it as long as you have it reserved.[†]

The Internet gets its cost advantage over traditional telephone service by sharing telephone lines. If data networking required placing a long-distance phone call every time a computer wanted to use a resource elsewhere, it would be prohibitively expensive—much more expensive than the network of high-speed leased lines that is currently in place. The problem with sharing resources is that things can get busy. When a network like the Internet gets busy, data just moves more slowly. There's no such thing as a busy signal. If you're FTPing a file or using a Telnet server somewhere, it isn't a problem. But real-time applications can't deal with slow-downs. A video playback application needs some number of frames per second, regardless of what else is happening in the world. You would be very annoyed if your networked video conference suddenly went into slow motion (to say nothing of the technical problems this would cause).

It's generally accepted that if many people tried to do live audio or video, the Internet would get really slow, really fast. There is, however, a lot of research on two topics, resource reservation and multicasting, to try and expand the usability of the Internet to these areas.

---

[*] Technically, these are known as isochronous applications. They require a steady stream of equally spaced information.

[†] That's no longer quite true. However, if you're a stickler for accuracy, you don't have to think back too far to get to a time when it was true.

Resource reservation is just what it sounds like: allowing someone to pay for a dedicated piece of the Internet for a while. You might be doing a video conference with someone and would like to tell your service provider "I'd be willing to pay five dollars per minute for a guaranteed television channel between here and Stanford."

Multicasting involves using the lines you have wisely. Imagine doing a three-way video conference with sites in London, Washington, D.C., and New York. The obvious way to set up the conference would be to open three channels, one between each site. There are two problems with this. One is that as the number of sites goes up, the number of channels goes up faster. The second is that some channels are more expensive than others. It would be much more cost-effective for London to open one channel to the U.S., and have the channel duplicated once it crossed the ocean. One of the copies would be sent to Washington and one to New York, thereby saving a transoceanic channel.

To be network-literate, you should know about multicasting—but you probably can't use it. It's still experimental, and most Internet service providers don't support it. However, there are two techniques for audio and video that you can play with: CU-SeeMe and RealAudio.

CU-SeeMe

CU-SeeMe is an up-and-coming video conferencing application being developed by Cornell University's Information Technology organization and White Pine Software. It runs on both Windows and Macintosh platforms and allows participants to simultaneously exchange video, audio, and text on a one-to-one basis, or, by using a "reflector," it allows many users to communicate with each other. The usefulness of this application lies in the "reflector" concept. Instead of every conference participant making a direct connection with every other, each makes a single connection to one machine, the reflector, which transmits all the outgoing signals. It acts very much like an IRC or MUD server with each participant running a client program.

To send your own video and sound, you will need additional hardware, specifically a camera and a plug-in video board, capable of sending a 4-bit greyscale digital video signal. As you may have guessed, this equipment can be pretty expensive. A company called Connectix makes a popular $99 camera for the Mac, and will soon release one for the PC. The QuickCam is a Plug-and-Play device that does not require a separate video capture board and comes with video software for Windows. There are many other camera and video board combinations out there that will run CU-SeeMe on the PC, but since the software is not yet mature, you will have to play around with your system to get it to work. The CU-SeeMe FAQ lists all known compatible PC hardware for CU-SeeMe (**http://cu-seeme.cornell.edu/**).

CU-SeeMe doesn't provide perfect live video communication across the Net, but it's okay, and the program is free. The picture is clear, but the motion is jerky—only 3 to 7 frames per second even at transmission speeds around 120 KBPS. CU-SeeMe is marginally useful with a fast dial-up connection (28.8 kbps); it will be better if you're on a LAN with a high-speed link to the Net or ISDN. The audio is improving (current Windows versions have trouble receiving audio), and if you can't support sound, there's always good old text to communicate with (unless you want to mime). Even without a high-speed connection, CU-SeeMe is worth experimenting with, if you're the sort that's inclined to tinker. Keep in mind, however, that any video conferencing software is a heavy bandwidth user. The CU-SeeMe software is constantly improving on performance in terms network usage, but it will still be quite a load on your network. You should use it only at appropriate times.

The CU-SeeMe program is still in its early stages. White Pine Software has been licensed by Cornell to produce enhanced versions of CU-SeeMe for commercial and non-commercial use (**http://www.wpine.com/cuseeme**.html). The program is expected to be out of its beta versions towards the end of 1995. Many other real-time video conferencing applications are being developed around the world as well, so keep your eye out for them.

RealAudio

RealAudio is a Web-based, pseudo real-time audio application. It comes bundled with Microsoft Explorer in the Plus! package. You can also download the player from **http://www.realaudio.com**. I say "pseudo real-time" because RealAudio isn't used for direct communications. Instead, it is used to play audio files on the Web directly as they're loaded from a remote server. This replaces the mechanism of having to download an entire audio file onto your machine and then open a separate application for playback. As you may know, it takes much longer to download an audio file than to play it.

RealAudio plays the file as it loads. It does this by directly reading the data stream (the bits of the sound file that are traveling across the network to your machine). As the stream is read by the program, the bits are decoded and played back immediately—no waiting! RealAudio uses a small buffer which saves a portion of the file prior to playing it, so that network slow-downs will have less of a chance to produce skips. Figure 14-4 shows the RealAudio play window.

One of the neat features of RealAudio is that it lets you skip around an audio file and get instant playback as fast as you can skip to tracks on regular audio CDs—all while receiving the data stream from the remote server. The RealAudio encoding format and its specialized server allow for additional requests from the user during playback. All you do is move the playbar forward or back to where you want in the track, and the program sends the server a request. The server can locate any specific point in the file and send it beginning at that point. You can also pause the track, replay it from the beginning, or stop it.

The RealAudio home page contains many samples and links to other sites that are serving audio programs in RealAudio format. ABC and NPR serve regularly

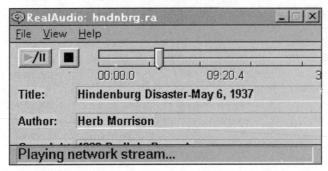

Figure 14-4: RealAudio program window

updated news programs at their sites. Several radio stations offer special interviews and programs in RealAudio at their Web sites as well.

PGP—Privacy and Encryption

For any number of reasons, you may want to keep your communications and information protected from prying eyes. You probably have security measures set up on your computer system to prevent unauthorized use of your files, but communications like e-mail are available for virtually anyone to read or tamper with when sent out over the Net. Cryptography is one of the best ways to ensure that your information is seen only by the intended audience—those who can decrypt the message. Strong encryption programs used to be available only for governments and large corporations, but now it is available for everyone via programs such as PGP, which stands for "Pretty Good Privacy."

PGP is a sophisticated encryption program written by Phil Zimmerman. You can use PGP to encrypt files on your computer with a password so that no one else can read them, encrypt your e-mail so that no one other than the intended recipient can read it, and you can sign documents with a tamper-proof digital signature to prevent someone from forging a document in your name or modifying a document that you have signed.

PGP uses *public key cryptography* to encode and decode messages. Public key cryptography differs from what you would think of as "traditional" cryptography in which a message is encoded with a specific "key" (e.g., a scheme replacing every letter of the alphabet with a unique number) and then decoded with the same key. In PGP, you have both a public key and a private, secret key. You distribute your public key to friends and colleagues, and they use that key to encrypt messages that they send to you. Only your secret key can decrypt a message that was encrypted with your public key. As long as you keep your secret key secret, the messages sent to you cannot be read by anyone else.

You can sign your messages (even if you don't encrypt them; for instance, when posting to USENET) by using your secret key to produce a digital signature. This digital signature enables you to verify your identity and determine whether or not your message has been tampered with. PGP does this by using a function to distill the message into one large number. This number is then encrypted with your secret key to create the signature, which will look something like this at the end of the message:

```
-----BEGIN PGP SIGNATURE-----
Version 2.6

iQB1AgUBLhwFvnOD8bPZas15AQF4VwL+NfmyMPYDmlXs7j0AoWPecC1I0b5fpGZa
SQx3bHV1sdEaLF7eEQVTa+C85cfPMmXi9c0yDmv/IB4xrX8q652IGWuAwn+xa2EF
5xE9QEOIfhpfaC9UVVZCykU4SjVrWuyU
=2Qe4
-----END PGP SIGNATURE-----
```

Only your public key can decrypt this signature and verify that you sent this message and that it is unaltered.

This scheme does rely on one risky factor, however, and that is trust. How do you know that a public key belongs to the person it claims it does? It is up to you to verify the public keys you keep and use. You can do this easily for people that you know personally and trust, and you can in fact certify the validity of this key. You may even want to add your signature to another person's public key. Then, if someone receives a public key with your signature on it, he can decide how much he trusts you to see if he will trust the key's validity. The scheme goes on like this, creating a "web of trust" on which you can base your faith in other people's public keys.

PGP is an extensive program that provides excellent information security. There are several places on the Internet where you can get it, but there are also restrictions. Versions 2.6 and higher are available to US citizens for use in the US. (Canadian citizens may use this version too.) PGP is an encryption program under US export control, and if you send or take it outside the borders, you are breaking the law and could be subject to severe penalties. The encryption algorithm in the program is patented by RSA Security, and this adds even more restrictions on PGP's use. You will find out all the details about legal usage at the sites where you can download the program.

You can get a copy of PGP via the World Wide Web at the site **http://web.mit.edu/network/pgp.html**. You can also use FTP (**net-dist.mit.edu** in *pub/PGP*), but the process is much easier using the Web. Here you will need to read the RSA license agreement and fill out a form. Then you are allowed to download the program. PGP is available in source code, where you will have to compile it yourself; a UNIX executable; a DOS executable; and a Macintosh executable. There is no Windows-only version of the program, so you must get the DOS version. To use this version in Windows you must create your messages as text files and then go to the DOS shell to encrypt them. The files can then be put into your mail and news programs for sending.

There are an increasing number of programs available on the Net that incorporate DOS PGP into Windows applications. You will probably find it easier to use PGP in conjunction with your communications programs with one of these applications. WinPGP is a shareware program that you can find at **ftp.firstnet.net** in the directory *pub/windows/winpgp*. Another application to check out is Private Idaho at **http://mail.eskimo.com/~joelm/**. Many popular mail and news programs have begun to incorporate PGP functionality; the MIT PGP page is a good source of information on new PGP developments.

For a detailed description of the program, its use, and its intriguing history, see the Nutshell Handbook *PGP: Pretty Good Privacy* by Simson Garfinkel, published by O'Reilly & Associates.

## CHAPTER FIFTEEN

DEALING WITH PROBLEMS

The Ground Rules
Gather Baseline Information
The Battle Plan
Talking to Operations Personnel

The network is not infallible. Eventually, when you click on the Exchange icon, you'll see the message in Figure 15-1.

You could not be logged on to mail server: ruby.ora.com

Be sure your account information for this server is accurate.
If this problem persists, contact your Internet Service Provider.

OK

Figure 15-1: What's up?

Now what?

You don't have to be an ace network technician to deal with this situation, but you do need some guidance about managing in the face of adversity. First, we'll talk about what usually breaks, then about what you need to know to attack a problem. After that, we'll give you a reasonable approach to dealing with common network problems. It's not an exhaustive guide. We could easily construct scenarios that would lead you astray with this approach, but they would not be common in real life.

If you are easily offended, you may be upset by some of the suggestions in this chapter. Don't be. When the pressure is on, people lose common sense. If you read this chapter when there is nothing wrong (and you should), you might think

"I'm not stupid. Of course I'd check the power cord." We don't think you are dumb. When you are in the swamp up over your knees, it's very easy to forget the most common-sense trouble spots.[*]

The Ground Rules

When you're thinking about what's wrong with the network, there are two rules to keep in mind:

- The cheaper the component, the more likely it is to fail and the less likely it is to be noticed by someone who is able to fix it.

- You need to know what's right before you can figure out what's wrong.

What do these rules mean? The Internet is frequently described as an amorphous cloud, as in Figure 15-2.

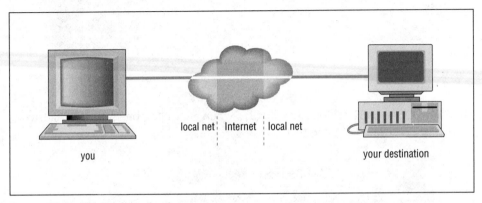

local net ¦ Internet ¦ local net

you   your destination

Figure 15–2: The Internet cloud

Think about this cloud in the context of the first rule. As you move away from your computer, you know less and less about what happens to your packets; you enter the cloud. As you get closer to the cloud, components get more expensive. Inside the cloud are a bunch of expensive computers and telephone lines. If one of them fails, a lot of people could be affected: a campus or even an entire country could be disconnected. So the cloud is monitored continuously and built as redundantly as possible. If something goes wrong, technicians notice and take corrective action immediately.

On the other extreme, you are probably sitting at a computer that costs under $3000 talking to a network over a $150 modem that is connected to your computer and telephone by under $10 worth of cable. If you're connected to the Internet through a LAN, the components are somewhat different, but the costs are likely to

---

* You might also be offended if you're an experienced administrator; a lot of the solutions here are, admittedly, simplistic. Remember that this chapter isn't for you.

be only slightly higher. If something happens to these, no one except you will notice.

In between, in an area of reduced visibility, there is a campus network, a corporate network, or a service provider connecting you to the Internet cloud. It is medium-priced, fairly well protected, and frequently monitored during business hours.

Most unexpected network outages occur fairly close to the ends: either around your computer or the one you are trying to reach. It may be in your computer or between your computer and the wall, but the closer you get to the cloud, the less likely the problem is to occur. This doesn't mean that problems are "always your fault." There is a destination computer sitting just as far from the cloud as you are, somewhere else in the world. The problem is just as likely to be on the other end. And, on rare occasions, there are problems in the cloud itself. But that should be your last assumption, not your first.

When something goes wrong, your major goal often isn't fixing the problem. If you can, great, but more often than not, the problem will be something you can't control. This is where the cloud starts: wherever the network gets beyond your control. In that case, your goal becomes figuring out when you can expect it to be fixed. Do you sit at your computer at midnight banging on the ENTER key, or do you go into the living room (or go home, if you're at an office) and watch David Letterman? If it's 10 P.M. and you deduce that the problem's a bad cable, you can probably go watch Letterman; you probably will not be successful in finding a replacement cable before morning. If you learn that you're accessing a service that's temporarily off-line until 11 P.M., you might stay at your computer and play some network chess.

Now we start getting into the second rule. You need to learn a little about the network while the network is running correctly. When things go wrong, a few simple tests will show you what's changed. You don't need anything special for these tests. You already have the tools you need: Telnet or another program which came with Windows 95: Ping.

Gather Baseline Information

To do any reasonable amount of network troubleshooting, you need to push the cloud back a bit. You need some information on your local connection to the network and, if there is one, the router that connects you to the rest of the Internet. If you push back the cloud, every network in the world looks something like Figure 15-3. The precise character of the connection may vary, but in every case, some kind of wire connects your computer to something else. You need to find out a little about both yourself and the "something elses": who is responsible for them and how fast they respond. So right now, go shopping for the following items:

- The IP address of your computer, if you have a constant IP address. In some cases, your IP address may be dynamically assigned at the beginning of each session. So, this may not be possible.

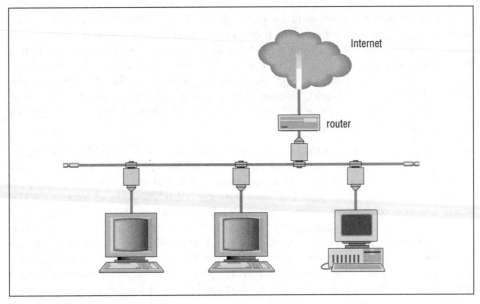

Figure 15–3: Network schematic

- If you're on a LAN, the IP address of another computer on the same LAN. If you're a dial-up user, the IP address of your service provider's terminal server. (Or, try the host which is listed on the **Gateway** tab in the TCP/IP configuration **Properties** menu).

- The IP address of the router or gateway closest to your computer that is responsible for connecting you to something larger (the router in Figure 15-3). If you're a dial-up user, get the address of your service provider's router

- Depending on your setup, a list of whom to call for particular problems at particular times. If you're a dial-up user who is connected to a commercial service provider, that's who you should call for problems not due to your hardware. If you're in a more sophisticated network environment, there is probably a system administrator who can either deal with the problem for you or give you a good sense of whom to call for what kinds of problems.

- The state of the status lights on any networking equipment you have access to. If you're a dial-up user, the state of the status indicators on your modem and the transitions they go through while you are making a connection.

In almost every case, the information required is quite manageable, but you need to modify the shopping list based on how your connection is made. For really large sites, the network infrastructure may be complicated, but so is the support structure. The heartening thing is that the more complex your network is, the more local help you are likely to find. In a really large network, "who to call" is probably a single phone number, answered 24 hours per day, seven days a week.

Don't underestimate the importance of the first three items: the numeric Internet addresses of your system, a neighbor's, and the closest router. Elsewhere, we've always used computer names to contact things, rather than IP addresses. Troubleshooting is the exception to this rule. In order to use a name to make contact, your computer may automatically seek out a Domain Name Server to convert the name to an address. This requires a healthy network. If your network is in sad shape, it won't be able to do this; the tests you run using a name will be meaningless. An IP address is immediately usable, so it eliminates one source of error.

The Battle Plan

Let's get back to the task at hand. You go to your computer to work on the big project at 10 P.M., and you can't connect to the "Federal Information Exchange." So let's look at the problem. Throughout this discussion, we need to assume that your connection has been working and just quit.[*]

Know the Hours of Operation

The computers that provide network resources range from personal computers to gigantic mainframes. Most of these, along with the network control computers, require some periodic maintenance. Most sites schedule maintenance during odd hours, like 2 A.M. Saturday, when the network load is usually light. However, scheduled "down time" varies from resource to resource. If you use a resource regularly, you should try to find out what its hours are supposed to be. You may save yourself a midnight attempt to access a resource that isn't available, anyway. Also, remember that the Internet is worldwide. Friday during business hours in the United States is 2 A.M. Saturday in Japan.

If you are trying sources randomly, you won't be aware of the site's schedule. If you try in the middle of the night, you may get better response time, but you run a greater risk of finding a computer out of service. The computer may be down for scheduled maintenance, or it may have crashed, and no one is around to bring it back up. Remember, many resources are volunteer efforts. If the last volunteer locks up the office and goes home at 5:00, it could be the next morning before someone can restart a crashed application.

---

[*] Initially configuring a system is dealt with in Appendix B, *Setting Up Your Internet Connection.*

Did You Change Anything?

If you've ever used a computer, or helped others use computers, the following dialog should come as no surprise:

> "It stopped working."
> "Did you change anything?"
> "No, it was working yesterday and then it just stopped."
> "You're sure?"
> "Well, I did change the screen color in my configuration file,
>   but that wouldn't affect it."

If it worked yesterday and doesn't work today, something has changed. It may be your computer, it may be the network, it may be the destination. Changes you've made are the easiest to undo, but the hardest to acknowledge as a problem. People change things on their computers because they're trying to accomplish something. If I tell you that your changes caused a problem, you'll probably think that I'm trying to impede progress. But in many cases, your recent changes probably did cause the problem. If you have changed anything—a file or some hardware thingy—and your network connection hasn't worked right since, don't consider it unrelated, even if the relationship appears remote. Before looking anywhere else, try to undo the change.

A good rule of thumb is to assume that the problem is at your end of the connection before you suspect problems at the other end. Make sure your end is working correctly before looking elsewhere. "Why?" you ask. "Didn't you say that the problem is equally likely to be at the far end?" Yes, that's true. But think about this: the far end is as likely to be in Japan as in Chicago, and almost certainly isn't close to you. Before making a long-distance phone call to Japan, make sure that the problem's not on your end.

Read the Error Message

When some people get an error message, they become so flustered that they only see:

```
ERROR - glitzfrick framus gobbledegook
```

Relax, read the error closely, and write it down. You need to write it down so that if you have to report it to someone, you have the exact text of the message. Nothing is more frustrating, for both the technical support person and the network victim, than a message like "It said 'error something something something'." And if you take time to look at the error message carefully before you start calling out the troops, you might be able to fix your own problem. Even if you don't understand the whole message, you should be able to pick out a couple of words to help you along.

Windows 95 error messages are big on helpful advice in plain English, but some of the suggestions can be misleading. The actual problem that produced the message in Figure 15-1 was a temporary network outage; the account information was fine. Don't focus too much on the possibilities suggested by the error messages; they may keep you from finding out what's really wrong.

Look Around Your Computer

Now, assume that the finger of Murphy's law is pointing directly at you—or your computer. It's time to start looking around your home or office. In World War II, the problem was gremlins. They caused bombs not to explode, engines to stop, etc., all for unknown causes. For a computer, the problem is usually people: if you're in an office, there are cleaning personnel, officemates, and you; if you're at home, there are you, your family and your pets. It's amazing how many computer and networking problems are caused by damage to the cable between your computer and your modem, or between your modem and the telephone. Janitors knock it out with a broom, or you roll over it a hundred times with a chair wheel and cut it. If you find something obviously wrong, fix it (or get someone to fix it).

Recognize When Things Happen

To use the Internet, a number of things need to happen in sequence.

1. You initiate a dial-up connection.

2. Your machine connects, gets authorized, and negotiates a number of parameters.

3. You attempt to contact a site.

4. Your machine turns a name into an address.

5. It contacts that remote computer and does good stuff.

Along the way, the computer tells you things either through dialog boxes or on status lines near the top or bottom of the window. Get familiar with how and when these things change. If they change in unfamiliar ways, they offer clues as to where the problem lies. Certain messages occur at certain times and knowing when a message occurs in relation to others can be quite revealing.

For example, if you say "connect to **ux1.cso.uiuc.edu**" and your computer responds "Trying 128.174.5.50", that tells you quite a bit. It tells you that your computer is connected to the Internet, and that you have successfully contacted the domain name system and converted the name into an address. So if you fail after that point, you probably should look more at problems with your application or the site you are trying to contact than at how your modem is configured.

Establishing Your Connection

First things first. You need to connect to your provider. (If you are not using PPP over a modem this doesn't apply.) You will open your **Dial-up Networking** icon and click on an icon which you have configured to call your Internet provider. It

will show you a dialog box and you press **Connect**.[*] (Make sure you've configured Windows 95 to bring up a terminal window while dialing; you need to be
able to see what's going on.) The next thing that happens is that your modem
should dial. This should be accompanied by a progress box which says it's dialing.
If you don't hear it dial and the lights on the modem don't flash, there is a problem with how your modem is talking to your computer. Check the cables and
whether it is connected to the port (COM1 or COM2) you thought it was.

If that was successful, eventually your provider should answer and the modem
should start hissing and whistling at you. This is good. It is the modems on each
end trying to decide how fast they can talk to each other.

Once the modems are talking, it is time for account numbers and passwords to be
passed along. If something goes wrong here, check the documentation that is provided by your provider and make sure you got the upper and lowercase correct; it
does make a difference. If it all looks OK, there is no recourse but to give your
provider a call.

When that hurdle is crossed, your machine tries to negotiate a number of issues
with your provider. Usually the biggest issue here is who is going to supply the IP
address for your computer. Some providers will provide you with a static IP
address which you need to enter, the same as if you had a LAN connection. Other
providers send your machine a temporary IP address when you connect. If you
get this wrong, it will give you an "Incompatible connection" error message.

Finally, if you made it this far you will be connected and will get the box shown
in Figure 15-4.

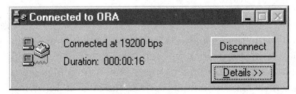

Figure 15–4: Connection status box

This tells you connection is achieved and gives a running total of how much time
you have spent.

Some Hints About Dial-ups

There are two very common problems which occur when you try to dial in: the
phone never answers or it answers and doesn't talk. Let's look at these problems
in detail.

---

[*] This, again, is described in Appendix B.

Ring, no answer

Check the number you dialed. Was it correct? If you dialed correctly and the remote system doesn't answer, that system may be down, or its modem may be bad. Check the published hours of operation to make sure it should be up. If it should be working, try the same phone number a few times. Better yet, if you have any alternate numbers, try them. If you have two phone lines available, try dialing the number with a phone on the line that doesn't have the modem. While it is ringing, dial with your modem phone and see if it gets through. (Sometimes if there are multiple phone lines through one number, one bad line will always answer the call. If you keep it busy with another phone, your modem call might get to a good one.) Even if you get through eventually, call your service provider and report the problem so it can be fixed.

Answer, then nothing

Here's one common scenario: the modem dials correctly, the remote system answers, and then everything goes dead. This usually points to a problem with your service provider's gear. Either the provider's modem is bad, or the port on the computer it is connected to is bad. Either way, the only thing you can do is call in and report it. You might try again. If you have an alternate number, try it—getting a different modem to answer might bypass the problem.

There's one other possibility. There are certain modems that "don't like to talk to each other," particularly if they're made by different manufacturers (and particularly particularly if they are 28.8kbps modems). However, we're assuming that you're troubleshooting a connection that has worked for you in the past. Unless you've just bought a new modem, incompatible modems probably aren't the problem.

Problems While Connected

Now you're connected, but you aren't home free. There are still pot holes, but you have more tools to help you figure out what the problem is. When dealing with your connection, it either works or it doesn't. It's mostly trial and error. If you're using Internet Explorer and see the error shown in Figure 15-5, you have a little more information to work with. You can also try a different site and see if you have better luck.

Remember that each application and each site uses a slightly different path through your computer and the Internet. So, if you click on **http://www.gnn.com/** and it doesn't work, you might just try **http://whitehouse.gov** (any of your favorite sites would do) or check your e-mail. The odds are slim that both of these sites are down at the same time. If the second one works, it's not your problem.

Internet sites and Web pages will occasionally just vanish. The best resources in many areas are maintained by students who grow up and graduate. When this happens, the resource often disappears. That's life on the Net.

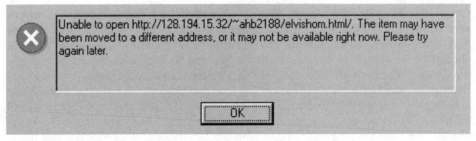

Unable to open http://128.194.15.32/~ahb2188/elvishom.html/. The item may have been moved to a different address, or it may not be available right now. Please try again later.

OK

Figure 15–5: Feeling Rejected

When something happens unexpectedly, several words and phrases often crop up in network error messages: "unknown," "unreachable," "refused," "not responding," and "timed out." Let's try and deal with each of these, mapping them into some telephone-call scenarios.

unknown

You called directory assistance and asked for Willie Martin's phone number. The operator responded "I'm sorry; there is no listing for Willie Martin." This problem usually shows up when your computer tries to convert a name into an IP address. You told the computer to call **ux1.cso.uiuc.edu**. It tried to find the address, but was told that the computer didn't exist. Either you misspecified the name (e.g., spelled it wrong) or the computer couldn't convert it. There could also be a problem with the Domain Name System. This last problem is almost certainly something you can't handle; get on the phone. In a pinch, if someone can tell you the IP address you need, you can use it and bypass this problem.

unreachable

You dialed the number and got the message "I'm sorry; the number you have reached is out of service." This is a real network problem. A portion of the network is down. The network is telling you, "I know where you want to go, but you can't get there from here." If this happens, there is nothing you can do but call for help.

refused

You tried to make a person-to-person call and got the correct number, but the person you want is not there. The computer at the far end needs to accept connections for a particular service (e.g., anonymous FTP). Your computer successfully contacted the destination computer and asked to make the connection to a service, but the destination said "no." There are several possible reasons for this. The computer may be running, but not available for user access. This is frequently the case during maintenance periods or while doing filesystem dumps. It's also possible that the service has been cancelled: i.e., the system's manager has decided not to provide it. For example, you might hear that a great game is available if you Telnet to **game.edu** at port 5000.

When you try this, you get a "connection refused" message. This probably means that the computer's owner decided not to allow game playing anymore.

timed out

This may mean that you called and no one answered, or that you were put on hold indefinitely. When TCP sends messages to a remote computer, through whichever application you are using, the local TCP process expects responses in a reasonable amount of time, usually a few minutes. If it doesn't get a response, it gives up and sends you this message. Usually, that means the destination computer or a piece of the network is dead. This can happen in the middle of a conversation. Try again in about ten minutes—long enough for most systems to recover from a crash automatically, if they are going to. If it still doesn't work, investigate further. (You would get this message if the modem cable or the network cable suddenly fell off your computer.)

not responding

This is very similar to a timed-out message, but the conversation is happening with UDP rather than TCP. (Different applications use different protocols. From your point of view, it shouldn't matter.) It does mean that packets were sent to the remote site and nothing came back. As with the timed-out message, try again in about ten minutes. If it still doesn't work, investigate further. (Again, you'd get this message if the modem cable or network cable suddenly fell off your computer.)

You may find that everything works, but only sort-of. Everything's slow as molasses, the lights on your modem blink in strange ways, and the modem occasionally disconnects. A common cause for this is a local noisy line. To test this theory, try to "ping" your Internet service provider's terminal server, or some other system on his network. (How to do this is covered in the next section.) Long round-trip times point to a bad phone line.

Try to Reach a Local System

On the shopping list, we told you to try to get the IP address of another computer on the same local network—or the address of some machine on the provider's network (ideally, the terminal server you connect to) if you're a dial-up customer.

Here's where you use that information. Find the Ping utility that came with Windows 95. It's probably in the *c:\windows* directory; you can search for it with the **Find File** function if need be, or you can get the WS_ping client (developed by John Junod), which is available via anonymous FTP. Use Ping to probe a few remote computers; you'll quickly narrow down where the problem lies:

- If you can't Ping other systems on your local network, your network (or your provider's network) is down.

- If you can Ping other systems on your local network, but can't Ping your gateway or router, you know that the router is down. You're connected to a single network on the Internet, but not to the Internet as a whole.

- If you can't Ping the remote computer you need to reach, but can **ping** another remote computer, the remote computer that you want to reach is down.

- If you can successfully Ping the remote computer you've been trying to reach, it indicates that the remote computer is working. If you continue to have difficulty connecting to it, it indicates that the computer is temporarily busy or has no additional connections available.

- If you can't successfully Ping any other computer, the problem lies with your computer and its connection to the Internet.

To use Ping, open a MS-DOS window and type in **ping** followed by the name or address of the machine you are trying to contact. For example, if we were having trouble contacting **www.gnn.com** we could try:

```
C:\WINDOWS> ping 204.148.101.51

Pinging 204.148.101.51 with 32 bytes of data:

Reply from 204.148.101.51: bytes=32 time=50ms TTL=236
Reply from 204.148.101.51: bytes=32 time=45ms TTL=236
```

This sends a 32-character packet to that computer, whose IP address is 204.148.101.51. We used the numeric IP address because that eliminates the possibility that something is wrong with address translation. It took 50 milliseconds for the first packet to return and 45 milliseconds for the second. Ping keeps sending packets every few seconds until you manually stop it with a CTRL-C. This proves you can contact **www.gnn.com**, and that (therefore) a lot of the Net is more-or-less working. If the times reported are very long, or Ping reports that packets are dropped, you might suspect that:

- The Internet is very heavily loaded (try again later), or

- There's noise on your local phone line (dial-up) or your local network that's damaging packets in transit. Good luck dealing with your local phone company. You'll need it.

Some Consolation

It may sound like there's not much you can do. In some sense, that's true. Think of your washer, dryer, or VCR. If they break, you can make sure all the plugs and hoses are tight, or maybe pull out a jammed cassette. There are a few things you can fix. But, much of the time, there is nothing you can do but call up the lonesome Maytag repairman and talk about the problem knowledgeably. Even if you can't solve the problem yourself, the more information you can gather, the better service you'll get.

Talking to Operations Personnel

Whenever pilots talk on the radio to air traffic controllers, they are taught that every message should say:

- Who you are

- Where you are

- What you want to do

These same guidelines apply to calling network operators. First, they need to know who you are—otherwise, they can't ask you for more information, or tell you that they've solved the problem. Where you are (the name of your computer and possibly its IP address) and what you want to do (the name of the remote computer and the service you want to get) allow operators to figure out the path your communications should take. This is the essential data necessary to diagnose and solve a problem. However, it is only the minimum. In addition, keep in mind why you've called the network operators. If you've followed our short procedure above, remember what you've done, why you did it, and what the results were. Why are you convinced that the problem isn't on your desktop? The answer to this question contains very important clues about the nature of the problem.

The operator you call should be the one running the network closest to you. Your local network operators are the only ones who monitor connections to your campus or building. It isn't like calling up the president of GM to get action on your car. In the network world, a national operator only knows about his network's connection to regional networks. Once he or she determines that MCI, or Sprint, or whatever isn't at fault, they will call the regional network responsible for your connection. In turn, the regional network will call your campus, corporate networking center or Internet service provider. Very likely, they will then call you. Save yourself some time: start at the bottom.

THE WHOLE
INTERNET

CATALOG

RESOURCES ON THE INTERNET

Stalking the Wild Resource
A Few Special Resources
How We Did It
Using the Catalog

Up to this point, you've been given a lot of "how to" advice. Now it's time to discuss "to what?" There are lots of resources out there—but there's no official list. Anyone who has an Internet connection can put a new resource on line at any moment without telling anyone—and they do. So the trick is finding out what's available, which is the purpose of this section of the book. We will show you how to use the tools we've already covered to find resources on your own. We will also talk about some special resources on the Internet that help you get to the information you are interested in. And finally, we have the *Resource Catalog*, a very special list of Internet resources categorized under a wide variety of topics that may interest you. The *Resource Catalog* printed in this book is an excerpt of the catalog kept on-line by the *Global Network Navigator (GNN)*:

```
http://gnn.com/gnn/wic/index.html
```

Remember, the Internet is dynamic. The half-life of an Internet resource is about four years.[*] Translated into practical terms, this means that given any index of network resources, in the next year about a quarter of them will change in such a way that the index's information about them is unusable. That's as true of the *Resource Catalog* in this book as it is for any (and every) other resource list out there. Lately, there has been an increase in the number of resource lists on the World Wide Web. These on-line directories can be selective or exhaustive, but they are the most up-to-date information sources available. Many of these lists seek submissions of new resources from users and often provide search capabilities for their resource databases. The quality and usefulness of these resources vary by who is maintaining them—some are simply long lists of addresses, some contain commentary on each resource, and others have introduced rating systems. How the list is presented and how well it is maintained are the important qualities of a good resource directory.

---

[*] It's probably not a coincidence that this is also the average time a student, whether undergraduate or graduate, remains at the same institution.

Another problem is that quality of network resources varies greatly. While many resource lists try to focus on the "best" resources they can find, it's certainly true that beauty is in the eye of the beholder. (On the other hand, there are a few very popular World Wide Web sites that are in the business of compiling the worst and most useless resources out there.) To become truly fluent in using the Net, you must learn how to find your own truffles amid the muck.

You will probably notice that in this edition of the catalog, there are a lot more World Wide Web resources. The explosive popularity of the Web has not slowed since the introduction of Mosaic in 1993. It is the fastest-growing part of the Net, and soon it will be the largest part of it as well. Most new resources on the Net are put up as WWW resources now, but do not forget that there are other parts of the Net besides the Web.

Stalking the Wild Resource

In the chapter on Gopher and WAIS, I drew some analogies between the Internet and a library without a card catalog. It's time to start thinking about that again. You may be without an official card catalog, but you are not without tools. The major tools at your disposal are your friends, network news, mailing lists, and the Archie, Gopher, WAIS, and World Wide Web services. Let's look at how each of these may be used to find the resource of your dreams.

Friends

Your friends are your friends because you have interests in common with them. In addition to your real-life ("RL") friends, you will make a set of network friends through e-mail. These friends may be looking for the same things you are; or even if their interests differ, they may be aware of resources that you want. In the real world, a friend who knows you are into female mystery writers might tell you "Sara Paretsky has a new book out," because he knows you are interested and will appreciate the tip. In the network world, a friend who knows you are interested in agriculture resources might send you a message saying "Have you seen *Not Just Cows*, the Internet ag resources guide?" He, being a pencil collector, would love to hear from you if you found a complete pencil-pricing database. Life on the network is not all that different from real life.

Network News and Mailing Lists

Network news and mailing lists are resources themselves and quite naturally lead you to other resources on a particular topic. Almost every newsgroup has a FAQ, or list of frequently asked questions. The FAQ is posted regularly to the newsgroup and to *news.answers*, usually monthly. Most FAQs contain a list of Internet resources related to the newsgroup topic. All FAQ files are archived and can be obtained via anonymous FTP from **rtfm.mit.edu** in *pub/usenet/ news.answers*. Newsgroups are shown in the catalog by topic.

Mailing lists are another great resource for discussion of a particular topic. If you are interested in pencil collecting and follow the pencil-collecting mailing list for a while, someone will invariably announce a great find, like "Pencil Collecting Database Found," or they will announce that they have created their own. Many public mailing lists are archived, so if you've just joined you can catch up on previous discussions. The official list of publically accessible mailing lists (currently numbering around 1300) is posted regularly to *news.answers* and is also archived at **rtfm**.**mit.edu** in */pub/usenet/news.answers/mail*.

If you don't find what you want in a FAQ or an archive, you can "go fishing" for an answer. For example, write a posting to the pencil-collecting newsgroup (or mailing list) asking "Does anyone have a database of current pencil prices?" It is easy to cast out and see what you can catch.

The World Wide Web

Due to its hypertext nature, the World Wide Web is a great way to find useful resources. Not only does it have resources of its own, but many Web pages also contain links to other related resources. Many people include their hotlists or bookmarks on their personal pages, and if you share common interests with a person, chances are that their lists of links will interest you.

The WWW has many searching services available that allow you to conduct wide-ranging, detailed searches of the Web, Gopher, and numerous specialized databases and archives. A comprehensive list of WWW search engines is available at **http://cuiwww.unige.ch/meta-index.html**.

One nice thing about the Web is once you find a page which you like, it is likely to have links to other pages on the same topic. Once you get a nibble, the whole fish will likely follow.

Another great place for finding WWW resources is the ever-present e-mail or posting signature. Many people use a line of their signature to display the URL for their own personal page or their organization's Web site. With so many Web resources out there, most don't end up in the big catalogs. Personal pages often have the most obscure and interesting links, so don't be afraid to do a little surfing.

Archie

Archie is primarily a service for locating files by name. It makes a slight attempt to allow searches by topic, but this facility is limited and dated. However, in reality Archie is more general-purpose than this description implies. People who maintain anonymous FTP servers try to name things logically. Frequently, they use the structure of a filesystem to be organized: related files are stored in the same directory, which will probably have a useful name. In these cases, Archie doesn't tell you exactly what you want to know, but gives you an idea where you might look. For example, to search for pencil-collecting information, you might try the search string "pencil" and get the following result:

```
Host blandsworth.usnd.edu
    Location: /pub
        DIRECTORY drwxr-xr-x    512  May 17 05:19  pencils
```

You didn't search for a particular topic, you searched for a file starting with "pencil." What Archie found was not a file, but a directory named */pub/pencils*, on the computer **blandsworth.usnd.edu**.

At this point, you don't know if there is anything useful to you on that computer or not. But—let's face it—how many people would create a directory named *pencils* for numerical analysis software? Not many. There's a good chance that this directory will contain something to do with pencils—maybe not exactly what you're looking for, but probably something interesting. All you need to do is **ftp** to **blandsworth.usnd.edu**, login as "anonymous," **cd pub/pencils**, and do a **dir**. Poke around a bit. It may contain good stuff, and it may not. It is a reasonable place to start.

Gopher

Gopher can be used to access other resource finders like Archie and WAIS. It can also be used by itself; Gopher menus are themselves pointers to resources. When looking for resources with Gopher, there are two particularly useful ways to start hunting: read the list of all the Gopher servers in the world, or start searching for particular menus with Veronica.

There are getting to be more and more specialized Gopher servers around. Someone sees the power Gopher could bring to a community, so she builds a Gopher server tailored to that community. The person responsible for the server is on the lookout for more information sources in the area of interest. If you can find a Gopher server that has a collection you like, you can stay up-to-date by dropping into that server every now and then. To find a server that appears to have similar leanings to your own, just start from any server, find the list of "other Gopher servers," and page through it. There are lots of them, but if you are lucky and patient, you might find the University of Minnesota Pencil Collection Gopher. That might be pushing it a bit, but there are already specialized Gopher servers for soil science, history of science, birdwatching, and law. Pencil collecting can't be far behind.

If you can't find a specialized server to your liking, use Veronica to search for a couple of keywords that are relevant to your quest. Remember that if you find an interesting resource through a Gopher server, you can either continue to use that resource through Gopher (set a bookmark to come back again easily), or you can ask Gopher how to access the resource directly.[*] If Gopher accesses the resource through Telnet, you can just start **telnet** manually and skip the Gopher menus.

---

[*] If you're using the ASCII ("curses") **gopher** client, use the = command.

WAIS

The directory of servers makes it easy to find any WAIS service. Some of the servers are actually indexes into other services. For example, the whole of the Archie database or the archives of many newsgroups can be searched through WAIS. This allows you to use the extended search capabilities of WAIS to look for things you might want.

A Few Special Resources

We tried to be selective in choosing resources for our catalog; we definitely didn't list every file that's available, or every site that has collections of files. It seems to have worked out very well, if we do say so ourselves. There are a few resources that are so exciting or important that we thought we would highlight them here.

The Global Network Navigator

The Global Network Navigator (GNN) was one of the first attempts to commercialize World Wide Web technology. You might think of GNN as an on-line magazine, but it's probably better to think of it as an information service. Its news stories and features include links to the services being described, so you can think of it as a kind of "information interface" to the Net.

GNN is a great place to start exploring the Net. It includes an expanded on-line version of the *Resource Catalog*. Instead of typing in a command to access the service being described, you can just click on a hypertext link to reach it. The on-line version of the catalog is updated regularly; you can check in at any time to find new resources. It's also a good way to track down resources that have changed or been reorganized since the last printed edition of the catalog.

In addition to the *Resource Catalog*, you can also navigate the Net with GNN's Best of the Net Awards and Netizens. The Best of the Net lists the Net sites chosen by the GNN staff to be the best out there. Netizens is a collection of personal home pages showing the people behind the Web. Make sure to add yours to the list.

GNN also has several special publications that center on such topics as travel, education, personal finance, and sports. *Book Story* is a section which features weekly excerpts from new fiction and non-fiction as well as interviews with the authors. WebReview is a new on-line magazine that focuses on the latest developments in the World Wide Web community. GNN also has an extensive marketplace section, with links to many commercial sites on the Web with on-line ordering capability.

You can get information about subscribing by pointing your Web browser at **http://gnn.com/**.

Yahoo

Yahoo is a popular on-line catalog on the World Wide Web. It was started as a hobby by two Stanford students, David Yang and Jerry Filo, and in April 1995 they turned it into a company. According to their FAQ page, Yahoo stands for "*Yet Another Hierarchical Officious Oracle.*" (Alternative words for "Officious" are listed as "Obstreperous," "Oderiferous," and "Organized.") Yahoo is one of the most extensive catalogs of World Wide Web resources. It currently lists around 50,000 Web sites and adds several hundred more every day. The catalog is extremely well organized into a wide range of categories and subcategories, and finding a resource is easy using Yahoo's search facility.

Yahoo collects its entries through Web searches done by the Yahoo staff and by soliciting new sites from users. The Yahoo directory has a form-based page where users can request that a new site be added. Users are asked to indicate which categories the new site may fall under and to provide a brief description. The Yahoo staff reviews the information and checks to make sure the site is working, and then adds it to the catalog. If you create a new Web site, getting it listed in Yahoo is a good way to publicize it. There is also a page for making suggestions. Here you can inform Yahoo of changes in site information, problems with listed sites, or any other comment you'd like to make about the catalog. The ease and encouragement of user input really help to make the Yahoo directory one of the most up-to-date Web resource centers.

There are many ways to look through the Yahoo listings. The simplest ways are through a search or by clicking through the category listings. You can view new entries in the daily "What's New" list. Favorite picks of the Yahoo staff can be found in the "What's Cool" list. You can view the most frequently accessed sites in the catalog in "What's Popular," and if you're not particular at all, you may choose "A Random Link" from the catalog. Yahoo can be accessed using the World Wide Web at **http://www.yahoo.com**.

Other Subject-Oriented Catalogs

There are a number of resource directories on the Internet, and it doesn't hurt to use more than one. Here are some catalogs that we think are worth mentioning:

- The WWW Virtual Library, maintained by the W3 Organization, is a distributed resource catalog in that different subjects are handled by different sites.

    ```
    www http://www.w3.org/hypertext/DataSources/bySubject/Overview.html
    ```

- EINet Galaxy is one of the original on-line resource catalogs. It uses "guest editors" to manage different areas of the catalog and provides an excellent search facility.

    ```
    www http://www.einet.net/galaxy.html
    ```

- Gopher Jewels is a catalog of Gopher resources. It organizes resources from around the world into a subject-oriented gopher directory tree. The catalog is searchable, and it now has a WWW interface located at EINet Galaxy.

  ```
  gopher cwis.usc.edu /Other_Gophers_and_Information_Resources/Gophers_
      by_Subject/Gopher_Jewels
  ```

- The Planet Earth Home Page Virtual Library is another excellent resource database. You can navigate the library either through a standard text listing of subjects, through imagemaps of the library's "floorplan," or through a comprehensive imagemap containing listings for the entire catalog.

  ```
  www http://www.nosc.mil/planet_earth/info.html
  ```

U.S. Government Resources

The U.S. government (like many governments worldwide) issues tremendous amounts of information on just about every topic imaginable, ranging from economic statistics to hints on home maintenance. In the past, a lot of this information has been hard to get; often, it has been very expensive; even if it hasn't been expensive, it's been hard to find.

One of the Clinton administration's goals is to release as much of this information as possible through the Internet. One of the biggest conduits for releasing information is the Extension Service of the U.S. Department of Agriculture (**esusda.gov**), partnering with universities in every state and territory across the nation. Don't let the name fool you; it isn't just soybeans and hog bellies. How about:

- Distance education (education at remote locations, through correspondence, video, etc.)
- Problems of large cities
- Ethnic diversity
- Children and families
- Sustainable agriculture
- Economics of communities
- NAFTA accord
- National Performance Review
- National Health Care Reform Report
- National Water Quality Information Database
- National Family Life Database
- International Food and Nutrition Database
- White House press reports

There's a lot more; these are a few of the highlights. Some of these resources are listed in the *Resource Catalog*, but what's there is expanding all the time. If you are interested in information like this, your best bet is to get a catalog right from the source.

Most of these resources are provided by Almanac servers, which are like list-servers. (How to use them was explained in Chapter 7, *Network News*). There are any number of servers, each of which has its own collection of information. To get detailed information about how to use Almanac servers, send the one-line e-mail message **send guide** to **almanac@esusda.gov**. For a catalog of what's available on any one server, send the one-line message **send catalog** to that server. For further information on a specific topic listed in the catalog, send the message **send** *topic* **catalog**.

Here's a short—and, no doubt, already incomplete—list of Almanac servers.

Table 1: Almanac Servers

Location	Address
Americans Communicating Electronically	almanac@ace.esusda.gov
Auburn University	almanac@acenet.auburn.edu
Cornell University	almanac@cce.cornell.edu
Extension Service-USDA	almanac@esusda.gov
National Ag Library	almanac@cyfer.esusda.gov
North Carolina State University	almanac@ces.ncsu.edu
Oregon State University	almanac@oes.orst.edu
Purdue University	almanac@ecn.purdue.edu
University of Missouri	almanac@ext.missouri.edu
University of Wisconsin	almanac@joe.uwex.edu
	almanac@wisplan.uwex.edu

Domain Name Lookup

Throughout this book, we've talked in terms of these nice, memorable "domain names." Maybe you don't find them memorable, but they're certainly nicer than the alternative: addresses like 143.209.24.92. In Chapter 3, *How the Internet Works*, we described the Domain Name System, which translates names into addresses.

Sometimes things go wrong. There are those unfortunate times when you don't have access to your Domain Name Server, or it is not working properly. This is a problem that should be remedied by a system administrator or a service provider—but when things are broken, sometimes you don't have the option of waiting until they're fixed. If you're in this situation, take heart: there is a way out! There are a few services for looking up numeric addresses "by hand;" once you've done that, you can use the numeric address instead of the name. None of the tools we've discussed (except for e-mail) care which you use—even the Web browsers!

Just substitute a numeric address for the Internet name in the URL, and you can use it.

One such service is available via electronic mail. The name server you use depends on where you are; it is best to use the server closest to you. In the U.S., use the address **resolve@cs.widener.edu** and include the message "site *internet-name*". Outside the U.S., use the address **dns@grasp.insa-lyon.fr** and include the message "ip internet-name".

For example, to find out the address of **ftp.uu.net**, send the message **ip ftp.uu.net** to **dns@grasp.insa-lyon.fr**; equivalently, send the message "site ftp.uu.net" to **resolve@cs.widener.edu**. You'll get a message back looking like this:

```
Return-Path: <dns-request@grasp.insa-lyon.fr>
Date: Tue, 1 Mar 1995 20:17:33 GMT
From: dns@grasp.insa-lyon.fr (Mail Name Server)
Subject: Reply to your queries

you> ip ftp.uu.net

Officiel hostname:  ftp.uu.net
Registered addresse(s):
       192.48.96.9
```

You may wonder why you can use an e-mail address like **dns-request@grasp.insa-lyon.fr**, when you can't use other Internet addresses. Unlike the other services, electronic mail is a "store and forward" service. Your own computer doesn't necessarily need to look up domain names; it can send the mail on to a "smarter" computer that knows how to interrogate the Domain Name System. So you can often use e-mail addresses even when you can't use domain names.

How We Did It

How did we create our resource catalog? What techniques did we use? We did all of the following:

- We listened to newsgroups and mailing lists looking for interesting announcements.

- We used what we learned to find other lists and used their information.

- We looked for sparse areas in the catalog and used Archie to perform subject searches. With that information, we then looked at the anonymous FTP servers to see if there was anything interesting in them.

- We performed searches on the World Wide Web.

- We visited a number of Gopher servers and tried to list any unique services we found.

- We were happy to hear about neat resources other people have used, found, or created. If you find a new one, mail us at **wic@ora.com**, and we'll take a look.

What Is a Resource?

What we included as a resource varies from subject to subject. There are subjects, like the Internet itself and computer science, where thousands of important files are scattered throughout the Internet, almost randomly. We chose not to include such resources; anyone can find these with Gopher or WAIS. There are other groups for which the sole motivation to be on the Internet might be to access one particular file; we tried to include these. In general, we included the most unique and interesting things we could find. Within each subject, resources were "graded on the curve." There was no absolute measure for what we considered interesting.

We biased our choices in favor of resources that anyone could use, or that could be used on the spur of the moment from the network. A prime example of this would be computational resources. We didn't list the NSF supercomputer centers, even though they were one of the prime reasons why the network became ubiquitous. Anyone who wants to do heavy-duty research computing can request time on a supercomputer, but they are not for everyone to use. If you are a valid user, each center will supply you with lots of documentation about how to use it. You can't just decide "I think I'll play on a Cray today."

On the other hand, there are a few sites that offer free UNIX computing. That is, anyone can **telnet** to them and run selected programs. With the emphasis on "anyone," we included such resources.

Finally, we tried to be broad rather than deep. In one respect, this book is an argument about why you should use the Internet. And the simplest argument for using the Net is that there are loads of resources interesting to all sorts of people, not just "geeks with pocket protectors." To prove this, we've tried to hit as many different and diverse topics as possible. If we've succeeded, even Internet veterans should be surprised at what we've found.

Accuracy and Permissions

We verified that every listed resource was working and available at some time when we were gathering information. That doesn't mean that these resources are still available, or that the usage information is still the same. There were times when the access information changed in the two weeks between the time we discovered the resource and the time we actually tried it. If we could figure out how to use a resource, we included it; if not, we chucked it.

For this reason, we included references to other resource directories and guides. They have the advantage of being on-line, hence easily updatable. This doesn't mean they actually are updated frequently. There's really no way to tell whether any on-line database is more or less up-to-date than this catalog. On-line indexes are usually maintained by volunteer effort; you never know how much effort the volunteer has to expend.

Remember: a resource that is publicly accessible isn't necessarily a public resource. This caused me a bit of trouble. If I stumbled upon a good resource, how could I decide if it was intended to be public? The rule of thumb I used was that a public resource had to fall into one of these categories:

- Commonly known within the community (e.g., frequently mentioned and discussed in newsgroups)

- Listed in other resource guides or catalogs

- Easily found with public index utilities (e.g., Gopher, WAIS)

We ran across a few resources that didn't fall into these categories, were subject to restrictions, or seemed "dangerous" to the offerer. In these cases, we asked the owner if he would like to see the resource listed. Usually the answer was "yes." If the answer was "no," the resources are still available on the Internet, but you aren't hearing about them from me.

Using the Catalog

We tried to group the resources into the areas where they belonged, but then what do we know?* If you already know the name of a resource and would like to see if it's listed, you might start at the Index to the *Resource Catalog*. All the entries in the resource guide are listed there, so if you have a resource that you like, and you want to see where I put it, work backwards.

After a description of the resource, we tell you how to access the resource. We'll show you what kind of resource is listed (FTP, Telnet, Gopher, or World Wide Web), followed by the site's Internet address, followed by any other information you need: how to log in, what directory to **cd** to, what port to use (if it's non-standard).

The descriptions for Gopher and World Wide Web servers get a little more complicated. For Gopher servers, the catalog shows which server to connect to, followed by the menu items to select. For the Flybase Gopher server (which contains information about fruit flies), the catalog shows the following entry:

```
gopher ftp.bio.indiana.edu /Flybase
```

This means to point your Gopher client at the server **ftp.bio.indiana.edu**, and then select the "Flybase" item from its root menu. To get to this server, you can either put its address on the command line, or search through a menu of Gopher servers until you find it.

---

* I'm not the only one who doesn't know about this. Cataloging of on-line resources is a really hot area of research in the library science community.

A typical World Wide Web entry looks like this:

    www http://www.nr.no/ordbok

This resource is an on-line dictionary of Norwegian (listed under "Norway" in the "International Interest" section of the *Resource Catalog*). To access this resource, just open the URL or location **http://www.nr.no/ordbok** in your browser. It's a lot of typing—and this is a short URL. Unfortunately, there's really no other way to describe a Web resource.

Of course, you may not be using a program that's exactly equivalent to the one we list. Don't let that bother you. There are many World Wide Web clients; you may be using Lynx or any of a number of other browsers. Don't let that confuse you; they all know how to use the address you give them.

There are no WAIS resources in the catalog. We thought that was redundant as all WAIS resources should be accessible through the unified directory of servers. (Yes, there are WAIS resources that aren't in the directory of servers, but we didn't want to encourage the practice.) Don't forget WAIS resources just because they don't have a home in the catalog; I wouldn't consider any Internet search finished until I had tried WAIS.

Remember that the Internet is always changing. Servers get reorganized, and the resources that are already there move around. If you can't find something, look around a bit; the server that provides the information may have undergone some "housecleaning," and you'll find what you want elsewhere.

AERONAUTICS & ASTRONAUTICS

Newsgroups:
sci.space, sci.astro, sci.aeronautics

NASA Spacelink

Entries about the history, current state, and future of NASA and space flight, provided by the NASA Marshall Space Flight Center. Also, some classroom materials and information on space technology transfer. This is a particularly valuable resource for educators.

Access via:
www *http://spacelink.msfc.nasa.gov/*

Shuttle and Satellite Images

The following sites make available photographs and other images taken from the Space Shuttle, Magellan and Viking missions, and other good stuff. The data formats vary; be sure to read any available README files.

Access via:
www *http://ceps.nasm.edu:2020/RPIF/SSPR.html*
Notes: Space Shuttle Photograph Repository

www *http://nssdc.gsfc.nasa.gov/photo_gallery/photogallery.html*
Notes: NSSDC Photo Gallery

www *http://www.jpl.nasa.gov:80/sircxsar/*
Notes: Space radar images of Earth from SIR-C/X-SAR

www *http://fi-www.arc.nasa.gov/fia/projects/bayes-group/Atlas/Mars/*

Notes: Atlas of Mars and Viking Orbiter image-finder

ftp *explorer.arc.nasa.gov;* login *anonymous;* cd *pub/SPACE*

Notes: Images are in GIF and JPEG directories

AGRICULTURE

Newsgroups:
alt.agriculture[fruit, misc], misc.rural

AgriGator Agriculture Information Index

A rich collection of Internet sites and sources related to agriculture. Maintained at the University of Florida, AgriGator is hampered only by its over-reliance on slow-to-load graphics. Material covered here is broken down into nine categories: an agricultural conference list, international locations, commercial groups, U.S. Government sites, U.S. state sites, almanac servers, publications, list servers, and marketing services.

Access via:
www *http://gnv.ifas.ufl.edu/WWW/AGATOR/HTM/AG.HTM*

Not Just Cows

A guide to resources on the Internet and BITNET that cover agriculture and related subjects, as compiled by Wilfred (Bill) Drew.

Access via:
www *http://www.lib.lsu.edu/sci/njc.html*

ftp *ftp.sura.net;* login *anonymous;* cd *pub/nic;* get *agricultural.list*

USDA Extension Service Gopher

A "master gopher" for the U.S. Department of Agriculture's activities and extension services. Visitors will find information about the extension service, policies of the USDA and extension services, educational (and other) projects of the extension service, disaster relief information, and many pointers to other government resources. The About the Extension Service file (accessible from the main menu) is a helpful guide to the services offered.

Access via:
gopher esusda.gov

ARCHAEOLOGY

Newsgroups:
sci.archaeology

ArchNet

ArchNet, at the University of Connecticut Department of Anthropology, provides links to archaeology sites worldwide.

Access via:
www http://www.lib.uconn.edu/ArchNet/ArchNet.html

gopher spirit.lib.uconn.edu/academic/Anthropology/archnet/

Archaeological Fieldwork Server

A service for those seeking archaeological fieldwork opportunities, this server offers detailed descriptions of planned research trips. Also listed are archaeological contractors, and links to other Internet resources that pertain to archaeology. The Archaeological Fieldwork Server is maintained by Ken Stuart of Cornell University.

Access via:
www http://durendal.cit.cornell.edu/TestPit.html

Classics & Mediterranean Archaeology

An index to archaeology resources on the Net, sponsored by the Department of Classical Studies, University of Michigan.

Access via:
www http://rome.classics.lsa.umich.edu/welcome.html

ART HISTORY

Newsgroups:
alt.architecture, rec.arts.fine

ArchiGopher

ArchiGopher advertises itself as a server dedicated to the dissemination of architectural knowledge, but actually covers more than that. There are links to a small archive of Kandinsky paintings, a small sample of drawings of Andrea Palladio's architectural projects, a collection of CAD computer models, and other possibly interesting items.

Access via:
gopher libra.arch.umich.edu

ArtServe

An art history server at Australian National University, created by professor Michael Greenhalgh. ArtServe springs from Greenhalgh's interest in discovering computing applications for students of the humanities. The site features 2,800 images of prints, largely from the 15th century to the end of the 19th century, and 2,500 images of mainly classical architecture and architectural sculpture from around the Mediterranean. There is also an exhibit of contemporary architecture from Hong Kong.

Access via:
www http://rubens.anu.edu.au/

Asian Arts

A large collection of images from exhibits of Asian art at museums and galleries worldwide. Among the exhibitions currently available are "Mongolia: The Legacy of Chinggis Khan" from the Asian Art Museum, San Francisco, and "Images of Faith" from the John Eskenazi Gallery in London. Asian Arts is published on-line by Web Arts Publishing. An index of links to other Asian art sites and a calendar of events are also available.

Access via:
www *http://www.webart.com/asianart/index.html*

Frank Lloyd Wright in Wisconsin

A tour of eight Wisconsin buildings that represent the accomplishments of Frank Lloyd Wright's 70-year career. Frank Lloyd Wright in Wisconsin works well as a virtual tour and includes images from the architect's home state. It can also serve as a planning guide for a real-life tour of these structures, which are all in the southern third of Wisconsin and open to the public.

Access via:
www *http://flw.badgernet.com:2080/*

Japanese Art

A directory of GIF prints in the Ukiyo-e style (17th - 19th centuries). Ukiyo-e, meaning "Pictures of the Floating World," was a dying art in Japan until the late nineteenth century. At that time, Japan was using woodblock prints merely as packing paper in the export of porcelain, then in vogue in turn-of-the- century France. In this way, the French discovered and fell in love with Ukiyo-e, and the art form was resurrected.

Access via:
ftp *ftp.uwtc.washington.edu;* login *anonymous;* cd *pub/Japanese/Pictures/Ukiyo-e/*

Leonardo da Vinci Museum

A small collection of Leonardo da Vinci's work, put together by Jim Pickrell of Leonardo Internet. Divided into three "wings," the museum features images of the *Mona Lisa* and *The Last Supper*, a short biography of Leonardo, and shots of some of his futuristic designs, including the menacing "Giant Crossbow."

Access via:
www *http://www.leonardo.net/main.html*

Mexican Painters and Muralists

Image files of paintings and murals by 15 renowned Mexican artists, including Rufino Tamayo, Diego Rivera, and Jose Clemente Orozco. Each artist is represented by two or more works. The exhibit is presented by the University of Guadalajara.

Access via:
gopher *unicornio.cencar.udg.mx/cultura/pintores*

National Museum of American Art

The on-line home of the Smithsonian Institution's National Museum of American Art. The inaugural Internet exhibition is "The White House Collection of American Crafts," a rich multimedia presentation of 72 works by contemporary American craft artists. The exhibit features scores of images, videos, and sound files. Take the virtual tour, which presents pictures of the works as they were exhibited in the White House. The interviews with the artists are also a nice touch. Other resources here include a gallery of GIF images of famous paintings in the museum collection ("Highlights of the Permanent Collection"), and a catalog of museum publications, including excerpts and images.

Access via:
www *http://www.nmaa.si.edu/*

Sistine Chapel

Breathtaking images from the Sistine Chapel. This site, developed by Michael Olteanu at the Christus Rex Web site, features a well-organized archive of 325 JPEG images, including full representations of Michelangelo's chapel ceiling and his *Last Judgment* mural. Although it would be nice to have more descriptions and background information on the works, they speak nicely for themselves.

Access via:
www *http://www.christusrex.org/www1/sistine/0-Tour.html*

Vatican City

A rich visual tour of Vatican City, from San Pietro Basilica to the Pontifical Palaces. Images are in JPEG format. The tour was created by Christus Rex, a "non-profit organization dedicated to the dissemination of information on works of art preserved in churches, cathedrals and monasteries all over the world." A jump up a level to the Christus Rex home page ("overview") provides access to tours of the Sistine Chapel and the Vatican museums.

Access via:
www *http://www.christusrex.org/www1/citta/0-Citta.html*

Vatican Exhibit

Images and text from a recent exhibition at the Library of Congress, including manuscripts from the Vatican Library in all areas of historical interest. Images are *large*, but provided in JPEG compression format.

Access via:
www *http://sunsite.unc.edu/expo/vatican.exhibit/Vatican.exhibit.html*

ftp *ftp.loc.gov;* login *anonymous;* cd *pub/exhibit.images/vatican.exhibit*

World Arts Resources

An impressive site and the best index to arts resources on the Net. Organized by the Ohio State University (at Newark) Art Gallery, World Arts Resources features links to hundreds of museums, publications, institutions, and commercial resources.

Access via:
www *www.concourse.com/wwar/default.html*

ASTRONOMY

Newsgroups:
sci.[astro, astrol.fits, astro.hubble, astro.planetarium]

National Space Science Data Center

This site features links to a variety of NASA and space science resources.

Access via:
www *http://nssdc.gsfc.nasa.gov*

telnet *nssdca.gsfc.nasa.gov;* login *nodis*

The Nine Planets

An exciting and comprehensive tour of our solar system, written in non-technical language. The Nine Planets site is loaded with interesting information, including history, current theories, mythology, and data garnered by spacecraft. The Nine Planets is well organized and easy to navigate and includes lots of images, some animation and sound files, and a glossary of terms. The is an excellent resource for general statistical research, as well as casual browsing. Take the express tour, or work your way systematically through the hierarchically organized data.

Access via:
www *http://seds.lpl.arizona.edu/
nineplanets/nineplanets/nineplanets.html*

Views of the Solar System

Use your mouse to explore space. You can travel to each of the planets, where you can visit asteroids, comets, meteors, and moons. The site offers fine graphics and a wealth of information, but it is often presented in a highly technical manner. Compiled by Calvin J. Hamilton of Los Alamos National Laboratory, Views also offers dozens of links to other space-related sites.

Access via:
www *http://www.c3.lanl.gov/~cjhamil/
SolarSystem/homepage.html*

The Web Nebulae

Stunning images of gaseous nebulae, from the Pleiades to the Horsehead Nebula. Each image is accompanied by a brief information file, although creator Bill Arnett (of The Nine Planets fame) advises visitors, "The emphasis here is on aesthetics, not science."

Access via:
www *http://seds.lpl.arizona.edu/billa/twn/*

AVIATION

Newsgroups:
rec.aviation.*

Aviation Enthusiasts Corner

An extensive reference guide to aircraft types and specifications, museums and displays, and air shows, maintained by volunteers at Brooklyn College.

Access via:
www *http://www.brooklyn.cuny.edu/rec/
air/air.html*

DUAT

Pilot flight services via the Internet. It provides pilots with weather briefings and flight planning services. You must be a pilot to use this resource.

Access via:
telnet *duat.gtefsd.com*

General Aviation Servers

An elegantly arranged collection of over 50 WWW links to aviation resources on the Net, maintained cooperatively by the Aviation Server Administrators. Resources listed here cover such topics as soaring, air shows, ballooning, hang gliding, helicopters, aerobatics, and skydiving.

Access via:
www *http://acro.harvard.edu/GA/
ga_servers.html*

BIOLOGY

Newsgroups:
sci.bio.[ecology, ethology, evolution, herp, technology], bionet.[cellbiol, general, molbio]

Biological Collections Gopher

Run by Harvard University's Herbarium, this site has information on Museum, Herbarium, and Arboretum collection catalogs, biodiversity information resources, and other directories, publications, and software.

Access via:
gopher *huh.harvard.edu*

Human Genome Project Information

The Human Genome Project was created to increase our understanding of human genetics and biology by determining the genetic code for the human genome, and is currently focusing on mapping the location of genes and on the development of technology that will allow the rapid determination of DNA sequence. (Review courtesy of Michael Cherry, Department of Genetics, Stanford University School of Medicine.)

Access via:
www *http://www.ornl.gov/TechResources/ Human_Genome/home.html*

Johns Hopkins Bioinformatics Web Server

This creative WWW server provides a collection of interconnected protein sequence, structure, and enzyme function databases. These protein databases also include links to other information, including bibliographic citations from MEDLINE and pictures of three-dimensional crystal structures from the Brookhaven structural database. Electronic publications for biology include the Primer on Molecular Genetics, genomic information databases such as the Mouse Locus Catalog (with a fetching portrait of its subject), and links to other resources.

Access via:
www *http://www.gdb.org/hopkins.html*

National Center for Biotechnology Information

The NCBI maintains the GenBank DNA sequence database, as well as several other specialized DNA databases. A subset of the MEDLINE bibliographic database is provided by the NCBI via WWW. The MEDLINE and GenBack entries are cross-referenced. (Review courtesy of Michael Cherry, Department of Genetics, Stanford University School of Medicine.)

Access via:
www *http://www.ncbi.nlm.nih.gov/*

Virtual FlyLab

Budding research geneticists and mad scientists will be equally drawn to this site, which allows users to virtually "breed" fruit flies in search of the secrets of genetic inheritance. The FlyLab is well documented and illustrated, making it a pleasure to use for those who aren't squeamish about drawings of forked fruit fly bristles. This "virtual application" was designed by the Electronic Desktop Project at California State University, Los Angeles.

Access via:
www *http://vflylab.calstatela.edu/edesktop/ VirtApps/VflyLab/IntroVflyLab.html*

WWW Virtual Library: Biosciences

A massive index to the bioscience resources on the Net, maintained by Keith Robison of the Harvard University Biological Laboratories. Subjects covered include biological molecules, biotechnology, genetics, immunology, plant biology, and many, many more.

Access via:
www *http://golgi.harvard.edu/ biopages.html*

BUSINESS

Newsgroups:
biz.*, comp.newprod, misc.jobs.[offered, wanted]

American Stock Exchange

As the first U.S. stock market on the Web, AMEX is a source for daily market summaries, equity and option information, and exchange-related news clips. An extensive introduction to the Exchange's derivative services (geared for a professional audience) may make for fine bedtime reading for gung-ho individual investors. An interactive information exchange that "will regularly offer insights from influential business leaders on major issues tied to the capital markets" is under development.

Access via:
www *http://www.amex.com/*

Business Resource Center

Maintained by Khera Communications, this center contains information about starting a new business, managing that business, and marketing products and services. The information, in the form of articles, is probably most useful to those who are new to the world of business.

Access via:
www *http://www.kciLink.com:80/sbhc/*

CareerMosaic

An employment information service operated by Bernard Hodes Advertising, "the largest human resources and employment communications agency in the world." The service has five main sections: Employers, College Connection, Jobs Offered, Special Features, and an Info Center. Though the name of the site would lead you to believe that its primary function is to help readers identify job opportunities, and perhaps to give job-hunting advice, CareerMosaic is not exclusively (or even primarily) focused on career help. The Employers section of CareerMosaic does contain employment information, but each employer section reads more like a marketing piece for the company, with product descriptions given at least as much space as employment opportunities.

Access via:
www *http://www.careermosaic.com/cm/*

Chicago Mercantile Exchange Web Page

The Chicago Mercantile Exchange (CME) is a trillion-dollar marketplace for commodity,

stock index, currency, and interest rate futures. Its Web page is a promotional vehicle for the exchange. Among the interesting items visitors will find are a chronological history of the CME and a 75-item glossary of futures and options terms.

Access via:
www *http://www.interaccess.com:80/cme/*

CommerceNet

A nonprofit information network designed to promote electronic commerce among Silicon Valley companies. Over 50 companies now participate, including IBM, Federal Express, Intel, and Wells Fargo.

Access via:
www *http://www.commerce.net/*

Consumer Information Center

Don't let the innocuous name fool you: This is one of the best sites on the Internet for basic personal finance information. The CIC is a U.S. Government organization that distributes pamphlets on consumer issues. Until recently, CIC publications were only available via government BBS or by mail. Now Net users have access to megabytes of information from the CIC catalog. The publications are arranged by subject; visitors to the Money section of the site will find information on credit cards, investment fraud, and financial planning. Accessing the on-line publications is free, despite the costs listed below the links. Other useful sections within the CIC site include Housing, Employment, Cars, and Small Business.

Access via:
www *http://www.gsa.gov/staff/pa/cic/cic.html*

FinanCenter Home Loan Department

FinanCenter is a commercial personal-finance resource developed by Banker's Portfolio

Exchange, Inc. Among the useful resources in the Home Loan Department are current mortgage rate data, informational reports on different aspects of home finance, two glossaries of home-loan terms, and a nice set of forms for making on-line loan and mortgage calculations.

Access via:
www http://www.financenter.com/ resources/homeloan/index.html

Highest Nationwide Bank Rates

A daily listing of the highest FDIC-insured bank rates in the United States, provided to the Global Network Navigator by Market Rates Insight, Inc. Use the rates as a guide when you shop for a CD. They also serve as an effective benchmark for evaluating the returns on market investments.

Access via:
www http://gnn.com/gnn/meta/finance/ res/mri.html

Home Business Review

This commercially sponsored on-line magazine is published monthly by the Ad Box Network. Each issue of HBR features 10 or more articles on home-based business topics, including starting a small business, tax planning, marketing strategies, and bookkeeping.

Access via:
www http://www.tab.com/Home.Business/

Interactive Age

The self-proclaimed "Newspaper for Electronic Commerce" features daily news and the full text of the biweekly print edition of *Interactive Age*. Emphasis is on the World Wide Web and Web-based commerce. Particularly impressive are the daily news stories, which run several paragraphs in length and are accompanied by linked URLs. An archive of past news items is also available, as is a collection of links to the top 100 business sites on the Web.

Access via:
www http://techweb.cmp.com:80/ia/ current/

Internet Advertising Resource Guide

If you're thinking about advertising on the Net, or if you're just curious about what advertisers are up to, the Internet Advertising Resource Guide is worth a visit. The site is principally made up of links to other sites around the Net, arranged by subject. The subjects covered include "Print Publications on Advertising on the Internet," "Business Presence on the Internet," and "Acceptable Advertising Practices on the Internet." The Internet Advertising Resource Guide is maintained by Hairong Li of the Missouri School of Journalism.

Access via:
www http://www.missouri.edu/ internet-advertising-guide.html

Internet Business Center

A useful primer for businesses considering a launch into cyberspace. The Internet Business Center offers ground-level information about the Net and how to use it for business. The Center includes demographic data and market segments, as well as examples of highly rated business sites. Perhaps most valuable is a section on how to create an Internet publishing system. A lighter side is the After Hours section, with links to entertaining sites from HotWired to the Louvre.

Access via:
www http://www.tig.com/IBC/

Internet Marketing Archives

Insider discussion of marketing and commerce on the Net. The Internet Marketing Archives is a compendium of postings to the popular Internet Marketing mailing list (which boasts 600 postings a month), moderated by Glenn Fleishman of the Point of Presence Company. The majority of postings come from site maintainers, Internet consultants, and marketers, making the archives lively and educational. This is a great place to build your Net business savvy.

Access via:
www http://galaxy.einet.net/hypermail/inet-marketing/

Investment FAQ

The best introduction to investing available on the Internet. The FAQ covers over 60 subject areas dealing with investment, with a focus on stock market information. The FAQ is regularly updated and expanded by its compiler, Christopher Lott.

Access via:
www http://www.cis.ohio-state.edu/hypertext/faq/bngusenet/misc/invest/top.html

Investor in Touch

A comprehensive directory of more than 15,000 public companies, including descriptions, addresses, officers, earnings estimates, and stock quotes. Links to other investor relations and corporate home pages are provided.

Access via:
www http://www.money.com/ssnhome.html

Job Search and Employment Opportunities: Best Bets from the Net

A collection of annotated links to job search sites on the Internet, arranged according to job type. The collection is maintained by Phil Ray and Brad Taylor of the University of Michigan, who hope to give job hunters a boost by making all the best sites accessible from a single location.

Access via:
www http://www.lib.umich.edu/chdocs/employment/

NASDAQ Financial Executive Journal

An electronic version of a quarterly sent free of charge to NASDAQ National Market company chief financial officers and to others by subscription. This is a joint project of the Legal Information Institute at Cornell Law School and the NASDAQ Stock Market. As of July 1995, there were five back issues available.

Access via:
www http://www.law.cornell.edu/nasdaq/nasdtoc.html

National Technology Transfer Center

The hub of a national network that links U.S. companies with federal laboratories to turn government research results into practical, commercially relevant technology. The Center operates the Gateway Service, a free telephone service that provides contacts between the private sector and various branches of the federal laboratory system. The Center also runs Business Gold, a bulletin board for activities and information relating to technology transfer opportunities.

Access via:
www http://iridium.nttc.edu/nttc.html

gopher iron.nttc.edu

ftp iron.nttc.edu; login *anonymous*
Notes: See "file_list" for contents

NETWorth

An excellent commercially sponsored investment information service presented by GALT Technologies. Visitors to NETWorth will find a 15-minute-delayed stock quote server, mutual fund NAVs, fund ratings from Morningstar, and links to other investment sites on the Web. *Note:* Although the service is free, some areas of NETWorth require user registration.

Access via:
www http://networth.galt.com/

Online Career Center

A resource for people who are recruiting employees or looking for jobs. It includes its own job listings and resumes, plus excerpts from other sources of job listings. There is also general corporate information, plus information about professional organizations, outplacement, and "employment events."

Access via:
www http://www.occ.com/occ/

gopher garnet.msen.com

Publishers' Catalogs Home Page

An international directory of links to publishing companies on the Web, created by Northern Lights Internet Solutions. Companies are listed by country. The 300-plus links in the directory range from Nedbook International in the Netherlands to the Knopf Publishing Group in the United States.

Access via:
www http://www.lights.com/publisher/

Small Business Administration Web Server

On-line help for small businesses, including lists of SBA offices and the Service Corps of Retired Executives (SCORE), training aids, information on government contracting, and an explanation of loan programs.

Access via:
www http://www.sbaonline.sba.gov/

Security APL Quote Server

15-minute-delayed stock quotes. Security APL began this service with little fanfare in mid-May 1994. Aside from quotes for most listed securities (including end-of-day mutual fund NAVs), the Security APL Quote Server provides historical charts for both the S&P 500 Index and the DJIA. Quotes themselves are provided by the Data Transmission Network Corporation of Omaha, Nebraska.

Access via:
www http://www.secapl.com/cgi-bin/qs

Thomas Register of American Manufacturers

The Thomas Register is America's preeminent directory of commercial products and services. On-line, there's no need to worry about back strain or paper cuts. Select Thomas Register Supplier Finder, register (if you haven't already), and you're on your way. Access to the on-line directory is via a search engine; type in "chicken wire" or "plastic pipe," for example, and you're directed to a list of suppliers. The only hitch is that you can't limit your results by geographic area and you have to browse through the manufacturers one at a time. Perhaps this is intentional—no point in giving away the store when there are CD-ROMs to be sold.

Access via:
www http://www.thomasregister.com/home.html

WWW Business Yellow Pages

Another place to look for company sites on the Web. Although there's no search engine, the directory is organized into traditional Yellow Pages subject areas, making browsing simple. The WWW Business Yellow Pages are maintained by the University of Houston's College of Business Administration.

Businesses are invited to add their own listings.

Access via:
www http://www.cba.uh.edu/ylowpges/ylowpges.html

CHEMISTRY

Newsgroups:
sci.[chem, engr.chem, chem.organomet]

American Chemical Society Gopher

A catalog of journals and books published by the American Chemical Society.

Access via:
gopher infx.infor.COM/American Chemical Society—Publications/

Periodic Table of Elements

WebElements is a hypertext periodic table. The symbol for each element links to a page containing general information on the element and data on radii, valence, electronegativities, effective nuclear charge, phase change temperatures, etc.

Access via:
www http://www.cchem.berkeley.edu/Table/

gopher ucsbuxa.ucsb.edu

CLASSICAL LANGUAGES & LITERATURE

Newsgroups:
sci.classics

Bryn Mawr Classical Review

Mostly a review journal of Greek and Latin classics, this database also includes public interest articles on the topic.

Access via:
gopher gopher.lib.virginia.edu/alpha/BMCR

Electronic Antiquity: Communicating the Classics

An Australian electronic journal inspired by the Bryn Mawr Classical Review, carrying academic articles on Greek and Roman Antiquity. The editors have maintained a monthly schedule since June 1993.

Please try to connect during off hours in Tasmania (Britain is more or less 10 hours behind Tasmanian time; California, 18 hours; Japan, 2 hours).

Access via:
gopher info.utas.edu.au/Publications/ElectronicAntiquity:CommunicatingTheClassics/

ftp ftp.utas.edu.au; login anonymous; cd departments/classics/antiquity

Gesamtverzeichnis der griechischen Papyrusurkunden Aegyptens

This is an index of dated Greek papyri from Egypt, arranged by century. The contents of the documents are not included, but standard papyrological abbreviations point to the printed literature.

Access via:
www www.ub.uni-heidelberg.de/

Tables of Contents of Journals of Interest to Classicists

An extensive volunteer project to abstract the tables of contents of scholarly journals. You can search for the author or title of articles by topic (Archaeology, or Religion and Near Eastern Studies) but apparently not by field, although the files are marked up in such a way as to support such searching.

Access via:
gopher gopher.lib.virginia.edu /alpha/tocs

The Tech Classics Archive

A superb presentation using modern technology to access the wisdom of the classics. The site includes masterpieces such as Plato's *Republic,* Virgil's *Aeneid,* and Homer's *Iliad* and *Odyssey,* classics that have shaped Western thought, literature, politics, and society. The archive has a brilliant search engine that locates key words or phrases and cites where in the text they appear. In a search, you can browse through the works of any or all of the 17 authors cataloged. The site, compiled by Dan Stevenson (a sophomore physics major at MIT) contains translations of 184 works.

Access via:
www http://the-tech.mit.edu/Classics/

COMICS

Newsgroups:
alt.comics.*

Dilbert

The exploits of everybody's favorite nerd... available on a one-week delay at the Dilbert Zone. Scott Adams, the cartoonist, provides some hilarious background on the strip, from early rejections to photos of how he creates Dilbert.

Access via:
www http://www.unitedmedia.com/ comics/dilbert

WebComics Daily

A clever site that grabs the actual cartoons from over 50 daily and weekly comics sites on the Web and publishes them together in newspaper funny-page format. The only drawbacks are the long wait for images to be downloaded from around the Web, and the poor scans of some of the comics. No mere collection of links to other comics sites, David de Vitry's WebComics brings actual comics from around the Web together in one place.

Access via:
www http://www.cyberzine.com/ webcomics/

COMPUTING

Newsgroups:
comp.admin, comp.sys.[3b1, acorn, alliant, amiga.*, apollo, apple2, atari.*, att, cbm, cdc, concurrent, dec, encore, handhelds, hp48, hp, ibm.pc.*, ibm.ps2.*, intel, isis, laptops, m6809, m68k, m88k, mac.*, mentor, mips, misc, ncr, newton, next.*, northstar, novell, nsc, palmtops, pen, powerpc, prime, protean, pyramid, ridge, sequent, sgi, sun.*, super, tahoe, tandy, ti transputer, unisys, xerox, zenith], comp.[ai, arch, cogeng, compilers, compression, databases, dcom, editors, graphics, human-factors, lang, isi, multimedia, music, parallel, programming, protocols, realtime, research, robotics, security, simulation, specification, terminals, theory, windows]

CERT

CERT, the Computer Emergency Response Team, is a federally funded group charged with dealing with computer and network security problems. Their server has papers about security concerns, tools to evaluate security, and an archive of alerts about current break-in attempts.

Access via:
ftp cert.sei.cmu.edu; login *anonymous;* cd *pub*

CERT Security Advisories

 Security has become a really hot topic in the last five years. Whether you're trying to protect your system from bright high school "crackers" or professional spies, it's certainly something you should keep informed about. CERT, the Computer Emergency Response Team, is a national focal point for security-related problems. When the CERT finds a security-related problem, it issues warnings to various mail lists. This is an indexed resource of those warnings. All system administrators should be aware of this archive!

To receive advisories as they are issued, send e-mail to **cert@cert.sei.cmu.edu.**

CICA Windows Shareware Archives

A huge Windows shareware archive maintained by the Center for Innovative Computer Applications (CICA) at Indiana University. The archive is served via FTP, making it easy to navigate but a pain to learn about the program you want to download. If you want to know more than "3fish.zip," be sure to read the INDEX pages.

Access via:
ftp Boris.InfoMagic.com; login *anonymous;* cd *pub/mirrors/cica*
Notes: InfoMagic mirror

ftp archive.orst.edu; login *anonymous;* cd *pub/mirrors/ftp.cica.indiana.edu/win3*
www http://www.cica.indiana.edu/cgi-bin/checkftp
Notes: List of CICA mirror sites

ftp ftp.cica.indiana.edu; login *anonymous*

Compaq Web Server

Company, product, and service information from the Compaq Computer Corporation. The Service and Support area contains product support FAQs for laptops, desktops, and systems.

Access via:
www http://www.compaq.com/

Compression FAQ

A collection of frequently asked questions to the *comp.compression* USENET newsgroups. The most useful questions here may be, "What is this .xxx file type? Where can I find the corresponding compression program?"

Access via:
www http://www.cis.ohio-state.edu/hypertext/faq/usenet/compression-faq/top.html

Consummate Winsock Apps

Forrest Stroud maintains this regularly updated list of the full range of Winsock software applications, from browsers to servers to chat software. Each item listed features a link to a download site for the application, a star rating, and a rundown of the application's version number, size, cost (most are freeware or shareware), and author. Stroud also maintains the Critical Applications Distribution List, an e-mail newsletter that announces changes and additions to Consummate Winsock Apps.

Access via:
www http://cwsapps.texas.net

CSUSM Windows Shareware Archive

A glorified FTP server on the Web, this site contains hundreds of shareware programs, including address books, clocks, time-management tools, Microsoft Word and Excel macros, and other fun and/or useful stuff. The documents contain very short, sometimes cryptic descriptions of the software, so you won't know what many of the programs are until you get them.

Access via:
www http://coyote.csusm.edu/cwis/ winworld/winworld.html

Data Communications and Networking Links

From the ISDN User's Guide to the Cell-Relay (ATM) Archives, Don Joslyn's Data Communications page surveys the networking resources on the Net. Don is a software engineer at Racal-Datacom, the company that hosts the page, which has an especially good collection of links to other specialized collections of links.

Access via:
www http://www.racal.com/ networking.html

DEC Web Server

A huge site featuring everything imaginable about DEC computers: products and services, customer periodicals, new technology, and user support. There's even a greeting from Digital CEO Bob Palmer.

Access via:
www http://www.digital.com/home.html

Dell Computer

A rich site from Dell Computer, targeted to both businesses and individual consumers. The site features product specifications, various customer support resources, and corporate and employment information.

Access via:
www http://www.dell.com/

DeskTop Publishing Jumplist

An awesome collection of links to the desktop publishing resources of the Net, compiled by Purdue University's Geof Peters.

Access via:
www http://www.cs.purdue.edu/homes/ gwp/dtp/dtp.html

Directory of Computer and Communication Companies

A user-friendly collection of links to computer and communications businesses on the Net, with a search feature to help locate them. The Computer and Communication Companies directory is maintained by staff at the University of California's Lawrence Livermore National Laboratory.

Access via:
www http://www-atp.llnl.gov/atp/ companies.html

Directory of Servers

A useful master list of all the public WAIS libraries in existence.

Access via:
www http://www.wais.com/ newhomepages/wais-dbs.html

The Father of Shareware

A little history...and links to shareware archives, too! Jim Knopf wrote PC-File in 1982 and, along with Andrew Fluegelman, pioneered the shareware distribution model. You can read Jim's true story at The Father of Shareware or nix it and head for his collection of links to over 50 shareware sites. Especially valuable is his terrific list of links to sites run by shareware creators like Happy Puppy Software and Pinnacle Solutions.

Access via:
www http://www.halcyon.com/knopf/jim

Fractals

Collections of fractal images and movies. Some of these are purely mathematical (such as Mandelbrot and Julia sets); others are 3-D renderings and fly-bys through fractal landscapes both real and imagined.

Access via:
www http://www.cnam.fr/fractals.html
Notes: Fractal images & animations at CNAM

www http://spanky.triumf.ca/
Notes: Spanky Fractal Database

ftp ftp.cnam.fr; login *anonymous;* cd *pub/Fractals*

Free On-Line Dictionary of Computing

A searchable glossary of programming languages, architectures, networks, domain theory, mathematics, and other information relating to computing. This site also contains links to several other computing-oriented glossaries, lists, and compilations.

Access via:
www http://wombat.doc.ic.ac.uk/

Graphics FAQs

A page with links to 11 collections of frequently asked questions from computer graphics-related USENET groups, including the FAQs for *comp.graphics, comp.graphics.algorithms, comp.graphics.animation,* and *comp.graphics.opengl.*

Access via:
www http://www.cis.ohio-state.edu/ hypertext/faq/bngusenet/comp/graphics/ top.html

Graphics Viewers, Editors, Utilities and Information

Joseph Walker's collection of links to graphics shareware, demos, and information files available over the Net. Links to applications are accompanied by a platform designation (Windows, DOS, UNIX, Mac).

Access via:
www http://www2.ncsu.edu/bae/ people/faculty/walker/hotlist/graphics.html

Hewlett-Packard

A link to Access HP, Hewlett-Packard's outpost on the Web. The site presents an array of news and product and services information.

Access via:
www http://www.hp.com/home.html

IBM WWW Server

A well-designed resource that provides a rich array of information about IBM products and services. The site is updated regularly with product announcements, press releases, and conference reports.

Access via:
www http://www.ibm.com/

Index to Multimedia Information Sources

A substantial list of pointers to the multimedia resources on the Internet.

Access via:
www http://viswiz.gmd.de/MultimediaInfo/

Internet Resources for Windows Developers

Robert Mashlan's collection of links to Net resources useful to Windows product developers. Resource areas covered include FTP sites, FAQs, developer magazines, and mailing lists.

Access via:
www http://www.csn.net/~rmashlan/ windev/windev.html

LAN Magazine

No mere promotion for their print publication, *LAN Magazine*'s WWW server features a rich collection of articles and product reviews related to local area networks. Major departments include Features, News Link, LAN Insider, Fun & Games, Innovations, and Test Drives.

Access via:
www *http://www.lanmag.com/cover/cover.html*

The Linux Operating System

Resources here include an explanation of what Linux is, a Linux FAQ, a comprehensive list of USENET groups, the Linux manual pages, a list of other Linux Web servers, and a searchable Linux software map. The site was created by the Linux Organization, a not-for-profit group of Linux users. The server is maintained by Liem Bahnema, a student at the University of Washington.

Access via:
www *http://www.ssc.com/linux/linux.html*

Microsoft Corporation

Microsoft's own server, containing comprehensive information on their products. Various sections cover desktop applications, development tools, and operating systems, as well as corporate and product support. This looks like a good place to get the latest drivers, bug fixes, and utilities.

Access via:
www *http://www.microsoft.com/*

ftp *ftp.microsoft.com;* login *anonymous*

O'Reilly Windows Center

O'Reilly's source for information about Windows, Windows 95, and Windows NT. This site is maintained by Andrew Schulman, author of *Unauthorized Windows 95* and now an O'Reilly editor. It includes editorials, information about O'Reilly's Windows products, and pointers to other important Windows sites on the net.

Access via:
http://www.ora.com/windows/

PC World Online

An impressive site from the publisher of *PC World* magazine. PC World Online brings together feature articles, news, columns, and product reviews from the magazine, along with a terrific Hot Software download area. Another great feature is a searchable database of back issues of the magazine; a search on "Microsoft" retrieved links to 237 full-text documents. The Buyer's Guide is tremendously helpful for anyone shopping for a new PC. The only major flaw at PC World Online is the lack of publication dates.

Access via:
www *http://www.pcworld.com/toc/index.html*

RealAudio

If you're tired of downloading massive .WAV or .AU files to get sound over the Net, Progressive Networks' RealAudio may be the answer to your prayers. Supposedly, the RealAudio server can deliver real-time sound over connections as slow as 14.4 kbps. To use RealAudio, you have to download the RealAudio Player, and you'll need a hefty chunk of RAM. Once you have the software set up, you can access sound files from ABC News and NPR.

Access via:
www *http://www.realaudio.com/*
Notes: RealAudio home page

www *http://www.realaudio.com/*
othersites.html
Notes: Other sites with RealAudio sound

Silicon Graphics WWW Server

Silicon Graphics' Silicon Surf features product announcements, product and services information, technical information, and other resources.

Access via:
www *http://www.sgi.com/*

Sun Microsystems

Home of Sun Microsystems on the Net. The Sun page features information in four categories: Products and Solutions, Sales and Service, Technology and Developers, and Corporate Overview. A collection of links to SunSITE (Sun Information and Technology Exchange) servers worldwide is also available.

Access via:
www *http://www.sun.com/*

University of Florida's Perl Archive

A compact yet thorough introduction to the Perl scripting language. This archive also features a list of other Perl sites on the Internet.

Access via:
www *http://www.cis.ufl.edu/perl/*

UNIXhelp for Users

A hypertext guide to the UNIX operating system, intended for beginning users of UNIX. Includes descriptions of common commands, managing jobs, and using e-mail, as well as longer descriptions of common tools. This site has a cool command conversion chart for

those people switching from VMS or DOS to UNIX.

Access via:
www *http://www.nova.edu/Inter-Links/*
UNIXhelp/TOP_.html

Virtual Computer Library

This electronic library provides links to information sources on computers and computing. Subjects indexed include academic computing, FAQs, Internet information, publishers, and WWW information. The "What's New" section lists recent additions to the site. This resource is maintained by the University of Texas Computation Center.

Access via:
www *http://www.utexas.edu/computer/vcl/*

Virtual Shareware Library

Have you ever wanted to find a shareware program, but weren't quite sure of its name? This database will help you search the major Internet shareware archives for program descriptions that match the words you supply. If the search is successful, you get a list of links to all known mirror sites that archive that program (as well as an option to start an Archie search for other sources). At the time of this review, the library database knew of 90,000 files in 21 archives, containing software for UNIX, Macintosh, Windows, DOS, OS/2, and Amiga.

Access via:
www *http://vsl.cnet.com/*

Visual Basic Home Page

Carl 'n Gary's Visual Basic Home Page is a resource courtesy of Carl Franklin and Gary Wisniewski. As the guys will tell you, "Our ongoing mission is to create a virtual gathering place for Visual Basic programmers throughout the world.... This page is dedicated to the free exchange of software, ideas, and information."

Access via:
www http://www.apexsc.com/vb/

VRML Repository

A clearinghouse for information related to Virtual Reality Modeling Language (VRML), "a developing standard for describing interactive three-dimensional scenes delivered across the Internet." Materials available include specifications and a calendar of VRML events, along with links to example applications, software projects, and other sources of VRML information. The VRML repository is maintained by the San Diego Supercomputer Center.

Access via:
www http://www.sdsc.edu/vrml

Windows Utilities Report

A nicely organized, well-designed site offering useful tips on recently released shareware, freeware, and public domain software for Windows. Users can access the current Utility Report, previous issues, and Essential Apps (i.e., software "found to be so useful that…inclusion in the report is necessary").

Access via:
www http://www.peinet.pe.ca:2080/ Chorus/U_report/urep.html

COOKING

Newsgroups:
rec.food.[cooking, drink, recipes, restaurants, sourdough, veg], rec.crafts.brewing

Dining Out on the Web

What are we going to have for dinner? You may find the answer to this age-old question on the Net. Dining Out on the Web is an index of restaurant guides that can help you find the restaurant you're looking for, from San Francisco to Tokyo. Some of the guides use a search engine; others list restaurants by type or location. Dining Out on the Web is maintained by John Troyer and Dan Whaley.

Access via:
www http://www.ird.net/diningout.html

La Comida Mexicana

A collection of classic Mexican recipes from the University of Guadalajara Web site. The site's home page features an innovative image-mapped index. Appearing in the form of an open cookbook, the image map provides links to the various types of dishes found at the site, including Sopas (soups), Carnes (meats), Salsas (sauces), and Postres (pastries). In all, La Comida Mexicana contains over 100 different recipes.

Access via:
www http://www.udg.mx/Cocina/ menu.html
Notes: Recipes appear in Spanish.

Over the Coffee

Tim Nemec's impressive collection of coffee resources, including information on preparation, drinking, and vendors. Especially fun is the Coffee Reference Desk, where one will find a comprehensive list of "Coffee Varieties, Blends & Roasts," among other things.

Access via:
www http://www.cappuccino.com

Ragu Presents—Mama's Cucina

Don't miss this creative site, which features Mama's Italian Cookbook, contests, sound files to help you learn to say "Hey, pizza face!" in Italian, and sayings from Mama herself. There are even Goodies from Mama, including coupons for Ragu Products and a Ragu t-shirt.

Access via:
www http://www.eat.com

Recipe Archives

Recipe archives are proliferating; the largest are those containing recipes that have passed through the *rec.food.cooking* and *rec.food. recipes* newsgroups.

Access via:
www http://www.nova.edu/Inter-Links/ fun/food.html

www http://www.honors.indiana.edu/ ~veggie/recipes.cgi/
Notes: Vegetarian recipe archive

ftp gatekeeper.dec.com; login *anonymous;* cd *pub/recipes*
Notes: ftp archive, organized by title

Spencer's Beer Page

Spencer's Beer Page is a general-purpose all-round collection of resources for home-brewers, covering beer, ale, "kegging," and "wort chillers." The page is maintained by Spencer W. Thomas, of the University of Michigan.

Access via:
www http://www.umich.edu/~spencer/ beer/

The Virtual Pub

An Internet gathering place for beer connoisseurs, maintained by Joel Plutchak of Brown University. Although the site features a large catalog of images, files, and outside links, the gem here is the interactive beer tasting room. (Well, it's not entirely interactive; the introduction to the tasting room reminds visitors that "technology is still limited, so you have to go out and purchase the brew yourself.") Patrons of the tasting room are invited to use a form to register their opinions on the featured brew. Recent tasters found Sam Adams Lager "a decent brew" and Anchor Steam "complex and enjoyable."

Access via:
www http://lager.geo.brown.edu:8080/ virtual-pub/

Wine Page

This good-looking page is a great resource for wine lovers and those who want to learn more about wine. The tasting archive features an interactive tasting note compiler, which allows readers to send in their own tasting notes. A virtual tasting group, The Wine Net Newsletter Archive, an extensive FAQ on wine, and links to other wine pages on the Net round out this informative and enjoyable resource.

Access via:
www http://augustus.csscr.washington.edu/ personal/bigstar-mosaic/wine.html

World Guide to Vegetarianism

The World Guide to Vegetarianism is a straightforward, easy-to-follow listing of vegetarian and vegetarian-friendly restaurants, natural food stores, and organizations. The guide is organized by region (USA, Canada, Europe, Other, and California, which has enough listings to merit its own heading). Listings are guaranteed to stay up-to-date and impartial because the guide provides forms for users to submit their own reviews of restaurants, natural food stores, and vegetarian organizations. Even if you're not a vegetarian, you'll probably find this guide interesting; if you are a vegetarian and plan to travel to a city or country you've never visited before, you may find this guide invaluable.

Access via:
www http://catless.ncl.ac.uk/Vegetarian/ Guide/index.html

ECONOMICS

Newsgroups:
sci.econ

Economics Departments on the Internet

Ed Price's "extensive but not exhaustive" listing of home pages for U.S. departments of Economics (Price also provides a link to listings of international departments). Approximately 150 different departments are presented in an alphabetized table.

Access via:
www http://gopher.econ.lsa.umich.edu

Other Academic Economics Departments, Faculties & Centres

Lief Bluck and David Giles of the Department of Economics at the University of Victoria, Canada maintain this listing of hypertext-based WWW servers for non-U.S. departments of Economics.

Access via:
www http://sol.uvic.ca/econ/depts.html

The Information Economy

Hal Varian's collection of documents regarding the "information economy." This under-construction site maintains links to essays on such topics as intellectual property and electronic publishing, as well as a link to U.C. Berkeley's School of Information Management and Systems.

Access via:
www http://gopher.econ.lsa.umich.edu

EDUCATION

Newsgroups:
k12.ed.[art, business, comp.literary, life-skills, math, music, science, soc-studies, special, tag, tech], and k12.lang.[art, deutsch-eng, espeng, francais, russian]

Academe This Week

Excerpts from the *Chronicle of Higher Education,* the weekly tabloid that covers all aspects of the college and university business. Each week's issue features a well-organized listing of hundreds of teaching, research, and administrative jobs in higher education.

Access via:
www http://chronicle.merit.edu/

gopher chronicle.merit.edu

AdoptionNetwork

There were over 100,000 adoptions in the U.S. in 1990. AdoptionNetwork is an on-line volunteer effort to help serve the information needs of everyone involved in the process, from adoptive parents, to adoptees, to birth-mothers. No political agenda is apparent at the site. Resources available include directories of support groups and adoption agencies, various FAQs, and a collection of links to other adoption-related Web sites.

Access via:
www http://www.adoption.org/adopt/

Adolescence Directory On-Line

A large and well-structured collection of links to Internet resources related to adolescence and secondary education. Subject areas include Mental Health, Health Risk, Teens Only!, and Lesson Plans. The Adolescence Directory is maintained by the Center for Adolescent Studies at Indiana University. An archive of their publication *Teacher Talk* is also available at the site.

Access via:
www http://education.indiana.edu/cas/ adol/adol.html

The Ambitious Student's Guide to Financial Aid

An excellent introduction to financial aid, written by Robert and Anna Leider and presented on the Web by Signet Bank. At twenty-five chapters, the guide is remarkably comprehensive for a free resource.

Access via:
www http://www.infi.net/collegemoney/ toc2.html

Berit's Best Sites for Children

 This is what every "best sites" page should be like. Berit Erickson, who works for Cochran Interactive Inc., has organized dozens of sites by category, provided good descriptions about them, and rated each on a scale of one to five. There are tons of links here, from science and history sites to kids' magazines and home pages.

Access via:
www http://www.cochran.com/theosite/ KSites.html

Consortium for School Networking (CoSN)

This consortium (composed of businesses, organizations, schools, and individuals) calls itself "the national voice for advocating access to the emerging National Information Infrastructure in schools." Among the resources available from the CoSN home page is a Technology Resources Page, featuring a list of "Important Educational Technology Resources." Additional informa-tion on CoSN's work is available via the consortium's gopher server.

Access via:
www http://cosn.org/

English as a Second Language Home Page

This site uses the World Wide Web as an environment to help people learn to speak English. There are a variety of resources for students and teachers of ESL, including a collection of home pages created by ESL students.

Access via:
www http://www.ed.uiuc.edu/EdPsy-387/ Rongchang-Li/esl/index.html

Educom

Educom helps educational institutions stay on the cutting edge of information technology by showing them how to integrate information technology into classrooms, curricula, and research. Among other resources, visitors to the site will find current and past issues of EduPage, an information technology newslet-ter published three times per week via e-mail, Gopher, and the World Wide Web. EduPage summarizes printed news coverage of interest to the leaders and citizens of the Internet.

Access via:
www http://educom.edu/

EdWeb: The On-Line K–12 Resource Guide

EdWeb is a guide to the world of educational computing and networking maintained by Andy Carvin of the Corporation for Public Broadcasting. The site provides access to many useful resources for K–12 teachers— some interactive—including discussion groups, lesson plans, and stories about first-hand teaching experience. The interface is simple to use and offers access to an on-line technical dictionary on every page.

Access via:
www http://edweb.cnidr.org:90/

Financial Aid Information Page

Mark Kantrowitz, co-author of *The Prentice Hall Guide to Scholarships and Fellowships for Math and Science Students,* has compiled this collection of WWW links to financial aid information resources on the Internet. The Financial Aid Information page directs visitors to over 50 general and school-specific financial aid resources. The resources are relevant to graduate and undergraduate students, and cover science and liberal arts disciplines.

Access via:
www http://www.cs.cmu.edu/afs/cs/ user/mkant/Public/FinAid/finaid.html

HotList of K–12 Internet School Sites

A collection of links to U.S. primary and secondary schools with servers on the Internet, maintained by net-happenings guru Gleason Sackman. The list, which is strictly no-frills, is broken down according to state and type of school (elementary, middle, high school).

Access via:
www http://toons.cc.ndsu.nodak.edu/ ~sackmann/k12.html

The JASON Project

Teachers often wonder, "Where should we go for our next field trip?" How about Hawaii? Or the Galapagos Islands? Perhaps the Mediterranean Sea. Each year the JASON Project takes a select group of students and teachers to a remote area on a two-week scientific expedition. The trip, held from late February to early March, is broadcast in real-time, using state-of-the-art technology, to a network of educational, research, and cultural institutions. The results of the trips are cataloged at this site, so classes can visit

them anytime. The JASON Project was founded by Dr. Robert Ballard, who discovered the location of the sunken R.M.S. *Titanic.*

Access via:
www http://seawifs.gsfc.nasa.gov/scripts/ JASON.html

KIDLINK

"The goal of KIDLINK is to create a global dialog among the 10-to-15-year-old youth of the world." Visit the site to find out how to set up or join a KIDLINK project, and how Internet Relay Chat is used in on-line projects.

Access via:
www http://www.kidlink.org/

Kids' Space

A marvelous site for kids to share their artwork, music, and stories. My favorite area is the "Story Book," where kids are presented with a collection of five small images and invited to write and submit a story incorporating the images. The stories that have been collected so far include "The Big Tomato" from Kyle Owen (age 7), which begins, "One day a big red [tomato] came to my front door wearing a big yellow [hat]. My family opened the door and was surprised that a [tomato] was wearing a [hat]." Kids' Space was created by Sachiko Oba, a Doctoral student at Teachers College, Columbia University.

Access via:
www http://www.interport.net/kids_space

Pathways to School Improvement

A collaboration between educators, researchers, and community leaders, Pathways to School Improvement seeks to address critical issues in education. While still under development, Pathways to School Improvement provides some good ideas and resources for teachers and communities.

Access via:
*www http://www.ncrel.org/ncrel/sdrs/
pathwayg.html*

Peterson's Education Center

The on-line door to summer jobs, summer
programs for teens, and college knowledge
is open. Peterson's now provides on-line information on undergraduate colleges, graduate
study, summer programs for kids, and
summer camp jobs.

Access via:
www http://www.petersons.com

Quest: NASA's K–12 Internet Initiative

An ideal starting point for K–12 teachers who
want to use the Internet as an educational
tool. Quest, sponsored by NASA, offers tips
for bringing the Net into your school, training
and technical hints, and links to other education resources. Through this site, students can
get in touch with NASA scientists and "volunteer" on NASA projects. Quest also shows
how to contact other classrooms on the Net.

Access via:
www http://quest.arc.nasa.gov/

Research for Better Schools

Resources supporting rural and urban educational reform, provided by Research for Better
Schools, a private, nonprofit corporation.

Access via:
gopher gopher.rbs.org

Software and Aids for Teaching of Mathematics

A collection of software to aid in the teaching
of mathematics at the college and university
levels. Also includes newsletters, reprints, and
other material of interest in the area. Most of

the software is for IBM PC compatibles. Other
computers may be supported in the future.

Access via:
www http://archives.math.utk.edu/

gopher archives.math.utk.edu

ftp archives.math.utk.edu; login *anonymous*

The Student Guide 1995-1996: Financial Aid from the U.S. Department of Education

The U.S. Department of Education's Student
Guide was written to help parents and potential students make sense of U.S. Government
financial aid. The guide covers everything
from financial need to applications to dead-
lines. Specific information is available on
programs like Pell Grants, Direct and FFEL
Program Loans, Federal Work-Study, and
Federal Perkins Loans. If you don't like reading on-line, a 126K compressed ASCII version of the guide is available for download.

Access via:
*www http://www.ed.gov/prog_info/
SFA/StudentGuide/*

Teacher*Pages

A resource provided by Penn State University
for educators at all levels. Information is available for many different school levels, academic areas, and subject areas.

Access via:
telnet psupen.psu.edu; login *your two-letter
state abbreviation*

Test Prep Sites (SAT, GRE, LSAT, etc.)

Who'd a thunk it? Useful information, canny
advice, even genuine words of wisdom can
be found at the Kaplan and Princeton Review
sites. Both sites offer basic information on
preparing for standardized tests, including
the SAT, ACT, GMAT, GRE, LSAT, MCAT

and TOEFL. The sites go beyond trying to lure students to enroll in their courses—they offer helpful guidance to aspiring college students, from tips to getting financial aid to thoughtful career advice.

Access via:
www http://www.kaplan.com/
Notes: Kaplan OnLine

www http://www.review.com/index.html
Notes: Princeton Review Online

Virtual Schoolhouse

A large but somewhat jumbled collection of links to K–12 Internet sites compiled by the Cisco Educational Archive. Subject areas include Schools and Universities on the Internet, The Art Room, Virtual Field Trips, The Techie's Corner, and The Principal's Office.

Access via:
www http://sunsite.unc.edu/cisco/ schoolhouse.html

Yamada Language Guides

A large index to the language resources of the Net, compiled by the Yamada Language Center at the University of Oregon. Each of the 75+ languages covered by the index has its own page of links. A collection of non-English fonts for Macintosh computers is also available here.

Access via:
www http://babel.uoregon.edu/yamada/ guides.html

ELECTRONIC MAGAZINES (E-ZINES)

Newsgroups:
alt.[authorware, etext, motherjones, wired, zines], rec.mag

FEED

A monthly on-line magazine with a focus on arts, politics, and technoculture. The well-written articles are interesting and elegantly formatted. Among the highlights are a panel discussion of the merits of electronic text (with brilliant use of hypertext) and a dead-on commentary by David Greenberg on the Enola Gay controversy in Washington.

Access via:
www http://www.emedia.net/feed/ index.html

Fine Art Forum

A monthly magazine of arts announcements from people and organizations in the United States and Europe. Although the magazine itself is still only ASCII text, a Web front-end has been added, with pictures of the artists, their works, and links to other arts resources on the Net. Edited by Paul Brown of Griffith University, this site is one of the oldest network services for the arts.

Access via:
www http://www.msstate.edu/ Fineart_Online/home.html

gopher gopher.msstate.edu / Resources at MS State/fineart_online/

ftp ftp.msstate.edu; login anonymous; cd pub/archives/fineart_online

John Labovitz's E-ZINE-LIST

A directory of electronically accessible zines, often personal and esoteric.

Access via:
www http://www.meer.net/~johnl/ e-zine-list/

ftp etext.archive.umich.edu; login anonymous; cd pub/Zines; get e-zine-list

Netsurfer Digest

An extensive, unorthodox collection of links offered in a weekly e-zine from Netsurfer Communications, Inc. The latest issue of this nicely organized zine can be sent to your e-mail box, or you can check the Netsurfer site for back issues. The collection of links for a recent week ranged from conventional offerings (CBS, National Press Club) to software from Novell to "The School of Wisdom" for those seeking enlightenment. Categories include "Surfing Sites," "Online Travel," and "Flotsam and Jetsam."

Access via:
www *http://www.netsurf.com/nsd/ index.html*

ENGINEERING

Newsgroups:
sci.engr, sci.engr.[chem, biomed, civil, control, manufacturing, mech]

American Society for Engineering Education (ASEE)

In addition to general information about the ASEE, this site features an extraordinarily comprehensive list of resources useful to engineers and others. Included at the site are links to corporate home pages, university engineering departments, and research and development facilities such as national and corporate labs. ASEE is a nonprofit organization dedicated to improving engineering education.

Access via:
www *http://www.asee.org/*

Internet Connections for Engineering

An extensive index to the engineering resources of the Internet, compiled by the Engineering Library of Cornell University. The index is organized according to discipline.

Access via:
www *http://www.englib.cornell.edu/ice/ ice-index.html*

The Semiconductor Subway

A collection of links to semiconductor- and microsystems-related information, featuring a cool subway-layout imagemap to take you to the sites. The Semiconductor Subway is kept on schedule by Duane Boning of MIT.

Access via:
www *http://www-mtl.mit.edu/ semisubway.html*

ENVIRONMENTAL ISSUES

Newsgroups:
sci.[environment, bio.ecology], talk.environment

CIESIN Global Change Information Gateway

The Consortium for International Earth Science Information Network (CIESIN) provides information from the Socioeconomic Data and Application Center, CIESIN's gateway to the NASA Earth Observation System Data and Information System, and the Global Change Research Information Office, CIESIN's gateway to the U.S. Global Change Research Program.

Access via:
www *http://www.ciesin.org/*
gopher *gopher.ciesin.org*

Environmental Studies Resources Index

A comprehensive index of environmental resources.

Access via:
gopher *gopher.unr.edu /Selected/ Environmental Studies Resources*

EnviroWeb

A comprehensive on-line environmental information service provided by the EnviroLink Network, a non-profit organization based in Pittsburgh, Pennsylvania. Among other things, EnviroWeb features a nice collection of links to Internet Environmental Resources.

Access via:
www *http://envirolink.org/*

National Renewable Energy Laboratory

Part of the U.S. Department of Energy, the NREL's mission is to conduct and coordinate "renewable energy research and technology development that private industry cannot reasonably be expected to undertake." Check up on their alternative fuel, solar, and wind technology research at this well-organized site.

Access via:
www *http://www.nrel.gov/*

gopher *gopher.nrel.gov*

ftp *nrel.nrel.gov; login anonymous; cd pub*

FREE-NETS

Free-Nets and Community Networks

Free-Nets are grassroots efforts to provide networking services to an urban community, with access either at public libraries or by dialing in. It's also possible to access Free-Nets through the Internet. Free-Nets are usually organized around a model town that you "walk" through. You can stop at the "courthouse and government center" and discuss local issues with the mayor. Or, you can stop by the "medical arts building" and discuss health issues with a health professional. Aside from discussions, there are usually bulletin boards, electronic mail, and other information services.

There are real hidden gem resources on some Free-Nets. These are indexed separately. Anyone can use a Free-Net as a guest, but guest privileges are limited; for example, you can't use e-mail and a few other things. You can get further privileges by registering; registration is usually free to people within a certain district, and available at nominal charge to those outside. When you log in as a guest, you'll probably see a message telling you how to get registration information.

Free-Net software is menu-driven and designed for ease of use. Give them a try. If you think you'd like to organize a Free-Net for your town, contact Dr. T.M. Grundner at *tmg@nptn.org*.

The Buffalo free-net is a lively community network.
telnet *freenet.buffalo.edu; login freeport*

The Denver free-net is fairly strong on the fine arts.
telnet *freenet.hsc.colorado.edu; login guest*

The National Capital Area Public Access Network, or CapAccess, is a free-net for the Washington, D.C. metropolitan area. It concentrates on K–12 education, health and social services, library services, and government.
telnet *freenet.nsc.colorado.edu; login guest*

GARDENING

Newsgroups:
rec.gardens

The Garden Gate

Eventually every fanatical gardener has to face the age-old question: What to do when it's too dark or too cold outside to garden? Why not pull up a chair, grab your mouse, and stroll through the Garden Gate. From The Gardener's Reading Room to an excellent collection of links to Internet resources for gardeners, this page could keep you busy for hours. The Garden Gate's pages are created and maintained by Karen Fletcher.

Access via:
www http://www.prairienet.org/ag/garden/homepage.html

Master Gardener Information

This server (run by the Texas Agricultural Extension Service) offers information on fruits and nuts, flowering plants, annual and perennial ornamental trees and shrubs, turf grasses, and vegetables.

Access via:
www gopher://leviathan.tamu.edu/11s/mg

GEOGRAPHY

Geographic Information Server

An interface to data supplied by the U.S. Geodetic Survey and the U.S. Postal Service. Make requests by name (Sebastopol, for all cities named Sebastopol, or Sebastopol, CA, for all cities named Sebastopol within California); the server returns latitude, longitude, population, zipcode, elevation, etc.

Access via:
www http://www.mit.edu:8001/geo/
telnet martini.eecs.umich.edu; port 3000

Xerox PARC Map Viewer

From the research labs of the people who make machines that make copies, here's one of the most interactive applications on the Net. MapViewer is an application that dynamically renders a map based on user input. Click on a region and MapViewer will zoom in on it. You can also use a geographic name server to locate a particular location. Typing in San Jose, California, we find that it is the county seat, and had a population of 629,442 in 1980. Its location is given, and we can click on it to display a map of the U.S. and a map of Northern California, showing where San Jose is. The Geographic Name Server is located at the University of Buffalo.

Access via:
www http://pubweb.parc.xerox.com/map

GEOLOGY

Newsgroups:
sci.geo.geology

Earthquake Image Information System

The Earthquake Image Information System (EqIIS) provides Web access to thousands of photos of quake damage. The EqIIS database can be queried and browsed by date and location of quake, or by name of photographer. Over 80 quakes are covered, ranging around the world from the 1923 quake in Tokyo, Japan, to the Whittier Narrows, California earthquake of 1987. EqIIS was developed with support from the Federal Emergency Management Agency in cooperation with the University of California Museum Informatics Project.

Access via:
www http://nisee.ce.berkeley.edu/eqiis.html

Hydrology-Related Internet Resources

An impressive collection of links, maintained by Tim Scheibe of the Earth and Environmental Sciences Center at the Pacific Northwest Laboratory.

Access via:
www http://terrassa.pnl.gov:2080/ EESC/resourcelist/hydrology.html

U.S. Geological Survey

A service provided by the United States Geological Survey; information about the survey, resources they provide, software, and other services related to geology, hydrology, and cartography. Organized by topic, it includes audio and animated material as well as text and pictures.

Access via:
www http://www.usgs.gov/

U.S.G.S. Weekly Seismicity Reports

Weekly reports of seismic activity (earthquakes, volcanos, etc.) and maps for Northern California, the U.S., and the world.

Access via:
www http://quake.wr.usgs.gov/QUAKES/ WEEKREPS/weekly.html

VolcanoWorld

VolcanoWorld is a growing site that was created to educate students and others by delivering data, including high-quality remote sensing images, near real-time volcano information, and interactive experiments. The site includes links to Current and Recent Eruptions, Images of Volcanoes, and a Volcano Slide Show. You can also ask questions of volcano experts who will e-mail you a response. VolcanoWorld is the production of

a team of 12 experts, primarily from the University of North Dakota.

Access via:
www http://volcano.und.nodak.edu/

GOVERNMENT AND UNITED NATIONS

EUROPA (European Union)

A large collection of information about the European Union's "goals, institutions, and policies." Among interesting resources here are a "European Consumer Guide to the Single Market" (beneath the "Europe ABC" link) and a 19-question FAQ on the European Union (beneath the "European Union" link).

Access via:
www http://www.cec.lu/Welcome.html

Foreign Government Resources from MARVEL

A rich collection of gopher resources compiled for the U.S. Library of Congress MARVEL system.

Access via:
gopher marvel.loc.gov

International Government Resources from MARVEL

A large collection of gopher links to United Nations, NATO, treaty, and international relations resources. The collection is maintained by the MARVEL service of the U.S. Library of Congress.

Access via:
gopher marvel.loc.gov

NATO

Press releases, speeches by the Secretary General, a Fact Sheet, and electronic versions of the *NATO Handbook* and the *NATO Review*.

Access via:
gopher *gopher.inform.umd.edu/ Educational_Resources/ AcademicResourcesBy Topic/UnitedStatesAndWorld/ World/International_Agencies/NATO*

United Nations News

Compiled five days a week and digested monthly, the U.N. News covers areas of the globe and events that involve this international body. Mostly this means trouble areas, but the site also contains updates for other parts of the world in which the U.N. has been involved, but which are now relatively stable.

Access via:
gopher *gopher.undp.org /U.N. Current/*

World Constitutions

Over a dozen constitutions and similar documents from countries and would-be countries around the world.

Access via:
ftp *wiretap.spies.com;* login *anonymous;* cd *Gov/World*

U.S. GOVERNMENT

Americans with Disabilities Act Regulations

The Americans with Disabilities Act reaches into many aspects of daily life. This resource includes not only the text of regulations, sub-

divided by Federal agency, but also a wealth of supporting information and pointers to offline resources.

Access via:
gopher *gopher.inform.umd.edu/ Educational_Resources/ AcademicResourcesByTopic/ UnitedStatesAndWorld/United_States/ National_Agencies/ExecutiveBranch/ ADARegulation*

Congressional E-Mail Directory

A handy directory of e-mail addresses for U.S. Senators and Congressional Representatives, compiled by Jeffrey Hoffman. The directory is organized alphabetically by state; addresses are interactive, so you can send a message directly from your browser (if it has e-mail support). Many U.S. elected officials still lack e-mail accounts; if your representative is not listed in the directory, Mr. Hoffman recommends sending them snail mail "DEMANDING that they get e-mail NOW!"

Access via:
www *http://uptown.turnpike.net/J/ jhoffman/congress-email.html*

Environmental Protection Agency

The official information server of the EPA, containing basic information, press releases, a calendar of events, and the text of initiatives and regulations. The server also contains the EPA Journal, which discusses current issues facing the EPA. Also on the server is a report of pesticides being re-registered, a software archive for the Center for Exposure Assessment Modeling, and several speeches given on Earth Day in 1994.

Access via:
www *http://www.epa.gov/*

gopher *gopher.epa.gov*

ftp *ftp.epa.gov;* login *anonymous*

Federal Bureau of Investigation

As of December, 1994, there have been 438 fugitives on the 'Top Ten' list. Seven of these have been women. Also as of December, 1994, 412 individuals who have appeared on this list have been located, 129 of them as a direct result of citizen cooperation. — from the FBI's *Top Ten Most Wanted* FAQ.

An intriguing collection of information from the FBI, including a current Top Ten Most Wanted List and material on the Oklahoma City bombing and Unabomber cases.

Access via:
www http://www.fbi.gov/

Federal Legislation

Access to information about Federal legislation.

Access via:
telnet locis.loc.gov

Federal Web Locator

A hotlist of links to U.S. Government WWW resources, compiled by Kenneth P. Mortensen of the Villanova Center for Information Law and Policy.

Access via:
www http://www.law.vill.edu/
Fed-Agency/fedwebloc.html

Internal Revenue Service

The IRS Web site provides a complete set of federal tax forms, a sparse IRS FAQ, and information on where to file and where to get help. Within the "where to get help" area is a complete listing of the files and services available from Tele-Tax, the toll-free IRS automated information service. Tax forms are in PDF format, which requires the Adobe Acrobat Reader to display. (Fortunately, the Acrobat Reader is freeware, and versions for the major operating systems can be downloaded at the IRS site.)

Access via:
www http://www.ustreas.gov/treasury/
bureaus/irs/irs.html

NavyOnLine

The official starting point for people interested in finding on-line resources provided by the U.S. Department of the Navy. This service provides an index of links to all the Navy's on-line servers. Although the site includes a search mechanism, finding resources can be difficult if you're uncertain where to look.

Access via:
www http://www.navy.mil/

Proposed Federal Budget, 1996

A comprehensive look at the proposed 1996 Budget, with search engine.

Access via:
www http://www.doc.gov/inquery/
BudgetFY96/BudgetFY96.html

Social Security Administration Online

This site is a sign of the U.S. government's increased presence on the World Wide Web. According to its documentation, "SSA Online was developed by the Office of Policy and External Affairs to provide easy access to a large variety of information about our programs and activities..."

Access via:
www http://www.ssa.gov/SSA_Home.html/

THOMAS: Legislative Information on the Internet

Created "in the spirit of Thomas Jefferson," THOMAS is a Library of Congress server devoted to information on the U.S. Congress. Among other resources, visitors to THOMAS will find an article on "How Our Laws Are Made," a keyword searchable database of House and Senate bills, and a link to the C-SPAN gopher.

Access via:
www *http://thomas.loc.gov/*

U.S. Army Home Page

This is the jumping-off point to over 60 U.S. Army Web sites, including the Pentagon's Artificial Intelligence Center, the Tank-Automotive Research, Development and Engineering Center, and Syracuse University ROTC.

Access via:
www *http://www.army.mil/*

U.S. Census Information Server

The self-proclaimed "Factfinder for the Nation," the Census Bureau has created a model server for government agencies to follow. In short, it organizes information so that citizens can make their own use of it. You can get financial data on state and local governments, as well as schools. The Bureau's statistical briefs are PostScript documents describing poverty in the U.S., analyzing housing changes from 1981–1991, or profiling people of Asian and Pacific Islander heritage in the American population. In the Census Bureau Art Gallery, they even display posters used to promote participation in the census.

Although the actual census data is not available due to privacy laws, the Data Extraction System (also known as SIPP-On-Call) summarizes recent census data based on criteria you supply. Through a somewhat cumbersome interface, you can perform a search based on a huge number of variables and receive the results in your TELNET window, by e-mail, or by a temporary file stored at the Census FTP site.

Access via:
www *http://www.census.gov/*

gopher *census.gov*

ftp *ftp.census.gov;* login *anonymous*

telnet *gateway.census.gov;* login *desuser*

U.S. Department of Education

Provides information about the Department of Education's programs and staff, along with announcements, press releases, and pointers to other resources.

Access via:
www *http://www.ed.gov/*
gopher *gopher.ed.gov*

U.S. Federal Government WWW Servers (FEDIX)

A comprehensive list of U.S. Government servers. The list, which is maintained by Federal Information Exchange, Inc., is broken down into three areas: Multiple agency servers, single agency servers (including the executive and legislative branches), and government consortia servers.

Access via:
www *http://www.fie.com/www/ us_gov.html*

U.S. Government Information Servers

An impressively large index of annotated links to U.S. Government servers. The index is arranged according to subject (e.g., "Administration and Management," "Education and Humanities") rather than by government agency, a feature that makes this a unique search environment. U.S. Government Information Servers are maintained as a section of the NTIS/FedWorld WWW information server.

Access via:
www *http://www.fedworld.gov/#usgovt*

U.S. House WWW Server

The U.S. House server contains an impressive amount of information on the membership and activities of the U.S. House of Representatives. Visitors to the site will find Newt Gingrich's e-mail address (*georgia6 @hr.house.gov*), a history of the Committee on Science, Space, and Technology, and the weekly House floor schedule, among other resources.

Access via:
www http://www.house.gov/

Welcome to the White House

On October 20, 1994, the Clinton Administration continued its march into the 21st century by unveiling the new White House Web server, dubbed "Welcome to the White House: An Electronic Citizen's Handbook." The server features audio welcomes from President Clinton and Socks the cat, excellent new Web servers for FEMA and the SBA, a place to send e-mail to the Administration, Vice President Al Gore's favorite political cartoons, and a search-by-subject database of all the government information on the Internet (under the Executive Branch icon).

Access via:
www http://www.whitehouse.gov

HISTORY OF CIVILIZATION

Newsgroups:
soc.history, sci.classics

American Memory

Online archival collections presented by the Library of Congress. A search through the collection of 1,609 color photographs from the Farm Security Administration and the Office of War Information, ca. 1938–1944, turned up digital images of a 1940s' "juke joint" in Belle Glade, Florida, a Ferris wheel at the 1941 Vermont state fair, and women assembling a bomber plane at a Douglas Aircraft factory in Long Beach, California. Other notable collections include *Early Motion Pictures, 1897–1916,* and *Life History Manuscripts from the Folklore Project, WPA Federal Writers' Project, 1936–1940.*

Access via:
www http://rs6.loc.gov/amhome.html

The Art of Renaissance Science

This is that rarest of WWW sites, a complete, formatted work that takes advantage of hypertext and multimedia to present a body of knowledge. Professor Joseph Dauben (the work starts with a photo of the professor against a backdrop of the Tower of Pisa—you'll know why if you read through his introduction) takes us through a history of Galileo, astronomical, anatomical, and architectural knowledge in the Renaissance, and finally concludes with a two-part essay about the interaction of art and science. Along the way, he includes lots of images of Renaissance paintings and drawings and a few sound and animation files.

Access via:
www http://found.cs.nyu.edu/found.a/ CAT/misc/welz/setn/

A Cybrary of the Holocaust

We cannot bring back the dead—we can only remember. Compelling and comprehensive, this site lucidly conveys the horror of the Holocaust. The exhibit presents history, survivors' tales, images, and artwork to a devastating yet mindful effect. A Cybrary of the Holocaust was developed by an international team of educators and historians, and is available to teachers on CD-ROM.

Access via:
www http://www.best.com/~mddunn/ cybrary/

Information Servers at the Smithsonian Institution

A collection of links to servers maintained by the Smithsonian Institution in Washington, D.C. Among the resources available from the Information Servers at the Smithsonian Institution page are the Center for Earth and Planetary Studies, the Natural History Web, and the Smithsonian Institution Photo Server.

Access via:
www *http://www.si.edu/*

Oneida Indian Nation of New York

Resources and documents that explain the history of the Oneida Indian tribe. Most interesting is the Treaties Project, which lists, by treaty, the various false agreements they were forced to sign with the United States Government. Be sure to read the Little Known Historical Facts.

Access via:
www *http://nysernet.org/oneida/*

Soviet Archives

The Library of Congress has an exhibit of materials from the newly opened Soviet archives. There is information about life under the Soviet system, Chernobyl, the Cold War, Cuban missile crisis, and many other topics. Anyone interested in understanding recent history should know about this archive.

Access via:
www *http://sunsite.unc.edu/expo/ soviet.exhibit/soviet.archive.html*

ftp *ftp.loc.gov*; login *anonymous*; cd *pub/ exhibit.images/russian.archive.exhibit*

HOBBIES

Newsgroups:
alt.[aquaria, magic, sewing], rec.[antiques, aquaria, collecting, crafts.brewing, crafts.misc, crafts.textiles, folk-dancing, gambling, gardens, guns, juggling, models.rail-road, models.rc, models.rockets, photo, radio.amateur.misc, radio.amateur.packet, radio.amateur.policy, radio.cb, railroad, roller-coaster, woodworking]

Automobile-Related Home Pages

From Saturn Enthusiasts to Datsun's Z cars and the Honda Civic Homepage, this site lists dozens of auto-related pages, as well as links to other auto indexes and a collection of motor sports links. Acura fan David Hwang, who maintains the page, actively seeks new pages to add to the index.

Access via:
www *http://ganglion.anes.med.umich.edu/ NSX/misc/other-pages.html*

Chess

The Internet Chess Library is an excellent resource, featuring an archive of World Championship games, a collection of FAQs, ratings information, and a comprehensive list of Internet chess resources.

Access via:
www *http://caissa.onenet.net/chess/*

Cyberspace World Railroad

A rich on-line resource for train buffs, maintained by Daniel Dawdy. In addition to a collection of weekly news reports from the Association of American Railroads, there are longer stories in the Lounge Car, a huge collection of links in the Switch Track area, and a nifty collection of Railroad Clip Art.

Access via:
www *http://www.mcs.com/~dsdawdy/ cyberoad.html*

Dance Directory

A thorough and easy-to-use index to the dance resources of the Internet. The Dance Directory is maintained by Marv Vandehey, who has mined the Net for such gems as "Tango in Munich," "Ballet Terms," and "Folk Dance in South Hampshire."

Access via:
www http://www.cyberspace.com/ vandehey/dance.html

The Fishing Page

Mostly information about flyfishing, with images of fish and flies. There is the beginning of an extensive set of FAQs about flyfishing. Also contains a link to the WAIS database of the FLYFISH mailing list.

Access via:
www http://www.geo.mtu.edu/ ~jsuchosk/fish/fishpage/

ftp netsurf.geo.mtu.edu; login anonymous; cd pub/fishing
Notes: Images of fish and fishing

Games Domain

The largest games-related site on the WWW, the Games Domain features links to over 570 gaming resources, including FAQs, walkthroughs, information lists, charts, FTP sites, a huge games home-page catalog, and much more. Visitors will find everything from Doom to Darts, MUDs to Mortal Kombat, PBMs to PiD, EA to Epic. There are also links to over 1,100 games and demos for immediate download, and a magazine called GD Review that features news, previews, and reviews for the gaming community.

Access via:
www http://wcl-rs.bham.ac.uk/ GamesDomain

Ham Radio

Indexes for looking up hams by callsign, name, or area, information on newsgroups related to amateur radio, excerpts from FCC rules, FAQs, pointers to other sites, and a license exam quiz server.

Access via:
www http://www.ecst.csuchico.edu/ ~stefanis/call.html

www http://www.mit.edu:8001/callsign/

telnet callsign.cs.buffalo.edu2000

www http://www.mcc.ac.uk/OtherPages/ AmateurRadio.html

www http://www.acs.ncsu.edu/HamRadio/

www http://w3eax.umd.edu/w3eax.html

www http://www.acs.oakland.edu/ barc.html

ftp oak.oakland.edu; login anonymous; cd pub/hamradio

Internet Textiles Server

From knitting and crocheting to rug hooking, Diana Lane's Internet Textiles Server presents links to other textiles sites on the Net. The server also features two excellent local resources: a message bulletin board and a database of textiles stores worldwide.

Access via:
www http://www.textiles.org/crafts/

Joseph Wu's Origami Page

Joseph Wu's Origami Page provides some extraordinary examples of origami, the ancient art of paperfolding. Learn when and where the art originated (no, not Japan) and where the name "origami" comes from. This site would be more engaging if it had more instructions, particularly for beginners; however, it does have links to other origami sites. The page is maintained by Wu, a grad student at the University of British Columbia.

Access via:
www http://www.cs.ubc.ca/spider/jwu/origami.html

Motorcycle Links

Want to know what rides are coming up in New Jersey? What are the differences between early and later BMW R1100RSs? What to do if you're first on the scene of a motorcycle accident? The answers to these and other questions can be found through Motorcycle Links, which lists links to dozens of sites. Many are personal home pages, others are produced by motorcycle companies, and some, like the Motorcycle Safety and Survival Mailing List, are a public service. Personal pages are organized by country with separate categories for commercial links, mailing list home pages, and search engines.

Access via:
www http://jupiter.lfbs.rwth-aachen.de/~markolf/Moto_Links.html

Shortwave/Radio Catalog

A large amount of information and links to servers related to radio, including shortwave, ham, broadcast AM/FM, and satellite. Has links to home pages of broadcast stations, news organizations like the BBC and Voice of America, and technical information about operating transmitters.

Access via:
www http://itre.ncsu.edu/radio/

World Wide Quilting Page

Just about everything you ever wanted to know about quilting. The World Wide Quilting Page offers how-to advice, a history of quilting around the world, and info on where to find fabric and supplies. At the Design Board, you can see what fellow

quilters are doing; another site lists computer software for quilt designing. The site includes a FAQ page and links to other textile information on the Web.

Access via:
www http://ttsw.com/MainQuiltingPage.html

INTEREST GROUPS

Newsgroups:
soc.[answers, bi, college, couples, culture, feminism, men, motss, penpals, politics, religion, rights, roots, singles, veterans, women], talk.*

African Studies

The African Studies Web server is brought to the Net by the University of Pennsylvania. It represents a very large and growing body of information about the subject, and each country on the continent. The site includes information about the African Studies program at Penn, plus a bulletin board with extensive listings, including airfares, study-abroad programs, networks, bibliographies, events, pictures, lectures, and much more. There is also a section of pages for each African country, and a listing of Internet links to other Black/African-related resources.

Access via:
www http://www.sas.upenn.edu/African_Studies/AS.html

Alternative Sexuality/Sexual Politics Resource List

An index to documents, newsgroups, mailing lists, and Web sites related to alternative sexuality and sexual politics. Specific subject areas include body art, BDSM, polyamory, and gay and lesbian resources. The maintainer of the index invites suggestions for additions but notes, *"Sites should be resources not porn archives. Not that I have anything against smut, but that's not what this list is for."*

Access via:
www http://www.phantom.com:80/ ~reive/altsex.html

Queer Resources Directory

A good resource for the gay, lesbian, bisexual, and transgendered community. Has sections concerned with AIDS facts and treatments; resources and contact information for various support and activist groups; bibliography of publications, movies, radio, and other media of interest to the community; civil rights; and domestic partnerships. Also, has portions of the *GLAAD Newsletter* on-line.

Access via:
www http://www.qrd.org/qrd/

ftp vector.casti.com; login *anonymous;* cd *pub/QRD*

Universal Black Pages

An index of Black-related sites, from music to business, schools to professional organizations. Each category lists a collection of links. For example, under History you can find a link to a site about the Negro Leagues, which thrived until the integration of Major League Baseball after World War II. Developed by members of the Black Graduate Students Association at Georgia Institute of Technology, the goal of the Universal Black Pages is to provide a comprehensive listing of pan-African home pages at one site.

Access via:
www http://www.gatech.edu/bgsa blackpages.html

Vietnam Veterans Home Page

The Vietnam Veterans Home Page provides an interactive on-line forum for Vietnam Veterans and their families and friends to exchange information, stories, poems, songs, art, pictures, and experiences. The page pre-

sents views of the war through the eyes of those who served in it. The page also includes a listing of veterans organizations and support groups. The Vietnam Veterans Home Page is maintained by Bill McBride, a Vietnam veteran who served in the Marine Corps.

Access via:
www http://grunt.space.swri.edu/index.html

Women Homepage

A collection of links to on-line writings and resources by, about, and for women. Covers women in academics, science, technology, and health, as well as organizations for social change.

Access via:
www http://www.mit.edu:8001/people/ sorokin/women/index.html

Women in Computing

The Ada Project is a clearinghouse for information and resources relating to women in computing. Maintained by Elisabeth Freeman and Susanne Hupfer of Yale University, The Ada Project is mainly a collection of links to other on-line resources. There is an extensive bibliography of books and papers written on the topic of women and computing, a lengthy list of organizations and discussion groups, and a section devoted to short biographies. This site is under construction, but already contains a great deal of statistical and bibliographic reference material.

Access via:
www http://www.cs.yale.edu/HTML/ YALE/CS/HyPlans/tap/tap.html

INTERNET INFORMATION

All the FAQs

A FAQ is the first refuge of an Internet user. There are thousands of FAQs on as many different subjects, written by long time users who grew tired of answering the same questions over and over again. Thomas Fine has helped provide a better answer to the frequently asked question: How can I find the FAQ I need? He has created a hypertext database of FAQs and made them available through Ohio State University.

Access via:
www *http://www.cis/ohio-state.edu/ hypertext/faq/usenet/FAQ-List.html*

ftp *rtfm.mit.edu;* login *anonymous;* cd *pub/usenet/news.answers/get* index

Archie Request Form

A neat forms-based WWW gateway to a multitude of Archie servers; makes Archie really easy. Be careful not to overdo it! If an error occurs, try using another server.

Access via:
www *http://hoohoo.ncsa.uiuc.edu/ archie.html*

Clearinghouse for Subject-Oriented Internet Resource Guides

The Clearinghouse provides one-stop access to over 150 subject guides to Internet resources. Most of the guides have been compiled by academics, lending them authority that many Net guides lack. Subjects covered include Futurology, Theater, Tibetan Studies, Philosophy, and Aerospace Engineering. The big drawback here is that the majority of the guides are in ASCII text, with some, like Blake Gumprecht's "Internet Sources of Government Information," running over 100K in size. Fortunately for Web users, there is a growing collection of HTML versions.

Access via:
www *http://www.lib.umich.edu/ chhome.html*

Cryptography, PGP, and Your Privacy

Part of the WWW Virtual Library, this site contains a remarkable collection of links to information on the practical and philosophical aspects of encryption.

Access via:
www *http://draco.centerline.com:8080/ ~franl/crypto.html*

Domain Name Lookup

Resources to turn domain names like *wuarchive.wustl.edu* into a numeric address. These are particularly useful if you find yourself on a computer that doesn't participate in the domain name system.

Access via:
telnet *130.59.1.40;* login *lookup*

Inter-Network Mail Guide

A detailed description of how to address e-mail so it will get from any network to any other network. This list includes lots of small networks, special interest networks, and corporate networks, in addition to well-known networks such as MCI, CompuServe, etc. Updated monthly.

Access via:
www *http://alpha.acast.nova.edu/ cgi-bin/inmgq.pl*

ftp *csd4.csd.uwm.edu;* login *anonymous;* cd *pub; get internetwork-mail-guide*
Notes: (30K)

MBONE Information Web

Information and links related to the Virtual Internet Backbone for Multicast IP, or "MBONE." This page was created by Vinay

Kumar of Enterprise Integration Technologies, and is broken down into two primary areas: General Information and Resources.

Access via:
www http://www.eit.com/techinfo/ mbone/mbone.html

Netiquette Home Page

A concise guide to good citizenship on the Internet. The Netiquette Home Page is maintained by Arlene Rinaldi of Florida Atlantic University, and covers such topics as e-mail, FTP, TELNET, and discussion groups.

Access via:
www http://rs6000.adm.fau.edu/rinaldi/ netiquette.html

Publicly Accessible Mailing Lists

An index of e-mail lists available on the Internet, maintained by Stephanie da Silva. Among the hundreds of groups indexed here, you'll find Phonecard Collectors and Hockey-Goalies. The index can be browsed by name and subject.

Access via:
www http://www.NeoSoft.com:80/ internet/paml/

ftp rtfm.mit.edu; login *anonymous;* cd *pub/ usenet/news.answers/mail/mailing-lists*

RFCs (Requests for Comments)

RFCs are the documents that define the Internet—they talk about how it works, how to use it, and where it is going. There are over 1700 RFCs (most fairly technical), which can be distributed in either text or PostScript. The text documents have names of the form "rfcnnnn.txt"; PostScript RFCs are in files named "rfcnnnn.ps." In either case, nnnn is the number of the RFC you want.

Access via:
www http://ds.internic.net/ds/ dspg1intdoc.html

UNIX Security Information

An excellent library of links to UNIX, the Internet, and WWW security-related sites. The collection is maintained by Jessica Kelley of the National Institutes of Health Distributed Systems Section.

Access via:
www http://www.alw.nih.gov/Security/ security.html

INTERNET ORGANIZATIONS

Newsgroups:
news.[announce.important, announce.newusers, newusers.questions, answers, groups, future, lists, software.readers, sysadmin, misc]

Electronic Frontier Foundation

The EFF exists to promote existing academic and personal freedoms in the new worldwide computer society. It fights against things such as network censorship, and for such things as freely available information. Included on this server is information about the foundation (in the "EFF" directory) and the Computer and Academic Freedom Archives.

Access via:
www http://www.eff.org/

gopher gopher.eff.org

ftp ftp.eff.org; login *anonymous;* cd *pub*

Internet Society

The Internet Society is an international professional organization established to encourage the evolution, standardization, and dissemination of techniques and technologies which allow diverse information systems to communicate. The Society publishes newsletters, organizes conferences, and manages e-mail distribution lists to educate the worldwide community about the Internet. The Society sponsors the Internet Architecture Board and its Internet Engineering and Research Task Forces, and maintains liaisons with other international organizations and standards bodies as part of its effort to assist in the evolution and growth of the Internet.

Access via:
www *http://info.isoc.org/*

INTERNET SERVICES

Newsgroups:
news.[announce.important, announce.newusers, newusers.questions, answers, groups, future, lists, software.readers, sysadmin, misc]

ISDN (PacBell ISDN Page)

Up-to-date information on several aspects of ISDN technology, presented by those in the know—namely Pacific Bell and AT&T. This kind of site could easily slide towards the infomercial, and there are plenty of opportunities throughout to order your ISDN connection. However, Pac Bell realizes that an ISDN-literate public is in its best interest, and it rises to the occasion by providing plenty of concrete information.

Access via:
www *http://www.pacbell.com/isdn/isdn_home.html*

The List of Internet Service Providers

An invaluable directory of Internet service providers in the United States and around the world. Maintained by Colossus Inc., the directory can be accessed by country name or U.S. telephone area code. Clicking on an area code generates an alphabetical list of all the companies providing Internet connectivity for that area. The record for each company includes other area codes served, tele-

phone number, e-mail address, services, fees, and the URL for the company Web page. As of July 9, 1995, there were 797 service providers listed.

Access via:
www *http://thelist.com/*

LAW

Newsgroups:
misc.legal

Assault Prevention Information Network

Many of us live in an "invisible prison," limiting our choices about when and where we go. The Assault Prevention Information Network was created to help people overcome these limits with empowering techniques for self-defense and information about violent behavior. The site, compiled by Personal Power Assault Prevention Training of Austin, Texas, offers safety precautions, true self-defense success stories, strategies to protect children, and tools for evaluating a self-defense course.

Access via:
www *http://galaxy.einet.net/galaxy/Community/Safety/Assault-Prevention/apin/APINintro.html*

CopNet

An index to law enforcement sites on the Web, sponsored by the University of Wyoming Police Department. The index includes over 50 links to campus police departments, city and county police departments, and state and federal agencies. There is also a collection of "Misc Related Sites," which lists servers like the Missing Children

Network and the High Tech Crime Investigation Association.

Access via:
www *http://copnet.uwyo.edu/*

Corporation for Research and Educational Networking (CREN)

CREN is the corporation that runs BITNET. It has asked its attorneys to research their liability in using the network to access foreign countries. These files are specific to BITNET, but are probably applicable to the Internet as well.

Mail *listserv@bitnic.bitnet*; body of message should contain 3 lines:

get legal commerce
get legal gtda
get legal counsel

Criminal Justice Page

An impressive collection of links to criminal justice sites on the Net, from O.J. Central to the U.S. Constitution. The Criminal Justice Page is maintained by Cecil Greek of the Criminology Department of the University of South Florida.

Access via:
www *http://www.stpt.usf.edu/~greek/cj.html*

Supreme Court Rulings

Project Hermes makes the U.S. Supreme Court's opinions and rulings publicly available via the Internet. The information is posted worldwide electronically within 15 minutes of the Court's announcement in Washington, D.C. Opinions and decisions from the 1989 term to the present are available.

Hypertexted decisions (from 1991 onward) are prepared by the Legal Information Institute of Cornell Law School.

The original versions of the Supreme Court data are made available by a noncommercial, nonprofit consortium composed of Case Western Reserve University (CWRU), EDUCOM, and the National Public Telecomputing Network (NPTN). The files are organized by docket number, and are available in ASCII, ATEX, WordPerfect, and XYWrite formats.

Access via:
www *http://www.law.cornell.edu/supct/*

www *http://www.law.cornell.edu/syllabi*

ftp *ftp.cwru.edu;* login *anonymous;* cd *hermes*

U.S. Constitution

The text of the Constitution, in full or divided by Article and Amendment.

Access via:
www *http://www.law.cornell.edu/constitution/constitution.overview.html*

gopher
info.umd.edu/Educational_Resources/Academic_Resources/United_States/United_States/History/HistoricalDocuments/Constitution

West's Legal Directory

West's Legal Directory is a "comprehensive directory of law firms, government offices, corporate law offices, and lawyers" published by West Publishing Company of Eagan, Minnesota. A search on the small city of Petaluma (California) yielded over 50 listings, so their claim to comprehensiveness seems plausible. Searches can be run on any keyword or combination of keywords—read the "search methods" file for more information.

Access via:
www *http://www.westpub.com/WLDInfo/WLD.html*

LITERATURE

Newsgroups:
rec.arts. [books, sf, theatre, poems, prose]

Alex: A Catalogue of Electronic Texts on the Internet

The Internet has been called the most important innovation since the Gutenberg Press. Backing up this claim is Hunter Monroe's Alex, a combination WWW/gopher site that lists almost 1,800 on-line books, most of which are old enough to escape copyright restrictions. You can browse by author, subject, title, date, or language. Subjects range from fiction to philosophy; authors from Dickens to the Dalai Lama.

Access via:
www http://www.lib.ncsu.edu/stacks/ alex-index.html

British Poetry 1780–1910

An archive of poems from Coleridge, Keats, Shelley, Wilde, and other greats. This collection is hosted by the University of Virginia's Electronic Text Center.

Access via:
www http://www.lib.virginia.edu/etext/ britpo/britpo.html

Complete Works of William Shakespeare

The web of our life is of a mingled yarn, good and ill together: our virtues would be proud, if our faults whipped them not; and our crimes would despair, if they were not cherished by our virtues. — All's Well That Ends Well.

An on-line collection of Shakespeare's plays and poetry created by Jeremy Hylton, a graduate student with the Library 2000 project at MIT. Aside from allowing visitors to browse through Shakespeare's works, the site features a keyword search tool that lets users search for words or phrases in the database (like "web," for example). There's also a hypertext glossary built into each work.

Access via:
www http://the-tech.mit.edu/Shakespeare/ works.html

ftp sunsite.unc.edu; login *anonymous;* cd *pub/docs/books/shakespeare*

Electronic Poetry Center

A collection of links to Internet poetry resources, compiled by Kenneth Sherwood and Loss Glazier of the University of Buffalo. Local resources include the RIF/T poetry journal.

Access via:
www http://wings.buffalo.edu/epc

Elements of Style

The original 1918 edition of William Strunk's classic guide to effective writing, brought to the Web by Columbia University's Project Bartleby. Strunk focuses on the basics; the heart of the book consists of the chapters "Elementary Rules of Usage" and "Elementary Principles of Composition."

Access via:
www http://www.columbia.edu/~svl2/ strunk/

Internet Wiretap Book Collection

A rather large collection of electronic texts, including religious texts, fiction, nonfiction, and electronic texts available from other sources.

Access via:
gopher wiretap.spies.com/ Wiretap Online Library

Indexes of On-line Books

Hypertext indexes of books available on-line, from Carnegie-Mellon University.

Access via:
*www http://www.cs.cmu.edu/Web/
bookauthors.html*

*www http://www.cs.cmu.edu/Web/
booktitles.html*

Indigenous Peoples' Literature

A site that brings to life the traditions and philosophies of native peoples through stories, poetry, prayers, and quotations of tribal leaders. Indigenous Peoples' Literature is edited by computer programmer Glenn H. Welker of Virginia, who also maintains the Indigenous Peoples of Mexico Home Page.

Access via:
*www
http://kuhttp.cc.ukans.edu/~marc/natlit/
natlit.html*

Leaves of Grass by Walt Whitman

Project Bartleby's elegant on-line collection of the works of American poet Walt Whitman (1819-1892). Whitman's poems speak of the joys of being alive in a world of wonders. The collection can be accessed via the original table of contents or using the alphabetical or first-line indices. A set of photos of Whitman over the years can be found by selecting the Illustrations link.

Access via:
*www http://www.columbia.edu/~svl2/
whitman/*

Letters from an Iowa Soldier in the Civil War

An affecting and unusual resource, this site maintains a collection of letters written by Newton Scott, a private in the 36th Infantry, Iowa Volunteers, during the Civil War.

During the three years he served, Scott wrote letters to his sweetheart and parents. Here the letters are transcribed as written, without changes to the spelling or punctuation. Also included are Scott's service record, his obituary, and links to other Civil War information on the Net. This simple site is well designed and adds a very personal note to the many Civil War resources already available. Congratulations to William Scott Proudfoot, a librarian at West Valley College in Saratoga, California, who says he developed the project just "to see if I could do it!"

Access via:
*www http://www.ucsc.edu/
civil-war-letters/home.html*

Mark Twain Resources on the World Wide Web

"Get your facts first, and then you can distort them as much as you please." Thus spake Mark Twain. If you can't get enough Twainisms, you might enjoy a visit to this group of Mark Twain Resources on the Web, from Jim Zwick at Syracuse University. It's all here, from a large collection of Samuel Clemens' texts (including the entire *Adventures of Huckleberry Finn*) to an analysis of his character's appearance on "Star Trek: The Next Generation," and links to other Twain resources. You've got to wonder what Twain would have written about the Internet....

Access via:
*www http://web.syr.edu/~fjzwick/
twainwww.html*

Online Book Initiative

Electronic texts by many authors, from Emily Bronte to Karl Marx, along with electronic journals, excerpts from newsgroups, and pointers to other sources of electronic texts and other Internet resources. A major resource for literature—and all texts are freely redistributable.

Access via:

gopher gopher.std.com/obi/

ftp ftp.std.com; login *anonymous*; cd *obi*

Project Gutenberg

Project Gutenberg is an ambitious nonprofit and volunteer effort to get as much literature as possible into machine-readable form. Their holdings include the works of Shakespeare, lots of Lewis Carroll, Moby Dick, and a rapidly growing number of classic texts, speeches, and reference materials.

Access via:

www http://jg.cso.uiuc.edu/pg_home.html

gopher gopher.tc.umn.edu /Libraries/ Electronic_Books

ftp uiarchive.cso.uiuc.edu; login *anonymous*; cd /pub/etext/gutenberg

Science Fiction Resource Guide

From the Philip K. Dick FAQ to William Gibson's Alien 3 script, this is a gigantic collection of links to science fiction resources on the Net. The site is maintained by Chaz Baden.

Access via:

www http://sundry.hsc.usc.edu/hazel/ www/sfrg/sf-resource.guide.html

Society of Professional Journalists

SPJ's site includes an on-line version of *Quill* (SPJ's monthly magazine), a code of journalistic ethics, and a list of resources on Freedom of Information issues. The site also includes pointers to journalism publications and news media on-line.

Access via:

www http://town.hall.org/places/spj/ index.html

Writers' Resources On The Web

Debbie Ridpath Ohi's collection of links for writers. Subject areas covered include General Writing Resources, Style Guidelines, Writing for Children, Journalism, and Technical Writing.

Access via:

www http://www.interlog.com/~ohi/www/ writesource.html

MATHEMATICS

Newsgroups:
sci. [math, math.num-analysis, math.stat, math.symbolic, math.research], k12.ed.math

e-MATH

e-MATH is an Internet node that provides mathematicians with an expanding list of services that can be accessed electronically. e-MATH is intended as an electronic clearinghouse for timely research information in the mathematical sciences. Some of the current services are the American Mathematical Society membership database, employment opportunities, publication ordering, author lists, meeting notices, and a directory of journals and newsletters.

Access via:

www http://e-math.ams.org/

telnet e-math.ams.com; login *e-math*

GAMS (Guide to Available Mathematical Software)

The GAMS project of the National Institute of Standards and Technology studies techniques to provide scientists and engineers with improved access to reusable computer software, which is available to them for use in mathematical modeling and statistical analysis. One of the products of this work is an on-line cross-index of available mathematical software. This system also operates as a virtual software repository; that is, it provides centralized access to such items as abstracts, documentation, and source code of software modules that it catalogs. However, rather than operate a physical repository of its own, GAMS provides transparent access to multiple repositories operated by others. *(Review contributed by Talvinder Chawla of Florida State University.)*

Access via:
www http://gams.nist.gov/

The Geometry Center

Fascinating for both the mathematically inclined and the mathematically inept, this site is a gathering of geometry information funded by the National Science Foundation and located at the University of Minnesota. The Center's mission is to stimulate research in geometry and promote the development of computer tools for visualizing all those squares and parallelograms. This well-constructed site lists seminars, documents and images, geometry software, and a tag-along section for general Web navigation. A quick peek at the design-rich Geometry Picture Archive confirmed that there have been big-time changes in geometry lately—this stuff looks interesting!

Access via:
www http://www.geom.umn.edu/ welcome.html

History of Mathematics Archive

A nifty collection of one-page biographies on over 550 mathematicians, from Thales to Mandelbrot. The collection is well organized; biographies are accessible both chronologically and alphabetically. A short biographies index and a birthplace map are also available. The History of Mathematics Archive comes to the Net care of John O'Connor and

Edmund F. Robertson of the University of St. Andrews, Scotland.

Access via:
www http://www-groups.dcs.st-and.ac.uk/ ~history/

Mathematics Information Servers

A large collection of links to mathematics sites on the Net, maintained at Penn State University.

Access via:
www http://www.math.psu.edu/ OtherMath.html

MEDICINE

Newsgroups:
sci.med, sci.med.
[aids, dentistry, physics, pharmacy, nutrition, occupational, psychobiology, telemedicine]

Aesclepian Chronicles

Aesclepian Chronicles is a holistic medicine journal published monthly by the Synergistic Medicine Center of Chapel Hill, North Carolina. Articles are written for a general audience and tend to focus on the spiritual and psychological side of health and healing.

Access via:
www http://www.forthrt.com/~chronicl/ homepage.html

AL-ANON and ALATEEN

This site is a straightforward presentation of information from the AL-ANON and ALA-TEEN organizations, which are devoted to helping families and friends of alcoholics. The 12 steps and 12 traditions of Al-ANON are listed, as are the telephone numbers and addresses for AL-ANON offices all around the world. Probably the most useful document offered on this site is the 20-question questionnaire entitled "Are You Troubled by Someone's Drinking?," which is designed to help people decide if they need the services of AL-ANON.

Access via:
www http://solar.rtd.utk.edu/~al-anon/

The Arc (Mental Retardation)

This site maintains a compendium of resources and information for people with mental retardation and those concerned about them. The Arc, based in Arlington, Texas, publishes fact sheets on key topics, explains how to be an effective legislative advocate, and discusses the Americans with Disabilities Act. The Q&A page offers options for employment, education, and community living. The "Report Card to the Nation" evaluates inclusion of people with mental retardation in mainstream housing and workplaces.

Access via:
www http://fohnix.metronet.com/~thearc/ welcome.html

Blind Links

A large collection of links to Internet sites related to blindness, compiled by Ron Marriage for his Play Pen. Among the resources listed in the collection are Raised Dot Computing, the Interactive ASL & Braille Guide, and the American Foundation for the Blind server.

Access via:
www http://dialin.ind.net/~rmarriag/ rblind.html

Breast Cancer Information Clearinghouse

A comprehensive server containing practical information about breast cancer, including questions and answers about breast cancer, a breast self-exam (be patient; large graphics take a long time to load), listings of support groups in the United States, and sources for medical information. This site also maintains a summary of current events related to breast cancer, the White House position on breast cancer, and links to other cancer-related Internet resources.

Access via:
www http://nysernet.org/breast/ Default.html

gopher nysernet.org /Special: Breast Cancer

CancerGuide

I am convinced that researching my options has been an important factor in my survival. Naturally then, I am a strong advocate of patients doing their own research, including delving into the most recent technical literature on their disease. Helping you do that is what CancerGuide is all about. — Steve Dunn, on the pros of researching your cancer.

A guide for cancer patients who want to understand more about the disease and their treatment options. The author is a cancer survivor himself.

Access via:
www http://bcn.boulder.co.us/health/ cancer/canguide.html

CancerNet (NCI International Cancer Information Center)

The National Cancer Institute's Gopher and WWW server, with information for both physicians and patients.

Access via:
www http://biomed.nus.sg/Cancer/ welcome.html

gopher biomed.nus.sg / NUS-NCI-CancerNet/

Center for Food Safety and Applied Nutrition

Some people are also convinced that in children, sweets are a major culprit in causing hyperactivity and other behavior and cognitive (learning) problems. Recent evidence suggests that it's unlikely. — from Candy: How Sweet It Is!

The Center for Food Safety and Applied Nutrition (CFSAN) is a department of the FDA whose mission is "to promote and protect the public health and economic interest by ensuring that the food supply is safe, nutritious, wholesome, and honest, and that cosmetics are safe and properly labeled." The CFSAN WWW site provides access to a variety of FDA publications, covering such areas as food additives, biotechnology, food labeling, and foodborne illnesses.

Access via:
www http://vm.cfsan.fda.gov/list.html

Computer Related Repetitive Strain Injury

"Use a light touch when typing. Don't tightly squeeze the mouse. Take frequent breaks." These are among the tips found at this site for avoiding repetitive strain injury, which also offers diagrams of proper typing position and descriptions of the first warning signs of injuries. The author of the page is Paul Marxhausen, an engineering electronics technician who suffers from RSI.

Access via:
www http://engr-www.unl.edu/ee/ eeshop/rsi.html

Conversational Hypertext (via telnet)

The CHAT natural language information system. Be sure to check out T.E. Whalen's sex education program "Ask the Sexpert," winner of the 1994 Loebner Prize for the most human-like natural language program.

Access via:
telnet debra.doc.ca; port 3000

Deaf World Web

Deaf and hearing people alike can click into the world of the deaf at this expanding site. Deaf World Web has three main categories: Culture, Youths, and References. Culture includes articles, sports, quotations, history, and poems. The References area includes listings for organizations, arts, life, technology, and many other categories. The Youth section had only one listing at the time of this review. A survey in Deaf World shows deaf people prefer overwhelmingly the term "deaf" to "hearing impaired" or "hard of hearing."

Access via:
www http://deafworldweb.org/deafworld/

Depression FAQ

The Depression FAQ is a comprehensive list of resources for those combating depression. It includes typical symptoms, causes, types of depression, support groups, and other resources (including electronic ones), and ways to help yourself. There are also more than a dozen links for information on medication. Users can download the entire alt.support.depression FAQ as an ASCII file.

Access via:
www http://avocado.pc.helsinki.fi/ ~janne/asdfaq

Disability Resources on the Internet

Disability Resources on the Internet is an index compiled by Evan Kemp Associates, a company based in Washington, D.C. The site is well organized, with categories such as Disability Related Legal Resources and Health and Medicine Resources.

Access via:
www http://disability.com/cool.html

Facts for Families

Presented by the American Academy of Child and Adolescent Psychiatry, Facts for Families is a collection of 51 fact sheets covering the mental health issues faced by children and teens today. Among the topics covered in the collection are children and divorce, teenagers with eating disorders, and responding to child sexual abuse. Each fact sheet is written in an even and accessible style that explains the nature of each malady, its likely causes, and recommendations for treatment. Several fact sheets have been translated into Spanish.

Access via:
www http://www.psych.med.umich.edu/ web/aacap/factsFam/

HabitSmart

HabitSmart is a Web site created by the California-based outpatient facility of the same name. The Web site features thoughtful articles on a variety of issues related to substance abuse. Titles include "Coping with Addiction," "Kids Learn to Drink," "Moderation Training," and "Smoking Reduction."

Access via:
www http://www.cts.com/~habtsmrt/

Health Information Gopher

A collection of health information files from the University of Illinois' McKinley Health Center. Subjects covered include stress, sexuality, women's health, medications, and nutrition.

Access via:
gopher gopher.uiuc.edu /UI Campus Info/Campus Services/Health Services

Just Say Yes: Sex Ed for Teens

A healthy, non-judgmental look at sex from the Coalition for Positive Sexuality. Originally published in pamphlet form for Chicago high school students, Just Say Yes covers sex myths, respect, safe sex, birth control, STDs, and pregnancy.

Access via:
www http://www.webcom.com/ ~cps/jsy/jsy.html

International Food Information Council (IFIC)

According to the IFIC, this site is "the source on food-related issues." These people don't mess around; the site is packed with information about health and nutrition, most of it in the form of the on-line versions of IFIC pamphlets. The pamphlets are organized according to audience (parents, educators, consumers, etc.), and cover such subjects as caffeine, food coloring, biotechnology, pregnancy, hyperactivity, and aspartame.

Access via:
www http://ificinfo.health.org/

The Medicare and Medicaid Agency

Another U.S. governmental agency is now on-line. Although the documents here are often frustratingly dense, this is a good place to learn about the more intricate aspects of Medicare and Medicaid. Visitors to the Medicare and Medicaid site will find such resources as Healthcare Financing News, the

Medicare Q&A for 85 common questions, and a survey of research and demonstration initiatives.

Access via:
www *http://www.ssa.gov/hcfa/ hcfahp2.html*

Midwifery, Pregnancy, and Birth Related Information

If you, or someone you know, is considering homebirth or using a midwife to assist in a birth, this page could prove to be a valuable resource. Donna Dolezal Zelzer, who put this page together, has done a thoughtful job of compiling information on homebirth, midwives (including a history of midwifery), and other related topics, including breastfeeding, nutrition, and high-risk pregnancies.

Access via:
www *http://www.efn.org/~djz/birth/ birthindex.html*

MS Direct: Multiple Sclerosis Support

Pointers to Multiple Sclerosis resources on the Internet, compiled by Dean Sporleder. In his introduction to the page, Mr. Sporleder writes, "We can all use different forms of information and hopefully from that info some support. Thanks, and I hope this helps others too..."

Access via:
www *http://www.aquila.com/ dean.sporleder/ms_home/*

National Institute of Allergy and Infectious Diseases

Notable for its AIDS directory, this site also includes a lot of administrative information.

Access via:
gopher *gopher.niaid.nih.gov*

National Institutes of Health (NIH)

Information on and links to biomedical data, activities and grants of the NIH, and the NIH Library.

Access via:
www *http://www.nih.gov/*

gopher *gopher.nih.gov*

National Library of Medicine (NLM)

The NLM holds over 4.5 million records, including books, journals, reports, manuscripts, and audio-visual items, and offers on-line information on a variety of medical topics. HyperDOC, the Web server, is a well-organized collection of NLM and National Institutes of Health information, including a new exhibit of over 60,000 images of prints and photographs from the history of medicine.

Access via:
www *http://www.nlm.nih.gov/*

gopher *gopher.nlm.nih.gov*

ftp *ftp.nlm.nih.gov;* login *anonymous*

NicNet (Smoking)

An index ("NicNet Resources") to the smoking resources on the Net, maintained by the Arizona Program for Nicotine & Tobacco Research. Among sites in the index are the University of Pennsylvania's collection of smoking, tobacco, and cancer documents and a U.S. Department of Health and Human Services pamphlet called *Check Your Smoking I.Q.* There's also a nifty set of links to general and health sciences indexes with material on smoking.

Access via:
www *http://www.medlib.arizona.edu/ ~pubhlth/tobac.html*

Parkinson's Web

A vast collection of information resources for sufferers of Parkinson's disease and their friends and family. Subjects covered include treatment options, support groups, and coping with the disease. Parkinson's Web is hosted by Massachusetts General Hospital's Department of Neurology.

Access via:
www http://neuro-chief-e.mgh.harvard.edu/ parkinsonsweb/Main/PDmain.html

Points of Pediatric Interest

An index of links for pediatric physicians as well as for parents of young children. Categories include hospitals, parenting resources, and "fun stuff" on the Web for kids.

Access via:
www http://musom.mu.wvnet.edu/ 0u:/peds/poi.html

World Health Organization

A WWW service offering information on the WHO's major health programs, as well as press releases, e-mail/phone contacts, and general information about the organization.

Access via:
www http://www.who.ch

gopher gopher.who.ch

ftp ftp.who.ch; login *anonymous*

MOVIES

Newsgroups:
rec.arts. [animation, cinema, movies]

Internet Movie Database

A fantastic site that features information on thousands of movies. All cast and production information is hypertext linked, meaning you

can identify a director you like and quickly discover the names of his or her other films. Most films are also accompanied by a rating (on a scale of 1 to 10), created by averaging the votes of users of the site. (Formerly known as the Cardiff Movie Database.)

Access via:
www http://www.cm.cf.ac.uk/Movies/

Movie Studio Promotional Sites

Video previews, photos, and press kits are among the entertaining resources visitors will find at the movie studio sites listed below.

Access via:
www http://www.disney.com/
Notes: Buena Vista MoviePlex—Hollywood Pictures, Walt Disney Pictures, Touchstone Pictures

www http://www.mca.com/index.html
Notes: MCA/Universal Cyberwalk

www http://www.mgmua.com
Notes: MGM and United Artists

www http://cybertimes.com/NewLine/ Welcome.html
Notes: New Line Cinema

www http://www.spe.sony.com/Pictures/ SonyMovies/index.html
Notes: Sony Pictures

www http://www.paramount.com/
Notes: Paramount Pictures

www http://www2.interpath.net/ fineline/
Notes: Fine Line Features

Star Wars Home Page

It's been more than a decade since the last Star Wars movie, but you can still be with the Force. The newly revised, comprehensive Star Wars home page offers links to news, multimedia files, trivia, and information about current Star Wars events. Link to an interview with George Lucas or find out about plans for an upcoming trilogy of prequels to the originals. This page is maintained by Jason Ruspini, a student at the University of Pennsylvania.

Access via:
www http://stwing.resnet.upenn.edu:8001/ ~jruspini/starwars.html

MUSIC

Newsgroups:
alt.[emusic, exotic-music], k12.ed.music, rec.music.[afro-latin, a-cappela, beatle, bluenote, cd, celtic, christian, classical, compose, country, dementia, dylan, early, folk, funky.gaffa, gdead, indian, industrial, info, makers, marketplace, misc, newage, reggae, reviews, synth, video]

The Blue Highway

From Robert Johnson to John Lee Hooker, The Blue Highway leads you on a stroll through the lives and music of the blues masters. Over 20 great musicians are profiled in these pages, and although the profiles are brief, they are well written and complemented by pictures and sound samples (.WAV format). The Blue Highway was created by Curtis Hewston, who has also put together a Blues News area and a collection of links to other blues sites on the Net.

Access via:
www http://www.magicnet.net/~curtis/

Concert Schedules from POLLSTAR

Where is Pearl Jam playing this summer? Who's booked for your local theater? Who's coming to Akron this fall? Find out from POLLSTAR, a vast database of concert schedules. Searches can be run for bands, venues, and cities; select "Search Tour Database" from the home page to begin a query. Other services available at the POLLSTAR site include a list of the ten most-requested tour schedules and a selection of tour gossip.

Access via:
www http://www.pollstar.com/

Country Connection

Country music has long been under-represented on the Web, so it's great to see a hefty site like this. Hacked together by Michael Blanche, the site's chief strength is in its Artists Listings which, as of July 1995, contained information on 110 different artists. Some artist pages only had a smattering of lyrics or fan club information, others featured photos and sound files. Another nice resource at Country Connection is the collection of links to other country music sites on the Web, including Nashville On-line, Wayne's Country Music Pages, and Black Boot Records.

Access via:
www http://metro.turnpike.net/C/country/ index.html

Elvis Home Page

Andrea Berman's Elvis home page brings together images of Graceland, classic photos of Elvis, sound clips from his music, and even a link to a hysterical Ouiji board seance. This server leaves the fertile ground of posthumous Elvis sightings untouched, but the home page states that its intention is to honor Elvis's musical and cultural legacy, not to belittle or defame him. So why quibble? We love it.

Access via:
www http://sunsite.unc.edu/elvis/ elvishom.html

FolkBook

FolkBook offers a rich collection of information about folk music. Fans can find bios, discographies, and tour information for artists like the Indigo Girls and Mary Chapin Carpenter. Aspiring folk musicians will find links to the singer-songwriters' sites on the Net. FolkBook also has a comprehensive list of links to other music sites on the Web. Overall, this is a great place for the folka-holic to browse through: tons of information and a lot of fun.

Access via:
www *http://web.cgrg.ohio-state.edu:80/ folkbook/*

Grateful Dead Home Page

This Web server is for the Deadhead in all of us. Maintained by Mark Leone, this site is not an officially licensed Grateful Dead project; it's just out there for anyone "playin' in the heart of gold band." Leone maintains a lot of Jerry Garcia memorials, and a FAQ that answers everything from "How to do mail order?" to "How did Jerry lose his finger?" It's definitely worth adding to any Deadhead's hotlist.

Access via:
www *http://www.cs.cmu.edu/~mleone/ dead.html*

The Jazz Web

The complete Internet jazz resource. Visitors will find discographies, FAQs, and links to over 15 other jazz sites on the Net. This Web site is maintained by the staff of WNUR-FM of Evanston, Illinois.

Access via:
www *http://www.acns.nwu.edu/jazz/*

Music Resources on the Internet

This mind-boggling site contains links to every music site imaginable (and a few you would-n't have imagined). Meticulously maintained by some very cool people at the Indiana University Music Library, Music Resources on the Internet contains links to everything from the Pearl Jam home page to the Fractal Music Project. Web, Gopher, artist-specific, local music, and record label sites: they're all here. Set aside a few hours and check it out.

Access via:
www *http://www.music.indiana.edu/misc/ music_resources.html*

NEWS AND MAGAZINES

Business Update

A daily summary of business news presented by Reuters NewMedia and Internet MCI. Topics covered include investment markets, telecommunications, federal regulation, and economic news.

Access via:
www *http://www.fyionline.com/infoMCI/ update/BUSINESS-MCI.html*

Condé Nast Traveler Online

Condé Nast's new Web site is a welcome addition to the growing number of publications that are appearing on-line. Unlike many of them, CNT has embraced the Web in a creative and expansive way that goes beyond their traditional magazine offerings. They aren't simply regurgitating what they produce in print. At this site you'll find a huge number of selections and departments, some of which are interactive, and others that change daily. If you get tired of reading the articles and updates, there are forums and contests as well. Check it out.

Access via:
www *http://www.cntraveler.com/*

Electronic Newsstand

The Electronic Newsstand is a free service that publishes the full text of recent magazine and journal articles, among other things. How is this possible? Well, magazine publishers hope that Newsstand readers will become hooked on their publications and place a snail-mail subscription order. Among the magazines available from the Electronic Newsstand are *BusinessWeek, Computer Graphics World, The Economist, The Sporting News,* and *Telecommunications Week.*

Access via:
www *http://www.enews.com/*

The Financial Times

This venerable international newspaper goes on-line with a daily summary of top news stories as well as articles on the Americas, Europe, and the Asia/Pacific region. A 30-minute-delayed list of world stock market indices provides a nice complement to FT's solid reporting.

Access via:
www *http://www.ft.com/*

The Gate

The on-line service of the big San Francisco newspapers, the *Chronicle* and the *Examiner.* The Gate features a daily on-line edition of each paper, with news, sports, and weather. Visitors will find plenty of interesting information to keep them busy.

Access via:
www *http://sfgate.com/*

HotWired

HotWired is *Wired Magazine*'s home on the Internet. Although it takes a few minutes to register and get your bearings, HotWired is full of thought-provoking articles and engaging interactive resources. HotWired is also extremely image-intensive; users with dial-up Internet connections or non-graphic browsers may become bored or frustrated.

Access via:
www *http://www.hotwired.com*

The Irish Times on the Web

World Wide Web home of Dublin's *Irish Times.* The site presents news in six areas: Front, Home News, Sport, Opinion, Letters, and Finance. Updates appear each weekday. Articles are by *Times* correspondents and tend to be the equivalent of one or two text pages in length.

Access via:
www *http://www.irish-times.ie/ cgi-bin/IThome*

Mother Jones Magazine

Still carrying the torch of "progressive" politics, but now in hypertext.

Access via:
www *http://www.mojones.com/ motherjones.html*

gopher *gopher.mojones.com*

ftp *ftp.mojones.com;* login *anonymous*

The NandO Times

A great source for U.S. and international news. Most articles come from either Reuters or the Associated Press, with access to A.P. articles requiring a free registration. Major sections of the NandO Times include World, Nation, Sports, Politics, Business, and Entertainment. Each section features a news summary and links to longer stories. Published by the New Media Division of the News & Observer Publishing Co. in Raleigh, N.C.

Access via:
www *http://www2.nando.net/nt/nando.cgi*

NewsLink

NewsLink, Inc. has created excellent indexes to newspaper, magazine, and radio and TV station sites on the Web. Links to the indexes are found at the top of NewsLink's home page.

Access via:
www http://www.newslink.org/menu.html

NewsLink: Non-U.S. Newspapers

A handy index to selected non-U.S. on-line newspapers, compiled by NewsLink Associates, a research and consulting firm studying electronic publishing. Papers range from *De Financieel-Economische Tijd* in Antwerp, Belgium, to *El Periodico* in Barcelona, Spain.

Access via:
www http://www.newslink.org/nonus.html

Pathfinder from Time Warner

Pathfinder is home on the Net for the Time Warner Inc. publishing empire. Visitors to Pathfinder will find scores of articles and reviews from *LIFE, Sports Illustrated, Money, People, Time magazine, Entertainment Weekly,* and *Vibe,* as well as special features like daily news reports, chat bulletin boards, and "The Virtual Garden," an extensive collection of gardening information. The Pathfinder interface is attractive and easy to use, although browsing can be frustrating due to the time it takes to load its large image maps. Overall, this is an excellent site, well worth a visit. It's so good, in fact, that sometime soon you'll probably have to start paying to get it.

Access via:
www http://www.timeinc.com/pathfinder/

TechWeb

CMP Publications' TechWeb shows what can be accomplished when publishers go whole hog in their Internet publishing efforts. CMP publishes computer and on-line magazines like Communications Week, Information Week, and NetGuide. TechWeb presents selected articles from each publication, but its shining star is the full-text searching capability. The WAIS search engine lets you select any single publication or all of them, specify a range of dates, and search for specific titles, authors, sections, and columns. After your initial search, you can widen your inquiry by adding all of the words in one or more articles to your request. While the searching side is impressive, the Web front-end could use some design work; particularly irritating is the presence of graphics on the hit list document, which makes the user wait unnecessarily to see the results.

Access via:
www http://techweb.cmp.com/techweb/default.html

TimesFax: From the Pages of the New York Times

A daily eight-page digest of the *New York Times,* including highlights from different sections and a complete crossword puzzle. To view the digest, however, you'll first need to register and download Adobe Acrobat Reader.

Access via:
www http://nytimesfax.com/

OCEANOGRAPHY

Newsgroups:
sci.environment, sci.geo.oceanography

Ocean Information Center (OCEANIC)

The Ocean Information Center Bulletin Board is provided by the University of Delaware. The site features technical and organization-

al material about various oceanographic experiments, field trials, and meetings.

Access via:
www http://www.cms.udel.edu/

gopher gopher.cms.udel.edu

Ocean Planet

A fascinating, if time-consuming, tour. Presented by the Smithsonian Institution, Ocean Planet uses images, text, and walk-through environments to educate people about the environmental issues affecting the world's oceans. While intriguing, the viewer has to navigate through many links, which can be tedious. This is a nice presentation, but no substitute for the real exhibit.

Access via:
www http://seawifs.gsfc.nasa.gov/ ocean_planet.html

National Marine Fisheries Service

From the U.S. National Marine Fisheries Service comes a great server chock full of marine (ocean, not military) data. Coverage includes domestic and international marine fisheries programs, reports, graphics, sea temperature maps, audio clips of whale songs, assorted marine videos, and the obligatory links to related on-line information. This is a well-designed server, with an active What's New page and regular updates.

Access via:
www http://kingfish.ssp.nmfs.gov/home-page.html

National Oceanographic Data Center (NODC)

The NODC's global holdings of physical, chemical, and biological oceanographic data currently total over 60 gigabytes, making it the world's largest publicly available ocean data archive. This server provides access to those holdings, as well as other products and services.

Access via:
www http://www.nodc.noaa.gov/

gopher gopher.nodc.noaa.gov

Woods Hole Oceanographic Institution

No pictures of humpbacks breaching or sea otters swimming here. However, for the more scientifically minded, especially those interested in oceanography, this site provides extremely detailed information on myriad activities, projects, and programs at WHOI. Links to other oceanographic resources are included as well.

Access via:
www http://www.whoi.edu/index.html

PALEONTOLOGY

Newsgroups:
sci.archaeology

The Field Museum of Natural History

A tour through the prehistoric world of dinosaurs. With text and images, the Field Museum of Natural History offers a taste of its "Life Over Time" exhibit. Find out where dinosaurs lived, what they ate, and how they moved.

Access via:
www http://www.bvis.uic.edu/museum/ Dna_To_Dinosaurs.html

Honolulu Community College Dinosaur Exhibit

A fun, well-designed tour of the permanent dinosaur exhibit at Honolulu Community

College, complete with photographs, illustrations, movies, and even audio narration. The exhibits themselves are actually replicas from the originals at the American Museum of Natural History in New York City.

Access via:
www http://www.hcc.hawaii.edu/dinos/dinos.1.html

The Paleontology Server

The University of California Museum of Paleontology server is an interactive natural history museum available over the Internet. This museum without walls is well organized and makes interesting use of large graphics. You can learn about phylogeny, the "Tree of Life," or examine photographs of Great White Sharks off the California coast, which proves that paleontologists study living things as well as fossils.

Access via:
www http://ucmp1.berkeley.edu/welcome.html

www http://sunsite.unc.edu/expo/paleo.exhibit/paleo.html
Notes: EXPO, Fossil Life only

PETS

Newsgroups:
rec.pets, rec.pets. [birds, cats, dogs, herp]

Cat Fanciers' Home Page

Maintained with care by two ailurophiles (that's cat lovers!), Marie Lamb and Orca Starbuck, this site is packed with feline lore. There are many FAQs on exotic breeds—from Ragdolls (bred from a female Persian and male Birman) to Chartreux (known as the "blue cats of France"). You'll find more practical information here, too, on such subjects as feline leukemia virus and the overpopulation crisis. There are links to veterinary resources as well as to cat home pages; this is a site any cat lover should check out.

Access via:
www http://www.ai.mit.edu/fanciers/fanciers.html

Dog Homepage

Bryan Schumacher's home base for dog lovers. Visitors can search for Net-based information on specific breeds, peruse a collection of dog FAQs, and link to Usenet groups and other doggy sites on the Web.

Access via:
www http://www.sdsmt.edu/other/dogs/dogs.html

The Electronic Zoo

We first reviewed the Electronic Zoo back when it was a fledgling gopher site. Times have changed! Now on the Web, this site for animal lovers (compiled and maintained by veterinarian/computer nut Ken Boschert) is truly without peer. From amphibians to ruminants, catfish farming to Ferret Central, the Electronic Zoo has easy-to-navigate, comprehensive collections of Internet animal resources, grouped both by subject (animals, veterinary) and resource type (mailing lists, gopher and web sites). Sponsored by NetVet, the Zoo is a well-maintained site with a search facility, what's new list, and continual updates.

Access via:
www http://netvet.wustl.edu/e-zoo.html

FINS: Fish Information Service

An archive of information about aquariums, including general information about fish-keeping, discussion archives, images, and aquarium plans.

Access via:
www http://www.actwin.com/fish/

NetVet World Wide Web Server

NetVet Veterinary Resources is a comprehensive collection of on-line veterinary information. Among its offerings are the Electronic Zoo, the Missouri Association for Agriculture, Biomedical Research Education, the Animal Welfare Information Center, and American Academy of Veterinary Informatics. There are also general pointers to major Internet resources in veterinary medicine, agriculture, biology, environment and ecology, and medicine, as well as animal-related files, databases, FTP archive sites, and electronic publications.

Access via:
www http://netvet.wustl.edu/vet.html

gopher netvet.wustl.edu /NetVet Gopher/

PHILOSOPHY

Newsgroups:
sci.philosophy

American Philosophical Association

Serious information on serious subjects. Contains addresses, information on upcoming events, grants, fellowships and academic positions, bibliographies, and calls for papers.

Access via:
www http://www.oxy.edu/apa/apa.html

Journal of Buddhist Ethics

An on-line publication dedicated to scholarly papers and discussion of ethical considerations in Buddhism, with a focus on how Buddhism approaches modern ethical issues. The first issue was released in the Fall of 1994, and if it maintains its current level of clarity this journal will be worth the time for interested philosophers and students of Buddhism. The site also includes a list of related Net resources.

Access via:
www http://www.cac.psu.edu/jbe/jbe.html

PHOTOGRAPHY

Newsgroups:
rec.photo.*

Covington's Homeless: A Documentary

John Decker's documentary on drifters in Covington, Kentucky is an original and moving work, complete unto itself and wholly satisfying. There are four groupings: Backpack Bill, Patty and Art, Living in the Streets, and DJ's New Apartment. You can experience the photographs one at a time; there's just enough narrative to tie them together. In one photograph, homeless men are sitting in a line underneath a bridge overpass, each with a bottle in hand and wearing a baseball cap—they look like they are sitting in a dugout watching a ballgame.

Covington's Homeless is proof that the Web can be used for creative expression. You forget about being on the Net and find yourself drifting away, staring into these faces. Note: Be sure to use the "Next" button to move through the dozen or so photos in each grouping.

Access via:
www http://www.iia.org/~deckerj/

PHOTON

A monthly photography magazine based in the United Kingdom. "Arabian Wildlife Photographer of the Year" was the featured photo exhibit for June. The articles in PHOTON tend to be geared toward professionals and amateur enthusiasts and cover such topics as "Print cropping isn't lazy!" and "The Durst M370 Easycolor." Visitors shouldn't miss the PHOTONet Index, a regularly updated collection of links to photography sites on the Web.

Access via:
www http://www.scotborders.co.uk/ photon/index.html

Photo Perspectives

Photo Perspectives calls itself "a museum for the photographic examination of contemporary society and culture." The site is based on the exhibit model, with photos and text used to create a documentary on a particular topic. The inaugural exhibit (April 1995), "Faces of Sorrow: Agony in the Former Yugoslavia," is well crafted and devastatingly thorough. Future exhibits are planned on the American Ballet Theater and endangered wildlife.

Access via:
www http://www.i3tele.com/ photo_perspectives_museum/faces/ perspectives.home.html

PHYSICS

Newsgroups:
sci.physics. [accelerators, fusion, particle, research], sci.space

The American Physical Society

The home page of the editorial offices of the society. Contains files related to the Society's research journals and PACS (Physics and Astronomy Classification Scheme), as well as information about meetings and conferences.

Access via:
www http://aps.org/
ftp aps.org; login *anonymous;* cd *pub*

Los Alamos Physics Information Service

This server, maintained by the Los Alamos National Laboratory, contains links to archives for everything from high-energy physics to quantum cosmology to superconductivity.

Access via:
www http://xxx.lanl.gov/
gopher mentor.lanl.gov

Physics News

News and information related to physics, including links to other science news resources, and updates on Congressional action on science funding.

Access via:
www http://www.het.brown.edu/news/ index.html

Physics Servers and Services

A gigantic collection of links to the physics resources of the Internet. The site is maintained by Mikko Karttunen of the McGill University Department of Physics, and Gunther Nowotny of the Technical University of Vienna. Visitors will find links to preprint archives, labs, physics departments, and job listings.

Access via:
www http://www.physics.mcgill.ca/ deptdocs/physics_services.html

POLITICS

Newsgroups:
alt.activism, misc.activism.progressive, soc.politics

Abortion Rights Activist Home Page

A news and information resource devoted to the struggle to preserve abortion rights in the United States. Material is available in four categories: News, Clinic Violence, Information for Activists, and The Enemies of Choice. The Abortion Rights Activist Home Page is maintained bv Adam Guasch-Melendez.

Access via:
www http://www.cais.com/agm/index.html

Election '96

Will the Web provide a home for intelligent political discourse during the United States presidential election of 1996? Or will it be an arena for grandstanding and mudslinging? To keep track of the action, Netizens will have Michael Gonzalez's Election '96 site. Gonzales promises to maintain links to all candidate and voter education home pages, as well as to sites devoted to hot political issues.

Access via:
www http://dodo.crown.net/~mpg/election/96.html

The Human Rights Web

An excellent archive and research center for anyone interested in exploring or promoting this important topic. Although some links are out of date or don't work, there is plenty to start you learning. You can begin with the basics with the "What Are Human Rights?" area, and quickly advance to becoming an activist with "What Can I Do to Promote Human Rights?," "Human Rights Resources Page," and several other documents and sections.

Access via:
www http://www.traveller.com/~hrweb/hrweb.html

National Organization for Women

Find out what topics are on the forefront of NOW's agenda and learn how to become involved in the largest U.S. feminist organization. This site lists information about upcoming rallies, abortion rights, global feminism, and violence against women. Some of the most touching points are the personal stories, including the accounts of a rape survivor and a welfare mother. Also included are updates on legislation, information on reaching local chapters and joining NOW, and the latest issue of the *National NOW Times*. Links to resources for feminists are included.

Access via:
www http://now.org/now/home.html

Peace and Conflict Resolution WWW Resources

A solid collection of links from Wolfgang Schlor of the University of Pittsburgh International Affairs Network (IAN). Each site link, from the Stockholm International Peace Research Institute to the Human Rights and International Law Archive, is accompanied by a short description of the site and its resources.

Access via:
www http://www.pitt.edu/~ian/Resources/iat-peac.html

The Right Side of the Web

At last, a place on the Web to give equal time to make up for all of the socialism and moral anarchy (God bless 'em) you find on the Net. — from The Right Side of the Web home page.

Right wing attitude and Internet savvy. The Right Side of the Web presents both original material and links to other sources of information on the Net. Local resources include the Newt Gingrich WWW Fan Club page, a conservative comic strip called "DeMOCKracy," and a lovely image of Ronald Reagan.

Access via:
www http://www.clark.net/pub/jeffd/index.html

What's Newt

Left-of-center reports on the political machinations of Newt Gingrich. A recent visit to the site found information on the House Speaker's plan to single-handedly block funding for public broadcasting and two versions of "How the Gingrinch Stole Congress," poetry that would make Theodore Giesel proud. What's Newt is compiled by Dan Schueler, a software developer from Washington state's Puget Sound area.

Access via:
www http://www.wolfe.net/~danfs/newt.html

PSYCHOLOGY

Newsgroups:
sci.psychology

American Psychological Society (APS)

Information about the APS—membership, job postings, conferences, and research.

Access via:
www http://www.hanover.edu/psych/APS/aps.html

Cognitive and Psychological Sciences on the Internet

A library of links to psych resources on the Net, maintained by Scott Mainwaring of the Stanford Psychology Department. The collection presents over 100 links in the areas of academic programs, conferences, journals, discussion groups, publishers, and software.

Access via:
www http://matia.stanford.edu/cogsci/

Psycoloquy

An on-line academic journal about psychology, published by the American Psychological Association.

Access via:
www http://www.princeton.edu/~harnad/psyc.html

RECREATION

Newsgroups:
alt. [aquaria, magic, sewing], rec. [antiques, aquaria, collecting, crafts.brewing, crafts.misc, crafts.textiles, folk-dancing, gambling, gardens, guns, juggling, models.railroad, models.rc, models.rackets, photo, radio.amateur.misc, radio.amateur.packet, radio.amateur.policy, radio.cb, railroad, roller-coaster, woodworking]

Baseball Links

John Skilton's collection of links to baseball resources on the Net, including scores, stats, team pages, archives, and baseball newsgroups. Even the Class A Rancho Cucamonga Quakes have a home page!

Access via:
www http://ssnet.com/~skilton/baseball.html

Canonical Hockey Links Page

Doug Norris's page of links to hockey sites on the Web. The scope of the page is amazing, with links to every site from the Internet Hockey Quote Library to the Brazos Valley Roller Hockey League Page. Doug is also the maintainer of the Goaltender Home Page.

Access via:
www http://rowlf.cc.wwu.edu:8080/~n9143349/links.html

GolfWeb

If golf is your bag, this is the place for you. A very comprehensive and well-crafted site with extensive Library, Places to Stay, ProShop, and Tour Action sections. Within these are a surprising number of articles and reviews (from antiquities to equipment), courses, schools, tournaments, and much more.

Access via:
www http://www.golfweb.com/

GORP: Great Outdoor Recreation Pages

A well-designed and growing site made up of original documents and links to all manner of information for the outdoor enthusiast. Included are some descriptions of National Parks within the United States, all sorts of outdoor activities (mountain biking, boating, hiking, fishing, skiing) and how to find out more about them on the Internet. There is a general listing for other Internet locations, and sparse sections for Gear, Food, Health, and Clubs and Associations.

Access via:
www http://www.gorp.com/

Grand Canyon National Park

A superb experience for anyone interested in this most popular of National Parks. We especially like this site because it is nothing like some of the glossy and numbingly official tourist guides that appear on the Net. This site is authored by a private individual who knows and loves the park, and who has organized that knowledge and passion into an archive that is useful and a pleasure to navigate. If you go here, you'll get a quick history (check out the visitation figures), detailed maps, descriptions of trails, a listing of park services, a list of other sites worth visiting in the Grand Canyon area, and a short reminder of things to consider to make your trip there a Green one.

Access via:
www http://www.kbt.com/gc/gc_home.html

The Running Page

The Running Page lists running clubs, shows you where to run in 130 U.S. cities, and lists local races and marathons. The site also links to Recent Race Results, Cross Country Analysis, the *rec.running* FAQ, and others. The Running Page is maintained by Dennis G. Rears, a computer engineer at the U.S. Army Armaments Research and Development Center in New Jersey.

Access via:
www http://sunsite.unc.edu/drears/ running/running.html

The Sailing Page

A big page of pointers to Net sailing resources, including links to the Tall Ships FAQ, the International Lightning Page, and the Guide to Historic Wrecks of the United Kingdom. The Sailing Page is captained by Mark Rosenstein, who pilots a desk at Bellcore when he's not out on the open waters.

Access via:
www http://community.bellcore.com/mbr/ sailing-page.html

SkiWeb

The SkiWeb Home Page has mountains of information about ski areas, resorts, package tours, road conditions, and weather. Some areas depend on recent updates and can be spotty. The site contains info for cross-country skiers and snow boarders, too. Features include High Altitude Health and an insider's Newsletter. The site is well organized by region, from the Rockies to the Alps.

Access via:
www http://diamond.sierra.net/SkiWeb/

Soccer WWW Resources

Pure Web is a collection of links to the football (soccer, to most Americans) resources of the Internet. Visitors will find links to over fifty international resources, including Web pages maintained for club teams, national teams, leagues, and competitions. Pure Web was created by John Stringer and is now maintained by Gwen Garrett, a Computer Associate working in the Center for Atmospheric Science at Cambridge University.

Access via:
www http://www.atm.ch.cam.ac.uk/sports/ webs.html

Sports Information Service

This is a developing server that provides statistics, schedules, and some history of professional sports. Currently, there are sections on basketball, football, and hockey. The basketball server provides the latest NBA scores, a schedule of tonight's games, the league's current standings, box scores on all the season's games so far, player-by-player cumulative statistics for every team, and complete schedules for each team. In addition, you can get a history of NBA awards (Rookie of the Year, Most Valuable Player) and listings of the league's all-time leaders in scoring, rebounding, and assists.

Access via:
www http://www.netgen.com/sis/ sports.html

The Sports Server

Daily baseball, basketball, football, and hockey news from the New Media Division of the News & Observer Publishing Company. Stories and stats come from either Reuters or the Associated Press. Access to A.P. materials is restricted to folks who take a minute to fill

out the free registration form. This is a site worth returning to again and again.

Access via:
www http://www2.nando.net/SportServer/

Tennis Server

The Tennis Server, from the Racquet Workshop and the Tenagra Corporation, serves up a healthy slice of tennis information to the Internet. There are current and back issues of *Tennis News,* equipment and player tips of the month from tennis pros, rules and codes, and links to other on-line tennis news and tips.

Access via:
www http://arganet.tenagra.com/ Racquet_Workshop/Tennis.html

Windsurfing Resources on the WWW

Want to windsurf in Corpus Christi, Texas, or down the Columbia River Gorge? Looking for windsurfing shops and launch sites in the San Francisco Bay area? This information, along with phone numbers for various wind reporting stations, windsurfing pictures and videos, and hot topics of discussion, is located here.

Access via:
www http://www.dsg.cs.tcd.ie/dsg_people/ afcondon/windsurf/windsurf_home.html

ftp lemming.uvm.edu; login *anonymous;* cd *rec.windsurfing*

Women's Sports Page

The Women's Sports Page, put together by a grad student at the University of Texas, is a collection of women's sports resources on the Net that ranges from rugby to handball, with lots and lots of basketball pages. Some of the sites are collegiate, other links take you to the commercial on-line sports services that are starting to crop up on the Net. There is plenty of room to grow, but this is a good start.

Access via:
www http://fiat.gslis.utexas.edu/~lewisa/womsprt.html

REFERENCES

Acronym Dictionary

A searchable index of 6,000 acronyms.

Access via:
www http://curia.ucc.ie/info/net/acronyms/acro.html

American Library Association (ALA) Gopher

A large directory of information from the American Library Association. Much of the material here deals with the organization of the ALA, its bylines, and its publications. A collection of documents on intellectual freedom and regular editions of the ALA Washington Office Newsline are also available.

Access via:
gopher gopher.uic.edu /library/ala

AT&T 800 Directory

Let your mouse do the walking. You can find 800-numbers on-line using this AT&T-produced directory. Browse by category (like the Yellow Pages) or by name (white pages). This directory goes beyond printed versions with a string search that lets you find a listing even if you know only part of the company's name.

Access via:
www http://att.net/dir800

Bartlett's Familiar Quotations

Tap into the wisdom of great thinkers through Bartlett's Familiar Quotations. This site includes a search engine for words and authors, and a chronological list of primary authors. Don't expect to find any of your 20th Century favorites here—the collection ends with the 19th Century.

Access via:
www http://www.columbia.edu/~svl2/bartlett/

CIA World Factbook

The CIA maintains a detailed, encyclopedic dossier on every country, recognized island group, and certain regions. Each entry contains information about population, economic condition, trade, conflicts, and politics. There's lots of stuff you won't find here—such as the number of nuclear warheads aimed at the Pentagon. But there is information important to travelers, like weather, natural hazards, and severe weather seasons. There is also a good weights and measures table, a list of United Nations bodies, and a list of international organizations and groups.

Access via:
www http://www.odci.gov/94fact/fb94toc/fb94toc.html

gopher umslvma.umsl.edu /LIBRARY/GOVDOCS/WF93

Current Cites

A monthly publication of the University of California, Berkeley Library. It contains selected articles on electronic information technology.

Access via:
www http://www.lib.berkeley.edu/ISIS/current-cites/

Internet-Accessible Library Catalogs

Yale University maintains an index of the hundreds of on-line library catalogs available via the Internet.

Access via:
gopher libgopher.yale.edu

Library Information Servers via WWW

A large collection of links to library Web servers in the U.S., Canada, Europe, and Australia. A list of sites at library-related companies (Dialog, DRA, SilverPlatter) is also available here. The page is maintained by Thomas Dowling, a Networked Information Librarian at the University of Washington.

Access via:
www http://www.lib.washington.edu/~tdowling/libweb.html

Library-Oriented Lists and Electronic Serials

Mailing lists have not yet succumbed to the trend towards user-friendliness on the Internet. Library professionals are fortunate, therefore, that Ann Thornton and Steve Bonario of the University of Houston Libraries have created this index to library-related discussion lists and electronic serials. In addition to indexing mailing lists by subject, this resource walks users through the subscription process.

Access via:
www http://info.lib.uh.edu/liblists/home.html

MARVEL (Library of Congress)

This site is much more than just an on-line library catalog. MARVEL is the Library of Congress's Machine-Assisted Realization of the Virtual Electronic Library, which combines the information available at and about the Library of Congress with other Internet resources. It aims to serve the staff of the Library of Congress, the U.S. Congress, and constituents throughout the world. Most files are plain ASCII text.

Access via:
gopher marvel.loc.gov

On-Line Ready Reference

Whether you're tracking down geography facts or the current Vermont postal rates and mail codes, the On-Line Ready Reference at the SOLINET Gopher is prime hunting ground. A collection of desk references in Gopher space, the Ready Reference includes an acronym dictionary, almanacs, copyright law, the daily federal register, and a wide array of virtual reference desks.

Access via:
gopher sol1.solinet.net /SOLINETGopher/On-LineReadyReference

Roget's Thesaurus

One of the Project Gutenberg texts. Available as a searchable text through Gopher.

Access via:
gopher odie.niaid.nih.gov /Desk Reference

Telephone Area Codes

Where is telephone area code 203? What's the area code for Nashville, Tennessee? If you ever have questions like these, the Long Distance Area Decoder belongs on your hotlist. Using an on-line form, you enter the location or area code you're interested in—the Decoder responds by filling in the blanks. The Long Distance Area Decoder is provided as a promotion by AmeriCom, Inc.

Access via:
www *http://www.xmission.com/ ~americom/aclookup.html*

University of Illinois Grammar Handbook

"What do you want: good grammar or good taste?" asked the old TV commercial for Winston cigarettes. Winston gave us neither, but, happily, the Grammar Handbook provides both. Grammar tips are tastefully presented at this site, an English class project. It's especially useful for teachers, as teaching suggestions are offered in many sections. A couple of drawbacks: first, it is a gopher menu, so you often have to click several times to get to the document you want; second, the student writing is occasionally inconsistent.

Access via:
gopher *gopher.uiuc.edu /Libraries/ writers/GRAMMAR*

Virtual Reference Desk

A great collection of links to the reference sources of the Internet, compiled by Carl E. Snow of the Purdue University Library. Among the plums available here are the AT&T 800 Number Directory, a list of Internet Country Codes, and the College Slang Dictionary.

Access via:
www *http://thorplus.lib.purdue.edu/ reference/index.html*

Webster English Dictionary

A hypertext interface to the Webster English dictionary. All roots and words are linked to their definitions.

Access via:
www *http://c.gp.cs.cmu.edu:5103/prog/ webster*

RELIGION AND BELIEF

Newsgroups:
soc.religion. [bahai, christian, christian.bible-study, easter, islam, quaker], alt.atheism, alt.atheism.moderated, alt.hindu, alt.religion, talk.religion

Anders Magick Page

A library of links to mystical and occult resources on the Net, created by Anders Sandberg of Stockholm, Sweden. Anders captures the spirit of of the site in his introduction: "This page contains links to pages related to magick, mysticism, and similar matters. It's not sorted, it's under construction and it's filled with holes. A bit like reality, when you think of it."

Access via:
www *http://www.nada.kth.se/ ~nv91-asa/magick.html*

Bible

The Bible is accessible at a number of different sites. Versions include searchable texts and a number of different translations.

Access via:
www *http://www.mit.edu:8001/people/ aaronc/bibles.html*

www *http://www.calvin.edu/cgi-bin/bible*

ftp *nic.funet.fi;* login *anonymous;* cd *pub/doc/bible/texts*

Book of Mormon

The Book of Mormon, in text form.

Access via:
gopher *cs1.presby.edu /religion/Mormon*

Catholic Resources on the Net

A comprehensive collection of pointers maintained by John Ockerbloom of Carnegie-Mellon University.

Access via:
www http://www.cs.cmu.edu/Web/People/spok/catholic.html

I Ching

The I Ching ("Book of Changes") is an ancient Chinese system of divination. An oracle is cast by flipping coins or, more traditionally, by manipulating yarrow stalks. With this on-line version, there's no need to throw sticks or open the book. Just access the site and an I Ching reading will appear, including a judgment ("Modesty creates success..."), an image ("Within the earth, a mountain..."), and a display and description ("No boasting of wealth...") of the stalks. If you want a second opinion, just reload the page.

Access via:
www http://cad.ucla.edu:8001/iching

Islam

Resources for Muslims on the Net, including the Qur'an in English translation.

Access via:
gopher latif.com /RESOURCE/CYBER

www http://sparc.latif.com/welcome.html

Judaism and Jewish Resources

An excellent index maintained by Andrew Tannenbaum of Brookline, MA. Resource areas covered include Web sites, mailing lists, museums, and Israeli servers.

Access via:
www http://shamash.nysernet.org/trb/judaism.html

Not Just Bibles: A Guide to Christian Resources on the Internet

A comprehensive hypertext file of mailing lists, archive sites, Gopher and Web servers, bulletin boards, newsgroups, and other publications regarding Christianity, both historic and current.

Access via:
www http://www.iclnet.org/pub/resources/christian-resources.html

Sikhism

"Any human being who faithfully believes in: (i) One Immortal Being, (ii) Ten Gurus, from Guru Nanak Dev to Guru Gobind Singh, (iii) the Guru Granth Sahib, (iv) the utterances and teachings of the ten Gurus and, (v) the baptism bequeathed by the tenth Guru, and who does not owe allegiance to any other religion is a Sikh." — Sikh Code of Conduct

A large and well-designed collection of resources devoted to Sikhism, maintained by Sandeep Singh Brar.

Access via:
www http://www.io.org/~sandeep/sikhism.htm

Software for Theologians

Descriptions and sources for software of use in religious studies. Information is available on word processing in Greek and Hebrew; sources of biblical texts and databases available on-line and on disk; software to help in learning Greek, Latin, and Hebrew; and a bibliography of on-line and print publications related to Computing in Theology. This site also contains an archive of selected software.

Access via:
gopher delphi.dur.ac.uk /Academic/Departments P-T/Theology/Computing/Software

SPIRIT-WWW

A truly eclectic compilation of spiritual resources on the Net, from ancient Vedic wisdom to the latest theories on free energy and interdimensional travel. This site is maintained by Rene K. Muller, a noted contributor in this field, and it's rumored that simply focusing on the site's brilliant golden mastheads can raise you to a higher state of being (color monitors only).

Access via:
www *http://www.protree.com/Spirit.html*

Zen Page

"When the screen is rolled up the great sky opens,/ Yet the sky is not attuned to Zen./It is best to forget the great sky/And to retire from every wind." — from The *Gateless Gate.*

The focus of Ben Walters' *Zen@Sunsite* is on *The Gateless Gate,* a famous collection of Zen koans. In addition to browsing *The Gateless Gate* via its index page, visitors can choose to generate a random koan. Other resources available at this site include the **alt.zen** FAQ and a collection of links to other Zen sites on the Net.

Access via:
www *http://sunsite.unc.edu/zen/*

TELEVISION AND RADIO

Newsgroups:
alt.fan.*, rec.arts.*, rec.music.*, rec.arts.startrek

BBC Web Resources

The gateway to the British Broadcasting Corporation's resources on the WWW. Among the quirky and interesting gems to be found here are playlists from Radio 1, recipes from Madhur Jaffrey's Flavours of India, and schedules from "The Big Byte," a funky computer program on Radio 5.

Access via:
www *http://www.bbcnc.org.uk/*

CBS Eye on the Net

CBS Eye should be on the hotlist of every Letterman junkie. With daily updates of Top Ten lists, you need not fret about missing the best part of the show. A roster of upcoming guests lets you decide if it's really worth staying up. The site also contains nightly listings of CBS shows under the What's On heading. There's even a special home page for Tom Snyder's "Late Late Night" show, but unfortunately there's no contest or prize for counting the number of colors in his hair.

Access via:
www *http://www.cbs.com/*

National Public Radio Home Page

A fun site for NPR fans, including information on programming, member stations, and transcripts. Sadly, there is still no photograph of Click and Clack, the "Car Talk" guys.

Access via:
www *http://www.npr.org/*

Satellite TV

Pointers to useful information on the Net relating to satellite TV and radio, assembled by Jay Novello.

Access via:
www *http://itre.uncecs.edu/misc/sat.html*

Star Trek: Points of Interest

Chiefly a page of links to other Star Trek sites, including the "official" "Star Trek: Voyager" site, Orhan W.D. Ertughrul's Star Trek page, and the Star Trek Universe. Maintained by Marcus E. Hennecke.

Access via:
www *http://www.crc.ricoh.com/~marcush/startrek.html*

The Ultimate TV List

A massive collection of links to TV-show sites on the Internet. As of September 8, 1995, the list contained 1337 WWW, Gopher, FTP, and newsgroup links to information on 416 TV shows, including "Married with Children," "Star Trek," "Seinfeld," "E.R.," and "The Young and the Restless." Formerly a resident of The Creative Internet, The Ultimate TV List can now be found at TV Net.

Access via:
www *http://www.tvnet.com/UTVL/utvl.html*

THEATER

On Broadway

Heading to New York and looking to catch a show? The bright marquee of On Broadway offers listings on current and upcoming Broadway shows, gleaned from magazines that are in the know: *New York*, the *New Yorker*, and *Theatre Week*. These on-line playbills are bare bones—just text listings of the show title, theater address, play dates, and ticket prices. Two nice features are the links to related on-line listings of the shows and links to soundtracks for musicals.

Access via:
www *http://artsnet.heinz.cmu.edu:80/OnBroadway/*

Playbill On-Line

An informative, well-designed site that features remarkably comprehensive theater listings for New York, London, and regional touring companies, along with theater news, job listings, and trivia.

Access via:
www *http://webcom.com/~broadway/*

TRAVEL

Newsgroups:
rec.travel, rec.travel. [air, marketplace]

American Odyssey

Wherever I go in the world, people I meet say they dream of doing the ultimate road-trip—a drive through the United States of America. Whether you'd like to set off on your own and need a few good suggestions, or just want to read about someone else's experiences, Brett Leveridge's four-month American Odyssey is an excellent place to begin. It's well written, entertaining, funny—Brett has a way of exposing himself to local cultures that reveals as much about them as it reveals about him.

Access via:
www *http://www.timeinc.com/vibe/vibeart/brettnews/roadtoc.html*

Center for Disease Control

The Center for Disease Control offers reams of official information on diseases from around the world. Of interest to travelers is the Traveler's Health section, which lists countries and the diseases you may encounter, their prevention, symptoms, and remedies. Also listed are vaccine requirements, areas where outbreaks are occurring, as well as information on established diseases like malaria, dengue and yellow fevers, AIDS, cholera, rabies, and others.

Access via:
www *http://www.cdc.gov/cdc.html*

Council on International Educational Exchange

From the people who offer those handy International Student Identity Cards comes this Web site, where you can explore the possibilities of working, volunteering, and studying abroad. If you've got the time and an adventurous spirit, and don't need to make a lot of money, check this site out.

Access via:
www http://www.ciee.org/ciee.html

GNN Travel Center

The Global Network Navigator's on-line travel center features a large collection of travel writing in its Notes from the Road feature area.

Access via:
www http://gnn.com/gnn/meta/travel/index.html

Healthy Flying

Diana Fairechild knows the importance of flying healthfully. She flew 10 million miles as an international flight attendant before being grounded because of the damaging effects caused by the cabin environment. To help others avoid the stresses of international flying, she wrote *Jet Smart,* a welcome addition to any traveler's bookshelf. Diana has now put much of her collected wisdom on-line. You can learn about special meals, packing, jet lag, dehydration, sleeping, and adjusting to a new time zone. You can even ask Diana questions of your own.

Access via:
www http://www.maui.net/diana

Human Languages Page

An impressive archive of language resources on the Net, compiled by Tyler Jones, a student at Willamette University. Some of the resources, like the Glossary of Computer Terms in Vietnamese, are links to simple lists of words and their translations. Others, like the Russian and Eastern European Studies Home Page, offer general cultural information but little in the way of language primers or lessons. Versions of the Human Languages Page are also available in nine other languages, including Spanish, German, Russian, and French.

Access via:
www http://www.willamette.edu/~tjones/Language-Page.html

International Travelers Health Clinic

After years of working with travelers and answering their health and medical questions, Gary P. Barnas, M.D., of the Medical College of Wisconsin, decided to create a Web page. You will find some excellent information here, including what to pack in a medicine kit, advice on traveling while pregnant, a list of common diseases and how to avoid getting them, and advice on avoiding altitude sickness, motion sickness, and auto accidents.

Access via:
www http://www.intmed.mcw.edu/travel.html

Internet Guide to Hostelling

A very thorough and well-maintained WWW/FTP site that includes a Hostels FAQ, Worldwide Hostel Directory, The Backpackers Guide to Budget Guidebooks, and information about the creator of this site, Darren K. Overby, an avid hosteller and hostel owner in San Francisco.

Access via:
www http://www.hostels.com/hostels/

Lonely Planet Travel Guides

The Lonely Planet site offers text and tips for anyone thinking of venturing into the world. One of the best features of this site is the Health area, an archive of preventions, remedies, and cures for exotic and common maladies that lurk in the shadows.

Access via:
www http://www.lonelyplanet.com.au/lp.html

New Zealand Information

Perhaps you are traveling to New Zealand, or teaching a class about it. You don't even have to go there, but a server at Carnegie-Mellon University will tell you more than you might want to know. Want to know about the climate, or locate Auckland on a map of New Zealand? Listen to a speech in the native Maori language. Want to know what a tuatara is? You'll even find out that the main difference between Marmite and Vegemite, two types of yeast extract, is that the latter is Australian and tastes awful.

Access via:
www *http://nz.com/nz/*

Peace Corps

The Peace Corps, that venerable U.S. organization started by President Kennedy, is online with information on how U.S. citizens can join and serve abroad or domestically. Along with getting a feel for the organization and its goals, you can find out which occupational categories need filling, which countries need volunteers, how the interview process works, and where to get additional information. There is also an e-mail form for sending mail to the district office nearest you.

Access via:
www *http://www.clark.net/pub/peace/PeaceCorps.html*

Perry-Castaneda Library Map Collection

Housed at the University of Texas at Austin, this is a huge collection of country, city, and regional maps, most of which were created by the CIA. If you like to keep apprised of current events, be sure to check out the Electronic Maps of Current Interest section, where you will find maps for parts of the world that are currently in the news.

Access via:
www *http://www.lib.utexas.edu/Libs/PCL/Map_collection/Map_collection.html*

Shoestring Travel E-Zine

Composed of readers' e-mail submissions and good posts to various *rec.travel* newsgroups, Shoestring Travel is dedicated to helping budget travelers find the best cheap food, lodging, and transportation tips on the Net. Like so many sites, this one's under construction and changing frequently. At the time of this review, there were tips from Netizens who had recently visited Southeast Asia, Portugal, Mexico, Iceland, and a range of other intriguing destinations. There were also listings of cheap hotels in New York, San Francisco, and Boston, plus links to railroad timetable info, currency exchange rates, home exchange clubs, and other resources of interest to those traveling on the cheap.

Access via:
www *http://metro.turnpike.net/eadler/index.html*

Staying Healthy in Asia, Africa, and Latin America

Travel Health: Staying Healthy in Asia, Africa, and Latin America is brought to the Net by Moon Publications. This site contains information for travelers intent on getting off the beaten track and is divided into easy-to-negotiate headings: Before you Go, Arrival and Preventing Illness, Diagnosis and Treatment of Illness, After You Return Home, and Recommended Reading.

Access via:
www *http://www.moon.com*

Tips for Travelers

Contains thorough and practical information on traveling, including sections on "What to Take, What to Pack It In," and the essential "How to Get What You Take Into What You Take It In." This archive is growing, and will soon include practical information on air travel and passports.

Access via:
www *http://www.webfoot.com/travel/tips/tips.top.html*

ftp *ftp.netcom.com;* login *anonymous;*
cd *pub/ducky/docs/tips;* get *tips.top.html*

Travel Information Library

Includes information about travel modalities, destinations, and the like, along with pointers to other travel information resources; much of the contents seems to be derived from the newsgroup *rec.travel.*

Access via:
www *http://www.nectec.or.th/rec-travel/README.html*

ftp *ftp.cc.umanitoba.ca;* login *anonymous;*
cd *rec-travel*

U.S. State Department Travel Warnings and Consular Information Sheets

The latest U.S. State Department travel advisories for just about any country you're interested in visiting. The advisories provide background information about current U.S. relations with a particular country. Unfortunately, this information does not necessarily apply to foreign nationals, though it can be used as a guide. There is also information about medical facilities, crime, currency regulations, drug penalties, and embassy locations.

This resource, compiled by the people at St. Olaf College, in Northfield, Minnesota, also includes links to the CIA World Factbook and color representations of flags of various countries from around the world.

Access via:
www *http://www.stolaf.edu/network/travel-advisories.html*

gopher *gopher.stolaf.edu /
Internet_Resources/
US-State-Department-Travel-Advisories*

ftp *ftp.stolaf.edu;* login *anonymous;*
cd *pub/travel-advisories/advisories*

USA CityLink

Links to state and city pages across the U.S. Some are dull "Things to do...blah blah blah..." pages, others contain funky local information worthy of intensive surfing.

Access via:
www *http://www.NeoSoft.com/citylink/*

A Visit to Nepal

A superb visit to Nepal is in store for anyone who makes the trip to this site. Scott A. Yost's six-week trekking journey is meticulously recorded in text, annotated photos, and interactive maps. At the bottom of the main page are links to a variety of other sites that contain information on Nepal.

Access via:
www *http://enigma.phys.utk.edu/~syost/nepal.html*

Virtual Tourist

Connections to tourist guides for a number of locations, including Australia, Japan, New Zealand, many European countries, and many points in the United States. The Japanese tourist guide contains a number of maps, several audio files (including the national anthem), plus weather information, cultural information, etc.

Access via:
www *http://wings.buffalo.edu/world*

The WWW Speedtrap Registry

Andrew Warner maintains a list of speed traps by state, along with pages discussing police use of radar, a Lidar FAQ, and a

Driver's Chart describing whether detectors and scanners are legal in a particular state. You'll also find links to Reasonable Drivers Unanimous and the National Motorists Association.

Access via:
www *http://www.nashville.net/speedtrap/*

USENET

Newsgroups:
news.answers, news.newusers.questions, news.software, news.groups

DejaNews

A fantastic tool that allows users to search a vast archive of USENET news postings by keyword, author, and date. The archive is updated every two days to cover the past month's postings for hundreds of newsgroups (the alt.*, soc.*, talk,* and *.binaries groups are notable exceptions). Read the HELP documents to make full use of the search and retrieval functions.

Access via:
www *http://www.dejanews.com/*

USENET Periodic Posting Archives

A repository of the periodic informational postings of the newsgroups. There is a directory corresponding to each newsgroup name. The directory contains all regular postings to the newsgroups (including FAQ lists), as well as many other "general interest" postings that have sprung out of the newsgroups.

Access via:
ftp *rtfm.mit.edu;* login *anonymous;* cd *pub/usenet*

USENET Info Center Launch Pad

Formerly called "The Bible of USENET," this is a comprehensive list of answers to FAQs about USENET. The site includes documents for new users and the Newsgroup Info Center where you can browse the groups by category, or view the master list of USENET groups.

Access via:
www *http://sunsite.unc.edu/usenet-b/home.html*

What is USENET?

A long explanation for what the USENET news system is, how it's managed, and how it got to be that way.

Access via:
ftp *rtfm.mit.edu;* login *anonymous;* cd *pub/usenet-bygroup/news.answers/what_is_usenet?;* get *part1*

WEATHER

Newsgroups:
sci.geo.meteorology

Intellicast USA Weather

With its big and colorful national weather outlook map, the Intellicast weather page will make you feel like the meteorologist on your local TV station. Once you've finished with the outlook, you can call up a few satellite and radar images and then check the forecast for the metro area nearest you. For international weather conditions, select the AROUND THE WORLD link at the top of the page.

Access via:
www *http://www.intellicast.com/weather/usa/wxusa.html*

NCAR Data Support Section Server

The National Center for Atmospheric Research has a wide variety of data and programs available to aid meteorological research.

Access via:
www http://www.ucar.edu/ ResearchData.html

gopher gopher.ucar.edu

*ftp ncardata.ucar.edu; login anonymous;
cd pub/weather*

Purdue Weather Processor (WXP)

WXP, with sleek weather map graphics, is a general-purpose weather visualization tool for current and archived meteorological data. Developed at Purdue University, it includes satellite imagery, surface and upper air data, and radar info. There are forecast models and links to "Earth and Atmospheric" home pages.

Access via:
www http://thunder.atms.purdue.edu/

Weather Information Superhighway

You could call this index the Internet Weather Channel. Compiled by the National Weather Service, the Weather Information Super-highway lists dozens of sites for weather updates and climate pre-diction. The Weather Underground Section lists university weather services—another area offers regional climate centers and gives information on droughts, heat waves, hurricanes, and blizzards. You'll also find international weather, satellite images, and weather maps and movies.

Access via:
www http://thunder.met.fsu.edu:80/ nws/public_html/wxhwy.html

WHITE PAGES

Four11

If you have a hunch someone you know is rolling down the Infobahn, but you can't locate that person, you might try Four11 Directory Services. While the Internet has no central directory, Four11 has about 500,000 entries and a fast, custom database engine for searching. New listings are incorporated daily. You can search the directory by any combination of first name, last name, location, and old e-mail address. Four11 is a free service from SLED Corporation. (Note: New users will have to fill out a brief registration form before they can search the database.)

Access via:
www http://www.four11.com/Sled.html

Knowbot Information Service

The Knowbot Information Service is a "white pages" service that will search for a name through a large number of Internet databases. It's a great way to look up friends and acquaintances. It's not yet as convenient as it might be, but Knowbots are among the newest and most advanced services on the Internet; it's worth knowing about them.

Access via:
telnet info.cnri.reston.va.us; port 185

List of Internet Whois Servers

Lists of all of the known whois-style white pages servers on the Internet, and related information.

Access via:
*ftp rtfm.mit.edu; login anonymous;
cd pub/whois*

LookUP! Directory Services

A Web-based directory of over 600,000 e-mail addresses. Basic searches are free; advanced features require membership (also free as of June 10, 1995). While the advanced search has some cool features, the basic search works great for a straightforward name search.

Access via:
www http://www.lookup.com/

Netfind

A very persistent program that searches a variety of databases to help you find someone. Not very easy to use, but it may be easier than looking through several different white pages servers to find someone.

Access via:
telnet bruno.cs.colorado.edu; login *netfind*

telnet archie.au; login *netfind*

telnet dino.conicit.ve; login *netfind*

telnet ds.internic.net; login *netfind*

telnet mudhoney.micro.umn.edu; login *netfind*

telnet monolith.cc.ic.ac.uk; login *netfind*

Special Internet Connections (Yanoff List)

A voluntarily compiled list of Internet services, commonly referred to as the "Yanoff list." It gives a short description of each service and access.

Access via:
www http://www.uwm.edu/Mirror/ inet.services.html

ftp csd4.csd.uwm.edu; login *anonymous;* cd *pub;* get *inet.services.txt*

USENET Addresses

This is a list of all people who have posted to USENET newsgroups passing through MIT. This is an excellent way to find out a reasonably up-to-date address for many users of the Net. Note that the FTP server is often overloaded. For information by e-mail, send mail to *mail-server@ rtfn.mit.edu;* place "help" in the message body.

Access via:
ftp rtfn.mit.edu; login *anonymous;* cd *pub/usenet-addresses/lists*
Notes: filenames begin with "addresses," one for each month back to 1992 and for occasional months before that; they are very large, and the server is often overloaded.

The WWW Virtual Library

An amazing example of the collaborative power of the Net, the WWW Virtual Library consists of over 50 independently maintained subject indexes to Net resources. Although the WWW Virtual Library home page resides on the CERN server in Switzerland, most of the individual indexes are available from the home servers of their maintainers: the Anthropology index comes from USC, Cognitive Science from Brown University, Engineering from NASA. This is a terrific resource that will only get better as it grows with the Internet.

Access via:
www http://www.w3.org/hypertext/ DataSources/bySubject/Overview.html

Yahoo: A Guide to WWW

With over 40,000 entries, the Yahoo Guide is the Net's largest subject index of WWW resources. Given its size, Net users are fortunate that designers David Filo and Jerry Yang of Stanford University have created an index structure that is both easy and fun to browse. Aside from its subject listings, Yahoo features a search function and hotlists of "What's Cool" and "What's Popular" at the site.

Access via:
www http://www.yahoo.com/

WORLD WIDE WEB

ALL-IN-ONE Search Page

A page configured to run remote searches on over one hundred Internet resource databases. From the page, you can search WWW indexes, software repositories, e-mail addresses, and dictionaries. Although ALL-IN-ONE makes it easier to query Net databases, many of the databases themselves are incomplete and clunky, so be prepared for frustration. ALL-IN-ONE was created by William Cross.

Access via:
www http://www.albany.net/~wcross/all1srch.html

Beginner's Guide to HTML

Tap into "A Beginner's Guide to HTML" and learn everything you wanted to know and more about hypertext mark-up language, the tool you need to write Web documents. Well-organized and cogent, the Guide uses concise language to explain creation of HTML documents. Especially valuable for beginners are links to "The Minimal HTML Document" and "Linking to Other Documents." Other sections include troubleshooting, in-line images, and character formatting.

Access via:
www http://www.ncsa.uiuc.edu/General/Internet/WWW/HTMLPrimer.html

Guides to Writing HTML Documents

There's more to publishing on the Web than simply knowing how to do HTML coding. You must also think about interface design, consistency, differences between various Web browsers, and the type of information you're presenting. This growing resource points to many useful guides for anyone interested in designing Web documents. Some of the guides are general-purpose, giving hints about HTML coding that could apply to any document design. Others are oriented toward a specific project (NASA) or a particular field (law, science).

Access via:
www http://union.ncsa.uiuc.edu/HyperNews/get/www/html/guides.html

The Internet Sleuth

If you know your subject, the Internet Sleuth can help you find the information you need. The Sleuth links visitors to searchable Net resources in dozens of subject areas, from Agriculture to Veterinary Science. Most sites require a forms-capable browser.

Access via:
www http://www.intbc.com/sleuth

Links from the Underground

An enthralling tour of the darker side of Net culture, conducted by Justin Hall. Hall calls Links from the Underground "my interpretation of the waste vastland." Visitors will find hundreds of links and plenty of pithy commentary from Justin, who reminds us regularly that he takes no responsibility for what lies beyond the links.

Access via:
www http://www.links.net/

Lycos: Hunting WWW Information

Lycos is an Internet search tool from Carnegie-Mellon University. The Lycos system combines a search engine with a robot that goes out on the Net to collect data—over five million unique URLs were identified for the July 25, 1995 catalog. While Lycos tends to be fairly slow, it does provide lots of context for evaluating whether a document is relevant.

Access via:
www http://lycos.cs.cmu.edu/

Mirsky's Worst of the Web

Ironically, one of the best sites on the Web chronicles some of the worst. Mirsky provides astute commentary, a "Drunk Browsing Test," and Vermont Bob.

Access via:
www http://mirsky.turnpike.net/wow/Worst.html

NCSA Mosaic Home Page

Software and support from the developers of the Mosaic WWW browser. Information is available here on the three flavors of NCSA Mosaic: X Windows, Apple Macintosh, and Microsoft Windows. Helper applications like Acrobat, JPEGView, and Mpegplay are also available for download.

Access via:
www http://www.ncsa.uiuc.edu/SDG/Software/Mosaic/NCSAMosaicHome.html

NCSA What's New Page

The newest of the new WWW sites are announced here three times weekly. NCSA What's New makes a good launch point for a Web surf; it's also one of the best ways to track the evolution of the Internet.

Access via:
www http://www.ncsa.uiuc.edu/SDG/Software/Mosaic/Docs/whats-new.html

The Spot

If you're looking for a little slice of Melrose Place on the Web, take a look at The Spot. This cyberspace soap opera, about a group of remarkably good-looking twenty-somethings who live together in a beach house, is an interesting example of storytelling through hypertext. The different characters tell their stories from their point of view—even the dog gets his own page. It's already spawned a satire, The Squat, about a group of twenty-somethings living in a trailer park.

Access via:
www http://www.thespot.com

www http://theory.physics.missouri.edu/~georges/Josh/squat/

W3 and HTML Tools

To really do effective Web design, you need a good toolbox. Located at CERN (the Web's birthplace in Geneva), this guide to Web tools is the best place on the Web to start collecting the tools of your trade. Trying to publish files from your word processor? Look here for anything-to-HTML and HTML-to-anything scripts. You can make sure you're writing valid HTML by using HTML-checking tools. Or maybe you're tired of handwriting HTML code—here you'll find links to several HTML editors for various systems.

Access via:
www http://www.w3.org/hypertext/WWW/Tools/

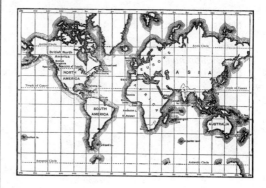

Wall O' Shame

The Wall O' Shame offers shameful (and hysterical) glimpses through the cracks in the facade of modern culture—from the Taco Bell manager who called security because he didn't believe two-dollar bills were real to what the Samburu tribesman is really saying in the Nike commercial. The Wall O' Shame is the creation of Dan Bornstein, a founder of Kaleida Labs.

Access via:
www *http://www.milk.com/wall-o-shame/*

WebChat

WebChat, created by Michael Fremont, is a significant improvement on traditional Internet Relay Chat (IRC). The Web environment tones down IRC's noisy cacophony into a simpler, more graphically rich environment. WebChat also has the capability to incorporate hyperlinks, which brings another dimension to chat. Fremont and his employer, the Internet Roundtable Society (an Internet marketing and consulting group) are also committed to taking WebChat in promising directions, such as using it as a forum for feature interviews with interesting personalities. If your Web browser supports forms, WebChat is worth a visit.

Access via:
www *http://www.irsociety.com/webchat/webchat.html*
Notes: WebChat at the Internet Roundtable Society

www *http://webchat.service.digital.com/*
Notes: WebChat on the Digital Server

www *http://www.acmeweb.com/webchat/webstation.html*
Notes: Links to WebChat sites worldwide

WebCrawler

The WebCrawler database was created by the WebCrawler robot, a software program that gathers and indexes URLs as it surfs the Web. As of November 1994, the database contained somewhere in the neighborhood of 350,000 separate entries—not as many as the Lycos database at Carnegie-Mellon University, but a significant number, nonetheless. Searches of the database are done by keyword, with results returned according to a WAIS scoring system. WebCrawler was developed by Brian Pinkerton of the University of Washington, who has included a helpful FAQ and a collection of hints for searchers at the site.

Access via:
www *http://webcrawler.com/*

Welcome to Netscape!

The Netscape browser from Netscape Communications Corp. has quickly become the most popular WWW browser on the Net. This Welcome page features a Netscape Handbook and information on how to download your own copy of the browser.

Access via:
www *http://www.netscape.com/home/welcome.html*

GETTING CONNECTED TO THE INTERNET

Grades of Service
Service Providers

No matter who you are, you get access to the Internet via a *service provider*. Service providers sell several different kinds of service, each with its own advantages and disadvantages. As with buying a car, you have to decide what features you want, how much you're willing to pay, and then go comparison shopping.

But before you even read the list of providers, there's one thing you should do. In Chapter 1, *What Is This Book About?*, we said that many, many people have access to the Internet and don't know it. Are you one of them? Find out. If your company or school is on the Internet, it almost certainly has better service than you can afford as an individual.

In other words, you may *already* have an Internet connection available to you. You don't need to go out and find a service provider, you don't need to pay any extra bills; you just need to use what you already have. If you're a student at a four-year college or university, you can almost assume that your school is on the Internet, and you can probably get access as a student. Many junior colleges and a growing number of secondary schools are on the Net. Go to your computer center or computer science department and ask around. Ask a number of places before giving up—many times the only people who are aware of the Internet are those people who actually use it. If you're no longer part of academia, the problem is a little more difficult.

How do you find out if your company has Internet access? Anyone who is responsible for managing computer systems or taking care of your corporate network should be able to tell you. If most of your computer systems run UNIX, there's a good chance that you're on the Internet or at least can exchange e-mail and USENET news with the Internet. For historical reasons, if your computers are running DOS and Windows, you probably aren't connected to the Internet—but Windows 95 should help to change this situation. Don't hesitate to dig some; if you're in marketing or accounting, you may not be aware of the nice Internet connection that the research or engineering group has been keeping to itself. If your company has a connection, but it's not in your department, your job is to ask "why?" Write a proposal and get it into next year's budget. Do whatever's necessary. If the resource already exists, it won't cost your company much more to give it to you.

And even if your company doesn't have a connection, it's still the best place to start. Find some other people who need Internet access, figure out how to justify it economically, and make a proposal.

If your company doesn't have a connection, and you're not a student, there are still two ways of coming by Internet access inexpensively. The first thing to do is check out the public library. Some libraries offer a service called a *Free-Net*. It is a community-based information and e-mail system which allows Internet access. You can either use the Free-Net from the library or dial in to it. Although only a few libraries provide this service at the moment, the number is growing. The Free-Nets we know about are listed in the *Resource Catalog* under "Free-Net."

The second way is to become a student. Find out whether or not your community college has an Internet connection. If it does, sign up for a course or two. At many community colleges it is cheaper to take a course than it would be to arrange Internet services with a service provider as an individual. Learn basketweaving, and you can have something to do when you go crazy because the network is down. Once you are enrolled, ask for Internet access. There's a need for a public archive of significant basket designs—isn't there?

Grades of Service

Well, you're still reading. So you probably didn't find any "free" Internet access points. Or perhaps someone said, "Sounds like a good idea. Why don't you do some research about what it will cost?" As we said, there are many different ways of connecting to the Internet. So, before you start your research, here's a summary of some types of connections that are available.

Dedicated Internet Access

Corporations and large institutions that want Internet access should look into dedicated network access. This gives you complete access to all of the Internet's facilities. A service provider leases a dedicated telephone line at a speed of your choosing (the faster the line speed, the more it costs), and places a special routing computer at your location. That router is responsible for taking communications from your site destined for somewhere else and sending them on their way (and vice versa). This is all quite expensive, running at least $2000 initially and several thousand dollars a year in monthly fees. However, once you've set up the connection, you can let as many computers as you like connect to the Internet—perhaps one computer in every classroom in your high school. To do so, you only need to place the computers on a local area network, along with the router.

Dedicated access offers the most flexible connection. Each computer is a full-fledged Internet member, capable of performing any network function. If there is some really neat new application you want to try, you only need to load the software and give it a whirl. It's essential if you want to provide information services.

However, since a dedicated connection is costly, it is most appropriate for a group setting, and impractical for home users.

Dedicated Internet access usually requires some support structure for your local network. The service provider will help you in the beginning, but once you get running, he is only responsible for the router and the phone line. What happens on your local network is your business. If you are responsible for the care and feeding of the LAN, this book won't be enough. The Nutshell Handbooks *Networking Personal Computers with TCP/IP* and *TCP/IP Network Administration*, both by Craig Hunt and published by O'Reilly & Associates, will help you to set up and run your local network. A class or two wouldn't hurt. And keep this book in mind; you may want to give it to users who keep bothering you with simple questions.

SLIP and PPP

In the past few years, some less expensive techniques for "almost-dedicated access" have appeared. These are called SLIP and PPP; they are versions of the Internet software that run over normal phone lines, using standard high-speed modems. PPP and SLIP software comes with Windows 95. You may have to buy a more expensive modem, but you won't have the very high connection costs.[*] You don't even have to use a "dedicated" phone line; you can use SLIP or PPP to dial in to your network when you want access, leaving the phone line free for other use when you don't need it. The real advantage of SLIP or PPP is that it allows a full-fledged connection to the Internet. You're not using someone else's system as an "access point" to the Net; you're on the Net yourself.

SLIP and PPP are very appropriate for connecting a home computer to a larger local network, which is in turn connected to the Internet. For example, you might use SLIP to connect your home computer to your company or campus network; then your home computer will have full Internet access, just as if it were on your company's Ethernet. SLIP and PPP are also appropriate for connecting a home computer (or perhaps a very small local network) to a service provider, who can give you full Internet access. They aren't appropriate for connecting a medium-sized or large network to the Internet; they can't talk fast enough to support many users at once. So if you have a medium or large network (or if you might have one in a few years), it's best to look into "real" dedicated access.

SLIP and PPP are moderate-cost options: they provide very good service and aren't terribly expensive, although prices for these services vary widely. You may find unlimited SLIP access for anywhere from $50 to $250. Alternatively, you may find a lower monthly charge but an additional hourly fee. You also have to worry

---

[*] By high-speed, we mean at least 9600 baud. A 28,800 baud modem is ideal. You could probably make SLIP work with a cheaper 2400-baud modem, but it would be painful. In any case, your service provider will be able to make recommendations about what to buy. Some service providers even sell modems; that's a good way to avoid problems. You will usually get a good price, and if you run into trouble, your provider can't tell you "Your modem isn't a type we support."

about the telephone bill. Many service providers provide 800 numbers or local access numbers in major urban areas to minimize this cost.

Installing SLIP or PPP, configuring them, and getting them running are covered in Appendix B, *Setting Up Your Internet Connection*. Also see the Nutshell Handbooks *TCP/IP Network Administration* and *Networking Personal Computers with TCP/IP* for more information about them.

ISDN Access

ISDN stands for "Integrated Services Digital Network." In essence, it means using a digital telephone line between your home or office and the telephone company's switching office (or "central office"). This might sound like a new technology, but it actually isn't. Although it's only now coming into common use in the United States, ISDN has been widely used in Europe for a number of years. ISDN access can be either dial-up (intermittent access, as needed), or dedicated (a permanent connection to the Internet).

The big advantage of ISDN is that it provides very high-speed access at relatively low cost. One ISDN channel includes two 56 or 64Kb digital channels (depending on the implementation your phone company uses). With a technique called "bonding," these channels can be combined to give you up to 128Kb. With access speeds like this, multimedia services really zip! You won't have to wait ten minutes to download someone's graphics-filled WWW home page.

Pricing is a big variable. It is almost certainly a lot less than a traditional dedicated line of the same speed would have cost a few years ago. Typical ISDN line charges are in the $20 to $50 per month range. Rates depend entirely on how the service is tariffed with the local public utilities commission. You may be able to save some money by using your ISDN line for your regular phone service, in addition to Internet access, but be careful. You can't use regular phones over an ISDN line, and ISDN phones cost hundreds of dollars. And sometimes, ISDN voice calls are billed at business rates, so your cost per call might be higher.

The disadvantage of ISDN that its availability in the U.S. is spotty. If you're in a big city, there's a good chance you can get it; if you're in a suburb, you probably can't; if you're in a rural area, forget it. No matter where you live, you may need to spend a week trying to find the one person at your local phone company who knows what ISDN is (and getting past the two hundred who don't and try to sell you something else).

Since there hasn't been a lot of ISDN service around, many Internet providers don't have the equipment to handle incoming ISDN calls. ISDN equipment used to be pretty scarce, but it is getting cheaper and more available as demand increases. You may need to shop around to find service, but you should eventually find it. The newsgroup *comp.dcom.isdn* can give you much helpful information and advice about ISDN.

Dial-Up Access

What if you can't afford dedicated access, and you don't want to experiment with SLIP or PPP? Is there any easy way to get network access? Yes—just get a time-sharing account on a computer that already has dedicated access. Then use your home computer to log in to this remote system, and do your network work there. Timesharing access is not quite as good as having your own connection, although it does give you powerful access to Internet services. It's also considerably easier to set up. You probably have all the hardware and software you need (i.e., a modem and a terminal emulation package).

With a dial-up service your computer doesn't actually become part of the Internet; it's just accessing a computer (probably a UNIX computer) that's permanently connected to the network. You can only do what the service provider allows. You may not be able to use all the services that the Internet has. There is probably no way to load a random nifty software application and use it; you have to appeal to the provider to add that service. You can't run fancy graphical applications, like Internet Explorer, because there's no standard way for transmitting the graphical display over the phone line (PPP and SLIP get around this problem). Some access providers may limit the amount of disk space you can use.

Access via Other Networks

Most networking services, like BITNET, CompuServe, America Online, and Prodigy, have set up *gateways* that allow you to exchange electronic mail with systems on the Internet. Some have set up gateways that let you read the Internet's bulletin boards (USENET news). And there are a few services scattered around that let you request a file via an electronic mail message; such services fetch the file and mail it to you automatically. This isn't as good as getting the file directly, but it works.

This may be all you need. But it's definitely not an Internet connection; you only have access to a few services. What you can do is fairly limited; there's a lot more out there waiting for you. However, these services have greatly expanded their Internet offerings in the past year (especially AOL), and we expect to see more in the future.

Telephone Connections

Whatever alternative you choose, you're going to need some kind of telephone connection— whether it's a very expensive T3 line or a standard voice line. Here's a summary of the most common service grades:

Table A–1: Telephone Line Options

Service Grade	Speed	Notes
Standard voice line	0 to 28.8Kbps	No extra cost; SLIP or dial-up connections
ISDN	56 - 128Kbps	Digital phone line; availability spotty; dedicated or dial-up
Leased line	56-64Kbps	Small dedicated link to a service provider
T1	1.544Mbps	Dedicated link with heavy use
T2	6Mbps	Not commonly used in networking
T3	45Mbps	Major networking artery for a large corporation or university

Service Providers

Internet service providers are participating in a competitive market. For any given kind of service, there are usually several providers available—and several different price structures. In the tables coming up, I've listed as many service providers as I could find. There are probably others. I can't tell you which ones are better than others; like the evolution of species, each has its own niche in the market. As you investigate, you'll certainly find different trade-offs you can make: quality of service versus price; initial cost versus monthly cost; 800-number access versus long-distance phone charges; and so on. However, I can give you some hints about how to shop.

POPs and 800 Numbers

One of the largest expenses in getting an Internet connection may be your phone bill. Service providers have come up with two approaches to this problem. One is to install 800 numbers that you can dial "for free." The other is to install local access numbers (called *points of presence*, or *POPs*), in major metropolitan areas. Providers like PSI and Netcom take the POP approach; AlterNet takes the 800-number approach. (These options are irrelevant to leased-line connections, which are negotiated separately with your phone company.)

Both approaches have obvious advantages and disadvantages. Dialing into a service provider can get very expensive, if it isn't a local phone call. The 800 number seems to be cheaper, but realize that someone still has to pay the bill, and that's going to be you. The provider may be able to get a better "bulk rate" for 800 service than you can for regular long-distance calls, but the difference won't be that substantial. You can expect service providers with 800 access to charge significantly higher monthly fees, or to have some kind of surcharge based on your connection time. Make sure to take that into account when doing a cost comparison.

Estimate the amount of time you're going to spend on the Net;[*] figure out how much this would cost in long-distance charges to a provider; and compare that with the charges for the equivalent 800-number service.

Getting access through a local POP is ideal—if you can find one. You'll only have local phone calls to deal with. Even if your Internet time rivals the time your teenage kids spend on the phone, there won't be any extra charges to surprise you. However, that's only an option if there really is a local POP. If you live just one town outside of a provider's local calling area, tough. (And if you live out in in the sticks, good luck!)

You should also consider how you will use your connection. If you are a traveling salesman driving from small town to small town, 800 service will probably be better, because you can call it from anywhere. If you travel between large cities, any national or international service provider with POPs will work, too. There will be a POP in every reasonable-sized city (populations above about 500,000, it appears). If you are looking for a cheap connection only to be used from home, you might check out the rash of local service providers. (In this case, you might try joining one of the "Internet Co-ops" that are starting up—particularly if you have some technical skills.)

There's No Such Thing as a Cheap Lunch

Since the first edition of this book, service providers have sprouted like weeds. And still there aren't enough of them. It's becoming clear, though, that there are wide differences in the quality of service that the providers offer. Some hold your hand while you get started, answer your questions, fix things quickly when they break, and so on. Others don't. That's not surprising—auto dealers, insurance agencies, and other businesses are the same. Most Internet service providers are extremely helpful (unlike insurance companies). Their biggest problem is that as a rule, they're too busy. But there are some service providers who will pocket your check and walk away. Some careful shopping will keep you out of trouble.

Here's one particular aspect of service you should think about. Lately, I've seen some very low-priced offers for true Internet connectivity (i.e., SLIP or PPP connections): in the range for $10 per month for unlimited access. That's certainly a good deal. If it really works—which it may. But it may not.

What's the problem? I suspect that these service providers are working on a "health club" model. For every person who buys a health club membership and works out faithfully, there are four or five who buy memberships and show up once or twice. If all the members worked out three times a week, the health club couldn't stay in business without drastically raising its prices and alienating its members . . . in which case, it would go out of business anyway. The same thing may be going on here. To offer unlimited access with very low monthly fees, the service provider must have a huge number of users and a relatively small number

---

[*] Be careful not to underestimate; networking often becomes addictive.

of phone lines and modems. The more users are sharing a limited bank of phones, the more likely you are to get a busy signal when you try to dial in. $10 per month is not a good price if all you're buying is a busy signal.

Keep in mind, though, that you might not have this problem. Nobody really knows how the service provider business will shake out. And getting people who use the Net for an hour every other month to subsidize your networking habit is great, but there's the risk that more people will actually make use of the service than you (and the service provider) are counting on. Just keep your eyes open and realize that there may be some drawbacks to offers that sound too good to be true.

Internet Co-Ops

One exciting development in the service provider arena has been the development of Internet cooperatives: groups of individuals and companies who buy a high-speed dedicated line from another service provider and then share it. As a result, the members get better service for less money than they could afford individually. Co-ops range from a few individuals sharing a PPP connection to elaborate arrangements for sharing leased T1 lines.

Since labor for running the coop (system administration, network administration, dealing with service providers and phone companies, billing) is often donated, members with technical skills are particularly valuable. Don't count yourself out if you're not a UNIX guru; other kinds of expertise are needed, too. Someone with a solid telecommunications background, or someone who can help support clients using Windows, would be very valuable to most co-ops. For that matter, few co-ops would sneer at a lawyer who could file incorporation papers or an accountant who could prepare financial statements.

A few of the providers we've listed are cooperatives. The more important question, though, is whether a cooperative is forming in your area—and there's no way we can tell you about that. Talk to your friends who are interested in the Internet; listen for rumors and investigate them; if you have access to USENET news, watch the newsgroups *alt.internet.access.wanted* and *alt.internet.services.* The first group consists mostly of people trying to find out how to get Internet access in a particular area. Don't just listen; get things started yourself by asking "Does anyone know how to get an Internet connection in Fargo, North Dakota?" You may find out about an active service provider in your neighborhood, a coop that's forming in your area, or other people who would like access with whom you can form a coop of your own.

Regional Versus National

Service providers within the U.S. and Canada tend to group themselves into two categories: national and regional. National providers market their services to anyone in their nation. Regional providers have staked out an area of their country and only market their services within that area. Of course, once you're connected to the Internet, you have access to the entire world. So the difference between national and regional providers depends on what you like. Regional providers would claim that they give better, "more personal" service, and that they can adapt more quickly to their clients' needs. (One regional provider helps its clients do teleconferencing, for example.) Nationwide providers would counter that claim by saying that they can bring more resources to bear to solve a particular client's problems.

International providers (providers that offer Internet connections in more than one country) are more difficult to categorize. One would assume that the national providers are ones who do international connections, too. This is true, but a number of regionals also do this. Many U.S. regional providers got dragged into providing international connections early in the Internet game, before most of the national providers existed, and they still have them today. So, if you are looking to connect from another country, you need to look at both national and regional provider tables.

Who you call depends on how and where you want to connect. How you should connect depends on the size of your connection. If you are an individual or really small business, you will probably be looking for providers of dial-up or SLIP/PPP services. Medium to large businesses should look to SLIP/PPP or dedicated services. Here are a few guidelines to help you in looking for a provider:

- If you want to connect a single site in one country to the Internet, or if you want to connect several sites in the same geographical area to the Internet, call either national or regional providers that offer suitable services. For example, if you want to connect several offices in New England to the Internet, you can contact either Northeast regional providers or national providers. Obviously, if you're only interested in connecting one site to the Internet, regional and national providers can serve you equally well; your choice will be based on price and the services that are available.

- If you want to connect several widely distributed sites within the same country to the Internet (e.g., offices in Washington D.C., Los Angles, and Chicago), talk to suitable national providers. If you try to do this with regional providers, you will probably end up dealing with multiple contracts, operations centers, etc. It's probably not worth the effort.

- If you want to connect sites in the U.S. and sites in other countries to the Internet (e.g., offices in Washington D.C. and London), talk to either a national provider or a regional provider with international connections on the coast closest to where you want to reach. It may be very hard to deal with a foreign bureaucracy; an experienced provider who is currently serving the country in question is valuable.

The Providers Themselves

Now we're through the preliminaries. Below, I give you a list of providers offering nationwide and regional service within the United States and Canada, followed by a list for the United Kingdom and Australia. But first, I'll tell you how to get your own information.

As with all other Internet resources, this list will be out of date in little time. Provider information will change, and many, many more providers will come into existence. As with other lists of Internet information, the most up-to-date versions can be found online. One of the most extensive lists of service providers I've found is *The List* from Collosus, Inc. You can find it on the World Wide Web at **http://thelist.com/**. Another excellent resource is an e-mail accessible list offered by ATrueStory. You simply send an e-mail message to **zahner@aimnet.com** with both the subject and text of the message reading "MY AREA CODE = *your area code*." You will receive an informative list of businesses offering Internet access in the area code you ask about. You should also note that the newsgroups *alt.internet.services* and *alt.internet.access.wanted* are well worth watching if you want to find out about Internet access opportunities.

A few notes on the North American list below. It is organized by major metropolitan area, and by the location of the provider's main office; a provider's POPs may very well extend beyond the metropolitan area they are listed in. Therefore, you may find it worthwhile to check all the providers in your state, and even in neighboring states. We have listed at least one provider per state (or Canadian province). This list is by no means exhaustive, nor does inclusion in this list imply advocacy on our behalf. A final note: most of the providers listed offer both individual/residential services and business services, but a number specialize in services marketed specifically for one or the other. Shop around in your area to find the best offers available to you locally.

All providers listed support PPP or SLIP connections, and thus should be compatible with Windows 95. An asterisk (*) indicates providers who also offer dedicated connections at T1 or higher levels, making good choices for LAN connections or other multi-user networks.

Table A–2: Regional and National Service Providers: U.S. and Canada

State/City/Provider	E-mail	Telephone
ALABAMA		
Birmingham		
Cheney Communications Company*	info@cheney.net	(800) CHENEY-1
The Matrix	webmaster@the-matrix.com	(205) 251-9347
SouthEast Information Systems	myoung@secis.com	(205) 678-9945
Viper Computer Systems, Inc.*	vipersys@viper.net	(205) 978-9850

Table A-2: Regional and National Service Providers: U.S. and Canada (continued)

State/City/Provider	E-mail	Telephone
ALABAMA (continued)		
Mobile		
Mobile Area Free-Net	info@maf.mobile.al.us	(334) 405-4600
WSNetwork Communications Services*	info@wsnet.com	(334) 263-5505
ALASKA		
All points		
Corcom, Inc.	support@corcom.com	(907) 563-1191
ImagiNEt, Inc.	coppick@imagi.net	(907) 455-9638
Internet Alaska*	info@alaska.net	(907) 562-4638
MicroNet Communications	info@lasertone.com	(907) 333-8663
PolarNet	help@polarnet.fnsb.ak.us	(907) 457-4929
ALBERTA		
Calgary		
AlphaCom Business Center	quint@alphacom.com	(403) 245-4512
Debug Computer Services	root@debug.cuc.ab.ca	(403) 248-5798
Nucleus Information Service	markm@nucleus.com	(403) 541-9470
OA Internet Inc.*	info@oanet.com	(403) 430-0811
Edmunton		
Alberta SuperNet, Inc.	info@supernet.ab.ca	(403) 441-3663
CCINet	info@ccinet.ab.ca	(403) 450-6787
ARIZONA		
Phoenix/Mesa		
Crossroads Communications*	info@xroads.com	(602) 813-9040
Evergreen Internet*	evergreen@enet.net	(602) 926-4500
GetNet International, Inc.*	info@getnet.com	(602) 943-3119
Internet Access	bang@neta.com	(602) 820-4000
Internet Direct, Inc.*	info@indirect.com	(602) 274-0100
NETWEST Communications, Inc.	webmaster@netwest.com	(602) 948-5052
Primenet*	info@primenet.com	(602) 395-1010
Systems Solutions Inc.*	webmaster@syspac.com	(602) 955-5566
Tuscon		
ACES Research*	sales@aces.com	(520) 322-6500
Internet Direct, Inc.*	info@indirect.com	(520) 324-0100
Opus One*	info@opus1.com	(520) 324-0494
ARKANSAS		
All points		
Axess Providers*	info@axs.net	(501) 225-6901
Information Galore!	info@elvis.infogo.com	(501) 862-0777
IntelliNet, LLC*	info@intellinet.com	(800) 290-7677

Table A–2: Regional and National Service Providers: U.S. and Canada (continued)

State/City/Provider	E-mail	Telephone
ARKANSAS (continued)		
All points (continued)		
world lynx	ivars@cei.net	(501) 562-8297
YourNET	newuser@yournet.com	(501) 988-9432
BRITISH COLUMBIA		
Vancouver		
auroraNET, Inc.*	sales@aurora.net	(604) 294-4357 x101
Cyberstore Systems, Inc.*	info@cyberstore.net	(604) 482-3400
Helix Internet*	info@helix.net	(604) 689-8544
ICE Online	info@iceonline.com	(604) 298-4346
Internet Direct	sales@direct.ca	(604) 691-1600
MIND LINK! Communication Corporation*	info@mindlink.net	(604) 668-5000
Wimsey Information Services Inc.*	info@wimsey.com	(604) 257-1111
All other points		
A&W Internet Inc.*	info@awinc.com	(604) 763-1176
Fairview Technology Centre Ltd.	bwklatt@ftcnet.com	(604) 498-4316
Island Net, AMT Solutions Group, Inc.	mark@islandnet.com	(604) 383-0096
NETinterior ComputerLinks, Ltd.	info@netinterior.com	(604) 851-9700
Okanagan Internet Junction*	info@junction.net	(604) 549-1036
Sunshine Net, Inc.	admin@sunshine.net	(604) 886-4120
UNIServe Online*	info@uniserve.com	(604) 856-6281
Whistler Networks*	webmaster@whistler.net	(604) 932-0606
CALIFORNIA		
Bakersfield		
Kern Internet Services	support@kern.com	(805) 397-4513
Lightspeed Net	hostmaster@lightspeed.net	(805) 324-4291
Fresno		
Cybergate Internet Services	info@cybergate.com	(209) 486-GATE
InfoNet Communications*	johnb@icinet.net	(209) 446-2360
ValleyNet Communications*	info@valleynet.com	(209) 486-VNET
Los Angeles		
Artnet Communications	info@artnet.net	(310) 659-0122
Cogent Software, Inc.*	info@cogsoft.com	(818) 585-2788
DigiLink Network Services	info@digilink.net	(310) 542-7421
DirectNet*	sales@directnet.com	(213) 383-3144
EarthLink Network	info@earthlink.net	(213) 644-9500
Flamingo Communications Inc.	sales@fcom.com	(310) 532-3533
LA Free-Net	info@lafn.org	(310) 724-8713

Table A–2: Regional and National Service Providers: U.S. and Canada (continued)

State/City/Provider	E-mail	Telephone
CALIFORNIA (continued)		
Los Angeles (continued)		
LA Internet	info@lainet.com	(310) 442-4670
Lightside, Inc.*	info@lightside.net	(818) 858-9261
The Loop Internet Switch Co.	info@loop.com	(213) 465-1311
PacificNet*	info@pacificnet.net	(818) 717-9500
ValNet	info@val.net	(818) 506-5757
Oakland		
Beckemeyer Development*	info@bdt.com	(510) 530-9637
Community ConneXion	info@c2.org	(510) 601-9777
Direct Network Access (DNAI)	info@dnai.com	(510) 649-6110
Idiom Consulting	info@idiom.com	(510) 644-0441
LanMinds, Inc.	info@lanminds.com	(510) 843-6389
Norcov Research	info@norcov.com	(510) 559-9645
Surf Communications, Inc.	info@expressway.com	(800) 499-1517
Orange County		
Delta Internet Services*	sales@delta.net	(714) 778-0370
Riverside/San Bernadino		
EmpireNet	support@empirenet.com	(909) 787-4969
PE.net	info@pe.net	(909) 320-7800
Sacramento/Yolo		
CalWeb Communications*	info@calweb.com	(916) 641-WEB0
Coastal Web Online	info@cwo.com	(916) 552-7922
mother.com, Inc.*	info@mother.com	(916) 757-8070
NSNet*	sales@ns.net	(916) 856-1530
ProMedia	info@promedia.net	(916) 853-5520
QuikNet*	sales@quiknet.com	(916) 773-0917
Sacramento Network Access, Inc.*	ghall@sna.com	(916) 565-4500
San Diego		
American Digital Network	info@adnc.com	(619) 576-4272
ConnectNet	sales@connectnet.com	(619) 450-0254
CTSNet*	info@cts.com	(619) 637-3637
Data Transfer Group	info@thegroup.net	(619) 220-8601
ElectriCiti	info@electriciti.com	(619) 338-9000
SuperSales Internet	wjnorris@supersales.com	(619) 220-2125
ZNet*	info@znet.com	(619) 755-7772
San Francisco		
Connex Communications	admin@connex.com	(415) 386-7734
CreativeNet	info@creative.net	(415) 495-1811 x14
Hooked	info@hooked.net	(415) 343-1233
The Little Garden/TLGnet*	info@tlg.net	(415) 487-1902

Table A–2: Regional and National Service Providers: U.S. and Canada (continued)

State/City/Provider	E-mail	Telephone
CALIFORNIA (continued)		
San Francisco (continued)		
QuakeNet Internet Services*	info@quake.net	(415) 655-6607
Sirius Connections	info@sirius.com	(415) 284-4700
SlipNET*	info@slip.net	(415) 281-3196
Televolve, Inc.	televolve@sfo.com	(415) 867-7712
San Jose/Palo Alto		
Ablecom	support@ablecom.net	(408) 280-1000
Aimnet Infomation Services*	info@aimnet.com	(408) 257-0900
Bay Area Internet Solutions*	info@bayarea.net	(408) 447-8690
InterNex Tiara*	info@internex.net	(408) 496-5466
InterServe Communications, Inc.*	info@interserve.com	(415) 328-4333
Internet Public Access Corporation*	info@ipac.net	(408) 532-1000
ISP Networks*	info@isp.net	(408) 653-0100
MediaCity	info@mediacity.com	(415) 321-6800
NETCOM On-Line Communication Services	info@netcom.com	(408) 983-5950
NetGate Communications*	info@netgate.net	(408) 565-9601
Silicon Valley Public Access Link	support@svpal.org	(408) 448-3071
West Coast Online*	info@wco.com	(800) 926-4683
Ventura		
FishNet Internet Services of Ventura	daveh@fishnet.net	(805) 650-1844
Internet Access of Ventura County	info@vcnet.com	(805) 383-3500
RAIN	rain@rain.org	(805) 650-5354
Silicon Beach Communications*	info@silcom.com	(805) 730-7740
WestNet Communications, Inc.	info@west.net	(805) 892-2133
COLORADO		
Denver/Boulder/Greeley		
Colorado Internet Cooperative Association*	info@coop.net	(303) 443-3786
Colorado SuperNet, Inc.*	info@csn.net	(303) 296-8202
Computer Systems Design Company*	support@csd.net	(303) 443-0808
DASH*	custserv@dash.com	(303) 674-9784
@denver.net	info@denver.net	(303) 973-7757
EnvisioNet	info@envisionet.net	(303) 770-2408
Indra's Net, Inc.	info@indra.com	(303) 546-9151
Colorado (southeast)		
Internet Express*	service@usa.net	(800) 592-1240
OldColo Company	dave@oldcolo.com	(719) 636-2040
Rocky Mountain Internet, Inc.*	info@rmii.com	(800) 900-RMII

Table A–2: Regional and National Service Providers: U.S. and Canada (continued)

State/City/Provider	E-mail	Telephone
CONNECTICUT		
Hartford		
imagine.com*	postmaster@imagine.com	(860) 293-3900
MiraCom*	sales@miracle.net	(860) 523-5677
NETPLEX*	info@ntplx.net	(860) 233-1111
North American Internet Company*	info@nai.net	(800) 952-INET
New Haven/Meriden		
CallNet Information Services	info@callnet.com	(203) 389-7130
PCNet	info@pcnet.com	(203) 250-7397
DELAWARE		
All points		
Business Data Systems, Inc.*	info@bdsnet.com	(302) 674-2840
DCANet*	info@dca.net	(302) 654-1019
iNET Communications*	info@inetcom.net	(302) 454-1780
Internet Delaware	delnet@mail.delnet.com	(302) 737-1001
The Magnetic Page	info@magpage.com	(302) 651-9753
SSNet, Inc.*	info@ssnet.com	(302) 378-1386
DISTRICT OF COLUMBIA		
All points		
Capital Area Internet Service*	info@cais.com	(703) 448-4470
ClarkNet*	info@clark.net	(410) 254-3900
CrossLink	sales@crosslink.net	(703) 642-1120 x175
digitalNATION	lori@csgi.com	(703) 642-2800
Internet Access Group, Inc.	info@iagi.net	(301) 652-0484
Internet Interstate	info@intr.net	(301) 652-4468
NetRail, Inc.*	info@netrail.net	(703) 524-4800
RadixNet*	info@radix.net	(301) 567-9831
USNet*	info@us.net	(301) 572-5926
Virginia Internet Services	info@vais.net	(703) 913-0823
World Web Limited*	info@worldweb.net	(703) 838-2000
FLORIDA		
Jacksonville		
First Coast Online	schuyler@moe.fcol.com	(904) 279-0009
Jacksonville Internet Services, Inc.	info@jax-inter.net	(904) 296-1201
Jax Gateway to the World*	sales@jax.gttw.com	(904) 730-7692
Southeast Network Services, Inc.*	sysop@jaxnet.com	(904) 260-6064
Miami/Fort Lauderdale		
Acquired Knowledge Systems, Inc.	info@aksi.net	(954) 525-2574
BridgeNet, LC	access@bridge.net	(305) 374-3031
Compass.Net	jason@compass.net	(954) 733-2556

Table A-2: Regional and National Service Providers: U.S. and Canada (continued)

State/City/Provider	E-mail	Telephone
FLORIDA (continued)		
Miami/Fort Lauderdale (continued)		
CyberGate*	sales@gate.net	(954) 428-4283
Internet Gateway Connections*	info@igc.net	(954) 430-3030
Neptune.com	mario@neptune.com	(305) 597-8226
NetPoint Communications, Inc.*	info@netpoint.net	(305) 891-1955
Paradise Communications	sales-info@paradise.net	(305) 598-4426
SatelNet Communications	info@satelnet.org	(954) 321-5660
Shadow Information Services, Inc.	admin@shadow.net	(305) 594-3450
World Information Network	info@winnet.net	(305) 535-3090
Orlando		
AccNet*	info@acc.net	(407) 834-2222
Global DataLink, Inc.	info@gdi4.gdi.net	(407) 841-3690
GS-Link Systems Inc.	info@gslink.net	(407) 671-8682
Infinite Space Systems Corporation	info@ispace.com	(407) 850-2404
Internet Access Group*	sales@iag.net	(407) 786-1145
MagicNet, Inc.*	info@magicnet.net	(407) 657-2202
Onet, Inc.	info@onetinc.com	(407) 291-7000
Online Orlando Internet Services	support@oo.com	(407) 647-7559
Sundial Internet Services	info@sundial.net	(407) 438-6710
World Ramp Inc.	info@worldramp.net	(407) 740-5987
Tampa/St. Petersburg/Clearwater		
Bay-A-Net*	info@bayanet.com	(813) 988-7772
Centurion Technology, Inc.	info@tpa.cent.com	(813) 538 1919
CFTnet*	info@cftnet.com	(813) 980 1317
Intelligence Network Online, Inc.*	info@intnet.net	(813) 442-0114
InterAccess	info@interaccess.com	(813) 254-9435
InterNet Integration, Inc.	info@icubed.net	(813) 633-9555
OpenNet*	info@opennet.com	(813) 446-6558
PacketWorks, Inc.	info@packet.net	(813) 446-8826
West Palm Beach/Boca Raton		
The EmiNet Domain*	info@emi.net	(407) 731-0222
Magg Information Services, Inc.*	help@magg.net	(407) 642-9841
Netline Communications, Inc.	info@netline.net	(800) 638-0023
StarDate Communications	info@stardate.com	(407) 683-3235
GEORGIA		
Atlanta		
America Net	sales@america.net	(770) 667-7200
Connect Atlanta	info@america.net	(770) 751-9425
CyberNet Communications	sfeingold@atlwin.com	(770) 518-5711
Digital Service Consultants	john@dscga.com	(770) 455-9022

Table A–2: Regional and National Service Providers: U.S. and Canada (continued)

State/City/Provider	E-mail	Telephone
GEORGIA (continued)		
Atlanta (continued)		
Intergate, Inc.*	info@intergate.net	(770) 429-9599
Internet Atlanta*	info@atlanta.com	(770) 410-9000
Internet Services of Atlanta (ISA)	info@is.net	(770) 662-1616
Lambda.Net Information Services	info@lambda.net	(770) 441-0265
Lyceum Internet Services	info@lyceum.com	(404) 248-1733
Mindspring*	info@mindspring.com	(800) 719-4332
Navigator Communications	sales@nav.com	(770) 441-4007
NetDepot, Inc.*	info@netdepot.com	(770) 434-5595
Random Access, Inc.*	marius@randomc.com	(770) 804-1190
Georgia (north)		
Internet CSRA	info@csra.net	(706) 724-1509
Znet*	info@znet.augusta.ga.us	(706) 722-2175
Georgia (south)		
Homenet Communications, Inc.	info@hom.net	(912) 329-8638
HAWAII		
All points		
1Source*	info@1source.com	(808) 293-0733
Data Plus Systems	hostmaster@dps.net	(808) 678-8989
FLEX INFORMATION NETWORK	postmaster@aloha.com	(808) 732-8849
Hawaii OnLine (HOL)*	info@aloha.net	(800) 207-1880
HulaNet	hulagirl@hula.net	(808) 524-7717
Interlink Hawaii	sales@ilhawaii.net	(808) 334-4000
Inter-Pacific Networks*	sysman@interpac.net	(808) 935-5550
LavaNet	info@lava.net	(808) 545-5282
Maui Global Communications Co.*	info@maui.net	(808) 875-2535
Pacific Information eXchange (PixiNet)*	info@pixi.com	(808) 596-7494
IDAHO		
All points		
Micron Internet Services*	info@micron.net	(208) 368-5400
NICOH Net	info@nicoh.com	(208) 233-5802
SRVnet, Inc.*	nlp@srv.net	(208) 524-6237
ILLINOIS		
Chicago/Gary/Kenosha		
American Information Systems*	info@ais.net	(312) 255-8500
CINnet*	sales@cin.net	(708) 310-1188
Crown.Net Inc.	info@crown.net	(219) 762-1431
InterAccess	info@interaccess.com	(708) 498-2542

Table A–2: Regional and National Service Providers: U.S. and Canada (continued)

State/City/Provider	E-mail	Telephone
ILLINOIS (continued)		
Chicago/Gary/Kenosha (continued)		
Interactive Network Systems	info@insnet.com	(312) 881-3039
Macro Computer Solutions, Inc.*	rate-request@mcs.net	(312) 248-8649
Millenia Services	sales@miint.net	(312) 341-0192
NetWave	info@maui.netwave.net	(800) 961-WAVE
OnRamp, Ltd.	info@theramp.net	(708) 222-6666
Ripco Communications, Inc.	info@ripco.com	(312) 665-0065
StarNet, Inc.	info@starnetinc.com	(708) 382-0099
Sun Valley SoftWare, Ltd.*	ken@svs.com	(708) 983-0889
Tezcat Communications*	info@tezcat.com	(312) 850-0181
ThoughtPort Authority of Chicago*	info@thoughtport.com	(312) 862-6870
Wink Communications*	sales@winkcomm.com	(708) 310-9465
WorldWide Access	info@wwa.com	(708) 367-1870
XNet Information Systems*	info@xnet.com	(708) 983-6064
East St. Louis		
see St. Louis, MISSOURI		
Illinois (central)		
Adams Networks	dley@golden.adams.net	(217) 696-4455
Cen-Com Internet*	info@cencom.net	(217) 793-2771
FGInet, Inc.	admin@fgi.net	(217) 787-2775
ICEnet	icenet@ice.net	(309) 454-4638
Itek*	jasegler@itek.net	(309) 691-6100
Prairienet, The East-Central Illinois FreeNet	info@prairienet.org	(217) 244-1962
Shouting Ground Technologies	admin@shout.net	(217) 351-7921
INDIANA		
Gary		
see Chicago, ILLINOIS		
Indianapolis		
IndyNet	support@indy.net	(317) 251-5208
Internet Indiana*	info@in.net	(317) 876-5NET
IQuest Network Services*	info@iquest.net	(800) 844-8649
Net Direct*	kat@inetdirect.net	(317) 251-5252
surf-ICI	sales@surf-ici.com	(317) 243-7888
IOWA		
Council Bluffs		
see Omaha, NEBRASKA		

Table A–2: Regional and National Service Providers: U.S. and Canada (continued)

State/City/Provider	E-mail	Telephone
IOWA (continued)		
Des Moines		
Des Moines Internet, Inc.*	brentf@dsmnet.com	(515) 270-9191
Freese-Notis WeatherNet*	info@weather.net	(515) 282-9310
INS Info Services*	info@netins.net	(515) 830-0110
JTM Multimedia, Inc.	jtm@ecity.net	(5155) 277-1990
KANSAS		
Kansas City		
see Kansas City, MISSOURI		
Wichita		
DTC Supernet	info@dtc.net	(316) 683-7272
Elysian Fields Inc.	info@elysian.net	(316) 267-2636
Future Net, Inc.	info@fn.net	(316) 652-0070
SouthWind Internet Access, Inc.*	info@southwind.net	(316) 263-7963
KENTUCKY		
Covington		
see Cincinatti, OHIO		
Louisville		
BluegrassNet*	info@bluegrass.net	(502) 589-INET
IgLou Internet Services	info@iglou.com	(502) 966-3848
The Point Internet Services	staff@thepoint.com	(812) 246-7187
LOUISIANA		
Baton Rouge		
Intersurf Online Inc.	info@intersurf.net	(504) 755-0500
Premier One*	info@premier.net	(504) 751-8080
New Orleans		
AccessCom Internet Providers*	info@accesscom.net	(504) 887-0022
CommNet Information	info@comm.net	(504) 836-2844
Communique, Inc.*	info@communique.net	(504) 527-6200
Cyberlink	cladmin@eayor.cyberlink-no.com	(504) 277-4186
Greater New Orleans Free-Net	info@gnofn.org	(504) 539-9239
MAINE		
All points		
AcadiaNet	support@acadia.net	(207) 288-5959
Agate Internet*	ais@agate.net	(207) 947-8248
Biddeford Internet*	info@biddeford.com	(207) 756-8770
Internet Maine Inc.*	mtenney@mainelink.net	(207) 780-0416
The Maine InternetWorks, Inc.*	info@mint.net	(207) 453-4000
MaineStreet Communications	cfm@maine.com	(207) 657-5078
Midcoast Internet Solutions	info@midcoast.com	(207) 594-8277

Table A-2: Regional and National Service Providers: U.S. and Canada (continued)

State/City/Provider	E-mail	Telephone
MANITOBA		
Winnipeg		
Astra Network, Inc.	sales@man.net	(204) 987-7050
Internet Solutions, Inc.*	info@solutions.net	(204) 982-1060
Gate West Communications	info@gatewest.net	(204) 663-2931
Magic Online Services Winnipeg, Inc.	info@magic.mb.ca	(204) 949-7777
All other points		
MTS Internet	registration@mts.net	(800) 280-7095
MARYLAND		
Baltimore		
ABSnet Internet Services, Inc.*	info@abs.net	(410) 361-8160
Charm Net*	info@charm.net	(410) 558-3900
Clark Internet Services, Inc.*	info@clark.net	(410) 254-3900
jaguNET	info@jagunet.com	(410) 931-3157
Maryland (west)		
ARInternet Corporation*	info@ari.net	(301) 459-7171
Digital Express Group–DIGEX*	info@digex.net	(800) 969-9090
EagleNet	info@eagle1.eaglenet.com	(301) 863-6992
Fred.Net*	info@fred.net	(301) 631-5300
Planetcom, Inc.	info@planetcom.com	(301) 258-2963
Tansin A. Darcos & Company	service@tdr.com	(800) TDARCOS
MASSACHUSETTS		
Boston/Worcester/Lawrence		
Blue Sky, Inc.*	info@bluesky.net	(617) 270-4747
CENTnet, Inc.	info@cent.net	(617) 492-6079
Channel 1	info@channel1.com	(800) 745-2747
COWZ Technologies	beef@cow.net	(617) COW-TOWN
CyberAccess Internet Communication, Inc.	info@cybercom.net	(617) 396-0491
North Shore Access	info@shore.net	(617) 593-3110
One World Network*	sales@oneworld.net	(617) 267-2440
Pioneer Global Telecommunications*	sales@pn.com	(617) 375-0200
Software Tool & Die	support@world.std.com	(617) 739-0202
TerraNet Internet Services*	info@terra.net	(617) 450-9000
TIAC	info_ma@tiac.net	(617) 276-7200
Wilder InterNet Gateway*	info@wing.net	(617) 932-8500
The Xensei Corporation	info@xensei.com	(617) 376-6342
Fall River		
see Providence, RHODE ISLAND		

Table A-2: Regional and National Service Providers: U.S. and Canada (continued)

State/City/Provider	E-mail	Telephone
MASSACHUSETTS (continued)		
Springfield		
MAP Internet Services*	info@map.com	(413) 732-0214
MICHIGAN		
Detroit/Ann Arbor/Flint		
Branch Internet Services Inc.*	info@branch.com	(800) 349-1747
CICNet*	info@cic.net	(313) 998-6703
Gateway Online	accounts@gatecom.com	(313) 291-2666
ICNet*	info@ic.net	(313) 998-0090
Isthmus Corporation	info@izzy.net	(313) 973-2100
Merit/MichNet*	info@merit.edu	(313) 764-9430
Msen*	service@msen.com	(313) 998-4562
O & E On-Line!	info@oeonline.com	(313) 591-2300
Michigan (central)		
Arrownet	info@arrownet.com	(800) 999-4409
Sojourn Systems Ltd.*	info@sojourn.com	(800) 949-3993
Michigan (west and north)		
Alliance Network, Inc.	info@alliance.net	(616) 774-3010
Freeway*	info@freeway.net	(616) 347-3175
Iserv*	info@iserv.net	(616) 847-5254
Novagate	info@novagate.com	(616) 847-0910
The Portage	fuzzy@portage1.portup.com	(906) 487-9832
MINNESOTA		
Minneapolis/St. Paul		
Bitstream Underground	gods@bitstream.net	(612) 321-9290
Digital Solutions, Inc.	info@solon.com	(612) 488-1740
gofast.net	info@gofast.net	(612) 647-6109
GoldenGate Internet Services, Inc.	timmc@goldengate.net	(612) 574-2200
InterNetwork Services*	info@proteon.inet-serv.com	(612) 391-7300
Millennium Communications, Inc.*	info@millcomm.com	(612) 338-8666
MinnNet*	info@minn.net	(612) 944-8660
Minneapolis Telecommunications Network	mtn@mtn.org	(612) 331-8575
Minnesota MicroNet	info@mm.com	(612) 882-7711
Minnesota Online*	sales@mn.state.net	(612) 225-1110
The Minnesota Regional Network*	info@mr.net	(612) 342-2570
Orbis Internet Services, Inc.	info@orbis.net	(612) 645-9663
pclink.com	infomatic@pclink.com	(612) 541-5656
Protocol Communications	info@protocol.com	(612) 541-9900
Sihope Communications	info@sihope.com	(612) 829-9667

Table A–2: Regional and National Service Providers: U.S. and Canada (continued)

State/City/Provider	E-mail	Telephone
MINNESOTA (continued)		
Minneapolis/St. Paul (continued)		
SkyPoint Communications, Inc.*	info@skypoint.com	(612) 475-2959
Vector Internet Services, Inc.*	info@visi.com	(612) 288-0880
Vitex Communications	info@vitex.com	(612) 822-1166
WaveFront Communications, Inc.*	info@wavefront.com	(612) 638-9594
WebSpan	info@webspan.com	(612) 333-LINK
Winternet (Startnet Communications)	info@winternet.com	(612) 941-9177
Minnesota (north)		
Computer Pro	info@computerpro.com	(218) 772-4245
Minnesota (south)		
Desktop Media*	isp@dm.deskmedia.com	(507) 373-2155
Information Superhighway Limited	info@isl.net	(507) 289-5543
Internet Connections, Inc.*	info@ic.mankato.mn.us	(507) 625-7320
Millennium Communications, Inc.*	info@millcomm.com	(507) 282-1004
MISSISSIPPI		
All points		
Aris Technologies*	info@aris.com	(601) 324 7638
Datasync Internet Services	info@datasync.com	(601) 872-0001
EBI Comm, Inc.*	hostmaster@ebicom.net	(601) 243-7075
Internet Doorway, Inc.*	info@netdoor.com	(800) 952-1570
InterSys Technologies, Inc.*	info@inst.com	(601) 949-6992
Southwind Technologies, Inc.	info@southwind.com	(601) 374-6510
TecLink*	info@teclink.net	(601) 949-6992
MISSOURI		
Kansas City		
AccuNet, Inc.*	dwhitten@accunet.com	(816) 246-9094
Databank, Inc.*	info@databank.com	(913) 842-6699
Internet Direct Communications	sales@idir.net	(913) 842-1100
Interstate Networking Corporation*	info@interstate.net	(816) 472-4949
Q-Net, Inc.	info@qni.com	(816) 795-1000
SkyNet*	info@sky.net	(816) 421-2626
Unicom Communications, Inc.*	fyi@unicom.net	(913) 383-8466
St. Louis		
Cybergate L.L.C.	info@cybergate.org	(314) 214-1013
iCON	info@icon-stl.net	(314) 241-ICON
Inlink	support@inlink.com	(314) 432-0149

Table A-2: Regional and National Service Providers: U.S. and Canada (continued)

State/City/Provider	E-mail	Telephone
MONTANA		
All points		
Avicom, Inc.	avicom@montana.avicom.net	(406) 587-6177
Cyberport Montana*	skippy@cyberport.net	(406) 863-3221
Internet Connect Services	ics@montana.com	(406) 721-4952
Internet Montana	support@imt.net	(406) 255-9699
Internet Services Montana, Inc.*	support@ism.net	(406) 542-0838
Montana Communications Network	info@mcn.net	(406) 254-9413
Netrix Internet System Design, Inc.*	leesa@netrix.net	(406) 257-4638
NEBRASKA		
Omaha		
Nebraska On-Ramp, Inc.	info@neonramp.com	(402) 339-6366
NFinity Systems	info@nfinity.com	(402) 551-3036
Nebraska (west)		
see NATIONAL COVERAGE		
NEVADA		
Las Vegas		
Access Nevada, Inc.*	info@accessnv.com	(702) 294-0480
InterMind*	info@intermind.net	(702)878-6111
@wizard.com*	george@wizard.com	(702) 871-4461
All other points		
Connectus*	info@connectus.com	(702) 323-2008
Great Basin Internet Services*	info@greatbasin.com	(702) 348-7299
NevadaNet	braddlee@nevada.edu	(702) 784-6861
Sierra-Net	info@sierra.net	(702) 832-6911
SourceNet*	info@source.net	(702) 832-7246
Tahoe On-Line	info@tol.net	(702) 588-0616
NEW BRUNSWICK		
All points		
Maritime Internet Services, Inc.	sales@mi.net	(506) 652-3624
NEWFOUNDLAND		
All points		
Data Bits, Inc.	info@databits.com	(709) 786 5660
NLnet	slipreq@nlnet.nf.ca	(709) 737-4555
NEW HAMPSHIRE		
All points		
The Destek Group, Inc.*	info@destek.net	(603) 635-3857
Empire.Net, Inc.	info@empire.net	(603) 889-1220
John Leslie Consulting	info@jlc.net	(603) 673-6132

Table A-2: Regional and National Service Providers: U.S. and Canada (continued)

State/City/Provider	E-mail	Telephone
NEW HAMPSHIRE (continued)		
All points (continued)		
Mainstream Electronic Information Services	info@mainstream.net	(603) 424-1497
MonadNet Corporation*	info@monad.net	(603) 352-7619
MV Communications, Inc.	info@mv.mv.com	(603) 429-2223
NETIS Public Access Internet	info@netis.com	(603) 437-1811
North Country Internet Access	ed@moose.ncia.net	(603) 752-1250
NEW JERSEY		
Bergen/Passaic		
Carroll-Net	info@carroll.com	(201) 488-1332
Interactive Networks, Inc.	info@interactive.net	(201) 881-1878
Internet Online Services	info@ios.com	(201) 928-1000
nic.com	info@nic.com	(201) 934-1445
Jersey City		
The Connection	info@cnct.com	(201) 435-4414
Mordor International	info@mordor.com	(201) 433-7343
Middlesex/Somerset/Hunterdon		
ECLIPSE Internet Access*	info@eclipse.net	(800) 483-1223
Internet For 'U'*	info@ifu.net	(908) 435-0600
Superlink*	info@superlink.net	(908) 828-8988
Texel International	info@texel.com	(908) 297-0290
Monmouth/Ocean		
Atlantic Internet Technologies, Inc.*	info@exit109.com	(908) 758-0505
Monmouth Internet	sales@shell.monmouth.com	(908) 389-6094
NEW MEXICO		
Albuquerque		
Internet Direct, Inc.*	info@indirect.com	(505) 888-4624
New Mexico Internet Access, Inc.*	info@nmia.com	(505) 877-0617
New Mexico Technet, Inc.*	granoff@technet.nm.org	(505) 345-6555
Rt66-Engineering International, Inc.*	info@rt66.com	(505) 343-1060
Southwest Cyberport	info@swcp.com	(505) 271-0009
Terra Communications	office@terra.com	(505) 256-1676
Santa Fe		
Roadrunner Communications*	sysop@roadrunner.com	(505) 988-9200
Studio X	info@nets.com	(505) 438-0505
All other points		
Community Internet Access	sysadm@cia-g.com	(505) 863-2424
CyberPort Station	info@cyberport.com	(505) 324-6400

Table A–2: Regional and National Service Providers: U.S. and Canada (continued)

State/City/Provider	E-mail	Telephone
NEW YORK		
Albany/Schenectady/Troy		
AlbanyNet*	info@albany.net	(518) 465-0873
Automatrix	info@automatrix.com	(518) 372-5583
Global One	info@globalone.net	(518) 452-1465
LogicalNet*	sales@logical.net	(518) 452-9090
NetHeaven	info@netheaven.com	(518) 885-1295
Wizvax Communications*	info@wizvax.net	(518) 273-4325
Nassau/Suffolk Counties		
Long Island Internet HQ & Pointblank BBS Ltd.	support@pb.net	(516) 549-2165
Long Island Information, Inc.	info@liii.com	(516) 248-5381
Long Island Net	info@li.net	(516) 265-0997
Network-USA	all-info@netusa.net	(516) 543-0240
North American Internet Services	info@nais.com	(516) 358-8204
Savvy Communications	info@savvy.com	(800) 275-7455
Sestran Industries, Inc.	info@sestran.com	(516) 253-3362
SpecNet	sysadmin@specdata.com	(516) 735-9678
New York City		
Angel Networks	info@angel.net	(212) 947-6507
Blythe Systems	accounts@blythe.org	(212) 979-0471
BrainLINK	info@brainlink.com	(718) 805-6559
bway.net (Outernet, Inc.)	info-bot@bway.net	(212) 982-9800
Calyx Internet Access*	info@calyx.net	(212) 475-5051
Cloud 9 Internet*	info@cloud9.net	(914) 682-0626
The Dorsai Embassy, Inc.	system@dorsai.org	(718) 392-3667
dx.com	info@dx.com	(212) 929-0566
elroNet	info@elron.net	(212) 935-3110
EscapeCom*	info@escape.com	(212) 888-8780
i-2000*	info@i-2000.com	(800) 464-3820
Ingress Communications, Inc.*	info@ingress.com	(212) 268-1100
Internet Channel*	info@inch.com	(212) 243-5200
Internet Exchange*	ksc@inx.net	(212) 935-3322
Internet Quicklink Corp.*	info@quicklink.com	(212) 307-1669
Interport Communications Corp.*	info@interport.net	(212) 989-1128
Maestro Technologies, Inc.*	info@maestro.com	(212) 240-9600
New York Net*	info@new-york.net	(718) 776-6811
The New York Web, Inc.*	nysurf@nyweb.com	(212) 748-7600
NY WEBB, Inc.	gwg7@webb.com	(212) 242-4912
Panix	info@panix.com	(212) 741-4400
PCW Internet Services*	sales@pcwnet.com	(718) 937-0380

Table A–2: Regional and National Service Providers: U.S. and Canada (continued)

State/City/Provider	E-mail	Telephone
NEW YORK (continued)		
New York City (continued)		
PFM Communications*	marc@pfmc.net	(212) 254-5300
Phantom Access Technologies, Inc. / MindVox	info@phantom.com	(212) 989-2418
Pipeline New York	info@nyc.pipeline.com	(212) 267-3636
RealNet*	reallife@walrus.com	(212) 366-4434
SenseNet, Inc.	sales@sensenet.com	(212) 824-5000
SILLY.COM	info@silly.com	(718) 229-7096
ThoughtPort Authority of NYC*	info@thoughtport.com	(212) 645-7970
TunaNet/InfoHouse	info@tunanet.com	(212) 229-8224
Rochester		
E-Znet, Inc.*	info@eznet.net	(716) 262-2485
ServiceTech, Inc.*	sales@servtech.com	(716) 263-3360
Vivanet	info@vivanet.com	(716) 272-9101
Syracuse		
Dreamscape	temerick@dreamscape.com	(315) 446-2626
EMI Communications*	info@emi.com	(800) 456-2001
Syracuse Internet	info@vcomm.net	(315) 233-1948
NORTH CAROLINA		
Charlotte/Gastonia/Rock Hill		
Cybernetx, Inc.*	info@cybernetics.net	(704) 561-7000
SunBelt.Net*	info@sunbelt.net	(800) 950-4726
Vnet Internet Access, Inc.	info@vnet.net	(800) 377-3282
Greensboro/Winston-Salem/High Point		
Kinetics, Inc.*	info@kinetics.net	(910) 370-1985
Online South	info@ols.net	(910) 983-7212
Red Barn Data Center	postmaster@rbdc.rbdc.com	(910) 774-1600
SpyderByte	info@spyder.net	(910) 643-6999
Raleigh/Durham/Chapel Hill		
Atlantic Internet Corporation*	info@ainet.net	(919) 833-1252
Interpath*	info@interpath.net	(800) 849-6305
NandO.Net	info@nando.net	(919) 836-2808
NC-REN Data Services*	info@ncren.net	(919) 248-1999
Network Data Link, Inc.	staff@nc.ndl.net	(919) 878-7701
NORTH DAKOTA		
All points		
Dakota Internet Access	admin@host1.dia.net	(701) 774-DIA1
Red River Net*	info@rrnet.com	(701) 232-2227
The Internet Connection. Inc.*	tic@emh1.tic.bismarck.nd.us	(701) 222-8356

Table A–2: Regional and National Service Providers: U.S. and Canada (continued)

State/City/Provider	E-mail	Telephone
NORTHWEST TERRITORIES		
All points		
Internet North	stevel@internorth.com	(403) 873-5975
Network North Communications, Ltd.	info@netnorth.com	(403) 873-2059
NOVA SCOTIA		
All points		
Atlantic Connect Inc.	info@atcon.com	(902) 429-0222
Internet Passport Services	sales@ips.ca	(902) INT-ERNET
internet services and information systems (isis) Inc.	info@isisnet.com	(902) 429-4747
North Shore Internet Services	support@north.nsis.com	(902) 928-0565
NSTN Incorporated*	info@nstn.ca	(902) 481-NSTN (6786)
OHIO		
Cincinnati/Hamilton		
Exodus Online Services	info@eos.net	(513) 522-0011
horanDATA	info@horandata.net	(513) 241-3282
Internet Access Cincinnati / M&M Engineering*	info@iac.net	(513) 887-8877
OneNet Communications*	info@one.net	(513) 326-6000
Premiere Internet Cincinnati*	pic@cinti.com	(513) 561-6245
Primax.Net	info@primax.net	(513) 772-1223
Cleveland/Akron		
APK*	info@apk.net	(216) 481-9428
BBS One OnLine Service	jimdief@bbsone.com	(216) 825-5217
CyberGate	info@cybergate.net	(216) 247-7660
ExchangeNet (EN)*	info@en.com	(216) 261-4593
GWIS	info@gwis.com	(216) 656-5511
Multiverse	noc@mail.multiverse.com	(216) 344-3080
New Age Consulting Services*	info@nacs.net	(216) 524-8388
Winfield Communication, Inc.	info@winc.com	(216) 867-2904
Columbus		
Global Access Network	info@ganet.net	(614) 766-1258
Infinet, Infinite Systems	info@infinet.com	(614) 268 9941
Internet Concourse	info@coil.com	(614) 242-3800
OARnet*	info@oar.net	(614) 728-8100
Dayton/Springfield		
Dayton Internet Services, Inc.*	info@dayton.net	(513) 643-0188
The Dayton Network Access Co.	info@dnaco.net	(513) 237-6868
DONet, Inc.	info@donet.com	(513) 256-7288

Table A-2: Regional and National Service Providers: U.S. and Canada (continued)

State/City/Provider	E-mail	Telephone
OHIO (continued)		
Dayton/Springfield (continued)		
EriNet Online Communications*	support@erinet.com	(513) 291-1995
HCST-Net*	info@hcst.com	(513) 390-7486
Youngstown/Warren		
CISNet, Inc.*	todd@cisnet.com	(216) 629-2691
OKLAHOMA		
Oklahoma City		
InterConnect On-Line*	info@icon.net	(405) 949-1800
Internet Oklahoma	info@ionet.net	(405) 721-1580
Keystone Technology	sales@keytech.com	(405) 848-9902
Tulsa		
Galaxy Star Systems*	info@galstar.com	(918) 835-3655
OKNET*	oksales@oknet.com	(918) 481-5899
ONTARIO		
Ottawa		
Achilles Internet Ltd.	info@achilles.net	(613) 723-6624
Channel One Internet Services*	getwired@sonetis.com	(613) 236-8601
Comnet Communications	info@comnet.ca	(613) 747-5555
Cyberus Online Inc.	info@cyberus.ca	(613) 233-1215
In@sec	info@inasec.ca	(613) 746-3200
info.web, A Division of MAGI Data Consulting Inc.	info@magi.com	(613) 225-3354
Interactive Telecom Inc.	info@intertel.net	(613) 727-5258
Internet Access Inc.*	info@ottawa.net	(613) 225-5595
Internet Connectivity, Inc.	helpdesk@icons.net	(613) 828-6221
Magma Communications Ltd.*	info@magmacom.com	(613) 228-3565
NewForce Communications	feedback@newforce.ca	(819) 682-9893
Resudox Online Services, Inc.	admin@2resudox.net	(613) 567-6925
Synapse Internet	info@synapse.net	(819) 561-1697
Trytel Internet, Inc.	dialup@trytel.com	(613) 722-6321
WorldLink Internet Services	info@worldlink.ca	(613) 233-7100
Toronto		
9 To 5 Communications	staff@inforamp.net	(416) 363-9100
All Systems Go	info@asgo.net	(416) 961-7399
CIMtegration Ltd.	info@cimtegration.com	(416) 665-3566
Enterprise Online	sales@enterprise.ca	(416) 932-3030
InfoRamp, Inc.	info@inforamp.net	(416) 363-9100
Interlog Internet Services	info@interlog.com	(416) 975-2655
Internet Front Inc.	support@internetfront.com	(416) 293-8539

Table A–2: Regional and National Service Providers: U.S. and Canada (continued)

State/City/Provider	E-mail	Telephone
ONTARIO (continued)		
Toronto (continued)		
Internet Light and Power	staff@ilap.com	(416) 502-1512
Internex Online	info@io.org	(416) 363-8676
ONet Networking*	info@onet.on.ca	(416) 978-4589
Pathway Communications	info@pathcom.com	(416) 214 6235
TerraPoint Online, Inc.	info@terraport.net	(416) 492-3050
UUNorth International	info@mail.north.net	(416) 225-8649
The Wire	info@the-wire.com	(416) 214-WIRE
World Wide Wave*	info@wwwave.com	(416) 499-7100
Xenon Laboratories	info@xe.net	(416) 214-5606
OREGON		
Portland/Salem		
aracnet.com	info@aracnet.com	(503) 626-7696
Autobahn Internet Services Inc.	info@northwest.com	(503) 775-9523
CenORneT	info@cenornet.com	(503) 557-9047
CyberNet NorthWest	sales@cybernw.com	(503) 256-5350
DTR Communications Services	info@dtr.com	(503) 252-5059
Europa	info@europa.com	(503) 222-9508
Hevanet Communications	info@hevanet.com	(503) 228-3520
Industrial	root@industrial.com	(503) 636-9931
NetRamp	info@netramp.com	(503) 650-8193
One World Internetworking, Inc.	info@oneworld.com	(503) 758-1112
Pacifier Online Data Service	sales@pacifier.com	(360) 693-2116
RainDrop Laboratories	info@agora.rdrop.com	(503) 293-1772
Spire Communications*	info@spiretech.com	(503) 222-3086
Structured Network Systems*	sales@structured.net	(503) 656-3530
Teleport Internet Services	info@teleport.com	(503) 223-0076
Transport Logic*	info@transport.com	(503) 243-1940
A World Locally	thorton@locally.com	(503) 251-2078
All other points		
BendNet	info@bendnet.com	(503) 385-3331
Data Research Group, Inc.	info@ordata.com	(503) 465-DATA
Empire Net, Inc.	webmaster@empnet.com	(503) 317-3437
InfoStructure	info@mind.net	(503) 488-1962
Magick Net, Inc.	peabody@magick.net	(503) 471-2542
mtjeff.com	info@mtjeff.com	(503) 475-6233
Northwest Internet Services	info@rio.com	(503) 485-7601
Open Door Networks, Inc.	info@opendoor.com	(503) 488-4127
RAINet	help@rain.net	(503) 227-5665

Table A-2: Regional and National Service Providers: U.S. and Canada (continued)

State/City/Provider	E-mail	Telephone
PENNSYLVANIA		
Allentown/Bethlehem/Easton		
Early Access	info@early.com	(610) 770-7800
Enter.Net*	info@enter.net	(610) 366-1300
Internet Tidal Wave	steve@itw.com	(610) 770-6187
Oasis Telecommunication, Inc.	info@ot.com	(610) 439-8560
You Tools Internet*	info@fast.net	(610) 954-5910
Harrisburg/Lebanon/Carlisle		
CPCNet	webmaster@news.cpcnet.com	(717) 393-2956
Keystone Information Access Systems	office@yrkpa.kias.com	(717) 741-2626
LebaNet*	office@leba.net	(717) 270-9790
SuperNet Interactive Services, Inc.*	info@success.net	(717) 393-7635
Philadelphia		
FishNet	info@pond.com	(610) 337-9994
Micro Control, Inc.	info@inet.micro-ctrl.com	(215) 321-7474
Net Access*	info@netaxs.com	(215) 576-8669
OpNet	info@op.net	(610) 520-2880
RE/COM - Reliable Communications*	sales@recom.com	(609) 225-3330
Voicenet*	info@voicenet.com	(800) 835-5710
Pittsburgh		
CityNet, Inc.*	info@city-net.com	(412) 481-5406
Nauticom	info@pgh.nauticom.net	(800) 746-6283
Pittsburgh OnLine, Inc.*	sales@pgh.net	(412) 681-6130
Stargate	info@sgi.net	(412) 942-4218
Telerama Public Access Internet*	info@telerama.lm.com	(412) 481-3505
ThoughtPort Authority of Pittsburgh	info@thoughtport.com	(412) 963-7099
USA OnRamp*	info@usaor.net	(412) 391-4382
Scranton/Wilkes-Barre/Hazelton		
The Internet Cafe, Scranton, PA*	info@lydian.scranton.com	(717) 344-1969
MicroServe Information Systems, Inc.*	helpdesk@admin.microserve.net	(717) 821-5964
QUEBEC		
Montreal		
Accent Internet	admin@accent.net	(514) 737-6077
CiteNet Telecom Inc.*	info@citenet.net	(514) 861-5050
Communications Accessibles Montreal	info@cam.org	(514) 288-2581
Connection MMIC, Inc.	michel@connectmmic.net	(514) 331-6642
Global Info Access	info@globale.net	(514) 737-2091
Infobahn	info@infobahnos.com	(514) 481-2585

Table A–2: Regional and National Service Providers: U.S. and Canada (continued)

State/City/Provider	E-mail	Telephone
QUEBEC (continued)		
Montreal (continued)		
NetAxis Inc. of Montreal	info@netaxis.qc.ca	(514) 482-8989
Odyssey Internet*	info@odyssee.net	(514) 861-3432
PubNIX Montreal*	info@PubNIX.net	(514) 990-5911
ZooNet	info@zoo.net	(514) 935-6225
All other points		
ClicNet Telecommunications Inc.	info@qbc.clic.net	(418) 686-CLIC
Valiquet Lamothe, Inc. (VLI)	info@vli.ca	(819) 776-4438
RHODE ISLAND		
Providence/Fall River/Warwick		
IDS World Network	info@ids.net	(401) 884-7856
Log On America	info@loa.com	(401) 453-6100
All other points		
Aquidneck Web Inc.	sysop@aqua.net	(401) 841-5WWW
brainiac services, inc.	info@brainiac.com	(401) 539-9050
SASKATCHEWAN		
All points		
SaskTel	info@www.sasknet.sk.ca	(800) 644-9205
SOUTH CAROLINA		
Charleston		
Horry Telephone Cooperative / Coastal Cruiser Internet Access	htc@sccoast.net	(803) 365-2155
SIMS, Inc.*	info@sims.com	(803) 853-4333
A World of Difference*	sales@awod.com	(803) 769-4488
Rock Hill		
see Charlotte, NORTH CAROLINA		
SOUTH DAKOTA		
All points		
Dakota Internet Services, Inc.	service@dakota.net	(605) 371-1962
Internet Services of the Black Hills, Inc.	rryan@blackhills.com	(605) 642-2244
RapidNet LLC	gary@rapidnet.com	(605) 341-3283
SoDak Net	info@sodak.net	(605) 582-2549
TENNESSEE		
Knoxville		
GoldSword Sys	info@goldsword.com	(423) 691-6498
Internet Communications Group	info@netgrp.net	(423) 691-1731
United States Internet, Inc.*	info@usit.net	(800) 218-USIT
World Net Communications	info@wncom.com	(423) 922-2326

Table A-2: Regional and National Service Providers: U.S. and Canada (continued)

State/City/Provider	E-mail	Telephone
TENNESSEE (continued)		
Memphis		
Magibox, Inc.	info@magibox.net	(901) 452-7555
NetLinx Technologies	sales@netlnx.com	(901) 757-5351
Synapse	info@syncentral.com	(901) 767-9926
World Spice	info@wsp1.wspice.com	(901) 454-5808
Nashville		
CoolBeans Network	leblanc@coolbeans.net	(615) 519-6832
Edge Internet Services*	info@edge.net	(615) 726-8700
ISDNet*	info@isdn.net	(615) 377-7672
Last Straw Communications	info@laststraw.com	(615) 519-6832
The Telalink Corporation*	info@telalink.net	(615) 321-9100
United States Internet, Inc.*	info@usit.net	(615) 259-2006
TEXAS		
Austin/San Marcos		
Commuter Communication Systems	info@commuter.net	(512) 257-CCSI
CyberTects	staff@einstein.ssz.com	(512) 832-4849
The Eden Matrix	info@eden.com	(512) 478-9900
Freeside Communications, Inc.	info@fc.net	(512) 339-6094
i-link	info@i-link.net	(512) 388-2393
Illuminati Online	info@io.com	(512) 462-0999
Moon Tower, Inc.	help@moontower.com	(512) 837-8670
Onramp Access, Inc.	info@onr.com	(512) 322-9200
OuterNet Connection Strategies	info@outer.net	(512) 345-3573
Real/Time Communications*	sales@bga.com	(512) 206-3124
@sig.net*	sales@sig.net	(512) 306-0700
Turning Point Information Services*	info@tpoint.net	(512) 499-8400
Zilker Internet Park	info@zilker.net	(512) 206-3850
Dallas/Fort Worth		
CompuNet*	info@computek.net	(214) 994-0190
Connect! On-Line*	info@online.com	(214) 396-0038
ConnectNet*	info@connect.net	(214) 490-7100
CyberRamp.net	admin@cyberramp.net	(214) 340-2020
Dallas Internet*	manager@dallas.net	(214) 881-9595
DFWNet*	info@dfw.net	(800) 2-DFW-NET
DFW VietNet, saomai.org	info@saomai.org	(214) 705-2900 x58
FastLane Communications, Inc.	info@fastlane.net	(817) 589-2400
Galaxy Access Network	info@gan.net	(214) 396-0038
Internet America	info@iadfw.net	(214) 491-7134
National Knowledge Networks, Inc.*	info@nkn.net	(214) 880-0700
On-Ramp Technologies, Inc.*	info@onramp.net	(214) 746-4710

Table A-2: Regional and National Service Providers: U.S. and Canada (continued)

State/City/Provider	E-mail	Telephone
TEXAS (continued)		
Dallas/Fort Worth (continued)		
PICnet	info@pic.net	(214) 789-0456
Plano Internet*	manager@plano.net	(214) 881-9595
Spindlemedia	info@spindle.net	(817) 332-5661
Texas Metronet, Inc.	info@metronet.com	(214) 705-2900
UniComp Technologies, Inc.	info@unicomp.net	(214) 663-3155
Why? Internet Services	info@whytel.com	(817) 795-1765
Houston/Galveston/Brazoria		
Access Communications	info@accesscomm.net	(713) 896-6556
Black Box	info@blkbox.com	(713) 480-2684
Centurion Technology-Houston	info@cent.com	(713) 878-9980
Compass Net, Inc.	info@compassnet.com	(713) 776-0022
Connections.Com, Inc.	info@concom.com	(713) 680-9333
CyberSim	cybersim@cybersim.com	(713) 229-9992
Digital MainStream, Inc.*	schmidt@main.com	(713) 364-1819
Electrotex	info@electrotex.com	(800) 460-1801
GHG Corporation	info@ghgcorp.com	(713) 488-8806
InfoCom Networks	info@infocom.net	(713) 286-0399
Info-Highway International, Inc.*	info@infohwy.com	(713) 447-7025
Insync Internet Services*	jimg@insync.net	(713) 961-4242
interGate	gcox@intergate.com	(713) 558-7200
IWL Net	info@iwl.net	(713) 992-4082
NeoSoft, Inc.*	info@neosoft.com	(713) 968-5800
NetOne	info@net1.net	(713) 688-9111
NetTap Data Services	helpdesk@nettap.com	(713) 482-3903
Phoenix DataNet*	helpdesk@mailserv.phoenix.net	(713) 486-8337
Sesquinet	info@sesqui.net	(713) 527-6038
South Coast Computing Services, Inc.	sales@sccsi.com	(713) 917-5000
United States Information Superhighway	info@usis.com	(713) 682-1666
Wantabe, Inc.	ggkelley@wantabe.com	(713) 493-0718
San Antonio		
Internet Direct	nerone@txdirect.net	(210) 308-9800
NetXpress	info@netxpress.com	(210) 822-7887
Salsa.Net	info@salsa.net	(210) 704-3770
South Texas Internet Connections	info@stic.net	(210) 828-4910
Texas Networking, Inc.	helpdesk@texas.net	(210) 272-8111

Table A–2: Regional and National Service Providers: U.S. and Canada (continued)

State/City/Provider	E-mail	Telephone
UTAH		
Salt Lake City/Ogden		
ArosNet*	info@aros.net	(801) 532-AROS
Internet Alliance*	adm@alinc.com	(801) 964-8490
KDC On-Line	support@kdcol.com	(801) 497-9931
ThoughtPort Authority of Salt Lake City*	info@thoughtport.com	(801) 596-2277
Utah Wired	pam@utw.com	(801) 532-1117
X-Mission*	support@xmission.com	(801) 539-0852
All other points		
AXXIS Internet Service*	webmaster@axxis.com	(801) 565-1443
CacheNET*	hal@cachenet.com	(801) 753-2199
DirecTell LC*	kathy@ditell.com	(801) 647-5838
Emery Telecommunications and Video	sales@etv.net	(801) 748-2388
Fibernet Corporation*	info@fiber.net	(801) 223-9939
Infonaut Communication Services	info@infonaut.com	(801) 370-3060
InfoWest*	info@infowest.com	(801) 674-0165
VERMONT		
All points		
SoVerNet	info@sover.net	(802) 463-2111
TGF Technologies, Inc.	info@together.net	(802) 862-2030
ValleyNet	info@valley.net	(802) 649-2200
VIRGINIA		
Norfolk/Virginia Beach/Newport News		
Exis Net, Inc.	support@exis.net	(804) 552-1009
InfiNet*	sales@infi.net	(804) 622-4289
Pinnacle Online	info@pinn.net	(804) 490-4509
Richmond/Petersburg		
Global Connect, Inc.	info@gc.net	(804) 229-4484
I 2020*	info@i2020.net	(804) 330-5555
Widomaker Communication Services	info@widomaker.com	(804) 253-7621
WASHINGTON		
Seattle/Tacoma		
Access One	info@accessone.com	(206) 827-5344
Alternate Access, Inc.*	info@aa.net	(206) 728-9585
Blarg! Online Services*	info@blarg.com	(206) 784-9681
Compumedia, Inc.*	support@compumedia.com	(206) 623-8065
Cyberspace	info@cyberspace.com	(206) 505-5577
Eskimo North*	nanook@eskimo.com	(206) FOREVER

Table A–2: Regional and National Service Providers: U.S. and Canada (continued)

State/City/Provider	E-mail	Telephone
WASHINGTON (continued)		
Seattle/Tacoma (continued)		
Interconnected Associates, Inc.*	info@ixa.com	(206) 622-7337
Northwest Link*	staff@nwlink.net	(206) 451-1151
Northwest Nexus, Inc.*	info@halcyon.com	(206) 455-3505
NWNet*	info@nwnet.net	(206) 562-3000
NWRAINET, Inc.*	info@nwrain.com	(206) 566-6800
Olympic Computing Solutions	ocs@oz.net	(206) 989-6698
Seanet*	seanet@seanet.com	(206) 343-7828
Seattle Community Network	help@scn.org	(206) 365-4528
TCM Communications	rgrothe@tcm.nbs.net	(206) 941-1474
WOLFE Internet Access, LLC*	info@wolfe.net	(206) 443-1397
Washington (east)		
AT-NET Connections, Inc.	support@atnet.net	(509) 766-7253
Blue Mountain Internet	info@bmi.net	(509) 522-5006
Cascade Connections, Inc.	root@cascade.net	(509) 663-4259
Computech*	admin@iea.com	(509) 624-6798
EagleNet*	info@soar.com	(509) 466-3535
Internet Connection	info@eznet.com	(509) 022-0417
Internet On-Ramp	info@on-ramp.ior.com	(509) 624-RAMP
One World Telecommunications, Inc.*	info@oneworld.owt.com	(509) 735-0408
Televar Northwest*	info@televar.com	(509) 664-9004
WEST VIRGINIA		
All points		
CityNet Corporation	info@citynet.net	(304) 342-5700
IANet	info@ianet.net	(304) 453-5757
Intrepid Technologies, Inc.*	info@intrepid.net	(304) 876-1199
MountainNet, Inc.*	info@mountain.net	(304) 594-9075
Ram Technologies	sales@ramlink.net	(304) 522-1726
WISCONSIN		
Kenosha		
see Chicago, ILLINOIS		
Milwaukee/Waukesha		
alpha.net*	info@alpha.net	(414) 274-7050
Exec-PC BBS	info@earth.execpc.com	(800) EXECPC-1
Great Lakes Area Commercial Internet Company	info@glaci.com	(414) 475-6388
I.Net Solutions, Inc.	info@mke.com	(414) 785-0920
Internet Connect, Inc.*	info@inc.net	(414) 476-ICON
MIX Communications	info@mixcom.com	(414) 351-1868

Table A–2: Regional and National Service Providers: U.S. and Canada (continued)

State/City/Provider	E-mail	Telephone
WYOMING		
All points		
NETConnect*	office@tcd.net	(307) 789-8001
Visionary Communications*	info@vcn.com	(307) 682-1884
wyoming.com LLC*	info@wyoming.com	(307) 332-3030
YUKON		
All points		
YKNet	yknet@yknet.yk.ca	(403) 668-8202
NATIONAL COVERAGE: U.S.		
ACM Network Services	account-info@acm.org	(817) 776-6876
Allied Access, Inc.	sales@intrnet.net	(800) 463-8366
AlterNet/UUNET	info@alter.net/info@uu.net	(800) 488-6384
BBN Planet Corporation*	net-info@bbnplanet.com	(800) 472-4565
CERFnet*	infoserv@cerf.net	(800) 876-2373
Cheney Communications Company	info@cheney.net	(800) CHENEY-1
CICNet*	info@cic.net	(800) 947-4754
Cogent Software, Inc.*	info@cogsoft.com	(818) 585-2788
CyberENET Network (KAPS, Inc.)	access-sales@cyberenet.net	(609) 753-9840
Databank, Inc.*	info@databank.com	(913) 842-6699
Delphi	info@delphi.com	(800) 695-4005
The Destek Group, Inc.*	info@destek.net	(603) 635-3857
EMI Communications*	info@emi.com	(800) 456-2001
free.org	info@free.org	(715) 743-1700
Futuris Networks, Inc.	info@futuris.net	(800) 976-2632
Global Enterprise Services, Inc.	info@jvnc.net	(800) 358-4437 x7325
HoloNet	info@holonet.net	(510) 704-0160
INS Info Services*	info@netins.net	(800) 546-6587
Institute for Global Communications	igc-info@igc.apc.org	(415) 442-0220
Interconnected Associates, Inc. (IXA)*	info@ixa.com	(800) IXA-8883
Internet America	info@iadfw.net	(800) BE-A-GEEK
Internet Connect, Inc.*	info@inc.net	(414) 476-ICON
Internet Direct Communications	sales@idir.net	(913) 842-1100
Internet Express*	service@usa.net	(800) 592-1240
Internet Online Services, Inc.*	info@ios.com	(201) 928-1000
Internet Texoma, Inc.	info@texoma.com	(800) 697-0206
INTERNExT*	info@internext.com	(703) 502-1899
Interpath*	info@interpath.net	(800) 849-6305
IONet	info@ionet.net	(405) 721-1580
Kallback	info@kallback.com	(206) 286-5200

Table A–2: Regional and National Service Providers: U.S. and Canada (continued)

State/City/Provider	E-mail	Telephone
NATIONAL COVERAGE: U.S. (continued)		
Midwest Internet	info@midwest.net	(800) 651-1599
Msen*	info@msen.com	(313) 998-4562
National Internet Source, Inc.*	info@nis.net	(201) 825-4600
New Mexico Technet, Inc.*	granoff@technet.nm.org	(505) 345-6555
Nothing But Net*	info@trey.com	(800) 951-7226
NovaLink Interactive Networks	info@novalink.com	(800) 274-2814
OARnet*	info@oar.net	(614) 728-8100
OnRamp, Ltd.	info@theramp.net	(708) 222-6666
Opus One*	info@opus1.com	(520) 324-0494
Pacific Rim Network, Inc.*	info@pacificrim.net	(360) 650-0442
PSI (Performance Systems International)	info@psi.com	(800) 82PSI82
The Point Internet Services, Inc.*	info@thepoint.net	(812) 246-7187
Portal Information Network	info@portal.com	(800) 433-6444
Protocol Communications, Inc.*	info@protocom.com	(612) 541-9900
Questar Microsystems, Inc.*	fbarrett@questar.com	(800) 925-2140
Random Access, Inc.*	marius@randomc.com	(800) 463-8366
Sacramento Network Access, Inc.*	ghall@sna.com	(916) 565-4500
ServiceTech, Inc.*	sales@servtech.com	(716) 263-3360
Synergy Communications*	sales@synergy.net	(402) 346-4638
Traders' Connection*	info@trader.com	(800) 753-4223
Turning Point Information Services, Inc.*	info@tpoint.net	(512) 499-8400
Viper Computer Systems, Inc.*	vipersys@viper.net	(800) VIPER-96
Voicenet*	info@voicenet.com	(800) 835-5710
The WELL	info@well.com	(415) 332-9200
WLN Internet Services*	info@wln.com	(800)-DIALWLN
Zocalo Engineering*	info@zocalo.net	(510) 540-8000
NATIONAL COVERAGE: CANADA		
Focus Technologies*	info@ftn.net	(800) FTN-INET
HoloNet	info@holonet.net	(510) 704-0160
HookUp Communications	info@hookup.net	(905) 847-8000
UUNET Canada*	info@uunet.ca	(800) 463-8123
see also NATIONAL COVERAGE: U.S.		

Table A-3: International Service Providers

Provider	E-mail	Telephone
UNITED KINGDOM		
AirTime Internet Resources Ltd UK	sales@airtime.co.uk	1254 676 921
Aladdin	info@aladdin.co.uk	1489 782 221
Almac	info@almac.co.uk	1324 666 336
Atlas InterNet	info@atlas.co.uk	171 312 0400
BBC Networking Club	info@bbcnc.org.uk	181 752 4159
Bournmouth Internet	sales@bournemouth-net.co.uk	1202 292 900
BTnet	internet@bt.net	345 585 110
Celtic Internet Services Limited	enquiry@celtic.co.uk	1633 811 825
CityScape	sales@ns.cityscape.co.uk	1223 566 950
CIX, (Compulink Information eXchange) Ltd	cixadmin@cix.compulink.co.uk	181 390 8446
Demon Internet, Ltd.*	internet@demon.net	181 371 1234
Direct Connection	sales@dircon.co.uk	181 297 2200
Dungeon Network Systems	info@dungeon.com	1473 621 217
Easynet	admin@easynet.co.uk	171 209 0990
Enterprise PLC	sales@enterprise.net	1624 677 666
EUnet GB Ltd	sales@Britain.EU.net	1227 266 466
FastNet	sales@fastnet.co.uk	1273 675 314
Foobar Internet	sales@foobar.co.uk	116 233 0033
Frontier Internet Services	info@ftech.net	171 242 3383
Gaiacom	info@gaiacom.co.uk	1732 351 111
GreenNet	support@gn.apc.org	171 713 1941
Hiway	info@inform.hiway.co.uk	1635 550 660
Internet Discovery	padds@idiscover.co.uk	181 694 2240
KENTnet	info@kentnet.co.uk	1580 890 089
Luna Internet	sales-uk@luna.net	1734 791 900
Magnum Network Services, Ltd.	sales@mag-net.co.uk	1908 216 699
Mistral Internet	info@mistral.co.uk	1273 708 866
NETHEAD	info@nethead.co.uk	171 207 1100
NetKonect	info@netkonect.net	171 345 7777
Nildram On-Line	info@nildram.co.uk	01442 891 331
Onyx	onyx-support@octacon.co.uk	1642 210 087
Paston Chase	info@paston.co.uk	1603 502 061
Pavillion Internet	info@pavillion.co.uk	1273 607 072
PC User Group/WinNET Communications	request@win-uk.net	181 863 1191
Pinnacle Internet Services	info@pncl.co.uk	1293 613 686
PIPEX (Public IP Exchange Limited)*	sales@pipex.com	500 646 566
Powernet	info@powernet.co.uk	1908 503 126
Primex Information Services	info@alpha.primex.co.uk	1908 313 163

Table A–3: International Service Providers (continued)

Provider	E-mail	Telephone
UNITED KINGDOM (continued)		
Pro-Net Internet Services	sales@pro-net.co.uk	181 200 3565
RedNet onLine	orders@rednet.co.uk	1494 513 333
Sound & Vision BBS (Worldspan Communications Ltd)	world@span.com	181 288 8555
Technocom	sales@technocom.co.uk	1753 673 200
Telecall	support@telecall.co.uk	117 941 4141
Total Connectivity Providers Ltd	sales@tcp.co.uk	1703 393 392
U-NET Limited	hi@u-net.com	1925 633 144
Wintermute Ltd.	info@wintermute.co.uk	1224 622 477
WinNet	info@win-uk.net	181 863 1191
ZETNET Services	info@zetnet.co.uk	1595 696 667
Zynet Ltd	zynet@zynet.net	1392 426 160
AUSTRALIA		
Access One	info@aone.net.au	1 800 818 391
APANA	propaganda@apana.org.au	02 635 1751
ASAHi Computer Systems	asahi@asahi.com.au	03 9429 6011
AUSNet Services Pty Ltd	sales@world.net	02 241 5888
Australia On Line	sales@ozonline.com.au	1 800 621 258
Ballarat NetConnect Pty Ltd	info@netconnect.com.au	53 322 140
BrisNet	dancer@mail.brisnet.org.au	07 3229 3229
connect.com.au pty ltd	connect@connect.com.au	03 528 2239
Cooee Communications	sysop@cooee.com.au	43 696 224
Cynergy	cynergy@cynergy.com.au	07 3357 1100
DIALix	info@dialix.com	1902 29 2004
Dynamite Internet	info@dynamite.com.au	06 242 8644
Geko	info@geko.com.au	02 439 1999
Highway 1	info@highway1.com.au	09 370 4584
iiNet Technologies Pty Ltd	iinet@iinet.net.au	09 307 1183
Informed Technology	info@it.com.au	09 245 2279
Intercom Pacific	info@ipacific.net.au	02 281 1111
InterConnect Australia Pty Ltd	info@interconnect.com.au	03 9528 2239
Internet Access Australia	accounts@iaccess.com.au	03 576 4222
Internet Interface Systems Pty Ltd	info@webnet.com.au	03 9525 0922
Kralizec Dialup Internet System	info@zeta.org.au	02 837 1397
Microplex Pty Ltd*	info@mpx.com.au	02 438 1234
Netcore Pty Ltd	info@netcore.com.au	03 9872 3821
Netro, Your Internet Connection	info@netro.com.au	02 876 8588
OzEmail	info@ozemail.aust.com	02 391 0480
Pegasus Networks	pegasus@peg.apc.org	07 3255 0255
Penrith NetCom	info@pnc.com.au	04 735 7000

Table A–3: International Service Providers (continued)

Provider	E-mail	Telephone
AUSTRALIA (continued)		
Really Useful Communications Company	info@rucc.net.au	03 9818 8711
Stour System Services	stour@stour.net.au	09 571 1949
TMX, The Message eXchange	info@tmx.com.au	02 550 4448
World Reach Pty Ltd	info@wr.com.au	02 436 3588
Zip Australia Pty. Ltd.	info@zip.com.au	02 482 7015
INTERNATIONAL/WORLDWIDE COVERAGE		
GeoAccess Network	sharpe@cafe.net	(604) 970-0049
IBM Global Network*	globalnetwork@info.ibm.com	*United States:* (800) 933-3997
		Canada: (800) 463-8331
		United Kingdom: 800 614 012
		Australia: 1 800 811 094

SETTING UP YOUR INTERNET CONNECTION

Microsoft Internet Jumpstart Kit
Windows 95 PPP
Windows 95 on a LAN
Microsoft Exchange

In terms of Internet access, the most important new feature of Windows 95 is its built-in network support, including support for TCP/IP and PPP. TCP/IP refers to the basic set of protocols that make the Internet work. PPP is a special-purpose protocol that lets you connect your computer to the Internet using a standard telephone line and high-speed modem. What this means for you is that Windows 95 is Internet-ready, whether you dial into a commercial Internet service provider from your home or you have access to the Internet through your corporate network using TCP/IP and a LAN adaptor.

This situation is a great improvement over Windows 3.1, where if you wanted to connect to the Internet, you needed to find your own TCP/IP protocol stack and applications. While this task wasn't too difficult, it did require more work, as well as knowledge about how Internet applications really work.

Now with Windows 95, you simply need to configure your system to use the built-in TCP/IP support. Then you have access to FTP and Telnet applications, provided with Windows 95. Using these tools, you can retrieve other Internet applications, such as a World Wide Web browser and a newsreader, from various Internet archives, as described earlier in this book.

Microsoft has developed some additional Internet tools that are not included as part of Windows 95. These tools are collectively packaged as the Internet Jumpstart Kit. This kit includes a Web browser called Internet Explorer, an Internet Setup Wizard that walks you through the setup process, and an additional driver for Microsoft Exchange that allows you to use it for reading Internet electronic mail.

You may already have the Internet Jumpstart Kit on your system. It is included as part of Microsoft Plus! for Windows 95. Plus! provides a number of other features, including a System Agent for scheduling tasks, enhanced disk compression tools, and a variety of desktop enhancements. The Internet Jumpstart Kit is also included on new computers that come with Windows 95 preinstalled. To see if you have the toolkit, click on the **Start** menu and select **Programs** followed by **Accessories**. If you see **Internet Tools** on this menu, you have the Internet Jumpstart Kit.

You can get startup tools for free over the Internet, but that probably doesn't do you a whole lot of good right now, if you're trying to set up your Internet access. But just so that you know, you can download the tools via anonymous FTP from **ftp.microsoft.com**. You want the file *msie10.exe* in */peropsys/ Win_News/Windows95Information/InternetExplorer*. You can also use the following URL if you have access to a Web browser:

```
http://www.windows.microsoft.com/windows/software/iexplorer.htm
```

After you've downloaded the tools, run the *msie10.exe* executable to install the Internet tools.

Since the Internet Jumpstart Kit is freely available, I'm going to start by describing how to use it to set up your Internet connection. The Internet Setup Wizard makes it quite easy to set up your connection; I highly recommend that you get it if at all possible. If it's not on your machine and you aren't willing to buy Plus!, you might try getting it on diskette from a friend or co-worker. If none of these avenues pan out, you'll have to skip the first section of this appendix and go to the explanation of how to set up Internet access with plain Windows 95.

Before you can set up your Internet connection, you need to know what kind of connection you'll have. Are you using a network adaptor to connect to a LAN that, in turn, is connected to the Internet. Or will you be dialing in to the Internet through a telephone line? If you're going to be using a modem and a telephone line to connect to the Internet, you'll need to use PPP. Since I expect that many of you will be dialing in from a home computer, I'll explain how to set up this kind of connection first. Then I'll talk about setting up Internet access via a LAN.

Microsoft Exchange is a multi-purpose communications tools that is included as part of Windows 95. By using the driver included as part of the Internet Jumpstart Kit, you can set up Exchange to send and receive e-mail through your Internet service provider. If you want to use Microsoft Exchange to read and send Internet e-mail, you'll need to follow the instructions provided in the section on configuring Exchange.

Setting up your Internet connection is actually quite easy. You're simply going to be using some applets from the **Control Panel** and entering information into various windows. Some of the information is about your hardware, but in many cases Windows 95 should be able to figure out what it needs to know about your particular hardware, so that should be painless. You'll also need to enter some information about your Internet access, but you should be able to get this information from either your Internet service provider or the network administrator for your LAN.

All of the explanations in this appendix assume that you are simply trying to connect your PC to the Internet. If you are responsible for networking a collection of

PCs and connecting them to the Internet, you'll certainly need more information than what is provided here. In that case, you should refer to *Networking Personal Computers with TCP/IP* from O'Reilly & Associates.

Microsoft Internet Jumpstart Kit

If you have the Microsoft Internet Jumpstart Kit, setting up your Internet access is quite simple. All you need to do is run the Internet Setup Wizard, which guides you through setting up your Internet connection. You can find the wizard from the **Start** menu, by using the following submenus: **Programs**, **Accessories**, and **Internet Tools**.

If you have a network adaptor installed on your PC, the Internet Setup Wizard should detect the adaptor and prompt you for the information it needs to set up Internet access through your local area network. Otherwise, the wizard assumes that you are going to use a dial-up connection to the Internet. In this case, you need to decide whether you are going to use an independent Internet service provider or the Microsoft Network for your Internet access. The following sections explain the setup process for each type of connection.

An Internet Service Provider

If you are using a dial-up connection to the Internet, the Internet Setup Wizard uses the window shown in Figure B-1 to find out how you want to connect to the Internet. To use an independent service provider, you need to have an account established before you continue with the setup process. You'll need the information listed in Figure B-2 before you can answer the wizard's questions; you can write the information for your account in the blank column. Make sure you check the box indicating that you want to use a different service provider in Figure B-1 and then click **Next**.

Now the Internet Setup Wizard prompts you for the name of your Internet service provider. This information is used as the name of your connection in the **Dial-Up Networking** folder; be sure to use a descriptive name, especially if you have a number of different Internet accounts. When you click **Next**, the wizard prompts you for the phone number of your service provider, as shown in Figure B-3.

Enter the phone number you dial to connect to the Internet in the **Area code** and **Telephone number** fields and make sure the correct country code is selected. Be sure to check the **Bring up terminal window after dialing** box, so that the system brings up a terminal window after connecting to your service provider, allowing you to enter the necessary information. Click **Next** again.

In the next window, the Internet Setup Wizard prompts you for your username and password. Enter this information and click **Next**. Figure B-4 shows the window used to request the IP address for your machine. The IP address uniquely identifies your computer on the Internet. Normally, your Internet service provider will assign you a permanent IP address and a "subnet mask." If so, check the

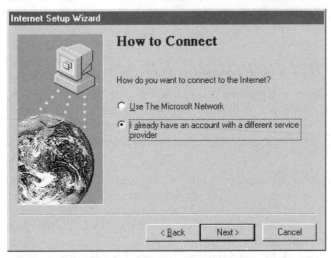

Figure B-1: Connecting with an Internet service provider

Information Necessary for Internet Setup	
• *your username*	
• *your password*	
• *phone number you dial to connect to internet*	
• *baud rate of service provider's modem*	
• *your host name*	
• *the domain name*	
• *your IP address* *(unless your provider uses the Dynamic Host Control Protocol)*	
• *the IP subnet mask*	
• *the gateway IP address*	
• *the IP address of the DNS server*	
• *any specific commands to log into the account*	
Information Necessary for Internet Electronic Mail	
• *your e-mail address*	
• *the name of your internet mail server*	

Figure B-2: What you need to know to connect with an Internet service provider

Always use the following box and fill in the **IP Address** and **Subnet Mask** fields with the appropriate values. Your service provider may use the Dynamic Host Control Protocol (DHCP) to assign you an IP address automatically. DHCP isn't

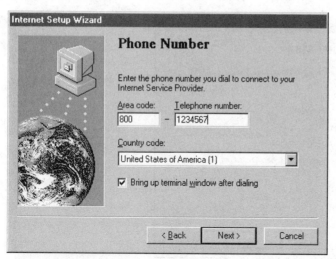

Figure B-3: Phone Number window

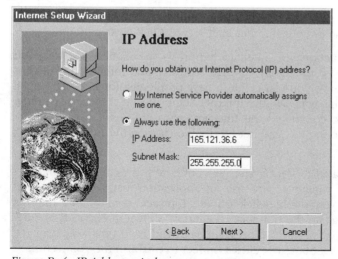

Figure B-4: IP Address window

widespread, but it should become more common. If this is the case, just check the **My Internet Service Provider automatically assigns me one** box. Now click **Next**.

The next window asks for the IP address of your Domain Name System (DNS) server. This machine is responsible for looking up Internet addresses and translating them into computer names. If your service provider has more than one machine that functions as a DNS server, you can enter the address of an alternate server as well. When you click **Next**, the wizard prompts you for information about your Internet e-mail access, as shown in Figure B-5. If you want to use

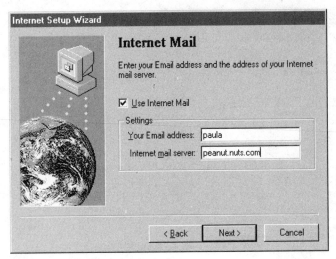

Figure B–5: Internet Mail window

Internet e-mail, make sure the **Use Internet Mail** box is checked, and fill in your e-mail address and the name of your Internet mail server. Click **Next**.

The final piece of information you need to supply is the name of a Microsoft Exchange profile to be used for Internet e-mail. You can add Internet e-mail support to an existing profile, or you can create a new profile just for Internet e-mail. When you click **Next** in this window, the Internet Setup Wizard displays a window telling you that you have completed the Internet setup process. Once you click **Finish**, you can start exploring the Internet by double-clicking the **Internet** icon on the desktop.

With the Internet Jumpstart Kit, your system is configured to establish an Internet connection automatically whenever you use an application that requires Internet access. For example, if you double-click on the **Internet** icon to start Internet Explorer, the system brings up the Connect To window shown in Figure B-6. Enter your password; if you don't want to type your password each time you connect, select the **Save password** option.* Now click **Connect** to establish the connection.

The system brings up a terminal window after dialing your service provider, as shown in Figure B-7. Enter the necessary login commands for your account when

---

* If the **Save password** option doesn't work, here's what you need to do to fix it. Select the **Network** icon from the **Control Panel** and click the **Add** button. Now highlight **Client** in the **Select Network Component Type** window and click **Add**. Select **Microsoft** from the **Manufacturers** list and then pick **Client for Microsoft Networks** from the **Network Clients** list. Click **OK** to add the client. When you get back to the **Network** applet, select the **Identification** tab and enter names for your computer and workgroup. After you click **OK**, you'll need to restart your system to have this setting take effect. Once you do, you'll be able to select the **Save password** option.

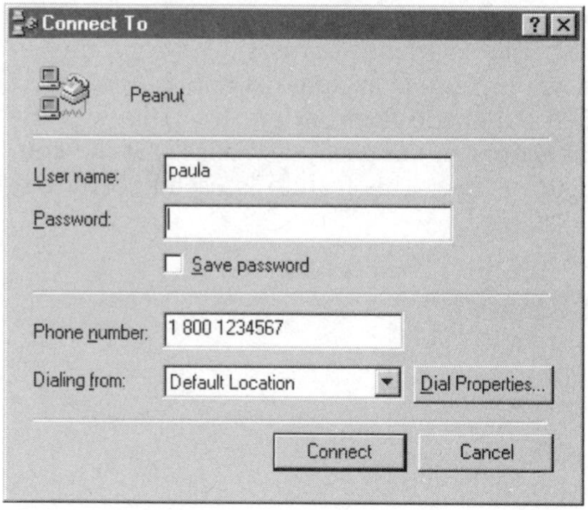

Figure B-6: Connect To window

the window appears and click **Continue**. You will need to give a username and a password.* You may also need to give a special command to start the PPP session; your service provider will give you that command, if one is needed. When the connection has been established, you'll see a window that provides status information. This window displays the amount of time you've been connected; it also contains a **Disconnect** button that you can use to end your connection.

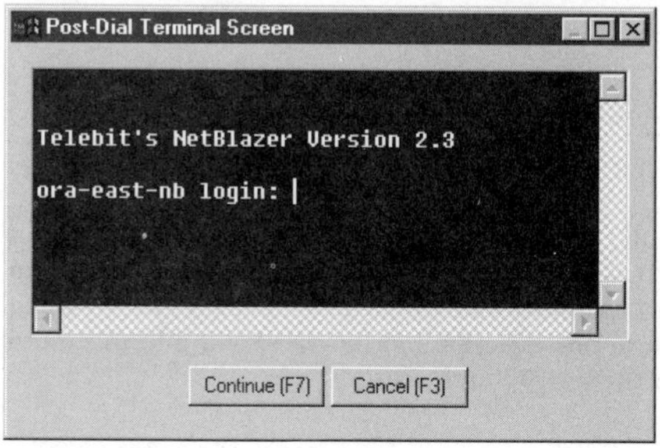

Figure B-7: Post-Dial terminal window

You can also bring up a connection manually by selecting the icon for the connection from the **Dial-Up Networking** folder in **My Computer**. If you have multiple

---

* Are you wondering why you need to enter your username and password in both the Connect To window and the terminal window? That's a good question; I'll answer it in the next section, "Automating the Login Process."

Internet access accounts, you can select the one that is dialed automatically using the **Internet** applet in the **Control Panel**. Figure B-8 shows the **AutoDial** tab of the **Internet** applet. The **Use AutoDial** box controls whether or not the system tries to connect automatically to the Internet when you use an Internet application. Select the connection you want to be dialed automatically from the list. This window also lets you specify that your system should disconnect automatically if the connection stays idle for a specified length of time. This feature is useful if you pay for your Internet access by the hour.

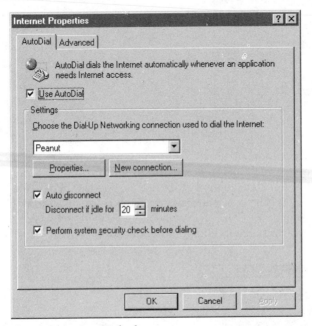

Figure B-8: AutoDial tab

Actually, the auto-dial feature only works with 32-bit Internet applications that have been designed to work with Windows 95. If you are using an older, 16-bit Internet application, you'll need to establish the connection manually before using the application. Some of the applications described in this book fall into that category, including winWAIS, WSGopher, and WSArchie.

Automating the Login Process

The CD-ROM version of Windows 95 includes a utility you can use to automate the process of logging into your service provider. The program is called the Dial-Up Scripting Tool. It's available from the **Start** menu; select **Programs, Accessories,** and then **Dial-Up Scripting Tool.**[*] The program allows you to attach a script to your dial-up connection; the script then controls the login process, so you don't have to deal with the terminal window.

Writing a login script

The first step in using the Dial-Up Scripting Tool is to write a script for your Internet connection. The script is simply a text file, so you'll use a text editor like Notepad to create it. Here's a sample script for a PPP login that you should be able to modify for your Internet connection:

```
;Sample PPP login script
;Begin the script
proc main

;Delay for 5 seconds to allow host time to respond
;Not needed by many providers -- enable if necessary
;delay 5

;Send ENTER if it's needed to start the login process
;Again, not needed by all providers -- enable if necessary
;transmit "<cr>"

;Wait for the login prompt
waitfor "ogin:"

;Send username and ENTER in response
;Value of $USERID comes from the connection dialog box
transmit $USERID
transmit "<cr>"

;Wait for the password prompt
waitfor "assword:"

;Send password and ENTER in response
;Value of $PASSWORD comes from the connection dialog box
transmit $PASSWORD
transmit "<cr>"

;Wait for service ready prompt
waitfor "eady>"

;Specify service, PPP, and send ENTER
transmit "PPP<cr>"
```

---

[*] If the Dial-Up Scripting Tool isn't there and you have the Windows 95 CD-ROM, use **Add/Remove Programs** from the **Control Panel** to install it. On the **Windows Setup** tab, click **Have Disk**. Assuming that your CD-ROM drive is D:, enter the following path, *d:\win95\admin\apptools\dscript*, and click **OK**. If you have Windows 95 on diskette, you can download the Dial-Up Scripting Tool over the Web using the following URL: http://download.windows.microsoft.com/windows/download/dscrpt.exe

```
;Finish the script
endproc
```

The script must start with the **proc main** command and end with **endproc**; these commands tell the system to start and stop the script. The two other basic commands are **transmit** and **waitfor**. Essentially, you tell the script to wait for a particular prompt from the remote system, and then send a response to that prompt.

To modify the above script for your connection, first change the **waitfor** commands to match the prompts used by your service provider. It is common practice to write scripts so that they only match the end of a prompt, as shown in this example. You don't need to modify the **transmit** commands because they use the values of the $USERID and $PASSWORD variables. When you type in your username and password in the Connect To window, the variables are assigned the appropriate values. If your service provider doesn't prompt you for the type of service, you can remove these lines from the script. By the same token, you can add another **waitfor/transmit** pair if you need to. When you are finished with the script, save it in the *Program Files\Accessories* folder, with a file extension of SCP (e.g. PPP.SCP).

If logging into your Internet connection requires more advanced input, such as menu selections, you should consult the file *Script.doc* in the *Program Files\Plus!* folder. This document describes the scripting command language in detail. There are also a few sample script files in *Program Files\Accessories* that you may want to look at.

Attaching a script to a connection

After you have written your login script, you need to attach it to your dial-up connection. This is where the Dial-Up Scripting Tool comes in. If you haven't already started the Dial-Up Scripting Tool, do so now. You should see the window shown in Figure B-9.

Your dial-up connection should be highlighted in the **Connections** list; if you have more than one connection, select the appropriate one from the list. Now click the **Browse** button to specify the script for the connection. If you saved the script in the *Accessories* folder, it should be listed in the Open dialog that appears. Select the script and click **Open**.

The first time you use your login script, I'd recommend that you troubleshoot the script by selecting the **Step through script** option. This option allows you to "step through" each line of the script and see the results in a terminal window. When you are certain the script is working properly, you can turn off this option and select **Start terminal screen minimized** to keep the script window minimized during the connection process. After you've set these options, click the **Apply** button to attach the script to your dial-up connection.

Before you try the script for the first time, there's one more important thing you need to do. Select the icon for your connection from the **Dial-Up Networking**

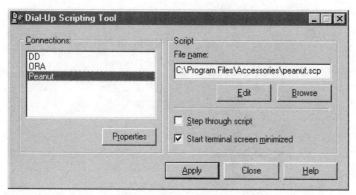

Figure B-9: Dial-Up Scripting Tool window

folder and then select **Properties** from the **File** menu. Click the **Configure** button to change your modem configuration. On the **Options** tab, make sure that neither of the items under **Connection Control** is selected. Even though you had **Bring up a terminal window after dialing** selected, the Dial-Up Scripting Tool opens its own terminal window. If you leave this option selected, your script won't work.

Now, if you select your connection from the **Dial-Up Networking** folder and click **Connect**, the Dial-Up Scripting Tool should handle the login process for you. Make sure you enter your username and password in the Connect To window, as your script uses these values to make the connection.

If you opted to step through the script, you'll see two windows during the connection process: a terminal window and a script window. You step through the script by clicking the **Step** button on the script window. The results are shown in the terminal window; pay close attention to the output to track down any errors in your script. After you are satisfied that your script works, turn off the **Step through script** option. You can also click the **Close** button to close the Dial-Up Scripting Tool. The tool does not need to be open for the script to run; the script runs automatically with your dial-up connection as long as it is attached correctly.

The Microsoft Network

If you want to use the Microsoft Network (MSN) to connect to the Internet, you need to select that option when the Internet Setup Wizard asks you how you want to connect (see Figure B-1). With the Microsoft Network, you don't need to have an account set up in advance; the Internet Setup Wizard will guide you through creating an MSN account. After you select **MSN** as your service provider and click **Next**, you'll see the window shown in Figure B-10a. If you are already a member of the Microsoft Network, you can indicate that here.

Assuming you're not a member, select **No: sign me up** and click **Next**. Now the Microsoft Network wizard takes over to help you create an MSN account. You

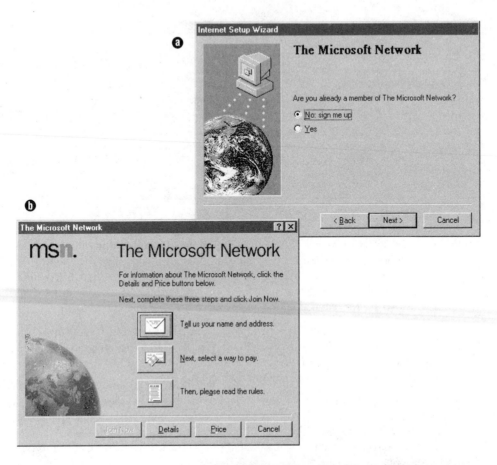

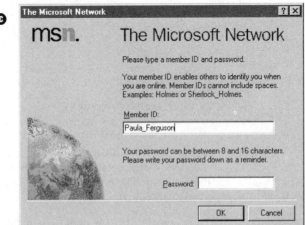

Figure B-10: Joining the Microsoft Network

should see a window that describes the features of the Microsoft Network; click **OK** to continue creating an account. In the next window, the wizard asks you for your area code and the first three digits of your phone number. When you enter this information and click **OK**, the MSN wizard connects to the Microsoft Network to get the latest product information and update its internal list of phone numbers. This step ensures that the wizard provides you with accurate information, and don't worry, there's no charge for the call. After the wizard retrieves the information, you'll see the window shown in Figure B-10b.

Follow the directions in this window to join the Microsoft Network. In the first step, you'll have to fill out a form with your name, address, and phone number. Next, you'll need to provide credit card information for billing purposes. Finally, you'll need to agree to the rules of the Microsoft Network. After you've completed all three steps, click **Join Now**. The MSN wizard will connect to the Microsoft Network and transmit the information you've provided. The next window, shown in Figure B-10c, asks you to select a member ID and password.

You're free to choose any name you'd like for your member ID; you can just use your name or you can come up with a creative pseudonym. But be aware that people will come to refer to you with your member ID, so you may not want to choose anything too outlandish. After you've entered a member ID and password, click **OK**. Now the MSN wizard will make sure that your member ID is unique; you cannot use a member ID that has already been choosen by another MSN member.

In the next window, the MSN wizard displays the phone numbers that your system will use to connect to the Internet. This window also lists your service type, which should be **Internet and The Microsoft Network**. This service type means that when you connect to the Microsoft Network, you have full access to the Internet, as well as to the various services of MSN. For more information about MSN services, see Appendix D, *The Microsoft Network*. After you confirm the phone numbers by clicking **OK**, the wizard displays a window telling you that you have completed the setup process.[*]

Now you are ready to start exploring the Internet. As an MSN member, you can explore the Internet using various MSN services, as described in Appendix D, but that's really not what this book is about. With Internet access through MSN, you can use Internet applications just as you would with an independent service provider. For example, double-click on the **Internet** icon on the desktop to start Internet Explorer. When you do, the system brings up the window shown in Fig-

---

[*] If you have previously set up your system to use another Internet service provider, you may see a dialog window asking you about the configuration of your DNS servers. To make Internet setup easy, MSN dynamically assigns you a DNS server when you log in. This may conflict with your existing settings. If so, the MSN setup wizard offers you the choice of keeping or removing the existing settings. If you want to use both MSN and your existing service provider, *do not* remove the existing settings. If, however, you want to use MSN exclusively, you can remove the existing settings.

Figure B-11: Connecting to the Microsoft Network

ure B-11 to establish your Internet connection. Enter your member ID and password and click **Connect**.

When the connection has been established, Internet Explorer will display its home page and you can start browsing the World Wide Web. You should also be connected to MSN Central, so you can access MSN services. You'll see an MSN icon on the far left side of the taskbar at the bottom of your screen. If you want to disconnect from the Microsoft Network, double-click on this icon. MSN is set up to automatically disconnect if the connection is idle for a specified length of time. You can adjust this time period using the **Internet** applet on the **Control Panel**. Select the **AutoDial** tab to adjust auto-dial features.

If you choose the Microsoft Network as your Internet provider, you'll find it quite easy to set up Internet access. You certainly have to enter a lot less information than with an independent service providers. However, there are a few caveats. Initially, MSN Internet access is limited to particular metropolitan areas as the network infrastructure is put in place, so there may not be a local access number in your area. Even if you can get access, the number of phone lines may be limited, which can lead to access problems.

You may also want to do a bit of comparison shopping. As the number of independent Internet service providers continues to grow, you may find that you can get better service and lower prices from an independent provider in your community. See Appendix A, *Getting Connected to the Internet*, for a list of providers in major metropolitan areas throughout the United States.

A Local Area Network

If your PC is connected to a LAN using a network adaptor, the Internet Setup Wizard should detect the adaptor. In this case, the wizard begins by asking you how you want to connect to the Internet, as shown in Figure B-12a. Just because your PC is connected to a LAN doesn't guarantee that the LAN is connected to the Internet, which is why the Internet Setup Wizard gives you the option to connect using your phone line. If your LAN is connected to the Internet, however, you should choose the second option, as that's the easiest way to connect to the Internet. Before you proceed any further, you need to get some information from your network administrator about how to access the Internet from your site.

Select the box indicating that you want to connect using your LAN and click **Next**. Now the Internet Setup Wizard asks you for the IP address of your Domain Name System (DNS) server, as shown in Figure B-12b. This machine is responsible for looking up Internet addresses. If your network has more than one machine that functions as a DNS server, you can enter the address of an alternate server as well. Your network administrator can give you the addresses of these servers.

When you click **Next**, the wizard prompts you for the IP address of the gateway for your network. The gateway machine is the one that connects your LAN to the rest of the Internet. Again, your network administrator should give you this address. Click **Next** again and the Internet Setup Wizard asks you for information about your Internet e-mail access. If you want to use Internet e-mail, make sure the **Use Internet Mail** box is checked, and fill in your e-mail address and the name of your Internet mail server. Click **Next**.

The last piece of information you need to provide is the name of a Microsoft Exchange profile to be used for Internet e-mail. You can add Internet e-mail support to an existing profile, or you can create a new profile for Internet e-mail. When you click **Next** in this window, the wizard displays a window informing you that you have completed the Internet setup process. Once you click **Finish**, you can start exploring the Internet by double-clicking the **Internet** icon on the desktop.

If your LAN is connected to the Internet through a firewall, you may have to do a bit more work to set up your Internet access. The Internet tools included in the Internet Jumpstart Kit support *proxy servers.* A proxy server acts as a barrier between the Internet and your LAN, protecting the information on your LAN. Your network administrator should tell you if you need to set up a proxy server. To do so, use the **Internet** applet on the **Control Panel** and select the **Advanced** tab.

Windows 95 PPP

If you've set up your Internet connection using the Internet Setup Wizard, you can skip the next two sections. You only need to read these sections if you are trying to set up your connection with plain Windows 95. Be sure to read the final section

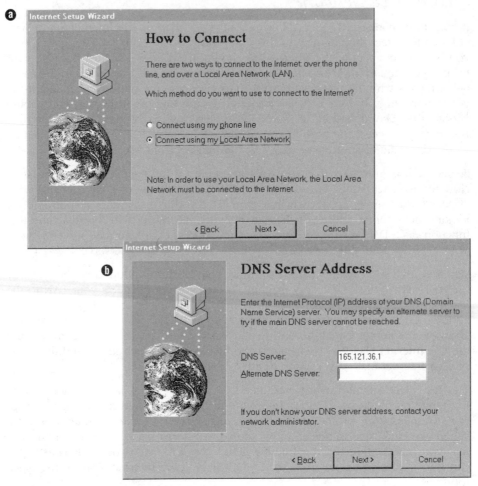

Figure B-12: Connecting via a LAN

on configuring Microsoft Exchange, however, if you want to use Exchange to send and receive Internet e-mail.

If you already have an account with an Internet service provider that uses the Serial Line Internet Protocol (SLIP), you need a special driver to use that account with Windows 95. This driver is only provided on the CD-ROM version of Windows 95. To see if the driver is installed, use **Add/Remove Programs** from the **Control Panel**. Select the **Install/Uninstall** tab and make sure **SLIP and Scripting for Dial-Up Networking** is in the list. If it isn't, use the **Windows Setup** tab to install it. Click **Have Disk** and assuming your CD-ROM drive is D:, enter the following path, *d:\win95\admin\apptools\dscript*, and click **OK**. Once the SLIP driver is installed, setting up your Internet access is the same as with PPP.

Windows 95 includes the Point-to-Point Protocol (PPP) for dial-up connections to the Internet. All you need is a standard phone line, a high-speed modem, and an account with an Internet service provider. Prior to installing PPP, you must contact a service provider and set up this account. When you do this, the service provider will give you a lot of configuration information. Figure B–13 gives the details; you can write the information for your account in the blank column.

Information Necessary for Installing PPP	
• *your username*	
• *your password*	
• *phone number you dial to connect to internet*	
• *baud rate of service provider's modem*	
• *your host name*	
• *the domain name*	
• *your IP address* *(unless your provider uses the Dynamic Host Control Protocol)*	
• *the IP subnet mask*	
• *the gateway IP address*	
• *the IP address of the DNS server*	
• *any specific commands to log into the account*	

Figure B–13: What you need to know for PPP or SLIP connections

Installing PPP

You install PPP using the **Network** applet in the **Control Panel**. Open the **Control Panel** by selecting it from the **Settings** menu that appears when you select the **Start** menu from the taskbar at the bottom of the screen. Open **Network** by double-clicking on the **Network** icon in the **Control Panel** window.

Figure B-14a shows the **Configuration** tab of the **Network** window after several network components, including TCP/IP, have been configured. (The first time you see this window on your system, the list may be empty.) The **Network** window is actually used for all network components, not just PPP and TCP/IP. So, for example, the **Identification** tab allows you to set the name and workgroup of your computer if it is connected to a network, while the **Access Control** tab lets you select the type of access control that is used. These tabs aren't important, however, if you are using a standalone PC to connect to the Internet.

To install PPP, you first need to install TCP/IP, since PPP is a dial-up adaptor layered over the TCP/IP support in Windows 95. To install TCP/IP, click on the **Add** button in the **Configuration** tab of the **Network** window. Another window, labeled **Select Network Component Type**, appears. Highlight **Protocol** in this new window

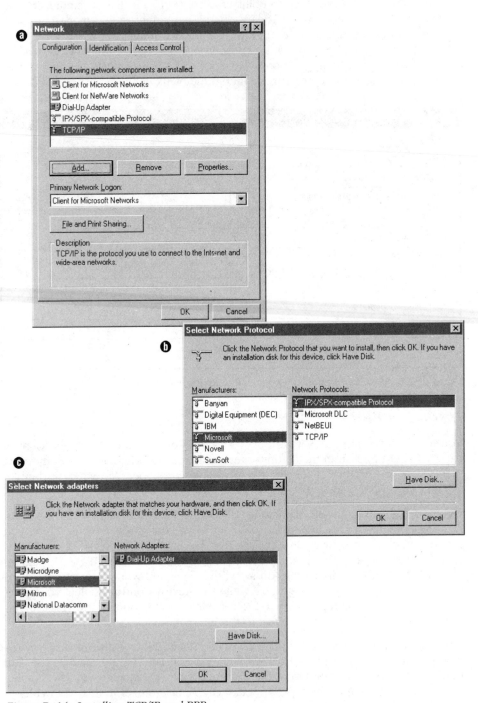

Figure B–14: Installing TCP/IP and PPP

and click **Add**. The window shown in Figure B-14b appears. In the **Select Network Protocol** window, highlight **Microsoft** in the **Manufacturers** listbox. When you do, a list of protocols appears in the **Network Protocols** listbox. One of these is TCP/IP. Highlight it and click **OK**.

Now Windows 95 asks you to select a network adaptor using the window shown in Figure B-14c. Since you are going to be using PPP to connect to the Internet, you need to select the dial-up adaptor. To do this, highlight **Microsoft** in the **Manufacturers** listbox. The only adaptor that appears in the **Models** listbox is the **Dial-Up Adaptor**; select it and click **OK**.

The system now returns to the **Network** window shown in Figure B-14a. If you click **OK** right now, you'll dismiss the **Network** applet. At this point, the system may prompt you to supply the Windows 95 CD-ROM or a number of Windows 95 diskettes, so that it can load the necessary software. When this process is complete, reboot the system and TCP/IP is installed. Of course, you still haven't configured TCP/IP and PPP, but you can do that simply by opening the **Network** applet again and selecting TCP/IP. Or you can keep the **Network** applet open, perform the configuration, and then dismiss the applet.

Configuring TCP/IP

The next step in the setup process is to configure TCP/IP for your particular Internet connection. At this point, you should have ready the information about your Internet account from your service provider. To setup TCP/IP, highlight TCP/IP in the **Network** window and click **Properties**. The **TCP/IP Properties** window, shown in Figure B-15a, appears.

This window contains six tabs. The **IP Address** tab, shown in Figure B-15a, is the tab you see first. The IP address uniquely identifies your computer on the Internet. Normally, your Internet service provider will assign you an IP address and a "subnet mask." If so, check the **Specify an IP address** box and fill in the **IP Address** and **Subnet Mask** fields.[*] Your service provider may use the Dynamic Host Control Protocol (DHCP) to assign the IP address automatically. DHCP isn't widespread, but it should become more common. If this is the case, just check the **Obtain an IP address from a DHCP server** box, and you're done with this tab.

Now choose the **DNS Configuration** tab, which is shown in Figure B-15b. Select **Enable DNS** to enable the Domain Name System, the system that translates computer names (like **acorn.nuts.com**) into numeric Internet addresses (like **165.121.36.6**) and vice-versa. Now enter the hostname for your computer in the **Host** field. This name is used to identify your PC; it may be assigned by your service provider, or you may be allowed to choose your own hostname. You also need to enter the domain name assigned by your service provider in the **Domain** field.

---

[*] If you've been using Trumpet Winsock, these values are the **IP Address** and **Netmask** values in the Trumpet Winsock Setup window.

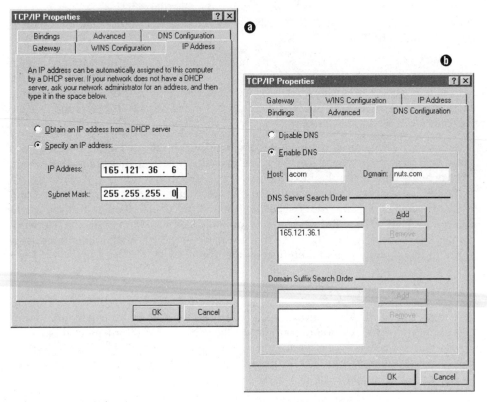

Figure B-15: TCP/IP Properties

Your Internet service provider should give you the IP address of one or more machines that will function as your DNS server. These machines are responsible for looking up Internet addresses. Enter the IP address of the first of these machines in the **DNS Server Search Order** field and click **Add.**[*] Then add the second and third DNS servers in the same way.

The **Domain Suffix Search Order** box at the bottom of the window defines the order in which domains are searched for host information. Normally the box is left blank, so unless your service provider tells you to fill in this information, just leave it empty.

The **Gateway** tab is the final one that is critical for your TCP/IP configuration. Select this tab and enter the IP address of the default gateway for your Internet

---

[*] With Trumpet Winsock, this is the **Name server** value in the Setup window.

connection in the **New gateway** field.[*] The gateway machine is the one that connects your Internet service provider to the rest of the Internet; your service provider should give you the address of the gateway. After you have entered the address, click **Add**.

The other three tabs on the **TCP/IP Properties** window, **Bindings**, **Advanced**, and **WINS Configuration**, don't contain any relevant settings for basic TCP/IP setup, so you can ignore them. However, you should check one setting on the **WINS Configuration** tab. Make sure the **Disable WINS Resolution** box is selected. WINS is a name server for another network protocol, called NetBIOS.[†]

Once you have finished setting up TCP/IP for your Internet connection, you can dismiss the **TCP/IP Properties** window by clicking **OK**. The system brings you back to the **Network** window shown in Figure B-14a.

Configuring PPP

Now you need to set up PPP to complete your Internet configuration. Highlight **Dial-Up Adaptor** in the **Network** window and click **Properties**. The **Dial-Up Adaptor Properties** window appears. The default values on all of the **Dial-Up Adapter Properties** tabs are probably just what you need. The one setting you should verify is on the **Bindings** tab; make sure that **TCP/IP** is checked on this tab. You can ignore the other tabs. Once everything is set the way you want it, click **OK**. If the system needs to install any software at this point, it may prompt you for the Windows 95 CD-ROM or a number of diskettes. After the necessary software is loaded, you'll be prompted to restart the system, so that your settings can take effect.

Making the PPP Connection

When the system restarts, it should install the **Dial-Up Networking** folder in **My Computer**. If **Dial-Up Networking** is not displayed in **My Computer**, use **Add/Remove Programs** from the **Control Panel** to install it. On the **Windows Setup** tab, select **Communications** and click **OK**. The system should now prompt you for the Windows 95 CD-ROM or several diskettes, so it can install the necessary communications software.

To setup your PPP network connection, open the **Dial-Up Networking** folder. The first time you open it, the modem installation wizard runs if a modem has not yet been installed. (A *wizard* is a program that simplifies the configuration of hardware and software. You can run the modem wizard any time you wish by opening **Modems** in the **Control Panel**.) The modem wizard automatically detects the type of modem connected to your system and configures it. If the wizard makes a mis-

---

[*] The **Default Gateway** value from the Trumpet Winsock Setup window.

[†] For more information about NetBIOS, see *Networking Personal Computers with TCP/IP* by Craig Hunt, from O'Reilly & Associates.

take detecting your modem, click the **Change** button and select the correct modem from the modem list.

After the modem driver is properly installed, the **Dial-Up Networking** folder opens to show the **Make New Connection** icon. Double-click the icon to run the "new connection" wizard. Figure B-16a shows the opening window of this wizard. Enter a unique name to identify your connection; use something descriptive. Click **Next** and enter the phone number your computer needs to call to access your PPP account in the appropriate boxes of the second window. That's all the information the wizard requests from you. Once you finish filling in the information, click **Finish**. The system creates a new icon in the **Dial-Up Networking** folder and labels it with the name you provided.

At this point, you should configure your modem for this connection. Select the icon for the connection in the **Dial-Up Networking** window and then choose **Properties** from the **File** menu. A general configuration window for your connection appears; you can use this window to change any of the information you provide. To review the modem configuration, click **Configure**. The modem configuration window shown in Figure B-16b appears.

This configuration window contains three tabs: **General**, **Connection**, and **Options**. The **General** tab is used to set the baud rate and the COM port for your modem. The COM port should be correctly set by the modem wizard. The baud rate, however, may need to set to match your service provider's modem. Your service provider should let you know the appropriate setting.

The **Connection** tab allows you to set the data bits and parity for your modem, which should always be **8** and **None** respectively for a PPP connection. Stop bits are usually 1. The **Advanced** button on this tab allows you to set the type of flow control being used, which must be either **Hardware (RTS/CTS)** or none for PPP. You can also choose whether or not error control and compression should be used. Error control is a safe bet for PPP connections, but data compression is debatable. Don't use modem data compression unless the serial port speed (the DTE speed) is greater than the modem speed (the DCE speed) at both ends. In other words, if you have a 9600 baud modem and the serial ports at each end are also set at 9600 baud, do not use data compression. It will actually slow things down. Use modem data compression when you have high speed serial ports, e.g., 38,400 bps, and a low speed link, e.g., 14,400 baud.

The most important item in the **Options** tab is labeled **Connection control**. It contains check boxes that allow you to bring up a terminal window before and after the computer dials your Internet service provider. Select the **Bring up terminal window after dialing** check box. You can then use the terminal window to key in the special instructions when you make the connection. When you have your modem set up the way you want, click **OK**.

Now you are back at the general configuration window for your connection. Click **Server Type** to bring up the server types window; there are a couple of settings you need to verify. Make sure that **PPP** is selected in the **Type of Dial-Up Server**

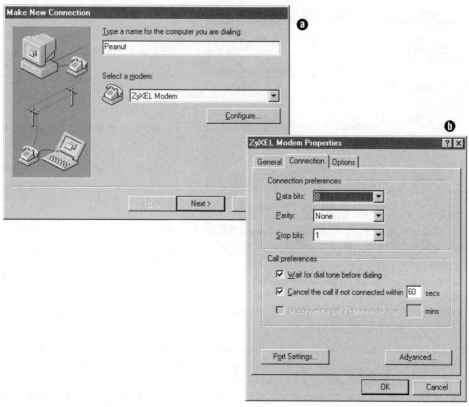

Figure B-16: Setting up a dial-up connection

combo box and that **TCP/IP** is checked in the **Allowed network protocols** section. Click **OK** once to dismiss the server types window and again to close the general configuration window.

Now you are ready to connect to the Internet. Double-click on the icon for your connection in the **Dial-Up Networking** window. The system prompts you for a username and password, using the window shown in Figure B-17. Enter your username and password; if you don't want to type your password each time you connect, select the **Save password** option. Now click **Connect**.

If the **Save password** option doesn't work, here's what you need to do to fix it. Select the **Network** applet from the **Control Panel**. If **Client for Microsoft Networks** appears in the list of components, select the **Identification** tab and enter names for your computer and workgroup. If this client is not in the list, you need to add it. Click the **Add** button, highlight **Client** in the **Select Network Component Type** window, and click **Add**. Select **Microsoft** from the **Manufacturers** list and then pick **Client for Microsoft Networks** from the **Network Clients** list. Click **OK** to add the

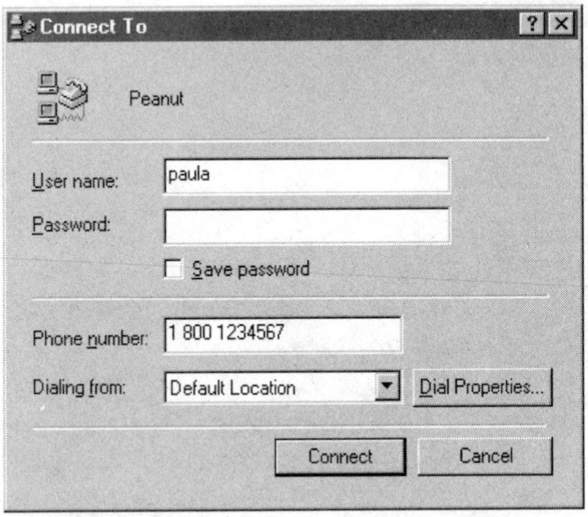

Figure B-17: PPP Connect To window

client. When you get back to the **Network** applet, select the **Identification** tab and enter names for your computer and workgroup. After you click **OK**, you'll need to restart your system to have this setting take effect. Once you do, you'll be able to select the **Save password** option.

Your computer will now dial your Internet service provider. A terminal window will appear after the computer has dialed. In this window, enter anything needed to start the PPP connection, and click **Continue**. You will need to give a username and a password. You may also need to give a special command to start the PPP session; your service provider will give you that command, if one is needed. When the connection process has been completed, you'll see a window that provides status information about the connection, including the amount of time you've been connected. This window also contains a **Disconnect** button that you can use to end your connection.

And now you're ready to start your exploration of the Internet. You may want to start by using FTP to download a more sophisticated Internet application, such as a World Wide Web browser like Internet Explorer or Netscape Navigator, as discussed in Chapter 6, *The World Wide Web*.

Whenever you want to use an Internet application, you need to bring up your Internet connection manually, as Windows 95 does not support an automatic connection mechanism. By the same token, once your machine is connected, it remains connected until you manually disconnect. If you pay for your Internet access by the hour, you'll need to make sure that you disconnect when you aren't using Internet applications, or your bill will quickly skyrocket.

Now that you have Internet access, you really should download the Microsoft Internet Jumpstart Kit. For one reason, these Internet tools provide auto-dial and auto-disconnect features, so you don't have to connect manually and you don't need to be as vigilant about disconnecting. As a reminder, you can download the tools via anonymous FTP from **ftp.microsoft.com**. You want the file *msie10.exe* in */peropsys/Win_News/Windows95Information/InternetExplorer*. Run the *msie10.exe* executable to install the tools

Now you should be able to use the **Internet** applet in the **Control Panel** to turn on the auto-dial functionality. You should also go back and follow the instructions in the "Automating the Login Process" section, so that you don't have to use a terminal window to establish your Internet connection.

Windows 95 on a LAN

If you are running Windows 95 on a networked PC, you should be able to access the Internet over your LAN (provided your LAN administrator has set up an Internet connection, which is another story). However, you may still need to install TCP/IP and a network adaptor, depending on how your system was set up. You'll also need some information about how to access the Internet from your site; you need to contact your network administrator to get this information.

Installing TCP/IP

You can see if TCP/IP is installed using the **Network** applet in the **Control Panel**. Open the **Control Panel** by selecting it from the **Settings** menu that appears when you click the **Start** menu on the Taskbar. Now open **Network** by double-clicking on the **Network** icon in the **Control Panel**. Figure B-18a shows the **Configuration** tab of the **Network** window after several network components have been configured. If TCP/IP is in the listbox in this window, then you can skip ahead to the section on "Configuring TCP/IP."

The **Network** window is used for all network components—it is not specific to TCP/IP:

- On the **Configuration** tab, the **File and Print Sharing** button brings up a window with check boxes that allow you to say whether or not you want this system to be able to offer file or printer sharing to other computers. The **Primary Network Logon** box on this window defines what server should validate the logon for this system. To validate the logon directly on the local host, choose **Windows Logon** from the pull-down list.

- The **Identification** tab is used to set the NetBIOS name and the NetBIOS workgroup.

- The **Access Control** tab is used to select whether the system should use share-level access control like Windows for Workgroups or user-level access control like Windows NT.

For more information about all of these different options, see *Networking Personal Computers with TCP/IP*, or ask your LAN administrator.

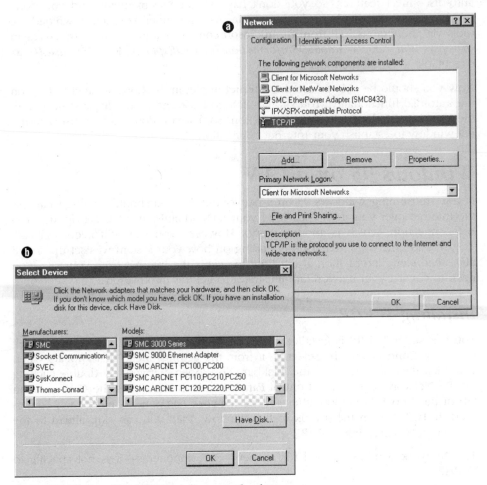

Figure B-18: Installing TCP/IP and a network adaptor

If TCP/IP is not installed on your system, you need to install it. To do so, click on the **Add** button in the **Configuration** tab of the **Network** window. Now a window labeled **Select Network Component Type** appears. Highlight **Protocol** in this new window and click **Add**. In the **Select Network Protocol** window that appears next, highlight **Microsoft** in the **Manufacturers** listbox. When you do, a list of protocols appears in the **Network Protocols** listbox. One of these is TCP/IP; highlight it and click **OK**.

If a network adaptor has not been configured for your system, Windows 95 now asks you to select an adaptor using the window shown in Figure B-18b. However, it is possible that Windows 95 detected and configured the network interface when the operating system was initially installed. If it did, you can skip the following step. Otherwise, select the manufacturer of your network adaptor from the

Manufacturers listbox, choose the appropriate model from the **Models** listbox, and then click **OK**.

Each of the adapters listed in this window has a driver included in the Windows 95 distribution. If your interface is not listed here, get the adapter manufacturer's software disk and click **Have Disk**. Vendors may not be shipping Windows 95 drivers yet. But that doesn't matter. If your adapter has a driver that can be installed under Windows 3.1, it will probably work with Windows 95. Simply provide Windows 95 with a disk that contains the OEMSETUP.INF file and the driver. Once the driver is loaded, you're prompted for the adapter configuration (IRQ, I/O Port, etc.), if one is required.

Configuring TCP/IP

The system now returns to the **Network** window shown in Figure B-18a. If you ever need to modify the adapter configuration, highlight the adapter in this window and click **Properties**. Likewise, to configure TCP/IP, highlight it and click **Properties**. The **TCP/IP Properties** window, shown earlier in Figure B-15, appears.

This window contains six tabs. Three of these tabs are critical for your TCP/IP configuration: **IP Address**, **Gateway**, and **DNS Configuration**. On the **IP Address** tab, make sure the **Specify an IP address** box is checked and fill in the **IP Address** and **Subnet Mask** fields with the values given to you by your network administrator.

The **Gateway** tab is used to enter the default gateway for your network. Enter the IP address of the default gateway for your LAN in the **New gateway** field and click **Add**. The gateway machine is the one that connects your LAN to the rest of the Internet. Your network administrator will tell you the gateway's address.

Now select the **DNS Configuration** tab and check **Enable DNS** to enable the Domain Name System. This system translates computer names into numeric Internet addresses and vice-versa. You need to enter the hostname for your computer in the **Host** field. This name is used to identify your PC; it may be assigned by your network administrator, or you may be allowed to choose your own hostname. You also need to type the domain name for your LAN in the **Domain** field. By now, you've guessed: ask your network administrator for the domain name.

Finally, enter the IP address of the machine that functions as your DNS server in the **DNS Server Search Order** field and click **Add**. This machine is responsible for looking up Internet addresses. If your network has more than one machine that functions as a DNS server, you should add all of the DNS servers in priority order. In other words, enter the most preferred server first, followed by the next most preferred server, and so on. Once again, your network administrator can give you the addresses of the DNS servers. The **Domain Suffix Search Order** box defines the order in which domains are searched for host information. Normally this box is left blank, so unless your network administrator tells you to fill in this information, just leave it empty.

The other three tabs on the **TCP/IP Properties** window are only important if your LAN is using other protocols besides TCP/IP, such as NetBIOS or NetBEIU. The **Advanced** tab is where you specify the default protocol for your system. With the **Bindings** tab, you can specify which network components communicate with TCP/IP. The **WINS Configuration** tab enables or disables WINS, which is a name server for NetBIOS names. You probably want WINS disabled; consult *Networking Personal Computers with TCP/IP* for more information.

When you have the configuration the way you want it, click **OK**. The system brings you back to the **Network** window. Click **OK** again to dismiss the **Network** applet. Depending on how your system was set up, at this point Windows 95 may prompt you to supply the Windows 95 CD-ROM or a number of diskettes, so that it can load the necessary software. You may also need to provide diskettes from your adaptor vendor. When this process is complete, reboot the system. Now the TCP/IP network is installed and you are ready to start exploring the Internet.

Microsoft Exchange

Before you try to configure Microsoft Exchange to send and receive Internet e-mail, you should make sure that your Internet connection is functioning properly. Troubleshooting can be difficult if you don't know what's working and what isn't.

Next you need to make sure that Exchange is installed on your system. Click the **Start** menu and select **Programs**; if you see **Microsoft Exchange** on this menu, you're all set. Otherwise, select **Add/Remove Programs** from the **Control Panel**. On the **Windows Setup** tab, select the **Microsoft Exchange** option. Now click **OK** and Windows 95 will install the program; have your CD-ROM or diskettes ready when the system prompts you for them.

If you don't yet have the Microsoft Internet Jumpstart Kit, you'll need to download it before you can proceed. This package contains an Internet e-mail driver for Exchange. Use the following URL with your Web browser:

```
http://www.windows.microsoft.com/windows/software/iexplorer.htm
```

After you have retrieved *msie10.exe*, run this executable to install the Internet tools.

If you've already run the Internet Setup Wizard as described earlier, the wizard should have prompted you for information about configuring Internet e-mail. If you chose not to use Internet e-mail at that time, you'll need to rerun the wizard and supply the necessary information. If you haven't run the wizard before, do so now. You'll be asked for your e-mail address and the name of your Internet mail server.

At this point, you should be able to read and send Internet e-mail with Microsoft Exchange. If everything doesn't work properly, however, you may need to change your configuration settings. Additionally, there are a few options you may want to set for your particular situation. To change your e-mail configuration, use the **Mail** and **Fax** applet on the **Control Panel**. When the MS Exchange Settings Properties window appears, select **Internet Mail** from the list of services and click **Properties**. Now you should see the window shown in Figure B-19a.

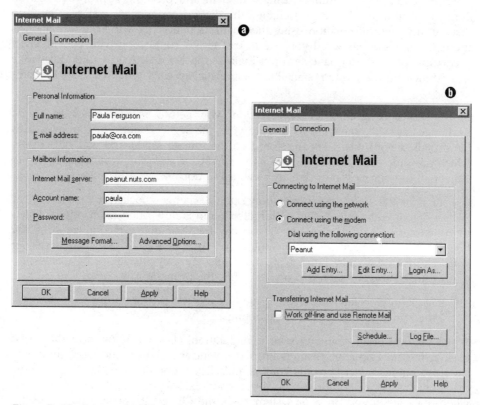

Figure B-19: Internet Mail information

Make sure the information in the **Personal Information** section is correct. If you need to change the name of your Internet mail server, enter your changes in the **Internet Mail server** field. You also need to supply your e-mail account name and password. If you are using a dial-up Internet connection, these may be the same as the username and password you use to connect to your Internet provider, but then again, they may not. Your service provider can give you this information. If you are using a LAN connection, you should know your username and password.

If you click the **Message Format** button on the **General** tab, you can decide whether or not to use the MIME format for sending messages. You almost certainly want to use MIME. This window also lets you specify the character set used for sending messages. The **Advanced Options** button on the **General** tab allows you to select a separate outgoing mail server for your e-mail. You probably don't need to set this option; your service provider or network administrator should tell you if you do.

Now select the **Connection** tab, which is shown in Figure B-19b. On this tab, you want to specify how Exchange should connect to your Internet mailbox. If you are using a LAN connection, select **Connect using the network**. If you're using a dial-up connection, select **Connect using a modem** and pick the appropriate dial-up connection from the list. If you change the dial-up connection, you may need to change the login information using the **Login As** button. This login information is the username and password you use to establish a connection with your Internet service provider. If you have set up a login script as I described earlier, Exchange will connect to your Internet mailbox automatically each time you start the program.

In the **Transferring Internet Mail** section, you get to specify whether or not Exchange uses Remote Mail to display your message headers. If you select this option, all of your messages are stored on the remote server and you can choose which messages you want to transfer to your PC. If you want your mail server to deliver all of your messages directly to your PC, don't select this option.

Use the **Schedule** button to specify how often Exchange checks for new messages. With a dial-up connection, this option also controls how often Exchange connects to your Internet service provider. If you pay for your Internet connection by the hour, you should be careful how often Exchange checks for new messages, or your bill may grow quite large. Note that Exchange only checks for new messages (and connects to your service provider) while the program is running.

The **Log File** button lets you create a file that records events during your mail sessions; this can be useful for troubleshooting.

When you are done changing your configuration, click **OK**. Now you should be back at the MS Exchange Settings Properies window. There's one more thing you should do here. Select **Personal Folders** and click **Properties**. You'll see a window that contains general information about your Exchange e-mail folders, such as where they are stored on your system. Click the **Change Password** button to set a password for your e-mail folders. This password protects your e-mail folders from being read by anyone else; Exchange will ask you for it each time you start the program. After you've entered a password, click **OK** once to return to the MS Exchange Settings Properties window, and once again to have your configuration changes take effect.

Now you should be ready to start using Exchange, as described in Chapter 5, *Electronic Mail*. Double-click on the **Inbox** icon on your desktop to open Exchange.

INTERNATIONAL NETWORK CONNECTIVITY

Country Codes and Connectivity

Outside of the United States, the top-level domains used in Internet addresses are two-letter country codes. The country codes (and their names) are defined in an International standards document called ISO 3166. The bulk of this appendix is a table, distributed by Lawrence Landweber and the Internet Society, that shows all of these codes.[*] The table also shows what kind of network connectivity each country has. They aren't all connected to the Internet, so services like the WWW and Telnet may not be available; but well over half have some kind of international network connectivity (whether BITNET, UUCP, Fidonet, or something else), so you can at least send e-mail.

The total number of entities with international network connectivity is 173. Figure C-1 summarizes the countries that have network connectivity, and the kind of connectivity they have.

Country Codes and Connectivity

Entries in the connectivity table look like this:

```
    BIUF AT        Austria
```

This entry means that AT is the top-level domain name for Austria; a domain name like **ffr.syh.at** is probably from an Internet site in Austria. The notation in the left column shows the kind of connectivity each country has, as shown in Table C-1.

Table C-1: Keys to Connectivity

Key	Type of Connectivity
----	No verified connectivity
B	Bitnet connectivity
I	Internet connectivity
U	UUCP connectivity
F	Fidonet connectivity

[*] The official and up-to-date version of this information may be found on the Internet Society Gopher: **gopher.isoc.org**. The name will be something like *ConnectivityChart*; the actual name varies with the version.

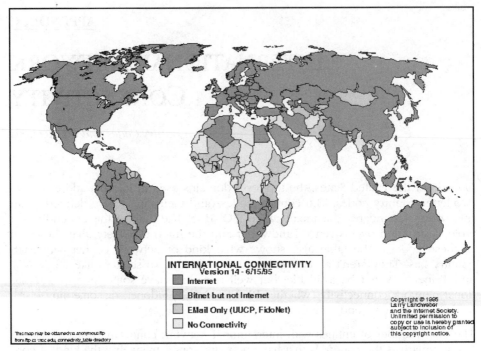

Figure C–1: International connectivity map

Lowercase letters indicate minimal connectivity; uppercase indicates widespread connectivity. The example entry indicates that Austria has BITNET, Internet, UUCP, and Fidonet connectivity—i.e., every kind of connectivity that's currently possible.

An entity is a geographical area that has an ISO two letter country code (ISO 3166). These country codes are included in the Table below for each entity. Note that the ISO codes do not always agree with the top level DNS (Domain Name) code(s) used for a particular entity. For example: Internet hosts in a number of countries have DNS names ending in .*net*. In the United Kingdom, UK is used while the official ISO code is GB. There are still some hosts in the former Soviet Union that use SU in their DNS names.

Haiti's u entry is based on a *ccmail* e-mail link. Restricted access or dial-up IP links exist in a number of countries. These are not included in the table as Internet connections. There are also a number of private Fidonet nodes that are used for specific projects or by designated groups. These are also not included.

----	AF	Afghanistan		---f	AO	Angola
----	AL	Albania		--u-	AI	Anguilla
-I--	DZ	Algeria		-I--	AQ	Antarctica
----	AS	American Samoa		-Iu-	AG	Antigua and Barbuda
----	AD	Andorra		BIUF	AR	Argentina

-IU-	AM	Armenia
---f	AW	Aruba
-IUF	AU	Australia
BIUF	AT	Austria
b-U-	AZ	Azerbaijan
--u-	BS	Bahamas
b---	BH	Bahrain
--U-	BD	Bangladesh
-Iu-	BB	Barbados
bIUF	BY	Belarus
bIUF	BE	Belgium
--U-	BZ	Belize
----	BJ	Benin
-IUf	BM	Bermuda
----	BT	Bhutan
--UF	BO	Bolivia
--u-	BA	Bosnia-Herzegovina
--uf	BW	Botswana
----	BV	Bouvet Island
BIUF	BR	Brazil
----	IO	British Indian Ocean Territory
----	BN	Brunei Darussalam
bIUF	BG	Bulgaria
--U-	BF	Burkina Faso
----	BI	Burundi
----	KH	Cambodia
--Uf	CM	Cameroon
BIUF	CA	Canada
----	CV	Cape Verde
----	KY	Cayman Islands
----	CF	Central African Republic
----	TD	Chad
BIUF	CL	Chile
-IuF	CN	China
----	CX	Christmas Island
----	CC	Cocos (Keeling) Islands
bIu-	CO	Colombia
----	KM	Comoros
--U-	CG	Congo
--u-	CK	Cook Islands
-Iuf	CR	Costa Rica
--Uf	CI	Cote d'Ivoire
bIuF	HR	Croatia
--U-	CU	Cuba
bI-f	CY	Cyprus
bIUF	CZ	Czech Republic
-IUF	DK	Denmark
----	DJ	Djibouti
----	DM	Dominica
-IUf	DO	Dominican Republic
----	TP	East Timor
-Iu-	EC	Ecuador
bIU-	EG	Egypt

--u-	SV	El Salvador
----	GQ	Equatorial Guinea
---f	ER	Eritrea
-IUF	EE	Estonia
---f	ET	Ethiopia
----	FK	Falkland Islands
-Iu-	FO	Faroe Islands
-Iu-	FJ	Fiji
BIUF	FI	Finland
bIUF	FR	France
--u-	GF	French Guiana
--u-	PF	French Polynesia
----	TF	French Southern Territories
----	GA	Gabon
---f	GM	Gambia
--UF	GE	Georgia
BIUF	DE	Germany
--UF	GH	Ghana
----	GI	Gibraltar
bIUF	GR	Greece
-I--	GL	Greenland
--u-	GD	Grenada
--uf	GP	Guadeloupe
-I-F	GU	Guam
--uf	GT	Guatemala
--u-	GN	Guinea
----	GW	Guinea-Bissau
--u-	GY	Guyana
--u-	HT	Haiti
----	HM	Heard and McDonald Islands
-I--	HN	Honduras
BI-F	HK	Hong Kong
BIUF	HU	Hungary
-IUF	IS	Iceland
bIUF	IN	India
-IUF	ID	Indonesia
bI--	IR	Iran
----	IQ	Iraq
bIUF	IE	Ireland
BIUF	IL	Israel
BIUF	IT	Italy
-Iu-	JM	Jamaica
BIUF	JP	Japan
---f	JO	Jordan
-IUF	KZ	Kazakhstan
--UF	KE	Kenya
--u-	KI	Kiribati
----	KP	Korea (People's Republic)
BIUF	KR	Korea (Republic)
-I--	KW	Kuwait
--U-	KG	Kyrgyz Republic
----	LA	Lao People's Democratic Republic
-IUF	LV	Latvia

--U-	LB	Lebanon	BIUF	PL	Poland
--u-	LS	Lesotho	bIUF	PT	Portugal
----	LR	Liberia	bIUF	PR	Puerto Rico
----	LY	Libyan Arab Jamahiriya	----	QA	Qatar
-I-F	LI	Liechtenstein	-Iu-	RE	Re'union
-IUF	LT	Lithuania	bIuF	RO	Romania
bIUF	LU	Luxembourg	bIUF	RU	Russian Federation
-I--	MO	Macau	----	RW	Rwanda
-Iu-	MK	Macedonia	----	SH	Saint Helena
--U-	MG	Madagascar	----	KN	Saint Kitts and Nevis
---f	MW	Malawi	--u-	LC	Saint Lucia
bIUF	MY	Malaysia	----	PM	Saint Pierre and Miquelon
----	MV	Maldives	--u-	VC	Saint Vincent and the Grenadines
--U-	ML	Mali	--u-	WS	Samoa
--uF	MT	Malta	----	SM	San Marino
--u-	MH	Marshall Islands	----	ST	Sao Tome and Principe
----	MQ	Martinique	B---	SA	Saudi Arabia
----	MR	Mauritania	--Uf	SN	Senegal
--uf	MU	Mauritius	--u-	SC	Seychelles
----	YT	Mayotte	---f	SL	Sierra Leone
bIuF	MX	Mexico	bIuF	SG	Singapore
----	FM	Micronesia	-IUF	SK	Slovakia
-IuF	MD	Moldova	-IUF	SI	Slovenia
-I--	MC	Monaco	--u-	SB	Solomon Islands
--u-	MN	Mongolia	----	SO	Somalia
----	MS	Montserrat	-IUF	ZA	South Africa
--Uf	MA	Morocco	BIUF	ES	Spain
-IUf	MZ	Mozambique	-IU-	LK	Sri Lanka
----	MM	Myanmar	----	SD	Sudan
--U-	NA	Namibia	--u-	SR	Suriname
--u-	NR	Nauru	-I--	SJ	Svalbard and Jan Mayen Islands
--u-	NP	Nepal	--u-	SZ	Swaziland
bIUF	NL	Netherlands	BIUF	SE	Sweden
--u-	AN	Netherlands Antilles	BIUF	CH	Switzerland
----	NT	Neutral Zone (Saudi Arabia/Iraq)	----	SY	Syria
--U-	NC	New Caledonia	BIuF	TW	Taiwan, Province of China
-IUF	NZ	New Zealand	--uf	TJ	Tajikistan
-Iu-	NI	Nicaragua	---f	TZ	Tanzania
--U-	NE	Niger	-IUF	TH	Thailand
--Uf	NG	Nigeria	--u-	TG	Togo
--u-	NU	Niue	----	TK	Tokelau
----	NF	Norfolk Island	--u-	TO	Tonga
----	MP	Northern Mariana Islands	--U-	TT	Trinidad and Tobago
bIUF	NO	Norway	-IUf	TN	Tunisia
----	OM	Oman	BI-F	TR	Turkey
--U-	PK	Pakistan	--u-	TM	Turkmenistan
----	PW	Palau	----	TC	Turks and Caicos Islands
-IuF	PA	Panama	--u-	TV	Tuvalu
--u-	PG	Papua New Guinea	---f	UG	Uganda
--u-	PY	Paraguay	-IUF	UA	Ukraine
-IUf	PE	Peru	-I--	AE	United Arab Emirates
-IuF	PH	Philippines	bIuF	UK	United Kingdom
----	PN	Pitcairn	BIUF	US	United States

```
---- UM  United States Minor Outlying Islands
-IUF UY  Uruguay
-IUF UZ  Uzbekistan
--u- VU  Vanuatu
---- VA  Vatican City State
-IUF VE  Venezuela
--U- VN  Vietnam
---- VG  Virgin Islands (British)
-I-f VI  Virgin Islands (U.S.)
---- WF  Wallis and Futuna Islands
---- EH  Western Sahara
---- YE  Yemen
--uf YU  Yugoslavia
---- ZR  Zaire
-I-f ZM  Zambia
-Iuf ZW  Zimbabwe
```

THE MICROSOFT NETWORK

Accessing the Microsoft Network
Exploring MSN
MSN and the Internet
Some Final Thoughts

The Microsoft Network (MSN) is a new on-line service that made its debut with Windows 95. MSN is really a hybrid, with two distinct parts. One part is a proprietary, value-added on-line service like America Online and CompuServe; the other a standard Internet service provider. MSN handles this dichotomy by providing two different *service types*. With the "MSN" service type, you get access to the proprietary on-line service, with its limited Internet services, and nothing more. However, with the "MSN and Internet" service type, MSN functions as an Internet service provider, giving you full Internet access.*

The proprietary part of the Microsoft Network provides the same types of services as the other on-line vendors. A *service* is defined as something you can do on MSN. For example, MSN offers bulletin board services, chat services, current news and weather reports, stock quote services, and reference material. This portion of MSN also offers you limited Internet access; you can send and receive electronic mail over the Internet and read Internet newsgroups. The interface for the Microsoft Network works just like the interface for Windows 95, so unlike other on-line services, you don't have to learn anything new to explore MSN.

The Microsoft Network can also act as an Internet service provider, giving you full access to all of the different Internet services that I've covered in this book. Appendix B describes how to set up your Internet connection using MSN as your service provider. If you are using MSN as an Internet provider, you also have access to the proprietary part of MSN, but it is important to note that you don't have to use it. You can do everything described in this book without once using the MSN on-line service.

This appendix describes how to use the MSN on-line service. While I'm not endorsing MSN, this book wouldn't be complete without a description of its

---

* To take advantage of the "MSN and Internet" service type, you need a new version of the MSN software; the version provided with Windows 95 only supports the "MSN" service type. You can get the new version of MSN (1.05) by purchasing Microsoft Plus! or downloading the Internet Jumpstart Kit, as described in Appendix B, *Setting Up Your Internet Connection*.

services. If you've found enough resources on the Internet to keep you busy and you aren't interested in an on-line service, you can stop reading right now. But if you want to see what MSN is all about, keep reading. I'll tell you how to access the Microsoft Network and give you a brief tour of its main services: bulletin boards, file libraries, and chat rooms. I'll also describe the limited Internet access provided through the on-line service. I'm not going to describe every feature of MSN; I'm just going to tell you what you need to know to explore it. Check the MSN on-line help system for more complete information, and feel free to experiment.

Accessing the Microsoft Network

Getting started with the Microsoft Network is simple; just double-click on **The Microsoft Network** icon on your desktop. If you've already signed up for MSN, you'll see the window in Figure D-1, prompting you for your member ID and password. If you've signed up with MSN as your Internet service provider, as described in Appendix B, you'll see this window as well.

Figure D−1: MSN sign in window

If you aren't a member of MSN, the first time you double-click on **The Microsoft Network**, you'll be given the option of joining. The MSN wizard walks you through the process of creating your account by prompting you for billing information, making sure you agree to the rules that govern MSN, and asking you to select a member ID. After you've created your MSN account, you should see the window in Figure D-1.

Enter your member ID and password and click **Connect**. If you don't want to type your password each time you connect to MSN, select the **Remember my password** option. When your system successfully connects to MSN, you'll see the MSN Central window shown in Figure D-2.

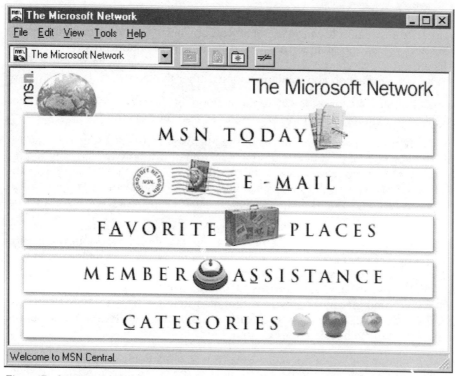

Figure D–2: MSN Central

You always begin your exploration of the Microsoft Network at MSN Central. If your MSN Central window doesn't have a toolbar like the window in Figure D-2, you can turn the toolbar on by selecting **Toolbar** from the **View** menu. I recommend using the toolbar; it makes navigating much easier.

The **MSN Today** button brings up the MSN Today window, which contains current news headlines and other interesting features, like interviews and discussions about current events. When you connect to MSN, this window is displayed automatically. If you want to read one of the articles or participate in a discussion, click on that area of the MSN Today window. The contents of this window are updated daily, so it's a good place to keep up with what's going on, both in the world and on the Microsoft Network.

Use the **E-mail** button to start Microsoft Exchange and read your e-mail. If you have new e-mail when you connect to MSN, you'll be asked if you want to start Exchange at that time. I'll talk more about MSN and e-mail later in this appendix.

As you explore MSN, you'll find places that you want to visit again. MSN makes it easy to keep track of these places using the concept of a "favorite place." When you find a favorite place, you mark it as such and MSN stores the location. To go to one of your favorite places, click the **Favorite Places** button from MSN Central and select the place. I'll describe how to mark your favorite places in the next section, once we start exploring MSN.

If you have a question about MSN, or if you are having a problem using one of the services, select the **Member Assistance** button. This button provides access to the Member Lobby, where you can get technical support, view the member directory, and get information about billing, among other things.

The final button, **Categories**, is where the majority of the services in MSN are kept. We'll begin our exploration of the Microsoft Network here shortly.

As you may have guessed, you navigate the Microsoft Network using your mouse. With the exception of the buttons on the MSN Central window, which only require a single-click, you move to a new area by double-clicking on its icon. For example, from the Member Lobby, you can double-click on the **Member Support** folder to open this area and then double-click on the **MSN Help Desk Icon** to see answers to frequently-asked questions.

There are a few other simple navigation tools you should know about before you start exploring. If you find you've opened an area that you aren't interested in, you can click the **Up One Level** button on the toolbar or select **Up One Level** from the **File** menu to move back. You can use this command repeatedly to return from whence you came. At any time, you can immediately get back to MSN Central by clicking the **Go to MSN Central** button on the toolbar or by selecting **Go to** on the **Edit** menu and then choosing **MSN Central**.

After you've connected to MSN, you should see an MSN icon on the far left side of the taskbar at the bottom of your screen, next to the clock. If you want to disconnect from the Microsoft Network, click on this icon with the right mouse button and select **Sign Out**. You can also select **Sign Out** from the toolbar or the **File** menu.

Exploring MSN

On the Microsoft Network, you have access to a variety of different services, including bulletin boards, file libraries, chat rooms, and reference information. These services are organized by subject area. For example, you'll find all of the bulletin boards and chat rooms for outdoor sports and recreation in the same location. MSN uses the concept of a *forum* for a collection of related services. A forum is represented graphically by a folder. When you select **Categories** from MSN Central, you'll see a number of folders on different topics, as shown in Figure D-3.

As you might imagine, there's a wealth of information in each of the forums in the **Categories** folder. Let's go exploring. Say you've got a couple of children, a young teenager and an eight-year old. You're interested in finding out what MSN has to

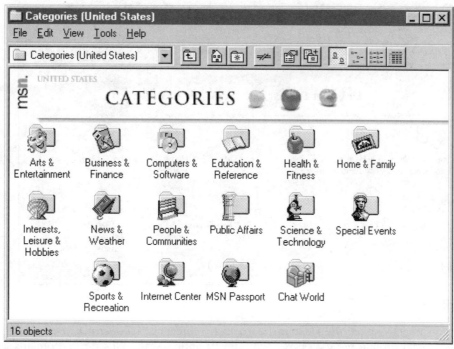

Figure D-3: Categories

offer the kids, as well as any useful information on parenting that might be available. The obvious place to start is the **Home & Family** folder. Double-click on it and you'll see the contents of the forum, as shown in Figure D-4.

In the **Home & Family** forum, you see more folders, this time with more specific topics. When you enter a new forum, you'll often see a folder with the information symbol, as you do in Figure D-4. This folder is an information center, or *kiosk*, for the forum. If you double-click on the **Home & Family InfoCenter** folder, you'll see current information about what's available in the **Home & Family** forum. I'll leave you to check out the kiosk on your own; for now let's go check out the **Parenting** forum. When you double-click on the **Parenting** icon, you'll see a number of forums on parenting. The **Parenting in the 90's Forum** looks interesting, so let's double-click on it. Now you should see something like the window shown in Figure D-5.

In Figure D-4, there are a number of new icons; these represent different kinds of MSN services. When you see an icon you don't recognize, there's an easy way to identify the service it represents. Simply click the **Details** button on the toolbar or select **Details** from the **View** menu to see a detailed listing of the contents of a forum.

Figure D–4: Home and Family folder

As you might expect, the bulletin board icon represents a *bulletin board* service, which is an on-line discussion service. The **Parenting in the 90's** forum contains a general bulletin board and several bulletin boards devoted to special topics. I'll describe how to use a bulletin board service shortly.

The caption bubble icon in Figure D-5, labeled **Parenting Chat**, is a *chat* service. This kind of service allows you to have real-time conversations with other MSN members. The conversations take place in a *chat room*. I'll talk more about participating in a chat in a little while.

The information icon in Figure D-5 represents another kiosk, or information center. If you double-click on this icon, you'll see a document that describes the purpose of the **Parenting in the 90's** forum. When you enter a new forum, it's a good idea to read this document, so that you can get a sense of what's going on.

If you think you've found a gold mine of resources in the **Parenting in the 90's** forum, you'll probably want to come back often. MSN provides two easy ways for you to keep track of places you want to visit frequently. First, you can mark the forum as one of your *favorite places*. To do so, select **Add to Favorite Places** from the **File** menu while you are in the forum. Now, when you click on the **Favorite Places** button in MSN Central, you'll see the forum in your **Favorite Places** folder.

The other option is to create a *shortcut* to the forum. When you create a shortcut, MSN puts an icon on your desktop that takes you directly to a particular location within MSN. If you double-click on the icon while you are connected to MSN, the system will open a new window and take you to the forum. If you aren't

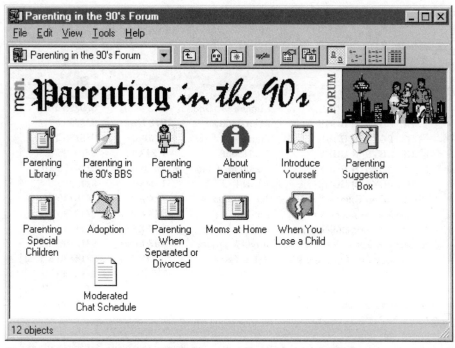

Figure D–5: Parenting in the 90's

connected, the system will establish a connection to MSN and take you directly to the forum. To create a shortcut, select **Create Shortcut** from the **File** menu.

Using Bulletin Boards

Let's take a look at one of the bulletin boards in the **Parenting in the 90's** forum. Double-click on the **Parenting in the 90's BBS** icon to open the bulletin board. Now you should see a list of messages posted to the bulletin board, as shown in Figure D-6. These messages have been posted by other MSN members; you are free to read the messages, respond to ones that interest you, and post your own messages.

When you open a bulletin board service for the first time, you'll see all of the messages that have been posted recently. The icons to the left of each message provide information about the message. If you haven't read a message, it will be marked with a right-pointing arrow and displayed in bold. After you read a message, the arrow is removed and the message is displayed with a plain typeface.

Figure D–6: Parenting in the 90's bulletin board

The bulletin board window

Messages in the bulletin board window can be displayed in one of three different views: a conversation, or thread, view, a list view, or a file view. In my opinion, bulletin board messages are easiest to deal with when they are organized by conversation, as they are in Figure D-6. This is the default view. A *thread* consists of an original message and all of the responses to it; MSN also refers to a thread as a *conversation*. (The thread concept in MSN bulletin board services is the same as with USENET newsgroups, if you are familiar with those; see Chapter 7, *Network News*.) List view shows the messages without regard to threads, so original messages and replies are all mixed together. File view only shows those messages that have attached files; this is most useful when you are downloading files, as we'll discuss in the next section.

If you want to change the view, you can do so using the **View** menu. The choices are: **Conversation**, **List**, and **Attached Files**. Use **Arrange Messages** on the **View** menu to sort the messages by subject, author, size, or date. You can also sort the messages by clicking on the appropriate header in the bulletin board window.

When you are using the conversation view, if a message is marked with a "plus" icon, there are replies to the message, but the replies are hidden. You can display all of the replies in the thread by clicking on the icon. When the replies are shown, the icon changes to a "minus" icon, as shown for the "BOYS 'N GUNS" thread in Figure D-6. To hide the replies again, click on the icon. You can also display all of the replies to all of the messages by selecting **Expand All Conversations** from the **View** menu. Use **Collapse All Conversations** to reverse the process. When a message has a text file icon next to it, there are no replies to that message.

Reading messages

But enough about how the messages are displayed. What you really want to know is how to read messages. It's easy; double-click on the message you want to read and it will be displayed in a separate window, as shown in Figure D-7.

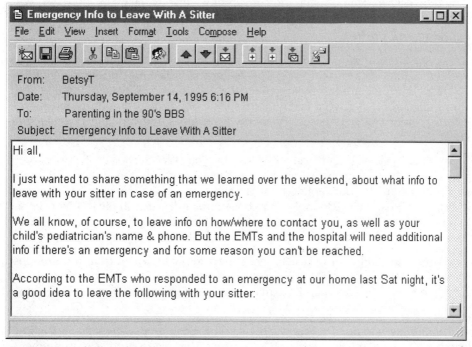

Figure D–7: A bulletin board message

From the viewing window, you can read view other messages by clicking the **Next Message** and **Previous Message** buttons on the toolbar. If you want to skip the replies to a particular message, use the **Next Conversation** and **Previous Conversation** buttons. The **Next Unread Message** and **Next Unread Conversation** buttons only show you messages that you haven't read before. All of these commands are also available on the **View** menu.

After you read a message, it is marked as such and displayed in a plain typeface (not bold). The next time you read the bulletin board, you'll find that MSN only shows you the messages you haven't read before. If you want to see all of the messages, select **Show All Messages** from the **Tools** menu. Messages eventually expire however, so if you want to keep a particular message, your best bet is to save it using **Save As** on the **File** menu.

If you read a number of different bulletin boards, you may find them taking up a fair bit of your time. Here's a technique that I find useful for managing messages. First, be sure to use the conversation view, so that messages and their replies are grouped together. After scanning the bulletin board listing, read any messages and replies that look interesting. Respond to any messages that warrant your input, as described in the next section. When you are done, select **Mark All Messages as Read** from the **Tools** menu. Now, the next time you check the bulletin board, you'll only see the new messages and any new replies to old messages, so it should be easy to keep up with the conversations that interest you.

Replying and posting

When you first join a new bulletin board, you may want to just read messages for a while to get a feel for the place. This is known as *lurking* and it's a highly recommended technique for learning about the culture of a particular bulletin board. Most bulletin boards have a certain atmosphere and tone; it's good to have a feel for this before you start posting your own messages and replying to other messages.

If you read a message and want to respond, you have a choice of posting your response to the bulletin board or sending e-mail directly to the author of the message. The nature of your reply often determines which type of response you want to make. To post your response to the bulletin board, select **Reply to BBS** from the **Compose** menu. When you do, MSN will display a composition window. Enter your response and select **Post Message** from the **File** menu.

If you want to send an e-mail response, select **Reply by E-mail** from the **Compose** window. In this case, MSN will start Microsoft Exchange, if the program isn't already running, and open an Exchange composition window. Type your response and click the **Send** button to send the e-mail message.

The final thing you need to know how to do is post your own message to a bulletin board. Again, this is quite easy; select **New Message** from the **Compose** menu. When the composition window appears, enter an appropriate subject in the **Subject** field and type your message. If you want to attach a file to your message, position the cursor where you want to put the file in the message window, choose **File** from the **Insert** menu, and select the file. Attaching a file is useful when you have something like a Word document that you want to share with others. When you are done, select **Post Message** from the **File** menu to post the message on the bulletin board.

Downloading Files

A *file library* is a special type of bulletin board that contains files, attached to messages, that you can copy to and from the bulletin board. In the **Computers & Software** forum, you'll find quite a few such libraries that contain different kinds of computer programs. For example, if you open the **Software** folder followed by the **Electronic Games** folder, you'll find the **Computer Games Forum**. This forum contains the **Computer Games File Library**; double-click on this item to open the library, which is shown in Figure D-8.

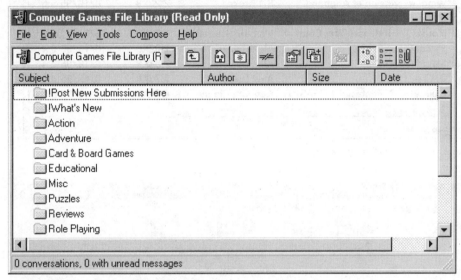

Figure D–8: Computer Games File Library

As you can see, the file library is divided into folders, with a different folder for each type of computer game. The library itself is read-only, which means that you cannot post messages to it. However, the **Post New Submissions Here** folder does allow you to post messages. If you've created a great new game that you think other people might be interested in, open this folder and read the submission guidelines posted there.

Let's look at how to download a file from the library. Double-click on **Role Playing** to open this portion of the library. You should see a window like the one in Figure D-9. The contents of the library are shown using the file view; the paper clip icon next to each item indicates that the message has an attached file.

To download an attached file, you have to read the message that contains the attachment. If you double-click on one of the messages shown in Figure D-9, you'll see a viewing window like the one shown in Figure D-10. The window should contain information about the game, as well as a file icon. This icon is the attached game.

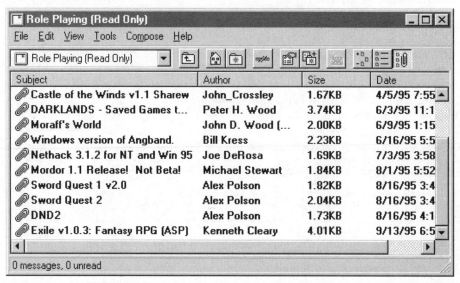

Figure D–9: Role Playing games

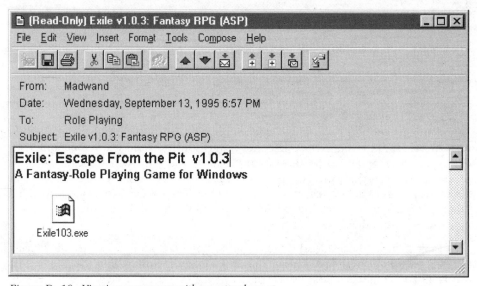

Figure D–10: Viewing a message with an attachment

Before you save the attached file, you should check its properties by double-clicking on the icon. MSN will display a window that contains information about the size of the file, the amount of time it will take to download it, and whether or not there is a fee for copying it. If you decide you want to save the game file, you can click on the **Download** button to start retrieving it immediately.

In addition, you can save the file by clicking on the icon for the file and selecting **Save** from the **File** menu. When the Save As window appears, select the **Attachments** option and specify a location for the saved file. Now click **OK**. This is the same process you would use to save a file attached to a message in a regular bulletin board; for example, a Word document that someone has attached to a message.

When you start downloading a file, MSN will display the File Transfer Status window. This window shows the status of files that are being downloaded and lets you control how files are transferred to your system. For example, while a file is being downloaded, you can select the file from the File Transfer Status window and click **Pause** on the toolbar to pause the transfer or **Remove** to stop the transfer altogether. If you select **Options** from the **Tools** menu in this window, you can change the default directory when files are copied, as well as control how compressed files are handled.

Chatting

As I mentioned earlier, a chat service allows you to have an interactive conversation with other MSN members. A chat is different than a bulletin board because all of the people participating in a chat have to be on-line, in the chat room, at the same time. A chat is quite similar to a conference call.

As you explore MSN, you'll come across chat services in the different forums; many chats are meant to be on a particular topic, like parenting in the 90's or the computer game Doom. MSN also has an entire area devoted to chatting. From the **Categories** folder, double-click on **Chat World** to enter this area, shown in Figure D-11.

There are countless chats accessible from **Chat World**, ranging in size from two participants to over twenty. A good place to try chatting for the first time is the **CW Lobby**. This chat room has a *host*, a member who moderates activities in the room, so it is a good place to get your feet wet and ask questions. To participate in the chat, double-click on the **CW Lobby** icon. MSN now opens a separate chat window, as shown in Figure D-12.

The chat window has three areas: a chat history area, a list of members in the chat room, and an area to compose your messages. As you can see in the chat history area, there can be a number of different conversations going on at the same time, especially in a room that can have over 25 participants. If the conversation you are interested in goes by too quickly, you can use the scroll bar to see what has been said.

The member list shows all of the MSN members who are in the chat room. The caption bubble icon next to a member ID indicates that the member is a *participant* in the chat; the member is free to read and send comments. The gavel icon is used to indicate a host. In some chat rooms, you aren't allowed to participate unless you are given permission by a host. In that case, you are known as a

Figure D–11: Chat World

spectator because you can only read comments. Members who are spectators are marked with a pair of sunglasses.

While some MSN members use their name as their member ID, many people do not. If you want to find out more about a particular member, select the member ID and click on the **Member Properties** button on the toolbar. MSN will display a window with that member's name and city of residence, among other things.

In the **CW Lobby** chat room, you should feel free to ask the host any questions you might have. To direct your question to the host, be sure you precede it with the string "Host:". Type your question in the composition area at the bottom of the window and press ENTER. You should see your question appear in the chat history almost immediately. If you want to type a question that is more than one line long, use CTRL-ENTER to start a new line in the composition area. Then click **Send** when you are ready to send your question.

Once you've been in a chat room for a few minutes, you should have a feel for the flow of conversation and you might want to join in. If you are feeling bold, you can even start a conversation with one of the other participants. If you are speaking to a particular member, be sure to address your comments to that person.

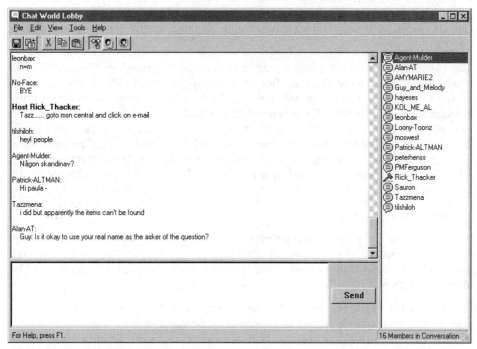

Figure D–12: Chat World Lobby

MSN and the Internet

So far, all of the services we've looked at in MSN have actually been a part of the Microsoft Network. But as I mentioned earlier, MSN also provides limited access to some services that are found on the Internet, rather than MSN proper. Most importantly, MSN allows you to send e-mail to anyone on the Internet, not just other MSN members. MSN also provides access to Internet newsgroups, which are like bulletin boards, except that anyone on the Internet can participate in the discussion.

The final Internet service is only available if you are using the "MSN and Internet" service type. With this service type, you have full Internet access. Consequently, you can browse the World Wide Web, either using a Web browser as described in Chapter 6, *The World Wide Web*, or by double-clicking on Internet shortcuts that you find while exploring MSN.

Electronic Mail

As a member of the Microsoft Network, you have the capability to send e-mail to anyone on the Internet, in addition to other MSN members. MSN uses Microsoft Exchange to handle e-mail, so if you click on the **E-mail** button in MSN Central, your system will start Exchange. When you connect to MSN, if you have new e-mail, you'll be asked whether or not you want to start Exchange to read it. You can also open Exchange directly by double-clicking on the **Inbox** icon on your desktop.

You use Exchange to compose e-mail messages as described in Chapter 5, *Electronic Mail*; select **New Message** from the **Compose** menu. While you are connected to MSN, you have access to the MSN address book, so you can look up the e-mail addresses of other MSN members. Select **Address Book** from the **Tools** menu to peruse the MSN address book. If you are sending e-mail to another MSN member, you can simply use their member ID in the "To:" field. If you are sending a message to someone on the Internet, you need to use their full Internet e-mail address. Internet users can send you mail through MSN using an address of the following form:

> *memberid*@msn.com

If you have set up your Exchange profile to handle both MSN mail and Internet mail, you'll need to specify how a particular message is sent. To send a message through MSN, select **Deliver Now Using** from the **Tools** menu and then choose **The Microsoft Network**.

Reading e-mail messages works just as described in Chapter 5. Make sure that your Exchange profile is set up to handle MSN e-mail. If it isn't, you can add MSN to your Exchange profile using the **Mail and Fax** icon on the **Control Panel**. Once you have your Exchange profile set up properly, reading mail is easy. If you want to, you can take advantage of Exchange's remote mail functionality, using the **Remote Mail** command on the **Tools** menu. You can also configure how Exchange downloads mail from MSN by selecting **Services** from the **Tools** menu.

Newsgroups

USENET newsgroups, also known as network news, are the Internet equivalent of MSN bulletin boards. While only MSN members can participate in a bulletin board, anyone on the Internet can take part in a newsgroup discussion. MSN provides access to Internet newsgroups using the bulletin board interface we saw earlier, so you don't have to learn anything new to join in on these Internet-wide discussions. I do, however, recommend that you read Chapter 7 to get an understanding of how Internet newsgroups work.

As you've explored MSN, you may have come across some Internet newsgroups in the various forums. Many forums contain links to related Internet newsgroups, often in a folder labeled **Related Internet Newsgroups** or **Internet Newsgroup Links**. So, for example, in **The Pets Forum**, you'll find links to a number of Internet newsgroups on different types of pets. This organization is useful, as there are thousands of newsgroups and finding the ones you are interested in can be somewhat overwhelming.

MSN also provides access to all of the Internet newsgroups in a single location, so that you don't have to hunt around for the groups you are looking for. To get to the comprehensive listing of newsgroups, select **Internet Center** from the **Categories** folder. As you can see in Figure D-13, this forum actually contains a wealth of information on the Internet. The **Core Rules of Netiquette** is an important document; you should read it to learn about what's appropriate on the Internet.

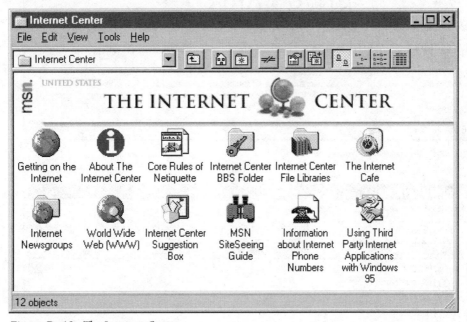

Figure D–13: The Internet Center

From the **Internet Center**, double-click on **Internet Newsgroups**. Now you should see the window shown in Figure D-14. Open the **USENET Newsgroups** folder to access the USENET portion of network news, with its seven well-managed newsgroup categories (described in Chapter 7). If you want access to the alternative newsgroups hierarchies, you'll need to open the **How to Access All Newsgroups** folder and follow the directions there.

When you open **USENET Newsgroups**, you'll see an icon for each of the seven newsgroups categories. Let's select **rec**, since we're looking for information about pets. Now you should see a listing like the one in Figure D-15. Each item in this listing represents a newsgroup or a collection of newsgroups. For example, if you select **rec.pets**, you'll see some additional folders that contain other newsgroups, as well as messages that have been posted to the group *rec.pets*.

Since we're looking for information about specific breeds of dogs, let's continue by selecting **rec.pets.dogs**. This brings us to yet another list, but now it looks like we're getting close. Double-click on **rec.pets.dogs.breeds** to open that newsgroup.

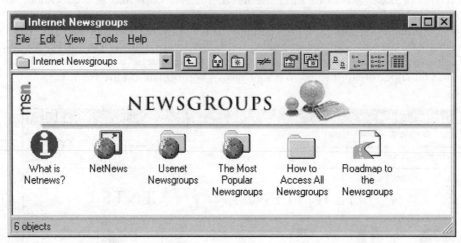

Figure D-14: Internet Newsgroups

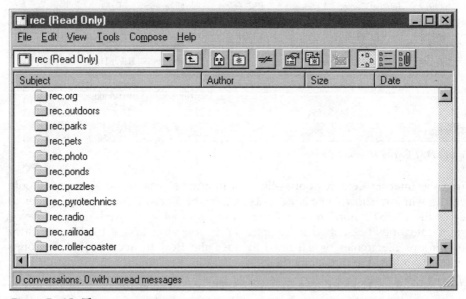

Figure D-15: The rec newsgroups

As you can see in Figure D-16, MSN uses its bulletin board interface for Internet newsgroups.

News postings are arranged by thread, just as with bulletin boards. You can read the messages, reply to the newsgroup or via e-mail, and post your own messages. Everything works just like it did with MSN bulletin boards, except that the audience is much larger. As you explore the Internet newsgroups, you'll find that there

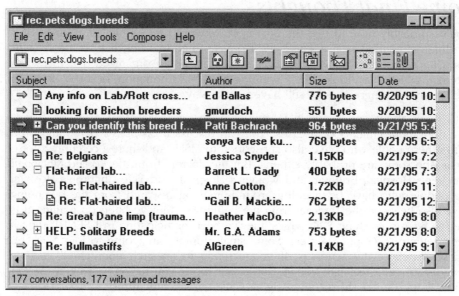

Figure D–16: The rec.pets.dogs.breeds newsgroup

are discussions on a wide variety of topics, from technical issues to social concerns. If you find a newsgroup that you particularly like, you may want to add it to your list of favorite places (**Add to Favorite Places** on the **File** menu), so that you can get to it easily.

The World Wide Web

Many of the MSN forums contain Internet shortcuts, which are links to documents on the World Wide Web. If you are using MSN as an Internet service provider, you can double-click on one of these shortcuts to start a Web browser and look at the document.* If you aren't using the "MSN and Internet" service type, you won't be able to look at Internet shortcuts. Internet shortcuts typically have a globe icon and the label often mentions the Web. For example, the **World Wide Web (WWW)** icon shown in Figure D-13 is an Internet shortcut to MSN's home page on the World Wide Web.

Now you may be wondering why you would want to use MSN to access documents on the World Wide Web. The only reason I can see is that a particular forum on MSN may have an interesting link to a Web document that you haven't seen before. Other than that, if you want to explore the Web, you'll be much better off using a Web browser, as described in Chapter 6.

---

* If Internet Explorer is the only Web browser on your system, MSN will start it. However, if you have more than one Web browser installed, MSN will start whichever one you installed last.

Some Final Thoughts

You've probably noticed that the Microsoft Network pretty much duplicates all of the Internet's services: in a sense, it's a private, mini-Internet that Microsoft owns. For a lot of people, this isn't bad. It's somewhat better organized that the whole Internet, which often looks like a seething mass of information, or an explosion in the Library of Congress. But I still have to ask: why?

Let's think about one example I brought up earlier: parenting. Say you have a question about childhood diseases. You can discuss it on MSN's parenting forum with other people who have also subscribed to MSN. And there's certainly a lot of them, and some are probably experts. But the doctors from the Ronald McDonald Children's Hospital, Brigham and Women's Hospital, and Yale Children's Hospital, the people who have been doing ground-breaking research from the beginning, have also been on the Internet from the beginning: they've been on mailing lists, they've been publishing Web pages, they've been participating in USENET, they've been setting up Gopher servers. Some small number are going to join MSN, but that's not where the action is. If you're trying to research your child's asthma, would you really feel like you've done your job if you haven't checked the On-Line Allergy Center (**http://www.sig.net/~allergy/welcome.html**)? If your teenager is suffering from depression, shouldn't you check the National Alliance for the Mentally Ill (**http://www.cais.com/vikings/nami/index.html**)? I could go on for hours. And that's precisely the point.

In Chapter 1, *What Is This Book About?*, I said that the Internet broke down barriers between different on-line services, between different operating systems. Anyone can take part. MSN (the proprietary part) just puts those barriers back up. If I told you "I only let Microsoft customers be my friends," you'd think I was pretty weird. But if you limit yourself to MSN's proprietary services, that's essentially what you're doing. If you want good information about pediatrics, you'd better not exclude all the doctors who use Macintosh computers—or, for that matter, all the doctors who don't upgrade to Windows 95. And you certainly don't want to eliminate the doctors who can't be bothered with the paperwork required to become an information provider on a proprietary network. On the Internet, everyone's allowed to participate—and that makes it a richer, more valuable environment than a proprietary on-line service can ever be.

The Microsoft Network is an interesting attempt to build a hybrid between the CompuServe-style on-line service and the Internet. Ultimately, though, what's interesting about it is the Internet. And you don't have to buy an Internet connection from Microsoft; there are over 1300 service providers competing for your business. MSN may be the best solution for you, but I'd be irresponsible not to tell you to do your homework first.

INTERNET EXPLORER 2.0 AND NETSCAPE NAVIGATOR 2.0

Internet Explorer 2.0
Netscape Navigator 2.0
Netscape Navigator Gold

This appendix describes the newest Web browsing tools from Microsoft and Netscape. As this book went to press, both companies announced new versions of their browsers. Internet Explorer 2.0 is currently available as a beta release, so the description of it here is based on beta functionality. Netscape Navigator 2.0 and Netscape Navigator Gold 2.0 are not yet available in beta form, so the discussion is solely based on Netscape's press release. By the time you read this, however, Netscape should have beta versions available.

Although the information here is mostly an overview of features, it should give you an idea of what to expect from the browsers. If you like playing with the latest "toys," you should probably check out the new versions of Internet Explorer and Netscape Navigator.

Internet Explorer 2.0

In September 1995, Microsoft announced version 2.0 of their Internet Explorer browser. This Web browser provides a number of new features, including improved security, better performance, and support for new HTML extensions. This section describes some of the new functionality in Internet Explorer 2.0. The description is based on a beta release; the functionality in the final release may differ from what is described here.

At this time, a beta release of Internet Explorer 2.0 is available at the following URL:

```
http://www.microsoft.com/windows/ie/beta.htm
```

If you want to check out this release, read the documents at this site and download the beta software.

After you've retrieved the software, run the executable to install the new version of Internet Explorer. Now double-click on **The Internet** icon on your desktop to try it out. You should see a window like the one in Figure E-1.

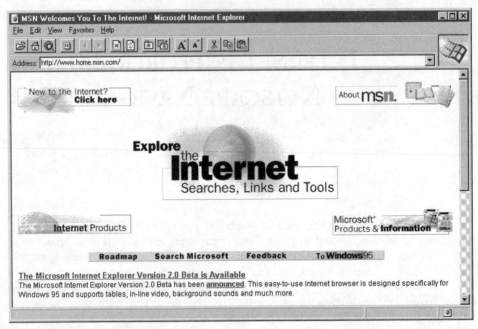

Figure E-1: Internet Explorer 2.0

The interface looks almost identical to the one for Internet Explorer 1.0; the only difference is that there are two new buttons on the toolbar. The **Open Search Page** button automatically opens Microsoft's search page, which is described in Chapter 6, *The World Wide Web*. You can configure Internet Explorer to use a different search page by selecting **Options** from the **View** menu and then using the **Start and Search Pages** tab.

The **Newsgroups** button on the toolbar allows you to view a list of Internet newsgroups, so that you can use Internet Explorer to read news. (See Chapter 7, *Network News*, for a complete explanation of news.) I describe this functionality in more detail shortly.

Mailing Shortcuts

Internet Explorer 1.0 lets you create shortcuts to Web documents using a number of techniques. When you add a Web document to your list of favorite places, you are really creating a shortcut to the document. You can also use drag-and-drop to create a shortcut on your desktop, as described in Chapter 6. Internet Explorer 2.0 expands on what you can do with shortcuts, allowing you to send a shortcut to a friend or colleague via e-mail.

If you are viewing a Web page that you want to send to a friend, select **Send Shortcut** from the **File** menu. Internet Explorer asks you to select an Exchange profile for sending the message, and then uses Exchange to open a New Message window. The shortcut is automatically included in the message; all you need to do is address the message and type any additional text. When you send the message, the shortcut is sent with the message as a MIME attachment. If the recipient is also using Exchange, he can click on the attachment to start Internet Explorer and view the document.

Reading News

In Chapter 6, I mentioned that a Web browser can be used as a rudimentary newsreader. Unfortunately, with Internet Explorer 1.0, this is not true. If you follow a link to a newsgroup, or enter a news URL, with version 1.0, you'll get an error saying that there was a problem accessing news.[*] Internet Explorer 2.0 fixes this problem by providing support for reading Internet newsgroups.

To use Internet Explorer 2.0 as a newsreader, you need to configure the browser to access your news server.[†] Your Internet service provider should provide you with the name of your news server; you need to supply this information to Internet Explorer for the news-reading functionality to work. Select **Options** from the **View** menu. On the **News** tab, select the **Use Internet Explorer to read Internet newsgroups** option and enter the name of the news server in the **NNTP server address** field.

Now you are ready to read news with Internet Explorer. To get a list of all the newsgroups available from your news server, click the **Newsgroups** button on the toolbar. You should see a long list of newsgroups. Each newsgroup name is a link to the actual postings for that group; click on the link to view the postings. You can also go directly to a newsgroup by selecting **Open** from the **File** menu and entering a news URL, which takes the following form:

    news:newsgroup-name

Figure E-2 shows some postings for the *rec.skiing.backcountry* newsgroup. As you can see, Internet Explorer shows an article number, the subject, and the author for each posting. These items are all links to the actual posting, so you can click on any of them to view the article.

When you read a news posting, you'll see that Internet Explorer provides links to the next posting and the previous posting, as well as a way to get back to the list of articles. Beyond these simple navigational links, however, many basic newsreader features are missing. For example, Internet Explorer doesn't support threading. And you can only read news with Internet Explorer; you can't post messages.

---

[*] This isn't exactly true. If you are using MSN as your Internet service provider, Internet Explorer will open the MSN **Newsgroups** forum, so you can use MSN to read news. But if you are using any other service provider, you cannot read news using Internet Explorer 1.0.

[†] If you don't tell Internet Explorer about your news server, the browser will continue to try to use MSN to provide news-reading functionality.

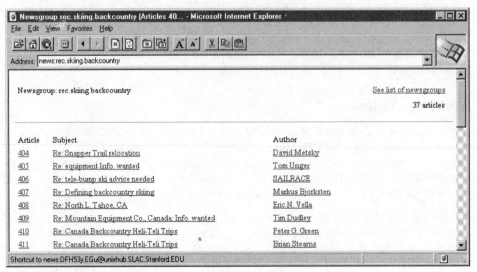

Figure E–2: Reading news with Internet Explorer

If you want to get the most out of news, you're better off using a program that is designed to read news.

Security

Internet Explorer 2.0 provides support for a number of different types of Web security. The Secure Sockets Layer (SSL) protocol ensures data security as data is transferred between an application protocol like HTTP or FTP and the underlying TCP/IP layer. Internet Explorer 2.0 supports this popular encryption standard, so it can protect transactions when dealing with a secure server.

The browser also has hooks for two new security mechanisms: Secure Transaction Technology (STT), which is being developed by Microsoft and Visa International for financial transactions, and Private Communication Technology (PCT), a new secure channel protocol. When these security protocols are implemented and available on Web servers, Internet Explorer will support them.

You can also configure Internet Explorer to warn you about transactions that are not secure. Select **Options** from the **View** menu and open the **Security** tab. This tab lets you control how "paranoid" Internet Explorer is when you send data across the Web.

HTML Extensions

Internet Explorer 2.0 supports a number of popular HTML 3.0 enhancements, including tables, centered and aligned text and graphics, background images, and text color and type face. These extensions give Web authors more control over the formatting of their Web documents and, as a result, their use is becoming widespread.

Internet Explorer also implements a few new HTML extensions. For example, the browser supports a new tag for marking text that is to be used as a scrolling marquee in a document. Internet Explorer also provides a way for a Web page to play background sounds and show inline video. For a demonstration of all these features, see the following demo document:

```
http://www.microsoft.com/windows/ie/iedemo.htm
```

VRML

Internet Explorer 2.0 is designed to be "VRML ready." Microsoft is working on a VRML browser that works with Internet Explorer. When this browser is available, Internet Explorer will use it to display VRML worlds inline in Web documents, so you can seamlessly browse VRML content.

Netscape Navigator 2.0

Netscape's announcement of Navigator 2.0 heralds it as "a major new release of the world's most popular Internet navigator."[*] What does this mean to you, aside from an improved bookmark? A fair amount, if Netscape fulfills its promise: optimized performance, an improved newsreader and mailer, enhanced security, and new design features.

The browser's performance will be enhanced and optimized to run smoothly over low-speed (14.4 kbps) modems. New support for the multiple streaming of audio and video should allow you to experience the effect of a page before it's been entirely downloaded. Similarly, the progressive JPEG file format loads images three times more quickly than images in the GIF format—and, according to Netscape, you should only need to load ten percent of an image before it becomes recognizable.

Additionally, Netscape promises improved and "integrated" e-mail and newsreading. You should be able to both send and read mail from within the browser. Since you could previously only send mail from Navigator, this is a significant addition. New features include a personal address book, the ability to include links and MIME attachments in multimedia messages, and enhanced mail security. The enhanced newsreader will have the same look and feel as the rest of the browser,

---

[*] http://home.netscape.com/comprod/products/navigator/version_2.0/index.html is the URL of the press release.

and will allow you to sort and list messages from subscribed newsgroups. MIME-compliant news reading and posting should allow for articles that include clickable URLs.

Netscape will also be adding additional security to the browser, through new protocols and new vendors. The Secure Courier open protocol provides for secure financial transactions, while the Secure MIME open protocol provides encryption and digital signatures for e-mail and newsgroups. Additionally, a company called VeriSign will be available to provide users with an on-line Digital ID; you'll be able to choose either the free, non-commercial version, or the commercially supported version for a very small fee. This ID should let you positively identify other Net users, and perhaps be authorized to access certain restricted sites.

Netscape also promises to support new programming features. Designers will be able to split a single screen into separate *frames*, each with its own URL. *Inline plug-ins* will let users view complicated multimedia objects without spawning an external viewer. Currently, if you wanted to view the New York TimesFax for the first time see the *Resource Catalog* under News & Magazines), you would first download the Adobe Acrobat reader, configure it for your system, go back to your browser and download that day's TimesFax, then open the imesFax file from within Acrobat to read it. Plug-ins let you read pages like TimesFax directly from Navigator. Additional programming features include support for the Java language (discussed very briefly in Chapter 6), and the Netscape Scripting Language, intended to allow less experienced designers to create more sophisticated pages.

Netscape Navigator Gold

Netscape Navigator Gold 2.0 has all the new features found in Netscape Navigator 2.0, plus a few more. If you're a relative novice to the Web who wants to start designing Web pages yourself, those features might be very important to you. Frankly, it's surprising that the Web has grown as quickly as it has, given the scarcity of editing and design tools. Navigator Gold promises to fulfill a big gap.

Netscape intends to make Web publishing easier by allowing real-time, WYSIWYG[*] editing. You'll be able to avoid many of the complexities of HTML (the usual method for composing Web documents) through an easy cut-and-paste, drag-and-drop process. Additionally, you'll be able to convert documents from formats including Microsoft Word, Novell WordPerfect, and FrameMaker; you'll also be able to convert images from formats including BMP, WMF, TIFF, PICT, and PCX. Netscape also plans to include features for more experienced designers, including a raw document and script editor. Finally, you'll be able to preview your documents from within Netscape Navigator Gold itself.

---

[*] WYSIWYG is an acronym, widely used in the computing world, that stands for "what you see is what you get."

GLOSSARY

application

(a) Software that performs a particular useful function for you. ("Do you have an electronic mail application installed on your computer?")

(b) The useful function itself (e.g., transferring files is a useful application of the Internet).

Archie

A system for locating files that are publicly available by anonymous FTP. Archie is described in Chapter 10, *Finding Files*.

ARPAnet

An experimental network established in the 70's where the theories and software on which the Internet is based were tested. No longer in existence.

bandwidth

The amount of data that can be transferred over a network connection. (Technically, it is the difference in Hertz between the highest and lowest frequencies of a transmission.) If you think of the network as a sewage pipe, the bandwidth can be thought of as the area of the cross-section: the wider the pipe, the faster "information" will flow. Many use the phrase *wasting bandwidth* to refer to "information" that takes up more flow than it deserves. (That was a better metaphor than the highway, wasn't it?)

baud

When transmitting data, the number of times the medium's "state" changes per second. For example: a 2400-baud modem changes the signal it sends on the phone line 2400 times per second. Since each change in state can correspond to multiple bits of data, the actual bit rate of data transfer may exceed the baud rate. Also, see "bits per second." Today, common modem speeds are 14,000, 19,600, and 28,000 bits per second.

BIND

The UNIX implementation of DNS (q.v.). It stands for "Berkeley Internet Name Domain."

bits per second (bps)

The speed at which bits are transmitted over a communications medium.

BTW

Common abbreviation in mail and news, meaning "by the way."

buffers

Areas of memory that provide temporary storage for input devices.

bulletin board service (BBS)

In on-line terms, an area where messages can be posted, read, and responded to in a non-real-time discussion. USENET newsgroups are basically bulletin boards. Traditionally, "BBS" has referred to a standalone computer or site where users can dial in and exchange messages and files, or access some other types of services (such as chat or mail). These "private" BBSs are self-contained services and are not part of the Internet, although many have gateway connections to the Net.

cache

Information saved in memory for later use. For example, Web browsers like Internet Explorer save recently viewed pages in a cache so the exact pages are not downloaded again, thereby saving Internet resources and time.

chat

A real-time conversation (in text, usually) among multiple users on-line. MSN and America Online have *chat rooms*, with discussions centered on a particular topic. Internet Relay Chat (IRC) is the analogous facility on the Internet.

CHAP

Challenge-Handshake Authentication Protocol. An authentication method that enables you to connect to your Internet service provider. It is a reasonably secure way to verify login and password access for dial-up Internet service.

CIX

Commercial Internet Exchange; an agreement among network providers that allows them to do accounting for commercial traffic. Although it has been discussed a lot in the press, it's primarily a concern for network providers.

client

A software application (q.v.) that works on your behalf to extract a service from a server somewhere on the network. Think of your telephone as a client and the telephone company as a server to get the idea.

COM port

A serial port on a PC. Serial ports have only one transmit line and one receive line. Data is thus sent over the line as a series of bits—hence the name "serial line."

datagram

A packet (q.v.) of information that is sent to the receiving computer without any prior warning. Conceptually, a "datagram" is somewhat like a telegram: it's a self-contained message that can arrive at any time, without notice. Datagrams are usually used in applications where the amount of information transfer is occasional and small.

DDN

Defense Data Network; a portion of the Internet which connects to U.S. military bases and contractors; used for non-secure communications. MILNET is one of the DDN networks. The DDN used to run "the NIC," which coordinated the Internet as a whole. However, the InterNIC (q.v.) has taken over that function; now the DDN NIC is responsible only for the DDN.

dial-up

(a) A connection to a computer made by calling the computer up on the telephone. Often, dial-up only refers to the kind of connection you make when using a terminal emulator and a regular modem. For the technoids: switched character-oriented asynchronous communication.

(b) A port (q.v.) that accepts dial-up connections. ("How many dial-up ports on your computer?")

DNS

The Domain Name System; a distributed database system for translating computer names (like **ruby.ora.com**) into numeric Internet addresses (like **194.56.78.2**), and vice-versa. DNS allows you to use the Internet without remembering long lists of numbers.

DoD

The (U.S.) Department of Defense, whose Advanced Research Projects Agency got the Internet started by funding the ARPAnet.

Domain name

The name given to a network or site that is connected to the Internet—e.g., **ora.com** is the domain name for O'Reilly & Associates.

EFF

Electronic Frontier Foundation. An organization founded to address the social and legal issues emerging from the increasing use of computers and their impact on society.

encryption

Encoding information so that only an intended recipient can read it. Encryption is used on the Internet for many things from basic network data packet transfers to the secure exchange of private e-mail. There are several different methods of encryption.

Ethernet

A kind of "local area network." It's a confusing concept, since there are several different kinds of wiring, which support communication speeds ranging from 2 to 10 million bits per second. What makes an Ethernet an Ethernet is the way the computers on the network decide whose turn it is to talk. Computers using TCP/IP are frequently connected to the Internet over an Ethernet.

FAQ

Either a frequently asked question, or a list of frequently asked questions and their answers. Many USENET newsgroups, and some non-USENET mailing lists, maintain FAQ lists (FAQs) so that participants don't spend lots of time answering the same set of questions.

flame

A virulent and (often) largely personal attack against the author of a USENET posting. "Flames" are unfortunately common. People who frequently write flames are known as "flamers."

followup

A response to a USENET posting (q.v.).

Frame Relay

A data communication technology that is sometimes used to provide higher speed (above 56Kb and less than 1.5Mb) for Internet connections. Its usual application is in connecting work groups rather than individuals.

Free-Net

An organization to provide free Internet access to people in a certain area, usually through public libraries.

FTP

(a) The File Transfer Protocol; a protocol that defines how to transfer files from one computer to another.

(b) An application program which moves files using the File Transfer Protocol. FTP is described in detail in Chapter 9, *Moving Files: FTP*.

FYI

(a) A common abbreviation in mail and news, meaning "for your information."

(b) A series of informative papers about the Internet; they're similar to RFCs (q.v.), but don't define new standards.

gateway

A computer system that transfers data between normally incompatible applications or networks. It reformats the data so that it is acceptable for the new network (or application) before passing it on. A gateway might connect two dissimilar networks, like DECnet and the Internet; or it might allow two incompatible applications to communicate over the same network (like mail systems with different message formats). The term is often used interchangeably with router (q.v.), but this usage is incorrect.

gif The Graphic Interchange Format standard; common file format used to exchange graphics over the Internet.

Gopher

A menu-based system for exploring Internet resources. Gopher is described in detail in Chapter 12, *Tunneling Through the Internet: Gopher*.

hostname

The name given to an individual computer attached to a network or the Internet (a host machine).

HTML

Hypertext markup language; the language in which World Wide Web documents are written.

hypermedia

A combination of hypertext (q.v.) and multimedia (q.v.).

hypertext

Documents that contain links to other documents; selecting a link automatically displays the second document.

IAB

The Internet Architecture Board; the "ruling council" that makes decisions about standards and other important issues.

IETF

The Internet Engineering Task Force; a volunteer group that investigates and solves technical problems and makes recommendations to the IAB (q.v.).

IMHO

Common abbreviation in mail and news, meaning "in my humble opinion."

Internet

(a) Generally (not capitalized), any collection of distinct networks working together as one.

(b) Specifically (capitalized), the worldwide "network of networks" that are connected to each other, using the IP protocol and other similar protocols. The Internet provides file transfer, remote login, electronic mail, news, and other services.

InterNIC

The combined name for the providers of registration, information, and database services to the Internet. The InterNIC is discussed in the "Introduction" to the *Resource Catalog*. It provides many network resources of its own.

IP The Internet Protocol; the most important of the protocols on which the Internet is based. It allows a packet to traverse multiple networks on the way to its final destination.

IP address

A 32-bit number defined by the Internet Protocol that uniquely identifies a resource on the Internet. It is usually shown in dotted-decimal or dotted-quad notation, which is four numbers separated by dots.

IRC

Internet Relay Chat. A client/server facility that allows large group conversations over the Internet.

ISDN

Integrated Services Digital Network; a digital telephone service. Essentially, with ISDN service, the phone lines to your house carry digital signals, rather than analog signals. If you have the appropriate hardware and software, if your local central office provides ISDN service, and if your service provider supports it, ISDN allows high-speed home access to the Internet (56Kb).

ISO

The International Organization for Standardization; an organization that has defined a different set of network protocols, called the ISO/OSI protocols. In theory, the ISO/OSI protocols will eventually replace the Internet Protocol. When and if this will actually happen is a hotly debated topic.

ISOC

The Internet Society; an organization whose members support a worldwide information network. It is also the governing body to which the IAB (q.v.) reports.

jpeg

The Joint Photographic Experts Group standard for encoding and compressing graphic images. A popular graphic file format on the Internet.

Jughead

A Gopher (q.v.) service similar to Veronica (q.v.), which searches Gopher menus on a particular set of Gopher servers.

leased line

A permanently connected private telephone line between two locations. Leased lines are typically used to connect a moderate-sized local network to an Internet service provider.

listserv

A popular software program used to create and manage Internet mailing lists. Mailing lists that run on Listserv are usually referred to as "Listservs."

mail reflector

A special mail address; electronic mail sent to this address is automatically forwarded to a set of other addresses. Typically, used to implement a mail discussion group.

Majordomo

A widely-used software program used to create and manage Internet mailing lists.

MILNET

One of the DDN networks that make up the Internet; devoted to non-classified military (U.S.) communications. It was built using the same technology as the ARPAnet, and remained in production when the ARPAnet was decommissioned.

MIME

Multimedia Internet Mail Extensions. A protocol that defines a number of content types and subtypes, which allow programs like Web browsers, newsreaders, and e-mail clients to recognize different kinds of files and deal with them appropriately. A MIME type specifies what media a file is, such as image, audio, or video, and a subtype identifies the precise file format.

mirror site

A computer that contains an exact replica of the directory structure of another computer to provide alternative access to information at a heavily accessed site. Mirror sites also provide geographically closer site access to save network resources. They are usually updated daily.

modem

A piece of equipment that connects a computer to a data transmission line (typically a telephone line of some sort). Most people use modems that transfer data at speeds ranging from 1200 bits per second (bps) to 28.8 Kbps. There are also modems providing higher speeds and supporting other media. These are used for special purposes—for example, to connect a large local network to its network provider over a leased line.

Mosaic

One particular World Wide Web browser that supports hypermedia.

mpeg

The Moving Pictures Experts Group standard for encoding and compressing moving video images.

MUD

Multi-User Dungeon; a group of role-playing games modeled on the original "Dungeons and Dragons" games. MUDs have also been used in other contexts; they have been used as conferencing tools and educational aids.

multimedia

Documents that include different kinds of data; for example, plain text and audio, or text in several different languages, or plain text and a spreadsheet.

netiquette

Network etiquette. A loose collection of undocumented rules that is supposed to govern acceptable social behavior on the Internet. Most of netiquette arises from simple politeness to other users, for example, not posting private e-mail without the sender's permission, or reading a FAQ (frequently asked questions) file before joining a USENET discussion on a topic that is new to you.

Netscape extensions

A set of HTML tags and HTTP functions that were developed for use with the popular Netscape Navigator Web browser. The extensions exist outside of current HTML and HTTP standards. Many other browsers are able to read them now due to their popular use in Web page design.

NIC

(a) Network Information Center; any organization that's responsible for supplying information about any network.

(b) The DDN's NIC, which plays an important role in overall Internet coordination.

NFS

The Network File System; a set of protocols that allows you to use files on other network machines *as if* they were local. So, rather than using FTP to transfer a file to your local computer, you can read it, write it, or edit it on the remote computer—using the same commands that you'd use locally. NFS was originally developed by Sun Microsystems, Inc., and is currently in widespread use.

NNTP

Network News Transfer Protocol; the protocol used to transfer USENET news articles between computers on the Internet.

NOC

Network Operations Center; a group which is responsible for the day-to-day care and feeding of a network. Each service provider usually has a separate NOC, so you need to know which one to call when you have problems.

NREN

The National Research and Education Network; a U.S. effort to combine networks operated by different federal agencies into a single high-speed network. While this transition will be of significant technical and historical importance, it should have no effect on the typical Internet user.

NSFNET

The National Science Foundation Network; the NSFNET is *not* the Internet. It's just one of the networks that make up the Internet.

NTP

Network Time Protocol; a protocol used to synchronize time between computers on the Internet.

octet

Internet standards-monger's lingo for a set of eight bits, i.e., a *byte*.

OSI

Open Systems Interconnect; another set of network protocols. See "ISO."

packet

A bundle of data. On the Internet, data is broken up into small chunks, called *packets*; each packet traverses the network independently. Packet sizes can vary from roughly 40 to 32,000 bytes, depending on network hardware and media, but packets are normally less than 1500 bytes long.

PGP

Pretty Good Privacy. A freely available program written by Phillip Zimmermann that provides very strong encryption to ensure the privacy and security of communications across computer networks for any user.

POP

The Post Office Protocol; a mail protocol that allows a remote mail client to read mail from a server.

port

(a) A number that identifies a particular Internet application. When your computer sends a packet to another computer, that packet contains information about what protocol it's using (e.g., TCP or UDP) and what application it's trying to communicate with. The port number identifies the application. (b) One of a computer's physical input/output channels (i.e., a plug on the back).

Unfortunately, these two meanings are completely unrelated. The first is more common when you're talking about the Internet (as in "**telnet** to port 1000"); the second is more common when you're talking about hardware ("connect your modem to the serial port on the back of your computer").

posting

An individual article sent to a USENET (q.v.) newsgroup; or the act of sending an article to a USENET newsgroup.

PPP

Point-to-Point Protocol; a protocol that allows a computer to use the TCP/IP (Internet) protocols (and become a full-fledged Internet member) with a standard telephone line and a high-speed modem.

protocol

A protocol is just a definition of how computers will act when talking to each other. Protocol definitions range from how bits are placed on a wire to the format of an electronic mail message. Standard protocols allow computers from different manufacturers to communicate; the computers can use completely different software, providing that the programs running on both ends agree on what the data means.

relevance feedback

The process of using a document you retrieved in a search to further refine your search. WAIS supports relevance feedback, though (currently) only through WAIS clients (and not all WAIS clients). Gateways between the World Wide Web and WAIS servers may support relevance feedback in the future.

RFC

Request for Comments; a set of papers in which the Internet's standards, proposed standards, and generally agreed-upon ideas are documented and published.

router

A system that transfers data between two networks that use the same protocols. The networks may differ in physical characteristics (e.g., a router may transfer data between an Ethernet and a leased telephone line).

RTFM

Common abbreviation in mail and news, meaning "read the . . . manual."

server

(a) Software that allows a computer to offer a service to another computer. Other computers contact the server program by means of matching client (q.v.) software.

(b) The computer on which the server software runs.

service provider

An organization that provides connections to a part of the Internet. If you want to connect your company's network, or even your personal computer, to the Internet, you have to talk to a service provider.

shell

On a UNIX system, software that accepts and processes command lines from your terminal. UNIX has multiple shells available (e.g., C shell, Bourne shell, Korn shell), each with slightly different command formats and facilities.

shortcut

A feature of Windows 95 that allows you to place an icon on the desktop or in a document and simply click on the icon to access a particular application.

signature

A file, typically about five lines long, that people often insert at the end of e-mail messages or USENET news articles. A signature contains, minimally, a name and an e-mail address. Signatures usually contain postal addresses, and frequently silly quotes, pictures, or other things. Some are very elaborate, though signatures of more than five or six lines are in questionable taste.

SLIP

Serial Line IP; a protocol that allows a computer to use the Internet protocols (and become a full-fledged Internet member) with a standard telephone line and a high-speed modem. SLIP is being superseded by PPP (q.v.), but is still in common use.

smiley

Smiling faces used in mail and news to indicate humor and irony. The most common smiley is :-). You'll also see :-(, meaning disappointment, and lots of other variations. Since the variations are so, er, "variant," it's not worth going into detail. You'll pick up their connotations with time.

SMTP

The Simple Mail Transfer Protocol; a protocol that is used to send mail over a TCP/IP network.

SRI

A California-based research institute that runs the Network Information Systems Center (NISC). The SRI has played an important role in coordinating the Internet.

subnet mask

An encoding for IP addresses (q.v.) that determines which parts of an IP address identify the network and which part identifies the host machine. It is only used internally on a network; your network administrator will supply you with the appropriate subnet mask if you need it.

switched access

A network connection that can be created and destroyed as needed. Dial-up connections are the simplest form of switched connections. SLIP and PPP also are commonly run over switched connections.

TCP

The Transmission Control Protocol. One of the protocols on which the Internet is based. For the technoids, TCP is a connection-oriented reliable protocol.

TCP/IP stack

The set of programs that connects your desktop to a TCP/IP network. It is composed of the different layers—TCP/IP software, sockets software, and hardware driver software—that data between your Internet application programs and the network must pass through.

Telnet

(a) A "terminal emulation" protocol that allows you to log in to other computer systems on the Internet.

(b) An application program that allows you to log in to another computer system using the Telnet protocol, described in detail in Chapter 8, *Remote Login*.

timeout

A timeout is what happens when two computers are "talking" and one computer—for any reason—fails to respond. The other computer will keep on trying for a certain amount of time, but will eventually "give up."

tn3270

A special version of the **telnet** program that interacts properly with IBM mainframes.

token ring

A technology for creating a local area network that may then be connected to the Internet. Token ring networks often use the TCP/IP protocols. See also "Ethernet."

UDP

The User Datagram Protocol. Another of the protocols on which the Internet is based. For the technoids, UDP is a connectionless unreliable protocol. If you're not a technoid, don't let the word "unreliable" worry you.

UNIX

A popular operating system that was very important in the development of the Internet. Contrary to rumor, though, you do NOT have to use UNIX to use the Internet. There are various flavors of UNIX. Two common ones are BSD and System V.

USENET

The USENET is an informal, rather anarchic, group of systems that exchange "news." News is essentially similar to "bulletin boards" on other networks. USENET actually predates the Internet, but these days, the Internet is used to transfer much of the USENET's traffic. USENET is described in detail in Chapter 7, *Network News*.

UUCP

UNIX-to-UNIX copy; a facility for copying files between UNIX systems, on which mail and USENET news services were built. While UUCP is still useful, the Internet provides a better way to do the same job.

Veronica

A service, very similar to Archie, that's built into Gopher. Just as Archie allows you to search all FTP sites for files, Veronica allows you to search all Gopher sites for menu items (files, directories, and other resources). Veronica is described in Chapter 12.

W3C

World Wide Web Consortium. A consortium of many companies and organizations that "exists to develop common standards for the evolution of the World Wide Web." It is run by a joint effort between the Laboratory for Computer Science at the Massachusetts Institute of Technology and CERN, the European Particle Physics Laboratory, where the WWW was first developed.

WAIS

Wide Area Information Service; a very powerful system for looking up information in databases (or libraries) across the Internet. WAIS is described in detail in Chapter 13, *Searching Indexed Databases: WAIS*.

White Pages

Lists of Internet users that are accessible through the Internet. There are several different kinds of white-pages servers and services, described in Chapter 11, *Finding Someone*.

Winsock

Common term for "Windows Sockets," which is the set of specifications that programmers must use to write TCP/IP software for Windows.

World Wide Web (WWW)

A hypertext-based system for finding and accessing Internet resources. WWW is described in Chapter 6, *The World Wide Web*.

INDEX

About the Authors

Raised in the Chicago area, **Ed Krol** went to the University of Illinois, got a degree in Computer Science, and never left.

In 1985, Krol became part of a networking group at the University of Illinois, where he became the network manager at the time the National Center for Supercomputer Applications was formed. It was there that he managed the installation of the original NSFnet. During the same period, he also wrote the "Hitchhiker's Guide to the Internet," because he had so much trouble getting information and was sick of telling the same story to everyone.

In 1989, Krol opted to leave the fast lane and returned to pastoral life on campus, where he remains to this day, Assistant Director for Network Information Services, Computing and Communications Service Office, University of Illinois, Urbana. He also writes a monthly column for *Network World*.

He has a wife and daughter (who is in the hacker's dictionary as the toddler responsible for "Mollyguards"). In his spare time Krol is a pilot and plays hockey.

Paula Ferguson is a writer for O'Reilly & Associates, as well as the editor of *The X Resource: A Practical Journal of the X Window System*. She has worked on a number of Internet projects, including *The Mosaic Handbook*. She has also updated various volumes in the X series, including *Volume 6A, Motif Reference Manual*. Before joining O'Reilly, Paula developed and taught courses on the Motif toolkit for the Open Software Foundation and worked on a variety of other interface design and software development projects.

Paula graduated from M.I.T. in 1990 with a B.S. in computer science and engineering. She currently lives in Boulder, Colorado with her black lab puppy, Obo, and her two cats. When she's not telecommuting from her home office, she's outside rock climbing, cycling, skiing, or mountaineering.

Colophon

Our look is the result of reader comments, our own experimentation, and feedback from distribution channels.

Distinctive covers complement our distinctive approach to technical topics, breathing personality and life into potentially dry subjects.

The image featured on the cover of *The Whole Internet for Windows 95: User's Guide & Catalog* is an alchemist. Alchemy, the precursor of modern chemistry, first appeared around 100 AD in Alexandria, Egypt—a product of the fusion of Greek and Oriental culture. The goal of this philosophic science was to achieve the transmutation of base metals into gold, regarded as the most perfect of metals.

Alchemy was based on three key precepts. The first was Aristotle's teachings that the basis for all material objects could be found in the four elements: fire, water, air, and earth. By altering the proportions in which the qualities were combined, elements could be changed into one another. The second precept arose from the philosophic thought of the time: metals, like all other substances, could be converted into one another. The third precept was taken from astrology: metals, like plants and animals, could be born, nourished, and caused to grow through imperfect stages into a final, perfect form.

Early alchemists were generally from artisan classes. As alchemy gained adherents, philosophers became more involved, and the cryptic language used by the early artisan-alchemists to protect trade secrets became virtually its own language, with symbols and fanciful terms. Over the centuries, the language of alchemy became ever more complex, reaching its height in Medieval Europe in the fourteenth and fifteenth centuries. Alchemy was superseded by the advent of modern chemistry at the end of the eighteenth century.

Edie Freedman designed this cover using an image adapted from a 19th-century engraving from the Dover Pictorial Archive. The cover layout was produced with Quark XPress 3.1 using the ITC Garamond font.

The inside formats were implemented in groff by Lenny Muellner. The text and heading fonts are ITC Garamond Light and Garamond Book Italic. The interior design was modified by Nancy Priest. The illustrations that appear in the book are a combination of figures created by Chris Reilley, and wood engravings from the Dover Pictorial Archive and the Ron Yablon Graphic Archives, and were created in Adobe PhotoShop and Macromedia Freehand.

INTERNET

Books from O'Reilly & Associates, Inc.

FALL/WINTER 1995-96

The Whole Internet User's Guide & Catalog

By Ed Krol
2nd Edition April 1994
574 pages, ISBN 1-56592-063-5

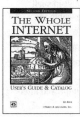

Still the best book on the Internet! This is the second edition of our comprehensive—and bestselling—introduction to the Internet, the international network that includes virtually every major computer site in the world. In addition to email, file transfer, remote login, and network news, this book pays special attention to some new tools for helping you find information. Useful to beginners and veterans alike, this book will help you explore what's possible on the Net. Also includes a pull-out quick-reference card.

"An ongoing classic."
—*Rochester Business Journal*

"The book against which all subsequent Internet guides are measured, Krol's work has emerged as an indispensable reference to beginners and seasoned travelers alike as they venture out on the data highway."
—*Microtimes*

"*The Whole Internet User's Guide & Catalog* will probably become the Internet user's bible because it provides comprehensive, easy instructions for those who want to get the most from this valuable electronic tool."
—David J. Buerger, Editor, *Communications Week*

The Whole Internet for Windows 95

By Ed Krol & Paula Ferguson
1st Edition October 1995
650 pages (est.), ISBN 1-56592-155-0

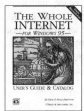

The best book on the Internet...now updated for Windows 95! *The Whole Internet for Windows 95* is the most comprehensive introduction to the Internet available today. For Windows users who in the past have struggled to take full advantage of the Internet's powerful utilities, Windows 95's built-in Internet support is a cause for celebration. And when you get online with Windows 95, this new edition of *The Whole Internet* will guide you every step of the way.

This book shows you how to use Microsoft Internet Explorer (the World Wide Web multimedia browser) and Microsoft Exchange (an email program). It also covers Netscape Navigator, the most popular Web browser on the market, and shows you how to use Usenet readers, file transfer tools, and database searching software.

But it does much more. You'll also want to take advantage of alternative popular free software programs that are downloadable from the Net. This book shows you where to find them and how to use them to save you time and money.

WebSite™ 1.1

By O'Reilly & Associates, Inc.
Documentation by Susan Peck
2nd Edition December 1995 (est.)
ISBN 1-56592-173-9
Includes three diskettes, 360-page book, and WebSite T-shirt

 WebSite 1.1 now makes it easier than
ever to start publishing on the Internet.
WebSite is a 32-bit multi-threaded World
Wide Web server that combines the power
and flexibility of a UNIX server with the
ease of use of a Windows application.
Its intuitive graphical interface and easy
install make it a natural for both Windows
NT and Windows 95 users.

WebSite provides a tree-like display of all the documents
and links on your server, with a simple solution for finding
and fixing broken links. Using CGI, you can run a desktop
application like Excel or Visual Basic from within a Web
document on WebSite. Its access authentication lets you
control which users have access to different parts of your
Web server. WebSite is a product of O'Reilly & Associates, Inc.
It is created in cooperation with Bob Denny and Enterprise
Integration Technologies, Inc. (EIT).

New features of WebSite 1.1 include: HTML editor, multiple
indexes, WebFind wizard, CGI with Visual Basic 4 framework
and server push support, graphical interface for creating virtual
servers, Windows 95 style install, logging reports for individual
documents, HTML-2 and -3 support, external image map support, self-registration of users, and EMosaic 2.1 Web browser.

Getting Connected:
Establishing a Presence on the Internet

By Kevin Dowd
1st Edition December 1995 (est.)
450 pages (est.), ISBN 1-56592-154-2

 A complete guide for businesses,
schools, and other organizations who
want to connect their computers to the
Internet. This book covers everything
you need to know to make informed
decisions, from helping you figure
out which services you really need to
providing down-to-earth explanations
of telecommunication options, such
as frame relay, ISDN, and leased lines. Once you're online,
it shows you how to set up basic Internet services, such as a
World Wide Web server. Tackles issues for the PC, Macintosh,
and UNIX platforms.

Internet In A Box,™ Version 2.0

Published by SPRY, Inc. (Product good only in U.S. and Canada)
2nd Edition June 1995
UPC 799364 012001
Two diskettes & a 528-page version of ***The Whole***
Internet Users Guide & Catalog *as documentation*

 Now there are more ways to connect
to the Internet—and you get to choose
the most economical plan based on
your dialing habits.

What will Internet In A Box *do for me?*

Internet In A Box is for PC users who want to connect to the
Internet. Quite simply, it solves Internet access problems for
individuals and small businesses without dedicated lines
and/or UNIX machines. Internet In A Box provides instant
connectivity, a multimedia Windows interface, and a full suite
of applications. This product is so easy to use, you need to
know only two things to get started: how to load software
onto your PC and how to use a mouse.

New features of version 2.0 include:

* More connectivity options with the CompuServe Network.
* With Spry Mosaic and Progressive Image Rendering,
  browsing the Internet has never been easier.
* SPRY Mail provides MIME support and a built-in spell
  checker. Mail and News are now available within the
  Mosaic Toolbar.
* You'll enjoy safe and secure shopping online with Secure HTTP.
* SPRY News offers offline support for viewing and sending
  individual articles.
* A Network File Manager means there's an improved inter-
  face for dealing with various Internet hosts.

Connecting to the Internet

By Susan Estrada
1st Edition August 1993
188 pages, ISBN 1-56592-061-9

 This book provides practical advice
on how to get an Internet connection.
It describes how to assess your needs
to determine the kind of Internet service
that is best for you and how to find a
local access provider and evaluate the
services they offer.

Knowing how to purchase the right kind
of Internet access can help you save money and avoid a lot of
frustration. This book is the fastest way for you to learn how
to get on the Internet. Then you can begin exploring one of
the world's most valuable resources.

The World Wide Web Journal

Edited by O'Reilly & Associates and the Web Consortium (W3C)
1st Edition January 1996 (est.)
800 pages (est.), ISBN 1-56592-169-0

The World Wide Web Journal is a quarterly publication that provides timely, in-depth coverage of the issues, techniques, and research developments in the World Wide Web. The Web Consortium (W3C), headed by Tim Berners-Lee, is the official standards body for the Web. Regular issues are thematically based and include interviews with experts, a roundtable discussion about current topics, perspectives on emergent Web research and development, and technical papers.

The December issue contains the Conference Proceeding papers that were chosen for the 4th International World Wide Web conference in Boston, MA. Out of the 197 papers that were submitted, 57 were accepted. These papers reflect the state-of-the-art of the Web right now. Some of the topics include strategies for creating quality graphics, accessing scientific data, describing an interactive, personalized newspaper, and bringing music to the web.

MH & xmh: Email for Users & Programmers

By Jerry Peek
3rd Edition April 1995
782 pages, ISBN 1-56592-093-7

There are lots of mail programs in use these days, but MH is one of the most durable and flexible. Best of all, it's available on almost all UNIX systems. It has spawned a number of interfaces that many users prefer. This book covers three popular interfaces: *xmh* (for the X environment), *exmh* (written with tcl/tk), and *mh-e* (for GNU Emacs users).

The book contains: a quick tour through MH, *xmh*, *exmh*, and *mh-e* for new users; configuration and customization information; lots of tips and techniques for programmers— and plenty of practical examples for everyone; information beyond the manual pages, explaining how to make MH do things you never thought an email program could do; and quick-reference pages in the back of the book.

In addition, the third edition describes the Multipurpose Internet Mail Extensions (MIME) and describes how to use it with these mail programs. MIME is an extension that allows users to send graphics, sound, and other multimedia formats through mail between otherwise incompatible systems.

Using Email Effectively

By Linda Lamb & Jerry Peek
1st Edition April 1995
160 pages, ISBN 1-56592-103-8

When you're new to email, you're usually shown what keystrokes to use to read and send a message. After using email for a few years, you learn from your own mistakes and from reading other people's mail. You learn:

- How to organize saved mail so that you can find it again

- When to include a previous message, and how much to include, so that your reader can quickly make sense of what's being discussed

- When a network address "looks right," so that more of your messages get through the first time

- When a "bounced" message will never be delivered and when the bounce merely indicates temporary network difficulties

- How to successfully subscribe and unsubscribe to a mailing list

With first-person anecdotes, examples, and general observations, *Using Email Effectively* shortens the learning-from-experience curve for all mailers, so you can quickly be productive and send email that looks intelligent to others.

The USENET Handbook

By Mark Harrison
1st Edition May 1995
388 pages, ISBN 1-56592-101-1

USENET, also called Netnews, is the world's largest discussion forum, encompassing the worldwide Internet and many other sites that aren't formally connected to any network. USENET provides a forum for asking and answering technical questions, arguing politics, religion, and society, or discussing most scientific, artistic, or humanistic disciplines. It's also a forum for distributing free software, as well as digitized pictures and sound.

This book unlocks USENET for you. It includes tutorials on the most popular newsreaders for UNIX and Windows (*tin, nn,* GNUS, and Trumpet). It's also a guide to the culture of the Net, giving you an introduction to etiquette, the private language, and some of the history.

Web Design for Designers

By Jennifer Niederst, Edie Freedman & Linda Mui
1st Edition December 1995 (est.)
120 pages (est.), ISBN 1-56592-165-8

 This book is for designers who need to hone their skills for the Web. It explains how to work with HTML documents from a designer's point of view, outlines special problems with presenting information online, and walks through incorporating images into Web pages, with emphasis on resolution and improving efficiency. Also discusses the different browsers available and how to make sure a document is most effective for a broad spectrum of browsers and platforms.

Marketing on the Internet

By Linda Lamb, Tim O'Reilly, Dale Dougherty & Brian Erwin
1st Edition January 1996 (est.)
170 pages (est.), ISBN 1-56592-105-4

 *Marketing on the Internet* tells you what you need to know to successfully use this new communication and sales channel to put product and sales information online, build relationships with customers, send targeted announcements, and answer product support questions. In short, how to use the Internet as part of your overall marketing mix. Written from a marketing, not technical, perspective.

Smileys

By David W. Sanderson
1st Edition March 1993
93 pages, ISBN 1-56592-041-4

 From the people who put an armadillo on the cover of a system administrator book comes this collection of the computer underground hieroglyphs called "smileys." Originally inserted into email messages to denote "said with a cynical smile" :-), smileys now run rampant throughout the electronic mail culture.

The Computer User's Survival Guide

By Joan Stigliani
1st Edition October 1995
296 pages, ISBN 1-56592-030-9

 The bad news: You can be hurt by working at a computer. The good news: Many of the factors that pose a risk are within your control. *The Computer User's Survival Guide* looks squarely at all the factors that affect your health on the job, including positioning, equipment, work habits, lighting, stress, radiation, and general health. It is not a book of gloom and doom. It is a guide to protecting yourself against health risks from your computer, while boosting your effectiveness and making your work more enjoyable.

This guide will teach you what's going on "under the skin" when your hands and arms spend much of the day mousing and typing, and what you can do to prevent overuse injuries. You'll learn various postures to help reduce stress; what you can do to prevent glare from modern office lighting; simple breathing techniques and stretches to keep your body well oxygenated and relaxed; and how to reduce eye strain. Also covers radiation issues and what electrical equipment is responsible for the most exposure.

HTML Handbook

By Chuck Musciano & Bill Kennedy
1st Edition February 1996 (est.)
350 pages (est.), ISBN 1-56592-175-5

 The *HTML Handbook* helps you become fluent in HTML, fully versed in the language's syntax, semantics, and elements of style. The book covers the most up-to-date version of the HTML standard, plus all the common extensions and, in particular, Netscape extensions. The authors cover each and every element of the currently accepted version of the language in detail, explaining how each element works and how it interacts with all the other elements. They've also included a style guide that helps you decide how to best use HTML to accomplish a variety of tasks, from simple online documentation to complex marketing and sales presentations.

Internet System Administration

PGP: Pretty Good Privacy

By Simson Garfinkel
1st Edition December 1994
430 pages, ISBN 1-56592-098-8

PGP is a freely available encryption program that protects the privacy of files and electronic mail. It uses powerful public key cryptography and works on virtually every platform. This book is both a readable technical user's guide and a fascinating behind-the-scenes look at cryptography and privacy. It describes how to use PGP and provides background on cryptography, PGP's history, battles over public key cryptography patents and U.S. government export restrictions, and public debates about privacy and free speech.

"I even learned a few things about PGP from Simson's informative book."—Phil Zimmermann, Author of PGP

"Since the release of PGP 2.0 from Europe in the fall of 1992, PGP's popularity and usage has grown to make it the de-facto standard for email encryption. Simson's book is an excellent overview of PGP and the history of cryptography in general. It should prove a useful addition to the resource library for any computer user, from the UNIX wizard to the PC novice."
—Derek Atkins, PGP Development Team, MIT

Building Internet Firewalls

By D. Brent Chapman & Elizabeth D. Zwicky
1st Edition September 1995
544 pages, ISBN 1-56592-124-0

Everyone is jumping on the Internet bandwagon, despite the fact that the security risks associated with connecting to the Net have never been greater. This book is a practical guide to building firewalls on the Internet. It describes a variety of firewall approaches and architectures and discusses how you can build packet filtering and proxying solutions at your site. It also contains a full discussion of how to configure Internet services (e.g., FTP, SMTP, Telnet) to work with a firewall, as well as a complete list of resources, including the location of many publicly available firewall construction tools.

Managing Internet Information Services

By Cricket Liu, Jerry Peek, Russ Jones, Bryan Buus & Adrian Nye
1st Edition December 1994
668 pages, ISBN 1-56592-062-7

This comprehensive guide describes how to set up information services and make them available over the Internet. It discusses why a company would want to offer Internet services, provides complete coverage of all popular services, and tells how to select which ones to provide. Most of the book describes how to set up Gopher, World Wide Web, FTP, and WAIS servers and email services.

Networking Personal Computers with TCP/IP

By Craig Hunt
1st Edition July 1995
408 pages, ISBN 1-56592-123-2

This book offers practical information as well as detailed instructions for attaching PCs to a TCP/IP network and its UNIX servers. It discusses the challenges you'll face and offers general advice on how to deal with them, provides basic TCP/IP configuration information for some of the popular PC operating systems, covers advanced configuration topics and configuration of specific applications such as email, and includes a chapter on NetWare, the most popular PC LAN system software.

TCP/IP Network Administration

By Craig Hunt
1st Edition August 1992
502 pages, ISBN 0-937175-82-X

A complete guide to setting up and running a TCP/IP network for practicing system administrators. *TCP/IP Network Administration* covers setting up your network, configuring important network applications including sendmail, and issues in troubleshooting and security. It covers both BSD and System V TCP/IP implementations.

FOR INFORMATION: **800-998-9938**, 707-829-0515; **INFO@ORA.COM**; **HTTP://WWW.ORA.COM/**

Internet Programming

CGI Scripting on the World Wide Web

By Shishir Gundavaram
1st Edition February 1996 (est.)
300 pages (est.), ISBN 1-56592-168-2, Includes CD-ROM

This book is a comprehensive explanation of CGI and related techniques for people who hold on to the dream of providing their own information servers on the Web. Gundavaram starts at the beginning, explaining the value of CGI and how it works, then moves swiftly into the subtle details of programming. The book offers a comprehensive look at the job of providing information dynamically on the Web. Includes CD-ROM with sample programs and NCSA server.

Learning Perl

By Randal L. Schwartz, Foreword by Larry Wall
1st Edition November 1993
274 pages, ISBN 1-56592-042-2

Learning Perl is a step-by-step, hands-on tutorial designed to get you writing useful Perl scripts as quickly as possible. In addition to countless code examples, there are numerous programming exercises, with full answers. For a comprehensive and detailed guide to advanced programming with Perl, read O'Reilly's companion book, *Programming perl*.

Programming perl

By Larry Wall & Randal L. Schwartz
1st Edition January 1991
482 pages, ISBN 0-937175-64-1

This is the authoritative guide to the hottest new UNIX utility in years, coauthored by its creator, Larry Wall. Perl is a language for easily manipulating text, files, and processes. Perl provides a more concise and readable way to do many jobs that were formerly accomplished (with difficulty) by programming in the C language or one of the shells.

Programming perl covers Perl syntax, functions, debugging, efficiency, the Perl library, and more, including real-world Perl programs dealing with such issues as system administration and text manipulation.

The World of the Internet

The Future Does Not Compute

By Stephen L. Talbott
1st Edition May 1995
502 pages, ISBN 1-56592-085-6

This book explores the networked computer as an expression of the darker, dimly conscious side of the human being. What we have been imparting to the Net—or what the Net has been eliciting from us—is a half-submerged, barely intended logic, contaminated by wishes and tendencies we prefer not to acknowledge. The urgent necessity is for us to wake up to what is most fully human and unmachinelike in ourselves, rather than yield to an ever more strangling embrace with our machines. The author's thesis is sure to raise a controversy among the millions of users now adapting themselves to the Net.

At Your Fingertips—
A COMPLETE GUIDE TO O'REILLY'S ONLINE SERVICES

O'Reilly & Associates offers extensive product and customer service information online. We invite you to come and explore our little neck-of-the-woods.

For product information and insight into new technologies, visit the O'Reilly Resource Center

Most comprehensive among our online offerings is the O'Reilly Resource Center. You'll find detailed information on all O'Reilly products, including titles, prices, tables of contents, indexes, author bios, software contents, and reviews. You can also view images of all our products. In addition, watch for informative articles that provide perspective on the technologies we write about. Interviews, excerpts, and bibliographies are also included.

After browsing online, it's easy to order, too, with GNN Direct or by sending email to **order@ora.com**. The O'Reilly Resource Center shows you how. Here's how to visit us online:

👉 *Via the World Wide Web*

If you are connected to the Internet, point your Web browser (e.g., `mosaic`, `netscape`, or `lynx`) to:

`http://www.ora.com/`

For the plaintext version, `telnet` to:
`www.ora.com` (login: `oraweb`)

👉 *Via Gopher*

If you have a Gopher program, our Gopher server has information in a menu format that some people prefer to the Web.

Connect your `gopher` to: `gopher.ora.com`
Or, point your Web browser to:
`gopher://gopher.ora.com/`

Or, you can `telnet` to: `gopher.ora.com`
(login: `gopher`)

A convenient way to stay informed: email mailing lists

An easy way to learn of the latest projects and products from O'Reilly & Associates is to subscribe to our mailing lists. We have email announcements and discussions on various topics, for example "ora-news," our electronic news service. Subscribers receive email as soon as the information breaks.

👉 *To join a mailing list:*

Send email to:
listproc@online.ora.com

Leave the message "subject" empty if possible.

If you know the name of the mailing list you want to subscribe to, put the following information on the first line of your message: `subscribe` "listname" "your name" `of` "your company."

For example: `subscribe ora-news Kris Webber of Fine Enterprises`

If you don't know the name of the mailing list, listproc will send you a listing of all the mailing lists. Put this word on the first line of the body: `lists`

To find out more about a particular list, send a message with this word as the first line of the body: `info` "listname"

For more information and help, send this message: `help`

For specific help, email to: **listmaster@online.ora.com**

The complete O'Reilly catalog is now available via email

You can now receive a text-only version of our complete catalog via email. It contains detailed information about all our products, so it's mighty big: over 200 kbytes, or 200,000 characters.

To get the whole catalog in one message, send an empty email message to: **catalog@online.ora.com**

If your email system can't handle large messages, you can get the catalog split into smaller messages. Send email to: **catalog-split@online.ora.com**

To receive a print catalog, send your snail mail address to: **catalog@ora.com**

Check out Web Review, our new publication on the Web

Web Review is our new magazine that offers fresh insights into the Web. The editorial mission of Web Review is to answer the question: How and where do you BEST spend your time online? Each issue contains reviews that look at the most interesting and creative sites on the Web. Visit us at **http://gnn.com/wr/**

Web Review is the product of the recently formed Songline Studios, a venture between O'Reilly and America Online.

Get the files you want with FTP

We have an archive of example files from our books, the covers of our books, and much more available by anonymous FTP.

ftp to:

ftp.ora.com (login: **anonymous** – use your email address as the password.)

Or, if you have a WWW browser, point it to:

ftp://ftp.ora.com/

FTPMAIL

The ftpmail service connects to O'Reilly's FTP server and sends the results (the files you want) by email. This service is for people who can't use FTP—but who can use email.

For help and examples, send an email message to:

ftpmail@online.ora.com

(In the message body, put the single word: **help**)

Helpful information is just an email message away

Many customer services are provided via email. Here are a few of the most popular and useful:

info@online.ora.com
> For a list of O'Reilly's online customer services.

info@ora.com
> For general questions and information.

bookquestions@ora.com
> For technical questions, or corrections, concerning book contents.

order@ora.com
> To order books online and for ordering questions.

catalog@online.ora.com
> To receive an online copy of our catalog.

catalog@ora.com
> To receive a free copy of *ora.com*, our combination magazine and catalog. Please include your snail mail address.

international@ora.com
> Comments or questions about international ordering or distribution.

xresource@ora.com
> To order or inquire about *The X Resource* journal.

proposals@ora.com
> To submit book proposals.

info@gnn.com
> To receive information about America Online's GNN (Global Network Navigator).™

O'Reilly & Associates, Inc.

103A Morris Street, Sebastopol, CA 95472
Inquiries: **707-829-0515, 800-998-9938**
Credit card orders: **800-889-8969** (Weekdays 6 A.M.- 5 P.M. PST)
FAX: **707-829-0104**

O'Reilly & Associates—
LISTING OF TITLES

INTERNET

CGI Scripting on the World Wide Web (Winter '95-96 est.)

Connecting to the Internet: An O'Reilly Buyer's Guide

Getting Connected (Winter '95-96 est.)

HTML Handbook (Winter '95-96 est.)

The Mosaic Handbook for Microsoft Windows

The Mosaic Handbook for the Macintosh

The Mosaic Handbook for the X Window System

Smileys

The USENET Handbook

The Whole Internet User's Guide & Catalog

The Whole Internet for Windows 95

Web Design for Designers (Winter '95-96 est.)

The World Wide Web Journal (Winter '95-96 est.)

SOFTWARE

Internet In A Box ™ Version 2.0

WebSite™ 1.1

WHAT YOU NEED TO KNOW SERIES

Using Email Effectively

Marketing on the Internet (Winter '95-96 est.)

When You Can't Find Your System Administrator

HEALTH, CAREER & BUSINESS

Building a Successful Software Business

The Computer User's Survival Guide

Dictionary of Computer Terms (Winter '95-96 est.)

The Future Does Not Compute

Love Your Job!

TWI Day Calendar - 1996

USING UNIX

BASICS

Learning GNU Emacs

Learning the bash Shell

Learning the Korn Shell

Learning the UNIX Operating System

Learning the vi Editor

MH & xmh: Email for Users & Programmers

SCO UNIX in a Nutshell

UNIX in a Nutshell: System V Edition

Using and Managing UUCP (Winter '95-96 est.)

Using csh and tcsh

ADVANCED

Exploring Expect

The Frame Handbook

Learning Perl

Making TeX Work

Programming perl

Running Linux

Running Linux Companion CD-ROM (Winter '95-96 est.)

sed & awk

UNIX Power Tools (with CD-ROM)

SYSTEM ADMINISTRATION

Building Internet Firewalls

Computer Crime: A Crimefighter's Handbook

Computer Security Basics

DNS and BIND

Essential System Administration

Linux Network Administrator's Guide

Managing Internet Information Services

Managing NFS and NIS

Managing UUCP and Usenet

Networking Personal Computers with TCP/IP

Practical UNIX Security

PGP: Pretty Good Privacy

sendmail

System Performance Tuning

TCP/IP Network Administration

termcap & terminfo

Volume 8 : X Window System Administrator's Guide

The X Companion CD for R6

PROGRAMMING

Applying RCS and SCCS

C++: The Core Language

Checking C Programs with lint

DCE Security Programming

Distributing Applications Across DCE and Windows NT

Encyclopedia of Graphics File Formats

Guide to Writing DCE Applications

High Performance Computing

lex & yacc

Managing Projects with make

Microsoft RPC Programming Guide

Migrating to Fortran 90

Multi-Platform Code Management

ORACLE Performance Tuning

ORACLE PL/SQL Programming

Porting UNIX Software

POSIX Programmer's Guide

POSIX.4: Programming for the Real World

Power Programming with RPC

Practical C Programming

Practical C++ Programming

Programming with curses

Programming with GNU Software (Winter '95-96 est.)

Programming with Pthreads (Winter '95-96 est.)

Software Portability with imake

Understanding and Using COFF

Understanding DCE

Understanding Japanese Information Processing

UNIX Systems Programming for SVR4 (Winter '95-96 est.)

Using C on the UNIX System

BERKELEY 4.4 SOFTWARE DISTRIBUTION

4.4BSD System Manager's Manual

4.4BSD User's Reference Manual

4.4BSD User's Supplementary Docs.

4.4BSD Programmer's Reference Man.

4.4BSD Programmer's Supp. Docs.

4.4BSD-Lite CD Companion

4.4BSD-Lite CD Companion: Int. Ver.

X PROGRAMMING

THE X WINDOW SYSTEM

Volume 0: X Protocol Reference Manual

Volume 1: Xlib Programming Manual

Volume 2: Xlib Reference Manual

Volume 3: X Window System User's Guide

Volume. 3M: X Window System User's Guide, Motif Ed.

Volume. 4: X Toolkit Intrinsics Programming Manual

Volume 4M: X Toolkit Intrinsics Programming Manual, Motif Ed.

Volume 5: X Toolkit Intrinsics Reference Manual

Volume 6A: Motif Programming Man.

Volume 6B: Motif Reference Manual

Volume 6C: Motif Tools

Volume 8 : X Window System Administrator's Guide

PEXlib Programming Manual

PEXlib Reference Manual

PHIGS Programming Manual

PHIGS Reference Manual

Programmer's Supplement for Release 6

The X Companion CD for R6

X User Tools (with CD-ROM)

The X Window System in a Nutshell

THE X RESOURCE

A QUARTERLY WORKING JOURNAL FOR X PROGRAMMERS

The X Resource: Issues 0 through 15

TRAVEL

Travelers' Tales France

Travelers' Tales Hong Kong (12/95 est.)

Travelers' Tales India

Travelers' Tales Mexico

Travelers' Tales Spain

Travelers' Tales Thailand

Travelers' Tales: A Woman's World

O'Reilly & Associates—
INTERNATIONAL DISTRIBUTORS

Customers outside North America can now order O'Reilly & Associates books through the following distributors. They offer our international customers faster order processing, more bookstores, increased representation at tradeshows worldwide, and the high-quality, responsive service our customers have come to expect.

EUROPE, MIDDLE EAST, AND AFRICA
(except Germany, Switzerland, and Austria)

INQUIRIES
International Thomson Publishing Europe
Berkshire House
168-173 High Holborn
London WC1V 7AA, United Kingdom
Telephone: 44-71-497-1422
Fax: 44-71-497-1426
Email: itpint@itps.co.uk

ORDERS
International Thomson Publishing Services, Ltd.
Cheriton House, North Way
Andover, Hampshire SP10 5BE, United Kingdom
Telephone: 44-264-342-832 (UK orders)
Telephone: 44-264-342-806 (outside UK)
Fax: 44-264-364418 (UK orders)
Fax: 44-264-342761 (outside UK)

GERMANY, SWITZERLAND, AND AUSTRIA

International Thomson Publishing GmbH
O'Reilly-International Thomson Verlag
Königswinterer Straße 418
53227 Bonn, Germany
Telephone: 49-228-97024 0
Fax: 49-228-441342
Email: anfragen@ora.de

ASIA *(except Japan)*

INQUIRIES
International Thomson Publishing Asia
221 Henderson Road
#08-03 Henderson Industrial Park
Singapore 0315
Telephone: 65-272-6496
Fax: 65-272-6498

ORDERS
Telephone: 65-268-7867
Fax: 65-268-6727

JAPAN
O'Reilly & Associates, Inc.
103A Morris Street
Sebastopol, CA 95472 U.S.A.
Telephone: 707-829-0515
Telephone: 800-998-9938 (U.S. & Canada)
Fax: 707-829-0104
Email: order@ora.com

AUSTRALIA
WoodsLane Pty. Ltd.
7/5 Vuko Place, Warriewood NSW 2102
P.O. Box 935, Mona Vale NSW 2103
Australia
Telephone: 02-970-5111
Fax: 02-970-5002
Email: woods@tmx.mhs.oz.au

NEW ZEALAND
WoodsLane New Zealand Ltd.
21 Cooks Street (P.O. Box 575)
Wanganui, New Zealand
Telephone: 64-6-347-6543
Fax: 64-6-345-4840
Email: woods@tmx.mhs.oz.au

THE AMERICAS
O'Reilly & Associates, Inc.
103A Morris Street
Sebastopol, CA 95472 U.S.A.
Telephone: 707-829-0515
Telephone: 800-998-9938 (U.S. & Canada)
Fax: 707-829-0104
Email: order@ora.com

Here's a page we encourage readers to tear out...

THE WHOLE INTERNET
for Windows 95

O'REILLY WOULD LIKE TO HEAR FROM YOU

Please send me the following:

❏ *ora.com*

O'Reilly's magazine/catalog, containing behind-the-scenes articles and interviews on the technology we write about, and a complete listing of O'Reilly books and products.

Thank you for purchasing *The Whole Internet for Windows 95*.

Where did you buy this book?
❏ Bookstore ❏ Direct from O'Reilly
❏ Bundled with hardware/software ❏ Class/seminar

Your job description: ❏ SysAdmin ❏ Programmer
❏ Other _____

Describe your operating system: _____
_____

Please print legibly

_____
Name

_____
Company/Organization Name

_____
Address

_____
City   State   Zip/Postal Code   Country

_____
Telephone   Internet or other email address (specify network)

Nineteenth century wood engraving
of an alchemist, from the O'Reilly
& Associates Nutshell Handbook®
The Whole Internet for Windows 95.

POST CARD

O'Reilly & Associates, Inc., 103A Morris Street, Sebastopol, CA 95472-9902

BUSINESS REPLY MAIL

FIRST CLASS MAIL   PERMIT NO. 80   SEBASTOPOL, CA

Postage will be paid by addressee

O'Reilly & Associates, Inc.

103A Morris Street
Sebastopol, CA 95472-9902